JOHN WILLIS

SCREEN WORLD

1999

VOLUME 50

ASSOCIATE EDITOR
BARRY MONUSH

NEW YORK • LONDON

Splendor in the Grass
1961

The Roman Spring of Mrs. Stone
1961

Kaleidoscope
1966

Bonnie and Clyde
1967

The Parallax View
1974

Shampoo
1975

The Fortune
1975

Heaven Can Wait
1978

Reds
1981

Dick Tracy
1990

Bugsy
1991

Bulworth
1998

To
WARREN BEATTY

whose work as an actor, director, producer and writer has infused the modern cinema with intelligence, insight, provocation, humor, and controversy without ever sacrificing the value of entertainment.

FILMS: *Splendor in the Grass* (1961), *The Roman Spring of Mrs. Stone* (1961), *All Fall Down* (1962), *Lilith* (1964), *Mickey One* (1965), *Promise Her Anything* (1966), *Kaleidoscope* (1966), *Bonnie and Clyde* (1967, and producer; Academy Award nominations for Best Actor and Picture), *The Only Game in Town* (1970), *McCabe and Mrs. Miller* (1971), *$* (1971), *The Parallax View* (1974), *Shampoo* (1975, and producer), *The Fortune* (1975), *Heaven Can Wait* (1978, and co-director, producer, co-writer; Academy Award nominations for Best Actor, Director, Adapted Screenplay, and Picture), *Reds* (1981, and director, producer, co-writer; Academy Award for Best Director; nominations for Best Actor, Original Screenplay, and Picture), *George Stevens: A Filmmaker's Journey* (1985), *Ishtar* (1987, and producer), *Dick Tracy* (1990, and director, producer), *Truth or Dare* (1991), *Bugsy* (1991, and producer; Academy Award nominations for Best Actor and Picture), *Love Affair* (1994, and producer, co-writer), *Bulworth* (1998, and director, producer, co-writer, Academy Award nomination for Best Original Screenplay), *Town and Country* (2000)

Tom Hanks in *Saving Private Ryan*
Academy Award Winner for Best Director
© DreamWorks/Paramount Pictures/Amblin Entertainment

CONTENTS

EDITOR: JOHN WILLIS

ASSOCIATE EDITOR: BARRY MONUSH

Staff: Marco Starr Boyajian, William Camp, Jim Hollifield, II,

Tom Lynch, John Sala

Acknowledgements: Tom Amorosi, Anthology Film Archives, Ed Arentz, Artistic License, Castle Hill, Castle Rock Entertainment, City Cinemas, Cline & White, Richard D'Attile, Dennis Davidson Associates, Alex Dawson, Samantha Dean, DreamWorks, Brian Durnin, The Film Forum, First Look, First Run Features, Fox Searchlight, Adrian Goycoolea, Gramercy Pictures, Seth Grossman, Khan & Jacobs, Kino International, Legacy Releasing, Leisure Time Features, LIVE Entertainment, Mike Maggiore, David Mazor, Robert Milite, Jr., Miramax Films,, New Line Cinema/Fine Line Features, New Yorker Films, Northern Arts Entertainment, October Films, PMK Publicity, Paramount Pictures, Phaedra Films, PolyGram, Quad Cinema, 7th Art Releasing, Sony Pictures Entertainment, Sheldon Stone, Strand Releasing, Paul Sugarman, Twentieth Century Fox, Universal Pictures, Richard Valley, Walt Disney Pictures, Robert Ward, Glenn Young, Zeitgeist Films.

1. Tom Hanks

2. Jim Carrey

3. Leonardo DiCaprio

4. Robin Williams

5. Meg Ryan

6. Mel Gibson

7. Adam Sandler

8. Eddie Murphy

9. Cameron Diaz

10. Julia Roberts

TOP BOX OFFICE STARS OF 1998

1998 RELEASES

January 1 Through December 31, 1998

Christian Slater, Morgan Freeman

HARD RAIN

(PARAMOUNT) formerly *The Flood;* Producers, Mark Gordon, Gary Levinsohn, Ian Bryce; Executive Producer, Allison Lyon Segan; Director, Mikael Salomon; Screenplay, Graham Yost; Photography, Peter Menzies, Jr.; Designer, J. Michael Riva; Editor, Paul Hirsch; Costumes, Kathleen Detoro; Co-Producer, Christian Slater; Casting, Risa Bramon Garcia, Randi Hiller; Stunts, Jeff Habberstad; Presented in association with Mutual Film Company; Dolby Stereo; Super 35 Widescreen; Deluxe color; Rated R; 96 minutes; January release

CAST

Jim	Morgan Freeman
Tom	Christian Slater
Sheriff	Randy Quaid
Karen	Minnie Driver
Charlie	Ed Asner
Kenny	Michael Goorjian
Mr. Mehlor	Dann Florek
Ray	Ricky Harris
Wayne	Mark Rolston
Phil	Peter Murnik
Hank	Wayne Duvall
Henry	Richard Dysart
Doreen	Betty White
Mayor	Ray Baker
Mayor's Wife	Lisa Fuhrman
Mr. Wellman	Jay Patterson
Father on Local News	Michael Monks
Baby on Local News	Mackenzie Bryce

During a devestating rain fall that floods the town of Huntingburg, an armored car driver is relentlessly pursued by a team of robbers seeking the $3 million dollars he has hidden from them.

©Paramount Pictures

Minnie Driver, Randy Quaid

Christian Slater

Christian Slater, Ed Asner

HALF BAKED

(UNIVERSAL) Producer, Robert Simonds; Director, Tamra Davis; Screenplay, Dave Chappelle, Neal Brennan; Photography, Steven Bernstein; Designer, Perry Andelin Blake; Editor, Don Zimmerman; Co-Producer, Ira Shuman; Associate Producers, Julia Dray, Rita Smith; Costumes, Vicki Graef; Music, Alf Clausen; Casting, Joanna Colbert; a Robert Simonds production; SDDS Stereo; Deluxe color; Rated R; 85 minutes; January release

CAST

Thurgood	Dave Chappelle
Scarface	Guillermo Diaz
Brian	Jim Breuer
Kenny	Harland Williams
Mary Jane	Rachel True
Samson Simpson	Clarence Williams III
Sir Smoka Lot	Dave Chappelle
Jan	Laura Silverman
Squirrel Master	Tommy Chong
Scientist	R.D. Reid
Potheads	Gregg Rogell, Kevin Brennan
Supply Clerk	Alice Poon
Nasty Nate	Rick Demas
Jerry Garcia	David Bluestein

and Kevin Duhaney (Young Thurgood), Matthew Raposo (Young Scarface), James Cooper (Young Brian), Michael Colton (Young Kenny), Paul Brogren (Burger Customer), Neal Brennan (Employee), Karen Waddell (Record Store Employee), Vincent Marino (Bodega Man), Domencio "Macio" Parrilla, Marcus Burrowes (Rasta Men), Mark Henriques (Delivery Guy), Jenni Burke (Overweight Woman), Gwenne Hudson (Bong Genie), David Mucci (Horse Cop), Reg Dreger (Judge), Kevin Rushton (Inmate), Paul Saunders (Doorman), Kyrin Hall, Joanna Bacalso, C.J. Fidler, Angelica Lisk, Jacqueline Anderson, Stephanie Bourgeois (Henchwomen), Ho Chow (Hot Dog Vendor), Rummy Bishop (Homeless Guy), Jon Stewart (Enhancement Smoker), Snoop Doggy Dogg (Scavenger Smoker), Stephen Baldwin (McGuyver Smoker), Marc Cohen (McGuyver Friend), Tracy Morgan (V.J.), David Edwards (Addict), Paulino Nunes (Swat Cop), Jason Blicker, Dave Nichols (Detectives), Sharon Brown (Talking Joint), Christopher Mugglebee, Raymond Hinton (Security Guards), David Sutcliffe (After School Dad), Daniel De Santo (After School Son), Gladys O'Connor (Grandma Smoker), Willie Nelson (Historian Smoker)

Three stoners hope to raise bail for their friend by selling pot stolen from a pharmaceutical lab.

©Universal Studios Inc.

Jim Breuer, Guillermo Diaz, Dave Chappelle

Denzel Washington, John Goodman

©Turner Pictures Worldwide, Inc.

FALLEN

(WARNER BROS.) Producers, Charles Roven, Dawn Steel; Executive Producers, Elon Dershowitz, Nicholas Kazan, Robert Cavallo, Ted Kurdyla; Director, Gregory Hoblit; Screenplay, Nicholas Kazan; Photography, Newton Thomas Sigel; Designer, Terence Marsh; Editor, Lawrence Jordan; Costumes, Colleen Atwood; Music, Tan Dun; Co-Producer, Kelley Smith-Wait; Associate Producers, Richard Suckle, Patricia Graf; Casting, David Rubin; a Turner Pictures presentation of an Atlas Entertainment production; Dolby; Panavision; Technicolor; Rated R; 124 minutes; January release

CAST

John Hobbes	Denzel Washington
Jonesy	John Goodman
Lieutenant Stanton	Donald Sutherland
Gretta Milano	Embeth Davidtz
Lou	James Gandolfini
Edgar Reese	Elias Koteas
Art	Gabriel Casseus
Sam	Michael J. Pagan
Charles	Robert Joy
Charles' Killer	Frank Medrano
Mini Golf Owner	Ronn Munro
Society Woman	Cynthia Hayden
Society Man	Ray Xifo
Toby	Tony Michael Donnelly

and Tara Carnes (Teenage Girl), Reno Wilson (Mike), Wendy Cutler (Denise), Aida Turturro (Tiffany), Jeff Tanner (Lawrence), Jerry Walsh (Fat Man), Bob Rumnock (Schoolteacher), Ellen Sheppard (Nun on Bus), Christian Aubert (Prof. Louders), Bill Clark (Det. Bill Clark), Allelon Ruggiero (Executioner), Jill Holden (Gracie), Drucie McDaniel (Vender), John Raphael Russell (Distinguished Gentleman), Lynn Wanlass (Complaining Woman), John Descano (Cab Driver), Cress Willias (Det. Joe), Rick Warner (Governor), Jim Grimshaw (Warden), Brandon Zitin (Muscle Builder), Rozwill Young, Michael Shamus Wiles, Frank Davis (Prison Guards), Barry "Sha Baka" Henley (Uniformed Cop), Mike Cicchetti (Mustache Man), William C. Jeffreys III (Transit Cop), Ben Siegler (Priest), Jason Winston George (College Kid), Anika Hawkins (Girlfriend), Stan Kang (Japanese Businessman), Thomas J. McCarthy, Sheila Bader (Witnesses), Elleanor Jean Hendley, Michael Aron, Byron Scott (Reporters), Pat Ciarrocchi, Steve Highsmith, Kent Manahan (Anchors)

Homicide detective John Hobbes apprehends serial killer Edgar Reese and sees him executed only to find that crimes similar to those perpetrated by Reese are being committed, leading him to suspect a supernatural occurance.

THE GINGERBREAD MAN

(POLYGRAM) Producer, Jeremy Tannenbaum; Executive Producers, Mark Burg, Glen A. Tobias, Todd Baker; Director, Robert Altman; Screenplay, Al Hayes; Based on an original story by John Grisham; Photography, Changwei Gu; Designer, Stephen Altman; Editor, Geraldine Peroni; Music, Mark Isham; Associate Producer, David Levy; an Island Pictures and Enchanter Entertainment production; Dolby; Panavision; Color; Rated R; 115 minutes; January release

Kenneth Branagh, Daryl Hannah, Embeth Davidtz

CAST

Rick Magruder .... Kenneth Branagh
Mallory Doss .... Embeth Davidtz
Clyde Pell .... Robert Downey, Jr.
Lois Harlan .... Daryl Hannah
Dixon Doss .... Robert Duvall
Pete Randle .... Tom Berenger
Leeanne .... Famke Janssen
Carl Alden .... Clyde Hayes
Libby .... Mae Whitman
Jeff .... Jesse James
Konnie Dugan .... Troy Beyer
Cassandra .... Julia R. Perce
Sheriff Hope .... Danny Darst
Phillip Dunson .... Sonny Seiler
Edmund Hess .... Walter Hartridge
Larry Benjamin .... Vernon E. Jordan, Jr.
Betty .... Lori Beth Sikes
Dr. Bernice Sampson .... Rosemary Newcott
Judge Russo .... Wilbur T. Fitzgerald
Tom Cherry .... David Hirsberg
Judge Cooper .... Paul Carden

and Michelle Benjamin-Cooper (Principal), Christine Seabrook (Secretary), Bob Minor (Mr. Pitney), Myrna White (Tax Clerk), Jim Grimshaw (Desk Cop), Stuart Greer (Detective Hal), Nita Hardy (Policewoman), Ferguson Reid (Detective Black), Benjamin T. Gay (Court Clerk), Mark Bednarz, Bill Cunningham, Chip Tootle (Effingham County Sheriffs), Sonny Shroyer, Mike Pniewski, Jay S. Pearson (Chatham County Sheriffs), L.H. Smith (Storm Evacuee), Wren Arthur (Barfly Robin), Angela Costrini (Barfly Wren), Gregory H. Alpert (Barfly Clark), Lydia Marlene (Tattooed Bartender), Bill Crabb (Huey), Jin Hi Soucy, Richie Dye, Chad Darnell (Huey's Patrons), Natalie Hendrix, Gregg Jarrett, Doug Weathers (Television Anchorpersons), Jeremy Cooper, Beth Eckard, Brad Huffines, Patrick Prokop (Television Weathercasters), Mike Manhattan, David Jordan, George Lyndel Brannen, Gregory F. Pallone, Alice Stewart, Vanessa Young (Television Field Reporters), Alyson E. Bealsey, Angela Beasley (Puppeteers), Scott Troughton (Dredge Worker), Grace Tootle (Gas Station Attendant), Shane James (Ricky Butch Banks), Herb Kelsey, William L. Thorp IV (Doss Gang Members)

Robert Duvall

Tom Berenger

Hot shot Southern attorney Rick Magruder is drawn into a dangerous web of deceit by a neurotic waitress who is seeking protection from her unhinged father.

©PolyGram Films

Robert Downey, Jr.

Embeth Davidtz, Kenneth Branagh

DESPERATE MEASURES

(TRISTAR) Producers, Barbet Schroeder, Susan Hoffman, Gary Foster, Lee Rich; Director, Barbet Schroeder; Screenplay, David Klass; Executive Producer, Jeffrey Chernov; Photography, Luciano Tovoli; Designer, Geoffrey Kirkland; Editor, Lee Percy; Costumes, Gary Jones; Music, Trevor Jones; Visual Effects Supervisor, Jim Rygiel; Casting, Howard Feuer; a Mandalay Entertainment presentation of an Eaglepoint/Schroeder/Hoffman production; Dolby; Technicolor; Rated R; 105 minutes; January release

CAST

Peter McCabe	Michael Keaton
Frank Conner	Andy Garcia
Jeremiah Cassidy	Brian Cox
Samantha Hawkins	Marcia Gay Harden
Nate Oliver	Erik King
Vargus	Efrain Figueroa
Matthew Conner	Joseph Cross
Sarah Davis	Janel Maloney
Ed Fayne	Richard Riehle
Medical Inmate	Tracey Walter
SWAT Team Commander	Peter Weireter
Wilson	Keith Diamond
Dr. Gosha	Steve Park
SWAT in Airduct	Steven Schub
Cell Guard	Neal Matarazzo
Pelican Bay Head Guard	Dennis Cockrum
Cigarette Guard	Charles Noland
Library Guard	Randy Thompson
Tough Inmate	Michael Shamus Wiles
Convoy Guards	Darren Pearce, Eric Tignini
Laser Technician	Billy Kane
Young ER Nurse	Christine Ashe
ER Nurse	Donna M. Duffy
Cop Escorting Frank	Troy Robinson
Security Booth Guard	Robert Baier
SWAT Sharpshooter in Street	David Flick
Doctor at Walkway	Joe Drago
SWAT Sniper on Roof	Josh Kemble

and Scott Colomby (Patrol Cop), Howard Meehan (Policeman on Street), Tim Kelleher (Helicopter Shooter), Cliff Fleming, Dirk Vahle, Craig Hoskings (SWAT Helicopter Pilots), Jack Gill, Scott Waugh, Danny Rogers (Motorcyclists), John Meier (Cop Shot in ER), Norm Howell, John Rottger (Burnt Cops), Donna Keegan (Burning Nurse)

Police officer Frank Connor hopes to save his son Matt through a bone marrow donation for which psychopathic killer Peter McCabe is the perfect DNA match. Complications arise when McCabe escapes from jail and Connor realizes he must track him down and bring him back unharmed.

©Mandalay Entertainment

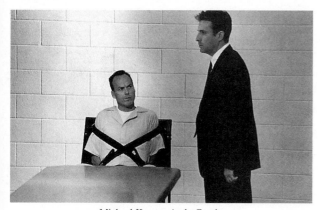

Michael Keaton, Andy Garcia

Famke Janssen, Treat Williams

Famke Janssen, Kevin J. O'Connor, Treat Williams,
Wes Studi, Anthony Heald

©Hollywood Pictures Company

DEEP RISING

(HOLLYWOOD PICTURES) Producers, Laurence Mark, John Baldecchi; Executive Producer, Barry Bernardi; Director/Screenplay, Stephen Sommers; Photography, Howard Atherton; Designer, Holger Gross; Editors, Bob Ducsay, John Wright; Music, Jerry Goldsmith; Visual Effects, Dream Quest Images; Creature Design, Rob Bottin; Costumes, Joseph Porro; Casting, Mary Goldberg; a Laurence Mark production; Distributed by Buena Vista Pictures; Dolby; Super 35 Widescreen; Technicolor; Rated R; 106 minutes; January release

CAST

Finnegan	Treat Williams
Trillian	Famke Janssen
Canton	Anthony Heald
Pantucci	Kevin J. O'Connor
Hanover	Wes Studi
Captain	Derrick O'Connor
Mulligan	Jason Flemyng
Mamooli	Cliff Curtis
Mason	Clifton Powell
T. Ray	Trevor Goddard
Vivo	Djimon Hounsou
Leila	Una Damon
Billy	Clint Curtis

and Warren T. Takeuchi (Radar Man), Linden Banks (Communications Officer), Jack Anker (Corpse), Anne-Simone (Video Vault Woman), Leanne Adachi (Toilet Lady), Melanie Carr (Dealer), Colin McCarlie (Sonar Man), Jim May (Mystery Man), Jana Sommers, Marti Baldecchi (Party Girls)

A team of thieves boards a disabled luxury cruise liner only to find that they are the designated prey of rampaging sea monsters.

Ethan Hawke, Gwyneth Paltrow

Jeremy James Kissner, Robert De Niro

GREAT EXPECTATIONS

(20TH CENTURY FOX) Producer, Art Linson; Executive Producer, Deborah Lee; Director, Alfonso Cuarón; Screenplay, Mitch Glazer; Based on the novel by Charles Dickens; Photography, Emmanuel Lubezki; Designer, Tony Burrough; Editor, Steven Weisberg; Music, Patrick Doyle; Co-Producer, John Linson; Costumes, Judianna Makovsky; Artwork, Francesco Clemente; Casting, Jill Greenberg; an Art Linson production; Dolby; Panavision; Deluxe color; Rated R; 111 minutes; January release

Anne Bancroft

CAST

Finnegan Bell	Ethan Hawke
Estella	Gwyneth Paltrow
Walter Plane	Hank Azaria
Joe	Chris Cooper
Ms. Dinsmoor	Anne Bancroft
Prisoner/Lustig	Robert De Niro
Jerry Ragno	Josh Mostel
Maggie	Kim Dickens
Erica Thrall	Nell Campbell
Owen	Gabriel Mick
Finnegan at age 10	Jeremy James Kissner
Estella at age 10	Raquel Beaudene
Carter Macleish	Stephen Spinella
Ruth Shepard	Marla Sucharetza
Lois Pope	Isabelle Anderson
Man on Phone	Peter Jacobson
Marcy	Drena De Niro
Anton Le Farge	Lance Reddick
Mr. Barrow	Craig Braun
Mrs. Barrow	Kim Snyder

and Nicholas Wolfert (Security Guard), Gerry Bamman (Ted Rabinowitz), Dorin Seymour (Senator Elwood), Clem Caserta, Frank Pietrangolare, Dennis Paladino, Clem Caserta, Jr. (Hitmen), Marc Macaulay (Cop on Boat), Ana Susana Gerardino (Clemma), Francis Dumaurier (Waiter), Pedro Barquin (Lover), Kendall Williamson (7 year old Girl), Shobha Jain (Singing Indian Woman), Aditi Jain (Singing Indian Girl), Margo Peace (Anchor Woman), Kimmy Suzuki (Waitress), John P. Casey (Doorman), Adusah Boakye (Taxi Driver), Dyan Kane (Gallery Waitress), Anne Ok (Gallery Receptionist), Alva Chinn, G.B. Thomas, Albert Zihenni, Fritz Michel, Lisa Herth, Nino Pepicelli, Wills Robbins, Jewel Turner, Jim Taylor McNickle, Martin Alvin, William Rothlein (Gallery Guests)

Young Finn is sent to play at the decaying mansion of the rich and eccentric Nora Dinsmoor. There he finds himself drawn to her niece, Estella, who continues to be an unobtainable object of passion even as Finn grows into a successful New York artist. Previous film versions of Charles Dickens' novel include those made in 1934 by Universal, featuring Phillips Holmes and Jane Wyatt; and by Cineguild-General Film Distributors in 1946 (released in the U.S. by Universal in 1947) with John Mills and Jean Simmons.

Robert De Niro, Ethan Hawke

ZERO EFFECT

(COLUMBIA) Producers, Lisa Henson, Janet Yang, Jake Kasdan; Executive Producers, Jim Behnke; Director/Screenplay, Jake Kasdan; Co-Producer, Naomi Despres; Photography, Bill Pope; Designer, Gary Frutkoff; Editor, Tara Timpone; Costumes, Kym Barrett; Music, The Greyboy Allstars; Casting, Mary Vernieu; a Castle Rock Entertainment presentation of a Manifest Film production; Dolby; Technicolor; Rated R; 115 minutes; January release

CAST

Daryl Zero	Bill Pullman
Steve Arlo	Ben Stiller
Gregory Stark	Ryan O'Neal
Gloria Sullivan	Kim Dickens
Jess	Angela Featherstone
Bill	Hugh Ross
Daisy	Sara Devincentis
Kragen Vincent	Matt O'Toole
Maid	Michele Mariana
Gerald Auerbach	Robert Katims
Staffers	Tyrone Henry, Aleta Barthell
Firefighter	Tapp Watkins
Motel Clerk	Wendy Westerwelle
Little Kid	Lauren Hasson
Rahim	Daniel Pershing
Officer Hagans	David Doty
Convention Employee	J.W. Crawford
Chuck	Fred Parnes
Waitress	Luisa Sermol
Astronomers	Marvin L. Sanders, Doug Baldwin
Paramedic #1	Robert Blanche
Clarissa Devereau	Margot Demeter

Daryl Zero, a neurotic, brilliant private detective who conducts his business through frontman and lawyer Steve Arlo, is hired by a blackmailed timber tycoon to help locate a missing set of keys to a safety deposit box.

Bill Pullman, Ben Stiller

Angela Featherstone, Ben Stiller

Ryan O'Neal

Kim Dickens, Bill Pullman

SWEPT FROM THE SEA

(TRISTAR) Producers, Polly Tapson, Charles Steel, Beeban Kidron; Director, Beeban Kidron; Screenplay, Tim Willocks; Based on the short story Amy Foster by Joseph Conrad; Photography, Dick Pope; Designer, Simon Holland; Costumes, Caroline Harris; Associate Producer, Devon Dickson; Executive Producers, Garth Thomas, Tim Willocks; Editors, Alex Mackie, Andrew Mondshein; Music, John Barry; a Phoenix Pictures presentation with the participation of The Greenlight Fund, of a Tapson Steel Films production; U.S.-British; Dolby; Super 35 Widescreen; Technicolor; Rated PG-13; 114 minutes; January release

CAST

Amy Foster	Rachel Weisz
Yanko	Vincent Perez
Dr. James Kennedy	Ian McKellen
Miss Swaffer	Kathy Bates
Mr. Swaffer	Joss Ackland
Mr. Smith	Tony Haygarth
Mrs. Smith	Fiona Victory
Isaac Foster	Tom Bell
Mary Foster	Zoë Wanamaker
Mr. Willcox	William Scott Masson
Mrs. Willcox	Eve Matheson
Jack Vincent	Dave Hill
Canon Van Stone	J.G.R. Ashton-Griffiths
Thackery	Matthew Scurfield
Widow Cree	Margery Withers

and Janine Duvitski (Mrs. Finn), Willie Ross (Preble), Janet Henfry (Mrs. Rigby), Paul Whitby (Stefan), Bob Smith (Nikolas), Angela Morant (Iryna), Gerardo Silano (Brother Bodan), Neil Rutherford (Brother Peter), Sandra Huggett (Brother Bodan's Wife), Frederique Feder (Peter's Wife), Ellis Fernandez (Amy's Son, Stefan)

A Ukranian adventurer, washed up on the shores of the Cornish coast after his ship capsizes, finds himself beginning a relationship with an outcast servant girl, much to the displeasure of the narrow-minded villagers.

©Phoenix Pictures

Vincent Perez, Rachel Weisz

Chow Yun-Fat, Mira Sorvino

©Columbia Pictures Industries, Inc.

THE REPLACEMENT KILLERS

(COLUMBIA) Producers, Brad Grey, Bernie Brillstein; Executive Producers, John Woo, Terence Chang, Christopher Godsick, Matthew Baer; Director, Antoine Fuqua; Screenplay, Ken Sanzel; Co-Producer, Michael McDonnell; Photography, Peter Lyons Collister; Designer, Naomi Shohan; Editor, Jay Cassidy; Music, Harry Gregson-Williams; Costumes, Arianne Phillips; Casting, Wendy Kurtzman; a Bernie Brillstein/Brad Grey production, a WCG Entertainment production; Dolby; Super 35 Widescreen; Technicolor; Rated R; 86 minutes; February release

CAST

John Lee	Chow Yun-Fat
Meg Coburn	Mira Sorvino
Stan "Zeedo" Zedkov	Michael Rooker
Terence Wei	Kenneth Tsang
Michael Kogan	Jurgen Prochnow
Ryker	Til Schweiger
Collins	Danny Trejo
Loco	Clifton Gonzalez Gonzalez
Hunt	Carlos Gomez
Rawlins	Frank Medrano
Lam	Leo Lee
Pryce	Patrick Kilpatrick
Alan Chan	Randall Duk Kim
Stevie	Andrew J. Marton
Sara	Sydney Coberly
Peter Wei	Yau-Gene Chan
Romero	Carlos Leon

and Nicki Micheaux (Technician), Max Daniels (Smuggler), James Wing Woo (Priest), Albert Wong (Old Man), Chris Doyle, Joey Bucaro III, Bob Apisa , Norm F. Compton (Thugs), Cle Shaheed Sloan, Paul Higgins (Bangers), James Lew (Bodyguard), Thomas Rosales Jr., Eddie Perez, Mario Roberts, Jimmy Ortega, Richard Duran (Gangsters)

When professional killer John Lee refuses to carry out a killing ordered by his underworld boss, he enlists the aide of passport forger Meg Coburn to help him prevent a retaliatory assassination of his family in Shanghai.

BLUES BROTHERS 2000

(**UNIVERSAL**) Producers, John Landis, Dan Aykroyd, Leslie Belzberg; Director, John Landis; Screenplay, Dan Aykroyd, John Landis, based on their screenplay and characters for The Blues Brothers; Photography, David Herrington; Designer, Bill Brodie; Editor, Dale Beldin; Associate Producer, Grace Gilroy; Costumes, Deborah Nadoolman; Music, Paul Shaffer; Choreographer, Barry Lather; Casting, Ross Clydesdale, Joanna Colbert; a Landis/Belzberg Film; DTS Digital Stereo; Deluxe color; Rated PG-13; 123 minutes; February release

CAST

Elwood Blues .... Dan Aykroyd
Mighty Mack McTeer .... John Goodman
Cabel Chamberlain .... Joe Morton
Buster .... J. Evan Bonifant
The Blues Brothers Band:
  Lead Guitar .... Steve "The Colonel" Cropper
  Bass Guitar .... Donald "Duck" Dunn
  Keyboards .... Murphy Dunne
  Drums .... Willie "Too Big" Hall
  Saxophone .... Lou "Blue Lou" Marini
  Trombone .... Tom "Bones" Malone
  Guitar .... Matt "Guitar" Murphy
  Trumpet .... Alan "Mr. Fabulous" Rubin
Mrs. Murphy .... Aretha Franklin
Reverend Cleophus James .... James Brown
Malvern Gasperson .... B.B. King
Lt. Elizondo .... Nia Peeples
Mother Mary Stigmata .... Kathleen Freeman
Reverend Morris .... Sam Moore
Mr. Pickett .... Wilson Pickett
Prison Warden .... Frank Oz
Ed .... Eddie Floyd
Ed's Love Exchange Janitor .... Jonny Lang
Maury Sline .... Steve Lawrence
Themselves .... Junior Wells, Lonnie Brooks
Blues Traveler (Motel Band) .... John Popper, Brendan Hill, Chan Kinchla, Bob Sheehan
Bob .... Jeff Morris
Matara .... Shann Johnson
Queen Mousette .... Erykah Badu
Robertson .... Darrell Hammond
The Tent Revival Choir .... Sharon Riley & Faith Corale
and Jeff Baxter, Gary U.S. Bonds, Eric Clapton, Clarence Clemons, Jack De Johnette, Bo Diddley, Jon Faddis, Isaac Hayes, Dr. John, Tommy "Pipes" McDonnell, Charlie Musselwhite, Billy Preston, Lou Rawls, Joshua Redman, Koko Taylor, Travis Tritt, Jimmie Vaughan, Grover Washington Jr., Willie Weeks, Steve Winwood (The Louisiana Gator Boys), Walter Levine (Same Guard), Tom Davis (Prison Clerk), Gloria Slade (Police Receptionist), Jennifer Irwin, Liz Gordon (Nuns), Leon Pendarvis, Steve Potts, Birch "Crimson Slide" Johnson, Demo Cates (Stripster Band), Michael Bodnar, Slavko Hochevar, Wally High, Richard Kruk, John Lyons (Russian Thugs), Igor Syyouk (Tstetsevkaya), Victor Pedtrchenko (Ivan), Esther Ridgeway, Gloria Ridgeway, Gracie Ridgeway (Mrs. Murphy's Friends), George Sperdakos (Priest), Jillian Hart (Phone Operator), Susan Davy, Soo Garay (Indiana State Troopers), Jeff Morris (Bob), Howard Hoover (F.B.I.), Chris Marshall (Skinhead), Nicholas Rice (County Fair Announcer), Max Landis (Ghostrider), Sandi Ross (Church Woman), Danny Ray (Deacon), Prakash John, Fred Keeler, Shiraz Tayyeb, John T. Davis (Tent Revival Band), Candide Franklin (Ton Tons Macoutes), Paul Shaffer (Marco), Patrick Patterson (Sheriff)

©Universal Studios Inc.

Elwood Blues, fresh out of prison, decides to recruit musicians to revive the Blues Brothers Band and winds up with both the Russian mafia and the police on his trail. Sequel to the 1980 Universal release The Blues Brothers *with Dan Aykroyd, Aretha Franklin, James Brown, Kathleen Freeman, Frank Oz, and Steve Lawrence reprising their roles.*

John Goodman, Dan Aykroyd, J. Evan Bonifant, Joe Morton

Paul Shaffer, Erykah Badu

Jonny Lang, Dan Aykroyd

Drew Barrymore, Christine Taylor

THE WEDDING SINGER

(NEW LINE CINEMA) Producers, Robert Simonds, Jack Giarraputo; Executive Producers, Brad Grey, Sandy Wernick; Director, Frank Coraci; Screenplay, Tim Herlihy; Co-Executive Producers, Brian Witten, Richard Brener; Co-Producer, Ira Shuman; Photography, Tim Suhrstedt; Designer, Perry Andelin Blake; Editor, Tom Lewis; Costumes, Mona May; Music, Teddy Castellucci; Casting, Roger Mussenden; a Robert Simonds/Brad Grey production; Dolby; CFI Color; Rated PG-13; 96 minutes; February release

CAST

Robbie Hart	Adam Sandler
Julia	Drew Barrymore
Holly	Christine Taylor
Sammy	Allen Covert
Glenn	Matthew Glave
Rosie	Ellen Albertini Dow
Linda	Angela Featherstone
George	Alexis Arquette
Angie	Christina Pickles
Kate	Jodi Thelen
Andy	Frank Sivero
Tyler	Patrick McTavish
Petey	Gemini Barnett
Robbie Hart Band	Teddy Castellucci, Randy Razz, John Vana
Himself	Billy Idol
Mr. Simms	Kevin Nealon
Joyce, Flight Attendant	Marnie Schneider
Old Man in Bar	Carmen Filpi
Andre	Robert Smigel
Jimmie Moore	Jon Lovitz
David	Steve Buscemi
Drunk Teenager	Todd Hurst
David's Friend	Peter Dante
Mrs. Harold Veltri	Phyllis Alia
Mr. Harold Veltri	Paul Thiele
Father of Groom	Jack Nisbet
Grandma Molly	Sally Pierce
Justice of the Peace	Earl Carroll

and Jenna Byrne (Cindy Castellucci), Jason Cottle (Scott Castellucci), Mark Lonow (Father of the Bride), Bill Elmer (Fat Man), Jackie R. Challet (Sideburns Lady), Jimmy Karz (Studliest Kid at Bar Mitzvah), Al Hopson (Grandpa at Bar Mitzvah), Michael Shuman (Bar Mitzvah Boy), Steven Brill (Glenn's Buddy), Angela Payton (Faye), Mike Thompson, Michael Jay, John Sawaski, Chris Alan, Kimberly Schwartz, Sanetta Y. Gipson (Jimmy Moore's Band), Timothy P. Herlihy (Rudy the Bartender), Matthew Kimble (Drunk at Bar), Sid Newman (Frank), Mark Beltzman (Vegas Air Ticket Agent), Andrew Shaifer, Shanna Moakler (Flight Attendants), Maree Cheatham (Nice Lady on Plane), Al Burke (Large Billy Idol Fan), Bob Hackl, Gabe Veltri, Josh Oppenheimer (David's Band)

Alexis Arquette, Adam Sandler

Wedding singer Robbie Hart, recently dumped by his fiancee, realizes that he is in love with waitress Julia who is already betrothed to a rich yuppie.

©New Line Cinema, Inc.

Allen Covert, Adam Sandler, Drew Barrymore

Ellen Albertini Dow

Brendan Sexton III, Isidra Vega

HURRICANE STREETS

(UNITED ARTISTS) Producers, Galt Niederhoffer, Gill Holland, Morgan J. Freeman; Executive Producers, L.M. Kit Carson, Cynthia Hargrave; Co-Producer, Nadia Leonelli; Director/Screenplay, Morgan J. Freeman; Photography, Enrique Chediak; Designer, Petra Barchi; Editor, Sabine Hoffmann; Music, Theodore Shapiro; Costumes, Nancy Brous; Casting, Susan Shopmaker; a (giv'en) production; Distributed by MGM Distribution; Ultra-Stereo; Technicolor; Rated R; 89 minutes; February release

CAST

Marcus Frederick...Brendan Sexton III
Paco ....Shawn Elliott
Chip ....David Roland Frank
Harold..Antoine McLean
Lucy...Lynn Cohen
Ashley ....Heather Matarazzo
Justin ....Damian Corrente
Mack ....L.M. Kit Carson
Kramer ....Jose Zuniga
Benny ....Carlo Alban
Louis ....Mtume Gant
Joanna...Edie Falco
Gloria ....Socorro Santiago
Shane...David Moscow
Melena ....Isidra Vega
Punk ....Adrian Grenier
Little Kid ....Andrew Ko
Duane ....Terry Alexander
Lee ....Jin S. Kim
Detectives..Preston B. Handy, Terry Sturiano
Social Worker ....Anna Basoli
Hank ....Richard Petrocelli
Police Man..Leslie Body

Fifteen-year-old Marcus, growing up in New York's Lower East Side, sees a ray of hope in his dead-end life when he falls in love with Melena, despite the interference of her disapproving father.

Brendan Sexton III, David Roland Frank

Brendan Sexton III, Jose Zuniga

Carlo Alban, Antoine McLean, David Roland Frank, Brendan Sexton III, Mtume Gant, Shawn Elliott (on floor)

PALMETTO

(COLUMBIA) Producer, Matthias Wendlandt; Executive Producers, Al Corley, Bart Rosenblatt, Eugene Musso; Director, Volker Schlondorff; Screenplay, E. Max Frye; Based on the novel Just Another Sucker by James Hadley Chase; Photography, Thomas Kloss; Designer, Claire Jenora Bowin; Editor, Peter Przygodda; Costumes, Terry Dresbach; Music, Klaus Doldinger; Casting, Dianne Crittenden; a Castle Rock Entertainment presentation of a Rialto Film production; Dolby; Super 35 Widescreen; Technicolor; Rated R; 113 minutes; February release

CAST

Harry Barber	Woody Harrelson
Mrs. Donnelly aka Rhea Malroux	Elisabeth Shue
Nina	Gina Gershon
Felix Malroux	Rolf Hoppe
Donnelly	Michael Rapaport
Odette	Chloe Sevigny
John Renick	Tom Wright
Miles Meadows	Marc Macaulay
Lawyer	Joe Hickey
Judge	Ralph Wilcox
Bartender	Peter Paul Deleo
Ed	Mal Jones
Driver	Salvador Levy
Billy Holden	Richard Booker
Alda	Mikki McKeever

and Bill Larson (Parking Lot Man), Tim W. Terry (Prison Guard), Jim Janey (Policeman), Brett Rice (Crash Site Cop), Vince Cecere (Tow Truck Driver), Don Bright (Crime Scene Cop), Ernie Garrett (TV Anchor), Karin J. Ivester (Forensic Detective), Marcus Thomas (Courtroom Photographer), Douglas J. Mann II (Courtroom Reporter), Jim Coleman, Victoria Tan (Reporters), Stephen McGruder (Convict), Annabelle Weenick (Ted), Wil Kilmer (Bungalow Cop), Ginger King (The Real Rhea), Corey Blevins (Motel Clerk), Duncan Chamberlain (Gallery Maitre D), Peggy Sheffield (Customer), Karen Fraction (Plainclothes Cop), Gary Lowe, Kenneth L. Bright, Jay Ridings, Graig Himes, James Gaunt (Boathouse Cops)

Ex-con Harry Barber returns to the Florida town of Palmetto where a mysterious woman offers to split some cash with him if he will help her scam her stingy husband out of $500,000.

Woody Harrelson, Elisabeth Shue, Michael Rapaport

Gina Gershon, Woody Harrelson

©Castle Entertainment

SPHERE

(WARNER BROS.) Producers, Barry Levinson, Michael Crichton, Andrew Wald; Director, Barry Levinson; Screenplay, Stephen Hauser, Paul Attanasio; Adaptation, Kurt Wimmer; Based on the novel by Michael Crichton; Executive Producer, Peter Giuliano; Photography, Adam Greenberg; Designer, Norman Reynolds; Editor, Stu Linder; Music, Elliot Goldenthal; Costumes, Gloria Gresham; Visual Effects Supervisor, Jeffrey A. Okun; Casting, Ellen Chenoweth; a Baltimore Pictures/Constant c Production in association with Punch Productions, Inc.; Dolby; Super 35 Widescreen; Color; Rated PG-13; 133 minutes; February release

CAST

Dr. Norman Goodman	Dustin Hoffman
Beth Halperin	Sharon Stone
Harry Adams	Samuel L. Jackson
Barnes	Peter Coyote
Ted Fielding	Liev Schreiber
Jane Edmunds	Marga Gomez
Helicopter Pilot	Huey Lewis
Seaman	Bernard Hocke
OSSA Instructor	James Pickens, Jr.
OSSA Officials	Michael Keys Hall, Ralph Tabakin

A trio of scientists assemble to investigate a mysterious spacecraft that appears to have being sitting, untouched, on the ocean floor for nearly 300 years.

©Warner Bros.

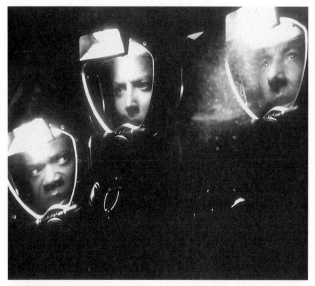

Samuel L. Jackson, Sharon Stone, Dustin Hoffman

SENSELESS

(DIMENSION) Producer, David Hoberman; Executive Producers, Bob Weinstein, Harvey Weinstein, Cary Granat, Eric L. Gold, Don Carmody; Director, Penelope Spheeris; Screenplay, Greg Erb, Craig Mazin; Co-Executive Producers, Peter Safran, Albert Beveridge; Photography, Daryn Okada; Designer, Peter Jamison; Editor, Ross Albert; Music, Yello; Costumes, Betsy Cox; Casting, Junie Lowry Johnson; a Mandeville Films, Gold/Miller production; Distributed by Miramax Films; Dolby; Color; Rated R; 88 minutes; February release

CAST

Darryl Witherspoon	Marlon Wayans
Scott Thorpe	David Spade
Tim LaFlour	Matthew Lillard
Randall Tyson	Rip Torn
Janice	Tamara Taylor
Dr. Wheedon	Brad Dourif
Robert Bellweather	Richard McGonagle
Denise Witherspoon	Esther Scott
Fertility Clinic Attendant	Debra Jo Rupp
Wig Shop Owner	Mark Christopher Lawrence
Economics Professor	John Ingle
Coach Brandau	Ernie Lively
Nurse Alvarez	Jennette Goldstein
Lorraine	Kenya Moore
Zestfully Clean Woman	Constance Zimmer
Dean Barlow	Ken Lerner
Waiters	Patrick O'Neill, Ross Rayburn
Banquet Guest	Jeanne Diehl
Pastry Chef	Jennie Vaughn
Tonya	Cee-Cee Harshaw
Chet	Michael Dean Ester
Steve	Greg Grunberg

and Mike Butters (Hockey Referee), Orlando Brown (Brandon Witherspoon), Angelique Parry (April Witherspoon), Tino Williams (Darius Witherspoon), Brenden Richard Jefferson (Lyndell Witherspoon), Greg Wilson (Monte Card Shark), Jeff Garlin (Arlo Vickers,) Patrick Ewing (Himself), Michelle Brookhurst, Alexander Enberg, Manu Intiraymi (Drug Intervention Students), Michael Weatherred (Kern), Vicellous Shannon (Carter), Kevin Cooney (Mr. Thorpe), Ivar Brogger (Economics Coach), Cyia Batten (Punk Waitress), Jack Shearer (Vice Chair Federal Reserve), Joe Basile (Security Guard), Darrel Heath (Shady Guy), Thom Gossom, Jr. (Clothing Salesman), Sierra Pasteur (Smythe-Bates Receptionist), Len Costenza (Board Member), Jeremy Paul Meldrum, Kevin Downes, Branden Morgan (Smythe-Bates Finalists), Sherman Hemsley (Smythe-Bates Doorman)

Hoping to win the cash prize in a college competition, overworked student Darryl Witherspoon agrees to be the guinea pig for a scientific experiment that will heighten his every bodily sensation.

Richard McGonagle, Rip Torn, David Spade, Marlon Wayans

Brad Dourif, Marlon Wayans

Tamara Taylor, Marlon Wayans

©Dimension Films

MOON OVER BROADWAY

(ARTISTIC LICENSE) Producers, Fazer Pennebaker, Wendy Ettinger; Directors/Editors, D.A. Pennebaker, Chris Hegedus; Photography, D.A. Pennebaker, Nick Doob, James Desmond; Color; Not rated; 92 minutes; February release. A behind-the-scenes look at the making of the 1995 Broadway production Moon Over Buffalo by Ken Ludwig, featuring Carol Burnett, Philip Bosco, Ken Ludwig, Tom Moore, Elizabeth Williams, Rocco Landesman, Heidi Ettinger, Jane Connell, Randy Graff, Andy Taylor, Kate Miller, Dennis Ryan, James Valentine, Bob Mackie, Dom DeLuise, Bernadette Peters, Carroll O'Connor, Matthew Broderick.

Philip Bosco, Carol Burnett

DANGEROUS BEAUTY

(WARNER BROS.) Producer, Marshall Herskovitz, Edward Zwick, Arnon Milchan, Sarah Caplan; Executive Producers, Michael Nathanson, Stephen Randall; Director, Marshall Herskovitz; Screenplay, Jeannine Dominy; Based on the biography The Honest Courtesan by Margaret Rosenthal; Photography, Bojan Bazelli; Designer, Norman Garwood; Editors, Steven Rosenblum, Arthur Coburn; Costumes, Gabriella Pescucci; Music, George Fenton; Casting, Mindy Marin, Wendy Kurtzman, Mary Selway; a Regency Enterprises presentation of an Arnon Milchan/Bedford Falls production; Dolby; Super 35 Widescreen; Technicolor; Rated R; 114 minutes; February release

CAST

Veronica Franco	Catherine McCormack
Marco Venier	Rufus Sewell
Maffio Venier	Oliver Platt
Beatrice Venier	Moira Kelly
Giulia De Lezze	Naomi Watts
Domenico Venier	Fred Ward
Paola Franco	Jacqueline Bisset
Pietro Venier	Jeroen Krabbé
Laura Venier	Joanna Cassidy
Livia	Melina Kanakaredes
Serafino Franco	Daniel LaPaine
Elena Franco	Justine Miceli
King Henry	Jake Weber
Minister Ramberti	Simon Dutton
Francesco Martenengo	Grant Russell
The Doge	Peter Eyre

and Carla Cassola (Caterina), Gianny Musy (Joseph), Michael Culkin (Bishop De La Torre), Ralph Riach (Lorenzo Gritti), Charlotte Randle (Francesca), Alberto Rossatti (Andrea Tron), Anna Sozzani (Marina), Luis Moltena (Giacomo Baballi), Tim McMullan, Richard O'Callaghan (Zealots), Lenore Lohman, Maud Bonanni, Gaia Zoppi (Venetian Wives), Roberto Corbiletto (Tailor), Annelie Harryson (Fanatic Woman), David Gant (Bolognetti), Daniele Ciampi (Naked Workman), Elena Mita, Federico Mita (Elena's Children), Francesca Lucidi, Simona Nobili, Lena Guthorsen, Valentina Ardeatini, Tiziana Della Spina, Anna Maria Minati, Ilaria De Vincenzis, Cristina Rinaldi, Garmy Sall, Flaminia Fegarotti, Federica Federici, Angela Camuso, Patrizia Leonet, Elide Marigliani, Natascia Pastorello, Barbara Di Dio, Fulvia Lorenzetti, Olfa Ben Romdane, Laura Tedesco, Emy Kay (Courtesans)

In 16th-Century Venice, Veronica Franco, realizing that her low station in life will never allow her to marry her lover Marco, decides to become a courtesan, giving her power, education and stature in society.

Jason Lee, Mili Avital, David Schwimmer

©Universal Studios Inc.

Catherine McCormack, Moira Kelly

Catherine McCormack, Rufus Sewell

©Monarchy Enterprises / Regency Entertainment

KISSING A FOOL

(UNIVERSAL) Producers, Tag Mendillo, Andrew Form, Rick Lashbrook; Executive Producers, David Schwimmer, Stephen Levinson; Director, Doug Ellin; Screenplay, James Frey, Doug Ellin; Story, James Frey; Photography, Thomas Del Ruth; Designer, Charles Breen; Editor, David Finfer; Music, Joseph Vitarelli; Casting, Ferne Cassel; a Tag Mendillo/Andrew Form production, presented in association with R.L. Entertainment and Largo Entertaiment; Dolby; Deluxe color; Rated R; 93 minutes; February release

CAST

Max Abbitt	David Schwimmer
Jay Murphy	Jason Lee
Samantha Andrews	Mili Avital
Linda	Bonnie Hunt
Natasha	Vanessa Angel
Dara	Kari Wuhrer
Cliff Randal	Frank Medrano
Vicki Pelam	Bitty Schram
Andrea	Judy Greer
Priest	Ron Beattie
Bartender/Springer Guest	Doug Ellin
Wedding Guest at Bar/Springer Guest	Tag Mendillo

and Justine Bentley (Beautiful Woman at Bar), Liza Cruzat, Jessica Mills (Dara's Friends), Sammy Sosa, Jerry Springer (Themselves), Mike Squire (Spanish Man in Bed), Marco Siviero (French Man in Bed), Steve Seagren (Heckler), Philip R. Smith (Fan on the Street), Jayson Fate (Rudolpho), Ross Bon (Blue Kings Lead Singer), Antimo Fiore (Tony)

Womanizing sportscaster Max Abbitt, worried about committing to marriage with Samantha Andrews, asks his best friend Jay to test her fidelity by trying to seduce her.

Rufus Sewell

William Hurt

DARK CITY

(NEW LINE CINEMA) Producers, Andrew Mason, Alex Proyas; Executive Producers, Michael De Luca, Brian Witten; Director/Story, Alex Proyas; Screenplay, Alex Proyas, Lem Dobbs, David S. Goyer; Line Producer, Barbara Gibbs; Photography, Dariusz Wolski; Designer, Patrick Tatopoulos; Designer, George Liddle; Editor, Dov Hoenig; Costumes, Liz Keogh; Music, Trevor Jones; Visual Effects Supervisors & Producers, Mara Bryan, Arthur Windus, Andrew Mason; Casting, Valerie McCaffrey, Shauna Wolifson, Vanessa Pereira; a Mystery Clock production; Dolby; Super 35 Widescreen; Deluxe color; Rated R; 101 minutes; February release

Richard O'Brien

CAST

John Murdoch	Rufus Sewell
Inspector Frank Bumstead	William Hurt
Dr. Daniel Schreber	Kiefer Sutherland
Emma Murdoch	Jennifer Connelly
Mr. Hand	Richard O'Brien
Mr. Book	Ian Richardson
Mr. Wall	Bruce Spence
Walenski	Colin Friels
Karl Harris	John Bluthal
Husselbeck	Mitchell Butel
May	Mellisa George
Stromboli	Frank Gallacher
Hotel Manager/Vendor	Ritchie Singer
Taxi Driver	Justin Monjo
Mr. Rain	Nicholas Bell
Mr. Sleep	Satya Gumbert
Mr. Quick	Frederick Miragliotta

and Peter Sommerfeld, Timothy Jones, Jeanette Cronin (Strangers), Paul Livingston, Michael Lake (Assistant Strangers), David Wenham (Schreber's Assistant), Alan Cinis, Bill Highfield (Automat Cops), Terry Bader (Mr. Goodwin), Rosemary Traynor (Mrs. Goodwin), Edward Grant II (Hotel Manager), Maureen O'Shaughnessy (Kate Walenski), Deobie Oparei (Train Passenger), Marcus Johnson (Station Master), Doug Scroope (Desk Sergeant), Cinzia Coassin (Waitress), Tyson McCarthy (Murdoch—Age 10), Luke Styles (Murdoch—Teenager), Anthony Kierann (Murdoch's Father), Laura Keneally (Murdoch's Mother), Natalie Bollard (Naked Woman), Eliot Paton (Matthew Goodwin), Naomi Van Der Velden (Jane Goodwin), Peter Callan (Taxi Driver), Mark Hedges (Emma's Lover), Darren Gilshenan (Fingerprint Cop), Ray Rizzo (Policeman), Bill Rutherford (Police Officer), Marin Mimica (Hotel Lobby Cop), Tony Mosley, Glenford O. Richards, Stanley Steer, Greg Tell (Four Piece Band), William Upjohn (Forensic Cop), Avril Wynne (Telephone Booth Woman)

Kiefer Sutherland

John Murdoch awakens to discover that he is wanted for murder but finds that almost all of his memories have vanished. He discovers that the mystery lies with a weird underground group called The Strangers who have the ability to stop time and alter physical reality.

Matthew Modine, Catherine Keener

©Paramount Pictures

THE REAL BLONDE

(PARAMOUNT) Producers, Marcus Viscidi, Tom Rosenberg; Executive Producers, Sigurjon Sighvatsson, Ted Tannebaum, Terry McKay; Director/Screenplay, Tom DiCillo; Photography, Frank Prinzi; Designer, Christopher Nowak; Editors, Camilla Toniolo, Keiko Deguchi; Costumes, Jennifer von Mayrhauser; Music, Jim Farmer; Co-Producer, Meredith Zamsky; Casting, Avy Kaufman; a Lakeshore Entertainment presentation of a Marcus Viscidi production; Dolby; Deluxe color; Rated R; 107 minutes; February release

CAST

Joe	Matthew Modine
Mary	Catherine Keener
Kelly	Daryl Hannah
Bob	Maxwell Caulfield
Tina	Elizabeth Berkley
Blair	Marlo Thomas
Sahara	Bridgette Wilson
Dr. Leuter	Buck Henry
Ernst	Christopher Lloyd
Dee Dee Taylor	Kathleen Turner
Doug	Denis Leary
Wilma	Beatrice Winde
Chang	Schecter Lee
Harassing Man	John Tormey
Blair's Assistant	Wayne Parent
Biker Boy Pete	Peter Rex
Biker Boy Ken	Kendall Knights
Kiki	Daniela Olivieri
Rubio	Bronson Picket
Javier	Arturo Fresolone
Dirty Old Man	Ray Trail
Porno Clerk	Joe D'Angerio
Playful Waiter	Kedar Brown
Alex	David Thornton
Raina	Alexandra Wentworth

and Sheila Hewlett (Waitress in Restaurant), Timm Zemanek (Man in Restaurant), Joan Heney (Wife in Restaurant), Jonathan Wilson (Young Man in Restaurant), Deborah Swanson (Young Woman in Restaurant), Moynan King, Gloria Slade, Kathryn Haggis, Dawn Roach (Biker Chicks), Debra McGrath (Cis), Tony Hendra (Soap Director), Jim Fyfe (Roy), Sean Orr (Stagehand), Tom Harvey (Whipped Cream Man), Nahanni Johnstone (Young Woman), Alex Appel (Sheila), Djanet Sears (Chantal), Steve Buscemi (Nick), Dave Chappelle (Zee), Landy Cannon (Beach Boy), Katie Griffin (Empty V Interviewer), Brian Frank (Chet), Vincent Laresca (Trey), Missy Yager (Lisa), Karen Woolridge (Nadia), Peter Keleghan (Successful Actor), Daniel Von Bargen (Devon), Colin Mocherie (Renny)

Joe, a struggling actor-waiter, tries to maintain his integrity while unsuccessfully searching for work as an actor. Meanwhile, fellow actor-waiter Bob obsessess over his quest to find a genuine "blonde" in an increasingly phoney world.

Christopher Lloyd, Matthew Modine

Elizabeth Berkley, Matthew Modine

Maxwell Caulfield, Daryl Hannah

KRIPPENDORF'S TRIBE

(TOUCHSTONE) Producer, Larry Brezner; Executive Producers, Whitney Green, Ross Canter; Director, Todd Holland; Screenplay, Charlie Peters; Based upon the book by Frank Parkin; Photography, Dean Cundey; Designer, Scott Chambliss; Editor, Jon Poll; Costumes, Isis Mussenden; Music, Bruce Broughton; Titles, Pablo Ferro; Special Tribal Makeup, David L. Anderson; Casting, Jackie Burch; a Morra-Brezner-Steinberg-Tenenbaum/Dreyfuss-James production; Distributed by Buena Vista Pictures; Dolby; Technicolor; Rated PG-13; 94 minutes; February release

CAST

James Krippendorf	Richard Dreyfuss
Veronica Micelli	Jenna Elfman
Shelly Krippendorf	Natasha Lyonne
Mickey Krippendorf	Gregory Smith
Edmund Krippendorf	Carl Michael Linder
Young Edmund	Jacob Handy, Zachary Handy
Ruth Allen	Lily Tomlin
Gerald Adams	Stephen Root
President Porter	Doris Belack
Simon Alonso	Julio Oscar Mechoso
Lori Hayward	Siobhan Fallon
Gladys Schmades	Amzie Strickland
Dr. Harvey	Phil Leeds
Edith Proxmire	Frances Bay
Mrs. O'Brien	Susan Ruttan
Jennifer Krippendorf	Barbara Williams
Irene	Elaine Stritch
Gordon	Tom Poston
Sulukim	Zakes Mokae
Henry Spivey	David Ogden Stiers

and Sandy Martin (Nurse), Lance Kinsey (Principal Reese), Mila Kunis (Abbey Tournquist), Robin Karfo (Mrs. Tournquist), Tim Halligan (Mr. Tournquist), Peter Tilden (Larry Swift), Shashawnee Hall (Mabu), Timothy Wells (Ruth's Guide), Kari Leigh Floyd (Party Guest), Michael Steve Jones (Alcove Man), Ian Busch (Flagpole Boy), Grace Lee, Todd Cattell (College Students), Chris Duque (Outpost Man), Valerie Reid (Divorced Woman), Rachel Winfree, Suanne Spoke, Catherine Paolone (Lecture Women), Bill Rosier, Robb Derringer (TV Store Customers), Laura Cayouette (TV Studio Woman), China Brezner (Elevator Teen), Bruce Jarchow (Andrews), Wendy Worthington (Secretary)

Anthropologist James Krippendorf, living off grant money to study an undiscovered New Guinea tribe, realizes he must come up with documentation for his upcoming lecture and fakes it by filming his own family dressed in primitive makeup.

Coolio, Eric Idle, Chuck D

©Cinergi Pictures

Jenna Elfman, Richard Dreyfuss, Peter Tilden

©Touchstone Pictures

AN ALAN SMITHEE FILM: BURN HOLLYWOOD BURN

(HOLLYWOOD PICTURES) Producer, Ben Myron; Executive Producer, Andrew G. Vajna; Director, Alan Smithee (Arthur Hiller); Screenplay, Joe Eszterhas; Co-Producer, Fred Caruso; Associate Producer, Michael Sloan; Photography, Reynaldo Villalobos; Designer, David L. Snyder; Editors, Marcus Manton, Jim Langlois; Costumes, Laura Cunningham-Bauer; Music, Chuck D and Gary G-Wiz; Graffiti Art, In Creative Unity; Casting, Nancy Foy; an Andrew J. Vajna presentation in association with Jose Eszterhas of a Cinergi production; Distributed by Buena Vista Pictures; Dolby; Technicolor; Rated R; 86 minutes; February release

CAST

James Edmunds	Ryan O'Neal
Dion Brothers	Coolio
Leon Brothers	Chuck D
Alan Smithee	Eric Idle
Jerry Glover	Richard Jeni
Michelle Rafferty	Leslie Stefanson
Ann Glover	Sandra Bernhard
Myrna Smithee	Cheri Lunghi
Sam Rizzo	Harvey Weinstein
Gary Samuels	Gavin Palone
Sister Il Lumumba	MC Lite
Stagger Lee	Marcello Thedford
Aloe Vera	Nicole Nagel
Bill Bardo	Stephen Tobolowsky
Wayne Jackson	Erik King
Themselves	Sylvester Stallone, Whoopi Goldberg, Jackie Chan

and Jim Piddock, Naomi Campbell (Attendants), Marianne Muellerleile (Sheila Caslin), Suli McCullough (S.L.A.), Dina Spybey (Allessandra), Robert Littman (Cousin Andrew), Doug Walker (Photographer), Robin Chivers & Robin Dugger (Bonnie N' Clyde), Leslie Segar (Big Lez), Duane Davis (Policeman), Hideo Kimura, Earl Kim Shiroma (Japanese Businessman), Jesse Rambis (Lakers Fan), Christopher Kelley (British Bartender), Robert Evans, Joe Eszterhas, Robert Shapiro, Naomi Eszterhas, Linnell Shapiro, Larry King, Grant Shapiro, Peter Bart, Brent Shapiro, Dominick Dunne, Shane Black, Billy Bob Thornton, Jeremy Baka, Billy Barty, Mario Machado, Norman Jewison, Lisa Canning, Victor Drai, Gary Franklin, Stanley Ralph Ross, John Corcoran, Alan Smith (Themselves)

When director Alan Smithee has his big budget movie "Trio" tampered with by the studio, he finds that he cannot have his name removed from the finished product since it happens to be the same name as the pseudonymn specified by the Directors Guild for any directors who doesn't want credit for his work. Ironically this movie's director, Arthur Hiller, had his name removed from the finished production, and thereby the credit goes to "Alan Smithee."

23

TWILIGHT

(PARAMOUNT) formerly *The Magic Hour*; Producers, Arlene Donovan, Scott Rudin; Director, Robert Benton; Screenplay, Robert Benton, Richard Russo; Photography, Piotr Sobocinski; Designer, David Gropman; Editor, Carol Littleton; Music, Elmer Bernstein; Costumes, Joseph G. Aulisi; Executive Producer, Michael Hausman; Casting, Ilene Starger; a Cinehaus production; Dolby; Deluxe color; Rated R; 96 minutes; March release

Paul Newman, James Garner

CAST

Harry Ross	Paul Newman
Catherine Ames	Susan Sarandon
Jack Ames	Gene Hackman
Mel Ames	Reese Witherspoon
Verna	Stockard Channing
Raymond Hope	James Garner
Reuben	Giancarlo Esposito
Jeff Willis	Liev Schreiber
Gloria Lamar	Margo Martindale
Captain Phil Egan	John Spencer
Lester Ivar	M. Emmet Walsh
Verna's Partner	Peter Gregory
Mexican Bartender	Rene Mujica
Young Cops	Jason Clarke, Neil Mather
Younger Cop	Patrick Y. Malone
Water Pistol Man	Lewis Arquette
Garvey's Bartender	Michael Brockman
Police Stenographer	April Grace
EMS Worker	Clint Howard
Paramedic	John J. Cappon
Crime Scene Detective	Ronald C. Sanchez
Interrogation Officer	Jack Wallace
Carl	Jeff Joy
Cop	Jonathan Scarfo

Retired investigator Harry Ross agrees to do a favor for friends Jack and Catherine Ames and finds himself involved in a murder that opens up past secrets.

©Paramount Pictures

Paul Newman, Stockard Channing

Paul Newman, Susan Sarandon

24

U.S. MARSHALS

(WARNER BROS.) Producers, Arnold Kopelson, Anne Kopelson; Executive Producers, Keith Barish, Roy Huggins; Co-Executive Producer, Wolfgang Glattes; Director, Stuart Baird; Screenplay, John Pogue; Based on characters created by Roy Huggins; Photography, Andrzej Bartkowiak; Designer, Maher Ahmad; Editor, Terry Rawlings; Co-Producer, Stephen Brown; Music, Jerry Goldsmith; Costumes, Louise Frogley; Visual Effects Supervisor, Peter Donen; Casting, Amanda Mackey Johnson, Cathy Sandrich; a Kopelson Entertainment/Keith Barish production; Dolby; Technicolor; Rated PG-13; 133 minutes; March release

CAST

Chief Deputy Marshal Samuel Gerard	Tommy Lee Jones
Sheridan	Wesley Snipes
John Royce	Robert Downey, Jr.
Deputy Marshal Cosmo Renfro	Joe Pantoliano
Biggs	Daniel Roebuck
Newman	Tom Wood
Cooper	Latanya Richardson
Marie	Irene Jacob
U.S. Marshal Walsh	Kate Nelligan
Lamb	Patrick Malahide
Barrows	Rick Snyder
Chen	Michael Paul Chan
Deputy Henry	Johnny Lee Davenport
Detective Kim	Donald Li
Deputy Jackson	Marc Vann
Distracted Driver	Michael Guido
Young Cop	Robert Mohler
Fireman	Richard Lexsee
Cop	Dado
Hospital Cashier	Karen Vaccaro
Desk Sergeant	David Kersnar
Greg Conroy	Tony Fitzpatrick
Mike Conroy	Don Gibb
Mama Conroy	Cynthia S. Baker

and Susan Hart (Greg's Girlfriend), Vaitiare Bandera (Stacia Vela), Don Herion (Detective Caldwell), Len Bajenski (Deputy Hollander), Matt DeCaro (Deputy Stern), Thomas Rosales, Jr. (727 Prisoner), James Sie (Ling), Christian Payton (727 Deputy #5), Steve King (727 Pilot), Tracy Letts (Sheriff Poe), Mark Morettini (Cop #1), Kent Reed (Trooper with Dogs), Ray Toler (Earl), Brenda Pickleman (Martha), Max Maxwell (Roadblock Trooper), Peter Burns (State Trooper Captain), Roy Hytower (Tracker), Ian Barford (Royce's Guide), Robert Kurcz (Kidnapped Man), Rose M. Abdoo (Donna), Lorenzo Clemons (Stark), Stephen A. Cinabro (Undercover Deputy), Clifford T. Frazier (Minister), Mindy Bell (Deputy Holt), Richard Thomsen (Doorman), Yasen Peyankov (Janitor), Meg Thalken (Saks Saleswoman), Lennox Brown (Man in Green Cap), Varen Black (Network Reporter), Ammar Daraiseh (Drugstore Clerk), Romanos Isaac (Ship's First Officer), Richard Pickren (Prosecutor), Lynn Wilde (Caldwell's Wife), Amy E. Jacobson (New York Reporter), Cliff Teinert (Swamp Tracker), Vince DeMentri, Louis Young, Ellen Hearn (Reporters), Janet Contursi (Chicago Nurse), George J. Hynek, Jr., Wendell Thomas (New York Paramedics), E. Glenn Ward, Jr., Marie Ware (Elderly Residents), Rick LeFevour, Jim Fierro (Deputies), Michael Braun (727 Co-Pilot), Perry D. Sullivan (727 Navigator), Terry G. Rochford (NTSB Agent), Tony Paris (Newman's Guide), Ed Fernandez, Richard Wilkie (Detectives), Rick Edwards (727 Deputy #7), Dale Chick Bernhardt (Royce's Guide), Tressana Alouane (Mike's Girlfriend), Ralph J. Lucci (Bartender), David A. Bales (Man in Taxi), Chris Bean (Bar Patron)

© Warner Bros.

U.S. Marshal Sam Gerard and government agent John Royce reluctantly team to capture a mysterious "assassin" who, while on the run, is trying to find out who framed him for a pair of murders in New York City. Sequel to the 1993 Warner Bros. film The Fugitive *with Tommy Lee Jones, Joe Pantoliano, Daniel Roebuck, and Tom Wood repeating their roles.*

Robert Downey Jr., Tommy Lee Jones

Wesley Snipes, Tommy Lee Jones

Tommy Lee Jones, Wesley Snipes

Jeff Bridges, Steve Buscemi, John Goodman

John Turturro

John Goodman

Jeff Bridges, Sam Elliott

THE BIG LEBOWSKI

(GRAMERCY) Producer, Ethan Coen; Executive Producers, Tim Bevan, Eric Fellner; Director, Joel Coen; Screenplay, Joel Coen, Ethan Coen; Line Producer, John Cameron; Photography, Roger Deakins; Designer, Rick Heinrichs; Costumes, Mary Zophres; Music, Carter Burwell; Editors, Roderick Jaynes, Tricia Cooke; Visual Effects Supervisor, Janek Sirrs; Choreographers, Bill and Jacqui Landrum; Casting, John Lyons; a PolyGram Filmed Entertainment presentation of a Working Title production; Dolby; Color; Rated R; 117 minutes; March release

Jeff Bridges, Julianne Moore

CAST

The Dude (Jeff Lebowski)	Jeff Bridges
Walter Sobchak	John Goodman
Maude Lebowski	Julianne Moore
Donny	Steve Buscemi
The Big Lebowski	David Huddleston
Brandt	Philip Seymour Hoffman
Bunny Lebowski	Tara Reid
Knox Harrington	David Thewlis
The Stranger	Sam Elliott
Jackie Treehorn	Ben Gazzara
Treehorn Thugs	Philip Moon, Mark Pellegrino
Nihilists	Peter Stormare, Flea, Torsten Voges
Smokey	Jimmie Dale Gilmore
Dude's Landlord	Jack Kehler
Jesus Quintana	John Turturro
Quintana's Partner	James G. Hoosier
Maude's Thugs	Carlos Leon, Terrance Burton
Older Cop	Richard Gant
Younger Cop	Christian Clemenson
Tony the Chauffeur	Dom Irrera
Lebowski's Chauffeur	Gerard L'Heureux
Coffee Shop Waitress	Lu Elrod
Auto Circus Cop	Michael Gomez
Gary the Bartender	Pete Siragusa

and Marshall Manesh (Doctor), Mary Bugin (Arthur Digby Sellers), Jesse Flanagan (Little Larry Sellers), Irene Olga Lopez (Pilar), Luis Colina (Corvette Owner), Leon Russom (Malibu Police Chief), Ajgie Kirkland (Cab Driver), Jon Polito (Private Snoop), Aimee Mann (Nihilist Woman), Jerry Haleva (Saddam), Jennifer Lamb (Pancacke Waitress), Warren David Keith (Funeral Director)

Jeff Bridges

Laid-back, burnt out Jeff Lebowski finds himself involved in a nightmare of extortion, embezzlement and danger when he is mistaken for a Pasadena millionaire whose daughter has been kidnapped.

© Gramercy Pictures

Jeff Bridges, John Goodman

Torsten Voges, Peter Stormare, Flea

HUSH

(TRISTAR) Producer, Douglas Wick; Director/Story, Jonathan Darby; Screenplay, Jonathan Darby, Jane Rusconi; Co-Producer, Ginny Nugent; Photography, Andrew Dunn; Designers, Thomas A. Walsh, Michael Johnston; Editors, Dan Rae, Lynzee Klingman, Robert Leighton; Costumes, Ann Roth; Music, Christopher Young; Casting, Heidi Levitt, Billy Hopkins; a Douglas Wick production; Dolby; Technicolor; Rated PG-13; 93 minutes; March release

CAST

Martha Baring	Jessica Lange
Helen	Gwyneth Paltrow
Jackson Baring	Johnathon Schaech
Alice Baring	Nina Foch
Lisa	Debi Mazar
Sister O'Shaughnessy	Kaiulani Lee
Gavin	David Thornton
Dr. Hill	Hal Holbrook
Hal Bentall	Richard Lineback
Clayton Richards	Richard Kohn
Georgina Richards	Faith Potts
Priest	Tom Story
Church Warden	Jolene Carroll
Usher	Jacob Press
Doctor	Joe Inscoe
Nurse	Catherine Shaffner
Paramedic	Lenny Steinline

and Rick Gray (Banker), Tom Holmes (Auctioneer), Owen Valentine (Official), Ricardo Miguel Young, Woody Robertson Jr. (Policemen), Charles Thomas Baxter (Racing Enthusiast), Jayne Hess (Nursing Home Nun), Sarah Elspas, Rebecca Elspas, Jacob Elspas (Helen's Baby)

Jackson Baring brings his new girlfriend Helen home for the holidays only to have the young woman scorned by his jealous and dangerously over-bearing mother.

Gwyneth Paltrow, Jessica Lange

Federico Luppi, Dan Rivera González

MEN WITH GUNS

(SONY PICTURES CLASSICS) Producers, R. Paul Miller, Maggie Renzi; Executive Producers, Jody Patton, Lou Gonda, John Sloss; Director/Screenplay/Editor, John Sayles; Photography, Slawomir Idziak; Designer, Felipe Fernández Del Paso; Costumes, Mayes C. Rubeo; Music, Mason Daring; Casting, Lizzie Curry Martinez; Co-Producer, Bertha Navarro; a Lexington Road Productions and Clear Blue Sky Productions in association with the Independent Film Channel and Anarchists' Convention presentation; a U.S. film in Spanish with subtitles; Dolby Stereo; Color; Rated R; 126 minutes; March release

CAST

Dr. Humberto Fuentes	Federico Luppi
Domingo, the Soldier	Damián Delgado
Conejo, the Boy	Dan Rivera González
Graciela, The Mute Girl	Tania Cruz
Padre Portillo, The Priest	Damián Alcázar
Andrew	Mandy Patinkin
Harriet	Kathryn Grody
Mother	Iguandili López
Daughter	Nandi Luna Ramírez
General	Rafael De Quevedo
Angela, Dr. Fuentes' Daughter	Carmen Madrid
Raúl, Angela's Fiance	Esteban Soberanes
Carlos, Dr. Fuentes' Son	Alejandro Springall
Rich Ladies	Maricruz Najera, Jacqueline Walters Voltaire
Bravo	Roberto Sosa
Cienfuegos	Iván Arango
Montoya	Lizzie Curry Martínez
Hidalgo	Luis Ramírez
De Soto	Humberto Romero
Echevarría	Gabriel Cosme
Arenas	Horacio Trujillo

and Efrine Elfaro, Pedro Hernández (Kokal Drivers), Dionisios (Salt Man), Loló Navarro (Blind Woman), Maggie Renzi, Shari Gray (Tourists by Pool), Paco Mauri (Captain), Gilma Tuyub Castillo (Mother with Baby), Armando Martínez Velásquez (Vendor), Luis Felipe Tovar (Barber), Fernando Medel (Barber's Client), David Villalpando, Raúl Sánchez (Gum People), Diego Méndez Guzmán (Moisés), Mariano López De La Cruz (Gonzalo), Antonio De La Torré López (Isidro), Ermenehildo Sáenz Guzmán (Sixto), Cristóbal Guzmán Mesa (Artemio), Domingo Pérez Sánchez (Junípero), Oscar García Ortega (Sergeant), Miguel Xocua (Modelo Boy), Guadalupe Xocua (Modelo Woman), Celeste Cornelio Sánchez (Raped Girl), Nazario Montiel, Francisco Váldez, José Alberto Acosta (Guerillas)

Dr. Fuentes, on the verge of retirement, journeys across his country to visit his student proteges only to find that they have been slain by unspecified "men with guns."

John Malkovich, Gerard Depardieu, Gabriel Byrne, Jeremy Irons

Leonardo DiCaprio, Gabriel Byrne, Edward Atterton

Leonardo DiCaprio

Leonardo DiCaprio, Judith Godreche

THE MAN IN THE IRON MASK

(UNITED ARTISTS) Producers, Randall Wallace, Russell Smith; Executive Producer, Alan Ladd, Jr.; Co-Producers, Paul Hitchcock, Rene Dupont; Director/Screenplay, Randall Wallace; Based upon the novel by Alexandre Dumas; Photography, Peter Suschitzky; Designer, Anthony Pratt; Editor, William Hoy; Costumes, James Acheson; Music, Nick Glennie-Smith; Casting, Amanda Mackey Johnson, Cathy Sandrich; Distributed by MGM Distribution Co.; DTS Stereo; Deluxe color; Rated PG-13; 132 minutes; March release

CAST

King Louis XIV/Phillippe............................Leonardo DiCaprio
Aramis ....Jeremy Irons
Athos ....John Malkovich
Porthos...Gerard Depardieu
D'Artagnan ....Gabriel Byrne
Queen Anne ....Anne Parillaud
Christine ....Judith Godreche
Lieutenant Andre ....Edward Atterton
Raoul ....Peter Sarsgaard
King's Advisors ....Hugh Laurie, David Lowe
Madame Rotund ....Brigitte Boucher
Assassin ....Matthew Jocelyn
Wench ....Karine Belly
King's Friend ....Emmanuel Guttierez
Ballroom Guard...................................Christian Erickson
Blond Musketeer...................................Francois Montagut
Peasant Boy ....Andrew Wallace
Serving Women ....Cecile Auclert, Sonia Backers
Customer ....Vincent Nemeth
Fortress Keeper.....................................Joe Sheridan
Fortress Head Guard ....Olivier Hemon
Bastille Gate Guard ....Michael Morris
Fortress Guard ....Emmanuel Patron
Ballroom Beauty...................................Leonor Varela
and Michael Hofland (Ruffian), Laura Fraser (Bedroom Beauty), Brigitte Auber (Queen Anne's Attendant), Jean-Pol Brissart (Monk)

The aging Musketeers reunite to free a mysterious prisoner from the Bastille and put him on the throne in place of the tyrannical King Louis XIV. Previous versions were filmed in 1928 (as The Iron Mask) with Douglas Fairbanks; 1939, with Louis Hayward; 1998, with Edward Albert.

PRIMARY COLORS

(**UNIVERSAL**) Producer/Director, Mike Nichols; Executive Producers, Neil Machlis, Jonathan D. Krane; Screenplay, Elaine May; Based on the novel by Anonymous (Joe Klein); Photography, Michael Ballhaus; Designer, Bo Welch; Editor, Arthur Schmidt; Music, Ry Cooder; Costumes, Ann Roth; Casting, Juliet Taylor, Ellen Lewis, Juel Bestrop; a Mutual Film Company presentation of an Icarus production; Dolby; Super 35 Widescreen; Deluxe color; Rated R; 143 minutes; March release

CAST

Governor Jack Stanton	John Travolta
Susan Stanton	Emma Thompson
Richard Jemmons	Billy Bob Thornton
Libby Holden	Kathy Bates
Henry Burton	Adrian Lester
Daisy	Maura Tierney
Governor Fred Picker	Larry Hagman
Mamma Stanton	Diane Ladd
Howard Ferguson	Paul Guilfoyle
March	Rebecca Walker
Lucille Kaufman	Caroline Aaron
Fat Willie	Tommy Hollis
Izzy Rosenblatt	Rob Reiner
Arlen Sporken	Ben Jones
Uncle Charlie	J.C. Quinn
Miss Walsh	Allison Janney
Norman Asher	Robert Klein
Dewayne Smith	Mykelti Williamson
Mitch	Jamie Denton
Ruby	Leontine Guilliard
Tawana Carter	Monique K. Ridge
Brad Lieberman	Ned Eisenberg
Randy Culligan	Brian Markinson
Themselves	Geraldo Rivera, Charlie Rose, Larry King, Bill Maher
Sailorman Shoreson	O'Neal Compton
Lawrence Harris	Kevin Cooney
Martha Harris	Bonnie Bartlett
Elegant Woman	Cynthia O'Neal
Charlie Martin	Chelcie Ross
Lorenzo Delgado	John Vargas
Eddie Reyes	Tony Shalhoub
Loretta	Bianca Lawson
Jimmy Ozio	Robert Cicchini
Jack Mandela Washington	Stan Davis

and Harrison Young (Sam), Rolando Molina (Anthony Ramirez), Ross Benjamin (Peter Goldsmith), Stacy Edwards (Jennifer Rogers), Kristoffer Ryan Winters (Terry Hicks), Susan Kussman (Ella Louise), Vickilyn Reynolds (Amalee), Robert Symonds (Bart Nilson), Gia Carides (Cashmere McLeod), Robert Easton (Dr. Beauregard), Scott Burkholder (Danny Scanlon), Lu Elrod (Chubby Woman), R.M. Haley (Shipyard Announcer), Henry Woronicz (Pundit), Darice Richman (Linda Feldstein), Rosalie Peck (Retiree), Susan Forristal (Bugger Bugger Woman), James Earl Jones (CNN Voiceover)

Political strategist Henry Burton is reluctantly pursuaded by charismatic Governor Jack Stanton to join his team as he prepares to run for office of the President of the United States. This film received Oscar nominations for supporting actress (Kathy Bates) and screenplay adaptation.

©Universal Studios Inc.

Adrian Lester, John Travolta

John Travolta

Emma Thompson

Emma Thompson, John Travolta

Kathy Bates

Billy Bob Thornton

Adrian Lester

John Travolta

Neve Campbell, Denise Richards

Kevin Bacon, Denise Richards

Matt Dillon, Neve Campbell

Matt Dillon, Denise Richards

Denise Richards, Neve Campbell

Theresa Russell

Matt Dillon, Bill Murray

©Mandalay Entertainment

Neve Campbell, Kevin Bacon

Daphne Rubin-Vega

Robert Wagner

WILD THINGS

(COLUMBIA) Producers, Rodney Liber, Steven A. Jones; Executive Producer, Kevin Bacon; Director, John McNaughton; Screenplay, Stephen Peters; Photography, Jeffrey L. Kimball; Music, George S. Clinton; Designer, Edward T. McAvoy; Editor, Elena Maganini; Costumes, Kimberly A. Tillman; Casting, Linda Lowry, John Brace; a Mandalay Entertainment presentation; Dolby; Panavision; Technicolor; Rated R; 113 minutes; March release

CAST

Ray Duquette	Kevin Bacon
Sam Lombardo	Matt Dillon
Suzie Toller	Neve Campbell
Sandra Van Ryan	Theresa Russell
Kelly Van Ryan	Denise Richards
Gloria Perez	Daphne Rubin-Vega
Tom Baxter	Robert Wagner
Ken Bowden	Bill Murray
Ruby	Carrie Snodgress
Bryce Hunter	Jeff Perry
Jimmy Leach	Cory Pendergast
Walter	Marc Macaulay
Nicole	Toi Svane
Art Maddox	Dennis Neal
School Secretary	Diane Admas
Kirk	Paulo Benedeti
Frankie Condo	Eduardo Yañez
Barbara Baxter	Jennifer Bini
Judge	Victoria Bass

and Ted Bartsch (Bailliff), Leonor Anthony (Ken's Secretary), Antoni Cornacchione (Police Chief), Robert Deacon (Prisoner), Tony Giaimo (Dave), Manny Suarez (Georgie), Janet Bushor (Barmaid), Gina LaMarca (Hooker), Nancy Duerr, Margo Peace, Keith Wilson (Reporters), Nelson Oramos, Michael Dean Walker, Jesse Muson (Policemen), Kimberly Lamaze, Rebecca White (Policewomen)

A scandal erupts in Blue Bay, Florida, when teenagers Kelly Van Ryan and Suzie Toller both come forward with the claim that high school guidance counselor Sam Lombardo has raped them.

Denise Richards, Matt Dillon

WIDE AWAKE

(MIRAMAX) Producers, Cary Woods, Cathy Konrad; Executive Producers, Bob Weinstein, Harvey Weinstein, Meryl Poster, Randy Ostrow; Co-Producer, James Bigwood; Director/Screenplay, M. Night Shyamalan; Photography, Adam Holender; Editor, Andrew Mondshein; Music, Edmund Choi; Designer, Michael Johnston; Costumes, Bridget Kelly; Casting, Avy Kaufman; a Woods Entertainment production; Dolby Stereo; Technicolor; Rated PG; 90 minutes; March release

CAST

Joshua Beal..Joseph Cross
Dave O'Hara...Timothy Reifsnyder
Mrs. Beal...Dana Delany
Mr. Beal..Denis Leary
Grandpa Beal..Robert Loggia
Sister Terry...Rosie O'Donnell
Sister Sophia...Camryn Manheim
Sister Beatrice...Vicki Giunta
Neena Beal...Julia Stiles
Hope ....Heather Casler
Father Peters..Dan Lauria
Frank Benton...Stefan Niemczyk
Freddie Waltman..Michael Pacienza
Robert Brickman...Michael Shulman
and Jaret Ross Barron (Dan), Jarrett Abello (John), Joseph Melito, Jr. (Billy), Peter A. Urban, Jr. (Newman), Jahmal Curtis (Student), Michael Craig Bigwood (Little Boy), Gil Robbins (Cardinal Geary), Marc H. Glick (Father Sebastian), Robert K. O'Neill (Young Priest), Deborah Stern (Mrs. Waltman), Joey Perillo (Mr. Waltman), Jerry Walsh (Football Coach), Liam Mitchell (Gym Teacher), Charles Techman (Janitor), Antoine McLean (Wilson), Arleen Goman (Mrs. Pitman), Mets Suber (Race Starter)

Months after the death of his beloved grandfather, ten-year-old Joshua Beal decides that he is going to find the answers about heaven, God and his place in the universe.

Joseph Cross, Rosie O'Donnell

Denis Leary, Joseph Cross, Julia Stiles, Dana Delany

©Miramax Films

NIAGARA, NIAGARA

(THE SHOOTING GALLERY) Producer, David L. Bushell; Executive Producer, Larry Meistrich; Director, Bob Gosse; Screenplay, Matthew Weiss; Photography, Michael Spiller; Designer, Clark Hunter; Editor, Rachel Warden; Music, Michael Timmins, Jeff Bird; Casting, Sheila Jaffe, Georgianne Walken; from LIVE Entertainment; Dolby Stereo; Technicolor; Rated R; 96 minutes; March release

CAST

Marcy..Robin Tunney
Seth..Henry Thomas
Walter...Michael Parks
Claude (Pharmacist)...Stephen Lang
Seth's Father...John MacKay
Sanitation Lot Cop..Alan Pottinger
Pawn Broker..Sol Frieder
Sally..Candy Clark
Sally's Policeman ....Andrew L. Phillips
Liquor Store Clerk..Jeffrey Howard
Lead High School Punk..Shawn Hatosy
Doug...John Ventimiglia
and Adam T. Lauricella (High School Punk #2), Jaime Lynn O'Hara (High School Girl), Clea DuVall (Convenience Store Clerk), Mark Chandler Bailey (Toystore Employee), Dwight Ewell (Toystore Manager), Larry Meistrich, Michael D. Rath (Police Officers), Matthew Weiss (Target Practice Cop)

Robin Tunney, Henry Thomas

©The Shooting Gallery Inc.

Loner Seth meets up with fellow-shoplifter Marcy, a teen who suffers from Tourette syndrome, and the pair take off on the road to Toronto in hopes of finding a rare doll.

A PRICE ABOVE RUBIES

(MIRAMAX) Producers, Lawrence Bender, John Penotti; Executive Producers, Bob Weinstein, Harvey Weinstein; Co-Producer, Joann Fregalette Jansen; Director/Screenplay, Boaz Yakin; Line Producer, Adam Brightman; Photography, Adam Holender; Designer, Dan Leigh; Editor, Arthur Coburn; Music, Lesley Barber; Costumes, Ellen Lutter; Casting, Douglas Aibel; Presented in association with Pandora Cinema and Channel Four Films; Dolby; Deluxe color; Rated R; 117 minutes; March release

Renée Zellweger, Christopher Eccleston

CAST

Sonia	Renée Zellweger
Sender	Christopher Eccleston
Rachel	Julianna Margulies
Ramon	Allen Payne
Mendel	Glenn Fitzgerald
Rebbitzn	Kim Hunter
Rebbe	John Randolph
Beggar Woman	Kathleen Chalfant
Schmuel	Peter Jacobson
Felga	Edie Falco
Dr. Bauer	Tim Jerome
Mrs. Gelbart	Phyllis Newman
Shaindy	Joyce Reehling
Yossi	Shelton Dane
Young Sonia	Jackie Ryan
Hrundi Kapoor	Faran Tahir

and Martin Shakar (Mr. Berman), Teodorina Bello (Mrs. Garcia), Glenn Flesher (Chief Gabbal), Adam Dannheisser (Young Gabbal #1), Stephen Singer, Marvin Einhorn (Gabbals), Mark Zimmerman (Doctor), Richard "Izzy" Lifshutz (The Moel), David Deblinger (Baruch), Sam Jennings (Heshle), Erin Rakow (Tsipi), Asher Tabak (Yechlel), Allen Swift (Mr. Fishbeln), Daryl Edwards (Nelson), Peter Slutsker (Mr. Sugarman), Lauren Klein (Sonia's Mother), Tonye Patano (Earring Woman), Don Wallace (Ty), Asia Minor, Roseanna Plasencia (Homegirls), Jerry Matz (Mr. Engelberg), Michael Sthulbarg (Young Hassid), Karen Contreras (Young Woman), Wai Ching Ho (Vendor), Mel Duane Gionson (Paranoid Vendor), Paul J.Q. Lee (Smooth Vendor), Leyla Aalam (Israeli Woman)

Julianna Margulies, Renée Zellweger

When her husband accepts an appointment to a prestigious Yeshiva, Sonia moves to Brooklyn's Hasidic community where she finds her freedom stifled until her brother-in-law encourages her to fight for her independence.

Renée Zellweger, Allen Payne

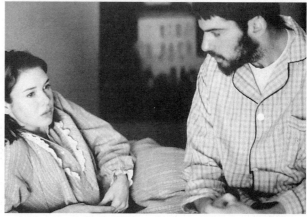

Renée Zellweger, Glenn Fitzgerald

Ethan Hawke, Matthew McConaughey

Vincent D'Onofrio

Julianna Margulies, Matthew McConaughey

THE NEWTON BOYS

(20TH CENTURY FOX) Producer, Anne Walker-McBay; Executive Producer, John Sloss; Director, Richard Linklater; Screenplay, Richard Linklater, Claude Stanush, Clark Lee Walker; Based on the book The Newton Boys: Portrait of an Outlaw Gang by Claude Stanush; Photography, Peter James; Designer, Catherine Hardwicke; Editor, Sandra Adair; Costumes, Shelley Komarov; Co-Producer, Clark Lee Walker; Associate Producer, Keith Fletcher; Music, Bad Livers, Edward D. Barnes; Casting, Don Phillips; a Detour Filmproduction; Dolby; Panavision; Deluxe color; Rated PG-13; 113 minutes; March release

CAST

Willis Newton	Matthew McConaughey
Jess Newton	Ethan Hawke
Dock Newton	Vincent D'Onofrio
Joe Newton	Skeet Ulrich
Louise Brown	Julianna Margulies
Brentwood Glasscock	Dwight Yoakam
Avis Glasscock	Chloe Webb
Slim	Charles Gunning
K.P. Aldrich	Bo Hopkins
Ma Newton	Gail Cronauer
Orphan Singers	Jena Karam, Casey McAuliffe
Orphan Fiddler	Regina Mae Matthews
Waiter	Lew Temple
Farmer Williams	Glynn Williams
Bank Teller	Charles "Chip" Bray
Crooked Banker	Gary Moody
Tailor	Robert Iannaccone
Catherine	Jennifer Miriam
Madeline	Anne Stedman
Old Woman	Marjorie Carroll

and Katie Gratson (Young Hotel Clerk), Angie Chase (Kat), Lynn Mathis (Arthur Adams), Becket Gremmels (Lewis), Ed Dollison (Night Guard), Boots Southerland (Wagon Driver), Tommy Townsend (Omaha Detective), Mary Love (Hotel Maid), A.G. Zeke Mills (Old Usher), Abra Moore (Argosy Ballroom Singer), Lori Heuring (Flapper), Joe Stevens (Bank Association President), Eddie Matthews, Scott Roland, J.P. Schwan (Bank Messengers), Rooster McConaughey (Tool Pusher), Bo Franks (Barker), Ali Nazary (Thug), Ron De Roxtra (Murray), David Jensen (William Fahy), Brad Arrington (Hobo), Richard A. Jones (Engineer), Randy Stripling (Fireman), Harold Suggs (Old Brakeman), Chamblee Ferguson (Head Postal Clerk), F.W. Post (Postal Turkey), Grant James (Gangland Doctor), Mark Fickert (Chicago Sergeant), Kerry Tartack (Chicago Detective), Luke Askew (Chief Schoemaker), Blue McDonnell (Nurse), Eduardo Cavazos Garza (Mexican Cab Driver), Ken Farmer (Frank Hamer), Daniel T. Kamin (District Attorney), Ross Sears (Judge)

The true story of America's most successful bank robbers who stole from over eighty banks from Texas to Canada during the period from 1919 to 1924.

©Twentieth Century Fox

Skeet Ulrich, Dwight Yoakam, Matthew McConaughey

Madeleine Stowe, Kenneth Branagh

Neil Patrick Harris, Madeleine Stowe

Blythe Danner, William Hurt

THE PROPOSITION

(POLYGRAM) Producers, Ted Field, Diane Nabatoff, Scott Kroopf; Executive Producer, Lata Ryan; Director, Lesli Linka Glatter; Screenplay, Rick Ramage; Co-Executive Producer, Alessandro F. Uzielli; Photography, Peter Sova; Designer, David Brisbin; Editor, Jacqueline Camabs; Costumes, Anna Sheppard; Music, Stephen Endelman; Casting, Johanna Ray, Elaine J. Huzzar; a PolyGram Filmed Entertainment presentation of an Interscope Communications production; Dolby Stereo; Technicolor; Rated R; 110 minutes; March release

CAST

Father Michael McKinnon	Kenneth Branagh
Eleanor Barret	Madeleine Stowe
Arthur Barret	William Hurt
Roger Martin	Neil Patrick Harris
Hannibal Thurman	Robert Loggia
Syril Danning	Blythe Danner
Father Dryer	Josef Sommer
Sister Mary Frances	Bronia Wheeler
Wayne Fenton	Ken Cheeseman
Timothy	Jim Chiros
Susan Vicar	Dee Nelson
Skip Taylor	Pamela Hart
Maid	Wendy Feign
Hannibal's Secretary	Dossy Peabody
Torrey Harrington	Tom Downey
Arthur's Chauffeur	Tom Kemp
Father Frank Timothy	Father Frank Toste, CSC
Dr. Jenkins	David Byrd
Butler Captain	Lawrence Bull
Butler	Michael Bradshaw
Andre	Willy O'Donnell
Coroner	Frank T. Wells

When Arthur Barret realizes he cannot help his wife conceive a child they hire a young law student to serve as sexual surrogate with tragic results.

NO LOOKING BACK

(GRAMERCY) Producers, Ted Hope, Michael Nozik, Edward Burns; Executive Producer, Robert Redford; Director/Screenplay, Edward Burns; Co-Executive Producer, John Sloss; Line Producer, Alysse Bezahler; Photography, Frank Prinzi; Editor, Susan Graef; Music, Joe Delia; Designer, Thérèse DePrez; Costumes, Sara Jane Slotnick; Casting, Laura Rosenthal; a PolyGram Filmed Entertainment presentation of a Marlboro Road Gang/Good Machine/South Fork Pictures production; Dolby Stereo; Technicolor; Rated R; 96 minutes; March release

Lauren Holly, Edward Burns

CAST

Claudia	Lauren Holly
Charlie	Edward Burns
Michael	Jon Bon Jovi
Kelly	Connie Britton
Claudia's Mom	Blythe Danner
Mrs. Ryan	Kathleen Doyle
Teresa	Jennifer Esposito
Goldie	Nick Sandow
Alice	Kaili Vernoff
Shari	Shari Albert
Marcia	Marcia Debonis
Bugsy	Matty Delia
Leah	Leah Gray
Sco	Kevin Heffernan
Waitress	Ellen McElduff
Chris	Chris McGovern
Maggie	Margaret O'Neill
Annie	Susan Pratt
The Foot	Stuart Rudin
Glenn	Glenn D. Sanford
Bno	Mark Schulte
Tony	John Ventimiglia
Missy	Welker White

Waitress Claudia finds her seemingly ideal relationship with Michael disrupted when her former boyfriend Charlie returns to her life, hoping to win her back.

©Gramercy Pictures

Jon Bon Jovi, Lauren Holly

Jon Bon Jovi, Lauren Holly, Connie Britton, Blythe Danner

Jack Johnson, Robot

LOST IN SPACE

(NEW LINE CINEMA) Producers, Mark W. Koch, Stephen Hopkins, Akiva Goldsman, Carla Fry; Executive Producers, Mace Neufeld, Bob Rehme, Richard Saperstein, Michael DeLuca; Co-Executive Producer, Michael Ilitch, Jr.; Director, Stephen Hopkins; Screenplay, Akiva Goldsman; Based on the television series created by Irwin Allen; Photography, Peter Levy; Designer, Norman Garwood; Editor, Ray Lovejoy; Music, Bruce Broughton; Visual Effects Supervisor, Angus Bickerton; Animatronic Creatures, Jim Henson's Creature Shop; Co-Producers, Tim Hampton, Kris Wiseman; Space Costumes Designer, Vin Burnham; Earth Costumes Designers, Robert Bell, Gilly Hebden; Casting, Mike Fenton, Allison Cowitt, Mary Selway; a Prelude Pictures production in association with Irwin Allen Productions; Dolby; Panavision; Rank color; Rated PG-13; 122 minutes; April release

Heather Graham, Mimi Rogers, Gary Oldman

Jack Johnson, Matt LeBlanc

CAST

John Robinson..William Hurt
Maureen Robinson...Mimi Rogers
Judy Robinson ....Heather Graham
Penny Robinson...Lacey Chabert
Will Robinson..Jack Johnson
Dr. Smith/Spider Smith ....Gary Oldman
Don West ....Matt LeBlanc
Older Will ....Jared Harris
General ....Mark Goddard
Jeb Walker ....Lennie James
Reporters ....Marta Kristen, Angela Cartwright
Principal...June Lockhart
Business Man..Edward Fox
Lab Technician ....Adam Sims
Noah Freeman ....John Sharian
Annie Tech..Abigail Canton
Attack Pilot ....Richard Saperstein
Voice of Robot ....Dick Tufeld

The Robinsons, the first family selected to colonize in space, find themselves thrown off course and lost in space after a saboteur ends up on board, intent on foiling their mission. Based on the CBS television series that ran from 1965-68; four original cast members from the series, June Lockhart, Mark Goddard, Angela Cartwright, and Marta Kristen, appear in this film. Dick Tufeld, who supplied the voice of the Robot in the series, repeats that duty here.

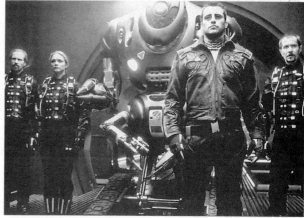

William Hurt, Heather Graham, Matt LeBlanc, Gary Oldman

Bruce Willis, Miko Hughes

Bruce Willis, Miko Hughes

MERCURY RISING

(UNIVERSAL) Producers, Brian Grazer, Karen Kehela; Executive Producers, Joseph M. Singer, Ric Kidney; Director, Harold Becker; Screenplay, Lawrence Konner, Mark Rosenthal; Based on the novel Simple Simon by Ryne Douglas Pearson; Photography, Michael Seresin; Designer, Patrizia von Brandenstein; Editor, Peter Honess; Co-Producers, Maureen Peyrot, Paul Neesan; Costumes, Betsy Heimann; Music, John Barry; Casting, Nancy Klopper; an Imagine Entertainment presentation of a Brian Grazer production; Dolby; Panavision; Deluxe color; Rated R; 112 minutes; April release

Alec Baldwin

Miko Hughes

CAST

Art Jeffries	Bruce Willis
Lt. Col. Nicholas Kudrow	Alec Baldwin
Simon	Miko Hughes
Tommy B. Jordan	Chi McBride
Stacey	Kim Dickens
Dean Crandell	Robert Stanton
Leo Pedranski	Bodhi Pine Elfman
Emily Lang	Carrie Preston
Burrell	L.L. Ginter
Shayes	Peter Stormare
Lomax	Kevin Conway
Martin Lynch	John Carroll Lynch
Jenny Lynch	Kelley Hazen
Supervisor Hartley	John Doman
Edgar Halstrom	Richard Riehle
James	Chad Lindberg
Isaac	Hank Harris
SWAT Team Leader Francis	James MacDonald
Dr. London	Camryn Manheim
Detective Nichols	Jack Conley
Charlayne	Maricela Ochoa
Pasquale	Peter Fontana

and Kirk B.R. Woller (Lieutenant), Kristina Eliot Johnson, Betsy Brantley (Special Ed Teacher #2), Ashley Knutson (Samantha), Tom Gallop (Medic), Margaret Travolta (Autism Expert Nurse), Tiffany Fraser (Night Nurse), Koko Taylor (Koko Taylor), Matt Levert (Tommy Jordan, Jr.), Lisa Summerour (Dana Jordan), Barbara Alexander (Librarian), Gwen McGee (Security Woman), Ned Schmidtke (Senator), James Krag (Rookie Agent Roger), Wadell Brown (Bank Security Guard), Tim Grimm (Ted—Security Guard), John Scanlon (South Dakota Helicopter Pilot), Annabel Armour (Ruth), Brent Freeman (Marine Guard), Gary Hand (Kudrow's Assistant), Michael Chieffo (Hostage), Steve Key (Cop at Lynch House), Darryl Alan Reed (Ambulance Driver), Steve Rankin (WGEX Helicopter Pilot), Maureen Gallagher (Flea Market Lady), Mark Collins (Train Conductor), Denise Woods (Nurse in Elevator), Kim Robillard (Motorman)

FBI Agent Art Jeffries takes it upon himself to save the life of an autistic boy who has become the target of the National Security Agency after inadvertently cracking a top-secret military code.

Bruce Willis, Miko Hughes

THE SPANISH PRISONER

(SONY PICTURES CLASSICS) Producer, Jean Doumanian; Executive Producer, J.E. Beaucaire; Director/Screenplay, David Mamet; Co-Executive Producer, Letty Aronson; Co-Producer, Sarah Green; Photography, Gabriel Beristain; Editor, Barbara Tulliver; Designer, Tim Galvin; Costumes, Susan Lyall; Music, Carter Burwell; Casting, Billy Hopkins, Suzanne Smith, Kerry Barden; a Sweetland Films presentation of a Jean Doumanian production; Dolby Stereo; Color; Rated PG; 112 minutes; April release

CAST

Joe Ross	Campbell Scott
Susan Ricci	Rebecca Pidgeon
Jimmy Dell	Steve Martin
Klein	Ben Gazzara
George Lang	Ricky Jay
McCune	Felicity Huffman
Businessmen	Richard L. Freidman, Jerry Graff, G. Roy Levin
Resort Concierge	Hilary Hinckle
Resort Manager	David Pittu
Dell's Bodyguard	Christopher Kaldor
Ticket Agent	Gary McDonald
Security Person	Michael Robinson
Flight Attendant	Olivia Tecosky
Bookstore Woman	Charlotte Potok
Bookbinder	Paul Butler
Doorman	J.J. Johnston
Secretary	Emily Weisberg
Receptionist	Stephanie Ross
Antique Car Dealer	Elliot Cuker
Car Dealer's Assistant	Scott Zigler
Restaurant Manager	Steven Hawley

and Jordan Lage (Maitre'd), Steven Goldstein, Jonathan Katz (Lawyers), Paul Dunn III (Jailer), Tony Mamet (FBI Agent Levy), Jack Wallace (Sanitation Man), Ed O'Neill (FBI Team Leader), Clark Gregg (FBI Sniper), Lionel Mark Smith (Det. Jones), Jim Frangione (Det. Luzzio), Allen Soule (Fingerprint Technician), Mary McCann (Policewoman), Gus Johnson (Property Clerk), Isiah Whitlock, Jr. (Trooper) Harriet Voyt (Airline Employee), Kristin Reddick (Airport Mother), Andrew Murphy (Airport Child), Jeremy Geidt (Timid Man), Carolyn "Coco" Kallis (Timid Woman), Neil Pepe (Airport Security), Charles Stransky (Deckhand), Takeo Matsushita, Seiko Yoshida (U.S. Marshals), Mimi Jo Katano (Japanese Tour Guide)

Joe Ross, the inventor of a valuable scientific formula known as "the Process," realizes he is being shut out of the profits on his creation and befriends a mysterious millionaire he hopes can help him out.

Ben Gazzara

Campbell Scott, Rebecca Pidgeon

Campbell Scott, Ricky Jay

Campbell Scott, Steve Martin

CITY OF ANGELS

(WARNER BROS.) Producers, Dawn Steel, Charles Roven; Executive Producers, Arnon Milchan, Robert Cavallo, Charles Newirth; Director, Brad Silberling; Screenplay, Dana Stevens; Based on the film Wings of Desire directed by Wim Wenders, and written by Wim Wenders, Richard Reitinger, and Peter Handke; Photography, John Seale; Designer, Lilly Kilvert; Editor, Lynzee Klingman; Special Visual Effects, Sony Picture Imageworks Inc.; Co-Producers, Douglas Segal, Kelley Smith-Wait; Music, Gabriel Yared; Costumes, Shay Cunliffe; Casting, David Rubin; an Atlas Entertainment production, presented in association with Regency Pictures; Dolby; Panavision; Technicolor; Rated PG-13; 117 minutes; April release

Nicolas Cage, Meg Ryan

CAST

Seth	Nicolas Cage
Dr. Maggie Rice	Meg Ryan
Cassiel	Andre Braugher
Nathaniel Messinger	Dennis Franz
Jordan	Colm Feore
Anne	Robin Bartlett
Teresa	Joanna Merlin
Susan	Sarah Dampf
Susan's Mother	Rhonda Dotson
Doctor	Nigel Gibbs
Man in Car	John Putch
Woman in Car	Lauri Johnson
Foreign Visitor in Car	Christian Aubert
Air Traffic Controller	Jay Patterson
Anesthesiologist	Shishir Kurup
Surgical Fellow	Brian Markinson

and Hector Velasquez (Scrub Nurse), Marlene Kanter, Bernard White (Circulating Nurses), Dan Desmond (Mr. Balford), Deirdre O'Connell (Mrs. Balford), Kim Murphy (Balford's Daughter), Chad Lindberg (Balford's Son), Alexander Folk (Convenience Store Clerk), Rainbow Borden (Hold-Up Man), Harper Roisman (Old Man in Library), Sid Hillman (Librarian), Wanda-Lee Evans (Nurse in Messinger's Room), Wanadchristine (Station Nurse), E.J. Callahan (Waiter at Johnnie's), Tudi Roche (Messinger's Daughter), David Moreland (Husband Frank), Kristina Malota (Hannah), Stan Davis (Construction Foreman), Mik Scriba, Nick Offerman (Construction Workers), Kieu-Chinh (Asian Woman), Geoffrey A. Thorne (Big Orderly), Peter Spellos (Mac Truck Driver), Jim Kline (Store Clerk), Cherene Snow (Woman Sewing)

Andre Braugher

A restless angel encounters a doctor who has lost a patient and finds himself drawn to her, longing to be a part of the mortal world he can observe but not experience. Remake of the German film Wings of Desire which was released in the U.S. in 1988 by Orion Classics.

Dennis Franz, Meg Ryan

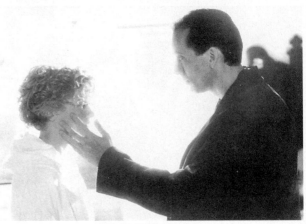

Meg Ryan, Nicolas Cage

THE ODD COUPLE II

(PARAMOUNT) Producers, Neil Simon, Robert W. Cort, David Madden; Director, Howard Deutch; Screenplay, Neil Simon; Photography, Jamie Anderson; Designer, Dan Bishop; Editor, Seth Flaum; Costumes, Lisa Jensen; Associate Producer, Elena Spiotta; Music, Alan Silvestri; Casting, Jane Shannon-Smith, Alex Rosenberg; a Cort/Madden production; Dolby Stereo; Super 35 Widescreen; Deluxe color; Rated PG-13; 96 minutes; April release

Christine Baranski, Walter Matthau, Jean Smart, Jack Lemmon

CAST

Felix Ungar	Jack Lemmon
Oscar Madison	Walter Matthau
Thelma	Christine Baranski
Beaumont	Barnard Hughes
Brucey Madison	Jonathan Silverman
Holly	Jean Smart
Hannah Ungar	Lisa Waltz
Felice	Mary Beth Peil
Blanche Madison Povitch	Doris Belack
Frances Ungar Melnick	Ellen Geer
Leroy	Jay O. Sanders
JayJay	Rex Linn
Detective	Richard Riehle
Abe	Lou Cutell
Flossie	Mary Fogarty
Esther	Alice Ghostley
Millie	Peggy Miley
Wanda	Rebecca Schull
Hattie	Florence Stanley

and Estelle Harris (Flirting Woman), Joaquin Martinez (Truck Driver), Amy Yasbeck (Stewardess), Francesca P. Roberts (Passenger), Amy Parrish (Computer Girl), Liz Torres (Maria), Myles Jeffrey (Little Boy), Carmen Mormino, Chuck Montgomery (California Troopers), Earl Boen (Fred), Ron Harper (Jack), Edmund Shaff (Ralph), Daisy Velez (Conchita), Beecey Carlson (Waitress), Terry L. Rose (Bartender), Alfred Dennis (Morton), Armando Ortega (Detective #2), Peter Renaday (Justice of the Peace), David Jean-Thomas (Bus Driver), Daniel Zacapa (Lead Cop), Cliff Bemis (Dance Partner), Frank Roman (Bellman), Lonnie McCullough (Roadblock Officer), Matt McKenzie (Pilot), Heath Hyche (Policeman), Irene Olga Lopez (Cafe Waitress), Jerry Rector (Detective), Martin Grey (Immigration Officer), Michelle Johnston (Bridesmaid/Airline Employee), Michelle Matthow (Wedding Guest), Mark McGee (Wedding Bartender), Barry Thompson, Joanna Sanchez, Catherine Paolone (Passengers), Laura Russo (Stewardess #2)

Jack Lemmon, Francesca P. Roberts

A series of mishaps ensue when former roommates Felix Ungar and Oscar Madison reunite to journey to the wedding of their offspring. Sequel to the 1968 Paramount film The Odd Couple which also starred Lemmon and Matthau (with Matthau repeating his role from the original 1965 Broadway production).

© Paramount Pictures

Walter Matthau, Jack Lemmon

Walter Matthau

MY GIANT

(COLUMBIA) Producer, Billy Crystal; Executive Producer, Peter Schindler; Director, Michael Lehmann; Screenplay, David Seltzer; Story, Billy Crystal, David Seltzer; Photography, Michael Coulter; Designer, Jackson DeGovia; Costumes, Rita Ryack; Editor, Stephen Semel; Music, Marc Shaiman; Casting, Pam Dixon Mickelson; a Castle Rock Entertainment presentation of a Face Production; Dolby; Technicolor; Rated PG; 97 minutes; April release

CAST

Sammy	Billy Crystal
Serena	Kathleen Quinlan
Max	Gheorghe Muresan
Lilliana	Joanna Pacula
Nick	Zane Carney
Weller	Jere Burns
Milt	Harold Gould
Partlow	Dan Castellaneta
Eddie	Raymond O'Connor
Justin	Rider Strong
Rose	Doris Roberts
Rabbi	Carl Ballantine
Young Sammy	Eric Lloyd
Jay	Jay Black
Joanne	Lorna Luft

and Tony Belton (Man on Street), Lindsay Crystal (Stephanie), Peter Schindler (Don), Martin Falty'n (Cinema Manager), Miroslav Dubsky (Cameraman), Dale Wyatt (Dialogue Coach), David Steinberg, Steven Seagal (Themselves), Ajay Naidu (Hot Dog Vendor), Estelle Harris (Aunt Pearl), Elaine Kagan (Myrna), Philip Sterling (Uncle Nate), Max Goldblatt (Jerry), E.E. Bell (Ring Announcer), Michael Papajohn, Lincoln Simonds (Tough Guys), Heather Thomas (Showgirl), Rick Overton (Director), Richard Portno (Producer), Nikki Micheaux (P.A. Jeannie), Lawrence Pressman (Doctor), Yvonne de la Paix (Cleaning Woman), Miroslava Baburkova, Zoja Oubramova (Peasant Women), Vaclav Kotva (Max's Father), Lena Birkova (Max's Mother)

A second-rate talent agent stumbles across a 7'7" giant in Romania and believes he has found his ticket out of obscurity.

©Castle Rock Entertainment

Billy Crystal, Gheorghe Muresan

Billy Crystal, Kathleen Quinlan

Billy Crystal, Steven Seagal

Gheorghe Muresan

THE BIG ONE

(MIRAMAX) Producer, Kathleen Glynn; Executive Producers, David Mortimer, Jeremy Gibson; Director/Screenplay, Michael Moore; Photography, Brian Danitz, Chris Smith; Editor, Meg Reticker; Line Producer, Jim Czarnecki; Music, World Famous Blue Jays; Coordinating Producer, Tia Lessin; Presented in association with Mayfair Entertainment International, BBC Production and Dog Eat Dog Films; U.S. - British; Dolby Stereo; Color; Rated PG-13; 96 minutes; April release

WITH

Michael Moore, Rick Nielsen, Garrison Keillor, Phil Knight, Studs Terkel.

While on a promotion tour for his book Downsize This! *writer-director Michael Moore investigates the shady financial dealings of various American corporations.*

Phil Knight, Michael Moore

©Miramax Films

Jamie Foxx, LisaRaye

Bernie Mac

©NewLine Cinema

THE PLAYERS CLUB

(NEW LINE CINEMA) Producers, Patricia Charbonnet, Carl Craig; Executive Producer/Director/Screenplay, Ice Cube; Photography, Malik Sayeed; Designer, Dina Lipton; Editor, Suzanne Hines; Costumes, Dahlia Foroutan; Music, Hidden Faces; Casting, Kimberly Hardin; an Ice Cube/Pat Charbonnet production; Dolby; Deluxe color; Rated R; 104 minutes; April release

CAST

Diana Armstrong/Diamond	LisaRaye
Ebony	Monica Calhoun
Dollar Bill	Bernie Mac
Blue	Jamie Foxx
Ronnie	Chrystale Wilson
Tricks	Adele Givens
Li'l Man	A.J. Johnson
Reggie	Ice Cube
Clyde	Alex Thomas
Peters	Faizon Love
Brooklyn	Charles O. Murphy
Tina	Tracy C. Jones
K.C.	Terence Howard
St. Louis	Larry McCoy
Professor Mills	Ronn Riser
Mr. Armstrong	Dick Anthony Williams
The Doctor	Badja Djola
XL	Tiny Lister
Freeman	John Amos

and Judy Ann Elder (Mrs. Armstrong), Jimmy Woodard (Miron), Monte Russell (Lance), Oren Williams (Jamal at 4 years), Jossie Harris, Lalanya Masters (Strippers), Ursula Y. Houston (Dancer #2), Annie O'Donnell (Lady), Satari (Girl), Bettina Rae (Vanilla), Big Boy (Joe), Gregg McDonald (Cop) Brett Wagner (Guy—Cop Party), Kenya Williams (Student), Nigel Thatch (Morehouse Guy), Big Mike Duncan (Bodyguard), Luther Campbell (Luke), Samuel Monroe, Jr. (Junior), Master P (Guy), Keith Burke (Guy at Party)

While hoping to get a college degree and become a broadcast journalist, single mother Diana Armstrong takes a job as a stripper at the Players Club.

SOUR GRAPES

(COLUMBIA) Producer, Laurie Lennard; Executive Producer, Barry Berg; Director/Screenplay, Larry Davis; Photography, Victor Hammer; Designer, Charles Rosen; Editor, Priscilla Nedd-Friendly; Costumes, Debra McGuire; Casting, Liberman/Hirschfeld Casting; a Castle Rock Entertainment presentation; Dolby Stereo; Technicolor; Rated R; 92 minutes; April release

CAST

Evan	Steven Weber
Richie	Craig Bierko
Danny Pepper	Matt Keeslar
Joan	Karen Sillas
Roberta	Robyn Peterman
Selma	Viola Harris
Digby	Orlando Jones
Eulogist	Jack Burns
Teenage Richie	Scott Erik
Teenage Evan	Michael Resnick
Millie	Jennifer Leigh Warren

and Anthony Parziale (Blackjack Dealer), Abraham Kessler (Crap Dealer), Fred Goehner (Floor Manager), Amy Hohn (Waitress), Denise Bessette (Cocktail Waitress), Angelo Tiffe (Chauffeur), Bari K. Willerford (Truck Driver), Alan Wilder (Irwin), Hiram Kasten, Kari Coleman (Co-Workers), Rosanna Huffman (Mr. Bell's Assist.), Philip Baker Hall (Mr. Bell), Harry Murphy, Tucker Smallwood (Anesthesiologist #1), Deirdre Lovejoy (Nurse Wells), Iqbal Theba (Dr. Alagappan), Tamara Clatterbuck (Nurse Donator), Helen Anzalone (Nurse Jamison), Richard Gant (Det. Crouch), James MacDonald (Det. Frehill), Ann Guilbert (Mrs. Drier), Harper Roisman (Mr. Drier), Edith Varon (Fran), Jack Kehler (Jack), John Toles-Bey (Lee), Michael Krawic (Larry), Sonya Eddy (Nurse Loder), Jill Talley (Lois), Bryan Gordon (Doug), Rachel Crane (Allie), Julie Claire (Matisse), Patrick Fabian (Palmer), Kevin Shinick (Conner), Meredith Salenger (Degan), Kristin Davis (Riggs), Larry David, Jon Hayman, Linda Wallem (TV Producers), Ron West (Dr. Isner), Bruce Jarchow (Dr. Dean), Marvin Braverman (Bartender), Arthur Chobanian (Man in Bar), Jack O'Connell (Homeless Man), Mark Chaet (Dr. Michaels), Rande Leaman (Hospital Worker), Larry Brandenburg (Landlord), James Gallery (Mr. Lesser), Tom Dahlgren (Mr. Havelock).

After Richie hits the jackpot at a slot machine, his cousin Evan feels he is entitled to two-thirds of the payoff, having lent Richie two of the three quarters needed to play.

©Castle Rock Entertainment

Steven Weber, Craig Bierko

Ewan McGregor, Patricia Arquette

Nick Nolte, John C. Reilly

NIGHTWATCH

(DIMENSION) Producer, Michael Obel; Executive Producers, Bob Weinstein, Harvey Weinstein, Cary Granat; Director, Ole Bornedal; Screenplay, Ole Bornedal, Steven Soderbergh; Based on the film *Nattevagten* by Ole Bornedal; Photography, Dan Laustsen; Designer, Richard Hoover; Editor, Sally Menke; Costumes, Louise Mingenbach; Music, Joachim Holbek; Line Producer, Daniel Lupi; a Michael Obel production; Distributed by Miramax Films; Dolby; Super 35 Widescreen; Color; Rated R; 101 minutes; April release

CAST

Martin Bells	Ewan McGregor
Inspector Cray	Nick Nolte
James	Josh Brolin
Marie	Lauren Graham
Katherine	Patricia Arquette
Deputy Inspector Bill	John C. Reilly
Newscaster	Erich Anderson
Old Watchman	Lonny Chapman
College Professor	Scott Burkholder
Duty Doctor	Brad Dourif
Guy in Pub	Michael Matthys
Girl Friend of Guy in Pub	Alison Gale
Pub Thugs	Robert Lasardo, Mongo

and Candy Brown Houston (Paramedic), Michelle Csitos (Leanne Singer), Alix Koromzay (Joyce), Larry Cedar (Waiter), Lennie Loftin (Man in Theater), Bradley Gregg (Theatre Actor), Nicholas Sadler (Theater Director), Jeff Davis (Stagehand), Nicholas Cascone (Paramedic)

Law student Martin Bells takes a part-time job as a nightwatchman at a morgue only to find himself the chief suspect in a series of serial murders that have put the city in panic. Remake of the 1995 Dutch film Nattevagten which was also directed by Ole Bornedal.

Hallie Kate Eisenberg, Paulie

Paulie, Bruce Davison

Cheech Marin, Paulie

Jay Mohr, Buddy Hackett, Paulie

Paulie, Tony Shalhoub

PAULIE

(DREAMWORKS) Producers, Mark Gordon, Gary Levinsohn, Allison Lyon Segan; Executive Producer, Ginny Nugent; Director, John Roberts; Screenplay, Laurie Craig; Photography, Tony Pierce-Roberts; Designer, Dennis Washington; Editor, Bruce Cannon; Costumes, Mary Zophres; Music, John Debney; Animal Stunt Coordinator, Boone Narr; Animatronic Characters, Stan Winston; a Mutual Film Company production; Dolby Stereo; Color; Rated PG; 91 minutes; April release

CAST

Ivy	Gena Rowlands
Misha	Tony Shalhoub
Ignacio	Cheech Marin
Dr. Reingold	Bruce Davison
Voice of Paulie/Benny	Jay Mohr
Adult Marie	Trini Alvarado
Artie	Buddy Hackett
Marie	Hallie Kate Eisenberg
Warren	Matt Craven
Virgil	Bill Cobbs
Ruby/Lupe	Tia Texada
Lila	Laura Harrington
Gerald	Charles Parks
Grad Students	Peter Basch, Emily Mura-Smith
Grandpa	Hal Robinson
Jeremy	Seth Mumy
Molly	Francesca Federico-O'Murchú
Mr. Tauper	Jerry Winsett

and Dig Wayne, Michael Leydon Campbell (Research Assistants), Nicole Chamberlain (Shirley), Tamara Zook (Speech Therapist). Kristie Transeau (Veterinarian #2)

While caged in the basement of a research lab, a parrot tells a kindly janitor the story of how he came to be there as he was passed from owner to owner over the course of several years.

THE OBJECT OF MY AFFECTION

(20TH CENTURY FOX) Producer, Laurence Mark; Director, Nicholas Hytner; Screenplay, Wendy Wasserstein; Based upon the novel by Stephen McCauley; Photography, Oliver Stapleton; Designer, Jane Musky; Editor, Tariq Anwar; Co-Producer, Diana Pokorny; Music, George Fenton; Costumes, John Dunn; Casting, Daniel Swee; a Laurence Mark production; Dolby Stereo; DuArt color; Rated R; 112 minutes; April release

CAST

Nina Borowski	Jennifer Aniston
George Hanson	Paul Rudd
Vince McBride	John Pankow
Sidney Miller	Alan Alda
Dr. Robert Joley	Tim Daly
Rodney Fraser	Nigel Hawthorne
Constance Miller	Allison Janney
Paul James	Amo Gulinello
Melissa Marx	Kali Rocha
Frank Hanson	Steve Zahn
Sally Miller	Lauren Varija Pratt
Mermaid	Hayden Panettiere
Violin Player	Lauren Chen
Nathan	Liam Aiken
Stephen Saint	Bradley White
Mrs. Sarni	Marilyn Dobrin
Nina's Colleague	Midori Nakamura
Madame Reynolds	Joan Copeland
Kennedy	Kate Jennings Grant
Dr. Goldstein	Bruce Altman
Mr. Shapiro	Salem Ludwig
Mrs. Ochoa	Antonia Rey
Nina's Dance Partner	Danny Darrow
Suni	Samia Shoaib

and Douglas Wert (Father), Michael Phelan (Son), Edward James Hyland (Doctor), Gabriel Macht (Steve Casillo), Miguel Maldonado (Colin Powell), Peter Maloney (Desk Clerk), Bette Henritze (Mrs. Skinner), Iraida Polanco (Carmelita), Kevin Carroll (Louis Crowley), Sarah Knowlton (Caroline Colucci), Lena Cardwell, Natalie B. Kikkenborg (Girls at Community Center), Janet Zarish, Ellen Tobie, Virl Andrick, Robert C. Lee (Dinner Guests), Sean Rademaker, Heather Thompson (School Children), Mary McIlvaine, Lisa-Erin Allen (Nurses), John Roland, Rosanna Scotto (TV Anchors), Steven Ochoa (Waiter), Kia Joy Goodwin (Juliet), Daniel Cosgrove (Trotter Bull), Damian Young (Romeo & Juliet Director), Rebecca Eichenberger, Jane Bodle (Wedding Guests), Audra McDonald (Wedding Singer), Fanni Green (Nurse), Sarah Hyland (Molly), Paz de la Huerta (13-year-old Sally), Jeffrey Marchett, Susan Bradford (Parents), Christopher Durang (Man in Audience)

After George Hanson is dumped by his boyfriend, a new acquaintance, Nina Borowski, invites him to move in with her, beginning a very special, albeit troublesome, relationship between the two.

Paul Rudd, Jennifer Aniston

Paul Rudd, Jennifer Aniston

Amo Gulinello, Paul Rudd

Alan Alda, Allison Janney

Jennifer Aniston, Paul Rudd

Nigel Hawthorne, Paul Rudd, Jennifer Aniston

Paul Rudd, Jennifer Aniston

Tim Daly, Paul Rudd

Paul Rudd, Jennifer Aniston, John Pankow

Woody Allen, Soon-Yi Previn

Woody Allen

Woody Allen, Eddy Davis

Woody Allen, Soon-Yi Previn

©Fine Line Features

WILD MAN BLUES

(FINE LINE FEATURES) Producer, Jean Doumanian; Executive Producer, J.E. Beaucaire; Director, Barbara Kopple; Photography, Tom Hurwitz; Editor, Lawrence Silk; Associate Producer, Kathleen Bambrick Meier; a Sweetland Films presentation of a Jean Doumanian production; Dolby Stereo; DuArt Color; Rated PG; 105 minutes; April release. Documentary covering the 1996 European tour of Woody Allen and his New Orleans Jazz Band.

WITH

Woody Allen (clarinet), Dan Barrett (trombone), Simon Wettenhall (trumpet), John Gill (drums), Cynthia Sayer (piano), Greg Cohen (bass), Eddy Davis (banjo and band leader), John Doumanian (road manager), Richard Jones (tour manager/sound engineer), Soon-Yi Previn, Letty Aronson, Martin Konigsberg, Nettie Konigsberg.

Dan Barrett, Simon Wettenhall, Woody Allen

Jay Mohr

©Live Entertainment Inc.

SUICIDE KINGS

(ARTISAN ENTERTAINMENT) Producers, Wayne Rice, Morrie Eisenman; Executive Producer, Stephen Drimmer; Co-Executive Producer, Rick Mischel; Director, Peter O'Fallon; Screenplay, Josh McKinney, Gina Goldman, Wayne Rice; Based on the short story The Hostage by Don Stanford; Co-Producer, Patrick Peach; Photography, Christopher Baffa; Designer, Clark Hunter; Music, Graeme Revell; Editor, Chris Peppe; Associate Producers, Charles A. Chiara, Adam Mills; Casting, Wendy Kurtzman, Roger Mussenden; a Wayne Rice/Dinamo Entertainment production in association with Artisan Film and Mediaworks; Dolby Stereo; Deluxe color; Rated R; 106 minutes; April release

CAST

Carlo Bartolucci (Charlie Barrett)	Christopher Walken
Lono Vecchio	Denis Leary
Max Minot	Sean Patrick Flanery
Ira Reder	Johnny Galecki
Brett Campbell	Jay Mohr
T.K.	Jeremy Sisto
Avery Chasten	Henry Thomas
Marty	Cliff DeYoung
Lydia	Laura San Giacomo
Doorman	Mark Watson
Jennifer	Nina Siemaszko
Bartender	Jay Fiondella
Marcus	Nathan Dana
Heckle	Frank Medrano
Jeckyll	Brad Garrett
Maitre D'	Trent Bross
Marty's Wife	Lisanne Falk
Mickey	Louis Lombardi
Window Washer	Barry Sherman
Barrio Bennie	Lenny Citrano
Elise "Lisa" Chasten	Laura Harris
Nick the Nose	Joseph Calli
Harry	Joseph Whipp
Widowmaker	Sean Whalen

and James Peter "JP" O'Fallon, Jr., Nicholas Huttloff (Kids), Spike Silver, Corey Eubanks (Masked Men), Kevin Crowley (Security Guard), Karen Rosin (Emergency Room Nurse), Bryan Swerling (Doctor), Will Klipstine (Protesting Orderly)

A group of prep school buddies kidnap Mafia kingpin Charlie Barrett hoping to get him to pay a $2 million dollar ransom for the recently kidnapped sister of one of the boys.

Henry Thomas, Jay Mohr, Johnny Galecki,
Sean Patrick Flanery, Jeremy Sisto

Denis Leary, Christopher Walken

Jeremy Sisto

51

Bokeem Woodbine, Lou Diamond Phillips,
Mark Wahlberg, Antonio Sabato, Jr.

Mark Wahlberg, Lela Rochon

China Chow, Bokeem Woodbine

Christina Applegate, Mark Wahlberg, Lainie Kazan, Elliott Gould

THE BIG HIT

(TRISTAR) Producers, Warren Zide, Wesley Snipes; Executive Producers, John Woo, Terence Chang, John M. Eckert; Director, Che-Kirk Wong; Screenplay, Ben Ramsey; Photography, Danny Nowak; Designer, Taavo Soodor; Editors, Robin Russell, Pietro Scalia; Music, Graeme Revell; Costumes, Margaret Mohr; Co-Producers, Craig Perry, Victor McGauley, Roger Garcia; Casting, Roger Mussenden; an Amen Ra Films/Zide-Perry/Lion Rock production; Dolby Stereo; Deluxe color; Rated R; 99 minutes; April release

CAST

Melvin Smiley ....Mark Wahlberg
Cisco...Lou Diamond Phillips
Pam Shulman...Christina Applegate
Paris...Avery Brooks
Crunch...Bokeem Woodbine
Vince...Antonio Sabato, Jr.
Jeanne Shulman ....Lainie Kazan
Morton Shulman...Elliott Gould
Jiro Nishi...Sab Shimono
Gump, The Stutterer ....Robin Dunne
Chantel...Lela Rochon
Keiko Nishi ....China Chow
Video Store Kid ....Danny Smith
Lance...Joshua Peace
Sergio...David Usher
Accountant...Hardee T. Lineham
Slave Trader..Gerry Mendocino
and Robert Veron Eaton, John Stoneham Sr. (Pimps), Nicola Jones (Blonde), Alexa Gilmour (Aly, Keiko's Friend), John Stoker (Sid Mussberger, The Neighbor), Cotton Mather (Moe), Derek Peels (Windbush), Tig Fong (Kaya), Danny Lima (Aaron the Limo Driver), Morgan Freeman (Boy in Hotel Lobby), Giovahann White (Paris' Son), Bobby Hannah (Paris' Driver)

Hitman Melvin Smiley talks his associates into a kidnapping plot that goes horribly wrong on the same weekend that his fiancee's parents show up for a visit.

I THINK I DO

(STRAND) Producer, Jane Janger; Executive Producers, Jon Gerrans, Marcus Hu, Robert Miller, Daryl Roth; Director/Screenplay, Brian Sloan; Photography, Milton Kam; Designer, Debbie Devilla; Editor, Francois Keraudren; Costumes, Kevin Donaldson, Victoria Farell; Casting, Stephanie Corsalini; Presented in association with Robert Miller, Danger Filmworks/House of Pain Productions, Sauce Entertainment and Daryl Roth Productions; Color; Not rated; 91 minutes; April release

CAST

Bob	Alexis Arquette
Beth	Maddie Corman
Eric	Guillermo Diaz
Sarah	Marianne Hagan
Matt	Jamie Harrold
Brendan	Christian Maelen
Carol	Lauren Vélez
Sterling Scott	Tuc Watkins
Mrs. Gonzalez	Patricia Mauceri
Aunt Alice	Marni Nixon
Celia	Elizabeth Rodriguez
Photographer	Dechen Thurman

Five years after his friendship with Brendan fell apart, Bob and his new lover Sterling show up at a friend's wedding, making Brendan question why he had previously rejected Bob's advances.

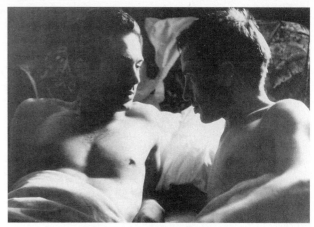

Christian Maelen, Alexis Arquette

Jamie Harrold, Lauren Vélez

©Strand Releasing

Natasha Gregson Wagner, Robert Downey Jr., Heather Graham

©Twentieth Century Fox

TWO GIRLS AND A GUY

(FOX SEARCHLIGHT) Producers, Edward R. Pressman, Chris Hanley; Executive Producers, Michael Mailer, Daniel Bigel; Director/Screenplay, James Toback; Photography, Barry Markowitz; Designer, Kevin Thompson; Editor, Alan Oxman; Line Producer, Gretchen McGowan; Wardrobe, Renata Chaplynsky; Casting, Sheila Jaffe, Georgianne Walken; an Edward R. Pressman production produced in association with Muse Productions; Dolby; Color; Rated R; 92 minutes; April release

CAST

Blake	Robert Downey, Jr.
Carla	Heather Graham
Lou	Natasha Gregson Wagner
Tommy	Angel David
Carol	Frederique Van Der Wal

When strangers Lou and Carla realize they are both romantically involved with Blake, they decide to wait for him at his apartment and confront him about the deception.

DÉJÀ VU

(RAINBOW) Producer, John Goldstone; Director/Editor, Henry Jaglom; Screenplay, Henry Jaglom, Victoria Foyt; Photography, Hanania Baer; Music, Gaili Schoen; Designer, Helen Scott; Costumes, Rhona Russell; Co-Producer, Judith Wolinsky; Casting, Irene Lamb; a Rainbow/Revere production of a Jagtoria Film; Stereo; Color; Not rated; 116 minutes; April release

CAST

Sean	Stephen Dillane
Dana	Victoria Foyt
Skelly	Vanessa Redgrave
Claire	Glyis Barber
Alex	Michael Brandon
Konstantine	Vernon Dobtcheff
Dana's Father	Graydon Gould
John	Noel Harrison
Woman in Cafe	Aviva Marks
Fern	Anna Massey
Skelly's Mother	Rachel Kempson

An attempt to return a piece of jewelry to a passing acquaintance causes Dana to make a detour on her trip to visit her fiancee, a journey that takes her to the town of Dover where she finds herself drawn to a man named Sean.

Victoria Foyt, Stephen Dillane

Victoria Foyt, Stephen Dillane

Vanessa Redgrave

Stephen Dillane, Victoria Foyt

Vanessa Redgrave, Anna Massey

Denzel Washington, Ray Allen

Rosario Dawson, Ray Allen

HE GOT GAME

(TOUCHSTONE) Producers, Jon Kilik, Spike Lee; Director/Screenplay, Spike Lee; Photography, Malik Hassan Sayeed; Designer, Wynn Thomas; Editor, Barry Alexander Brown; Costumes, Sandra Hernandez; Music, Aaron Copland; Songs, Public Enemy; Casting, Aisha Coley; a 40 Acres and a Mule Filmworks production; Distributed by Buena Vista; Dolby; Technicolor; Rated R; 134 minutes; May release

CAST

Jake Shuttlesworth	Denzel Washington
Jesus Shuttlesworth	Ray Allen
Dakota Burns	Milla Jovovich
Lala Bonilla	Rosario Dawson
Coleman "Booger" Sykes	Hill Harper
Mary Shuttlesworth	Zelda Harris
Warden Wyatt	Ned Beatty
Spivey	Jim Brown
Crudup	Joseph Lyle Taylor
Uncle Bubba	Bill Nunn
Aunt Sally	Michele Shay
Sweetness	Thomas Jefferson Byrd
Big Time Willie	Roger Guenveur Smith
Coach Billy Sunday	John Turturro
Martha Shuttlesworth	Lonette McKee
Coach Cincotta	Arthur J. Nascarella
Sip	Travis Best
Mance	Walter McCarty
Lonnie	John Wallace
Chick Deagan	Rick Fox
Dom Pagnotti	Al Palagonia
D'Andre Mackey	Leonard Roberts

and Saul Stein (Prison Guard Books), Ron Cephas Jones (Prison Guard Burwell), Jade Yorker (Jesus Shuttlesworth— age 12), Shortee Red (Booger—age 12), Quinn Harris (Mary Shuttlesworth—age 6), Coach Dean Smith, Coach John Chaney, Coach Roy Williams, Coach Denny Crum, Coach Clem Haskins, Coach Jim Boeheim, Coach Robert "Bobby" Cremins, Bill Walton, Reggie Miller, Scottie Pippen, Coach Lute Olson, Coach John Thompson, Coach Nolan Richardson, Coach Tom Davis, Coach George Karl, Coach Rick Pitino, Dick Vitale, Shaquille O'Neal, Charles Barkley, Michael Jordan, Robin Roberts (Themselves), Gus Johnson (PSAL Announcer), Stuart Scott (TV Announcer), Ray Clay (Tech U Announcer), J.C. Mackenzie (Doctor Cone), Coati Mundi (Clerk in Motel), Avery Glymph (Sneaker Clerk), Ciara A. Shields (Mary's Friend), Lin Que Ayoung, Dionne D. Phillips, Jamie Hector, Kelli-Lin McMillan, Angela Meryl, Gary Frith, Harry Philippe, Lamar Tookes ("I Love You" Leeches), Mark Breland (Man with Gat), Heather Hunter (Female in Sex Montage), Christopher Wynkoop (The John), Alonzo Scales (Goose), Lori Rom (June), Kim Director (Lynn), Felicia Finley (Molly), Tiffany Jones (Buffy), Jill Kelly (Suzie), Jennifer Esposito (Ms. Janus), Tony Paige (Correction Officer)

Jake Shuttlesworth is temporarily paroled in hopes that he can persuade his estranged son Jesus - the top high school basketball player in the country - to sign with the governor's alma mater, Big State.

©Touchstone Pictures

Denzel Washington, Ray Allen, Zelda Harris

Milla Jovovich, Denzel Washington

LES MISÉRABLES

Liam Neeson, Claire Danes

Uma Thurman

(COLUMBIA) Producers, Sarah Radclyffe, James Gorman; Director, Bille August; Screenplay, Rafael Yglesias; Based on the novel by Victor Hugo; Photography, Jørgen Persson; Designer, Anna Asp; Editor, Janus Billeskov-Jansen; Costumes, Gabriella Pescucci; Music, Basil Poledouris; Co-Producer, Caroline Hewitt; Casting, Leonora Davis; a Mandalay Entertainment presentation of a Sarah Radclyffe production/a James Gorman production; Dolby; Panavision; Technicolor; Rated PG-13; 131 minutes; May release

CAST

Jean Valjean ....Liam Neeson
Javert...Geoffrey Rush
Fantine...Uma Thurman
Cosette ....Claire Danes
Marius...Hans Matheson
Captain Beauvais ....Reine Brynolfsson
Bishop ....Peter Vaughan
Bertin ....Christopher Adamson
Lafitte ....Tim Barlow
Banker ....Timothy Bateson
Azelma...Veronika Bendová
Courfeyrac ....David Birkin
Toussaint ....Patsy Byrne
Mother Superior ....Kathleen Byron
André ....Václav Chalupa
Feuilly...Ian Cregg
Grantier...Ben Crompton
Peasant ....Zdenek David
Forewoman ....Paola Dionisotti
Old Woman ....Edna Dore
Letter Reader ....Louis Hammond
Mme Thenardier ....Gillian Hanna
Mme Gilot..Janet Henfrey
Gavroche ....Shane Hervey
Foreman ....Zdenek Hess
Digne Gendarme ....Gerard Horan
Mme Victurien...Kelly Hunter
and Lennie James (Enjolras), Toby Jones (Doorkeeper), Jon Kenny (Thenardier), Pavel Koci (Coachdriver), Sylvie Koblizkova (Eponine), Jane Kuzelka (Furniture Dealer), Peter Mackriel (Doctor), Margery Mason (Nursing Nun), Shannon McCormick (Redheaded Gendarme), John McGlynn (Carnot), Philip McGough (Judge), David McKay (Informer), Mimi Newman (Cosette—aged 8), Alex Norton (General), Ralph Nossek (Clerk), Frank O'Sullivan (Brevet), Zoja Oubramová (Old Woman), Jiri Patocka (Old Man), Petr Penkava (Beggar Child), Julian Rhind-Tutt (Bamatabois), Milan Riehs (Priest), James Saxon (Chabouillet), Petr Strnad (Young Homeless Boy), John Surman (Stonemason), Miroslav Taborsky (Gendarme), Terry Taplin (Prosecutor), Richard Toth (Gendarme), Edward Tudor Pole (Landlord), Zdenek Vencl (Messenger), Tony Vogel (Lombard), Pavel Vokoun (Sergeant), Jan Unger (Officer), Joshua Wren (Old Homeless Boy), Libor Zídek (Wig Maker)

Jean Valjean, unjustly imprisoned for stealing a loaf of bread, encounters a bishop whose kindness encourages him to change his life for the better. Meanwhile, determined policeman Javert vows to find Valjean and bring him back to jail. Previous versions of Hugo's novel include those done in 1935 (20th Century, with Fredric March and Charles Laughton), 1952 (20th Century Fox, Michael Rennie and Robert Newton), and 1995 (Warner Bros., Jean-Paul Belmondo).

©Mandalay Entertainment

Geoffrey Rush, Liam Neeson

DANCER, TEXAS POP. 81

(TRISTAR)) Producers, Chase Foster, Peter White, Dana Shaffer; Executive Producers, Michael Burns, Leanna Creel; Director/Screenplay, Tim McCanlies; Photography, Andrew Dintenfass; Designer, Dawn Snyder; Editor, Rob Kobrin; Music, Steve Dorff; Costumes, Susan Matheson; Co-Producers, Tina Brawner, Jeff Rice; Associate Producers, David Prybil, Jacqueline Anderson; Casting, Laurel Smith, Michael Testa; an HSX Films production in association with Chase Productions and Caribou Pictures; Dolby; Technicolor; Rated PG; 95 minutes; May release

CAST

Keller	Breckin Meyer
Terrell Lee	Peter Facinelli
John	Eddie Mills
Squirrel	Ethan Embry
Josie	Ashley Johnson
Mrs. Lusk	Patricia Wettig
Mr. Lusk	Michael O'Neill
Earl	Eddie Jones
Keller's Grandfather	Wayne Tippit
Vivian	Alexandra Holden
Squirrel's Father	Keith Szarabajka
Sue Ann	Shawn Weatherly
Mr. Hemphill	Michael Crabtree
Mrs. Hemphill	LaShawn McIvor

and Joe Stevens (Leon), Tommy G. Kendrick (Rusty), Steven Bland (Wayne), Craig Carter (Guy), Tennessee (Old Fart Rancher), Mary Ann Luedecke (Betty Sue), Bill Brooks (Reverend), Felipe De Ortego y Gasca (Principal), Kessia Kordelle (Jean), Kendra Payne (Loretta), Jack Vaden (Harvey), Lynn Carter (Another Rancher), Jon Bergholz (Bus Driver), Lucy Jacobson (Flora), Lisa Billing (Sandra), Emilie B. Severin (Mrs. Caldwell), Leigh Eaton (Mrs. Hufheinz), Billie Craddock (Mrs. Garcia)

On the eve of graduation four high school friends wonder if they will follow through on their pledge to leave their sleepy Texas town and find better lives in the outside world.

Breckin Meyer, Ethan Embry, Peter Facinelli, Eddie Mills

©TriStar Pictures

CLOCKWATCHERS

(ARTISTIC LICENSE/BMG) Producer, Gina Resnick; Executive Producer, John Flock; Director, Jill Sprecher; Screenplay, Jill Sprecher, Karen Sprecher; Co-Executive Producer, Guy Collins; Photography, Jim Denault; Editor, Steven Mirrione; Designer, Pamela Marcotte; Costumes, Edi Giguere; Music, Mader, Joey Altruda; Co-Producer, Karen Sprecher; Line Producer, W. Mark McNair; Casting, Jeanne McCarthy; a Goldcrest Films International presentation of a Gina Resnick production; Dolby; Color; Rated PG-13; 105 minutes; May release

CAST

Iris	Toni Collette
Margaret	Parker Posey
Paula	Lisa Kudrow
Jane	Alanna Ubach
Cleo	Helen Fitzgerald
Art	Stanley DeSantis
Eddie	Jamie Kennedy
MacNamee	David James Elliott
Barbara	Debra Jo Rupp
Mr. Kilmer	Kevin Cooney
Milton Lasky	Bob Balaban
Bud Chapman	Paul Dooley
Jack Shoberg	Scott Mosenson

and Irene Olga Lopez (Coffee Lady), Joshua Malina (Receptionist), O-Lan Jones (Madame Debbie), Joe Chrest (Detective), Patrice Pitman Quinn (Woman in Office), Michelle Arthur (Dianne the Shoe Lady), Athena Ulbach (Jane's Sister), Lynn Tufeld (Woman Missing Watch), Jennifer Balgobin (Attractive Woman), Chuck Borden (Guard), Gregg Daniel (Policeman), Tim Hutchinson (Businessman), Sully Diaz (Waitress), Jim Wise (Man in Bar), Wendy Pitts (Saleslady), Patti Yasotake (Theater Woman), Steve Rodriguez (Lobby Guard), Constance Forshind (Flight Attendant), Jaime Gomez (Derrick), Bridget Sienna (Woman with Cop), Terri Hoyos (Executive), Brodie Nelson (Copy Repairman)

Four women working as temps at a credit agency become friends while hoping to find themselves better careers.

Jamie Kennedy, Parker Posey, Toni Collette, Lisa Kudrow,
Alanna Ubach, Debra Jo Rupp

©Goldcrest Films Intl./ BMG Independents

DEEP IMPACT

(PARAMOUNT/DREAMWORKS) Producers, Richard D. Zanuck, David Brown; Executive Producers, Steven Spielberg, Walter Parkes, Joan Bradshaw; Director, Mimi Leder; Screenplay, Bruce Joel Rubin, Michael Tolkin; Photography, Dietrich Lohmann; Designer, Leslie Dilley; Editor, David Rosenbloom; Costumes, Ruth Myers; Visual Effects Supervisor, Scott Farrar; Music, James Horner; Casting, Allison Jones; Stunts, M. James Arnett, Charles Croughwell; a Zanuck/Brown production; Dolby; Super 35 Widescreen; Deluxe color; Rated PG-13; 120 minutes; May release

Morgan Freeman, Téa Leoni

CAST

Spurgeon Tanner	Robert Duvall
Jenny Lerner	Téa Leoni
Leo Biederman	Elijah Wood
Robin Lerner	Vanessa Redgrave
President Tom Beck	Morgan Freeman
Jordan Lerner	Maximilian Schell
Alan Rittenhouse	James Cromwell
Oren Monash	Ron Eldard
Gus Partenza	Jon Favreau
Beth Stanley	Laura Innes
Andrea Baker	Mary McCormack
Don Biederman	Richard Schiff
Sarah Hotchner	Leelee Sobieski
Mark Simon	Blair Underwood
Eric Vennekor	Dougray Scott
Chuck Hotchner	Gary Werntz
Stuart Caley	Bruce Weitz
Ellen Biederman	Betsy Brantley
Morton Entrekin	O'Neal Compton
Chloe	Rya Kihlstedt
Boris Tulchinsky	Alexander Baluev
Caitlin Stanley	Caitlin Fein, Amanda Fein
Ira Moskatel	Joseph Urla
Marianne Duclos	Una Damon
Tim Urbanska	Mark Moses
Theo Van Sertema	Derek de Lint
Jeff Worth	Charles Dumas
Jenny's Assistant	Suzy Nakamura
Bobby Rhue	Almi Ballard
Marcus Wolf	Charles Martin Smith
Jane Biederman	Katie Hagan
Vicky Hotchner	Denise Crosby
Priest	Frank Whiteman
Harold	Jason Dohring
Kid	Jasmine Harrison
Student	Rahi Azizi
Holly Rittenhouse	Hannah Werntz
Ivan Bronsky	Tucker Smallwood
Sheila Bradley	Merrin Dungey
Wendy Mogel	Kimberly Huie

Leelee Sobieski, Elijah Wood

and William Fair (Grey Man), Francis X. McCarthy (General Scot), Ellen Bry (Stofsky), Lisa Ann Grant (Reporter), Leslie Dilley (Waiter), Concetta Tomei (Patricia Ruiz), Mike O'Malley (Mike Perry), Kurtwood Smith (Otis Hefte), Gerry Griffin (NASA Official), Charlie Hartsock (David Baker), Jennifer Jostyn (Mariette Monash), Don Handfield (Dwight Tanner), Jason Frasca (Steve Tanner), Cynthia Ettinger (Pretty Woman), Benjamin Stralka (Little Boy), Stephanie Patton (Brittany Baker), Michael Winters (NASA Guy), John Ducey (Young Lieutenant), Christopher Darga (Section Leader), Joshua Colwell (CAPCOM), Cornelius Lewis (Bus Sergeant), Kevin LaRosa (Pilot)

When scientists discover a comet hurtling towards earth with enough force to cause total destruction, a team of astronauts is sent into space in hopes of obliterating the comet before it is too late.

Alexander Baluev, Jon Favreau

Blair Underwood, Alexander Baluev, Robert Duvall, Mary McCormack, Ron Eldard

Vanessa Redgrave

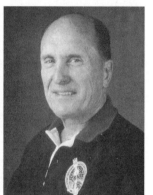

Robert Duvall

Elijah Wood, Leelee Sobieski

Jon Favreau, Mary McCormack, Alexander Baluev, Ron Eldard, Robert Duvall, Blair Underwood

Oliver Platt, Warren Beatty

Paul Sorvino

Ariyan Johnson, Michele Morgan

Don Cheadle

Richard Sarafian, Jack Warden

Warren Beatty

BULWORTH

Warren Beatty

(20TH CENTURY FOX) Producers, Warren Beatty, Pieter Jan Brugge; Executive Producer, Lauren Shuler Donner; Director/Story, Warren Beatty; Screenplay, Warren Beatty, Jeremy Pikser; Photography, Vittorio Storaro; Designer, Dean Tavoularis; Editors, Robert C. Jones, Billy Weber; Costumes, Milena Canonero; Co-Producers, Victoria Thomas, Frank Capra III; Music, Ennio Morricone; Executive Soundtrack Producer, Karyn Richtman; Music Designer, Bob Badami; Dolby; Technicolor; Rated R; 107 minutes; May release

CAST

Jay Bulworth	Warren Beatty
Nina	Halle Berry
Dennis Murphy	Oliver Platt
L.D.	Don Cheadle
Graham Crockett	Paul Sorvino
Eddie Davers	Jack Warden
Constance Bulworth	Christine Baranski
Feldman	Joshua Malina
Vinnie	Richard Sarafian
Darnell	Isaiah Washington
Homeless Man (Rastaman)	Amiri Baraka
Gary	Sean Astin
Mimi	Laurie Metcalf
Fred	Wendell Pierce
Cheryl	Michele Morgan
Tanya	Ariyan Johnson
Denisha	Kimberly Deauna Adams
Debate Director	Vinny Argiro
Debate Producer	Kirk Baltz
Leroy	Ernie Banks
Mrs. Brown	Adilah Barnes
Man with Dark Glasses	Graham Beckel
Uncle Rafeeq	Thomas Jefferson Byrd
Anthony	J. Kenneth Campbell
Head Valet	Scott Michael Campbell
Rev. Wilberforce	Kevin Cooney
Manny Liebowitz	Stanley DeSantis
Missy Berliner	Nora Dunn
Man with Blunt	Dartanyan Edmonds
Mr. Sasser	Edward J. Etherson

and V.J. Foster (Photographer), Leon Curtis Frierson (Osgood), George Furth (Older Man), Robin Gammell (Geoffrey), Life Garland (Darnell's Bud), Jackie Gayle (Macavoy), Jim Haynie (Bill Stone), Randee Heller (Mrs. Tannenbaum), Barry Shabaka Henley (Man at Frankie's), Brian Hooks (Marcus Garvey), Mario Jackson (Snag), James Keane (American Politics Director), Mimi Lieber (Mrs. Liebowitz), Elizabeth Lindsey (American Politics Host), Helen Martin (Momma Doll), Armelia McQueen (Ruthie), Debra Monk (Helen), Michael "Big Mike" Duncan, Brandon N. Bowlin, Larry Mark, Gary H. Walton (Bouncers), Andrew Warne, Xiomara Cuevas Galindo, Ava Rivera, Kerry Catanese (Video Reporters), Jann Carl, Dave Allen Clark, Jerry Dunphy, Larry King (Themselves), Kenn Whitaker, Terry Cooley (Henchmen), Christopher Curry, James Hill, Robert Scheer (Journalists), Kene Holliday, Lee Weaver (Men in Church), Michael Kaufman, Deborah Lacey, Terri Hoyos, Tom Kelly, Brooke Skulski, Robert Soto (Reporters), Myra J., Jedda Jones (Women in Church), Michael Milhoan, Chris Mulkey (Cops), Jamal Mixon, Jerod Mixon, Jonathan Roger Neal, Kenneth Randle, Tony Tomas Randle, Arthur Reggie III (Little Gangstas), Patrick Morgan (Studio Employee), Juli Mortz (Larry King's Assistant), Scott Mosenson (Video Cameraman), Paul Motley (Janitor in Senate Office), Lou Myers (Uncle Tyrone), Shawna Nagler (Technical Director), Ron Ostrow (Staff Member), Norman Parker (Irwin Tannenbaum), James Pickens, Jr. (Uncle David), Adrian Ricard (Aunt Alice), Sam Shamshak (Fundraiser Guest), Sarah Silverman (2nd American Politics Assistant), Bee-Be Smith (Aunt Harriet), Florence Stanley (Dobish), Quinn Sullivan (Fundraiser Server), JoAnn D. Thomas (Rapper), Robin Thomas (Reporter in Hallway), Sheryl Underwood (Woman in Frankie's), Jermaine Williams (Paul Robeson), John Witherspoon (Reverend Morris), Sumiko Telljohn (Lady at Banquet), Paul Mazursky (Party Guest), George Hamilton (Himself), William Baldwin (Constance's Lover)

Halle Berry, Warren Beatty

Incumbent U.S. Senator Jay Bulworth finds himself on the verge of a nervous breakdown because of all the political promises left unfulfilled during his term in office. As a result he arranges for his own assassination, a move which unleashes from within him a freedom to honestly speak his mind to the public. This film received an Oscar nomination for original screenplay.

©Twentieth Century Fox

Joshua Malina, Jackie Gayle, Oliver Platt

Robert Redford

Kristin Scott Thomas, Robert Redford

THE HORSE WHISPERER

(TOUCHSTONE) Producers, Robert Redford, Patrick Markey; Director, Robert Redford; Screenplay, Eric Roth, Richard LaGravenese; Based upon the novel by Nicholas Evans; Photography, Robert Richardson; Designer, Jon Hutman; Editors, Tom Rolf, Freeman Davies, Hank Corwin; Costumes, Judy L. Ruskin, Bernie Pollack; Music, Thomas Newman; Song: "A Soft Place to Fall" by Allison Moorer and Gwil Owen; Executive Producer, Rachel Pfeffer; Co-Producer, Joseph Reidy; Associate Producer, Karen Tenkoff; Visual Effects Supervisors, Peter Donen, Peter Crosman; Casting, Ellen Chenoweth, Gretchen Rennell Court; a Wildwood Enterprises production; Distributed by Buena Vista Pictures; Dolby; Panavision; Technicolor; Rated PG-13; 168 minutes; May release

CAST

Tom Booker	Robert Redford
Annie MacLean	Kristin Scott Thomas
Robert MacLean	Sam Neill
Diane Booker	Dianne Wiest
Grace MacLean	Scarlett Johansson
Frank Booker	Chris Cooper
Liz Hammond	Cherry Jones
Joe Booker	Ty Hillman
Judith	Catherine Bosworth
Twins	Austin Schwarz, Dustin Schwarz
Ellen Booker	Jeanette Nolan
Hank	Steve Frye
Smokey	Don Edwards
Lucy	Jessalyn Gilsig
Lester Petersen	William "Buddy" Byrd
Local Tracker	John Hogarty
Park Ranger	Mike La Londe
Doctor	C.J. Byrnes
Nurses	Kathy Baldwin Keenan, Kelley Sweeney
Barn Dance Vocalist	Allison Moorer
Truck Driver	George Sack, Jr.
David Gottschalk (V.O.)	Stephen Pearlman
Office Workers	Joelle Carter, Sunny Chae, Anne Joyce
Schoolgirls	Tara Sobeck, Kristy Ann Servidio
Neighbor	Marie Engle
Handsome Cowboy	Curt Pate
Ranch Hand	Steven Brian Conard
Roper	Tammy Pate

Successful New York magazine editor Annie MacLean hires famed horse trainer Tom Booker hoping that he will heal her daughter who has been severely traumatized by a riding accident that killed her best friend and left her prize horse physically scarred. This film received an Oscar nomination for original song ("A Soft Place to Fall").

©Touchstone Pictures

Scarlett Johansson, Robert Redford

Dianne Wiest, Chris Cooper

Robert Redford, Scarlett Johansson

Robert Redford

Dianne Wiest

Sam Neill

Kristin Scott Thomas, Robert Redford

Harry Shearer, Maria Pitillo

Kevin Dunn, Doug Savant

Jean Reno, Matthew Broderick

Michael Lerner, Lorry Goldman

Hank Azaria

GODZILLA

(TRISTAR) Producer, Dean Devlin; Director, Roland Emmerich; Screenplay, Dean Devlin, Roland Emmerich; Story, Ted Elliott, Terry Rossio, Dean Devlin, Roland Emmerich; Based on the character owned and created by Toho Co. Ltd.; Executive Producers, Roland Emmerich, Ute Emmerich, William Fay; Photography, Ueli Steiger; Designer, Oliver Scholl; Editors, Peter Amundson, David J. Siegel; Music, David Arnold; Co-Producers, Peter Winther, Kelly Van Horn; Co-Executive Producers, Robert N. Fried, Cary Woods; Visual Effects Supervisor, Volker Engel; Godzilla Designer and Supervisor, Patrick Tatopoulos; Costumes, Joseph Porro; Visual Effects Producer, Terry C. Clotiaux; Digital Effects and Digital Creature Animation, Centropolis Effects; Casting, April Webster, David Bloch; a Centropolis Entertainment production; a Fried Films and Independent Pictures production; Dolby; Super 35 Widescreen; Technicolor; Rated PG-13; 139 minutes; May release

Matthew Broderick, Maria Pitillo

CAST

Dr. Niko Tatopoulos	Matthew Broderick
Philippe Roaché	Jean Reno
Audrey Timmonds	Maria Pitillo
Victor "Animal" Palotti	Hank Azaria
Colonel Hicks	Kevin Dunn
Mayor Ebert	Michael Lerner
Charles Caiman	Harry Shearer
Lucy Palotti	Arabella Field
Dr. Elsie Chapman	Vicki Lewis
Sergeant O'Neal	Doug Savant
Dr. Mendel Craven	Malcolm Danare
Gene—Mayor's Aide	Lorry Goldman
Jean-Luc	Christian Aubert
Jean-Claude	Philippe Bergeron
Jean-Pierre	Frank Bruynbroek
Jean-Philippe	Francois Giroday
Ed	Nicholas J. Giangiulio
Murray	Robert Lesser
Old Fisherman	Ralph Manza
Governor	Greg Callahan
General Anderson	Chris Ellis
Caiman's Secretary	Nancy Cartwright
Admiral Phelps	Richard E. Gant
Leonard	Jack Moore
Jules	Steve Giannelli
Arthur	Brian Farabaugh
Lt. Anderson	Stephen Xavier Lee
Freddie	Bodhi Elfman
Jimmy	Rich Battista

and Lloyd Kino (Japanese Tanker Cook), Toshi Toda (Japanese Tanker Captain), Clyde Kusatsu (Japanese Tanker Skipper), Masaya Kato (Japanese Tanker Crew Member), Glenn Morshower (Kyle Terrington),Lola Pashalinski (Pharmacist), Rob Fukuzaki (WIDF Co-Anchor), Dale Harimoto (WKXI Anchor), Gary Cruz (WFKK Anchor), Derek Webster (Utah Captain), Stuart Fratkin (Utah Ensign), David Pressman (Anchorage Captain), Frank Cilberg, Jason Edward Jones, Roger McIntyre (Utah Sailors), Robert Faltisco, Chris Maleki, Scott Lusby (Anchorage Ensigns), Alex Dodd (Anchorage Sailor), Terence Winter, Kirk Geiger, Pat Mastroianni, Eric Saiet, Burt Bulos, Robert Floyd, Seth Peterson (Apache Pilots), Jamison Yang, Nathan Anderson, Mark Munafo, Dwight Schmidt (F-18 Pilots), Dwayne Swingler (Raven Pilot #2), Lawton Paseka (Officer), Greg Collins (Soldier on Bridge), James Black, Thomas Giuseppe Giantonelli, Paul Ware (Soldiers), Monte Russell (Soldier on Plane), Christopher Carruthers, Daniel Pearce (Radio Technicians), Mark Fite (Radio Operator), Craig A. Castaldo (Radio Man), Eric Paskel (Rodgers), Lee Weaver, Leonard Termo (Homeless Guys), Joshua Taylor (Spotter), Al Sapienza (Taxi Cab Driver), Stoney Westmoreland (Tunnel Guard), Gary Warner (Gun Technician), Ed Wheeler (New York Cop), Bill Hoag (New Jersey Cop), Joe Badalucco, Jr. (Forklift Driver), Jonathan Dienst (Field Reporter), Benjamin V. Baird, Madeline McFadden, Julian M. Phillips, Raymond Ramos (Reporters)

Matthew Broderick

A gigantic reptilian monster arises from the sea and sets its sights on New York City where it proceeds to cause untold carnage as scientist Nick Tatopoulos, a French insurance investigator, and the U.S. military try to stop the rampaging beast. The character of Godzilla was first introduced in the 1954 Japanese-Toho feature Gojira, *which debuted in America in 1956 under the title* Godzilla, King of the Monsters. *This was followed by a long series of Japanese Godzilla films produced by Toho.*

©TriStar Pictures

QUEST FOR CAMELOT

(WARNER BROS.) Producer, Dalisa Cooper Cohen; Director, Frederik Du Chau; Screenplay, Kirk DeMicco, William Schifrin, Jacqueline Feather, David Seidler; Based on the novel The King's Damosel by Vera Chapman; Music, Patrick Doyle; Songs by David Foster, Carole Bayer Sager; Designer, Steve Pilcher; Editor, Stanford C. Allen; Associate Producer, Zahra Dowlatabadi; Lead Animator, Alyson Hamilton; Art Directors, Carl Kieffer Police, J. Michael Spooner; Creative Consultant, Mike Ockrent; Choreographer, Kenny Ortega; Additional Clean-Up Animation, Theresa Smythe; Casting, Julie Hughes, Barry Moss; Dolby; Technicolor; Rated G; 85 minutes; May release

VOICE CAST

Kayley (speaking voice) ....Jessalyn Gilsig
Kayley (singing voice)...Andrea Corr
Garrett (speaking voice) ....Cary Elwes
Garrett (singing voice)..Bryan White
Ruber ....Gary Oldman
Devon ....Eric Idle
Cornwall ....Don Rickles
Juliana (speaking voice) ....Jane Seymour
Juliana (singing voice)..Celine Dion
King Arthur (speaking voice) ....Pierce Brosnan
King Arthur (singing voice) ....Steve Perry
Griffin ....Bronson Pinchot
Bladebeak ....Jaleel White
Lionel...Gabriel Byrne
Merlin ....Sir John Gielgud
Ayden ....Frank Welker
Young Kayley ....Sarah Rayne

Kayley, who dreams of becoming a knight of the Round Table, embarks on a quest to retrieve King Arthur's sword Excalibur after it is stolen by the evil Ruber. This film received an Oscar nomination for original song ("The Prayer").

Devon & Cornwall, Kayley, Garrett

Griffin, Ruber

OFF THE MENU: THE LAST DAYS OF CHASEN'S

(NORTHERN ARTS) Producer, Julia Strohm; Executive Producers, Diandra Douglas, Alicia Sams; Co-Executive Producer, James Kimsey; Directors, Shari Springer Berman, Robert Pulcini; Photography, Ken Kobland, Sandra Chandler; Editor, Robert Pulcini; Music, Mark Suozzo; from A La Carte Film Inc. and Lobo Grande Pictures Inc.; Color; Not rated; 90 minutes; May release. Documentary about the final two weeks of Hollywood's last golden age restaurant, Chasen's.

WITH

Steve Allen, Army Archerd, Maureen Arthur, James Bacon, Angela Bassett, Jeff Berg, David Brown, Brett Butler, Gary Coleman, Jackie Collins, Pierre Cossette, Billy Davis Jr., Bo Derek, Angie Dickinson, Matt Dillon, Cristina Ferrari, Betty Ford, Gerald Ford, Jodie Foster, Michael J. Fox, Chuck Fries, Ava Fries, David Frost, Elmer Fudd, Neal Gabler, Hugh Grant, Merv Griffin, Monty Hall, Charlton Heston, Bob Hope, Holly Hunter, Elizabeth Hurley, Samuel L. Jackson, Jennifer Jones, Jessica Lange, Ethel Kennedy, Quincy Jones, Sally Kellerman, Nastassja Kinski, Sally Kirkland, Martin Landau, Jack Lemmon, Jay Leno, Michael Lerner, Art Linkletter, Courtney Love, A.C. Lyles, Carol Lynley, Madonna, Johnny Mathis, Marilyn McCoo, Ed McMahon, Jayne Meadows, Margaret O'Brien, Dale Olson, Chazz Palminteri, Sarah Jessica Parker, Suzanne Pleshette, Colin Powell, Kelly Preston, Nancy Reagan, Miranda Richardson, Don Rickles, Tom Snyder, Rod Steiger, Sharon Stone, Donna Summer, Quentin Tarantino, Jennifer Tilly, John Travolta, Mrs. Rudy Vallee, Robert Wagner, Lew Wasserman, Dianne Wiest, Norm Winter, Fay Wray, Jane Wyman, Yanni

Pepe Ruiz

FEAR AND LOATHING IN LAS VEGAS

(UNIVERSAL) Producers, Laila Nabulsi, Patrick Cassavetti, Stephen Nemeth; Executive Producers, Harold Bronson, Richard Foos; Director, Terry Gilliam; Screenplay, Terry Gilliam, Tony Grisoni, Tod Davies, Alex Cox; Based on the book by Hunter S. Thompson; Photography, Nicola Pecorini; Designer, Alex McDowell; Editor, Lesley Walker; Costumes, Julie Weiss; Co-Producer, Elliot Lewis Rosenblatt; Lounge Lizards Designer, Rob Bottin; Visual Effects Supervisor, Kent Houston; Casting, Margery Simkin; a Rhino Films/Laila Nabulsi production; Dolby; Super 35 Widescreen; Rank color; Rated R; 119 minutes; May release

Benicio Del Toro, Johnny Depp

CAST

Raoul Duke	Johnny Depp
Dr. Gonzo	Benicio Del Toro
Hitchhiker	Tobey Maguire
Uniformed Dwarf	Michael Lee Gogin
Carl Rental Agent (Los Angeles)	Larry Cedar
Parking Attendant	Brian LeBaron
Reservations Clerk	Katherine Helmond
Bell Boy	Michael Warwick
Lacerda	Craig Bierko
Magazine Reporter	Mark Harmon
Reporter	Tyde Kierney
Hoodlum	Tim Thomerson
Dune Buggy Driver	Richard Riehle
Dune Buggy Passengers	Ransom Gates, Frank Romano
Desert Room Doormen	Gil Boccaccio, Gary Bruno
Wine Colored Tuxedo	Richard Portnow
Voice of Debbie Reynolds	Debbie Reynolds
Goon	Steve Schirripa
Wee Waiter	Verne J. Troya
The Black Guy	Will Blount
Clown Barker	Ben Yeager
Carnie Talker	Penn Jillette
Bazooka Circus Waitress	Christopher Callen
Blonde TV Reporter	Cameron Diaz
TV Crew Man	Ben Van der Veen
Road Person	Lyle Lovett
Musician	Flea
Stockbroker	Alex Craig Mann
Clerk at Mint Hotel	Gregory Itzin
Highway Patrolman	Gary Busey
Police Chief	Troy Evans
Police Chief's Wife	Gale Baker
Clerk at Flamingo Hotel	Chris Meloni
Lucy	Christina Ricci
Executive Director	Chris Hendrie
Cop in Black	Larry Brandenburg
L. Ron Bumquist	Michael Jeter
Voice of Film Narrator	Donald Morrow
Judge	Harry Dean Stanton
Maid	Jenette Goldstein
Human Cannonball	Stephen Bridgewater
North Star Waitress	Ellen Barkin

and Buck Holland, Mary Gillis, Jennifer Elise Cox (the Shoppers), Robert Allen (Car Rental Agent—Las Vegas), David Brisbin (Man in Car), James O'Sullivan, Milt Tarver (TV Newsmen), Kathryn Alexander, Mia Babalis, Kristin Draudt, Kim Flowers, Nan Friedman, Trudi Forristal, Judith Lieff, Tane McClure, Diana Mehoudar, Geoffrey B. Nimmer (Lizard Performers), Marlene Bologna, Chobi Gyorgy, Karen E. Castoldi, Lisa S. Hoyle, Joseph S. Griffo (Trapeze Artists)

Johnny Depp

Raoul Duke and his buddy Dr. Gonzo take off for a drug-induced journey to Las Vegas where their "tripping" becomes a haze of surreal imagery.

©Universal City Studios Productions Inc.

Johnny Depp, Benicio Del Toro

Christina Ricci

Lisa Kudrow, Lyle Lovett

Christina Ricci, Ivan Sergei

Martin Donovan, Johnny Galecki

©Sony Pictures Entertainment

THE OPPOSITE OF SEX

(SONY PICTURES CLASSICS) Producers, David Kirkpatrick, Michael Besman; Executive Producers, Jim Lotfi, Steve Danton; Director/Screenplay, Don Roos; Photography, Hubert Taczanowski; Designer, Michael Clausen; Editor, David Codron; Music, Mason Daring; Costumes, Peter Mitchell; a David Kirkpatrick/Michael Besman production; Dolby; Color; Rated R; 105 minutes; May release

CAST

Dedee Truitt	Christina Ricci
Bill Truitt	Martin Donovan
Lucia Dalury	Lisa Kudrow
Carl Tippett	Lyle Lovett
Jason Bock	Johnny Galecki
Randy	William Scott Lee
Matt Mateo	Ivan Sergei
Bobette	Megan Blake
Tom Dalury	Colin Ferguson
Timothy	Dan Bucatinsky
Joe	Chauncey Leopardi
Ty	Rodney Eastman
Jennifer	Heather Fairfield
TV Reporter	Amy Atkins
Student	Leslie Grossman
Marcia	Emily Newman
Medical Examiner	Harrison Young
Police Officer	Pancho Demmings
Harley Men	Terry L. Rose, Richard Moore
Policewoman Judy Zale	Susan Leslie

and Marguax St. Ledger (Reporter), Leslie Bevis (World NewsReporter) Nicole Tocantins (Bobette's Lawyer), Becky Wahlstrom (Cashier), Peter Spears (Dr. Allen), Kristine Keever (Nurse), David Phelps-Williams (School Principal), Todd Eckert (Parole Officer)

Eternally bored teen Dedee Truitt runs away from home, moves in with her brother Bill and proceeds to seduce Bill's dim-witted boyfriend.

HOPE FLOATS

(20TH CENTURY FOX) Producer, Lynda Obst; Executive Producers, Mary McLaglen, Sandra Bullock; Director, Forest Whitaker; Screenplay, Steven Rogers; Photography, Caleb Deschanel; Designer, Larry Fulton; Costumes, Susie DeSanto; Editor, Richard Chew; Executive Soundtrack Producers, Don Was, Forest Whitaker; Music, Dave Grusin; Casting, Ronnie Yeskel; a Lynda Obst production in association with Fortis Films; Dolby; Deluxe color; Rated PG-13; 114 minutes; May release

Harry Connick Jr., Sandra Bullock

CAST

Birdee Pruitt	Sandra Bullock
Justin Matisse	Harry Connick, Jr.
Ramona Calvert	Gena Rowlands
Bernice Pruitt	Mae Whitman
Bill Pruitt	Michael Paré
Travis	Cameron Finley
Toni Post	Kathy Najimy
Nurse	Bill Cobbs
Bobbi-Claire	Connie Ray
Teacher	Mona Lee Fultz
Orange Julia	Sydney Berry
Big Dolores	Rachel Lena Snow
Kristen	Christina Stojanovich
Debbie Reissen	Allisa Alban
Dot	Dee Hennigan
Waitress	Martha Long
Mr. Davis	Norman Bennett
Harry Calvert	James N. Harrell
P.E. Teacher	Chris Drewy
Young Man at Dance	Meason Wiley
Suzy	Tisa Hibbs
Bartender	Art Michael Tamez
Volleyball Captain	Jeanette Sieh
Young Birdee	Tara Price
Priest	Richard Nance
Connie	Rosanna Arquette

Sandra Bullock, Mae Whitman

After her husband dumps her for her best friend, Birdee Pruitt takes her young daughter and moves back to the town in which she grew up, hoping to start life anew.

©Twentieth Century Fox

Mae Whitman, Sandra Bullock, Gena Rowlands

Harry Connick, Jr.

Chris Eigeman, Kate Beckinsale, Mackenzie Astin,
Matt Ross, Chloë Sevigny

Chloë Sevigny, Chris Eigeman

THE LAST DAYS OF DISCO

(GRAMERCY) Producer/Director/Screenplay, Whit Stillman; Photography, John Thomas; Editors, Andrew Hafitz, Jay Pires; Co-Producers, Cecilia Kate Roque, Edmon Roch; Executive Producer, John Sloss; Costumes, Sarah Edwards; Designer, Ginger Tougas; Music, Mark Suozzo; Choreographer, John Carrafa; Casting, Billy Hopkins, Suzanne Smith, Kerry Barden; a Castle Rock Entertaiment presentation; Dolby; Color; Rated R; 112 minutes; May release

CAST

Alice	Chloë Sevigny
Charlotte	Kate Beckinsale
Des	Chris Eigeman
Jimmy	Mackenzie Astin
Josh	Matt Keeslar
Tom	Robert Sean Leonard
Nina	Jennifer Beals
Dan	Matthew Ross
Holly	Tara Subkoff

At the Club:

Van	Burr Steers
Bernie	David Thornton
Tiger Lady	Jaid Barrymore
Diana	Sonsee Ahray
Victor	Edoardo Ballerini
Adam	Scott Beehner
Backdoorman	Zachary Taylor
Rick	Neil Butterfield

Clients & Models:

Hap	Michael Weatherly
Marshall	James Murtagh
Steve	John C. Havens
Models	Amanda Harker, Brandi Seymor

and *Publishing House*: Leslie Lyles (Sally), Cate Smit (Helen), Kathleen Chalfant (Zenia), Jan Austell (Bob), Robin Miles (Josephine); *from "Metropolitan"*: Carolyn Farina (Audrey Rouget), Taylor Nichols (Charlie), Bryan Leder (Fred), Dylan Hundley (Sally Fowler); *from "Barcelona"*: Taylor Nichols (Ted Boynton), Debbon Ayer (Betty); *Elsewhere*: Mark McKinney (Rex), Linda Pierce (Real Estate Lady), Carlos Jacott (Dog Walker), Sharon Scruggs (Justine Prashker), Ajay Mehta (Pharmacist), Norma Quarles (Anti-Disco Rally Reporter); and George Plimpton, Anthony Haden-Guest, Kimball Chen, Desiree Von La Valette, Ivy Supersonic & the Groovy Girls, Bunny Beekman, Inmaculada De Habsburgo, Redman Maxfield, Jack Staub, Elizabeth Strong Cuevas, Isabelle Townsend (Clubgoers)

In the early 1980s, Alice and Charlotte, a pair of recent Hampshire College grads working at a publishing house, take up residence with a third roommate in Manhattan, where they hope to expand their social life at a popular dance club.

Robert Sean Leonard, Kate Beckinsale, Chloë Sevigny

Matt Keeslar, Chloë Sevigny, Kate Beckinsale

LITTLE BOY BLUE

(**CASTLE HILL**) Producer, Amedeo Ursini; Executive Producer, Virginia Giritlian; Director, Antonio Tibaldi; Screenplay, Michael Boston; Photography, Ron Hagen; Designer, John Frick; Editors, Antonio Tibaldi, Tobin Taylor; Music, Stewart Copeland; Costumes, April Ferry; Casting, Michelle Guillermin; a Jazz Pictures presentation; Dolby; Color; Rated R; 107 minutes; May release

CAST

Jimmy West/Danny Knight	Ryan Phillippe
Kate West	Nastassja Kinski
Ray West	John Savage
Doris Knight	Shirley Knight
Nate Carr	Tyrin Turner
Traci Connor	Jenny Lewis
Tom	Brent Jennings
Andy Berg	John Doman
Mark West	Devon Michael
Mikey West	Adam Burke
Young Doris	Kaitlin Hopkins
Sgt. Phillips	Dennis Letts
Det. Fleaharty	Jerry Cotton
Leo Dalt	Michael Boston
Motel Clerk	Gail Cronaur
Paramedic	Carine Chalfoun

Nineteen-year-old Jimmy West tries to protect his younger brothers and his mom from the hellish existence caused by his war-scarred, emotionally unbalanced father.

©Castle Hill/Alan Pappé

John Savage, Nastassja Kinski, Ryan Phillippe

Ryan Phillippe, John Savage

Eric Stoltz, Annabella Sciorra

©Lions Gate Films

MR. JEALOUSY

(**LIONS GATE**) Producer, Joel Castleberg; Executive Producer, Eric Stoltz; Director/Screenplay, Noah Baumbach; Photography, Steven Bernstein; Designer, Anne Stuhler; Music, Luna, Robert Een; Editor, J. Kathleen Gibson; Costumes, Katherine Jane Bryant; Line Producer, Victoria McGarry; a Joel Castleberg production; Dolby; Color; Rated R; 105 minutes; June release

CAST

Lester Grimm	Eric Stoltz
Ramona Ray	Annabella Sciorra
Dashiell Frank	Chris Eigeman
Vince	Carlos Jacott
Lucretia	Marianne Jean-Baptiste
Stephen	Brian Kerwin
Dr. Poke	Peter Bogdanovich
Irene	Bridget Fonda
Lint	John Lehr

and Vincent Polidoro (Young Lester), Yvette Brooks Grant (Paulina), Jose Soto (Club Promoter), Delanie Yates (Ariana), Nico Baumbach (Ex-Boyfriend), Joel Castleberg (Curt), Dean Wareham (Music Video Director), Leigh Zimmerman (Lois), Patricia Towers (Museum Woman), Helen Hanft (Millie); Group: Andrew Mills (Trey), James P. Engel (Harold), Martha Gehman (Josselyn), Lauren Katz (Maria), Michelle Blakely (Imogen), Matthew Kaplan (Omar), Jonathan Baumbach (Marlon), Julie Jacott (Amy), Noah Baumbach (Arliss), Eddie Kaye Thomas (Nat), Laurie Durning (Waitress), Chris Reed (Classmate)

Irrationally jealous of his girlfriend Ramona's previous relationship with Dashiell Frank, Lester Grimm joins Dashiell's group therapy session to find out more about Ramona.

Jim Carrey

Holland Taylor, Jim Carrey, Laura Linney

Ed Harris

THE TRUMAN SHOW

(PARAMOUNT) Producers, Scott Rudin, Andrew Niccol, Edward S. Feldman, Adam Schroeder; Executive Producer, Lynn Pleshette; Director, Peter Weir; Screenplay, Andrew Niccol; Photography, Peter Biziou; Designer, Dennis Gassner; Editors, William Anderson, Lee Smith; Music, Burkhard Dallwitz; Additional Original Music, Philip Glass; Costumes, Marilyn Matthews; Visual Effects Supervisor, Michael J. McAlister; Co-Producer, Richard Luke Rothschild; Casting, Howard Feuer; a Scott Rudin production; Dolby; Deluxe color; Rated PG; 102 minutes; June release

CAST

Truman's World
Truman Burbank ....Jim Carrey
Meryl ....Laura Linney
Marlon ....Noah Emmerich
Lauren/Sylvia ....Natascha McElhone
Truman's Mother ....Holland Taylor
Truman's Father ....Brian Delate
Young Truman ....Blair Slater
Lawrence ....Peter Krause
Vivien ....Heidi Schanz
Ron and Don ....Ron Taylor, Don Taylor
Spencer ....Ted Raymond
Travel Agent..Judy Clayton
and Fritz Dominique, Angel Schmiedt, Nastassja Schmeidt (Truman's Neighbors), Muriel Moore (Teacher), Mal Jones (News Vendor), Judson Vaughn (Insurance Co-Worker), Earl Hilliard, Jr. (Ferry Worker), David Andrew Nash (Bus Driver/Ferry Captain), Jim Towers (Bus Supervisor), Savannah Swafford (Little Girl in Bus), Antoni Corone, Mario Ernesto Sanchez (Security Guards), John Roselius (Man at Beach), Kade Coates (Truman—4 years), Marcia DeBonis (Nurse), Sam Kitchin (Surgeon), Sebastian Youngblood (Orderly), Dave Corey (Hospital Security Guard), Mark Alan Gillott (Policeman at Power Plant), Jay Saiter, Tony Todd (Policemen at Truman's House), Marco Rubeo (Man in Christmas Box), Daryl Davis, Robert Davis (Couple at Picnic Table), R.J. Murdock (Production Assistant), Matthew McDonoguh, Larry McDowell (Men at Newstand), Joseph Lucus (Ticket Taker), Logan Kirksey (TV Host)

Christof's World
Christof ....Ed Harris
Control Room Directors ....Paul Giamatti, Adam Tomei
Mike Michaelson ....Harry Shearer
Chloe...Una Damon
Network Executives ....Philip Baker Hall, John Pleshette
Keyboard Artists ....Philip Glass, John Pramik
The Viewers
Bar Waitresses......................................O-Lan Jones, Krista Lynn Landolfi
Bartender...Joe Minjares
Bar Patrons ....Al Foster, Zouanne LeRoy, Millie Slavin
Man in Bathtub..Terry Camilleri
Senior Citizens...Dona Hardy, Jeanette Miller
Garage Attendants.........................Joel McKinnon Miller, Tom Simmons
Mother ....Susan Angelo
Daughter...Carly Smiga
Japanese Family ....Yuji Okumoto, Kiyoko Yamaguchi, Saemi Nakamura

Truman Burbank leads a happy existence in the picture-perfect town of Seahaven, unaware that his life is a 24-hour-a-day television show, staged in a monitored and controlled environment by a God-like director named Christof. This film received Oscar nominations for supporting actor (Ed Harris), director, and original screenplay.

©Paramount Pictures

Laura Linney, Jim Carrey

Jim Carrey

Natascha McElhone

Jim Carrey

Noah Emmerich, Jim Carrey

A PERFECT MURDER

(WARNER BROS.) Producers, Arnold Kopelson, Anne Kopelson, Christopher Mankiewicz, Peter MacGregor-Scott; Executive Producer, Stephen Brown; Director, Andrew Davis; Screenplay, Patrick Smith Kelly; Based upon the play Dial M for Murder by Frederick Knott; Photography, Dariusz Wolski; Designer, Philip Rosenberg; Editors, Dennis Virkler, Dov Hoenig; Music, James Newton Howard; Costumes, Ellen Mirojnick; Co-Producers, Nana Greenwald, Mitchell Dauterive; Associate Producers, Lowell Blank, Lisa Reardon, Teresa Tucker-Davies; Casting, Amanda Mackey Johnson, Cathy Sandrich; a Kopelson Entertainment production; Dolby; Technicolor; Rated R; 105 minutes; June release

Gwyneth Paltrow, Michael Douglas

CAST

Steven Taylor ....Michael Douglas
Emily Bradford Taylor ....Gwyneth Paltrow
David Shaw ....Viggo Mortensen
Mohamed Karaman ....David Suchet
Raquel Martinez...Sarita Choudhury
Bobby Fain ....Michael P. Moran
Ambassador Alice Wills..Novella Nelson
Sandra Bradford...Constance Towers
Jason Gates...Will Lyman
Ann Gates ....Maeve McGuire
Effete Man at Met...Stephen Singer
Met Women...Laurinda Barrett, Aideen O'Kelly
and Reed Birney, Robert Vincent Smith, Bill Ambrozy, George S. Blumenthal (Merchant Princes), Iris Alten, Marion Blumenthal, Andrew Sussman, Robynn N. Sussman, Radney Tucker, Beverly Tucker, Bradford Billet (Guests at Met), Robert Bosco Cokljat (Croation Delegate), Marat Yusim (Russian Delegate), Lee Wong (Japanese Diplomat), Roberta Orlan (Italian Diplomat), Francis Dumaurier (French Delegate), Deen Badarou (African Delegate), Peter Benson (Hansen), Jeff Williams (Nolan), David Eigenberg (Stein), Jean Debaer (Secretary), Michel Moinot (Maitre d'), Gerrit Vooren (Waiter), Monica Parker (Janice Moran), Michael H. Ingram (Albert), Scott Dillin (Detective Scott), Starla Benford (Police Technician), Bob Bowersox (Police Photographer), Joanna P. Adler (Vyczowski), James Georgiades, Jose Ramon Rosario (Policemen), Gerry Becker (Roger Brill), William Bogert (Harrington), Adrian Martinez (Young Tough), Dexter Brown (Porter)

Realizing that his beautiful young wife Emily is carrying on with another man, millionaire Steven Taylor offers his rival money if he will agree to murder Emily. Remake of the 1954 Warner Bros. film Dial M for Murder which starred Ray Milland and Grace Kelly.

©Warner Bros.

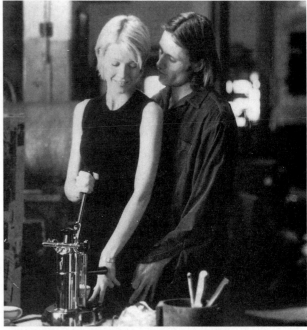

Gwyneth Paltrow, Viggo Mortensen

Michael Douglas

Michael Douglas, Gwyneth Paltrow

COUSIN BETTE

(FOX SEARCHLIGHT) Producer, Sarah Radclyffe; Executive Producers, Susan Tarr, Lynn Siefert, Rob Scheidlinger; Director, Des McAnuff; Screenplay, Lynn Siefert, Susan Tarr; Based upon a portion of the novel Le Comedie Humaine by Honoré de Balzac; Co-Producer, Philippe Guez; Photography, Andrzej Sekula; Designer, Hugo Luczyc-Wyhowski; Costumes, Gabriella Pescucci; Editors, Tariq Anwar, Barry Alexander Brown; Music, Simon Boswell; Casting, Mary Margiotta, Karen Margiotta, Liora Reich; Dolby; Panavision; Color; Rated R; 108 minutes; June release

CAST

Bette	Jessica Lange
Jenny Cadine	Elisabeth Shue
Crevel	Bob Hoskins
Hector Hulot	Hugh Laurie
Wenceslas	Aden Young
Hortense	Kelly MacDonald
Adeline	Geraldine Chaplin
Victorin	Toby Stephens
Dr. Bianchon	John Benfield
Priest	Paul Bandey
Mariette	Laura Fraser
Célestine	Janie Hargreaves
Portress	Gillian Martell
Musical Director	John Sessions
Baritone	Henrik Wagner
Elderly Aristocrat	John Quentin
Stidmann	Jefferson Mays
De Forzheim	Tim Barlow
Nucingen	Heathcote Williams
De Wissembourg	Philip Jackson
Gentlemen in Café des Artistes	Toby Jones, Kenneth Jay
Vauvinet	Simon McBurney
Duelmaster	Geoffrey Carey
Chief Gendarme	Dermot Keaney

Bette, a bitter spinster, hopes to gain the affections of a starving artist whom she has rescued only to find him plucked away by her cousin. As revenge, Bette seeks the help of performer Jenny Cadine to seduce the man and hopefully destroy his life.

Jessica Lange, Elisabeth Shue

Jessica Lange, Elisabeth Shue

©Twentieth Century Fox

THE FARM: ANGOLA USA

(GABRIEL FILMS) Producers/Directors, Jonathan Stack, Liz Garbus; Co-Director, Wilbert Rideau; Photography, Samuel Henriques, Bob Perrin; Music, Curtis Lundy; Editors, Mona Davis, Mary Manhardt; Narrator, Bernard Addison; Color; Not rated; 93 minutes; June release. Documentary on Angola, America's largest maximum security prison, located on Louisian's Mississippi River

FEATURING

Warden Burl Cain, Vincent Simmons, Ashanti Witherspoon, Bishop Tannehill, George Crawford, John Brown, Bones Theriot.

This film received an Oscar nomination for feature documentary.

George Crawford

Lauren Ambrose, Seth Green

Ethan Embry, Jennifer Love Hewitt

CAN'T HARDLY WAIT

(COLUMBIA) formerly *The Party*; Producers, Jenno Topping, Betty Thomas; Directors/Screenplay, Harry Elfont, Deborah Kaplan; Photography, Lloyd Ahern; Designer, Marcia Hinds-Johnson; Editor, Michael Jablow; Music, David Kitay, Matthew Sweet; Costumes, Mark Bridges; Co-Producer, Karen Koch; Casting, Mary Vernieu, Anne McCarthy; a Tall Trees production; Dolby; Technicolor; Rated PG-13; 98 minutes; June release

CAST

Amanda Beckett	Jennifer Love Hewitt
Preston Meyers	Ethan Embry
William Lichter	Charlie Korsmo
Denise Fleming	Lauren Ambrose
Mike Dexter	Peter Facinelli
Kenny Fisher	Seth Green
Girl Whose Party It Is	Michelle Brookhurst
Exchange Student	Alexander Martin
Cousin Ron	Erik Palladino
Jocks	Channon Roe, Sean Patrick Thomas, Freddy Rodriguez
X-Philes	Joel Michaely, Jay Paulson
The Angel	Jenna Elfman
Trip McNeely	Jerry O'Connell
Yearbook Girl	Melissa Joan Hart
Real Homeboy	Brian Hall
Homeboys	Branden Williams, Bobby Jacoby
Guitar Player	Johnny Zander
Drummer	Donald Faison
Bass Player	Alaa Khaled
Girlfriends	Jamie Pressly, Tamala Jones, Jennifer Lyons
Keg Guy	Seth Peterson
Beer Drinkers	Angelo Vacco, Nick Paulos
Klepto Kid	Chris Owen
Reddi Whip Kid	Vicellous Shannon
Reminiscing Guy	Victor Togunde

and Monica McSwain, Marisol Nichols (Groupies), Liz Stauber (Gossipy Girl), Nicole Bilderback (Ready to Have Sex Girl), Jason Segel (Watermelon Guy), Paige Moss (Ashley), Clea Duvall (Jana), Leslie Grossman (Ready to Have Sex's Friend), Ali MacLean (Language Lab Girl), Brian Klugman (Stoner Guy), Meadow Sisto (Hippie Girl), Eric Balfour (Hippie Guy), Selma Blair, Jennifer Paz (Girls Mike Hits On), Sara Rue (Earth Girl), Nils Larsen (Skinny Guy), Steve Monroe (Headbanger), Eric Brice Scott (Hockey Guy), Chris Wiehl (Horny Guy), John Patrick White (Tassel Guy), Jamie Donnelly (Teacher), Reni Santoni, Rob Roy Fitzgerald, Corinne Reilly (Cops)

Jenna Elfman, Ethan Embry

At the big graduation party for Huntington High, shy aspiring writer Preston Meyers tries to seize his last chance to tell the girl of his dreams, popular and pretty Amanda Beckett, that he has been in love with her all during high school.

Charlie Korsmo, Peter Facinelli, Freddy Rodriguez

SIX DAYS SEVEN NIGHTS

(TOUCHSTONE) Producers, Ivan Reitman, Wallis Nicita, Roger Birnbaum; Executive Producers, Joe Medjuck, Daniel Goldberg, Julie Bergman Sender; Director, Ivan Reitman; Screenplay, Michael Browning; Co-Producers, Gordon Webb, Sheldon Kahn; Photography, Michael Chapman; Designer, J. Michael Riva; Editors, Sheldon Kahn, Wendy Greene Bricmont; Costumes, Gloria Gresham; Music, Randy Edelman; Casting, Michael Chinich, Bonnie Timmerman; a Roger Birnbaum/Northern Lights Entertainment production, presented in association with Caravan Pictures; Distributed by Buena Vista; Dolby; Panavision; Technicolor; Rated PG-13; 101 minutes; June release

Anne Heche, Harrison Ford

CAST

Quinn Harris	Harrison Ford
Robin Monroe	Anne Heche
Frank Martin	David Schwimmer
Angelica	Jacqueline Obradors
Jager	Temuera Morrison
Marjorie	Allison Janney
Phillippe	Douglas Weston
Kip	Cliff Curtis
Pierce	Danny Trejo
Helicopter Pilot	Ben Bodé
Ricky	Derek Basco
Robin's Secretary	Amy Sedaris
Handsome Mechanic	Michael Chapman
Tahitian Priest	E. Kalani Flores
Infirmary Oderly	Ping Wu
Photographer	Greg Gorman

and Long Nguyen, Jake Feagai, John Koyama, Jen Sung Outerbridge (Pirates), Hoyt Richards, Odile Broulard (Models), Cynthia Langbridge (Resort Greeter), Jody Kono (Hotel Clerk), Michael Lushing (Front Desk Clerk), Pua Kaholokula (Waitress), Ron Dinson Jr., Don Nahaku (Bellboys), Priscilla Lee Taylor (Bathing Suit Girl), Reri Tava Jobe, Natalie Goss (Flight Attendants), Christian Martson, James Edward Sclafani (French Airport Security), Jason S. Nichols (Runway Traffic), Taj Mahal (Himself), Fred Lunt, Kester Smith, Wayne Jacintho, Rudy Costa, Carlos Andrade, Pat Cockett, Michael Barretto, Pancho Graham (Band Members)

Magazine editor Robin Monroe, on holiday with her fiancee, enlists the aide of cargo pilot Quinn Harris to fly her to Tahiti for an assignment, only to have their plane crash land on a deserted island.

David Schwimmer, Jacqueline Obradors

Anne Heche, Harrison Ford

Harrison Ford, Anne Heche

THE X-FILES

(20TH CENTURY FOX) Producers, Chris Carter, Daniel Sackheim; Executive Producer, Lata Ryan; Director, Rob Bowman; Screenplay, Chris Carter; Story, Chris Carter, Frank Spotnitz; Photography, Ward Russell; Designer, Christopher Nowak; Editor, Stephen Mark; Music, Mark Snow; Costumes, Marlene Stewart; Special Make-up Effects, Alec Gillis, Tom Woodruff, Jr.; Visual Effects Supervisor, Mat Beck; Casting, Liberman/Hirschfeld Casting; a Ten Thirteen production; Dolby; Super 35 Widescreen; Deluxe color; Rated PG-13; 120 minutes; June release

Gillian Anderson, David Duchovny

CAST

Agent Fox Mulder ....David Duchovny
Agent Dana Scully...Gillian Anderson
The Well-Manicured Man...John Neville
The Cigarette-Smoking Man..William B. Davis
Kurtzweil..Martin Landau
Assistant Director Walter Skinner...Mitch Pileggi
Bronschweig ....Jeffrey De Munn
Cassidy..Blythe Danner
Michaud..Terry O'Quinn
Strughold..Armin Mueller-Stahl
Stevie..Lucas Black
Boys ....Chris Fennell, Cody Newton, Blake Stokes
The Lone Gunmen:
    Langly...Dean Haglund
    Byers..Bruce Harwood
    Frohike..Tom Braidwood
Group Elder ....Don S. Williams
2nd Elder..George Murdock
Black-Haired Man ....Michael Shamus Wiles
Primitives...Craig Davis, Carrick O'Quinn
Creatures ....Tom Woodruff, Jr., Gregory B. Ballora
FBI Agent on Roof ....T.W. King
FBI Agent ....Luis Beckford
and Steve Rankin (Field Agent), Gary Grubbs (Fire Captain Cooles), Steven M. Gagnon (Last Agent Out), Lawrence Joshua, Glendon Rich (DC Cops), Gunther Jensen (Security Guard), Scott Smith (Technician), Ian Ruskin (Well-Manicured Man's Valet), Paul Welterlen (Control Room Operator), Joel Traywick (Young Naval Guard), Milton Johns (British Valet), Paul Tuerpi, Michael A. Krawic (Paramedics), Larry Rippenkroeger (Towncar Driver), Josh McLaglen (Buzz Mihoe), Randy Hall (Windbreaker Agent), T.C. Badalato (Fireman), Amine Zary (Tunisian)

John Neville, Armin Mueller-Stahl, William B. Davis

When a small boy succumbs to a strange virus, government officials seize the site of the occurance, causing FBI agent Mulder to suspect some kind of coverup involving alien activity. David Duchovny and Gillian Anderson repeat their roles from the Fox television series which premiered in 1993.

©Twentieth Century Fox

Dean Haglund, Tom Braidwood, Bruce Harwood

Martin Landau, David Duchovny

James Urbaniak, Thomas Jay Ryan

HENRY FOOL

(SONY PICTURES CLASSICS) Producer/Director/Screenplay/Music,
Hal Hartley; Executive Producers, Larry Meistrich, Daniel J. Victor, Keith
Abell; Photography, Mike Spiller; Designer, Steve Rosenzweig; Editor,
Steve Hamilton; Costumes, Jocelyn Joson; Casting, Chelsea Fuhrer; a
True Fiction Pictures and the Shooting Gallery presentation; Dolby; Color;
Rated R; 137 minutes; June release

CAST

Henry Fool	Thomas Jay Ryan
Simon Grim	James Urbaniak
Fay	Parker Posey
Mary	Maria Porter
Mr. Deng	James Saito
Warren	Kevin Corrigan
Ned	Liam Aiken
Gnoc Deng	Miho Nikaido
Officer Buñuel	Gene Ruffini
Father Hawkes	Nicholas Hope
Amy	Diana Ruppe
Laura	Veanne Cox
Vicky	Jan Leslie Harding
Pearl (age 7)	Chaylee Worrall
Pearl (age 14)	Christy Romano
Angus James	Chuck Montgomery
Go-Go Dancers	Melanie Vesey, Denise Morgan
Afternoon Table Dancer	Jill Morley
Steve	Paul Boocock
Barry	David Latham
Newspaper Reporter	Marissa Chibas
Woman Outside Store	Julie Anderson
Anchorman	Reggie Harris
Owen Feer	Don Creech

and Camile Paglia (Herself), Maraya Chase (TV Reporter), Shoshana Ami (Young Woman in
Library), Karen DiConcetto, Tiffany Sampson, Rachel Miner (Girls in Library), Paul Lazar
(Doctor), Gretchen Krich (Nurse), Valorie Hubbard (Patty the Bartender), Dave Simonds (Bill),
Fay Ann Lee (Lawyer), Paul Greco (Concierge), Blake Willett, Raymond Cassar (Cops), Katreen
Hardt (Airline Ticket Clerk), Rebecca Nelson (Flight Attendant Lucy), Paul Albe (Angry
Customer), Vivian Bang, Brandon Boey, Claire Ritchie, Herbie Duarte, Toy Connor (Teenagers at
World of Donuts)

*Simon, a garbage man who supports his mother and sister, finds his life
disrupted when the egotistical and vulgar Henry Fool shows up one day
and takes up residence in the family's basement.*

©Sony Pictures Entertainment Inc.

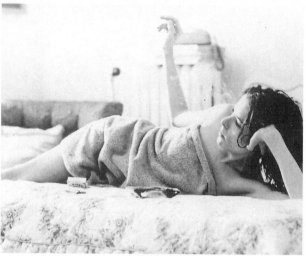

Parker Posey

Thomas Jay Ryan, James Urbaniak

Thomas Jay Ryan, Parker Posey

79

Mulan

Fa Zhou, Mulan

Mushu, Cri-Kee

Shan-Yu

Mulan, Shang

MULAN

(WALT DISNEY PICTURES) Producer, Pam Coats; Directors, Barry Cook, Tony Bancroft; Screenplay, Rita Hsiao, Christopher Sanders, Philip Lazebnik, Raymond Singer, Eugenia Bostwick-Singer; Story, Robert D. San Souci; Original Songs, Matthew Wilder (music), David Zippel (lyrics); Music, Jerry Goldsmith; Associate Producers, Kendra Haaland, Robert S. Garber; Designer, Hans Bacher; Art Director, Ric Sluiter; Editor, Michael Kelly; Artistic Supervisors: Story, Christopher Sanders; Character Design, Chen-Yi Chang; Layout, Robert Walker; Background, Robert E. Stanton; Clean-Up, Ruben Procopio; Visual Effects, David Tidgwell; Computer Animation, Eric Guaglione; Artistic Coordinator, Jeff Dutton; Distributed by Buena Vista; Dolby; Technicolor; Rated G; 87 minutes; June release

Mulan, Shang

VOICE CAST

Shan-Yu	Miguel Ferrer
Yao	Harvey Fierstein
Fa Li	Freda Foh Shen
Grandmother Fa	June Foray
Chi Fu	James Hong
The Matchmaker	Miriam Margolyes
The Emperor	Pat Morita
Mushu	Eddie Murphy
Singing Voice of Grandmother Fa	Marni Nixon
Fa Zhou	Soon-Tek Oh
Singing Voice of Shang	Donny Osmond
Singing Voice of Mulan	Lea Salonga
General Li	James Shigeta
First Ancestor	George Takei
Chien-Po	Jerry S. Tondo
Ling	Gedde Watanabe
Khan	Frank Welker
Mulan	Ming-Na Wen
Singing Voice of Ling	Matthew Wilder
Shang	B.D. Wong

Ling, Mulan, Yao, Chien-Po

and Tom Amundsen, Arminae Austen, Mary Kay Bergman, Susan Boyd, Julianne Buescher, Steve Bullen, Corey Burton, Mitch Carter, Robert Clotworthy, David Cowgill, Sally Dworsky, Beth Fowler, Don Fullilove, Elisa Gabrielli, Jack Gilpin, Sandie Hall, Richard S. Horvitz, Linda Kerns, Matthew Labyorteaux, Conan Lee, Dana Lee, Edie Lehmann-Boddicker, Luisa Leschin, Christina Ma, Susan McBride, Huanani Minn, Edie Mirman, Mark Moseley, Patrick Pinney, Peter Renaday, Maurita Thornburg-Phillips, John Walcutt, Claudette Wells (Additional Voices)

When her ailing father is commanded to join the Chinese army to do battle against the ruthless Hun leader Shan-Yu, young Mulan disguises herself as a man and joins the military in his place. This film received an Oscar nomination for original score—musical or comedy.

©Disney Enterprises, Inc.

Mushu, Mulan

Shan-Yu, Mushu, Mulan

HAV PLENTY

(MIRAMAX) Producers, Christopher Scott Cherot, Robyn M. Greene; Executive Producers, Tracy E. Edmonds, Kenneth "Babyface" Edmonds, Bridget D. Davis, S.J. Cherot; Director/Screenplay/Editor, Christopher Scott Cherot; Co-Producer, Dana Offenbach; Photography, Kerwin Devonish; Music, Wendy Melvoin, Lisa Coleman; Presented in association with Wanderlust Pictures Inc. and e2 Filmworks; Dolby; Color; Rated R; 92 minutes; June release

CAST

Lee Plenty .... Christopher Scott Cherot
Havilland Savage ....Chenoa Maxwell
Michael Simmons ....Hill Harper
Caroline Gooden ....Tammi Katherine Jones
Leigh Darling...Robinne Lee
Felix Darling...Reginald James
Alexandria Beaumont...Margie St. Juste
Mr. Savage ....Chuck Baron
Bobby Montgomery ....Kim Harris
Grandma Moore ....Betty Vaughn
Sylvia Savage ....Michele Turner
Evelyn ....P.G. Reese
and Wanda Candelario (Girl in Gas Station), Nia Long (Trudy), Shemar Moore (Chris), Lauryn Hill (Debra), Chilli (Kris), Mekhi Phifer (Harold), Leslie "Big Lez" Segar (Jane), Christopher Batyr (Emcee), Melissa Brooks, Juana Cullen, Marco Materassi, Celia Didier, Vincent Nolasco (Hav's Co-Workers), Shontonette Crawford, Reginald Bruce, Alaina Irizarry (Spectator), Keith Hudson (Festival Participant), Tracey E. Edmonds (Amy Madison), Kenneth "Babyface" Edmonds (Lloyd Banks), Bridget D. Davis, Shara P. Fleming, Patrik Ian Polk (Caprice Films Entourage)

Lee Plenty, a struggling writer, agrees to spend New Year's Eve at the home of his friend Havilland Savage where he finds himself in the midst of various romantic endeavors and desires.

©Miramax Films

(clockwise from left) Robinne Lee, Christopher Scott Cherot, Chenoa Maxwell, Tammi Katherine Jones

Vincent Gallo

Christina Ricci

BUFFALO 66

(LIONS GATE) Producer, Chris Hanley; Executive Producers, Michael Paseornek, Jeff Sackman; Director/Screenplay/Music, Vincent Gallo; Photography, Lance Acord; Designer, Gideon Ponte; Editor, Curtiss Clayton; Dolby; Color; Not rated; 112 minutes; June release

CAST

Billy Brown...Vincent Gallo
Layla..Christina Ricci
Janet Brown...Anjelica Huston
Jimmy Brown ....Ben Gazzara
Goon ....Kevin Corrigan
Bookie ....Mickey Rourke
Wendy ....Rosanna Arquette
Sonny...Jan-Michael Vincent
TV Sportscasters ....Alex Karras, Kevin Pollak
and John Sansone (Little Billy), Manny Fried (The Donut Clerk), John Rummel (Don Shanks), Bob Wahl (Scott Woods), Penny Wolfgang (The Judge), Anthony Mydcarz (The Motel Clerk), Michael Caciejewski (The Guy in the Bathroom), Jack Claxton (The Denny's Host), Dominic Telesco (The Prison Guard), Carl Marchi (The Cafe Owner), Kim Krah (The Denny's Waitress), Julius DeGennaro (The Info Booth Clerk), Terry Braunstein (The Tap Teacher), Jack Hunter (The Gas Station Clerk), Norma Gelose (The Bus Station Woman), Jamie and Janel King (The Tap Dance Kids)

Billy Brown kidnaps Layla and forces her to masquerade as his wife on one of his hellish visits to his parents' house.

DR. DOLITTLE

(20TH CENTURY FOX) Producers, John Davis, Joseph M. Singer, David T. Friendly; Executive Producers, Sue Baden-Powell, Jenno Topping; Director, Betty Thomas; Screenplay, Nat Mauldin, Larry Levin; Based upon the Doctor Dolittle stories by Hugh Lofting; Photography, Russell Boyd; Designer, William Elliott; Editor, Peter Teschner; Visual Effects Supervisor, Jon Farhat; Music, Richard Gibbs; Costumes, Sharen Davis; Animatronic Creatures, Jim Henson's Creature Shop; Casting, Nancy Foy; a Davis Entertainment Company/Joseph M. Singer Entertainment production; Dolby; Deluxe color; Rated PG-13; 85 minutes; June release

Eddie Murphy

CAST

Dr. John Dolittle	Eddie Murphy
Archer Dolittle	Ossie Davis
Dr. Mark Weller	Oliver Platt
Calloway	Peter Boyle
Dr. Gene Reiss	Richard Schiff
Lisa Dolittle	Kristen Wilson
Dr. Fish	Jeffrey Tambor
Maya Dolittle	Kyla Pratt
Charisse Dolittle	Raven-Symoné
Dr. Litvack	Steven Gilborn
Jeremy	Erik Todd Dellums
Diane	June Christopher
Mrs. Parkus	Cherie Franklin
Intern	Mark Adair-Rios

and Don Calfa (Patient at Hammersmith), Arnold F. Turner (Animal Control Officer), Kay Yamamoto (Receptionist), Kellye Nakahara-Wallett (Beagle Woman), Beth Grant (Woman), Yule Caise (Vet's Assistant), Brian Kwan (Busboy), L. Peter Callender (Policeman), Charles A. Branklyn (Security Guard), Cliff McLaughlin (Mounted Policeman), Richard Penn (Principal), John LaFayette (Reverend), Raymond Matthew Mason (3 Year-old Dolittle), Dari Gerard Smith (5 Year-old Dolittle), Karl T. Wright (Reporter), Stan Sellers, Ming Lo (Cops). VOICE CAST: Norm McDonald (Lucky), Albert Brooks (Tiger), Chris Rock (Rodney), Reni Santoni, John Leguizamo (Rats), Julie Kavner, Garry Shandling (Pigeons), Ellen DeGeneres (Prologue Dog), Brian Doyle-Murray (Old Beagle), Phil Proctor (Drunk Monkey), Jenna Elfman (Owl), Gilbert Gottfried (Compulsive Dog), Phyllis Katz (Goat), Douglas Shamburger (Pound Dog), Jeff Doucette (Possum), Archie Hahn (Heavy Woman's Dog), Tom Towles (German Shepherd), Eddie Frierson (Skunk), Paul Reubens (Racoon), Royce D. Applegate ("I Love You" Dog), James F. Dean (Orangutan), Chad Einbinder (Bettleheim the Cat), Jonathan Lipnicki (Baby Tiger), Hamilton Camp (Pig), Kerrigan Mahan (Penguin).

Ossie Davis, Raven-Symoné, Kyla Pratt, Kristen Wilson

Mild-mannered San Francisco doctor John Dolittle finds his career changed when he discovers that he can communicate with animals, prompting him to become a veterinarian. Previous film version was released by 20th Century-Fox in 1967 and starred Rex Harrison.

©Twentieth Century Fox

Eddie Murphy, Lucky, Jeffrey Tambor

Eddie Murphy

Ving Rhames, George Clooney

Jennifer Lopez, George Clooney

©Universal City Studios

OUT OF SIGHT

(UNIVERSAL) Producers, Danny DeVito, Michael Shamberg, Stacey Sher; Executive Producers, Barry Sonnenfeld, John Hardy; Director, Steven Soberbergh; Screenplay, Scott Frank; Based on the novel by Elmore Leonard; Photography, Elliot Davis; Designer, Gary Frutkoff; Editor, Anne V. Coates; Music, David Holmes; Costumes, Betsy Heimann; Casting, Francine Maisler; a Jersey Films; Dolby; Deluxe color; Rated R; 122 minutes; June release

George Clooney, Jennifer Lopez

CAST

Jack Foley	George Clooney
Karen Sisco	Jennifer Lopez
Buddy Bragg	Ving Rhames
Maurice "Snoopy" Miller	Don Cheadle
Marshall Sisco	Dennis Farina
Richard Ripley	Albert Brooks
Midge	Nancy Allen
Adele	Catherine Keener
Kenneth	Isaiah Washington
Glenn Michaels	Steve Zahn
Chino	Luis Guzman
White Boy Bob	Keith Loneker
Bank Employee	Jim Robinson
Bank Customer	Elgin Marlow
Teller/Loretta	Donna Frenzel
Cops—Bank	Manny Suarez, Keith Hudson
Lulu	Paul Soileau
Pup	Scott Allen
Parking Lot Woman	Susan Hatfield
White Boxer	Brad Martin
Himey	James Black
Daniel Burdon—FBI	Wendell B. Harris, Jr.
Library Guard	Chuck Castleberry
Fourth FBI Man	Chic Daniel
Old Elevator Lady	Connie Sawyer
Old Elevator Gent	Phil Perlman
Raymond Cruz	Paul Calderon
Officer Grant	Gregory H. Alpert

and Viola Davis (Moselle), Mark Brown (Ripley Personnel), Sandra Ives (Receptionist), Joe Hess (Ripley Guard), Betsy Monroe (Waitress—Celeste), Wayne Pere (Executive Guy—Philip), Joe Chrest (Executive Guy—Andy), Joe Coyle (Executive Guy #3), Stephen M. Horn (Federal Marshal), Michael Keaton (Ray Nicolet), Samuel L. Jackson (Hejira)

Ving Rhames, George Clooney, Isaiah Washington, Steve Zahn,
Don Cheadle, Keith Loneker

Deputy Federal Marshal Karen Sisco shows up outside the correctional facility during Jack Foley's prison break and finds herself being taken hostage by Jack and his partner Buddy Bragg. This film received an Oscar nomination for screenplay adaptation.

SMOKE SIGNALS

(MIRAMAX) Producers, Larry Estes, Scott Rosenfelt; Executive Producers, David Skinner, Carl Bressler; Director, Chris Eyre; Screenplay, Sherman Alexie, based on stories from his book *The Lone Ranger and Tonto Fistfight in Heaven*; Line Producer, Brent Morris; Photography, Brian Capener; Designer, Charles Armstrong; Costumes, Ron Leamon; Editor, Brian Berdan; Music, BC Smith; Associate Producers, Roger Baerwolf, Randy Suhr; a ShadowCatcher Entertainment production in association with Sherman Alexie; Dolby; Color; Rated PG-13; 89 minutes; June release

CAST

Victor Joseph	Adam Beach
Thomas Builds-the-Fire	Evan Adams
Suzy Song	Irene Bedard
Arnold Joseph	Gary Farmer
Arlene Joseph	Tantoo Cardinal
Young Victor Joseph	Cody Lightning
Young Thomas Builds-the-Fire	Simon Baker
Grandma Builds-the-Fire	Monica Mojica
Randy Peone	John Trudell
Lester Fallsapart	Leonard George
Junior Polatkin	Michael Greyeyes
Boo	Darwin Haine
Velma	Michelle St. John
Lucy	Elaine Miles
Cathy the Gymnast	Cynthia Geary
Cowboy	Gary Taylor
Holly	Perrey Reeves
Julie	Nicolette Vajtay
Penny	Molly Cheek
Burt	Robert Miano
Police Chief	Tom Skerritt
Jesuit #1	Todd Jamieson

Victor Joseph reluctantly travels to Phoenix to claim the remains of his father who had deserted him ten years before. Accompanying him is oddball Thomas Builds-the-Fire who feels a debt to Victor for having saved his life as a baby.

©Miramax Films

Cody Lightning, Adam Beach

Irene Bedard, Adam Beach

Tantoo Cardinal

Adam Beach, Evan Adams

ARMAGEDDON

(TOUCHSTONE) Producers, Jerry Bruckheimer, Gale Anne Hurd, Michael Bay; Executive Producers, Jonathan Hensleigh, Jim Van Wyck, Chad Oman; Director, Michael Bay; Screenplay, Jonathan Hensleigh, J.J. Abrams; Story, Robert Roy Pool, Jonathan Hensleigh; Adaptation, Tony Gilroy, Shane Salerno; Photography, John Schwartzman; Designer, Michael White; Editors, Mark Goldblatt, Chris Lebenzon, Glen Scantlebury; Costumes, Michael Kaplan; Music, Trevor Rabin; Visual Effects Supervisors, Pat McClung, Richard Hoover; Casting, Bonnie Timmermann; a Jerry Bruckheimer production in association with Valhalla Motion Pictures; Distributed by Buena Vista Pictures; Dolby; Panavision; Technicolor; Rated PG-13; 150 minutes; July release

CAST

Harry S. Stamper	Bruce Willis
Dan Truman	Billy Bob Thornton
A.J. Frost	Ben Affleck
Grace Stamper	Liv Tyler
General Kimsey	Keith David
Walter Clark	Chris Ellis
Ronald Quincy	Jason Isaacs
Charles "Chick" Chapple	Will Patton
Rockhound	Steve Buscemi
Max Lennert	Ken Campbell
Colonel William Sharp	William Fichtner
Co-Pilot Jennifer Watts	Jessica Steen
Gruber	Grayson McCouch
Oscar Choi	Owen Wilson
Freddy Noonan	Clark Brolly
Jayotis "Bear" Kurleenbear	Michael Clarke Duncan
Lev Andropov	Peter Stormare
Colonel Davis	Marshall Teague
Co-Pilot Tucker	Anthony Guidera
Lt. Halsey	Greg Collins
General Boffer	J. Patrick McCormack
NASA Tech #5	Michael Kaplan
Astronaut Pete Shelby	Ian Quinn
Operators	Christopher Worret, Adam C. Smith
Karl	John Mahon
Dottie	Grace Zabriskie
Samoan	K.C. Leomiti
Little Guy	Eddie Griffin
New York Guy	Mark Boone Junior
President	Stanley Anderson
Admiral Kelso	James Harper
Helga the Nurse	Ellen Cleghorne
Psychologist	Udo Kier
Dr. Banks	John Aylward
Stu the Cabbie	Mark Curry

and Deborah Nishimura, Albert Wong, Jim Ishida (Clients), Seiko Matsuda (Asian Tourist), Harry Humphries (Chuck Jr.), Dyllan Christopher (Tommy), Judith Hoag (Denise), Sage Allen (Max's Mom), Lawrence Tierney (Hollis Vernon "Grap" Stamper), Judith Drake (Grap's Nurse), Steven Ford (Nuke Tech), Christian Clemenson (Droning Guy), Duke Valenti, Michael "Bear" Taliferro, Billy Devlin (Roughnecks), Frank Van Keeken (NASA Planner #1), Kathleen Matthews, J.C. Hayward, Andrew Glassman (Newscasters), Shawnee Smith (Redhead), Dwight Hicks (FBI Agent #1), Odile Broulard (Geo Tech #1), Vic Manni (Loanshark), Jim Maniaci (Biker Customer), Layla Roberts (Molly Mounds), Joe Allen (Kennedy Launch), Bodhi Elfman (Math Guy), Alexander Johnson (Newscaster), Kathy Neff (Reporter #1), Victor Vinson (Sector Director), Joseph Patrick Kelly (Marine #1), Peter White (Secretary of Defense), Rudy Mettia (G-Man), Frederick Weller, Googy Gress, H. Richard Greene, Peter Murnik, Andrew Heckler, Jeff Austin, Matt Malloy, Brian Brophy, Brian Hayes Currie, Andy Milder (NASA Techs), Patrick Richwood (Dr. Nerd), Brian Mulligan (Dr. Nerd), Greg Warmoth (KSC News Reporter), John H. Johnson (Pad Director), Charles Stewart (Vacuum Chamber Tech), Scarlet Forge (Young Grace), John Frazier (Priest), Frankie (Little Richard), Charlton Heston (Narrator)

Bruce Willis, Ben Affleck

Billy Bob Thornton

When a massive asteroid is predicted to hit Earth at 22,000 mph, NASA enlists the aide of deep core driller Harry Stamper and a team of misfits to destroy it. This film received Oscar nominations for visual effects, sound, and sound effects editing.

Bruce Willis

Owen Wilson, Anthony Guidera, Ben Affleck, Greg Collins, Steve Buscemi, Ken Campbell,
Bruce Willis, Michael Duncan, Will Patton, Grayson McCouch, Clark Brolly

Liv Tyler, Ben Affleck

William Fichtner

Billy Bob Thornton, Bruce Willis

Frances McDormand, Hatty Jones

Hatty Jones, Kristian De La Osa

MADELINE

(TRISTAR) Producers, Saul Cooper, Pancho Kohner, Allyn Stewart; Executive Producer, Stanley R. Jaffe; Director, Daisy von Scherler Mayer; Screenplay, Mark Levin, Jennifer Flackett; Screen Story, Malia Scotch Marmo, Mark Levin, Jennifer Flackett; Based on the book *Madeline* by Ludwig Bemelmans; Photography, Pierre Aim; Designer, Hugo Luczyc-Wyhowski; Editor, Jeffrey Wolf; Costumes, Michael Clancy; Music, Michel Legrand; Casting, Karen Lindsay-Stewart, Pat McCorkle, Sylvie Brocheré; a Jaffilms Production of a Pancho Kohner/Saul Cooper Production; Dolby; Technicolor; Rated PG; 90 minutes; July release

CAST

Miss Clavel	Frances McDormand
Lord Covington	Nigel Hawthorne
Madeline	Hatty Jones
Leopold the Tutor	Ben Daniels
Lady Covington	Stéphane Audran
Mr. Spanish Ambassador	Arturo Venegas
Mrs. Spanish Ambassador	Katia Caballero
Helene the Cook	Chantal Neuwirth
Pepito	Kristian De La Osa
Aggie	Clare Thomas
Victoria	Bianca Ströhman
Chantal	Christina Mangani
Lucinda	Rachel Dennis
Beatrice	Pilar Garrard
Serena	Jessica Mason
Lolo	Alix Ponchon
Elizabeth	Emilie Jessula
Sylvette	Eloïse Eonnet
Veronica	Alice Lavaud
Marie-Odile	Morgane Farçat
Louis the Painter	Alexis Desseaux
Mr. Liberian Ambassador	George Harris
Mrs. Liberian Ambassador	Marie-Noëlle Eusebe
Mr. Indian Ambassador	Ash Varrez
Mrs. Indian Ambassador	Vayu Naidu
Mr. Uzbekhistani Ambassador	Alexandre Arbatt
Mrs. Uzbekhistani Ambassador	Katia Tchenko

and Julien Maurel, Raphaël Beauville, Choukri Gabteni (Idiots Popopov), Luc Florian (Chief Gendarme), Luca Vellani (Chauffeur), Emile Abossolo M'Bo (Circus Barker), Marianne Groves (Admitting Nurse), Christian Mulot (Hospital Doctor), Christophe Guybet (Paramedic), Nani (Genevieve)

Frances McDormand (in rear) and the girls

The future of the school where young Madeline and her eleven friends live is threatened when the stuffy Lord Covington decides to sell it.

©TriStar Pictures

Nigel Hawthorne

LETHAL WEAPON 4

(WARNER BROS.) Producers, Joel Silver, Richard Donner; Executive Producers, Steve Perry, Jim Van Wyck; Co-Producers, J. Mills Goodloe, Dan Cracchiolo; Director, Richard Donner; Screenplay, Channing Gibson; Story, Jonathan Lemkin, Alfred Gough, Miles Millar; Based on characters created by Shane Black; Photography, Andrzej Bartkowiak; Designer, J. Michael Riva; Costumes, Ha Nguyen; Editors, Frank J. Urioste, Dallas Puett; Music, Michael Kamen, Eric Clapton, David Sanborn; Martial Arts Choreographers, Cory Yen, Huen Chiu Ku, Chi Wah Ling; Special Effects Coordinator, Jon Belyeu; Casting, Marion Dougherty; a Silver Pictures production in association with Doshudo Prods.; Dolby; Panavision; Technicolor; Rated R; 127 minutes; July release

Mel Gibson, Danny Glover

CAST

Martin Riggs	Mel Gibson
Roger Murtaugh	Danny Glover
Leo Getz	Joe Pesci
Lorna Cole	Rene Russo
Lee Butters	Chris Rock
Wah Sing Ku	Jet Li
Capt. Ed Murphy	Steve Kahan
Uncle Benny	Kim Chan
Trish Murtaugh	Darlene Love
Rianne	Traci Wolfe
Hong	Eddy Ko
Man from State Department	Jack Kehler
Nick Murtaugh	Damon Hines
Carrie Murtaugh	Ebonie Smith
Dr. Stephanie Woods	Mary Ellen Trainor
Ping	Steven Lam
Benny's Assistant	Michael Chow
Ng's Partner	Tony Keyes
INS Agent	Richard Riehle
Yee	Phil Chong
Chu	Roger Yuan
Thugs	Jeff Imada, Simon Rhee
Uncle Chung	Zo-Wu Qian
Gomez	Danny Arroyo
Cheng's Receptionist	Jennie Lew Tugend
Hong's Wife	Elizabeth Sung
Little Girl	Jessica Jann
Human Tank	Danny Wynands

and Paul Tuerpe (Helicopter Co-Pilot), James Lew (Freighter's Captain), Conan Lee, James Wing Woo, Raymond Moy, François Chau (Four Fathers), Stephen Liska, Robin Link, Roland Kickinger, Benjamin King, John Harms, Al Sapienza, Darren Peel, Jamie Donovan, Shawn Michaels, Paul Bollen (Detectives), Ray Chang (Ping's Father), Jeanne Chin (Ping's Mother), Ryan C. Benson, Daniel Getzoff, Theodore Johnson, Jr. (Construction Workers), Richard Libertini (Rabbi), George Cheung (Fan), Dana Lee (General), Edward J. Rosen, Jay Fiondella, J. Matthew Jordan, Lisa Rhianna Smith (Murtaugh's Neighbors), Marian Collier, Cece Neber Labao (Maternity Workers), Barret Swatek, Kerry Kletter, Joyce Ingalls, Joan Frasco (Nurses), Glenn Tannous, Larkin Campbell (Patrolmen), Doug Weaver, Glenn Friedman (Police Officers), Brittany Gamble, James Oliver, Rick Hoffman (Police Officers at Port), Sarah Sullivan (News Reporter), Tim Coooney (News Cameraman), Bill Henderson (Angry Patient), Philip Tan (Waiter), Judith Woodbury (Question Lady), Jey Wada (Master Printer), Wally Gudgell (ATF Officer), Gary Hand (Coroner's Assistant), Nicole Rosenfield (Candy Striper), Kenneth Jackman (Hospital Employee), Nancy Hopewell (Patient with I.V.), Christina Orchid, Bruce R. Orchid (News Crew), Richard M. Steker (Motorcycle Officer), Jen Wey Chang (Bicycle Guy)

Chris Rock, Joe Pesci

Detectives Martin Riggs and Roger Murtaugh investigate a group of Chinese gangsters who are smuggling families from China into America. The fourth film in the Warner Bros. series all of which featured Mel Gibson, Danny Glover, Darlene Love, Steve Kahan, Tracy Wolfe, Ebonie Smith and Damon Hines. Joe Pesci returns for the third time; Rene Russo for the second.

©Warner Bros.

Jet Li, Mel Gibson

SMALL SOLDIERS

Archer, Chip Hazard

(DREAMWORKS/UNIVERSAL) Producers, Michael Finnell, Colin Wilson; Executive Producer, Walter Parkes; Director, Joe Dante; Screenplay, Gavin Scott, Adam Rifkin, Ted Elliott, Terry Rossio; Photography, Jamie Anderson; Designer, William Sandell; Editor, Marshall Harvey; Costumes, Carole Brown-James; Animation Supervisor, David Andrews; Visual Effects Supervisor, Stefen Fangmeier; Action Figures and Animatronics Designer, Stan Winston; Music, Jerry Goldsmith; Casting, Denise Chamian; Dolby; Super 35 Widescreen Technicolor; Rated PG-13; 99 minutes; July release

CAST

Christy Fimple	Kirsten Dunst
Alan Abernathy	Gregory Smith
Larry Benson	Jay Mohr
Phil Fimple	Phil Hartman
Stuart Abernathy	Kevin Dunn
Irwin Wayfair	David Cross
Irene Abernathy	Ann Magnuson
Gil Mars	Denis Leary
Joe	Dick Miller
Marion Fimple	Wendy Schaal
Clean Room Technician	Robert Picardo
The Voices:	
Chip Hazard	Tommy Lee Jones
Archer	Frank Langella
Kip Killagin	Ernest Borgnine
Butch Meathook	Jim Brown
Brick Bazooka	George Kennedy
Nick Nitro	Clint Walker
Link Static	Bruce Dern
Slamfist/Scratch-It	Christopher Guest
Insaniac/Freakenstein	Michael McKean
Punch-It	Harry Shearer
Gwendy Dolls	Sarah Michelle Gellar, Christina Ricci

and Alexandra Wilson (Ms. Kegel), Gregory Itzin (Mr. Florens), Jacob Smith (Timmy Fimple), Jonathan David Bouck (Brad), Archie Hahn III (Satellite Dish Installer), Julius Tennon (Toy World Supervisor), Belinda Balaski (Neighbor), Rance Howard (Husband), Jackie Joseph (Wife)

A greedy toy manufacturer secretly installs advanced military microchips into a collection of Commando Elite action figures causing them to come alive and do battle with their sworn enemies, the Gorgonites. This marked the final film appearance of actor Phil Hartman who was murdered on May 28, 1998.

Gregory Smith

Phil Hartman, Kirsten Dunst

Brick Bazooka, Butch Meathook, Kip Killagin, Chip Hazard, Link Static

π

(**ARTISAN ENTERTAINMENT**) Producer, Eric Watson; Executive Producer, Randy Simon; Director/Screenplay, Darren Aronofsky; Co-Producer, Scott Vogel; Co-Executive Producers, Tyler Brodie, David Godbout, Jonah Smith; Photography, Matthew Libatique; Designer, Matthew Maraffi; Editor, Oren Sarch; Music, Clint Mansell; Casting, Denise Fitzgerald; a Harvest Film Works Truth & Soul and Plantain Films presentation; Black and white; Rated R; 85 minutes; July release

Sean Gullette

CAST

Maximillian Cohen	Sean Gullette
Sol Robeson	Mark Margolis
Lenny Meyer	Ben Shenkman
Marcy Dawson	Pamela Hart
Rabbi Cohen	Stephen Pearlman
Devi	Samia Shoaib
Farrouhk	Ajay Naidu
Jenna	Kristyn Mae-Anne Lao
Jenna's Mom	Espher Lao Nieves
Jenny Robeson	Lauren Fox
Mrs. Ovadia	Joanne Gordon

and Stanley Herman (Moustacheless Man), Clint Mansell (Photographer), Tom Tumminello (Ephraim), Ari Handel, Oren Sarch, Lloyd Schwartz, Richard Lifschutz, David Strahlberg, Peter Cheyenne (Brad), David Tawil (Jake), J.C. Islander (Man Presenting Suitcase), Abraham Aronofsky (Man Delivering Suitcase), Ray Seiden, Scott Franklin (Transit Cops), Chris Johnson (Limo Driver), Sal Monte (King Neptune)

A troubled mathmatical genius attempts to decode a numerical pattern revealing the chaotic state of the stock market. As a result he finds himself being pursued by a Wall Street firm set on domination and a Kabbalah sect hoping to unlock secrets behind their ancient holy texts.

Pamela Hart, Sean Gullette

©Artisan Entertainment

WHATEVER

(**SONY PICTURES CLASSICS**) Producers, Ellin Baumel, Michelle Yahn, Kevin Segalla, Susan Skoog; Executive Producers, Jim Pedas, Ted Pedas, Irwin Young, Bill Durkin, George P. Pelecanos; Director/Screenplay, Susan Skoog; Photography, Michael Barrow, Michael Mayers; Designer, Dina Goldman; Editor, Sandi Guthrie; Casting, Adrienne Stern; a Circle/Duart Films and Anyway Productions presentation; Dolby; DuArt color; Rated R; 112 minutes; July release

Liza Weil

CAST

Anna Stockard	Liza Weil
Brenda Talbot	Chad Morgan
Carol Stockard	Kathryn Rossetter
Mr. Chaminsky	Frederic Forrest
Eddie	Gary Wolf
Zak	Dan Montano
Martin	Marc Riffon
John Woods	John G. Connolly
Mr. Stanley	Tony Torn
Sam	Trey Compton
Chris	Joe Mantranga
Tony	Matt Rumbaugh
Rob	Jim Neville
Joe	Garret Spencer

and Destiny Matranga (Lynn), Mary Jo Roth (Amy Peck), Evie Mazzone (Mrs. Wilson), Michelle Yahn, Lenora Nemetz (Principals), Peter Gannon (Henry Talbot), Jean Cardello (Karen Talbot), Harold Herthum (Howard), Sean O'Brien (Mr. Tibbets), Frank Licato (Real Estate Agent), Charlie Schroeder (Tom), Zach Chapman (Gus), Susan Skoog (Roxanne), Ed Mattson (Danny Boy)

Chad Morgan, Liza Weil

©Sony Pictures Entertainment

A look into the lives of a pair of sexually anxious and confused teenage girls growing up in suburban New Jersey in the early 1980s.

Cameron Diaz

Matt Dillon

THERE'S SOMETHING ABOUT MARY

(20TH CENTURY FOX) Producers, Frank Beddor, Michael Steinberg, Charles B. Wessler, Bradley Thomas; Executive Producers/Directors, Bobby Farrelly, Peter Farrelly; Screenplay, Ed Decter, John J. Strauss, Peter Farrelly, Bobby Farrelly; Story, Ed Decter, John J. Strauss; Photography, Mark Irwin; Designer, Arlan Jay Vetter; Editor, Christopher Greenbury; Costumes, Mary Zophres; Co-Producers, Marc S. Fischer, James B. Rogers; Associate Producers, Mark Charpentier, Patrick Healy; Music, Jonathan Richman; Title song by Jonathan Richman/performed by Jonathan Richman and Tommy Larkins; Casting, Rick Montgomery; a Farrelly Brothers Movie; Dolby; Color; Rated R; 118 minutes; July release

CAST

Mary Jenson	Cameron Diaz
Pat Healy	Matt Dillon
Ted Stroehmann	Ben Stiller
Tucker	Lee Evans
Dom	Chris Elliott
Magda	Lin Shaye
Sully	Jeffrey Tambor
Mary's Mom	Markie Post
Mary's Stepdad	Keith David
Warren	W. Earl Brown
Jonathan	Jonathan Richman
Drummer	Tommy Larkins
Brenda	Sarah Silverman
Joanie	Khandi Alexander
Lisa	Marnie Alexenburg
Boss' Brother	Dan Murphy
Detective Krevoy	Richard M. Tyson
Detective Stabler	Rob Moran
South Carolina Police	Jackie Flynn
Dom's Wife	Hillary Matthews
Dr. Zit Face/High School Pal	Willie Garson
Coconut Guy	David Shackelford

and David Goryl (Petey), Lori Glick (Friend #3), Jeffrey P. Lerner, Cory Pendergast (Car Hood Kids), Brett Favre (Himself), Warren Tashjian (Freddie), Kelly Roarke (Girl), Herbie Flynn (Homeless Man), Caryl West (Medical Assistant #1), Ken Rogerson (Pants at Ankles Guy), Brad Blank (Paramedic), Steve Sweeney (Police Officer), Cindy Oliver (Renise), Will Coogan (Smokey), Steve Tyler (TV News Reporter), Maureen Griffin (Wine Waitress), The Artist Formerly Known as Docky (Hot Dog Stud), Mariann Farrelly (Driving Range Sweetie), Lenny Clarke (Fireman), Daniel Greene (Pizza House Man), Lagena Greene (Pizza House Wife), Michael Budge (Joey Bishop Look-alike), James Gifford (Jimmy), Sean P. Gildea (Prison Warden), Zen Gesner (Bartender), Tracy Anne George (Dancer), Jesse & Anna Farrelly (Dom's Kids), Zack Lee (Mary's Little Friend), Valerie Bruce (Nimrod's Cafe Patron), Kelly O'Brien (Office Assistant), Mike Charpentier, Peter Grundy, Michael Gannon, Peter Conway, Ann Conway, Susan O'Day, Heather Rosbeck (Hot Club Patrons), Jack Shields, Fallon Shields, Bob Grundy (Hot Club Barkeeps), Nancy Farrelly (Boardroom Babe), Billy Beauchene, Kathy Beauchene, Manny Barrows (Insurance Spitballers), Michael Murphy, Sheila Mone (Office Workers), Barbara O'Connor (Ashtray Babe), Tim Sheehan (Camera Hog), Richie Balsbaugh (Cigar Smoker), Jim "Sunshine" Blake, Tim Robbie, Providence Wissel, Ruth Michelle Meyer, Billy Meyer, Brian McGlaughlin, Brian Mone, John Strochman, Pete Anicelli (Architect Partiers), Duana Knight, Kelley Schneider, Meda Thomas (Architect Babes), Steve & Kenny, Pat & Mike, Larry & Sam, Ernie & Tom, Chris & Rosie (Rest Stop Couples), Jeanie Flynn, Kevin Civali, Tom Leasca, Mercy Lopez (Cuban Dancers), Scott Rosenberg, Michael Cheney (Cell Block Bitch), Scott Rosenberg, George Bedard, Terry Mullany, Rick Coleman, Michael Burke, Kris Meyer, Emilio Diaz, Billy Smith, Ed Nelson, Brian Stube, Don Daley (Jail Birds), Celm Franek, Julia Hissom, Spórt Ahern, Robin Gau (Strip Club Perverts), Paul & Monique Pelletier (Cordosa Gawkers), Johnny Mone (Comic Book Kid), Nick & Andrew Greenbury (Fish Hook Kids), Phil Rosenberg (Cell Block Masseuse), John-Eliot Jordan, John Adamonis, Kyle Adamonis, Neil Pomfret, Ruth Pomfret, Josh Miller (Buttercup Singers)

Perennial loser Ted Stroehmann, hopelessly stuck on Mary Jenson since high school, hires a private detective to track her down only to have the sleazy investigator fall for Mary himself.

©Twentieth Century Fox

Chris Elliott, Ben Stiller

Jonathan Richman, Tommy Larkins

Ben Stiller, Lenny Clarke, Keith David, Markie Post

Lin Shaye

Ben Stiller, Matt Dillon, Cameron Diaz, Chris Elliott, Lee Evans

Antonio Banderas

Antonio Banderas, Catherine Zeta-Jones

Anthony Hopkins

Stuart Wilson, Matt Letscher

THE MASK OF ZORRO

(TRISTAR) Producers, Doug Claybourne, David Foster; Executive Producers, Steven Spielberg, Walter F. Parkes, Laurie MacDonald; Director, Martin Campbell; Screenplay, John Eskow, Ted Elliott, Terry Rossio; Story, Ted Elliott, Terry Rossio, Randall Jahnson; Based on the character created by Johnston MCulley; Photography, Phil Meheux; Designer, Cecilia Montiel; Editor, Thom Noble; Costumes, Graciela Mazon; Music, James Horner; Co-Producer, John Gertz; Casting, Pam Dixon Mickelson; 2nd Unit/Stunts, Glenn Randall, Jr.; Sword Master, Robert Anderson; an Amblin Entertainment production; Dolby; Panavision; Technicolor; Rated PG-13; 136 minutes; July release

Antonio Banderas

CAST

Alejandro Murrieta (Zorro)	Antonio Banderas
Don Diego de la Vega (Zorro)	Anthony Hopkins
Elena Montero	Catherine Zeta-Jones
Don Rafael Montero	Stuart Wilson
Captain Harrison Love	Matt Letscher
Prison Warden	Maury Chaykin
Don Luiz	Tony Amendola
Don Pedro	Pedro Armendariz
Three-Fingered Jack	L.Q. Jones
Fray Felipe	William Marquez
Corporal Armando Garcia	Jose Perez
Joaquin Murrieta	Victor Rivers
Esperanza de la Vega	Julieta Rosen
Young Alejandro Murrieta	Jose Maria De Tavira
Young Joaquin Murrieta	Diego Sieres
Boy Crying	Emiliano Guerra
Woman Crying	Yolanda Orizaga
Undertaker	Paco Morayta
Squad Leader	Pedro Altamirano
Nanny	Luisa Huertas
Baby Elena de la Vega	Maria & Monica Fernandez Cruz
Heavyset Lieutenant	Raul Martinez
Soldier Holding "Wanted" Poster	Tony Cabral
Watering Station Owner	Tony Genaro
Small Boy at Watering Station	Ivan Rafael
Stupid Soldier	David Villalpando
Prison Guard	Paul Ganus
Leper Zorro	Sergio Espinosa
Black Zorro	Conrad Roberts
Anicent Zorro	Abel Woolrich

and Moises Suarez (Don Hector), Humberto Elizondo (Don Julio), Fernando Becerril, Alberto Carrera, Eduardo Lopez, Gonzalo Lora, Rudy Miller, Manolo Pastor (The Six Dons), Diego Sandoval, Enrike Palma (Bartender), Erika Carlson (Don Pedro's Wife), Manuel de Jesus Vasquez Morales (Guitar-Playing Soldier), Oscar Zerafin Gonzalez (Giant Soldier), Vanessa Bauche (Indian Girl), Kelsie Kimberli Garcia, Kaylissa Keli Garcia (Baby Joaquin)

Antonio Banderas, Catherine Zeta-Jones

Zorro, escaping from prison after twenty years, enlists bandit Alejandro Murrieta to become his successor to fight Spanish opression in Alta California and take revenge on Don Rafael Montero who had stolen Zorro's daughter away and raised her as his own. Previous Zorro films include The Mark of Zorro (UA, 1920) starring Douglas Fairbanks; The Bold Caballero (Republic, 1936), with Robert Livingston; the serial Zorro Rides Again (Republic, 1937) with John Carroll; The Mark of Zorro (20th, 1940) with Tyrone Power; and Zorro (released in the U.S. by Allied Artists, 1977) with Alain Delon. This film received Oscar nominations for sound and sound effects editing.

Anthony Hopkins

Tom Hanks, Matt Damon

Tom Hanks

Jeremy Davies

SAVING PRIVATE RYAN

(DREAMWORKS/PARAMOUNT) Producers, Steven Spielberg, Ian Bryce, Mark Gordon, Gary Levinsohn; Director, Steven Spielberg; Screenplay, Robert Rodat; Photography, Janusz Kaminski; Designer, Tom Sanders; Editor, Michael Kahn, Music, John Williams; Costumes, Joanna Johnston; Co-Producers, Bonnie Curtis, Allison Lyon Segan; Special Effects Supervisor, Neil Corbould; Casting, Denise Chamian; Stunts, Simon Crane; an Amblin Entertainment production in association with Mutual Film Company; Dolby; Technicolor; Rated R; 169 minutes; July release

CAST

Captain John Miller	Tom Hanks
Sergeant Horvath	Tom Sizemore
Private Reiben	Edward Burns
Private Jackson	Barry Pepper
Private Mellish	Adam Goldberg
Private Caparzo	Vin Diesel
T/4 Medic Wade	Giovanni Ribisi
Corporal Upham	Jeremy Davies
Private Ryan	Matt Damon
Captain Hamill	Ted Danson
Sergeant Hill	Paul Giamatti
Lieutenant Colonel Anderson	Dennis Farina
Steamboat Willie	Joerg Stadler
Toynbe	Dylan Bruno
Weller	Daniel Cerqueira
Parker	Demetri Goritsas
Trask	Ian Porter
Rice	Gary Sefton
Garrity	Julian Spencer
Wilson	Steve Griffin
Lyle	William Marsh
Fallon	Marc Cass
Major Hoess	Markus Napier
Ramelle Paratroopers	Neil Finnighan, Peter Miles
Field HQ Major	Paul Garcia
Field HQ Aide	Seamus McQuade
General Marshall	Harve Presnell
Coxswain	Ronald Longridge
Delancey	Adam Shaw

and Rolf Saxon (Lieutenant Briggs), Corey Johnson (Radioman), John Sharian (Corporal), Glenn Wrage (Boyle), Crofton Hardester (Senior Medical Officer), Martin Hub (Czech Wermacht Soldier), Raph Taylor (Goldman), Nigel Whitmey (Private Boyd), Loclann Aiken, John Barnett, MacLean Burke, Victor Burke, Aiden Condron, Paschal Friel, Shane Hagan, Paul Hickey, Shane Johnson, Laird MacIntosh, Brian Maynard, Martin McDougall, Mark Phillips, Lee Rosen, Andrew Scott, Matthew Sharp, Vincent Walsh, Grahame Wood (Soldiers on the Beach), Sam Ellis (Private Hastings), Erich Redman, Tilo Keiner (Germans), Stephan Grothgar (German #3/Voice on Bullhorn), Stephan Cornicard (Jean), Michelle Evans (Jean's Wife), Martin Beaton (Jean's Son), Anna Maguire (Jean's Daughter), Nathan Fillion (Minnesota Ryan), Leland Orser (Lieutenant DeWindt), Michael Mantas (Paratrooper Lieutenant), David Vegh (Paratrooper Oliver), Ryan Hurst (Paratrooper Michaelson), Nick Brooks (Paratrooper Joe), Sam Scudder (Paratrooper #1), John Walters (Old French Man), Dorothy Grumbar (Old French Woman), James Innes-Smith (MP Lieutenant), Dale Dye, Bryan Cranston (War Department Colonels), David Wohl (War Department Captain), Eric Loren (War Department Lieutenant), Valerie Colgan (War Department Clerk), Amanda Boxer (Mrs. Margaret Ryan), Harrison Young (Ryan as Old Man), Kathleen Byron (Old Mrs. Ryan), Rob Freeman (Ryan's Son), Thomas Gizbert (Ryan's Grandson)

Following the bloody D-Day invasion, Captain Miller and a small squadron of men are assigned to go behind enemy lines to locate and bring back Private James Ryan whose three brothers have all been killed in battle. 1998 Academy Award-winner for Best Director, Cinematography, Editing, Sound, and Sound Effects Editing. The film received additional nominations for picture, actor (Tom Hanks), original screenplay, original dramatic score, makeup, and art direction. This film became the highest-grossing picture released in 1998.

©DreamWorks/Paramount/Amblin

Edward Burns

Vin Diesel

Jeremy Davies

Tom Sizemore

Tom Hanks, Giovanni Ribisi, Tom Sizemore

Barry Pepper

Matt Damon

Giovanni Ribisi

Adam Goldberg

97

Christina Applegate, Jay Mohr

Blake Hammond

JANE AUSTEN'S MAFIA!

(TOUCHSTONE) Producer, Bill Badalato; Executive Producers, Peter Abrams, Robert L. Levy; Director, Jim Abrahams; Screenplay, Jim Abrahams, Greg Norberg, Michael McManus; Photography, Pierre Letarte; Designer, William Elliott; Editor, Terry Stokes; Costumes, Mary Malin; Music, Gianni Frizzelli; Co-Producers, Greg Norberg, Michael McManus; Associate Producers, Jack Bernstein, Jennifer Gibgot; Casting, Jackie Burch; a Tapestry Films production; Distributed by Buena Vista Pictures; Dolby; Technicolor; Rated PG-13; 84 minutes; July release

CAST

Anthony Cortino	Jay Mohr
Joey Cortino	Billy Burke
Diane	Christina Applegate
Pepper Gianini	Pamela Gidley
Sophia	Olympia Dukakis
Vincenzo Cortino	Lloyd Bridges
Young Vincenzo	Jason Fuchs
Clamato	Joe Viterelli
Marzoni	Tony Lo Bianco
Fatso Paulie Orsatti	Blake Hammond
Frankie Totino	Phil Suriano
Gorgoni	Vincent Pastore
Carla	Marisol Nichols
Clamato's Wife	Carol Ann Susi
Bonifcaio	Gregory Sierra
Rosa Cortino	Vera Lockwood
Jimmy Big Features	Martin Charles Warner
Willy Denunzio	Joseph Jumbo Rufo

and Tyler Daniel Wenz (Toddler), Jason Davis (Geno), T.J. Cannata (The Boy Diane), Louis Mandylor (Middle-Aged Vincenzo), Georgia Simon (Middle-Aged Rosa), Joey Dente (Middle-Aged Clamato), Sebastian Aza (Young Joey), Seth Adkins (Tiny Anthony), Andreas Katsulas (Narducci), Joseph R. Sicari (Rizzo), Allyson Call (Jenny), Monica Mikala (Young Rosa), Anthony Jesse Cruz (Young Clamato), James Costa (Immigration Thug), Mark Goldstein (Clerk), Stefan Lysenko (Ruffo), Sofia Milos (Young Sophia), Anthony Crivello (Luigi Cortino), Saverio Carubia (Villager), Bill Livingston (Gues the Number Croupier), Gerald Emerick (Guess the Number Player), Frankie Como (Waiter), Brian Tahash (Bodyguard), Richard Abraham (Evil Priest), Frank Birney (Wedding Priest), Don Bovingloh (Funeral Priest), Henry Harris (Nonchalant Guy), Karen Leigh Hopkins (Nurse), Dan Klein (Judas), Pat Harvey (Newscaster), Jerry Haleva (Saddam Hussein), Mr. Oh (Korean Soldier), Trinity Dance Troupe (Irish Dancers), Jack Bernstein (ATM Man with Double Chin), Isabell Sanford, Sherman Hemsley (The Jeffersons), Alex Trebek (Himself)

Anthony Cortino looks back on how he went from being a war hero to the head of the powerful Cortino crime family.

Lloyd Bridges

Jay Mohr, Pamela Gidley

BILLY'S HOLLYWOOD SCREEN KISS

(TRIMARK) Producer, David Moseley; Director/Screenplay, Tommy O'Haver; Photography, Mark Mervis; Designer, Franco-Giacomo Carbone; Costumes, Julia Bartholomew; Editor, Jeff Betancourt; Associate Producer, Marcus Hu; Co-Producers, Meredith Scott Lynn, Irene Turner; Line Producer, Irene Turner; Music, Alan Ari Lazar; Casting, Robert McGee; a Revolutionary Eye production; Dolby; Panavision; FotoKem color; Rated R; 92 minutes; July release

CAST

Billy Collier	Sean P. Hayes
Gabriel	Brad Rowe
Perry	Richard Ganoung
Georgiana	Meredith Scott Lynn
Rex Webster	Paul Bartel
Gundy	Carmine Giovinazzo
Fernando	Armando Valdes-Kennedy
Les	Les Borsay
Holly	Holly Woodlawn
Deidre	Niles Jenson
Andrew	Christopher Bradley
Peter	Mark Anderson
Donna	Kimiko Gelman

and Mr. Dan (Drag Queen), Chad Boardman, Rodney Chester, Eric Davenport (Drag Chorus), Shanti Reinhardt (Ju-Ju, the Performance Artist), Kiff Scholl (Rio, the Performance Artist), Shawn Nicholson (Young Billy), Jaime Spencer (Kent Bartlett), Michelle Karen (Billy's Mom), Aaron Wilde (Chris Jungblut), Annabelle Gurwitch (Gallery Owner), Matthew Ashford (Whitey), Bonnie Biehl (Connie Rogers), Jason-Shane Scott (Brad), Kim Campoli (Natalie), Mark Conley (Raymond), Robbie Cain (Joshua)

Billy, a gay photographer whose project it is to recreate famous Hollywood loves scenes with male couples, comes to Los Angeles to establish himself and falls madly in love with one of his models, Gabriel, who claims he is straight.

Brad Rowe, Sean P. Hayes

Brad Rowe, Sean P. Hayes

HANDS ON A HARD BODY

(LEGACY) Producers, Kevin Morris, Chapin John Wilson, S.R. Bindler; Director/Editor, S.R. Bindler; Photography, Michael Nickles, Chapin John Wilson, S.R. Bindler; Associate Producer, Julia Wall; Music, Neil Kassanoff; from J.K. Livin Productions, in association with Idea Entertainment and Wessex Entertainment Group; Color; Not rated; 95 minutes; July release. Documentary about an annual contest held in Longview, Texas, in which the participant who keeps one hand on a brand new Nissan pickup for the longest period of time gets to keep the vehicle.

The Contestants

©Legacy Releasing

Lindsay Lohan, Lindsay Lohan

Natasha Richardson, Lindsay Lohan

Lindsay Lohan, Elaine Mendrix, Lindsay Lohan

Natasha Richardson, Dennis Quaid

THE PARENT TRAP

(WALT DISNEY PICTURES) Producer, Charles Shyer; Director, Nancy Meyers; Screenplay, David Swift, Nancy Meyers, Charles Shyer; Co-Producer, Bruce Block; Photography, Dean Cundey; Designer, Dean Tavoularis; Editor, Stephen A. Rotter; Music, Alan Silvestri; Costumes, Penny Rose; Casting, Ilene Starger; Special Visual Effects, CIS Hollywood; Distributed by Buena Vista Pictures; Dolby; Technicolor; Rated PG; 127 minutes; July release

CAST

Hallie Parker and Annie James	Lindsay Lohan
Nick Parker	Dennis Quaid
Elizabeth James	Natasha Richardson
Meredith Blake	Elaine Hendrix
Chessy	Lisa Ann Walter
Martin	Simon Kunz
Marva Kulp, Sr.	Polly Holliday
Marva Kulp, Jr.	Maggie Wheeler
Grandfather	Ronnie Stevens
Hallie/Annie Acting Double	Erin Mackey
Vicki Blake	Joanna Barnes
Lindsay	Hallie Meyers-Shyer
Zoe	Maggie Emma Thomas
Nicole	Courtney Woods
Jackie	Katerina Graham
Lost Boy at Camp	Michael Lohan
Bugler	Lisa Iverson
Gareth, the James' Chauffeur	John Atterbury
Photographer	Hamish McColl
Bridal Gown Model	Vendela K. Thommessen

and Rachel Sullivan, Katie Deshan, Brighton Hertford, Jennifer Lin, Amy Centner, Mia Tramz (Navajo Bunk Girls), Christina Toral, Dana Ponder, Brianne Mercier (Cell Phone Girls), Danielle Sherman, Natasha Melnick, Amanda Hampton (Girls at Poker Game), Lisa Cloud, Kellie Foster, Heidi Boren (Camp Counselors), Marissa Leigh, Heather Wayrock (Fencing Girls), Alexander Cole (Richard, Meredith's Assistant), J. Patrick McCormack (Les Blake), William Akey (Bellhop with Flowers), David Doty (Hotel Bartender), Roshanna Baron (Lady at Pool), Annie Meyers-Shyer (Towel Girl), Brian Fenwick (Desk Clerk), Jonneine Hellerstein (Ship Photographer), Troy Christian, Denise Holland (QE2 Dancers), Terry Kerr (Living Statue), Bruce Block (Tourist), Bob (Sammy the Dog)

A pair of identical twins, raised by their divorced parents on separate continents, meet at summer camp and hatch a scheme to pose as one another in order to bring their parents back together again. Remake of the 1961 Disney film which starred Hayley Mills, Maureen O'Hara and Brian Keith. Joanna Barnes, who appeared in the original film, appears here in the role of the mother of the equivalent character she played the first time out.

©Disney Enterprises

THE NEGOTIATOR

(WARNER BROS.) Producers, David Hoberman, Arnon Milchan; Executive Producers, David Nicksay, Robert Stone, Webster Stone; Director, F. Gary Gray; Screenplay, James DeMonaco, Kevin Fox; Photography, Russell Carpenter; Designer, Holger Gross; Editor, Christian Wagner; Music, Graeme Revell; Co-Producer, Albert Beveridge; Costumes, Francine Jamison-Tanchuck; Casting, David Rubin; a Regency Enterprises presentation of a Mandeville Films/New Regency production; Dolby; Super 35 Widescreen; Technicolor; Rated R; 138 minutes; July release

Samuel L. Jackson, J.T. Walsh

CAST

Danny Roman	Samuel L. Jackson
Chris Sabian	Kevin Spacey
Adam Beck	David Morse
Grant Frost	Ron Rifkin
Chief Al Travis	John Spencer
Terence Niebaum	J.T. Walsh
Maggie	Siobahn Fallon
Rudy	Paul Giamatti
Karen Roman	Regina Taylor
Markus	Bruce Beatty
Palermo	Michael Cudlitz
Eagle	Carlos Gomez
Argento	Tim Kelleher
Scott	Dean Norris
Hellman	Nestor Serrano
Tonray	Doug Spinuzza
Allen	Leonard Thomas
Farley	Stephen Lee

and Lily Nicksay (Omar's Daughter), Lauri Johnson (Chief's Wife), Sabi Dorr (Bartender), Gene Wolande (Morewitz), Rhonda Dotson (Linda Roenick), Donald Korte, Anthony T. Petrusonis (Officers at funeral), John McDonald (Pipes and Drums Leader), Jack McLaughlin Gray (Priest), John Lordon (Linda's Attorney), Jack Shearer (D.A. Young), Donna Ponterotto (Secretary), Michael Shamus Wiles (Taylor), Mik Scriba (Bell), Joey Perillo (Tech #1), Mary Page Keller (Lisa Sabian), Kelsey Mulrooney (Stacy Sabian), Brad Blaisdell (FBI Agent Grey), Bruce Wright (FBI Agent Moran), Robert David Hall (Cale Wangro), Guy Van Swearingen (Officer), Bernard Hocke (Sniper), Tony Mockus, Jr. (Agent), Carol-Anne Touchberry, Robert Jordan, Geoff Morrell, Janna Tetzlaff, Millie Santiago, Mike Leiderman, Jay Levine, Mark Giangrego, Rick Scarry, Mary Ingersoll, McNally Sagal, Mary Major, Lynn Rondell, Edwina Moore, Lynn Forslund (Reporters), Muriel Clair, Mary Ann Childers, Diann Burns, Carla Sanchez (News Anchors), Charles Valentino (FBI Agent), Robert Baier (Officer at HBT), Ted Montue (Officer at IAB), John Buckley, Darius Aubry (Detectives), Steven Mainz (TAC Officer), Max Caine, (Raoul)

Falsely accused of murder, Chicago Police officer and hostage negotiator Danny Roman brings attention to his dilemma by holding the chief of the Internal Affairs Division hostage.

©Monarchy Enterprises/Regency Entertainment

Samuel L. Jackson

John Spencer, David Morse

John Spencer, Kevin Spacey, David Morse

EVER AFTER: A CINDERELLA STORY

(20TH CENTURY FOX) Producers, Mireille Soria, Tracey Trench; Director, Andy Tennant; Screenplay, Susannah Grant, Andy Tennant, Rick Parks; Photography, Andrew Dunn; Designer, Michael Howells; Editor, Roger Bondelli; Costumes, Jenny Beavan; Co-Producers, Kevin Reidy, Timothy M. Bourne; Music, George Fenton; Casting, Priscilla John, Lucinda Syson; a Mireille Soria production; Dolby;Super 35 Widescreen; Color; Rated PG-13; 122 minutes; July release

Drew Barrymore, Dougray Scott

CAST

Danielle	Drew Barrymore
Rodmilla	Anjelica Huston
Prince Henry	Dougray Scott
Leonardo	Patrick Godfrey
Marguerite	Megan Dodds
Jacqueline	Melanie Lynskey
King Francis	Timothy West
Queen Marie	Judy Parfitt
Auguste	Jeroen Krabbé
Gustave	Lee Ingleby
Paulette	Kate Lansbury
Louise	Matyelok Gibbs
Maurice	Walter Sparrow
Grande Dame	Jeanne Moreau
Young Danielle	Anna Maguire
Pierre Le Pieu	Richard O'Brien
Capt. Laurent	Peter Gunn
Wilhelm Grimm	Joerg Stadler
Jacob Grimm	Andrew Henderson
Royal Page	Toby Jones
Princess Gertrude	Virginia Garcia
Cargomaster	Al Hunter Ashton
Gypsy Leader	Mark Lewis
Jeweller	Howard Attfield
Young Gustave	Ricki Cuttell
Cracked Skull	Ricardo Cruz

and John Walters (Butler), Elizabeth Earl (Young Marguerite), Alex Pooley (Young Jacqueline), Janet Henfrey (Celeste), Ursula Jones (Isabella), Amanda Walker (Old Noblewoman), Rupam Maxwell (Marquis de Limoges), Tony Doyle (Driver—Royal Carriage), Christian Marc (King of Spain), Elvira Stevenson (Queen of Spain), Erick Awanzino (Short Bald Man), Susan Field (Laundry Supervisor), François Velter, Dominc Rols (Choirmen) Jean-Pierre Mazieres (Cardinal)

Drew Barrymore, Anjelica Huston

Young Danielle, raised to live a life of drudgery by her unsympathetic stepmother, finds herself falling in love with a prince.

©Twentieth Century Fox

Megan Dodds, Melanie Lynskey

Jeanne Moreau

SAFE MEN

(OCTOBER) Producers, Andrew Hauptman, Ellen Bronfman, Jeffrey Clifford, Jonathan Cohen; Director/Screenplay, John Hamburg; Photography, Michael Barrett; Designer, Anthony Gasparro; Associate Producer, Rain Kramer; Line Producer, Eva Kolodner; Editor, Suzanne Pillsbury; Costumes, Cat Thomas; Music, Theodore Shapiro; Casting, Avy Kaufman; an Andell Entertainment production in association with Blue Guitar; Dolby; Color; Rated R; 94 minutes; August release

CAST

Sam	Sam Rockwell
Eddie	Steve Zahn
Veal Chop	Paul Giamatti
Bernie Jr.	Michael Schmidt
Big Fat Bernie Gayle	Michael Lerner
Frank	Mark Ruffalo
Hannah	Christina Kirk
Mitchell	Josh Pais
Leo	Harvey Feinstein
Party Coordinator	Mark Shanahan
Barber	Raymond Serra
Swoop	Ray Iannicelli
Cousin Ira	Jacob Reynolds

and Peter Dinklage (Leflore), Michael Showalter (Larry), Adam Morenoff (Victor), John Tormey (Older Guy), Don Picard (Gunter), Carl Don (Hyman), Allen Swift (Sol)

Two hopelessly inept singers are mistaken for master safe crackers and find themselves being employed by some leading members of Providence, Rhode Island's Jewish Mafia.

Sam Rockwell, Steve Zahn

Sam Rockwell, Christina Kirk

©October Films

FIRST LOVE, LAST RITES

(STRAND) Producers, Scott Macaulay, Robin O'Hara, Herbert Beigel; Executive Producers, Jeffrey Levy-Hinte, Amanda Temple; Director, Jesse Peretz; Screenplay, David Ryan; Story Adaptation, David Ryan, Jesse Peretz; Based on the short story by Ian McEwan; Photography, Tom Richmond; Designer, Dan Estabrook; Editor, James Lyons; Music, Nathan Larson, Craig Wedren; Costumes, Yasmine Abraham; Casting, Billy Hopkins, Suzanne Smith, Kerry Barden, Pat Distefano; a Forensic Films Production; Ultra-Stereo; Color; Not rated; 93 minutes; August release

CAST

Joey	Giovanni Ribisi
Sissel	Natasha Gregson Wagner
Henry	Robert John Burke
Red	Donal Logue
Sissel's Mom	Jeannetta Arnette
Adrian	Eli Marienthal
Bob	Hugh Joseph Babin
Mitch	Earl S. Binninngs
Security Guard	Howard Barker
Restaurant Cook	Trang Thanh Le
Tattoo Artist	L. Christian Mixon

Giovanni Ribisi, Natasha Gregson Wagner

©Strand Releasing

A pair of young lovers enact an idyllic romance within the confines of a one-room shack in the Louisiana Bayou, hoping to shut out the rest of the world.

103

Nicolas Cage, Carla Gugino, Joel Fabiani

Nicolas Cage, Stan Shaw, Chip Zien

Nicolas Cage

Kevin Dunn, Gary Sinise

Nicolas Cage, Carla Gugino

SNAKE EYES

(PARAMOUNT) Producer/Director, Brian De Palma; Screenplay, David Koepp; Story, Brian De Palma, David Koepp; Executive Producer, Louis A. Stroller; Photography, Stephen H. Burum; Designer, Anne Pritchard; Editor, Bill Pankow; Music, Ryuichi Sakamoto; Special Visual Effects, Industrial Light & Magic; Associate Producer, Jeff Levine; Casting, Mary Colquhoun; a DeBart production; Dolby; Panavision; Deluxe color; Rated R; 99 minutes; August release

Nicolas Cage, Gary Sinise

CAST

Rick Santoro ....Nicolas Cage
Kevin Dunne ....Gary Sinise
Gilbert Powell ....John Heard
Julia Costello ....Carla Gugino
Lincoln Tyler ....Stan Shaw
Lou Logan ....Kevin Dunn
Jimmy George ....Michael Rispoli
Charles Kirkland ....Joel Fabiani
Cyrus ....Luis Guzman
Ned Campbell ....David Anthony Higgins
Walt McGahn ....Mike Starr
Anthea ....Tamara Tunie
Mickey Alter ....Chip Zien
Tyler's Bodyguard ....Jernard Burks
C.J. ....Mark Camacho
Ring Announcer ....Jean-Paul Chartrand
Zietz (Drunk) ....Chip Chuipka
Lady at Elevator ....Tara Ann Culp
Blonde Reporter ....Kelly Deadmon
Jose Pacifico Ruiz ....Adam C. Flores
Roundgirl ....Christina Fulton
Referee ....Kenneth Glegg
PPV Director ....Alain Goulem
Latecomer ....Dean Hagopian
Serena ....Jayne Heitmeyer
Rabat ....Eric Hoziel
Remote Producer ....Sylvain Landry
Powell's Aide ....Cary Lawrence
FBI Agent ....Robert Norman Lemieux
and Eva Tep, Michaella Bassey (Tyler's Party Girls), Paul Joseph Bernardo, Brian A. Wilson (Casino Security), Desmond Campbell, Deano Clavet (Arena Security), Frédérick DeGrandpré, Byron Johnson, Stephen Spreekmeester, Sebastien Delorme (College Boys), Guy Kelada, George Fourniotis (Blue Shirts), Richard Zeman, Richard Lemire (Agents), Jacynthe Rene, Christopher MacCabe (Couple), Sylvain Massé, John Thaddeus, Lance E. Nichols (Cops), Patrick F. McDade (Lawyer), William J. McKeon III (Anthea's Cameraman), Peter McRobbie (Pritzker), Christian Napoli (Michael Santoro), Jason Nuzzo (Coin Cup Grabber), Patrick Parent (Detective), Peter Patrikios (Coin Cup Decoy), James Whelan (Mayor), Gerard Max Désilus (Tyler's Party Crash Guy)

Carla Gugino

Following the assassination of the U.S. Secretary of Defense in the middle of a boxing match, Atlantic City police detective Rick Santoro has the arena sealed off so he can solve the murder and help salvage the career of his friend, defense staffer Kevin Dunne, on whose watch the killing occured.

©Paramount Pictures

John Heard, Joel Fabiani, Gary Sinise

Joaquin Phoenix, Vince Vaughn

Vince Vaughn, Anne Heche

Jada Pinkett Smith, Anne Heche

RETURN TO PARADISE

(POLYGRAM) Producers, Alain Bernheim, Steve Golin; Executive Producers, David Arnold, Ezra Swerdlow; Director, Joseph Ruben; Screenplay, Wesley Strick, Bruce Robinson; Photography, Reynaldo Villalobos; Designer, Bill Groom; Editors, Andrew Mondshein, Craig McKay; Music, Mark Mancina; a PolyGram Filmed Entertainment presentation of a Propaganda Films production in association with Tetragram; Dolby; Super 35 Widescreen; Color; Rated R; 109 minutes; August release

CAST

John Volgecherev ("Sheriff")...Vince Vaughn
Beth Eastern ....Anne Heche
Lewis...Joaquin Phoenix
Tony ....David Conrad
Kerrie ....Vera Farmiga
Ravitch...Nick Sandow
M.J. Major..Jada Pinkett Smith
Mr. Chandran ....Ming Lee
Mr. Doramin ....Joel De La Fuente
Prosecutor..Richard Chang
Famous Divorce Lawyer ....James Michael McCauley
Young Woman in Limo...Brettanya Friese
Woman in Bar..Deanna Yusoff
Construction Foreman...David Zayas
Ticket Agent...Amy Wong
Malaysian Woman in Hammock..Is Issariya
Features Editor ....Ed Hodson
Doormen ....Kevin Scullin, Glenn Patrick
and Yusmal Ghazali, Aril Izani, Kwak Wai (Scruffy Guys), Curzon Dobell (Client), Vincent Patrick (Tavern Waiter), Elizabeth Rodriguez (Gaby), Teoh Kah Yong (Chief Justice), Rebecca Saifer (Hotel Waitress), Rebecca Boyd (Restaurant Hostess), Woon-Kin Chin (Guard), Regina Wu (Bailiff)

Three years after a trip to Malaysia, Sheriff and Tony discover that their third travelling companion, Lewis, is about to face execution for a drug charge unless the two men return to the country and share responsibility for the crime.

©PolyGram Films

Joaquin Phoenix, Vince Vaughn, David Conrad

HOW STELLA GOT HER GROOVE BACK

(20TH CENTURY FOX) Producer, Deborah Schindler; Executive Producers, Terry McMillan, Ron Bass, Jennifer Ogden; Director, Kevin Rodney Sullivan; Screenplay, Terry McMillan, Ron Bass; Based on the novel by Terry McMillan; Photography, Jeffrey Jur; Designer, Chester Kaczenski; Editor, George Bowers; Music, Michel Colombier; Costumes, Ruth E. Carter; Casting, Francine Maisler; a Deborah Schindler production; Dolby; Color; Rated R; 124 minutes; August release

CAST

Stella	Angela Bassett
Winston	Taye Diggs
Delilah	Whoopi Goldberg
Vanessa	Regina King
Angela	Suzzanne Douglas
Quincy	Michael J. Pagan
Chantel	Sicily
Jack	Richard Lawson
Buddy	Barry "Shabaka" Henley
Nate	Lee Weaver
Dr. Shakespeare	Glynn Turman
Mrs. Shakespeare	Phyllis Yvonne Stickney
Ms. Thang	Denise Hunt
Abby	Lisa Hanna
Walter	James Pickens, Jr.
Kennedy	Philip Casnoff
Uncle Ollie	Lou Myers
Minister	D'Army Bailey
Dr. Steinberg	Art Metrano
Judge Boyle	Carl Lumbly
Leslie	Phina Oruche
Kitchen Worker	Tenny Miller
Buffet Server	Andrew Palmer

and Harold Dawkins, Kenneth Buckford, Simon Street (Upbeaters Band), Craig Blake (Winston's Friend), Elisabeth Granli (Girl in Jamaica Commerical), Steve Danton (Man in Commerical), Elly McGuire (Stella's Friend), Selma McPherson, Fern Ward (Friends at Party)

Stella, a forty-year-old, well-to-do single mother, finds her life in a rut until her friend Delilah convinces her to take a vacation in Jamaica where she meets a handsome, younger man who takes a deep interest in her.

©Twentieth Century Fox

Taye Diggs, Angela Bassett

Whoopi Goldberg, Angela Bassett

Regina King, Angela Bassett, Suzzanne Douglas

Angela Bassett, Taye Diggs

SLUMS OF BEVERLY HILLS

(FOX SEARCHLIGHT) Producers, Michael Nozik, Stan Wlodkowski; Executive Producer, Robert Redford; Director/Screenplay, Tamara Jenkins; Photography, Tom Richmond; Designer, Dena Roth; Costumes, Kirsten Everberg; Music, Rolfe Kent; Editor, Pamela Martin; Casting, Sheila Jaffe, Georgianne Walken; a South Fork Pictures production; Dolby; Color; Rated R; 91 minutes; August release

CAST

Vivian Abramowitz	Natasha Lyonne
Murray Abramowitz	Alan Arkin
Rita	Marisa Tomei
Eliot	Kevin Corrigan
Doris	Jessica Walter
Belle Abramowitz	Rita Moreno
Ben Abramowitz	David Krumholtz
Rickey Abramowitz	Eli Marienthal
Mickey Abramowitz	Carl Reiner
Saleslady	Bryna Weiss
Landlady	Charlotte Stewart
Cop in Station	Brendan Burns
Charlie the Cook	Harris Laskawy
Rachel	Mena Süväri
Brooke	Marley McClean
Mrs. Hoffman	Mary Portser
Man at Brymans	Jock McDonald
EMS Guys	Rich Willis, Rock Reiser
Cop #1	Jack Tracy
Dr. Grossman	Jay Patterson
Nurse Curtrell	Natalie Karp
Waitress	Sally Schaub

Looking back on 1976, Vivian Abramowitz recounts her life with her father and siblings as they move from one low-rent housing unit to the next, always within the city limits of Beverly Hills.

©Twentieth Century Fox

Marisa Tomei, Eli Marienthal, Alan Arkin, Natasha Lyonne, David Krumholtz

Alan Arkin, Natasha Lyonne, Jessica Walter

Eli Marienthal, Natasha Lyonne, Marisa Tomei

Marisa Tomei

THE AVENGERS

(WARNER BROS.) Producer, Jerry Weintraub; Director, Jeremiah Chechik; Screenplay, Don MacPherson; Executive Producer, Susan Ekins; Photography, Roger Pratt; Designer, Stuart Craig; Editor, Mick Audsley; Music, Joel McNeely; *The Avengers* Theme Composer, Laurie Johnson; Visual Effects Supervisor, Nick Davis; Costumes, Anthony Powell; Casting, Susie Figgis; a Jerry Weintraub production; Dolby; Technicolor; Rated PG-13; 89 minutes; August release

CAST

John Steed	Ralph Fiennes
Dr. Emma Peel	Uma Thurman
Sir August De Wynter	Sean Connery
Voice of Invisible Jones	Patrick Macnee
Mother	Jim Broadbent
Father	Fiona Shaw
Bailey	Eddie Izzard
Alice	Eileen Atkins
Trubshaw	John Wood
Brenda	Carmen Ejogo
Tamara	Keeley Hawes
Donavan	Shaun Ryder
Dr. Darling	Nicholas Woodeson
Butler	Michael Godley
Boodle's Porter	Richard Lumsden
Messenger	Daniel Crowder
World Council of Ministers	Nadim Sawalha, Christopher Godwin, David Webber

John Steed and Emma Peel are summoned by Britain's top-secret agency, The Ministry, to put a stop to the crazed Sir August De Winter's plan to control the weather. Based on the television series that ran in America from 1966 to 1969 on ABC and starred Patrick Macnee as Steed and Diana Rigg as Peel. Macnee's voice is heard in this film.

Ralph Fiennes, Uma Thurman

Uma Thurman, Sean Connery

UNMADE BEDS

(CHELSEA PICTURES) Producer, Steve Wax; Director/Screenplay, Nicholas Barker; Photography, William Rexer II; Editor, Paul Binns; Associate Producer, Sam Bickley; a co-production of BBC-Cinemax, Baltic Media and La Sept/Arte; U.S.-British; Color; Not rated; 105 minutes; August release. A look at the lives of four New York singles, playing themselves, with Brenda Monte, Michael DeStefano, Aimee Copp, Mikey Russo.

Aimee Copp

Ben Stiller, Aaron Eckhart, Jason Patric

Jason Patric, Nastassja Kinski

Amy Brenneman, Ben Stiller

YOUR FRIENDS & NEIGHBORS

(GRAMERCY) Producers, Steve Golin, Jason Patric; Executive Producers, Alix Madigan-Yorkin, Stephen Pevner; Co-Producer, Philip Steuer; Director/Screenplay, Neil LaBute; Photography, Nancy Schreiber; Designer, Charles Breen; Editor, Joel Plotch; Costumes, April Napier; Casting, Mali Finn; a PolyGram Filmed Entertainment presentation of a Propaganda Films/Fleece production; Dolby; Super 35 Widescreen; Deluxe color; Rated R; 99 minutes; August release

CAST

Mary...Amy Brenneman
Barry..Aaron Eckhart
Terri...Catherine Keener
Cheri...Nastassja Kinski
Cary...Jason Patric
Jerry..Ben Stiller

A look at the unhappy and bitter desires and sexual couplings of six thirtysomething men and women.

©Gramercy Pictures

Aaron Eckhart, Jason Patric, Ben Stiller

Nastassja Kinski, Catherine Keener

Hope Davis

Alan Gelfant, Cara Buono

NEXT STOP WONDERLAND

(MIRAMAX) Producer, Mitchell B. Robbins; Director/Editor, Brad Anderson; Screenplay, Brad Anderson, Lyn Vaus; Executive Producer, Mark Gill; Co-Producers, Laura Bernieri, Rachael Horovitz; Photography, Uta Briesewitz; Designer, Chad Detwiller; Music, Claudio Ragazzi; Casting, Sheila Jaffe, Georgianne Walken, Maura Tighe, Nancy Doyle; a Robbins Entertainment production; Dolby; Color; Rated R; 104 minutes; August release

CAST

Erin Castleton	Hope Davis
Alan Monteiro	Alan Gelfant
Frank	Victor Argo
Eric	Jon Benjamin
Julie	Cara Buono
Brett	Larry Gilliard, Jr.
Sean	Phil (Philip Seymour) Hoffman
Rory	Jason Lewis
Ray Thornback	Roger Rees
Kevin Monteiro	Sam Seder
Robert	Robert Stanton
Piper Castleton	Holland Taylor
Cricket	Callie Thorne
Lowrey the Bartender	Jimmy Tingle
Daryl	Lyn Vaus
Andre DeSilva	Jose Zuniga
Arty Lesser	Robert Klein

and Katherine Kerr (Candice), Paul Wagner (Bob), Ernest Thompson (Mathan), Charlie Broderick (Desmond), Bronwyn Sims (Traci), Paula Plum (Denise Shebola), Ken Cheeseman (Rick), Wayne Pretlow (Oliver), Pamela Hart (Berit), Diane Beckett (Seana), Neil Gustafson (Yuri Spinov), Luz Alexandra (Thalia), Kemp Harris (Ben), Dave Gilloran (Aquarium Volunteer), Emme Shaw (Bailey), Greg Watson (Frank's Crony), Robert Larkin (Arty Lesser's Crony), Elizabeth Lindsay (Lucy Bidwell), Jack Sweet (Sal), Jeremy Geidt (Bookseller), Paula Lyons (TV News Anchor), Arnie Reisman (Field Reporter), Renita Whited (Arizona Reporter), Alan Horwitz (Aquarium Guest), Todd Robinson (Society Photographer), Walter Krause (Pilot), Aleksander Wierzbicki (Barry), Andrea Grano (Pub Waitress), Lori Haims (Restaurant Waitress), Elizabeth Lindsay (Drunk Woman), Frank T. Wells (Alan's Father), Steve Sweeney (Cab Driver), James O'Connell (Linoleum Man), Melinda Lopez (Flight Attendant), Sandi Carroll (Woman on Plane); Phone Suitors: Ed Regine (Winston Bramen), Eric Roemele (Will Lebow), Daniel Ferrante (Tom Cotter), Eric Ruben (Charles Laquidara), Scott Richards (Ken Mason), Bob Druwing (Al Ducharme)

Philip Seymour Hoffman

Alan Gelfant, Hope Davis

A look at the lives of two lonely Bostonians, Erin and Alan, whose paths cross but never seem to meet as they search for fulfillment in the modern dating world.

DANCE WITH ME

(COLUMBIA) Producers, Lauren C. Weissman, Shinya Egawa, Randa Haines; Executive Producer, Ted Zachary; Director, Randa Haines; Screenplay, Daryl Matthews; Photography, Fred Murphy; Designer, Waldemar Kalinowski; Editor, Lisa Fruchtman; Costumes, Joe I. Tompkins; Choreographers, Daryl Matthews, Liz Curtis; Associate Producers, Aldric La'Auli Porter, Allan Wertheim; Music, Michael Convertino; Executive Music Producers, Joel Sill, Budd Carr; Casting, Lora Kennedy; a Mandalay Entertainment presentation of a Weissman/Egawa production; Dolby; CFI color; Rated PG; 126 minutes; August release

William Marquez, Joan Plowright

CAST

Ruby	Vanessa L. Williams
Rafael Infante	Chayanne
John Burnett	Kris Kristofferson
Bea	Joan Plowright
Patricia	Jane Krakowski
Jewel Lovejoy	Beth Grant
Michael Michaels	Harry Groener
Stefano	William Marquez
Steve	Scott Paetty
Julian	Rick Valenzuela
Peter	Chaz Oswill
Kim	Liz Curtis
Don Harrington	Bill Applebaum
Cuban Mailman	Angelo Pagan
Fernando	Victor Marcel
Fernando's Daughter	Ana Sofia Pomales
Fiance	Nelson Marquez

and Mike Gomez (Bartender), Charles Venturi (Waiter), Maurice Schwartzman (Man in Dance Club), Janette Valenzuela (Woman in Dance Club), Jim Mapp (Fisherman on Pier), Robert Pike Daniel (Emcee); Tony Meredith, Melanie LaPatin, Jean Marc Genereux, France Mousseau, James Kunitz, Janna Kunitz, Giacomo Steccaglia, Melissa Dexter, Eric Thomas Robinson, Maria Torres O'Connor (Professional Latin Finalists), Thomas A. Slater, Carol Bentley (Theater Arts Dancers), Jose Mesa Benjamin, Harry Bowens, Juan Carlois Cienfuegos, Leila Flores, Alicia Gomez, Raul Gomez, Monica Gonalez, Rudy Gonzalez, Ana Hernandez, Joel Hernandez, Erika Landin, Alyra Lennox, Rojelio Moreno, Anne Noelle, Piper Orr, Jacqueline Rios, Chantal Sagouspe, Marissa Soratorio, Albert Torres, Francisco Vazquez, Joby Vazquez, Luis Vazques, Roberto Villacorta (Salsa Club Dancers).

Rafael Infante arrives in Houston and lands a job at the Excelsior dance studio where he falls in love with dance instructor Ruby and helps bring new life to the fading business.

©Mandalay Entertainment

Vanessa L. Williams, Chayanne

Chayanne, Vanessa L. Williams

Jane Krakowski, Kris Kristofferson

BLADE

(NEW LINE CINEMA) Producers, Peter Frankfurt, Wesley Snipes, Robert Engelman; Executive Producers, Lynn Harris, Stan Lee, Avi Arad, Joseph Calamari; Director, Stephen Norrington; Screenplay, David S. Goyer; Based on the Blade and Deacon Frost Characters Created for Marvel Comics by Marv Wolfman and Gene Colan; Photography, Theo Van De Sande; Designer, Kirk M. Petruccelli; Editor, Paul Rubell; Costumes, Sanja Milkovic Hays; Music, Mark Isham; Co-Producers, Andrew J. Horne, Jon Divens; Make-Up Effects, Greg Cannom; Martial Arts Choreography, Jeff Ward, Wesley Snipes; Casting, Rachel Abroms, Jory Weitz; Stunts, Jeff Ward; an Amen Ra Films production in association with Peter Frankfurt; Dolby; Clairmont-Scope; Deluxe color; Rated R; 121 minutes; August release

Wesley Snipes, Stephen Dorff

CAST

Blade	Wesley Snipes
Deacon Frost	Stephen Dorff
Whistler	Kris Kristofferson
Karen	N'bushe Wright
Quinn	Donal Logue
Dragonetti	Udo Kier
Mercury	Arly Jover
Racquel	Tracy Lords
Krieger	Kevin Patrick Wells
Curtis Webb	Tim Guinee
Vanessa	Sanaa Lathan
Pearl	Eric Edwards
Nurse	Donna Wong
Senior Resident	Carmen Thomas
Resident	Shannon Lee
Heatseeking Dennis	Kenneth Johnson
Creepy Morgue Guy	Clint Curtis
Pallantine	Judson Scott
Japanese Doorman	Sidney Liufau
Kam	Keith Leon Williams

and Andray Johnson, Stephen R. Peluso (Paramedics), Marcus Aurelius (Pragmatic Policeman), John Enos III (Blood Club Bouncer), Eboni Adams (Martial Arts Kid), Lyle Conway (Reichardt), Freeman White III (Menacing Stud), DV DeVincentis (Vampire Underling), Marcus Salgado, Esau McKnight Jr. (Frost's Goons), ERL (Von Esper), Matt Schulze (Crease), Lennox Brown (Pleading Goon), Yvette Ocampo (Party Girl), Irenea Stepic (Slavic Vampire Lord), Jenya Lano (Russian Woman), Levani (Russian Vampire)

Vampire hunter Blade, who possesses the superhuman strength of his enemies, takes on his adversary, Deacon Frost, the vampire overlord who is intent on leading his minions to conquer mankind.

©New Line Cinema

Kris Kristofferson

Arly Jover, N'bushe Wright

Wesley Snipes

113

Lela Rochon, Halle Berry, Larenz Tate, Vivica A. Fox

WHY DO FOOLS FALL IN LOVE

(WARNER BROS.) Producers, Paul Hall, Stephen Nemeth; Executive Producers, Gregory Nava, Mark Allan, Harold Bronson; Director, Gregory Nava; Screenplay, Tina Andrews; Photography, Ed Lachman; Designer, Cary White; Editor, Nancy Richardson; Costumes, Elisabetta Beraldo; Music, Stephen James Taylor; Casting, Reuben Cannon; Title song written by Frankie Lymon and Morris Levy; a Rhino Films production; Dolby; Technicolor; Rated R; 115 minutes; August release

CAST

Zola Taylor	Halle Berry
Elizabeth Waters	Vivica A. Fox
Emira Eagle	Lela Rochon
Frankie Lymon	Larenz Tate
Morris Levy	Paul Mazursky
Himself	Little Richard
Herman Santiago	Alexis Cruz
Sherman	J. August Richards
Joe	Jon Huertas
Jimmy	Norris Young
Peter Markowitz	David Barry Gray
Ezra Grahme	Lane Smith
Lawrence Roberts	Clifton Powell
Judge Lambrey	Pamela Reed
Richard Barrett	Ben Vereen
Young Little Richard	Miguel A. Nunez, Jr.
Redd Foxx	Aries Spears
Paula King	Paula Jai Parker
Eddie Williams	Craig Kirkwood
Linda	Lucille M. Oliver
Jimmy Mac	Alex Thomas, Jr.

and Mary-Pat Green, Carlease Burke, Erik Dahlberg (Guards), Ray Laska (Bailiff), Renee Raudman (Waitress), Marcello Thedford ("Coop"), Frankie Jay Allison (Undercover Cop), Raymond O'Keefe (Desk Sgt.), Cerita Monet Bickelmann (Laura), Loretta Fox (Pam), Darrell Eisman, Sam Mountain, Ric Borelli, Douglas Seagraves (Control Room Workers), Mark Paulk, Martin Paulk, Ron Jaxson, Gary L. Neal (Platters), Yorgo Constantine (Announcer), Indira Tyler, Miya McGhee, Erica Cobbin Kenadie, Nanci Fletcher (Girl Group Singers), Shirley Caesar (Herself), James Gleason (Stage Manager), Brandon D. Morgan (Young Singer in Church Choir), Charles Walker (Driver), Kevin Fry (MP), Ray Proscia (Security Man), Keith Amos (Man in Hot Tub), J.W. Smith (Postman), Shashawnee Hall (Preacher), Shari Albert (Morris' Secretary), John West (Singer)

Three different women come forward claiming to be legitimate widow of singer-songwriter Frankie Lymon.

Larenz Tate

Vivica A. Fox, Halle Berry, Larenz Tate

Clifton Powell, Pamela Reed, Little Richard

(MIRAMAX) Producers, Richard N. Gladstein, Dolly Hall, Ira Deutchman; Executive Producers, Bob Weinstein, Harvey Weinstein, Bobby Cohen, Don Carmody; Director/Screenplay, Mark Christopher; Photography, Alexander Gruszynski; Designer, Kevin Thompson; Editor, Lee Percy; Costumes, Ellen Lutter; Music, Marco Beltrami; Music Supervisors, Susan Jacobs, Coati Mundi Hernandez; Associate Producer, Jonathan King; Casting, Billy Hopkins, Suzanne Smith, Kenny Barden; a Redeemable Features/Dollface/Filmcolony production; Dolby; Color; Rated R; 92 minutes; August release

Ryan Phillippe

CAST

Shane O'Shea ....Ryan Phillippe
Anita...Salma Hayek
Julie Black..Neve Campbell
Steve Rubell..Mike Myers
Billie Auster ....Sela Ward
Greg Randazzo ....Breckin Meyer
Viv ....Sherry Stringfield
Disco Dottie ....Ellen Albertini Dow
Atlanta ....Cameron Mathison
Romeo...Noam Jenkins
Buck..Jay Goede
Tarzan ....Patrick Taylor
Grace O'Shea ....Heather Matarazzo
Harlan O'Shea ....Skipp Sudduth
Kelly O'Shea...Aemilia Robinson
and Daniel Lapaine (Marc the Doorman), Erika Alexander (Ciel), Thelma Houston (Herself), Mary Griffin (Disco Star), Don Carrier (Julian), Domenick Lombardozzi (Kev), Mark Ruffalo (Ricko), Bruno Miguel (Boyd), Jason Andrews (Anthony), Laura Catalano (Rochelle), Kohl Sudduth (Rhett), Lorri Bagley (Patti), Lauren Hutton (Liz Vangelder), James Brinkley (Rubell's Bodyguard), Arthur Nascarella, John Himes (IRS Agents), Louis Negin (Truman Capote), Lena Vajakas (Conrows), Barbara Radecki (TV Host), Ron Jeremy (Ron), Sean Sullivan (Andy Warhol), Vieslav Krystyan (Photographer), Nick Holt (Alpine Inn Waitress), David Blacker (Bouncer), Bruce MacVittie (Music Producer), Emmanuel Mark (Talent Manager), Kabriel Lilly (Little Girl), Michael York (Ambassador), Morgan Freeman (Angelic Boy), Lina Felice (Nicaraguan Woman), Elio Fiorucci (Himself), Drake Alonso Thorens (Man on Horseback), Justin Tensun (Blond Busboy), Jason Fruitman (Bus Boy #1), Andy Grote (54 Waiter), Jordan Paige (Young Shane), Georgina Kess (Shane's Mom), Mario Bosco (Mario), Coati Mundi Hernandez, Victor Sutherland (DJs), Janine Longley, Michael Henderson, Chris Ingram (Kissing Trio), Cindy Crawford, Sheryl Crow, Donald Trump, Georgina Grenville, Cecilia Thomson, Ling, Frederique Van Der Wal, Heidi Klum, Victor Brown, Veronica Webb, Michel Van Der Wal, Sophie Rousseau (VIP Patrons), Art Garfunkel, Peter Bogdanovich, Lorna Luft, Valerie Perrine, Beverly Johnson, John Johnson, Bruce Jay Friedman, Andrea Bocaletti (Elaine's Patrons), Ultra Nate, Amber, Jocelyn Enriquez (Stars on 54)

Ryan Phillippe, Neve Campbell

Naive 19-year-old Shane O'Shea enters the world of the legendary disco Studio 54 where he lands a job as a bartender and becomes emeshed in a nightlife world of drugs, music and sex.

©Miramax Films

Mike Myers

Salma Hayek, Breckin Meyer

KNOCK OFF

(TRISTAR) Producer, Nansun Shi; Director, Tsui Hark; Screenplay, Steven E. DeSouza; Photography, Arthur Wong; Designers, James Leung, Bill Lui; Editor, Mak Chi Sin; Music, Ron Mael, Russell Mael; Associate Producers, Peter Nelson; Richard G. Murphy; Co-Producer, Raymond Fung; Casting, Illana Diamant, Lauris Freeman; a Knock Films, A.V.V. and MDP Worldwide presentation of a Film Workshop Company Ltd./Val D'Oro Entertainment production; U.S.-Hong Kong; Dolby; Super 35 Widescreen; Color; Rated R; 91 minutes; September release

CAST

Marcus Ray	Jean-Claude Van Damme
Tommy Hendricks	Rob Schneider
Karen Leigh	Lela Rochon
Harry Johansson	Paul Sorvino
Ling Ho	Carmen Lee
Eddie	Wyman Wong
Skinny	Glen Chin
Han	Michael Fitzgerald Wong
Office Fong	Moses Chan
Karl	Raymond Leslie Nicholas
Skaar	Jeff Joseph Wolfe

and Michael Miller (Tickler), Steve Brettingham (Hawkeye), Mark Haughton (Bear), Peter Nelson (Biff), Kim Maree Penn (Chip), Thomas Hudak (Kyle), Steve Nation (Kip), Rosa Librizzi (Buddha CIA), Noel Rands (Racemaster), Dennis Chan (Choy/Eddie Kid), William Chow (Papa Wang), Stuart Kavanagh (Col. Carrington), Noorie Razack (Fruit Market Old Man), Heung Hoi (Fruit Market Accountant), Cheung Simon (Supermarket Kid), Leslie Cheung (Young Worker—Skinny Freight), Matt Grant (Tarzan), Nyree Hansen (Jane), Kent Osborne (Pachy), Lynne Francis (V-Six Secretary), Cordelia Choy (Mel), Leon C. Somera, Jr. (Eddie's Ringer), Mathew Tang, Wong Yui Sang, Chan Man Cheong, Leung Yiu Hay, Roks Chik, Tse Wai Yin, Irene Luk (Han's Assistants), Kerrie Jordan, Bethany Wetjen, Dominique, Eniko Mayer, Anika Yuen, Anu Kattoor, Hanna Josesina Chaplain, Karin Holm, Amena Lee Schlaikjer, Helen Praetorius, Leta Chung, Belinka Polakova, Sinna Ping, Simone Lee, Irena Budayova, Marilka Aling (V-Six Models/Cheerleaders), Nina Mackenize, Trudy Jane Mansfield, Maria Butler (V-Six Office Girls), Denis Couprie, William Chan, Duane Davis (Skinny Bodyguards), Brad Warren, Tony Trimble, John Whitney, Max G., Michael Lambert, David Fiddes, Jason Todd Hancock, David Saunders, Ian Bruton, Phillip Duffy, Stuart Lee Markham, Jude Poyer, Jake Sear Jacob, Peter Kramer (Russian Mafia), Pascale Harris, Robert Baynton Eke, Alex Mazija (CIA Staff), Martyn A. Minns, Ian Clarke, Cesar Liesa, Kevin Butler, Melanie Page, Phil John Greatches, Ted Johan Michaels, Albert Dedem (Rickshaw Racers), Garry Beckhurst, Steve Syson, Ian Tang, David Rolls, Leon C. Somera Jr., Paolo Mario Moscardini, Barry Wensueen, Aaron Richardson, Au Man Leong, Yiu Shiu Chung (Rickshaw Passengers)

On the eve of Hong Kong's transition to Chinese Rule, V-Six jeans company rep Marcus Ray gets wind of a conspiracy by the Russian Mafia to bring a form of microbomb into the terrorist black market.

Jean-Claude Van Damme, Rob Schneider

©TriStar Pictures

Denis Leary, Famke Janssen

Martin Sheen, Ian Hart

©Lions Gate Films

MONUMENT AVE.

(LIONS GATE) formerly *Snitch*; Producer, Jim Serpico; Executive Producers, Joel Stillerman, Ted Demme; Director, Ted Demme; Screenplay, Mike Armstrong; Photography, Adam Kimmel; Designer, Ruth Ammon; Editor, Jeffrey Wolf; a Filmline International Films, Clinica Estetico and Tribeca Independent Films presentation of a Spanky Pictures/Apollo Production; Dolby; Color; Not rated; 93 minutes; September release

CAST

Seamus	Jason Barry
Teddy	Billy Crudup
Digger	John Diehl
Shang	Greg Dulli
Red	Noah Emmerch
Mouse	Ian Hart
Katy	Famke Janssen
Bobby O'Grady	Denis Leary
Jackie O'Hara	Colm Meaney
Hanlon	Martin Sheen
Annie	Jeanne Tripplehorn
Skunk	Lenny Clarke

and Kevin Chapman (Mickey Pat), George MacDonald (Gallivan), Lyndon Byers (Fitzie), Herbie Ade (Herbie), Melissa Fitzgerald (Sheila), Don Gavin (Brosnihan), Brian Goodman (Gavin), Victor Chan (Lee), Marilyn Murphy Meardon (Mrs. O'Grady), Bill McDonald (Father Donahue), Gene Boles (John Kelsey), Sandra Shippley (Mrs.Timmons), Karen White (Marcy), Francois Joseph (Kid), Sue McGinnis (Mrs. Turbody), Jackie Sullivan (Bar Owner)

In the Boston neighborhood of Charlestown, Bobby O'Grady and his fellow thieves agree not to identify the murderer of one of their members so not to incur the wrath of their mobster boss responsible for the killing.

SIMON BIRCH

(HOLLYWOOD PICTURES) Producers, Laurence Mark, Roger Birnbaum; Executive Producer, John Baldecchi; Director/Screenplay, Mark Steven Johnson; Suggested by the novel *A Prayer for Owen Meany* by John Irving; Co-Producer, Billy Higgins; Photography, Aaron E. Schneider; Designer, David Chapman; Editor, David Finfer; Costumes, Betsy Heimann, Abram Waterhouse; Music, Marc Shaiman; Casting, Mary Gail Artz, Barbara Cohen; a Roger Birnbaum and Laurence Mark production; Presented in association with Caravan Pictures; Distributed by Buena Vista; Dolby; Technicolor; Rated PG; 113 minutes; September release

Joseph Mazzello, Ian Michael Smith

CAST

Simon Birch	Ian Michael Smith
Joe Wenteworth	Joseph Mazzello
Rebecca Wenteworth	Ashley Judd
Ben Goodrich	Oliver Platt
Reverend Russell	David Strathairn
Grandmother Wenteworth	Dana Ivey
Hildie Grove	Beatrice Winde
Miss Leavey	Jan Hooks
Marjorie	Ceciley Carroll
Ann	Sumela-Rose Keramidopulos
Stuart	Sam Morton
Adult Joe Wenteworth	Jim Carrey
Simon Wenteworth	John Mazzello
Mrs. Birch	Holly Dennison
Mr. Birch	Peter MacNeil
Doctor Wells	Addison Bell
Coach Higgins	Roger McKeen
Chief Al Cork	Sean McCann
Mr. Baker	John Robinson
Janitor	Guy Sanvido
Eddie	Gil Filar
Howard Ellis	Marcello Meleca

and Tim Hall (Pitcher), Tom Redman (First Baseman), Mark Skrela (Third Baseman), Kevin White (Shortstop), Terry V. Hart, Alan Markfield (Umpires), Christopher Marren (Rival Baseball Coach), Tommy Dorrian, Justin Marangoni (Teammates), Tyler Cairns (Sheep), Gino Giacomini (Wise Man), Barbara Stewart (Delivery Room Nurse), David Rigby (Bus Driver), Sam Aaron, David Chapman (Old Men), Wendy Fleming (Mrs. Russell), Paul De Fibo, Dalton Rondell, Cameron Croughwell, Logan Holladay, Scott Leavenworth, Devon Alan, Joshua Titen, Tony Orr, Joshua Croughwell, Jeffrey Schoeny, Derek Montgomery, Sean Sullivan, Devon Borisoff, Taylor Emerson, Brian McLaughlin, Nicholas Andrew, Sean Flynn Amir, Patrick McTavish, Blake Hubbell, Cody Gill, Ramiro Gonzalez III, Mitchell Orr, Trevor Habberstad (Junior Lambs)

Joe Wenteworth looks back on the special friendship he had with an odd, undersized boy named Simon Birch who believed that his deformity and small stature meant he was destined to be a hero.

©Hollywood Pictures Company, Inc.

Ian Michael Smith, Ashley Judd

Joseph Mazzello, David Strathairn

Ian Michael Smith, Oliver Platt, Ashley Judd

Billy Crudup

Billy Crudup, Monica Potter

WITHOUT LIMITS

(WARNER BROS.) Producers, Tom Cruise, Paula Wagner; Executive Producers, Jonathan Sanger, Kenny Moore; Director, Robert Towne; Screenplay, Robert Towne, Kenny Moore; Photography, Conrad L. Hall; Designer, William Creber; Editors, Claire Simpson, Robert K. Lambert; Costumes, Grania Preston; Music, Randy Miller; Casting, Rick Pagano; a Cruise/Wagner production; Dolby; Super 35 Widescreen; Technicolor; Rated PG-13; 117 minutes; September release

CAST

Steve Prefontaine	Billy Crudup
Bill Bowerman	Donald Sutherland
Mary Marckx	Monica Potter
Frank Shorter	Jeremy Sisto
Kenny Moore	Billy Burke
Roscoe Devine	Matthew Lillard
Bill Dellinger	Dean Norris
Don Kardong	Gabriel Olds
Barbara Bowerman	Judith Ivey
Bob Peters	William Mapother
Mac Wilkins	Adam Setliff
Russ Francis	Nicholas Oleson
Iowa's Finest	Amy Jo Johnson
Elfriede Prefontaine	Lisa Banes
Fred Long	Frank Shorter
Himself	Charlie Jones
TV Director	William Friedkin
BBC Commentator	David Coleman
Pre at age 6	Jamie Schwering
George Young	Garth Granholm
Molly Cox	Karen Elliott

and Greg Foote (Walt McClure), Ryan S. Warren (Finnish Official), Ken Merckx (Eugene Register Reporter), Katharine Towne, Cassandra A. Coogan, Amy Erenberger (Coeds), Edwin L. Coleman II (Turn Judge), Jay Thorson (Pole Vaulter), John Roemer (German Guard), Wendy Ray (Hayward Field Announcer), Wade Bell (Starter), Coleman Dow (Bully), Kim Nickel (Flight Attendant), Jeffrey Atkinson (Steve Bence), James Howarth (Arne Kvalhiem), Avi Haas (Technical Director), Dawn Aotani, Jim Sevin (Control Room Assistants), Pat Porter (Lasse Viren), Steve Ave (Mohammed Gammoudi), Jonathan Pritchard (Dave Bedford), Tom Ansberry (Emiel Puttemans), Sol Alexis Sallos (Harold Norpoth), Thomas DeBacker (Juha Vaatinen), Ashley Johnson (Ian Stewart), Brad Hudson (Javier Alvarez), Todd D. Lewis (Frank Eisenberg), Tove Christensen (Per Halle), Chris Caldwell (Nikolay Sviridov), Paul Vincent (Ian McCafferty)

The true story of Olympic runner Steve Prefontaine whose career was tragically cut short by a car accident when he was only twenty-four. Previous film on the subject was Pre (Buena Vista, 1997) starring Jared Leto as Prefontaine.

©Warner Bros.

Donald Sutherland

Billy Crudup

ROUNDERS

(MIRAMAX) Producers, Joel Stillerman, Ted Demme; Executive Producers, Kerry Orent, Bob Weinstein, Harvey Weinstein, Bobby Cohen; Director, John Dahl; Screenplay, David Levien, Brian Koppelman; Associate Producers, Christopher Goode, Tracy Falco; Photography, Jean Yves Escoffier; Designer, Rob Pearson; Editor, Scott Chestnut; Costumes, Terry Dresbach; Music, Christopher Young; Casting, Avy Kaufman; a Spanky Pictures production; Dolby; Super 35 Widescreen; Deluxe color; Rated R; 120 minutes; September release

Edward Norton, Matt Damon, John Turturro

CAST

Mike McDermott	Matt Damon
Lester "Worm" Murphy	Edward Norton
Jo	Gretchen Mol
Teddy KGB	John Malkovich
Joey Knish	John Turturro
Professor Petrovsky	Martin Landau
Petra	Famke Janssen
Grama	Michael Rispoli
Russian Thugs	Paul Cicero, Jay Boryea
Kenny	Ray Iannicelli
Sy	Merwin Goldsmith
Tony	Sonny Zito
Zagosh	Josh Mostel
Irving	Mal Z. Lawrence
Savino	Lenny Clarke
Henry Lin	Peter Yoshida
Moogie	Lenny Venito
Professor Eisen	Richard Mawe
D.A. Shields	Michael Lombard
Judge Marinacci	Tom Aldredge
Judge Kaplan	Beeson Carroll
Professor Green	Matthew Yavne
Roy	Erik LaRay Harvey
Dowling	Dominic Marcus
Derald	Brian Anthony Wilson

and George Kmeck (Prison Guard), Joe Parisi (Property Guard), Melina Kanakaredes (Barbara), Kohl Sudduth (Wagner), Charlie Matthes (Birch), Hank Jacobs (Steiny), Chris Messina (Higgins), Michael Ryan Segal (Griggs), Kerry O'Malley (Kelly), Slava Schoot (Roman), Goran Visnjic (Maurice), Michele Zanes (Tai Dealer), Allan Havey (Guberman), Joe Vega (Freddy Face), Neal Hemphill (Claude), Vernon E. Jordan, Jr. (Judge McKinnon), Jon C. Chan (Johnny Chan), Lisa Gorlitsky (Sherry), John DiBenedetto (LaRossa), Nicole Brier (Sunshine), Bill Camp (Eisenberg), Tony Hoty (Taki), Mario Mendoza (Zizzo), Joe Zaloom (Cronos), Sal Richards (Johnny Gold), Josh Pais (Weitz), John Gallagher (Bartender), Adam LeFevre (Sean Frye), P.J. Brown (Vitter), David Zayas (Osborne), Michael Arkin (Bear), Murphy Guyer (Detweiler), Alan Davidson (Cabbie)

Matt Damon, Gretchen Mol

Mike McDermott, trying to carve out a legit life by attending law school, finds himself drawn back into the shady world of high stakes poker playing by his wastrel friend Worm.

©Miramax Films

Richard Mawe, Matt Damon, Martin Landau

John Malkovich

DIGGING TO CHINA

(MOONSTONE ENTERTAINMENT) Producers, Marilyn Vance, Alan Mruvka, John Davis, J. Todd Harris; Executive Producers, Etchie Stroh, David T. Friendly, Stephen Nemeth; Director, Timothy Hutton; Screenplay, Karen Janszen; Photography, Jörgen Persson; Editors, Dana Congdon, Alain Jakubowicz; Costumes, Mary Zophres; Music, Cynthia Millar; Presented in association with Davis Entertainment Classics & the Ministry of Film; Dolby; Color; Rated PG; 98 minutes; September release

CAST

Harriet Frankovitz	Evan Rachel Wood
Ricky	Kevin Bacon
Gwen	Mary Stuart Masterson
Leah	Marian Seldes
Mrs. Frankovitz	Cathy Moriarty
Sonia	Amanda Minikus
Miss Mosher	Nicole Burdette
Eric	Robert Putney
Young Harriet	Annie Jaynes

and Joanne Pankow (Nurse), Gareth Williams, Alan Mruvka (Tow Truck Drivers), J.C. Quinn (Minister), Keith Harris (Flirting Man), Nicole Namer (Girl in Classroom)

Young Harriet Frankovitz, who dreams of escaping her drab life at her family-run roadside motel, befriends a 30-year-old mentally retarded man who is staying at the facilities with his mother.

©Moonstone Entertainment

Kevin Bacon, Evan Rachel Wood

Mary Stuart Masterson, Evan Rachel Wood

Cathy Moriarty

Lana Tisdel, Brandon Teena

THE BRANDON TEENA STORY

(ZEITGEIST) Producers/Directors/Photography/Editors, Susan Muska, Gréta Olafsdóttir; Executive Producer, Jane Dekrone; Music, Lorrie Morgan, Dinah Washington, April Stevens, The Brown Brothers; Color; Not rated; 89 minutes; September release. Documentary on Brandon Teena who was brutally raped and murdered by two of his friends after they discovered "he" was a girl posing as a boy.

©Zeitgeist Films

A SOLDIER'S DAUGHTER NEVER CRIES

(OCTOBER) Producer, Ismail Merchant; Director, James Ivory; Screenplay, James Ivory, Ruth Prawer Jhabvala; Based on the novel by Kaylie Jones; Photography, Jean-Marc Fabre; Designers, Jacques Bufnoir, Pat Garner; Costumes, Carol Ramsey; Music, Richard Robbins; Editor, Noelle Boisson; Executive Producers, Richard Hawley, Nayeem Hafizka; Co-Producer, Paul Bradley; Casting, Annette Trumel, Tricia Tomey, Celestia Fox; a Merchant Ivory Productions presentation in association with Capitol Films, British Screen; Dolby; Color; Rated R; 127 minutes; September release

Kris Kristofferson, Barbara Hershey

CAST

Bill Willis	Kris Kristofferson
Marcella Willis	Barbara Hershey
Channe Willis	Leelee Sobieski
Mrs. Fortescue	Jane Birkin
Candida	Dominique Blanc
Billy Willis	Jesse Bradford
Billy's Mother	Virginie Ledoyen
Francis Fortescue	Anthony Roth Costanzo
Keith Carter	Harley Cross
Mamadou	Isaac de Bankolé
Madame Beauvier	Macha Méril
Mademoiselle Fournier	Nathalie Richard
Bob Smith	Bob Swaim
Young Channe	Luisa Conlon
Benoît/Young Billy	Samuel Gruen
Stéphane	Frédéric Da
Billy's Father	Antoine Chain
Miss O'Shaunessy	Michelle Fairley
Mademoiselle Devereux	Sarah Haxaire
Social Worker	Marie Henriau
Mr. Flowers	Pierre-Michel Sivadier
The Jock	Scott Thomas

The Willis family finds the social world they have created while spending years in France destroyed when their father, successful writer Bill Willis, announces that they will be returning to America.

©October Films

Barbara Hershey, Jesse Bradford

Jesse Bradford, Leelee Sobieski, Barbara Hershey

Anthony Roth Costanzo

Renée Zellweger, Meryl Streep

ONE TRUE THING

(UNIVERSAL) Producers, Jesse Beaton, Harry Ufland; Executive Producers, William W. Wilson III, Leslie Morgan; Director, Carl Franklin; Screenplay, Karen Croner; Based on the novel by Anna Quindlen; Photography, Declan Quinn; Designer, Paul Peters; Editor, Carole Kravetz; Costumes, Donna Zakowska; Music, Cliff Eidelman; Song: "My One True Friend" by Carole King, Carole Bayer Sager and David Foster/performed by Bette Midler; Casting, Rick Pagano; a Monarch Pictures/Ufland Production; Dolby; Deluxe color; Rated R; 127 minutes; September release

CAST

Kate Gulden	Meryl Streep
Ellen Gulden	Renée Zellweger
George Gulden	William Hurt
Brian Gulden	Tom Everett Scott
Jules	Lauren Graham
Jordan Belzer	Nicky Katt
District Attorney	James Eckhouse
Mr. Tweedy	Patrick Breen
Oliver Most	Gerrit Graham
Senator Sullivan	David Byron
Harold	Stephen Peabody
Dr. Cohen	Lizabeth MacKay

The Minnies:

Clarice	Mary Catherine Wright
Mrs. Best	Sloane Shelton
June	Michele Shay
Muriel	Bobo Lewis
Louisa	Marylouise Burke
Marcia	Marcia Jean Kurtz
Diana	Diana Canova

and John Deyle (Santa/Mayor), Hallee Hirsh (8-year-old Ellen), Jeffrey Scaperrotta (4-year-old Brian), Todd Cerveris (Casey), Anna Alvim (Nurse Teresa), Julie Janney (Hospital Nurse), Susan Stout (Tweedy's Secretary), Greg Hedtke, Christian James (Magazine Executives), Lauren Toub, Ashley Remy (Halloween Girls), Saul Stacey Williams (Graduate Student), Julianne Nicholson, Amber Kain (College Students), Yolande Bavan (Nari), Benjamin Andrews, Kathryn Walsh (Party Kids), James E. Graseck (Violinist), Doug Allen (Club Band Leader), Kirk Driscoll, Paul Pimsler, Scott Spray, Jay Stollman (Club Band Members), Cathy Comiskey, Ruth Egner, Phil Gamble, David Hutchings, Linda Hutchings, Wilbur Lewis, Rich Morin, Annette Mulholland, Rosemary Palmer, Gina Piccolo, Rebecca Raines, Barbara Russell, Joanna Hoty Russell, Barbara Savino, Normana Schaaf, Paul Schroeder, Mary G. Sims, Wolodymyr Smishkewych, Chris Sterling, Nancy Tkacs, Peter Zimmermann (Christmas Choir)

Journalist Ellen Gulden returns home to take a sabatical from her magazine job and finds herself asked to help look after her ailing mother whose simple and seemingly underwhelming life has always baffled her. This film received an Oscar nomination for actress (Meryl Streep).

Meryl Streep, William Hurt

William Hurt, Renée Zellweger

Meryl Streep, Renée Zellweger

Tom Everett Scott, Meryl Streep, William Hurt, Renée Zellweger

Meryl Streep

Meryl Streep, Renée Zellweger

Meryl Streep, Renée Zellweger

William Hurt, Meryl Streep

Chris Tucker, Jackie Chan

Chris Tucker

Chris Tucker, Elizabeth Peña

Chris Tucker, Jackie Chan

Jackie Chan

RUSH HOUR

(NEW LINE CINEMA) Producers, Roger Birnbaum, Arthur Sarkissian, Jonathan Glickman; Executive Producer, Jay Stern; Director, Brett Ratner; Screenplay, Jim Kouf, Ross LaManna; Story, Ross LaManna; Co-Executive Producer, Leon Dudevoir; Co-Producer, Art Schaeffer; Photography, Adam Greenberg; Designer, Robb Wilson King; Editor, Mark Helfrich; Music, Lalo Schifrin; Costumes, Sharen Davis; Casting, Matthew Barry, Nancy Green-Keyes; an Arthur Sarkissian and Roger Birnbaum production; Dolby; Panavision; Deluxe color; Rated PG-13; 98 minutes; September release

CAST

Lee	Jackie Chan
James Carter	Chris Tucker
Thomas Griffin/Juntao	Tom Wilkinson
Tania Johnson	Elizabeth Peña
Clive	Chris Penn
Consul Han	Tzi Ma
Sang	Ken Leung
Soo Yung	Julia Hsu
First Caucasian	Robert Littman
Dinner Guest	Michael Chow
Cops at Diner	Kai Lennox, Larry Sullivan Jr.
Consul Secretary	Yan Lin
Soo Yung's Bodyguard	Roger Fan
Soo Yung's Driver	George Cheung
Exposition Official	Lucy Lin
Agent Whitney	Rex Linn
Agent Russ	Mark Rolston
Captain Diel	Philip Baker Hall
Kid at Theatre	Jason Davis
Stucky	John Hawkes
Taxi Driver	Jean Lebell
Cigaweed Man	Wayne A. King
Bartender	Manny Perry
Pool Player	Kevin Jackson
Pool Hall Doorman	Ronald D. Brown
Luke	Clifton Powell
Market Clerk	Matt Barry
FBI Gate Guards	Stanley DeSantis, Dan Martin
Another Agent	Kevin Lowe
FBI Agent at Building	Billy Devlin
Bomb Practice Sergeant	Tommy Bush
Bobby	Barry Shabaka Henley
Chin	Albert Wong
Foo Chow Hostess	Ai Wan
Foo Chow Waitress	Lydia Look
Japanese Tourists	Sumiko "Osumi" Chan, Man Ching Chan
Socialite	Frances Fong
Convention Center Agent	Robert Kotecki

and Kenneth Houi Kang Low, Stuart Yee, Nicky Chung Chi Li, Andy Kai Chung Cheng, Man Ching Chan (Juntao's Men), Christine Ng Wing Mei, Mike Ashley, Ada Tai, Arlene Tai (Flight Attendants)

When Detective Inspector Lee of the Royal Hong Kong Police arrives in Los Angeles determined to rescue the Chinese Consul's kidnapped daughter, the FBI assigns arrogant, loud-mouthed agent James Carter to keep an eye on him.

Jackie Chan

Elizabeth Peña

Jackie Chan, Chris Tucker

SHADRACH

(COLUMBIA) Producers, Bridget Terry, John Thompson, Boaz Davidson; Executive Producers, Jonathan Demme, Steven Shareshian; Avi Lerner, Danny Dimbort, Trevor Short, Elie Samaha; Director, Susanna Styron; Screenplay, Susanna Styron, Bridget Terry; Based on a short story by William Styron; Photography, Hiro Narita; Editor, Colleen Sharp; Designer, Burton Rencher; Costumes, Dona Granata; Line Producer, Ric Rondell; Music, Van Dyke Parks; Casting, Tracy Kilpatrick; a Millennium Films presentation in association with Nu Image of a Bridget Terry production; Dolby; Fotokem color; Rated PG-13; 86 minutes; September release

CAST

Vernon Dabney	Harvey Keitel
Trixie Dabney	Andie MacDowell
Shadrach	John Franklin Sawyer
Paul Whitehurst	Scott Terra
Little Mole Dabney	Daniel Treat
Edmonia	Monica Bugajski
Lucinda	Erin Underwood
Middle Mole Dabney	Jonathan Parks Jordan
Mrs. Whitehurst	Deborah Hedwall
Mr. Whitehurst	Darrell Larson
Virginia	Ginnie Randall
Cloris	Alice Rogers
Smut	Michael Ruff
Captain	Muse Watson
Dock Worker	Doug Chancey
Presbyterian Minister	Rick Warner
Joe Thornton	Edward Bunker
Chapel Singer	Clarinda Hollmond
Earvin Williams	Melvin Cauthern
Seddon Washington	Richard Olsen
Sweet Betty	Olivia Bost
Fauntleroy	Bill Nelson
Preacher	Walter Hand
Narrator	Martin Sheen

In a small Tennessee town in 1935, Shadrach, a 99-year-old former slave, shows up at the Dabney family farm, the place where he had been born and plans to die.

Andie MacDowell, John Franklin Sawyer, Harvey Keitel

©Columbia Pictures Industries, Inc.

Ben Stiller

©Artisan Entertainment

PERMANENT MIDNIGHT

(ARTISAN ENTERTAINMENT) Producers, Jane Hamsher, Don Murphy; Director/Screenplay, David Veloz; Based upon the book by Jerry Stahl; Co-Producer, Robert Leveen; Photography, Robert Yeoman; Designer, Jerry Fleming; Editors, Steven Weisberg, Cara Silverman; Costumes, Louise Mingenbach, Lori Eskowitz; Music, Daniel Licht; Casting, Ronnie Yeskel; a Jane Hamsher—Don Murphy production; Dolby; Deluxe color; Rated R; 85 minutes; September release

CAST

Jerry Stahl	Ben Stiller
Sandra	Elizabeth Hurley
Kitty	Maria Bello
Nicky	Owen Wilson
Pamela Verlaine	Cheryl Ladd
Gus	Peter Greene
Jana	Janeane Garofalo
Phoenix Punk	Jay Paulson
Brad/Tim from Mr. Chompers	Spencer Garrett
Vola	Lourdes Benedicto
Craig Ziffer	Fred Willard
Jerry at 16	Chauncey Leopardi
Grandma Whittle	Mary Thompson
Dagmar	Connie Nielsen
Allen from Mr. Chompers	Charles Fleischer
Dita	Liz Torres
Miguel	Douglas Spain
Friend	Sandra Oh
Gary Warren	Scott Williamson
Dr. Murphy	Jerry Stahl
Nurse	Nancye Ferguson
Dr. Olsen	Sam Anderson
Scrub Nurse	Regina Nichols
Cop	John Prosky
Peter	Francois Giroday

Jerry Stahl recounts how he became a top television writer only to see his personal life and career destroyed by his dependency on drugs.

Robert De Niro

Stellan Skarsgård, Jonathan Pryce

Stellan Skarsgård, Jean Reno, Robert De Niro, Natascha McElhone

Jean Reno

RONIN

(UNITED ARTISTS) Producer, Frank Mancuso, Jr.; Executive Producer, Paul Kelmenson; Director, John Frankenheimer; Screenplay, J.D. Zeik, Richard Weisz; Story, J.D. Zeik; Photography, Robert Fraisse; Designer, Michael Z. Hanan; Costumes, May Routh; Editor, Tony Gibbs; Music, Elia Cmiral; Casting, Amanda Mackey Johnson, Cathy Sandrich, Margot Capelier; an FGM Entertainment production; Distributed by MGM; Dolby; Super 35 Widescreen; Deluxe color; Rated R: 118 minutes; September release

CAST

Sam ....Robert De Niro
Vincent ....Jean Reno
Deirdre ....Natascha McElhone
Gregor ....Stellan Skarsgård
Seamus ....Jonathan Pryce
Spence ....Sean Bean
Larry ....Skipp Sudduth
Jean-Pierre ....Michael Lonsdale
Dapper Gent ....Jan Triska
The Man with the Newspaper ....Ron Perkins
Mikhi ....Féodor Atkine
Natacha Kirilova...Katarina Witt
Sergi ....Bernard Bloch
Clown Iceskaters..........................Dominic Gugliametti, Alan Beckworth
Sergi's Accomplice ....Daniel Breton
Man at Exchange..Amidou Ben Messaoud
The "Boss" ....Tolsty
Tour Guide ....Gérard Moulevrier
The "Target" ....Lionel Vitrant
Arles Messenger..Vincent Schmitt
Arles Little Girls..Léopoldine Serre, Lou Maraval
and Frédéric Schmalzbauer (German Tour Guide), Julia Maraval (Girl Hostage), Laurent Spielvo-gel (Tourist in Nice), Ron Hiatt (Fishmonger), Steve Suissa (Waiter in Nice), Katia Tchenko (Woman Hostage), Dyna Gauzy (Little Screaming Girl), Lilly-Fleur Pointeaux, Amanda Spencer (Little Girls), Dimitri Rafalsky (Russian Interpreter), Vladimir Tchernine (Russian Mechanic), Gérard Touratier (Ice Rink Security Guard), Cyril Prentout (Mikhi's Bodyguard), Henry Moati (Bartender), Christophe Maratier (Armed Police Officer), Pierre Forest (C.R.S. Captain)

An international team of covert operatives set out to steal a mysterious briefcase, an operation that takes a dangerous turn when a member of the team tries to make off with the goods.

Christina Ricci, Edward Furlong

PECKER

(FINE LINE FEATURES) Producers, John Fiedler, Mark Tarlov; Executive Producers, Mark Ordesky, Jonathan Weisgal, Joe Revitte, Joe Caracciolo, Jr.; Director/Screenplay, John Waters; Photography, Robert Stevens; Designer, Vincent Peranio; Costumes, Van Smith; Editor, Janice Hampton; Music, Stewart Copeland; Casting, Pat Moran, Hopkins-Smith-Barden; a Polar Entertainment production; Dolby; Color; Rated R; 87 minutes; September release

CAST

Pecker	Edward Furlong
Shelley	Christina Ricci
Dr. Klompus	Bess Armstrong
Jimmy	Mark Joy
Joyce	Mary Kay Place
Tina	Martha Plimpton
Matt	Brendan Sexton III
Precinct Captain	Mink Stole
Rorey	Lili Taylor
Lynn Wentworth	Patricia Hearst
Memama	Jean Schertler
Little Chrissy	Lauren Hulsey
T-Bone	Maureen Fischer
Mr. Bozak	Donald Neal
Miss Betty	Carolyn Stayer
Outsider Al	Jack Webster
Mr. Nellbox	Alan J. Wendl

and Judith Knight Young ("Fat & Furious" Lady), Anthony Rogers (Death Row Dave), Billy Tolzman (Seafood Sam), Brian Thomas (Larry the Lughead), Tim Caggiano (Lester Hallbrook), Betsy Ames (Venetia Keydash), Scott Morgan (Jed Coleman), Valerie Karasek (Redd Larchmont), Cindy Sherman, Greg Gorman (Themselves), Joyce Flick Wendl (Street Lady), Liam Hughes (Wild Man of 22nd Street), Irving Jacobs (Guzzles), Mary Vivian Pearce (Homophobic Lady), Kennen Sisco, Jennifer Zakroff (Art Fans), Angela Calo (Pregnant Girl), Susan Duvall (Saleswoman), Ruth Lawson Walsh (Sneaky Customer), Adin Alai (Body Builder), Emmy Collins (Hippie), Brigid Berlin (Super Market Rich Lady), Kimberlee Suerth (Beautiful Girl), John Badila (Irate Manager), R. Scott Williams (Stylist), Susan Lowe (Hairdresser), Marisa Zalabak (Make-Up Artist), Andreas Kraemer (Junkie), Sharon Neisp (Bouncer), Delaney Williams (Construction Worker), Bobby Brown (Average Joe), Regi Davis (Cop A), Tyler Miller (Randy), Channing Wilroy (Wise Guy Neighbor), Rosemary Knower, Kate Kiley (Friends of Mary), Jack French (Old Fart Customer), Stan Brandorff (Geezer Customer), Doug Roberts (Death Row Dave's Father), Patsy Grady Abrams (Death Row Dave's Mother), Holly Twyford (Straight Lady), Joshua Shoemaker (Channel 11 Anchor), Sloane Brown (Channel 45 Anchor), Thomas Korzeniowski (Toupé Man), Susan Greenhill (Voice of Miraculous Virgin Mary), Lola Pashalinski (Voice of Pelt Room Announcer)

Lili Taylor

18-year-old amateur photographer "Pecker," who takes random snapshots of his Baltimore friends and neighbors, becomes a reluctant "instant celebrity" when a New York art dealer discovers his work.

©Fine Line Features

Edward Furlong

Martha Plimpton

Edward Furlong, Christina Ricci

Edward Furlong

Christina Ricci

Lili Taylor, Edward Furlong

Christina Ricci, Edward Furlong, Mary Kay Place, Jean Schertler, Mark Joy, Lauren Hulsey, Martha Plimpton, Brendan Sexton III

CLAY PIGEONS

(GRAMERCY) Producers, Ridley Scott, Christ Zarpas; Executive Producers, Tony Scott, Guy East, Nigel Sinclair; Director, David Dobkin; Screenplay, Matt Healy; Co-Producers, Carrie Morrow, Audrey Kelly; Photography, Eric Edwards; Designer, Clark Hunter; Editor, Stan Salfas; Costumes, Laura Goldsmith; Associate Producer, Hilarie Roope Benz; Music, John Lurie; Casting, Risa Bramon Garcia, Randi Hiller; a PolyGram Filmed Entertainment presentation in association with Intermedia Films of a Scott Free production; Dolby; Deluxe color; Rated R; 104 minutes; September release

CAST

Lester Long	Vince Vaughn
FBI Agent Dale Shelby	Janeane Garofalo
Clay Bidwell	Joaquin Phoenix
Amanda	Georgina Cates
Sheriff Mooney	Scott Wilson
Earl	Gregory Sporleder
Deputy Barney	Vince Vieluf
Minister	Wayne Brennan
Glen	Joseph D. Reitman
Gloria	Nikki Arlyn
Mark	Jeff Olson
Kimberly	Monica Moench
Bystander at Amanda's	Kevin Rahm
Dr. Jaffe	Jesse Bennett
Agent Reynard	Phil Morris
Dr. Buckley	Zane Parker
Pizza Delivery Kid	Ryan Mouritsen
Dolores	Kari Peterson
Bartender	Duane Stephens
Old Man Waiter	Steve Anderson

Clay Bidwell, whose best friend has committed suicide after finding out that Clay has been sleeping with his wife, disposes of the body only to find himself the chief suspect in a series of unrelated murders.

©Gramercy Pictures

Joaquin Phoenix, Vince Vaughn

Alicia Witt, Rebecca Gayheart

©TriStar Pictures Inc.

URBAN LEGEND

(TRISTAR) Producers, Neal H. Moritz, Gina Matthews, Michael McDonnell; Executive Producer, Brad Luff; Director, Jamie Blanks; Screenplay, Silvio Horta; Photography, James Chressanthis; Designer, Charles Breen; Editor, Jay Cassidy; Music, Christopher Young; Costumes, Mary Claire Hannan; Casting, John Papsidera; a Phoenix Pictures presentation of a Neal H. Moritz/Gina Matthews production; Dolby; Super 35 Widescreen; Technicolor; Rated R; 99 minutes; September release

CAST

Paul	Jared Leto
Natalie	Alicia Witt
Brenda	Rebecca Gayheart
Parker	Michael Rosenbaum
Reese	Loretta Devine
Damon	Joshua Jackson
Sasha	Tara Reid
Dean Adams	John Neville
Janitor	Julian Richings
Professor Wexler	Robert Englund
Tosh	Danielle Harris
Michelle Mancini	Natasha Gregson Wagner
Newsman	Gord Martineau
Library Attendant	Kay Hawtrey
Bitchy Girl	Angela Vint
Weather Woman	J.C. Kenny
David Evans	Vince Corrazza
Nerdy Guy	Balazs Koos
Felicia	Stephanie Mills

and Danny Comden (Blake), Nancy McAlear (Jenny), Shawn Mathieson (Hippie Guy), Cle Bennett (Dorky Guy), Danielle Brett (Trendy Girl), Roberta Angelica (Swimming Woman), Matt Birman (Killer)

In a New England college town, classic urban legends start becoming reality when various students and faculty begin dying in ways patterned after scary folk tales.

A NIGHT AT THE ROXBURY

(PARAMOUNT) Producers, Lorne Michaels, Amy Heckerling; Executive Producer, Robert K. Weiss; Director, John Fortenberry; Screenplay Steve Koren, Will Ferrell, Chris Kattan; Photography, Francis Kenny; Designer, Steven Jordan; Editor, Jay Kamen; Costumes, Mona May; Co-Producers, Marie Cantin, Steve Koren; Associate Producer, Erin Fraser; Music, David Kitay; Choreographer, Mary Ann Kellogg; Casting, Jeff Greenberg; a Lorne Michael and Amy Heckerling production, presented in association with SNL Studios; Dolby; Deluxe color; Rated PG-13; 82 minutes; October release

Will Ferrell, Gigi Rice, Chris Kattan, Elisa Donovan

CAST

Steve Butabi	Will Ferrell
Doug Butabi	Chris Kattan
Emily Sanderson	Molly Shannon
Kamehl Butabi	Dan Hedaya
Himself	Richard Grieco
Barbara Butabi	Loni Anderson
Cambi	Elisa Donovan
Vivica	Gigi Rice
Craig	Lochlyn Munro
Fred Sanderson	Dwayne Hickman
Credit Vixen	Meredith Scott Lynn
Dooey	Colin Quinn
Hottie Cop	Jennifer Coolidge
Roxbury Bouncer	Michael "Big Mike" Duncan
Zadir	Chazz Palminteri
Hot Girl	Raquel Gardner
Porsche Girls	Viveca Paulin, Paulette Braxton
Security Guards	Michael M. Horton, Richard Francese
Roxbury Club Girl	Trish Ramish
Saturday Night Fever Girl	Gina Mari
Flower Customers	Roy Jenkins, Kip King
Aerobics Instructor	Mary Ann Kellogg
Mabel Sanderson	Maree Cheatham

and Kristen Dalton (Grieco's Lady), Deborah Kellner (Topless Woman), Robin Krieger (Mrs. Manicotti), Betty Bridges-Nicasio (Zadir Receptionist), Yoshio Be, Victor Kobayashi (Japanese Men), Twink Caplan (Crying Flower Customer), Eva Mendez (Bridesmaid), Mark McKinney (Father Williams), Chad Bannon (New Club Bouncer), Jim Wise, Patrick Ferrell, Dorian Spencer (New Club Waiters), Tina Weisinger (New Club Waitress)

Molly Shannon, Chris Kattan, Will Ferrell

The Butabi Brothers, a pair of hopelessly "un-hip" swingers who comb the L.A. nightclub scene, make it their goal to get into the number one hot spot, the Roxbury.

©Paramount Pictures

Michael Duncan, Chris Kattan, Will Ferrell

Chris Kattan, Will Ferrell

ANTZ

(DREAMWORKS) Producers, Brad Lewis, Aron Warner, Patty Wooton; Executive Producers, Penney Finkelman Cox, Sandra Rabins, Carl Rosendahl; Director, Eric Darnell; Screenplay, Todd Alcott, Chris Weitz, Paul Weitz; Music, Harry Gregson-Williams, John Powell; Designer, John Bell; Art Director, Kendal Cronkhite; Editor, Stan Webb; Additional Sequences Director, Lawrence Guterman; Story Consultant, Zak Penn; Character Designer, Raman Hui; Key Conceptual Artist, Mary Grandpré; Modeling Supervisor, Konrad Dunton; Layout Supervisor, Simon J. Smith; Supervising Animators, Rex Grignon, Raman Hui; Casting, Leslee Feldman; a PDI presentation; Dolby; Technicolor; Rated PG; 83 minutes; October release

Z, Bala

VOICE CAST

Z ....Woody Allen
Chip...Dan Aykroyd
Queen..Anne Bancroft
Muffy...Jane Curtin
Barbatus...Danny Glover
General Mandible ....Gene Hackman
Azteca..Jennifer Lopez
Drunk Scout...John Mahoney
Psychologist ....Paul Mazursky
Foreman..Grant Shaud
Weaver...Sylvester Stallone
Princess Bala...Sharon Stone
Colonel Cutter ....Christopher Walken

Z, unhappy at being just one of a million worker ants, makes it his goal to woo and win the Princess Bala, much to the displeasure of the ambitious and dangerous General Mandible.

Z, Weaver

Queen, Bala, Azteca, Weaver, General Mandible, Colonel Cutter

Robin Williams, Annabella Sciorra

WHAT DREAMS MAY COME

(POLYGRAM) Producers, Stephen Simon, Barnet Bain; Executive Producers, Erica Huggins, Ron Bass, Ted Field, Scott Kroopf; Director, Vincent Ward; Screenplay, Ron Bass; Based upon the novel by Richard Matheson; Co-Producer, Alan C. Blomquist; Photography, Eduardo Serra; Designer, Eugenio Zanetti; Editors, David Brenner, Maysie Hoy; Costumes, Yvonne Blake; Music, Michael Kamen; Visual Effects Producer/Supervisor, Ellen M. Somers; Casting, Heidi Levitt; a PolyGram Filmed Entertainment presentation of an Interscope Communications production in association with Metafilmics; Dolby; Super 35 Widescreen; Technicolor; Rated PG-13; 113 minutes; October release

Robin Williams, Cuba Gooding Jr.

CAST

Chris Nielsen	Robin Williams
Albert	Cuba Gooding, Jr.
Annie Nielsen	Annabella Sciorra
The Tracker	Max von Sydow
Marie Nielsen	Jessica Brooks Grant
Ian Nielsen	Josh Paddock
Leona	Rosalind Chao
Mrs. Jacobs	Lucinda Jenney
Angie	Wilma Bonet
Stacey Jacobs	Maggie McCarthy
Reverend Hanley	Matt Salinger
Best Friend Cindy	Carin Sprague
Woman in Car Accident	June Lomena
Paramedic	Paul P. Card IV
Face	Werner Herzog
Emily	Clara Thomas
Billy	Benjamin Brock

Ending up in Paradise after he is killed in a freak accident, Chris Nielsen is devestated to discover that his widow has taken her own life in grief, prompting him to journey to the Underworld to find her. 1998 Academy Award-winner for Best Visual Effects. This film received an additional nomination for art direction.

©PolyGram Films

Robin Williams, Annabella Sciorra

Stanley Tucci, Oliver Platt

Alfred Molina, Campbell Scott, Tony Shalhoub

Oliver Platt, Billy Connolly

Hope Davis, Dana Ivey

Isabella Rossellini

THE IMPOSTORS

(FOX SEARCHLIGHT) formerly *Ship of Fools*; Producers, Elizabeth W. Alexander, Stanley Tucci; Executive Producer, Jonathan Filley; Director/Screenplay, Stanley Tucci; Photography, Ken Kelsch; Designer, Andrew Jackness; Music, Gary DeMichele; Editor, Suzy Elmiger; Costumes, Juliet Polcsa; Casting, Ellen Lewis; a First Cold Press production; Dolby; Technicolor; Rated R; 102 minutes; October release

CAST

Maurice	Oliver Platt
Arthur	Stanley Tucci
Sheik	Teagle F. Bougere
Pancetta Leaky	Elizabeth Bracco
Happy Franks	Steve Buscemi
Sparks	Billy Connolly
Captain	Allan Corduner
Emily	Hope Davis
Mrs. Essendine	Dana Ivey
Maxine (Maxi)	Allison Janney
Johnny (Frenchman)	Richard Jenkins
Marco	Matt McGrath
Jeremy Burtom	Alfred Molina
Queen (Veiled Woman)	Isabella Rossellini
Meistrich	Campbell Scott
First Mate	Tony Shalhoub
Lily	Lili Taylor
Maitre D'	Walker Jones
Attractive Woman	Jessica Walling
Baker	David Lipman
Gertrude	E. Katherine Kerr
Claudius	George Guidall
Bernardo	William Hill
Burtom's Assistant	Michael Emerson
Stage Manager	Jack O'Connell
Mike (Laertes)	Matt Malloy
Francisco	Ted Blumberg
Playwright	Woody Allen

and Arden Myrin (Stewardess with Luggage), Christopher Pomeroy (Steward), Sarah McCord (Stewardess with the Queen), Lewis J. Stadlen (Bandleader), Phyllis Somerville (Woman at Bar), Amy Hohn (Woman with Captain), Michael Higgins (Older Man), Ken Costigan (Bartender)

After insulting hammy thespian Jeremy Burtom, a pair of down-in-their-luck actors take flight and hide out aboard a luxury liner where they meet a variety of odd passengers and crew members.

©Fox Searchlight Pictures

Lili Taylor, Campbell Scott

Stanley Tucci, Oliver Platt

Allison Janney, Steve Buscemi, Stanley Tucci

Oliver Platt, Stanley Tucci

BAD MANNERS

(PHAEDRA CINEMA) Producers, J. Todd Harris, Stephen Nemeth, Alan Kaplan; Executive Producer, John Davis; Director, Jonathan Kaufer; Screenplay, David Gilman, based on his play *Ghost in the Machine*; Photography, Denis Maloney; Designer, Sharon Lomofsky; Costumes, Katherine Jane Bryant; Music, Ira Newborn; Editor, Robin Katz; Casting, Georgianne Walken, Sheila Jaffe; a Davis Entertainment Classics in association with Skyline Entertainment Partners, Wavecrest Pictures presentation of a J. Todd Harris/Stephen Nemeth production; Dolby; Color; Rated R; 88 minutes; October release

CAST

Wes Westlund	David Strathairn
Nancy Westlund	Bonnie Bedelia
Matt Carroll	Saul Rubinek
Kim Matthews	Caroleen Feeney
Professor Harper	Julie Harris
Musicologists	Robin Pooley, Daniel Koch
Coffeehouse Troubadour	Steve Forbert

A pair of academic couples engage in a vicious battle of verbal and psychological abuse when they spend a weekend together in Cambridge, Massachusetts.

©Phaedra Cinema

David Strathairn, Saul Rubinek

Caroleen Feeney, Saul Rubinek

Saul Williams

©Trimark Pictures

SLAM

(TRIMARK) Producers, Henri M. Kessler, Marc Levin, Richard Stratton; Executive Producers, David Peipers, Henri M. Kessler; Director, Marc Levin; Screenplay, Marc Levin, Bonz Malone, Sonja Sohn, Richard Stratton, Saul Williams; Story, Marc Levin, Richard Stratton; Photography, Mark Benjamin; Music, DJ Spooky; Editor, Emir Lewis; an Offline Entertainment Group & Slam Pictures presentation; Dolby; Color; Rated R; 100 minutes; October release

CAST

Raymond Joshua	Saul Williams
Lauren Bell	Sonja Sohn
Hopha	Bonz Malone
Jimmy Huang	Beau Sia
Big Mike	Lawrence Wilson
China	Andrew Taylor
Bay (Jail Rapper)	Momolu Stewart
Do Wop Cops	Ron Jones, Reamer Shedrick
Chief C.O.	Allan E. Lucas
Officer Dom	Dominic Chianese, Jr.
Jail Class Poet "Why"	Jerome Goldman
Party Poet "Diminuendo in Blue"	DJ Renegade
Slam Poet "Ice Cream"	Liza Jesse Peterson
Slam Poet "Like"	Taylor Mali
Slam M.C.	Bob Holman
Public Defender	Rhozier Brown
Prosecutor	Richard Stratton
Judge	Mayor Marion Barry, Jr.

With the help of a writing teacher, Ray Joshua, serving time for possession, discovers his knack for composing a form of spoken word poetry and rap called "slams."

HOLY MAN

(TOUCHSTONE) Producers, Roger Birnbaum, Stephen Herek; Executive Producers, Jeffrey Chernov, Jonathan Glickman; Director, Stephen Herek; Screenplay, Tom Schulman; Co-Producers, Ray Murphy, Rebekah Rudd; Photography, Adrian Biddle; Designer, Andrew McAlpine; Editor, Trudy Ship; Costumes, Aggie Guerard Rodgers; Music, Alan Silvestri; Casting, Amanda Mackey Johnson, Cathy Sandrich; a Roger Birnbaum production, presented in association with Caravan Pictures; Dolby; Panavision; Technicolor; Rated PG; 114 minutes; October release

Kelly Preston, Jeff Goldblum, Eddie Murphy

CAST

"G"	Eddie Murphy
Ricky Hayman	Jeff Goldblum
Kate Newell	Kelly Preston
McBainbridge	Robert Loggia
Barry	Jon Cryer
Scott Hawkes	Eric McCormack
Director	Sam Kitchin
Assistant Director	Robert Small
Cameraman (Brutus)	Marc Macaulay
Laundry Ladies	Mary Stout, Edie McClurg
Grace	Kim Staunton
Themselves	Morgan Fairchild, Betty White, Florence Henderson, James Brown, Soupy Sales, Dan Marino, Willard Scott, Nino Cerruti
Sunbathers	Barbara Hubbard Barron, Cristina Wilcox
TV Host	Clarence Reynolds
Elderly Couple	Mal Jones, Jody Wilson
Fresca, the Foot Model	Pamela West
Doctor Simon	Tim Powell
Nurses	Lori Viveros Herek, Angel Schmiedt
Laurie	Whitney Dupree
Hot Tub Girl	Jennifer Bini Taylor
Farmer	Robert Walker
Housekeeper	Elodia Riovega
Rabbi	Avrohom Horovitz
Moslem Theologian	Al Kamaar
Priest	Dan Fitzgerald
Grass Mat Salesman	Mark Brown
Bullet Proof Vest Man	Mike Benitez
Control Booth Technician	Deborah Magdalena
TV Hostesses	Adriana Catano, Andrea Lively

and Kim Alexis (Keratin Girls—Amber), Veronica Webb (Diandre), Lee Bryant (Money "Meg"), Nick Santa Maria (Sword Salesman), Aaron Elbaz (Glue-Gun Boy), Scotty Gallin, John Bosa (Jock Salesmen), Jeffrey Wetzel (Stage Manager), Erin Morrissey, Daryl Meyer, Ronda Pierson (Hosts), Brett Rice, John Archie (Detectives), Armando Ramos (Grace's Little Boy), Nancy Duerr, Tonya Oliver, Fred Workman, Jacqueline Chernov, Roger Reid (Reporters), Peter Paul DeLeo (Stagehand), Errol Smith (GBSN Staffer), Dave Corey (Announcer), Alejandro Acosta Fox (Flamenco Guitarist), Maria Alejandra Carpio (Flamenco Dancer), Laurie Wallace (Facial Mist Girl), Willie Gault (Nordic Track Guy), Amanda Lynn (Nordic Track Girl), Charlie Haugk (Party Animal), Margaret Muldoon (Attractive Party Guest), Mark Massar (Set Dresser), Toy Van Lierop ("G" Makeup Artist), Dana Hawkins, Denise Heinrich (Hair Chat Girls), Antoni Cornacchione (Chain Saw Host), Marc C. Geschwind (GBSN Electrician), A.J. Alexander O. Parhm (UPS Guy), Alan Jordan, Mike Kirton (Marksmen)

Jon Cryer

Robert Loggia

Good Buy Shopping Network executive Ricky Hayman, in danger of losing his job, meets up with an itinerant holy man named "G," giving Ricky the idea of putting the guru on television with his own show.

©Touchstone Pictures

Morgan Fairchild, Eddie Murphy

Sharon Stone

Kieran Culkin, Elden Henson

Elden Henson, Gena Rowlands, Kieran Culkin,
Sharon Stone, Harry Dean Stanton

Kieran Culkin, Elden Henson

THE MIGHTY

(MIRAMAX) Producer, Jane Startz, Simon Fields; Executive Producers, Bob Weinstein, Harvey Weinstein, Julie Goldstein; Director, Peter Chelsom; Screenplay, Charles Leavitt; Based on the novel *Freak the Mighty* by Rodman Philbrick; Co-Producer, Don Carmody; Co-Executive Producer, Chaos Productions; Photography, John De Borman; Designer, Caroline Hanania; Editor, Martin Walsh; Music, Trevor Jones; Costumes, Marie Sylvie Deveau; Casting, Barbara Cohen, Mary Gail Artz; a Scholastic Productions/Simon Fields production; Dolby; Deluxe color; Rated PG-13; 100 minutes; October release

CAST

Gwen Dillon	Sharon Stone
Maxwell Kane	Elden Henson
Kevin Dillon	Kieran Culkin
Gram	Gena Rowlands
Grim	Harry Dean Stanton
Loretta Lee	Gillian Anderson
Iggy	Meat Loaf
Kenny Kane	James Gandolfini
Blade	Joe Perrino
Homeless Man	Douglas Bisset
Doghouse Boys	Dov Tiefenbach, Michael Colton
Mrs. Donelli	Eve Crawford
Mr. Sacker	John Bourgeois
Officer	Bruce Tubbe
Mr. Hampton	Rudy Webb
Man in Diner	Ron Nigrini
Girl in Diner	Nadia Litz
Girl in Hall	Serena Pruyn
Boy in Hall	Telmo Miranda
Denardo	Jordan Hughes
Mrs. Addison	Jennfier Lewis

and Bryon Bully (Fat Boy), Charlaine Porter (Girl with Limp), Lisa Marie Chen (Girl in Cafeteria), Lisa Mininni (Cashier), Ann Chiu (Nurse), Carl Marotte (Doctor), Nora Sheehan (Police Woman), Sophie Bennett (Little Girl), William Van Allen (Laundry Worker)

Max, a hulking thirteen-year-old misfit, finds an unexpected friend in his next door neighbor Kevin, an intelligent, imaginative kid in leg braces who inspires Max to better his lot in life.

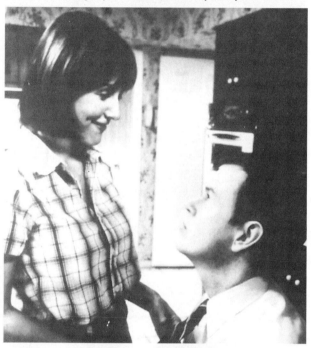

Philip Seymour Hoffman, Lara Flynn Boyle

Cynthia Stevenson, Dylan Baker

HAPPINESS

(GOOD MACHINE) Producers, Ted Hope, Christine Vachon; Executive Producers, David Linde, James Schamus; Director/Screenplay, Todd Solondz; Photography, Maryse Alberti; Editor, Alan Oxman; Music, Robbie Kondor; Designer, Therese Deprez; Costumes, Kathryn Nixon; Casting, Ann Goulder; a Good Machine/Killer Films production; Dolby; DuArt color; Rated R; 139 minutes; October release

CAST

Joy Jordan	Jane Adams
Andy Kornbluth	Jon Lovitz
Allen	Philip Seymour Hoffman
Bill Maplewood	Dylan Baker
Helen Jordan	Lara Flynn Boyle
Timmy Maplewood	Justin Elvin
Trish Maplewood	Cynthia Stevenson
Chloe Maplewood	Lila Glantzman-Leib
Psychiatrist	Gerry Becker
Billy Maplewood	Rufus Read
Mona Jordan	Louise Lasser
Lenny Jordan	Ben Gazzara
Kristina	Camryn Manheim
Detective Berman	Arthur Mascarella
Nancy	Molly Shannon
Kay	Ann Harada
Tom	Doug McGrath
Courteous Waiter	Dr. Eric Marcus
Rhonda	Anne Bobby
Vlad	Jared Harris
Joe Grasso	Dan Moran
Johnny Grasso	Evan Silverberg
Ann Chambeau	Marla Maples
Diane Freed	Elizabeth Ashley
Don	Dan Tedlie
Betty Grasso	Johann Carlo

and Kooki (Henry), Eytan Mirsky (Angry Picketer), Lisa Louise Langford (Radical Picketer), Socorro Santiago (Crying Teacher), Allison Furman (Consoling Teacher), Wai Ching Ho, Bina Sharif, Tsepo Mokone (Students), Hope Pomerance (Hysterical Woman), Matt Malloy (Doctor), Marina Gaizidorskaia (Zhenia), Joe Lisi (Police Detective), José Rabelo (Pedro), Diane Tyler (Janet), Olga Stepanova (Zhenia's Mother)

A look at the decidedly unhappy lives of three diverse sisters and the various people who interact with them.

©Good Machine

Jared Harris, Jane Adams

Camryn Manheim

139

BELOVED

(TOUCHSTONE) Producers, Edward Saxon, Jonathan Demme, Gary Goetzman, Oprah Winfrey, Kate Forte; Executive Producer, Ron Bozman; Director, Jonathan Demme; Screenplay, Akosua Busia, Richard LaGravenese, Adam Brooks; Based on the novel by Toni Morrison; Photography, Tak Fujimoto; Designer, Kristi Zea; Editors, Carol Littleton, Andy Keir; Music, Rachel Portman; Costumes, Colleen Atwood; Associate Producer, Steven Shareshian; Casting, Howard Feuer; a Harpo Films/Clinica Estetico production; Dolby; Technicolor; Rated R; 172 minutes; October release

CAST

Sethe ....Oprah Winfrey
Paul D ....Danny Glover
Beloved ....Thandie Newton
Denver ....Kimberly Elise
Baby Suggs ....Beah Richards
Younger Sethe ....Lisa Gay Hamilton
Stamp Paid ....Albert Hall
Ella ....Irma P. Hall
Janey Wagon ....Carol Jean Lewis
Amy Denver ....Kessia Kordelle
Schoolteacher..Jude Ciccolella
and Anthony Chisholm (Langhorne), Dorothy Love Coates (M. Lucille Williams), Jane White (Lady Jones), Yada Beener (Denver, aged 9), Emil Pinnock (Howard, aged 14), Calen Johnson (Buglar, aged 13), George E. Ray (Reverend Pike), Wes Bentley, Dashiell Eaves (Schoolteacher's Nephews), Tyler Hinson (Baby Beloved), Brian Hooks (Young Paul D), Angie Utt (Mrs. Garner), Hill Harper (Halle), Jim Roche (String Show Barker), Vertamae Grosvenor (Grace), Ramona Castle, Brooklyn James, Nora Marlowe (Carnival Kids), Frederick Strother (African Savage), Lillian Smith (Lemonade Server), Aliya Robinson (Denver's Carnival Friend), Joe Toutebon (Frenchie), Brittany Hawkins (Young Girl Sethe), Alerte Belance (Nan), Ayoka Dorsey (Sethe's Mother), Ashleigh Watson (Baby Denver), Dajon Matthews (Howard, aged 5), Norris Wiggins, Jr. (Buglar, aged 4), Harry Northup (Sheriff), Tracey Walter (Slave Catcher), Terel Gibson (Buglar, age 21), Damani Baker (Howard, aged 22), Robert Castle (Mr. Sawyer), Paul Lazar (General Store Proprietor), Leigh Smiley (General Store Helper), Jiggs Walker (Good Samaritan), Dan Olmstead (Policeman), Charles Glenn (Helpful Gentleman), Jason Robards (Mr. Bodwin), Anthony S. Calypso (Denver's Boyfriend), Ysaye M. Barnwell, Trazana M. Beverley, Cecelia Ann Birt, Grace Blake, Jordan Cael, Nitanju Bolade Casel, Edwidge Danticat, Yanick Etienne, Denise Gassant, Frances Gray, Thelma Houston, Louise Johnson, Aisha Kahlil, Carol Lynn Maillard, Dianne McIntyre, Gaynielle Neville, Madeline Preston, Matt Rochester, Millicent Sparks, Lisa Summerour, Ophelia M. Turner, Karen Lorraine Vicks, Willa Ward, Pauletta Washington, Jacqueline Celestin Fils-Aimé (The Thirty Women)

Sethe, a runaway slave trying to start life anew in 1873 Ohio, is visited by a bizarre, seemingly-possessed woman named Beloved. This film received an Oscar nomination for costume design.

©Touchstone Pictures

Kimberly Elise, Oprah Winfrey, Thandie Newton

Oprah Winfrey, Danny Glover

Beah Richards

Irma P. Hall, Lisa Gay Hamilton, Albert Hall

BRIDE OF CHUCKY

(UNIVERSAL) Producers, David Kirschner, Grace Gilroy; Executive Producers, Don Mancini, Corey Sienega; Director, Ronny Yu; Screenplay, Don Mancini; Based on his characters created for the film *Child's Play*; Photography, Peter Pau; Designer, Alicia Keywan; Editors, David Wu, Randolph K. Bricker; Chucky and Tiffany Puppet Effects Creator, Kevin Yagher; Chucky and Tiffany Dolls Creator, David Kirschner; Music, Graeme Revell; Costumes, Lynne MacKay; Casting, Joanna Colbert, Ross Clydesdale; Visual Effects Supervisor, Michael Muscal; a David Kirschner production; Dolby; Deluxe color; Rated R; 89 minutes; October release

CAST

Tiffany	Jennifer Tilly
Voice of Chucky	Brad Dourif
Jade	Katherine Heigl
Jesse	Nick Stabile
Damien	Alexis Arquette
David	Gordon Michael Woolvett
Chief Warren Kincaid	John Ritter
Lt. Preston	Lawrence Dane

and Michael Johnson (Norton), James Gallanders (Russ), Janet Kidder (Diane), Vincent Corazza (Bailey), Kathy Najimy (Motel Maid), Park Bench (Stoner), Emily Weedon (Girl at One-Stop), Ben Bass (Lt. Ellis), Roger McKeen (Justice of the Peace), Sandi Stahlbrand (Reporter)

The ex-girlfriend of a psycho whose soul was transferred into a doll, raises the doll back from the "dead" only to find herself murdered by the deadly toy. The fourth in the series following Child's Play *(UA, 1988),* Child's Play 2 *(Univ., 1990), and* Child's Play 3 *(Univ., 1991) all of which featured the voice of Brad Dourif as Chucky.*

©Universal City Studios

Alexis Arquette, Chucky, Jennifer Tilly

Alessandro Nivola

REACH THE ROCK

(GRAMERCY) Producers, John Hughes, Ricardo Mestres; Director, William Ryan; Screenplay, John Hughes; Executive Producer, Christopher Cronyn; Designer, Jeffrey Townsend; Editor, Jerry Greenberg; Associate Producer, James Giovannetti, Jr.; Music, John McEntire; Costumes, Ellen Ryba; Casting, Billy Hopkins, Suzanne Smith, Kerry Barden; Dolby; Deluxe Color; Rated R; 100 minutes; October release

CAST

Phil Quinn	William Sadler
Robin	Alessandro Nivola
Ernie	Bruce Norris
Donna	Karen Sillas
Lise	Brooke Langton
Ed	Richard Hamilton
Danny	Norman Reedus

Restless 21-year-old Robin winds up spending a night in jail where he is confronted by police sergeant Quinn who blames the young man for the death of his nephew.

©Gramercy Pictures

Chucky, Jennifer Tilly

141

PRACTICAL MAGIC

(WARNER BROS.) Producer, Denise Di Novi; Executive Producers, Mary McLaglen, Bruce Berman; Director, Griffin Dunne; Screenplay, Robin Swicord, Akiva Goldsman, Adam Brooks; Based on the novel by Alice Hoffman; Photography, Andrew Dunn; Designer, Robin Standefer; Editor, Elizabeth Kling; Co-Producer, Robin Swicord; Music, Alan Silvestri; Costumes, Judianna Makovsky; Special Effects Supervisor, Burt Dalton; Casting, Amanda Mackey Johnson, Cathy Sandrich; a Di Novi Pictures production in association with Fortis Films, presented in association with Village Roadshow Pictures; Dolby; Super 35 Widescreen; Technicolor; Rated PG-13; 105 minutes; October release

Sandra Bullock, Nicole Kidman

CAST

Sally Owens	Sandra Bullock
Gillian Owens	Nicole Kidman
Aunt Frances	Stockard Channing
Aunt Jet	Dianne Wiest
Jimmy Angelov	Goran Visnjic
Gary Hallet	Aidan Quinn
Kylie	Evan Rachel Wood
Antonia	Alexandra Artrip
Michael	Mark Feuerstein
Maria Owens	Caprice Benedetti
Lovelorn Lady	Annabella Price
Sally at age 11	Camilla Belle
Gillian at age 10	Lora Anne Criswell
Linda Bennett	Margo Martindale
Carla	Chloe Webb
Patty	Martha Gehman
Sara (adult)	Lucinda Jenney
Nan	Cordelia Richards
Debbie	Mary Gross
Old Man Wilkes	Jack Kirschke
Old Lady Wilkes	Herta Ware

and Ellen Geer (Pharmacist), Courtney Dettrich (Young Sara), John McLeod (Puritan Minister), Trevor Duncan (Sara's Boy), Colby Cochran (Ice Cream Boy), Caitlyn Holley (Ice Cream Girl), Ken Serratt, Jr. (Lovelorn's Lover), Rich Sickler (Dwight), Jeanne Robinson, Deborah Kancher (PTC Moms), Peter Shaw (Jack), Caralyn Kozlowski (Regina)

Goran Visnjic, Nicole Kidman

A pair of sisters, raised by their aunts to practice magic, realize that their abilities come at a price: the men they fall in love with are doomed to die.

©Warner Bros.

Nicole Kidman, Goran Visnjic, Sandra Bullock

Sandra Bullock, Aidan Quinn

THE ALARMIST

(LIONS GATE) formerly *Life During Wartime*; Producers, Dan Stone, Lisa Zimble; Executive Produers, Beau Flynn, Stefan Simchowitz, Matthias Emcke, Thomas Augsberger; Director/Screenplay, Evan Dunsky; Based on the play *Life During Wartime* by Keith Reddin; Co-Producer, Jonathan King; Photography, Alex Nepomniaschy; Designer, Amy B. Ancona; Costumes, Denise Wingate; Music, Christophe Beck; Editor, Norman Buckley; Casting, Carolyn Long, Concetta Di Matteo; a Key Entertainment in association with Bandeira Entertainment presentation of a Dan Stone, Flynn/Simchowitz production; Dolby; Color; Rated R; 92 minutes; October release

CAST

Tommy Hudler	David Arquette
Heinrich Grigoris	Stanley Tucci
Gale Ancona	Kate Capshaw
Sally	Mary McCormack
Howard Ancona	Ryan Reynolds
April	Tricia Vessey
Mrs. Fielding	Ruth Miller
Mr. Fielding	Hoke Howell
Beth Hudler	Michael Learned
Bruce Hudler	Lewis Arquette
Andrew Hudler	Richmond Arquette
Skippy Hudler	Gabriel Dell, Jr.

and Valerie Long (Doris), Kim Tobin (Bambi), Colin Campbell (Waiter), Eric Zivot (Shelly), Vincent J. Bilancio (Assistant Director), Clea DuVall (Suzy), David Brisbin (Detective Flinkman), Bradley J. Gorman (Grigoris Employee), Dennis Cockrum (Vendor), Matt Malloy (Morgue Technician), Alex Nepomniaschy (Installer)

A young man, selling burglar alarms door-to-door for a shady business-man who encourages him to prey on the paranoia of the population, meets an older woman with whom he begins an affair.

Stanley Tucci, Mary McCormack

David Arquette

Kate Capshaw

©Lions Gate Films

Timothy "Speed" Levitch

THE CRUISE

(ARTISAN ENTERTAINMENT) Producer/Director/Photography, Bennett Miller; Executive Producers, J.B. Miller, David Yamner, Teddy Miller, David Cohen; Editor, Michael Levine; Associate Producer, Kevin McLeod; Music, Marty Beller; a Charter Films presentation; Black and white; Not rated; 76 minutes; October release. Documentary on Timothy "Speed" Levitch, an irreverant and eccentric New York City tour bus guide.

Tobey Maguire, Reese Witherspoon

Reese Witherspoon, Paul Walker

Joan Allen, Reese Witherspoon

J.T. Walsh

Marley Shelton, Tobey Maguire

William H. Macy, Joan Allen

PLEASANTVILLE

(NEW LINE CINEMA) Producers, Jon Kilik, Robert J. Degus, Steven Soderbergh, Gary Ross; Executive Producers, Michael De Luca, Mary Parent; Director/Screenplay, Gary Ross; Photography, John Lindley; Designer, Jeannine Oppewall; Editor, William Goldenberg; Costumes, Judianna Makovsky; Visual Effects Supervisor, Chris Watts; Color Effects Designer, Michael Southard; Co-Producers, Allen Alsobrook, Allison Thomas, Edward Lynn; Music, Randy Newman; Casting, Ellen Lewis, Debra Zane; a Larger Than Life production; Dolby; Color/Black and white; Rated PG-13; 123 minutes; October release

Joan Allen, Tobey Maguire

CAST

David	Tobey Maguire
Mr. Johnson	Jeff Daniels
Betty Parker	Joan Allen
George Parker	William H. Macy
Big Bob	J.T. Walsh
TV Repairman	Don Knotts
Jennifer	Reese Witherspoon
Margaret	Marley Shelton
David's Mom	Jane Kaczmarek
Mary Sue	Natalie Ramsey
Bud	Kevin Connors
Girl in School Yard	Heather McGill
College Counselor	Paul Morgan Stetler
Health Teacher	Denise Dowse
Science Teacher	McNally Sagal
Howard	Giuseppe Andrews
Kimmy	Marissa Ribisi
Christin	Jenny Lewis
Mark	Justin Nimmo
Mark's Lackeys	Kai Lennox, Jason Behr
Commercial Announcer	Robin Bissell
Mr. Simpson	Harry Singleton
Firemen	John Ganun, Dan Gillies
Skip	Paul Walker
Betty Jean	Dawn Cody
Lisa Anne	Maggie Lawson
Peggy Jane	Andrea Taylor
Miss Peters	Lela Ivey
Tommy	Jim Patric
Basketball Hero	Marc Blucas
Coach	Stanton Rutledge
Paper Boy	Jason Maves
TV Weatherman	Gerald Emmerick
Dr. Henderson	Charles C. Stevenson, Jr.
Marge Jenkins	Nancy Lenehan
Gus	Weston Blakesley
Roy	Patrick T. O'Brien
Ralph	Jim Antonio
Juke Box Boy	Danny Strong
Mary	Kristin Rudrud
Bridge Club Lady	Laura Carney
Will	Erik MacArthur
Boy in Soda Shop	Adam Carter
Whitey	David Tom
Pete	Johnny Moran
Woman	Jeanine Jackson
Thug	J. Patrick Lawlor
Police Chief Dan	James Keane

Don Knotts

A pair of modern day teens find themselves magically zapped into reruns of an old fifties television show, "Pleasantville," where they are shocked at the purity and lack of complexity in this black and white world. This marked the final film of actor J.T. Walsh who died on Feb. 27, 1998. This film received Oscar nominations for original dramatic score, costume design, and art direction.

Jeff Daniels, Joan Allen

Ian McKellen, Brad Renfro

Brad Renfro, David Schwimmer

APT PUPIL

(TRISTAR) Producers, Jane Hamsher, Don Murphy, Bryan Singer; Executive Producer, Tim Harbert; Director, Bryan Singer; Screenplay, Brandon Boyce; Based on the novella by Stephen King; Co-Producer, Thomas DeSanto; Photography, Newton Thomas Sigel; Designer, Richard Hoover; Music/Editor, John Ottman; Casting, Francine Maisler, Kathryn Eisenstein; a Phoenix Pictures presentation of a Bad Hat Harry production; Dolby; Super 35 Widescreen; Technicolor; Rated R; 111 minutes; October release

CAST

Kurt Dussander	Ian McKellen
Todd Bowden	Brad Renfro
Richard Bowden	Bruce Davison
Archie	Elias Koteas
Dan Richler	Joe Morton
Isaac Weiskopf	Jan Triska
Ben Kramer	Michael Byrne
Becky Trask	Heather McComb
Monica Bowden	Ann Dowd
Joey	Joshua Jackson
Edward French	David Schwimmer
Sociology Teacher	Mickey Cottrell
Nightmare Victim	Michael Reid MacKay
Victor Bowden	James Karen
Agnes Bowden	Marjorie Lovett
Gym Teacher	David Cooley
Teammate	Blake Anthony Tibbetts
Student	Katherine Malone
Secretary	Grace Sinden
Umpire	Anthony Moore
Paramedic	Kevin Spirtas

and Danna Dennis (Nurse), Michael Artura (Detective Getty), Donna Marie Brown (Mother), Mark Flythe (Darren), Warren Wilson (Newscaster), Jill Harris (Reporter), Norbert D. Singer, Mildred Singer (Hospital Administrators), Mary Ottman (Doctor)

When 16-year-old Todd Bowden discovers that a Nazi war criminal has been hiding in his town, he demands that the man tell him stories of the atrocities committed during the war in exchange for the boy's silence regarding his true identity.

©TriStar Pictures Inc.

Ann Dowd, Bruce Davison

Brad Renfro, Joshua Jackson

SOLDIER

(**WARNER BROS.**) Producer, Jerry Weintraub; Executive Producers, James G. Robinson, R.J. Louis, Susan Ekins; Director, Paul Anderson; Screenplay, David Webb Peoples; Co-Producer, Jeremy Bolt; Photography, David Tattersall; Designer, David L. Snyder; Editor, Martin Hunter; Music, Joel McNeely; Visual Effects Supervisor, Ed Jones; Costumes, Erica Edell Phillips; Casting, Mindy Marin; a Jerry Weintraub production in association with Impact Pictures, presented in association with Morgan Creek; Dolby; Panavision; Technicolor; Rated R; 98 minutes; October release

Kurt Russell

CAST

Todd	Kurt Russell
Caine 607	Jason Scott Lee
Mekum	Jason Isaacs
Sandra	Connie Nielsen
Mace	Sean Pertwee
Nathan	Jared Thorne, Taylor Thorne
Rubrick	Mark Bringelson
Church	Gary Busey
Sloan	K.K. Dodds
Riley	James Black
Goines	Mark De Alessandro
Romero	Vladimir Orlov

and Carsten Norgaard (Green), Duffy Gaver (Chelsey), Brenda Wehle (Hawkins), Michael Chiklis (Jimmy Pig), Elizabeth Dennehy (Jimmy Pig's Wife), Paul Dillon (Slade), Max Daniels (Red), Paul Sklar (Melton 249), Jesse E. Goins (Chester), Ashley Winston Nolan (Judith), Ellen Crawford (Ilona), Don Pulford (Singh), Conni Marie Brazelton (Eva), Kyle Sullivan (Tommy), Corbin Bleu (Johnny), Danny Tucker (Omar), Patrick Tyler (Bucky), Sara Paxton (Angie), Elizabeth Huett (Janice), Janelle Ginestra (Sarah), Sydney Berry (Ellen), Jesse Littlejohn (Will), Shawn Manley (Sean), Jimmy Baker (8 year old Todd), Alex Mandelberg (11 year old Straggler), Wyatt Russell (11 year old Todd), Celina Muehlbauer (Crossfire Little Girl), M.G. Mills (Doctor), Laura Gray, Chandra Jones (Nurses), Alexander Denk (Military Observer), Shawn Quinn (Aggressive Kid)

A galactic soldier is deemed obsolete and sent to a garbage outpost where he befriends a colony of settlers who realize they must defend their home when the newer fighting machines attack the planet.

Jason Scott Lee, Kurt Russell

©Warner Bros./Morgan Creek Prods.

Lenny Bruce

LENNY BRUCE: SWEAR TO TELL THE TRUTH

(**WHYADUCK/HBO**) Producer/Director/Screenplay, Robert B. Weide; Executive Producer, Sheila Nevins; Supervising Producer, Anthony Radziwill; Editors, Geof Bartz, Robert B. Weide; a Whyaduck Production in association with HBO Documentary Films; Narrator, Robert De Niro; Color; Black and white; Not rated; 94 minutes; October release. Documentary on controversial stand-up comedian Lenny Bruce, including interviews with Sally Marr, Honey Bruce, Kitty Bruce, Martin Garbus, Paul Krassner, Nat Hentoff.

This film received an Oscar nomination for feature documentary.

AMERICAN HISTORY X

Edward Furlong, Edward Norton

Elliott Gould

(NEW LINE CINEMA) Producer, John Morrissey; Executive Producers, Lawrence Turman, Steve Tisch, Kearie Peak, Bill Carraro; Director/Photography, Tony Kaye; Screenplay, David McKenna; Designer, Jon Gary Steele; Editors, Jerry Greenberg, Alan Heim; Co-Executive Producers, Michael De Luca, Brian Witten; Co-Producers, Jon Hess, David McKenna; Music, Anne Dudley; Costumes, Doug Hall; Casting, Valerie McCaffrey; a Turman-Morrissey Company production; Dolby; Deluxe color/black and white; Rated R; 118 minutes; October release

CAST

Derek Vinyard	Edward Norton
Danny Vinyard	Edward Furlong
Doris Vinyard	Beverly D'Angelo
Bob Sweeney	Avery Brooks
Cameron	Stacy Keach
Stacey	Fairuza Balk
Davina Vinyard	Jennifer Lien
Murray	Elliott Gould
Lamont	Guy Torry
Seth	Ethan Suplee
Dennis Vinyard	William Russ
Rasmussen	Joe Cortese
Little Henry	Jason Bose-Smith
Lawrence	Antonio David Lyons
Mitch McCormick	Alex Sol
Chris	Keram Malicki-Sanchez
Jason	Giuseppe Andrews
Lizzy	Michelle Christine White
Jerome	Jonathan Fowler, Jr.
Daryl Dawson	Chris Masterson
Huge Aryan	Nicholas R. Oleson
Curtis	Jordan Marder
McMahon	Paul Le Mat
Cop #2	Tommy L. Bellissimo
Kammi	Cherish Lee
Dr. Aguilar	Sam Vlahos
Ally	Tara Blanchard
Cassandra	Anne Lambton
Reporter	Steve Wolford
Desk Sergeant	Richard Noyce
Buddy #1	Danso Gordon
Randy	Jim Norton
Guard	David Basulto
Young Ally	Alexis Rose Coen
Lawrence's Partner	Kiant Elam
Student	Paul Hopkins
Random Skinhead	Keith Odett
Stocky Buddy	Paul Short
Basketball Player	Nigel Miguel

Enraged by his father's murder, Derek Vinyard becomes the leader of a local white supremecy group, a move that has a powerful effect on his idolizing young brother Danny. This film received an Oscar nomination for actor (Edward Norton).

©New Line Cinema Inc.

Guy Torry, Edward Norton

Avery Brooks, Edward Norton

Beverly D'Angelo, Edward Norton

Edward Furlong, Edward Norton

Stacy Keach

Edward Norton

Edward Norton, Fairuza Balk

Jennifer Lien, Beverly D'Angelo, Edward Norton, Edward Furlong

Edward Furlong

Holly Hunter, Danny DeVito

Danny DeVito

Holly Hunter

Queen Latifah

Danny DeVito, Holly Hunter

LIVING OUT LOUD

(NEW LINE CINEMA) Producers, Danny DeVito, Michael Shamberg, Stacey Sher; Director/Screenplay, Richard LaGravenese; Co-Producer, Eric McLeod; Photography, John Bailey; Designer, Nelson Coates; Editors, Jon Gregory, Lynzee Klingman; Costumes, Jeffrey Kurland; Music, George Fenton; Casting, Margery Simkin; a Jersey Films production; Dolby; Panavision; Technicolor; Rated R; 100 minutes; October release

Holly Hunter, Danny DeVito

CAST

Judith Nelson	Holly Hunter
Pat Francato	Danny DeVito
Liz Bailey	Queen Latifah
Bob Nelson	Martin Donovan
Philly	Richard Schiff
The Kisser	Elias Koteas
Mary	Suzanne Shepherd
Donna	Mariangela Pino
The Masseur	Eddie Cibrian
Gary	Clark Anderson
Crying Woman	Ellen McElduff
Angry Boyfriend	Ivan Kronenfeld
Santi's Men	Fil Formicola, Nick Sandow
Fanny, Pat's Wife	Jenette Goldstein
Lisa's Nurse	Lin Shaye
Sid	John F. Donohue
Johnny	Fred Scialla
Mo	Anthony Russell
Lou	Sy Sher
Len	Sal Jenco
Lisa	Gina Philips
Diner	Kate McGregor-Stewart
Anchorman Voice-Over	Mitch Greenberg
Bob's Wife	Tamlyn Tomita
Fifth Avenue Parents	Henry Woronicz, Taylor Leigh
Jasper's House Band	Mervyn Warren (Piano), Reggie Hamilton (Bass)
	Peter Michael Escovedo (Drums)
	Mark Schulz (Guitar), Michael James (Guitar, Vocals)
	Gerald Albright (Alto Saxophone)
	Plas Johnson (Baritone Saxophone)
	Justo Almario (Tenor Saxophone)
	Vincent Trombetta Jr. (Tenor Saxophone)
Andy	Matthew McKane
Heckled Singer	Robin McDonald
Jasper's Waitress	Yolanda Snowball
Woman with Makeup	Deborah Geffner
Teenage Judith	Rachael Leigh Cook
Teenage Lover	Christian Hill
Formal Dress Man	Ed Fry
Formal Dress Woman	Judith Regan
Late Teenager	Sean Dooley

and Terry Rhoads (Across Hall Man), Susan Reno (Across Hall Woman), Claudia Shear (Drunken Fan), Mike G. Moyer (Jeweler), Sybil Azur, Carmit Bachar, Monique Chambers, Donielle Artese, Aisha Dubone, Shawnette Heard, Tanika Ray, Laurie Sposit, Adrian Young (Confessional Dancers), Roger Nehls, Mary Schmidtberger (Married Couple in Lawyer's Office), Lou Richards (Judith's Lawyer), Tom Howard (Bob's Lawyer), Michael Clair Miller (Couple's Lawyer), Willie Garson (Man in Elevator), Ellen Buckley (Pat & Judith's Waitress), Laura Salvato (Neo-Natal AIDS Volunteer), Hattie Winston (Hospital Nurse), Mario Piccirillo (Cousin Louie), Carole Ruggieri (Italian Girlfriend)

Holly Hunter

Judith Nelson, the wife of a rich New York doctor, finds she must start life anew after her husband dumps her for a younger woman.

©New Line Cinema

Queen Latifah

James Woods, Daniel Baldwin

Sheryl Lee

Tim Guinee

Thomas Ian Griffith

©Columbia Pictures Industries, Inc.

VAMPIRES

(COLUMBIA) Producer, Sandy King; Executive Producer, Barr Potter; Director/Music, John Carpenter; Screenplay/Co-Producer, Don Jakoby; Based on the novel *Vampire$* by John Steakley; Photography, Gary B. Kibbe; Designer, Thomas A. Walsh; Editor, Edward A. Warschilka; Costumes, Robin Michel Bush; Special Make-up Effects, Robert Kurtzman, Gregory Nicotero, Howard Berger; Special Effects Coordinator, Darrell D. Pritchett; Casting, Reuben Cannon, Eddie Dunlop; a Largo Entertainment presentation of a Storm King production; Dolby; Panavision; Fotokem color; Rated R; 107 minutes; October release

CAST

Jack Crow ....James Woods
Montoya ....Daniel Baldwin
Katrina ....Sheryl Lee
Valek...Thomas Ian Griffith
Cardinal Alba...Maximilian Schell
Father Adam Guiteau ....Tim Guinee
Catlin ....Mark Boone, Junior
Father Giovanni..Gregory Sierra
David Deyo ....Cary-Hiroyuki Tagawa
Ortega ....Tommy Rosales
Anthony...Henry Kingi
Bambi ....David Rowden
Davis ....Clarke Coleman
and Mark Sivertsen (Highway Patrolman), John Furlong (Father Molina), Angelina Calderon Torres (Cleaning Lady), Jimmy Ortega, Gilbert Rosales, Laura Cordova, Danielle Burgio (Vampires), Troy Robinson, Anita Hart, John Casino, Chad Stahelski, Steve Blalock, Marjean Holden, Cris Thomas Palomino (Masters), Julia McFerrin, Lori Dillen (Hookers), Jake Walker (County Sheriff), Michael Huddleston (Motel Owner), Todd Anderson (Deputy Sheriff), Steven Hartley (Clerk), Dennis E. Garber (Limousine Driver), Robert L. Bush (TV News Anchor), Frank Darabont (Man with Buick), Mona Garcia, Candice Kirkiles, Neva Lucero, Helen Moreno, Janice Richmond, Juanita Romano, Ann Romero, Elisa Valdez, April Winters (Hookers)

Vampire slayer Jack Crow and his team are ambushed by 600-year-old vampire Valek, causing the surviving members to take flight along with a prostitute who has been bitten but not yet "changed over."

THE SIEGE

(20TH CENTURY FOX) Producers, Lynda Obst, Edward Zwick; Executive Producer, Peter Schindler; Director, Edward Zwick; Screenplay, Lawrence Wright, Menno Meyjes, Edward Zwick; Story, Lawrence Wright; Photography, Roger Deakins; Designer, Lilly Kilvert; Editor, Steven Rosenblum; Music, Graeme Revell; Costumes, Ann Roth; Associate Producer, Robin Budd; Casting, Mary Goldberg, Mary Colquhoun; a Lynda Obst production; Dolby; Super 35 Widescreen; Deluxe color; Rated R; 116 minutes; November release

Annette Bening, Denzel Washington

CAST

Anthony Hubbard	Denzel Washington
Elise Kraft (Sharon Bridger)	Annette Bening
General William Devereaux	Bruce Willis
Frank Haddad	Tony Shalhoub
Samir Nazhde	Sami Bouajila
Sheik Ahmed Bin Talal	Ahmed Ben Larby
Muezzin	Mosleh Mohamed
Tina Osu	Liana Pai
Mike Johanssen	Mark Valley
Fred Darius	Jack Gwaltney
Danny Sussman	David Proval
Floyd Rose	Lance Reddick

and Jeremy Knaster (INS Official), William Hill (INS Uniform), Aasif Mandvi (Khalil Saleh), Frank DiElsi (Officer Williams), Wood Harris (Officer Henderson), Ellen Bethea (Anita), David Costabile (Fingerprint Expert), Glenn Kessler (Fiber Expert), Jeffrey Allan Waid (Video Agent), Tom McDermott (Phone Bank Agent), Sherry Ham-Bernard (Hub's Secretary), Joseph Hodge (Landlord), Joey Naber (Rashad), Said Faraj (Yousuf), Alex Dodd (Ali), Jacqueline Antaramian (Najiba Haddad), Helmi Kassim (Frank Haddad, Jr.), Ghoulam R. Rasoully (Frank Jr.'s Teacher), Joseph Badalucco, Jr. (EMT), Diana Naftal (Injured Woman), Insben Shenkman (Kaplan), A.A. Barton Tinapp (Mayoral), Neal Jones (NYPD Representative), Donna Hanover (District Attorney), Peter Schindler (Johnson, FAA), Hany Kamal (Arab Spokesman), Chip Zien (Chief of Staff), Dakin Matthews (Senator Wright), John Rothman (Congressman Marshall), John Henry Cox (Speaker of the House), E. Katherine Kerr (Attorney General), Jimmie Ray Weeks (Army General), Will Lyman (FBI Director), Ray Godshall (CIA Director), Victor Slezak (Colonel Hardwicke), Chris Messina (Corporal), Gilbert Rosales (Mechanic), Amro Salama (Tariq Husseini), Jim Shankman (ACLU Lawyer), Matt Servitto, Jourdan Fremin (Journalist), Anjua Warfield (March Organizer), Susie Essman (Protest Speaker), Rory J. Aylward (Lieutenant), Jeff Beatty (FBI Agent Undercover), Graham J. Larson (FBI Agent), Arianna Huffington, Robert Scheer, Matt MIller (Capitol Week Pundits), John F. Beard, Stan Brooks, Alex Chadwick, Epi Colon, Judy de Angelis, Luis Jimenez, Sean Hannity, Ronald Kuby, Daniel Schorr, Curtis Sliwa, Susan Stamberg, Mary Alice Williams (Newscasters)

After a group of Palestinian terrorists blow up a city bus full of hostages, FBI agent Anthony Hubbard is put on the case until further bombings force the President to declare a state of emergency and receive help from the military.

©Twentieth Century Fox

Bruce Willis

Tony Shalhoub, Denzel Washington

GODS AND MONSTERS

(LIONS GATE) Producers, Paul Colichman, Gregg Fienberg, Mark R. Harris; Executive Producers, Clive Barker, Stephen P. Jarchow; Co-Executive Producers, Valorie Massalas, Sam Irvin, Spencer Proffer; Director/Screenplay, Bill Condon; Based on the novel *Father of Frankenstein* by Christopher Bram; Line Producers, John Schouweiler, Lisa Levy; Photography, Stephen M. Katz; Designer, Richard Sherman; Costumes, Bruce Finlayson; Music, Carter Burwell; Editor, Virginia Katz; Casting, Valorie Massalas; a Showtime and Flashpoint presentation of a BBC Films and Regent Entertainment production; Dolby; Super 35 Widescreen; Color; Rated R; 105 minutes; November release

CAST

James Whale	Ian McKellen
Clayton Boone	Brendan Fraser
Hanna	Lynn Redgrave
Betty	Lolita Davidovich
Harry	Kevin J. O'Connor
David Lewis	David Dukes
Young Whale	Brandon Kleyla
Sarah Whale	Pamela Salem
William Whale	Michael O'Hagan
Edmund Kay	Jack Plotnick
Dwight	Mark Kiely
Dr. Payne	David Millbern
Kid Saylor	John Gatins
Young Karloff	Amir Aboulela
Elsa Lanchester	Rosalind Ayres
Jack Pierce	James Lecesne
Colin Clive	Matt McKenzie
George Cukor	Martin Ferrero
Princess Margaret	Cornelia Hayes O'Herlihy
Elder Karloff	Jack Betts
Ernest Thesiger	Arthur Dignam
Leonard Barnett	Todd Babcock
Assistant Director	Jesse Long
Camera Assistant	Owen Masterson
Librarian	Lisa Vastine
James Whale (25)	Kent George
Photographer	David Fabrizio
Michael Boone	Jesse James
Dana Boone	Lisa Darr
Sound Man	Paul Michael Sandberg
Young Man	Judson Mills
Liz Taylor	Marlon Braccia

In 1957, in the final days of his life, retired Hollywood director James Whale, tormented by images from his past and the effects of a mildly debilitating stroke, forms an unlikely friendship with Clayton Boone, a handsome young man employed as his gardener. 1998 Academy Award-winner for Best Screenplay Adaptation. This film received additional nominations for actor (Ian McKellen) and supporting actress (Lynn Redgrave).

©Lions Gate Films

Ian McKellen, Brendan Fraser

Brendan Fraser, Lynn Redgrave

Ian McKellen, Rosalind Ayres

Jack Betts, Ian McKellen, Rosalind Ayres

Brendan Fraser

Ian McKellen, Brendan Fraser

Brendan Fraser, Ian McKellen

Ewan McGregor

Toni Collette, Jonathan Rhys Meyers

Ewan McGregor, Jonathan Rhys Meyers

Jonathan Rhys Meyers

Christian Bale

Eddie Izzard

VELVET GOLDMINE

Christian Bale

(MIRAMAX) Producer, Christine Vachon; Executive Producers, Scott Meek, Michael Stipe, Sandy Stern; Co-Executive Producers, Chris J. Ball, William Tyrer; Director/Screenplay, Todd Haynes; Story, Todd Haynes, James Lyons; Co-Producer, Olivia Stewart; Photography, Maryse Alberti; Designer, Christopher Hobbs; Costumes, Sandy Powell; Editor, James Lyons; Hair and Makeup Designer, Peter King; Music, Carter Burwell; Music Supervisor, Randall Poster; Casting, Susie Figgis, Laura Rosenthal; a Zenith Productions/Killer Films production in association with Single Cell Pictures for Newmarket Capital Group, Goldwyn Films, Miramax Films, Film Four and Zenith; U.S.-British; Dolby; Color; Rated R; 120 minutes; November release

CAST

Curt Wild	Ewan McGregor
Brian Slade	Jonathan Rhys Meyers
Mandy Slade	Toni Collette
Arthur Stuart	Christian Bale
Jerry Divine	Eddie Izzard
Shannon	Emily Woof
Cecil	Michael Feast
Narrator	Janet McTeer
Wilde Housemaid	Maraid McKinley
Oscar Wilde (8)	Luke Morgan Oliver
Jack Fairy (7)	Osheen Jones
Jack Fairy	Micko Westmoreland
BBC Reporter	Damian Suchet
Kissing Sailor	Danny Nutt
Young Man	Wash Westmoreland
Lou	Don Fellows
Mary	Ganiat Kasumu
Murray	Ray Shell
Tommy Stone	Alastair Cumming
Girl on Subway	Zoe Boyce
Mr. Stuart	Jim Whelan
Mrs. Stuart	Sylvia Grant
Manchester Teacher	Tim Hans
Arthur's Brother	Ryan Pope
Boys in Record Shop	Stuart Callaghan, James Francis
Brian Slade (7)	Callum Hamilton
Pantomime Dame	Lindsay Kemp
Pianist	Carlos Miranda
Mod Girlfriend	Emma Handy
Mimosa	Matthew Glamour
Curt Wild (13)	Daniel Adams
Bartender	Brian Torfeh
Cooper	Joe Beattie
Angel	Sarah Cawood
Freddi	David Hoyle
Micky	Winston Austin
Cecil's Friends	Ivan Cartwright, Peter King
Rodney	Justin Salinger
Middle Age Man	Roger Alborough
30's Style Singer	Peter Bradley, Jr.
Reporters	Jonathan Cullen, William Key
U.S. Reporters	Vincent Marzello, Corey Skaggs, Nathan Osgood
Teenage Girl	Nadia Williams

and Flaming Creatures: Brian Molko (Malcolm), Anthony Langdon (Ray), Xaf (Pearl), Steve Hewitt (Billy); The Venus in Furs: Guy Leverton (Trevor), Vinney Reck (Reg), Keith-Lee Castle (Harley); The Wylde Rattz: Alan Fordham (Bass Guitar), Jono McGrath (Lead Guitar), Perry Clayton (Drummer); Polly Small's Band: Donna Matthews (Polly Small), Ritz (Lead Guitar), Stefan Olsday (Bass Guitar), Trevor Sharpe (Drummer)

In 1984 reporter Arthur Stuart is assigned to write a story on what happened to early seventies glam rock sensation Brian Slade, opening up a wealth of memories of when Arthur was a intrigued by the sexual freedom the movement promoted. This film received an Oscar nomination for costume design.

Jonathan Rhys Meyers

Toni Collette

Henry Winkler, Adam Sandler

Adam Sandler

Fairuza Balk, Adam Sandler

THE WATERBOY

(TOUCHSTONE) Producers, Robert Simonds, Jack Giarraputo; Director, Frank Coraci; Screenplay, Tim Herlihy, Adam Sandler; Co-Producer, Ira Shuman; Photography, Steven Bernstein; Designer, Perry Andelin Blake; Editor, Tom Lewis; Costumes, Tom Bronson; Music, Alan Pasqua; Casting, Roger Mussenden; Football Coordinator, Allan Graf; Distributed by Buena Vista Pictures; Dolby; Technicolor; Rated PG-13; 88 minutes; November release

CAST

Bobby Boucher	Adam Sandler
Mama Boucher	Kathy Bates
Coach Klein	Henry Winkler
Vicki Vallencourt	Fairuza Balk
Red Beaulieu	Jerry Reed
Derek Wallace	Larry Gilliard, Jr.
Farmer Fran	Blake Clark
Gee Grenouille	Peter Dante
Lyle Robideaux	Jonathan Loughran
Casey Bugge	Al Whiting
Paco	Clint Howard
Walter	Allen Covert
Townie	Rob Schneider
Greg Meaney	Todd Holland
Professor	Robert Kokol
Roberto	Frank Coraci
Rita	Jennfire Bini Taylor
West Mississippi Lineman	James Bates
Drunk Cheerleader	Kelly Hare
Red's Watergirl	Dawn Birch

and Steve Raulerson (Sheriff Loughran), Chris Mugglebee (Sheriff Jack), Brett Rice (Laski), John Farley (Tony Dodd), Kevin Farley (Jim Simonds), Lee Corso, Bill Cowher, Dan Fouts, Chris Fowler, Jimmy Johnson, Brent Musburger, Dan Patrick, Lynn Swann, Lawrence Taylor (Themselves), Paul "The Giant" Wight (Captain Insano), Jamie Williams (Young Bobby), Marc Kittay (Youngest Bobby), Matt Baylis (Student), Jack Carroll (Bible College Coach), Tom Nowicki (Community College Coach), Ric Swezey (Cheerleader), Matthew Lussier (Redneck), Haven Gaston (Tina), Michael Hold (Central Kentucky Quarterback), Kevin Reid (West Mississippi Quarterback), Mattie Wolf (Cajun Lady), Phyllis Alia (Assistant), Dave Wagner (Announcer), Tina Barr (Cheerleader), Michael Giarraputo (Bourbon Bowl Statistician), Marty Eli Schwartz (Moderator)

Bobby Boucher, a dim-witted, mother-dominated, 31-year-old waterboy, gets assigned to a washed-up football coach who realizes that Bobby has devestating abiltilies as a tackler when his inner rage is unleashed.

©Touchstone Pictures

Kathy Bates, Henry Winkler

Claire Forlani, Brad Pitt

Claire Forlani, Anthony Hopkins

©Universal City Studios

MEET JOE BLACK

(UNIVERSAL) Producer/Director, Martin Brest; Screenplay, Ron Osborn, Jeff Reno, Kevin Wade, Bo Goldman; Suggested by the play *Death Takes a Holiday* by Alberto Casella, as adapted into a film by Maxwell Anderson, Gladys Lehman, Walter Ferris; Executive Producer, Ronald L. Schwary; Photography, Emmanuel Lubezki; Designer, Dante Ferretti; Editors, Joe Hutshing, Michael Tronick; Co-Producer, David Wally; Music, Thomas Newman; Costumes, Aude Bronson-Howard, David C. Robinson; Casting, Juliet Taylor, Ellen Lewis; a City Lights Films production; Dolby; Deluxe color; Rated PG-13; 180 minutes; November release

CAST

Anthony Hopkins, Brad Pitt

Joe Black/Young Man in Coffee Shop	Brad Pitt
William Parrish	Anthony Hopkins
Susan Parrish	Claire Forlani
Drew	Jake Weber
Allison	Marcia Gay Harden
Quince	Jeffrey Tambor
Eddie Sloane	David S. Howard
Jamaican Woman	Lois Kelly-Miller
Jamaican Woman's Daughter	Jahnni St. John
Butler	Richard Clarke
Lillian	Marylouise Burke
Jennifer	Diane Kagan
Helen	June Squibb
Construction Foreman	Gene Canfield
Florist	Suzanne Hevner
Electrician	Steve Coats
Madeline	Madeline N. Balmaceda
Drew's Secretary	Julie Lund

and Kay Gaffney, Anthony Kane, Joe H. Lamb, Robert C. Lee, Jim McNickle, Hardy Phippen, Jr. (Boardmembers), Stephen Adly-Guirgis (Hospital Receptionist), Leo Marks (Party Waiter), Michelle Youell, Gene Leverone (Party Guests)

On the eve of his sixtieth birthday, millionaire William Parrish, a decent man who has led a charmed life, is visited by a mysterious young man who informs him that he is the angel of death, come to take Parrish to the afterlife. Previous version was Death Takes a Holiday (Paramount, 1934) starring Fredric March and Evelyn Venable.

Jeffrey Tambor, Marcia Gay Harden

I'LL BE HOME FOR CHRISTMAS

(WALT DISNEY PICTURES) Producers, David Hoberman, Tracey Trench; Executive Producer, Robin French; Director, Arlene Sanford; Screenplay, Harris Goldberg, Tom Nursall; Story, Michael Allin; Co-Producer, Justis Greene; Photography, Hiro Narita; Designer, Cynthia Charette; Editor, Anita Brandt-Burgoyne; Costumes, Maya Mani; Music, John Debney; Casting, Roger Mussenden, Karen Church; a Mandeville Films production; Dolby; Technicolor; Rated PG; 86 minutes; November release

CAST

Jake Wilkinson	Jonathan Taylor Thomas
Allie	Jessica Biel
Eddie	Adam Lavorgna
Jake's Dad	Gary Cole
Carolyn	Eve Gordon
Tracey	Lauren Maltby
Nolan Briggs	Andrew Lauer
Max	Sean O'Bryan
Marjorie	Lesley Boone
"Tom Tom Girl" Mary	Amzie Strickland
"Tom Tom Girl" Darlene	Natalie Barish
Esteban	Mark De La Cruz
"Tom Tom Girl" Gloria	Kathleen Freeman
Gabby	Jack Kenny
"Tom Tom Girl" Mama	Celia Kushner

and Blair Slater (Ian), P.J. Prinslow (The Brandt-Man), James Sherry (The Murph-Man), Kevin Hansen (The Ken-Man), Alexandra Mitchell (Little Girl in Hospital), Eric Pospisil (Little Boy at Bus Station), Cathy Weseluck (Wendy Richards), Peter Kelamis (Clyde), Betty Linde (Older Lady on the Bus), Awaovieyi Agie (Service Man), Brendan Beiser (Bellhop), Graeme Kingston (Pizza Eating Santa), Ian Robison (Mayor Wilson), Ernie Jackson (Kenyan Santa), Kurt Max Runte (Taxi Driver), Nicole Oliver (Ticket Agent), Tasha Simms (Parade Manager), Dimitry Chepovetsky (Angel), Dolores Drake (Fraulein Maid), Chris Willes (Race Official #1), Nick Misura (Groundskeeper)

Stranded in the California desert and glued into a Santa Claus suit by a vengeful college football team, Jake Wilkinson must find a way to get to New York by Christmas Eve and catch up with his girl who is taking a ride with another guy from school.

©Disney Enterprises, Inc.

Jennifer Love Hewitt, Brandy

I STILL KNOW WHAT YOU DID LAST SUMMER

(COLUMBIA) Producers, Neal H. Moritz, Erik Feig, Stokely Chaffin, William S. Beasley; Director, Danny Cannon; Screenplay, Trey Callaway; Photography, Vernon Layton; Designer, Doug Kraner; Editor, Peck Prior; Costumes, Dan Lester; Music, John Frizzell; Casting, Jackie Burch; a Neal H. Moritz production, presented in association with Mandalay Entertainment; Dolby; Panavision; Color; Rated R; 101 minutes; November release

CAST

Julie James	Jennifer Love Hewitt
Ray Bronson	Freddie Prinze, Jr.
Karla Wilson	Brandy
Tyrell	Mekhi Phifer
Ben Willis/Fisherman	Muse Watson
Estes	Bill Cobbs
Will Benson	Matthew Settle
Mr. Brooks	Jeffrey Combs
Nancy	Jennifer Esposito
Dave	John Hawkes
Olga	Ellerine!

and Benjamin Brown (Darick the Dockhand), Red West (Paulsen), Michael P. Byrne (Thurston), Michael Bryan French (Doctor), Dee Ann Helsel (Nurse), John Harrington (Todd), Mark Boone, Jr. (Pawn Shop Owner), Dan Priest (Professor), Sylvia Short (Old Woman)

Julie James, still tormented by having killed the evil fisherman who had been terrorizing her and her friends, takes a vacation with some of her college friends only to find herself running for her life again. Sequel to the 1997 Columbia film I Know What You Did Last Summer with Hewitt, Prinze and Watson repeating their roles.

Jessica Biel, Jonathan Taylor Thomas

THE RUGRATS MOVIE

(PARAMOUNT) Producers, Arlene Klasky, Gabor Csupo; Executive Producers, Albie Hecht, Debby Beece; Directors, Norton Virgien, Igor Kovalyov; Screenplay, David N. Weiss, J. David Stem; Co-Producers, Hal Waite, Eryk Casemiro, Julia Pistor; Supervising Editor, John Bryant; Music, Mark Mothersbaugh; a Nickelodeon Movies presentation of a Klasky/Csupo production; Color; Rated G; 79 minutes; November release

VOICE CAST

Tommy Pickles	E.G. Daily
Chuckie Finster	Christine Cavanaugh
Philip DeVille/Lillian DeVille/Betty DeVille	Kath Soucie
Didi Pickles	Melanie Chartoff
Howard DeVille	Phil Proctor
Susie Carmichael	Cree Summer
Grandpa Boris/Drew Pickles	Michael Bell
Charlotte Pickles	Tress MacNeille
Stu Pickles	Jack Riley
Reptar Wagon	Busta Rhymes
Grandpa Lou Pickles	Joe Alaskey
Angelica Pickles	Cheryl Chase
Dylan Pickles	Tara Charendoff
Rex Pester	Tim Curry
Ranger Margaret	Whoopi Goldberg
Ranger Frank	David Spade
Nurse	Edie McClurg
Dr. Lucy Carmichael	Hattie Winston

and Abe Benrubi (Serge), Charles Adler (United Express Driver), Roger Clinton (Air Crewman), Mary Gross, Andrea Martin (Aunt Miriam), Margaret Cho (Lt. Klann), Laurie Anderson, Beck, B-Real, Jakob Dylan, Phife, Gordon Gano, Iggy Pop, Lenny Kravitz, Lisa Loeb, Lou Rawls, Patti Smith, Dawn Robinson, Fred Sneider, Kate Pierson, Cindy Wilson (Newborn Babies), Steve Zirnkilton, Robin Groth, Angel Harper (Reporters)

The arrival of a new baby in the Pickles family prompts his brother Tommy and his friends to load the kid into Stu's "Reptar Wagon" and take off on an adventure to return the tot to the hospital. Based on the Nickelodeon series which premiered in 1991.

©Paramount Pictures/Viacom International

Stu Pickles, Tommy Pickles, Didi Pickles, Dil Pickles

Lil DeVille, Chuckie Finster, Tommy Pickles, Phil DeVille

Spike, Lil DeVille, Stu Pickles, Tommy Pickles, Didi Pickles, Chuckie Finster, Phil DeVille, Angelica Pickles

Will Smith, Gene Hackman

Barry Pepper, Ian Hart, Jake Busey

ENEMY OF THE STATE

(TOUCHSTONE) Producer, Jerry Bruckheimer; Executive Producers, Chad Oman, James W. Skotchdopole, Andrew Z. Davis; Director, Tony Scott; Screenplay, David Marconi; Photography, Dan Mindel; Designer, Benjamin Fernandez; Editor, Chris Lebenzon; Costumes, Marlene Stewart; Music, Trevor Rabin, Harry Gregson-Williams; Casting, Victoria Thomas; a Don Simpson/Jerry Bruckheimer production in association with Scott Free productions; Dolby; Panavision; Technicolor; Rated R; 127 minutes; November release

CAST

Robert Clayton Dean	Will Smith
Brill	Gene Hackman
Thomas Bryan Reynolds	Jon Voight
Rachel Banks	Lisa Bonet
Carla Dean	Regina King
Congressman Albert	Stuart Wilson
Christa Hawkins	Laura Cayouette
Hicks	Loren Dean
Pratt	Barry Pepper
Bingham	Ian Hart
Krug	Jake Busey
Jones	Scott Caan
Zavitz	Jason Lee
"Brill"	Gabriel Byrne
Jerry Miller	James Le Gros
Shaffer	Dan Butler
Fiedler	Jack Black
Jamie	Jamie Kennedy
Van	Bodhi Pine Elfman
Davis	Jacob Chambers
Martha	Alexandra Balahoutis
Emily Reynolds	Anna Gunn
Eric Dean	Jascha Washington
Marie the Nanny	Rebecca Silva
Dylan	Bobby Borriello
Mike (Law Firm)	Carl Mergenthaler
Gas Station Cashier	Mattias Kraemer
Young Worker	Lillo Brancato
Older Worker #1	John Capodice
Vic (Old Mobster)	Vic Manni
Cook	T.R. Richards
Ruby's Sales Clerk	Ivana Milavich
Accident Bystander	Patsy Grady Abrams
Reynold's Nanny	Beatriz Mayoral
Reynold's Daughter	Kasey Lynn Quinn

and Jason Robards (Congressman Hammersly), Seth Green (Selby), Philip Baker Hall (Silverberg), Brian Markinson (Brian), Tom Sizemore (Pintero), Elizabeth Berman (Ruthie), Donna Scott (Jenny), Allison Sie (Hotel Desk Clerk), Mike Andolini (Sal), Arthur Nascarella (Frankie), Grant Heslov (Lenny), John Cenatiempo (Young Mobster #1), Joyce Flick Wendl (Waitress), Frank Medrano (Bartender), Dennis S. Fahey (Cop with Ambulance), Albert Wong (Mr. Wu), Christopher B. Lawrence (Paramedic), John Haynes Walker, Joe Patrick Kelly (Firemen), Lennox Brown (Tunnel Maintenance Worker), Martin Bosworth (Bike Messenger), Nancy Yee (Mrs. Wu), Troy Anthony Cephers (ANA Hotel Security), Carlos Gomez (FBI Agents), Arnie Alpert (Robert Gersicoff), Greg Collins (FBI Supervisor), Doug Roberts (Hijacked Car Driver), Larry King, Chris Holt (Themselves), Warren Olney, Penny Griego (TV Anchors), Rhonda Overby, Mandy Kriss, Lillie Shaw Hamer, Brenna McDonough (Field Reporters), Eric Keung, David Han (Mambo Kitchen Workers), Noel Werking, Sam De Crispino (Reporters), Wayne A. Larrivey (Doorman), Callison Slater, Colin Brodie (Children), Daniel Cano (Hallway Lawyer), Joy Erhlich (Mom in Diner), Eric Olson, Thomas Troy, Adam Karkowsky (Aides), Steve Uhrig (Electronic Store Employee), Robyn Killian, Laura Eizenia, Angelica Pamintuan, Vené Arcoraci, Charlie Curtis (Models), Raichle Watt (Becky), Michael J. Walker (Union Official), Jackilynn Ward (Pintero's Sister), Jason Welch, Joshua Ward (Pintero Kids), Pete Sutton (Dean House Cop), Thomas M. Quinn (Tunnel Technician), Robert O'Rourke, John Allendorfer, Henry Sandler (FBI Observers)

Attorney Robert Clayton Dean's life is suddenly at stake after an old friend surreptitiously slips an incriminating tape to him containing evidence that a U.S. congressman was murdered.

©Touchstone Pictures/Jerry Bruckheimer, Inc.

Will Smith, Gabriel Byrne

Will Smith

Lisa Bonet, Will Smith

Will Smith, Jascha Washington, Regina King

Loren Dean, Jon Voight, Jack Black

Will Smith, Jason Lee

Kenneth Branagh, Charlize Theron, Anthony Mason

Kenneth Branagh, Winona Ryder

Sam Rockwell, Leonardo DiCaprio, Kenneth Branagh

Judy Davis, Aida Turturro

Kenneth Branagh, Joe Mantegna, Judy Davis

CELEBRITY

Melanie Griffith, Kenneth Branagh

(MIRAMAX) Producer, Jean Doumanian; Executive Producer, J.E. Beaucaire; Director/Screenplay, Woody Allen; Co-Executive Producers, Jack Rollins, Charles H. Joffe, Letty Aronson; Co-Producer, Richard Brick; Photography, Sven Nykvist; Designer, Santo Loquasto; Editor, Susan E. Morse; Costumes, Suzy Benzinger; Casting, Juliet Taylor, Laura Rosenthal; a Sweetland Films presentation of a Jean Doumanian production; Dolby; Black and white; Rated R; 114 minutes; November release

CAST

David	Hank Azaria
Lee Simon	Kenneth Branagh
Robin Simon	Judy Davis
Brandon Darrow	Leonardo DiCaprio
Nicole Oliver	Melanie Griffith
Bonnie	Famke Janssen
Dr. Lupus	Michael Lerner
Tony Gardella	Joe Mantegna
Hooker	Bebe Neuwirth
Nola	Winona Ryder
Supermodel	Charlize Theron

and Greg Mottola (Director), Jeff Mazzola (Assistant Director), Dick Mingalone (Camera Operator), Vladimir Bibic (Director of Photography), Francisco Quidjada (Erno Deluca), Aleska Palladino (Production Assistant), Dan Moran (Jackhammer Operator), Pete Castellotti (Sound Recordist), A. Lee Morris (Second Assistant Cameraperson), Douglas McGrath (Bill Gaines), Maurice Sonnenberg (Dalton Freed), Crag Ulmschneider (Production Assistant Daniel), Mina Bern (Elderly Homeowner), Janet Marlow (Singing Nun), Tommie Baxter (Second Nun), Kathleen Doyle, Arthur Berwick, Jodi Long (Father Gladen's Fans), John Carter (Father Gladen) Monique Fowler (Robin's Friend Jan), Mary Louise Burke, Peter Boyden, Peter McRobbie, Maureen McNamara (Father Gladden's Fans on Porch), Mary Catherine Wright (Pious Diner), J.K. Simmons (Souvenir Hawker), Dylan Baker (Priest at Catholic Retreat), Melinda Eng (Fashion Designer), Isaac Mizrahi (Bruce Bishop), Alma Cuervo, Roshumba Williams (Bruce Bishop's Admirers), Polly Adams, Brian McConnachie (Exercise Tape Fans), Irina Pantaeva, Mark Vanderloo, Frederique Van Der Wal (Friends of Supermodel), Michael Moon Band (El Flamingo Band), Anthony Mason, Mary Jo Buttafuoco, Joey Buttafuoco, Donald Trump (Themselves), Daisy Prince (Waiting Room Nurse), Tina Sloan, Dayle Haddon, Bill Gerber (Waiting Room Patients), Julie Halston (Patient with Jowls), Renee Lippin (Second Examining Room Patient), Kate Burton (Robin's Friend Cheryl), Reuben Jackson (Examining Room Patient), Debra Messing (Cameraperson at Lupus Office), Carmen Dell Orefice (TV Reporter at Lupus Office), Andre Gregory (John Papadakis), Skip Rose, Alicia Meer (Couple at Beach); Glenwood High Alumni: Becky Ann Baker (Doris), Michael Kell (Nat), Steve Mellor (Eddie), Gerry Becker (Jay Tepper), Ileen Getz (Reunion Announcer), Robert Cuccioli (Monroe Gordon), Larry Pine (Philip Datloff); Surinder Khosla (V.J. Rajnipal), Marian Seldes (Datloff Party Guest), Frederick Rolf (Book Reviewer), David Margulies (Counselor Adelman), Ramsey Faragallah (TV Program Director), William Addy, Patrick McCarthy (Klansmen), Bernard K. Addison (Minister Polynice), Mary Schmidberger, Sarah Buff (TV Production Assistants), Heather Marni (Teenage Obese Acrobat), Bruno Gioiello, Sean Daloise, Matthew Sweeney (Skinheads), Kyle Kulish (Overweight Achiever), Tony Sirico (Lou DeMarco), Kenneth Edelson (Rabbi Kaufman), Sam Gray (Tony's Father), Marilyn Raphael (Tony's Mother), Antoinette Schwartzberg (Tony's Grandma), Patti D'Arbanville (Iris), Frank Pellegrino (Frankie), Gabriel Millman (Ricky), Adam Sietz (Vince), Gretchen Mol (Vicky), Michael Crecco, Neal Arluck, Timothy Jerome, Joseph Tudisco (Hotel Clerks), Jim Moody, Robert Torres (Security Guards), Steven Randazzo, John Costelloe (Cops at Hotel), Adrian Grenier, Sam Rockwell, John Doumanian (Darrow Entourage), Lorri Bagley (Chekhov-Style Writer), Richard Mawe, Ted Neustadt, Bruce Jay Friedman, Erica Jong, Ned Eisenberg, Clebert Ford (Elaine's Book Party Guests), Ralph Pope (Comic's Agent), Rick Mowat, Tony Darrow, Victor Colicchio, Robert Cividanes (Moving Men in Loft), Donegal Fitzgerald (Moving Man on Street), Leslie Shenkel ("Manhattan Moods" Asst. Director), Donna Hanover ("Manhattan Moods" Anchor Woman), Allison Janney (Evelyn Isaacs), Howard Erskine (Senator Paley), Celia Weston (Dee Bartholomew), Wood Harris (Al Swayze), Ray Cohen (Pianist at Wedding), Angel Caban (Limo Driver), Aida Turturro (Psychic), Ingrid Rogers (Off-Off Broadway Actress), Jeffrey Wright (Off-Off Broadway Director), Karen Duffy (TV Reporter at Premiere), Brian McCormack (Phil), Gigi Williams (Fan of Robin Simon)

Kenneth Branagh, Leonardo DiCaprio, Gretchen Mol, Adrian Grenier

Recently divorced Lee and Robin Simon set out to establish new lives for themselves, as he becomes addicted to the superficial world of fame and she meets a television executive whom she hopes will give her stability.

Bebe Neuwirth, Judy Davis

A BUG'S LIFE

(WALT DISNEY PICTURES) Producers, Darla K. Anderson, Kevin Reher; Director, John Lasseter; Co-Director, Andrew Stanton; Screenplay, Andrew Stanton, Donald McEnery, Bob Shaw; Story, John Lasseter, Andrew Stanton, Joe Ranft; Music, Randy Newman; Song: *The Time of Your Life* written and performed by Randy Newman; Story Supervisor, Joe Ranft; Supervising Editor, Lee Unkrich; Photography, Sharon Calahan; Designer, William Cone; Art Directors, Tia W. Kratter, Bob Pauley; Supervising Animators, Glenn McQueen, Rich Quade; Supervising Layout Artist, Ewan Johnson; Story, Art & Layout, BZ Petroff; Casting, Ruth Lambert, Mary Hidalgo; a Pixar Animation Studios Film; Dolby; Cinemascope; Technicolor; Rated G; 96 minutes; November release

Hopper

VOICE CAST

Flik	Dave Foley
Hopper	Kevin Spacey
Princess Atta	Julia Louis-Dreyfus
Dot	Hayden Panettiere
Queen	Phyllis Diller
Molt	Richard Kind
Slim	David Hyde Pierce
Heimlich	Joe Ranft
Francis	Denis Leary
Manny	Jonathan Harris
Gypsy	Madeline Kahn
Rosie	Bonnie Hunt
Tuck & Roll	Michael McShane
P.T. Flea	John Ratzenberger
Dim	Brad Garrett
Mr. Soil	Roddy McDowall
Dr. Flora	Edie McClurg
Thorny	Alex Rocco
Cornelius	David Ossman

Terrified that he and his fellow ants will not have enough harvest to give to the greedy and manipulative grasshoppers, Flik seeks outside help and finds it in a gang of second-rate flea circus performers. This film received an Oscar nomination for original score—musical or comedy.

Tuck & Roll

Heimlich, Slim, Dim, Francis, Rosie, Tuck, Manny, Roll, Gypsy, Flik

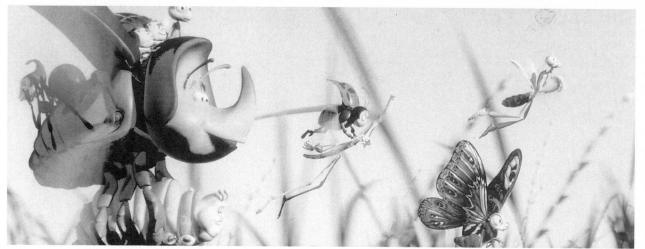

Rosie, Tuck & Rol, Flik (atop) Dim (holding) Heimlich, Francis (holding) Slim, Gypsy, Manny

Heimlich, Slim, Francis

Manny, Gypsy

Flik

THE SAVIOR

(LIONS GATE) Producers, Oliver Stone, Janet Yang; Executive Producer, Cindy Cowan; Director, Peter Antonijevic; Screenplay, Robert Orr; Photography, Ian Wilson; Co-Producers, Naomi Despres, Joseph Bruggeman; Associate Producers, Molly M. Mayeux, Scott Moore; Designer, Vladislav Lasic; Editors, Gabriella Cristiani, Ian Crafford; Music, David Robbins; Line Producer, Miryana Mijojlic; Costumes, Boris Caksiran; Casting, Mary Vernieu; an Initial Entertainment presentation of an Oliver Stone production; Dolby; Super 35 Widescreen; Deluxe color; Rated R; 103 minutes; November release

CAST

Joshua Rose/Guy	Dennis Quaid
Maria	Nastassja Kinski
Dominic	Stellan Skarsgård
Vera	Natasa Ninkovic
Goran	Sergej Trifunovic
Vera's Brother	Neboisa Glogovac
Woman on Bus	Vesna Trivalic
Paris Priest	Pascal Rollin
Christian Rose	Catlin Foster
Colonel	John McLaren
Drill Sergeant	Irfan Mensur

and Kosta Andrejevic (Boy on Bridge), Ljiljana Krstic (Old Lady), Sanja Zogovic (Girl on Bridge), Veljko Otasevic (Orthodox Priest), Marina Bukvicki (Muslim Girl), Dusan Perkovic (Uncle Ratko), Dajana Radevic, Sanja Borodenko, Aleksandra Bordenko, Toskovic Darka (Babies), Ljiljana Blagojevic (Vera's Mother), Modrag Krstovic (Vera's Father), Dusan Janicijevic (Old Man), Renata Ulmanski (Old Woman), Svetozar Cvetkovic (Croat Officer), Josif Tatic (Chief Executioner), Cedo Dragovic (Driver)

Joshua Rose, a U.S. mercenary fighting in Bosnia, finds his stony reserve tested when he helps a raped Serbian woman and the baby to whom she subsequently gives birth.

Dennis Quaid

©Savior Productions, Inc.

VERY BAD THINGS

(POLYGRAM) Producers, Michael Schiffer, Diane Nabatoff, Cindy Cowan; Executive Producers, Ted Field, Scott Kroopf, Michael Helfant, Christian Slater; Director/Screenplay, Peter Berg; Line Producer, Laura Greenlee; Photography, David Hennings; Designer, Dina Lipton; Editor, Dan Lebental; Music, Stewart Copeland; Costumes, Terry Dresbach; Presented in association with Initial Entertainment Group; an Interscope Communications production in association with Ballpark Productions; Dolby; Color; Rated R; 100 minutes; November release

CAST

Robert Boyd	Christian Slater
Laura Garrety	Cameron Diaz
Adam Berkow	Daniel Stern
Lois Berkow	Jeanne Tripplehorn
Kyle Fisher	Jon Favreau
Michael Berkow	Jeremy Piven
Charles Moore	Leland Orser
Man	Rob Brownstein
Adam Berkow, Jr.	Joey Zimmerman
Timmy Berkow	Tyler Malinger
Tina	Carla Scott
Security Guard	Russell B. McKenzie
Cop	Pancho Demings
Suit	Blake Gibbons
Clerk	Angelo Di Mascio, Jr.
Mr. Fisher	Lawrence Pressman
Cop at Hospital	Steve Fitchpatrick

and Brian Grandison, John Cappon, Linda Klein (Doctors), Byrne Piven (Rabbi), Bob Bancroft (Barry Morris), Trey Davis (Receptionist), Marilyn McIntyre (Judge Tower), Wrangler (Bunker the Dog—4 legs), Trooper (Bunker the Dog—3 legs)

Five friends go to Las Vegas for a bachelor party during which one of them accidentally kills a prostitute, an act the men try desperately to cover up.

(clockwise from top) Daniel Stern, Cameron Diaz, Jon Favreau, Leland Orser, Jeremy Piven, Christian Slater

©PolyGram Films

Bill Paxton, Billy Bob Thornton

Bridget Fonda, Bill Paxton

Billy Bob Thornton, Bill Paxton, Brent Briscoe

©Paramount Pictures

A SIMPLE PLAN

(PARAMOUNT) Producers, James Jacks, Adam Schroeder; Executive Producers, Gary Levinsohn, Mark Gordon; Director, Sam Raimi; Screenplay, Scott B. Smith, based on his novel; Co-Producer, Michael Polaire; Photography, Alar Kivilo; Designer, Patrizia von Brandenstein; Costumes, Julie Weiss; Editors, Arthur Coburn, Eric L. Beason; Music, Danny Elfman; a Mutual Film Company presentation in association with Savoy Pictures; Dolby; Color; Rated R; 121 minutes; December release

CAST

Hank	Bill Paxton
Sarah	Bridget Fonda
Jacob	Billy Bob Thornton
Lou	Brent Briscoe
Tom Butler	Jack Walsh
Carl	Chelcie Ross
Nancy	Becky Ann Baker
Baxter	Gary Cole
FBI Agent Renkins	Bob Davis
FBI Agent Freemont	Peter Syvertsen
Dwight Stephanson	Tom Carey
Mr. Schmitt	John Paxton
News Reporter	Marie Mathay
Anchorman	Paul Magers
Anchorwoman	Joan Steffand
Hospital Nurse	Jill Sayre
Bartender	Wayne A. Evenson
Drinker	Timothy Storms
Dead Pilot	Terry Hempleman
Bearded Man	Jay Gjernes

and Grant Curtis, Soloman Abrams, Nina Kaczorowski (Bar Patrons), Thomas Boedy (Priest), Mary Woolever (Linda), Rhiannon R. Savers (Girl on Sled), Christopher Gallus (Boy on Sled), Eric Cegon (Tommy), Robert Martin Halverson (Detective), Roger Watton (Barber)

Three men come upon a plane wreck containing four million dollars in cash and scheme to keep the money, a plan that leads to disaster. This film received Oscar nominations for supporting actor (Billy Bob Thornton) and screenplay adaptation.

Billy Bob Thornton, Bridget Fonda, Bill Paxton

HI-LIFE

(LIONS GATE) Producer, Erica Spellman-Silverman; Executive Producers, Michael Paseornek, Jeff Sackman, Steven C. Beer; Director/Screenplay, Roger Hedden; Photography, John Thomas; Designer, Sharon Lomofsky; Costumes, Isis Mussenden; Music, David Lawrence; Casting, Deborah Brown; a Silverman production, in association with Gun for Hire Films; Color; Not rated; 82 minutes; December release

CAST

Ray	Campbell Scott
Jimmy	Eric Stoltz
April	Katrin Cartlidge
Fatty	Charles Durning
Maggie	Daryl Hannah
Susan	Moira Kelly
Minor	Peter Riegert
Sherry	Anne DeSalvo
Elena	Saundra Santiago
Frankie	Kathleen Widdoes

and Bruce MacVittie (Cluck), Tegan West (Phil), Carlo Alban (Ricky), Dean Cameron (Santa), Tucker Smith (Adrien), Michelle Durning (Yale), David Aaron Baker (Cliff the Bartender), Steve Gilger (Bar Patron), Elizabeth Van Dyke (Charlotte the Bartender), Christina Santiago, Nicole Santiago (Twins), Marc Lovci (Head Caroler), James Curtin, Emilie Davezac, Kim Dooley, Nami Hirayanagi, Devon Sorrari (Carolers), J.R. Robinson (Ronny the Waiter), Allison Dougherty (Kristy), David Fuhrer (Henry), Spring Sutter (Subtle Cherry Wine Taster), Meg Hartig (Spit or Swallow Wine Taster), Columbia McCaleb (Coffee Bar Girl), Jeffrey V. Thompson (Cabbie), Cheryl Gaysunas (Maggie the Bartender), Jenna Lamia, Michael Pitt (Teens), Arnie Mazer (Chip), Lauren Wigo (Woman at Chip's Bar), Jordan Lage, Ray Anthony Thomas (Cops)

During Christmastime, Ray, an overly-generous bartender, is prodded by his sister Susan into collecting all the money he has lent to various fellow-bartenders on the Upper West Side.

Moira Kelly, Eric Stoltz, Daryl Hannah

JACK FROST

(WARNER BROS.) Producers, Mark Canton, Irving Azoff; Executive Producers, Matthew Baer, Jeff Barry, Richard Goldsmith, Michael Tadross; Director, Troy Miller; Screenplay, Mark Steven Johnson, Steve Bloom, Jonathan Roberts, Jeff Cesario; Photography, Laszlo Kovacs; Editor, Lawrence Jordan; Music, Trevor Rabin; Designer, Mayne Berke; Costumes, Sarah Edwards; Special Effects Supervisor, Steve Galich; Visual Effects Supervisor, Joe Letteri; an Azoff Entertainment/Canton Co. production; Dolby; Panavision; Technicolor; Rated PG; 95 minutes; December release

CAST

Jack Frost	Michael Keaton
Gabby Frost	Kelly Preston
Charlie Frost	Joseph Cross
Mac MacArthur	Mark Addy
Tuck Gronic	Andy Lawrence
Spencer	Eli Marienthal
Dennis	Will Rothhaar
Natalie	Mika Boorem
Alexander	Benjamin Brock
Rory Buck	Taylor Handley
Mitch	Joe Rokicki
Pudge	Cameron Ferre
Snowploy Driver	Ahmet Zappa
Audience Member	Paul F. Tompkins
Sid Gronic	Henry Rollins
John Kaplan	Dweezil Zappa

and Steve Giannelli (Referee), Jay Johnston (TV Weatherman), Jeff Cesario (Radio Announcer), Scott Thomson (Dennis's Dad), Jimmy Michaels (Devil's Goalie), Ajai Sanders (Interviewer), John Ennis (Truck Driver), Wayne Federman (Dave, Policeman), Golden Henning (Bank Customer), Pat Crawford Brown (Scorekeeper), Mr. Chips (Chester the Dog), Denise Cheshire, Bruce Lanoil (In Suit Performers); The Jack Frost Band: Trevor Rabin (Lead Guitar), Lili Haydn (Violin), Louis Molino III (Drummer), Scott Colomby (Bass)

A year after his death in a car accident, the spirit of musician Jack Frost comes to life within a snowman his son Charlie has built.

Jack Frost, Joseph Cross

STAR TREK: INSURRECTION

(PARAMOUNT) Producer, Rick Berman; Executive Producer, Martin Honrstein; Director, Jonathan Frakes; Screenplay, Michael Piller; Story, Rick Berman, Michael Piller; Based upon Star Trek created by Gene Roddenberry; Photography, Matthew F. Leonetti; Designer, Heran Zimmerman; Editor, Peter E. Berger; Associate Producer, Patrick Stewart; Co-Producer, Peter Lauritson; Music, Jerry Goldsmith; Costumes, Sanja Milkovic Hays; Casting, Junie Lowry-Johnson, Ron Surma; a Rick Berman production; Dolby; Panavision; Deluxe color; Rated PG; 100 minutes; December release

Brent Spiner, Donna Murphy, Patrick Stewart

CAST

Captain Jean-Luc Picard	Patrick Stewart
Commander William Riker	Jonathan Frakes
Lt. Commander Data	Brent Spiner
Lt. Commander Geordi La Forge	LeVar Burton
Lt. Commander Worf	Michael Dorn
Dr. Beverly C. Crusher	Gates McFadden
Lt. Commander Deanna Troi	Marina Sirtis
Ru'afo	F. Murray Abraham
Anij	Donna Murphy
Admiral Dougherty	Anthony Zerbe
Gallatin	Gregg Henry
Sojef	Daniel Hugh Kelly
Artim	Michael Welch
Tournel	Mark Deakins
Perim	Stephanie Niznik
Lt. Daniels	Michael Horton
Son'a Officers	Bruce French, Claudette Nevins, Joseph Ruskin
Lt. Curtis	Breon Gorman
Bolian Officer	John Hostetter
Elloran Officers	Rick Worthy, Greg Poland
Tarlac Officer	Larry Anderson

and D. Elliot Woods (Starfleet Officer), Jennfier Tung, Kenneth Lane Edwards (Ensigns), Raye Birk (Son'a Doctor), Peggy Miley (Regent Cuzar), Lee Arnone-Briggs (Librarian), Max Grodenchik (Alien Ensign), Zachary Williams (Ba'ku Child), McKenzie Westmore (Ba'ku Woman), Philip Glasser (Young Ru'afo)

The Son'a, an aging and dying race, scheme to evict the Ba'ku from their planet in order to use the planet's metaphysic radiation that reverses aging, a plot Captain Picard and the crew of the Starship Enterprises hope to stop. The third Paramount theatrical feature based on the series "Star Trek: The Next Generation" following Star Trek: Generations (1994), and Star Trek: First Contact (1996), with the same cast principles from those films appearing here as well.

©Paramount Pictures

F. Murray Abraham

Marina Sirtis, Jonathan Frakes

Gates McFadden, Patrick Stewart

RUSHMORE

(**TOUCHSTONE**) Producers, Barry Mendel, Paul Schiff; Executive Producers/Screenplay, Wes Anderson, Owen Wilson; Director, Wes Anderson; Photography, Robert Yeoman; Designer, David Wasco; Editor, David Moritz; Costumes, Karen Patch; Co-Producer, John Cameron; Music, Mark Mothersbaugh; Casting, Mary Gail Artz, Barbara Cohen; an American Empirical Pictures production; Distributed by Buena Vista Pictures; Dolby; Panavision; Eastman color; Rated R; 93 minutes; December release

Jason Schwartzman, Seymour Cassel

CAST

Max Fischer	Jason Schwartzman
Mr. Blume	Bill Murray
Miss Cross	Olivia Williams
Dr. Guggenheim	Brian Cox
Bert Fischer	Seymour Cassel
Dirk Calloway	Mason Gamble
Margaret Yang	Sara Tanaka
Magnus Buchan	Stephen McCole
Dr. Peter Flynn	Luke Wilson
Mr. Adams	Deepak Pallana
Coach Beck	Andrew Wilson
Mrs. Guggenheim	Marietta Marich
Ronnie Blume	Ronnie McCawley
Donny Blume	Keith McCawley
Alex	Hae Joon Lee
Mr. Obiamiwe	Adebayo Asabi
Mrs. Calloway	Connie Nielsen
Ernie	Al Fielder
Boy Portraying Frank Serpico	Colin Platt
O'Reilly	George Farish
Burnum	Frances Fernandez
Fields	McCauley Penderdast
Willie	Eric Weems
Wrestler	Dalton Tomlin
Referee	Wally Wolodarsky
Mrs. Blume	Kim Terry
Woman Back Stage	Ella Pryor
Waiter	Paul Schiff
Small Boy Artist	Antoni Scarano
Contractor	Brian Tenenbaum
School Reporter	Thayer McClanahan
Mrs. Whitney	Patricia Winkler
Mr. Holstead	Manning Mott
Woody	J.J. Stonebraker
40 Ounce	Donny Caicedo
Benjamin	Ali Ktiri
Concierge	Michael Maggart
Isaac	Robbie Lee
Bellman	Morgan Redmond
Security Guard	Ed Geldart
Dynamite Salesman	David Moritz
Tommy Stalling	J.J. Killalea
Mr. Yang	William Lau
Mrs. Yang	Lucille Sadikin
Tennis Pro	Steve Eckelman
Architect	Eric Anderson
Coach Fritz	Danny Fine
Regis	Kyle Ryan Urquhart
Mr. LittleJeans	Kumar Pallana
Reuben	Stephen Dignan

Bill Murray, Jason Schwartzman

Max Fischer, a 10th grader at Rushmore Academy with a heavy extra-cir-ricular schedule and terrible grades, asks steel tycoon Mr. Blume to help him raise money to impress a teacher he's in love with, only to have Blume fall for the same woman.

Olivia Williams, Jason Schwartzman

Bill Murray

Olivia Williams

Jason Schwartzman

Jason Schwartzman

Seymour Cassel

Mason Gamble

Brian Cox

Tom Hanks, Meg Ryan

Tom Hanks, Parker Posey

Tom Hanks, Dabney Coleman, John Randolph

Meg Ryan, Greg Kinnear

Meg Ryan (c)

YOU'VE GOT MAIL

(WARNER BROS.) Producers, Nora Ephron, Lauren Shuler Donner; Executive Producers, Delia Ephron, Julie Durk, G. Mac Brown; Co-Producer, Donald J. Lee, Jr.; Director, Nora Ephron; Screenplay, Nora Ephron, Delia Ephron; Based on the screenplay *The Shop Around the Corner* by Samson Raphaelson, from the play *Parfumerie* by Miklos Laszlo; Photography, John Lindley; Designer, Dan Davis; Editor, Richard Marks; Music, George Fenton; Costumes, Albert Wolsky; Casting, Francine Maisler; a Lauren Shuler Donner production; Dolby; Technicolor; Rated PG-13; 119 minutes; December release

Meg Ryan, Tom Hanks

CAST

Joe Fox	Tom Hanks
Kathleen Kelly	Meg Ryan
Frank Navasky	Greg Kinnear
Patricia Eden	Parker Posey
Christina	Heather Burns
George Pappas	Steve Zahn
Birdie	Jean Stapleton
Kevin Scanlon	David Chappelle
Nelson Fox	Dabney Coleman
Schuyler Fox	John Randolph
Annabel	Hallee Hirsh
Matt	Jeffrey Scaperrotta
Gillian	Cara Seymour
Maureen	Katie Finneran
Charlie	Michael Badalucco
Veronica Grant	Deborah Rush
Miranda Margulies	Veanne Cox
Vince Mancini	Bruce Jay Friedman
Zabars Cashier	Sara Ramirez
Zabars Shoppers	Howard Spiegel, Diane Sokolow, Julie Kass
Thanksgiving Guest	Reiko Aylesworth
Young Kathleen Kelly	Katie Sagona
Cecilia Kelly	Kathryn Meisle
TV Reporter	Nina Zoie Lam
Theatre Patron	Maggie Murphy
Shoppers	Michelle Blakely, Meredith White, Dianne Dreyer, Julie Galdieri, Leila Nichols
Fox Books Shopper	Mary Kelly
Fox Salesperson	Chris Messina
Man at Cafe Lalo	Ronobir Lahiri
Waiter at Lalo	André Sogliuzzo
Capeman	Petre A. Mian
Starbucks Customers	Richard Cohen, Enzo Angileri
Juggler	Nick Brown
Sarah Mancini	Ann Fleuchaus
Party Guests	Neil Bonin, Bill McHugh
Decorator	Santiago Quinones
Yvette Fox	Lynn Grossman
Mother of Twins	Dolores Sirianni
Florist	Nicole Bernadette
Brinkley	Bonnie & Clovis
Dog in Elevator	Lucy

Tom Hanks, Meg Ryan

Kathleen Kelly and Joe Fox become enemies when his huge chain book store threatens to put her small neighborhood shop out of business, all the while not realizing they have been communicating anonymously on the internet where they've formed a friendship. Previous film version was The Shop Around the Corner (MGM, 1940) with James Stewart and Margaret Sullavan.

Tom Hanks, Greg Kinnear, Meg Ryan

THE PRINCE OF EGYPT

(DREAMWORKS) Producers, Penney Finkelman Cox, Sandra Rabins; Executive Producer, Jeffrey Katzenberg; Directors, Brenda Chapman, Steve Hickner, Simon Wells; Associate Producer, Ron Rocha; Art Directors, Kathy Altieri, Richard Chavez; Designer, Darek Gogol; Supervising Editor, Nick Fletcher; Songs, Stephen Schwartz; Music Score, Hans Zimmer; Artistic Supervisors: Story, Kelly Asbury, Lorna Cook; Layout, Lorenzo E. Martinez; Background, Paul LaSaine, Ron Lukas; Visual Effects, Don Paul, Dan Philips; Scene Planning, David Morehead; Color Models, David Svend Karoll; Scanning, Stuart Campbell; Animation/Digital/Final Check, Pat Sito, Shauna Stevens; Digital Paint, Jillian Tudor; Music, Marylata E. Jacob; Casting, Leslee Feldman; Costume Designer, Kelly Kimball; Dolby; Technicolor; Rated PG; 97 minutes; December release

Rameses, Moses

VOICE CAST

Moses	Val Kilmer
Rameses	Ralph Fiennes
Tzipporah	Michelle Pfeiffer
Miriam	Sandra Bullock
Aaron	Jeff Goldblum
Jethro	Danny Glover
Seti	Patrick Stewart
The Queen	Helen Mirren
Hotep	Steve Martin
Huy	Martin Short
Yocheved	Ofra Haza

and James Avery, Aria Noelle Curzon, Stephanie Sawyer, Francesca Smith (Additional Voices)

Moses, adopted and raised as the son of the Pharoah, comes to the realization that his destiny in life is to lead the enslaved Jews of Egypt out of bondage. Previous film versions of the story were The Ten Commandments *(1923 and 1956), both released by Paramount and directed by Cecil B. DeMille. 1998 Academy Award-winner for Best Original Song ("When You Believe"). This film received an additional nomination for original score—musical or comedy.*

©DreamWorks LLC

Moses, Jethro, Tzipporah

Tzipporah, Moses, Miriam, Aaron

RED MEAT

(PENINSULA) Producers, Oliver Eberle, Marco Weber; Executive Producer, Fuminori Hayashida; Director/Screenplay, Allison Burnett; Co-Producer, Traci Lind; Co-Executive Producer, Kikuo Kawasaki; Photography, Charlie Lieberman; Editor, Sloane Klevin; Costumes, Michele Michel; Music, The Blue Hawaiians; Designer, Frank Bollinger, Clare Brown; Line Producer, Jeff Kirshbaum; a Treehouse Films presentation of a Treehouse/Imec production; Ultra-Stereo; Color; Not rated; 95 minutes; December release

CAST

Ruth	Lara Flynn Boyle
Victor	James Frain
Candace	Jennifer Grey
Connie the Waitress	Traci Lind
Chris	Stephen Mailer
Stefan	John Slattery
Prostitute	Dee Freeman
Ula	Anna Karin
Mia	Heidi Lenhart
Donna	Billie Neal
Isis	Julia Pearlstein
Nan	Andrea Roth

Three friends gather each Sunday to discuss women and their sex lives, a ritual that unleashes a lot of harsh feelings and opens old wounds.

John Slattery, Traci Lind, James Frain, Stephen Mailer

THE FACULTY

(DIMENSION) Producers, Elizabeth Avellan, Robert Rodriguez; Executive Producers, Bob Weinstein, Harvey Weinstein; Director/Editor, Robert Rodriguez; Screenplay, Kevin Williamson; Story, David Wechter, Bruce Kimmel; Photography, Enrique Chediak; Designer, Cary White; Music, Marco Beltrami; Costumes, Michael T. Boyd; Special Make-Up and Creature Effects, KNB-FX; Visual Effects Supervisor, Brian Jennings; Casting, Mary Vernieu, Anne McCarthy; a Los Hooligans production; Distributed by Miramax Films; Dolby; Technicolor; Rated R; 102 minutes; December release

CAST

Delilah	Jordana Brewster
Stokely	Clea DuVall
Marybeth	Laura Harris
Zeke	Josh Hartnett
Stan	Shawn Hatosy
Nurse Harper	Salma Hayek
Miss Burke	Famke Janssen
Mrs. Olson	Piper Laurie
Casey's Dad	Chris McDonald
Principal Drake	Bebe Neuwirth
Coach Willis	Robert Patrick
Gabe	Usher Raymond
Mr. Furlong	Jon Stewart
Mr. Tate	Daniel von Bargen
Casey	Elijah Wood

and Summer Phoenix (Fuck You Girl), Jon Abrahams (Fuck You Boy), Susan Willis (Mrs. Brummel), Pete Janssen (Meat), Christina Rodriguez (Tattoo Girl), Danny Masterson, Wiley Wiggins (Fuck Ups), Harry Knowles (Mr. Knowles), Donna Casey (Tina), Louis Black (Mr. Lewis), Eric Jungmann, Chris Viteychuk (Freshmen), Jim Johnston (P.E. Teacher), Libby Villari (Casey's Mom), Duane Martin, Katherine Willis (Officers), Mike Lutz (Hornet Mascot), Doug Aarniokoski (Brun Coach)

A group of students at Herrington High come to the realization that some of their teachers are actually aliens bent on taking over the rest of the town.

Piper Laurie, Salma Hayek, Robert Patrick

Shawn Hatosy, Laura Harris, Josh Hartnett, Jordana Brewster,
Clea DuVall, Elijah Wood

Sean Penn

John Savage

THE THIN RED LINE

(20TH CENTURY FOX) Producers, Robert Michael Geisler, John Roberdeau, Grant Hill; Executive Producer, George Stevens, Jr.; Director/Screenplay, Terrence Malick; Based upon the novel by James Jones; Photography, John Toll; Designer, Jack Fisk; Editors, Billy Weber, Leslie Jones, Saar Klein; Music, Hans Zimmer; Costumes, Margot Wilson; Associate Producer, Michael Stevens; Casting, Dianne Crittenden; a Fox 2000 Pictures presentation from Phoenix Pictures in association with George Stevens, Jr. of a Geisler-Roberdeau production; Dolby; Panavision; Technicolor; Rated R; 170 minutes; December release

CAST

Pvt. Tella	Kirk Acevedo
Lt. Col. Billig	Simon Billig
Pvt. Peale	Mark Boone Junior
Cpl. Fife	Adrien Brody
Pvt. Henry	Norman Patrick Brown
Pvt. Witt	Jim Caviezel
Pvt. Bell	Ben Chaplin
Capt. Bosche	George Clooney
Capt. Gaff	John Cusack
Cpl. Thorne	Jarrod Dean
Pvt. Coombs	Matt Doran
Pvt. Weld	Travis Fine
1st Lt. Band	Paul Gleeson
Sgt. Keck	Woody Harrelson
Cpl. Queen	David Harrod
Sgt. Becker	Don Harvey
Pvt. Carni	Danny Hoch
Pvt. Sico	Robert Roy Hofmo
Pvt. Ash	Tom Jane
Capt. Staros	Elias Koteas
2nd Lt. Whyte	Jared Leto
Pvt. 1cl. Earl	Gordon MacDonald
Pvt. Floyd	Michael McGrady
Pvt. 1cl. Doll	Dash Mihok
Pvt. Tills	Tim Blake Nelson
Lt. Col. Tall	Nick Nolte
1st Sgt. Welsh	Sean Penn
Sgt. Storm	John C. Reilly
Pvt. Mazzi	Larry Romano
Sgt. McCron	John Savage
Pvt. Train	John Dee Smith
Cpl. Jenks	Stephen Spacek
Pvt. 1cl. Bead	Nick Stahl
Brig. Gen. Quintard	John Travolta
Pvt. 1cl. Dale	Arie Verveen
2nd Lt. Gore	Steven Vidler
Pvt. Hoke	Will Wallace

and Penny Allen (Witt's Mother), Benjamin, Jimmy (Melanesian Villagers), Kengo Hasuo, Kazuyoshi Sakai (Japanese Prisoners), Ben Hines (Asst. Pilot), Jack (Melanesian Man Walking), Polyn Leona (Melanesian Woman w/Child), Dan Wyllie, Simon Lyndon (Medics), Kazuki Maehara, Tomohiro Tanji, Kouji Suzuki, Ryushi Mizukami, Terutake Tsuji, Taiju Okayasu, Hiroya Sugisaki (Japanese Pvts.), Marina Malota (Marina), Ken Mitsuishi, Masayuki Shida, Joe Watanabe (Japanese Officers), Larry Neuhaus (Crewman), Takamitsu Okubo (Japanese Soldier), Miranda Otto (Marty Bell), Minoru Toyoshima (Japanese Sgt.), Vincent (Melanesian Guide), Todd Wallace (Pilot), Simon Westaway (First Scout), Yasuomi Yoshino (Young Japanese)

C-for-Charlie company descends on Guadalcanal to engage in one of the bloodiest battles of World War II. Previous film version was released in 1964 by Allied Artists and starred Keir Dullea and Jack Weston. This film received Oscar nominations for picture, director, screenplay adaptation, cinematography, editing, sound, and original dramatic score.

©Twentieth Century Fox

Nick Nolte

Jim Caviezel

George Clooney

Ben Chaplin, Woody Harrelson

Ben Chaplin, John Cusack, Jim Caviezel

Elias Koteas

Adrien Brody

MIGHTY JOE YOUNG

(WALT DISNEY PICTURES) Producers, Ted Hartley, Tom Jacobson; Executive Producer, Gail Katz; Director, Ron Underwood; Screenplay, Mark Rosenthal, Lawrence Konner; Based on a screenplay by Ruth Rose and a story by Merian C. Cooper; Co-Executive Producers, Mark Lisson, Gary Stutman; Supervising Producer, Ralph Winter; Photography, Don Peterman, Oliver Wood; Designer, Michael Corenblith; Editor, Paul Hirsch; Mighty Joe Young Creature Designer/Producer, Rick Baker; Visual Effects Supervisor, Hoyt Yeatman; Music, James Horner; Costumes, Molly Maginnis; Casting, Pam Dixon Mickelson; an RKO Pictures production in association with the Jacobson Company; Dolby; Eastman color; Rated PG; 114 minutes; December release

CAST

Jill Young	Charlize Theron
Gregg O'Hara	Bill Paxton
Strasser	Rade Sherbedgia
Garth	Peter Firth
Harry Ruben	David Paymer
Cecily Banks	Regina King
Kweli	Robert Wisdom
Pindi	Naveen Andrews
Dr. Baker	Lawrence Pressman
Dr. Ruth Young	Linda Purl
Young Jill	Mika Boorem
Vern	Geoffrey Blake
Jack	Christian Clemenson
Jason	Cory Buck

Joe Young, Charlize Theron, Bill Paxton

and Liz Georges (Jason's Mother), Richard Riehle (Commander Gorman), Cynthia Allison, Ken Taylor (News Reporters), Ray Harryhausen (Gentleman at Party), Terry Moore (Elegant Woman at Party) Judson Mills (Impatient Driver), Tony Genaro (Boxer Shorts Man), Flo Di Re (Bambi's Owner), Kaylan Romero, Hernan Ruiz, Jenilee Deal, Matt Deal (Street Kids), Bethany Bassler, Vicki Davis, Deborah Kellner, Marguerite Moreau (Cabriolet Girls), Tracey Walter (Conservancy Guard), Larry Brandenburg (Animal Control Duty Officer), Damien Leake, Neal Kopit (Cops), Janet Eilber (Concerned Mother), Wiley Pickett (Police Sharpshooter), John T. Bower (Carjack Man), Hannah Swanson (Toddler), Laurie Kilpatrick (Toddler's Mom), Richard McGonagle (Panda Owner), Reno Wilson (Poacher), Theodore R. Hartley (Society Man), Dina Merrill (Society Woman), Lily Mariye (Ticket Clerk), Gary Hecker (Special Vocal Effects), John Alexander (Joe Young).

To save him from poachers, Jill Young reluctantly agrees to let zoologist Gregg O'Hara transport her 15-foot gorilla Joe to a California animal conservancy. Remake of the 1949 RKO film Mighty Joe Young which starred Terry Moore and Ben Johnson. Moore (as well as that film's special effects creator, Ray Harryhausen) make cameo appearances in this film. This film received an Oscar nomination for visual effects.

©Disney Enterprises, Inc.

Rade Sherbedgia, Charlize Theron, Peter Firth

Joe Young

Joe Young

Susan Sarandon, Julia Roberts

Liam Aiken, Susan Sarandon

STEPMOM

(COLUMBIA) Producers, Wendy Finerman, Mark Radcliffe, Michael Barnathan; Executive Producers, Julia Roberts, Susan Sarandon, Pliny Porter, Patrick McCormick, Ron Bass, Margaret French Isaac; Director, Chris Columbus; Screenplay, Gigi Levangie, Jessie Nelson, Steven Rogers, Karen Leigh Hopkins, Ron Bass; Story, Gigi Levangie; Photography, Donald M. McAlpine; Designer, Stuart Wurtzel; Editor, Neil Travis; Music, John Williams; Costumes, Joseph G. Aulisi; Casting, Ellen Lewis; a Wendy Finerman production/a 1492 production; Dolby; Panavision; Technicolor; Rated PG-13; 124 minutes; December release

Ed Harris, Julia Roberts

CAST

Isabel Kelly	Julia Roberts
Jackie Harrison	Susan Sarandon
Luke Harrison	Ed Harris
Anna Harrison	Jena Malone
Ben Harrison	Liam Aiken
Dr. Sweikert	Lynn Whitfield
Duncan Samuels	Darrell Larson
School Counselor	Mary Louise Wilson
Cooper	Andre Blake
Photo Assistant	Russell Harper
Craft Service Man	Jack Eagle
Rapunzel	Mark Gilchrist
Prince	Dylan Michaels
Policemen	David Zayas, Jose Ramon Rosario
Desk Sergeant	Lee Shepherd

and Lu Celania Sierra, Lauma Zemzare, Holly Schenck, Michelle Stone, Annett Esser, Monique Rodrique (Photo Shoot Models), Sal Mistretta, Rex Hays, Alice Liu, Chuck Montgomery (Ad Executives), George Masters (Maitre'd), Anthony Grasso (Waiter), Robert F. Alvarado (Soccer Coach), Sebastian Rand (Tucker), Michelle Hurst (Nurse), Jason Maves (Brad Kovitsky), Julie Lancaster (Flight Attendant), Charlie Christman (Stone Fox), Amina Asep, Naama Katz, Jennifer Best, Robin Fusco, Jessica M. Osias, Electra Telesford, Michelle L. Brady (Anna's Friends), Zachary M. Hasak, Jordan Gochros, Rob London, James Ostrofsky, Chad Lavinio (Brad's Friends), John Sadowski, Matthew Doudounis (Ben's Friends), Andrea Dolloff (Cocktail Waitress)

Jackie Harrison's resentment of Isabel Kelly, the younger woman her ex-husband Luke has taken up with, is similarly reflected in her two children who have little affection for their "stepmother."

©Columbia Pictures Industries, Inc.

Liam Aiken, Ed Harris, Jena Malone

John Travolta, Robert Duvall, Bruce Norris, John Lithgow

James Gandolfini, Kathleen Quinlan

John Travolta, Dan Hedaya

John Travolta, William H. Macy, Tony Shalhoub, Zeljko Ivanek

John Travolta

A CIVIL ACTION

Robert Duvall, John Travolta

(TOUCHSTONE/PARAMOUNT) Producers, Scott Rudin, Robert Redford, Rachel Pfeffer; Executive Producers, Steven Zaillian, David Wisnievitz; Director/Screenplay, Steven Zaillian; Based on the book by Jonathan Harr; Photography, Conrad L. Hall; Designer, David Gropman; Editor, Wayne Wahrman; Music, Danny Elfman; Costumes, Shay Cunliffe; Casting, Avy Kaufman; Dolby; Technicolor; Rated PG-13; 112 minutes; December release

CAST

Jan Schlichtmann	John Travolta
Jerome Facher	Robert Duvall
Kevin Conway	Tony Shalhoub
James Gordon	William H. Macy
Bill Crowley	Zeljko Ivanek
William Cheeseman	Bruce Norris
Judge Skinner	John Lithgow
Anne Anderson	Kathleen Quinlan
Neil Jacobs	Peter Jacobson
Kathy Boyer	Mary Mara
Al Love	James Gandolfini
Pinder	Stephen Fry
John Riley	Dan Hedaya
Richard Aufiero	David Thornton
Al Eustis	Sydney Pollack
Uncle Pete	Ned Eisenberg
Donna Robbins	Margot Rose
Mr. Granger	Daniel Von Bargen
Evelyn Love	Caroline Carrigan
Shalline	Paul Desmond
Barbas	Michael P. Byrne
Grace Workers	Tracy Miller, Paul Hewitt, Clayton Landey
Pasqueriella	Paul Ben-Victor
Lauren Aufiero	Elizabeth Burnette
Insurance Lawyers	Alan Wilder, Gregg Joseph Monk, Harout Beshlian
Law Clerk	Josh Pais
Courtroom #7 Clerk	Haskell Vaughn Anderson III
Mrs. Granger	Kaiulani Lee
Radio Talk Show Host	Howie Carr
Judge	Denise Dowse
Court Clerk	Pearline Fergerson
PI Lawyers	Scott Weintraub, Robert Cicchini
Insurance Plaintiff	Christopher Stevenson
Waiter	Kevin Fry
Mover	Brian Turk
TV Reporter	Rikki Klieman

and David Barrett, Ryan Janis, Rob McElhenney (Teenagers on Property), Mike Biase (Market Clerk), Richard Calnan (Woburn Traffic Cop), Gene Wolande (Hotel Clerk), Sam Travolta (Grace Attorney), Gregg Shawzin, Juli Donald, Sayda Alan, Catherine Leahan (Reporters), Bruce Holman (Federal Marshall), John LaFayette, Charles Levin, Byron Jennings, Jay Patterson (Geologists), Charlie Stavola (Detective), Kathy Bates (Bankruptcy Judge)

John Travolta

A group of concerned parents who believe their children have died because of poisoned drinking water, contact hot shot lawyer Jan Schlichtmann to prosecute the culprit. The initially disinterested attorney decides to take the case to court when he discovers that the companies responsible, W. R. Grace & Co. and Beatrice Foods, are two of the country's largest and most powerful corporations. This film received Oscar nominations for supporting actor (Robert Duvall) and cinematography.

Tony Shalhoub, Zeljko Ivanek, Mary Mara, William H. Macy

Sean Penn, Robin Wright Penn

Garry Shandling

Meg Ryan

Kevin Spacey, Anna Paquin, Sean Penn

HURLYBURLY

(FINE LINE FEATURES) Producers, Anthony Drazan, Richard N. Gladstein, David S. Hamburger; Executive Producers, H. Michael Heuser, Frederick Zollo, Nicholas Paleologos, Carl Colpaert; Director, Anthony Drazan; Screenplay, David Rabe, based on his play; Photography, Changwei Gu; Designer, Michael Haller; Costumes, Mary Claire Hannan; Editor, Dylan Tichenor; Music, David Baerwald; Casting, David Rubin; Dolby; CFI color; Rated R; 122 minutes; December release

CAST

Eddie ....Sean Penn
Mickey ....Kevin Spacey
Darlene ....Robin Wright Penn
Phil ....Chazz Palminteri
Artie ....Garry Shandling
Donna ....Anna Paquin
Bonnie ....Meg Ryan
and Gianna Renaudo (Susie), David Fabrizio (Store Manager), Kenny Vance (Singer), Michaline Babich (Receptionist), Elaine Corral, Frank Sommerville (TV Anchors), Sharon Tay (TV Reporter), Bob Jimenez (Newscaster), Piers Mackenzie (Dry Cleaner), Lisa Ristorucci (Cashier), Igor Hiller (Little Billy), Curt Skaggs (Cowboy), Nathalie Lake (Miranda), Bud Cox (Priest), Peter Siteri (Poet), Laura Brownson (Vicki)

Eddie, a high powered Hollywood casting director, begins to question his shallow existence of drugs, sex and partying.

©Fine Line Features

Chazz Palminteri

DOWN IN THE DELTA

(MIRAMAX) Producers, Rick Rosenberg, Bob Christiansen, Victor McGauley, Wesley Snipes, Reuben Cannon; Director, Maya Angelou; Screenplay, Myron Goble; Photography, William Wages; Designer, Lindsey Hermer-Bell; Editor, Nancy Richardson; Co-Producers, Terri Farnsworth, Myron Goble, Alfre Woodard; Music, Stanley Clarke; Casting, Reuben Cannon & Associates; a Showtime presentation of an Amen Ra Films and Chris/Rose productions; Dolby; Deluxe color; Rated PG-13; 111 minutes; December release

CAST

Loretta	Alfre Woodard
Earl	Al Freeman, Jr.
Rosa Lynn	Mary Alice
Annie	Esther Rolle
Zenia	Loretta Devine
Will	Wesley Snipes
Thomas	Mpho Koaho
Tracy	Kulani Hassen
Monica	Anne Marie Johnson
Dr. Rainey	Justin Lord
Marco	Richard Yearwood
Volunteer	Sandra Caldwell
Tourists	Colleen Williams, Richard Blackburn
Manager	Philip Akin
Drug Addict	Mary Fallick
Pawnbroker	Sandi Ross
Prim Woman	Barbara Barnes Hopkins
Prim Sister	Marium Carvell
Gina	Quancetia Hamilton
Isabelle	Kim Roberts

and DeFoy Glenn (Reverend Floyd), Jeff Jones (Man in Congregation), Michelyn Emelle (Dozing Woman), Johnie Chase (Grinning Man), Andrea Lewis (Cassandra), Nigel Shawn-Williams (Carl), Bernard Browne, Alison Sealy-Smith (Diners), Eugene Clarke, Chris Benson (Citizens), Carol Anderson (Jesse's Wife), Neville Edwards (Slave Man), Yanna McIntosh (Slave Woman), Troy Seivwright-Adams (Collin), Kevin Duhaney (Justin), Joel Gordon (Jesse 1865—17 years old), Phil Jarrett (Jesse 1890—42 years old), Clinton Green (Soloist in Church)

Seeing Loretta succumb to drugs and alcohol, her mother pawns a valuable family heirloom and moves Loretta and her children from Chicago to their ancestral home in the Mississippi Delta.

©Miramax Films

Al Freeman Jr., Wesley Snipes, Alfre Woodard

Alfre Woodard

Mary Alice, Kulani Hassen, Mpho Koaho, Alfre Woodard

Loretta Devine, Alfre Woodard

PATCH ADAMS

Robin Williams, Monica Potter

Robin Williams

(UNIVERSAL) Producers, Barry Kemp, Mike Farrell, Marvin Minoff, Charles Newirth; Executive Producers, Marsha Garces Williams, Tom Shadyac; Director, Tom Shadyac; Screenplay, Steve Oedekerk; Based on the book *Gesundheit: Good Health is a Laughing Matter* by Hunter Doherty Adams, with Maureen Mylander; Photography, Phedon Papamichael; Designer, Linda DeScenna; Editor, Don Zimmerman; Co-Producers, Steve Oedekerk, Devorah Moos-Hankin; Music, Marc Shaiman; Costumes, Judy Ruskin-Howell; a Blue Wolf-Farrell/Minoff-Bungalow 78 production; Dolby; Panavision; Deluxe color; Rated PG-13; 114 minutes; December release

CAST

Hunter "Patch" Adams	Robin Williams
Truman	Daniel London
Carin	Monica Potter
Mitch	Philip Seymour Hoffman
Dean Walcott	Bob Gunton
Dr. Eaton	Josef Sommer
Joletta	Irma P. Hall
Judy	Frances Lee McCain
Dean Anderson	Harve Presnell
Adelane	Daniella Kuhn
Bryan	Jake Bowen
Bill Davis	Peter Coyote
Bile	James Greene
Rudy	Michael Jeter
Arthur Mendelson	Harold Gould
Trevor Beene	Bruce Bohne
Dr. Prack	Harry Groener
Emmet	Barry "Shabaka" Henley
Charlie	Stephen Anthony Jones
Dr. Titan	Richard Kiley
Larry	Douglas Roberts
Aggie	Ellen Albertini Dow
Everton	Alan Tudyk
Neil	Ryan Hurst
Chess Man	Peter Siiteri
Scared Customer	Tim Wiggins
Feeble Woman	Helen Tourtillott
Instructor	On West
Passerby	Domenique Lozano
Organzier	Ralph Peduto
Big Texan	Ken Hoffman

and Jim Antonio, Roy Conrad (E.R. Doctors), Jay Jacobus (Jack Walton), Dot-Marie Jones (Miss Meat), Geoff Fiorito, Samuel Sheng (3rd Year Students), Kathleen Stefano (Margery), Piers Mackenzie (Dr. Hashman), Alex Gonzalez (Hispanic Boy), Ismael "East" Carlo (Hispanic Father)Wanda Christine (Nurse Klegg), Lorri Holt (Pediatric Nurse), Stephanie Smith (Laughing Nurse), Cameron Brooke Stanley, Jamieson G. Downes, Jena Marie Thomas, Wesley G. Haines (Children's Ward Patients), Richard J. Silberg, William Joseph Scharff, James Anthony Cotton, Michael Rae Sommers, Howard Allison Williams, David Fine, James Carraway, J. Stephen Coyle (Psych Patients), Wanda McCaddon (Woman in Lobby), Mary Delorenzo (Nurse), Vivis (Hysterical Woman), Donna Kimball (Waitress), Norman Alden (Truck Driver), Lydell M. Cheshier (Younger Man), Diane Amos, Sonya Eddy (Older Waitresses), Kelvin Yee (Orderly), Doreen Chou Croft (Asian Woman), Bill Roberson (Fred Jarvis), Randy Oglesby (Pinstriped Man), Vilma Vitanza (Maria), Bonnie Johnson (Walcott's Secretary), Jack Ford (Lecturer), Christine Pineda (Hispanic Girl), Karen Michel (Mrs. Davis), James Allen (Ed), Katherine A. Fitzhugh (Mrs. O'Bannon), Kyle Timothy Smith, Jonathan Holder (Davis Sons), Renee Rogers, Shanón Orrock (Receptionists), Don Rizzo (Minister), Andrew Clement (Puppeteer), George Lee Masters, Daniel P. Hannafin, Roger W. Durrett (Boardroom Doctors), Richard C. Adkins, Ralph David Westfall, Bob Feaster, Thom McIntyre, Alfred Salley, Michael Kennedy (Gynecologists)

Following a stay in a sanitarium, Patch Adams decides to study medicine and prove that those in the medical profession can treat their patients on a more personal and humane level. This film received an Oscar nomination for original score—musical or comedy.

©Universal City Studios Prods.

Robin Williams and Children

Nick Nolte, James Coburn

Nick Nolte, Sissy Spacek

Nick Nolte, James Coburn, Willem Dafoe, Sissy Spacek

AFFLICTION

(LIONS GATE) Producer, Linda Reisman; Executive Producers, Nick Nolte, Barr Potter; Director/Screenplay, Paul Schrader; Based on the novel by Russell Banks; Co-Producers, Eric Berg, Frank K. Isaac; Line Producer, Josette Perrotta; Photography, Paul Sarossy; Designer, Anne Pritchard; Editor, Jay Rabinowitz; Music, Michael Brook; Costumes, Francois LaPlante; Casting, Ellen Chenoweth, Kathleen Chopin; a Largo Entertainment presentation of a Reisman/Kingsgate production; Dolby; Color; Rated R; 114 minutes; December release

0CAST

Wade Whitehouse	Nick Nolte
Margie Fogg	Sissy Spacek
Glen Whitehouse	James Coburn
Rolfe Whitehouse	Willem Dafoe
Lillian	Mary Beth Hurt
Jack Hewitt	Jim True
Alma Pittman	Marian Seldes
Gordon LaRiviere	Holmes Osborne
Jill	Brigid Tierney
Evan Twombley	Sean McCann
Nick Wickham	Wayne Robson
Chick Ward	Tim Post
Frankie Lacoy	Christopher Heyerdahl
Hettie	Janine Theriault
Homer	Paul Stewart
Lugene Brooks	Sheena Larkin
Driver	Penny Mancuso
Elaine	Danielle Desormeaux
Jimmy Dane	Charles Powell
Short-Haired Local	Donovan Reiter
Young Wade	Brawley Notle
Young Rolfe	Michael Caloz
Sally Whitehouse	Joanna Noyes

and Marcel Jeannin (State Trooper), Susie Almgren (Mrs. Gordon), Steve Adams (Mel Gordon), Martha-Marie Kleinhans (Lena), Mark Camacho (Clyde), Ralph Allison (Reverend Doughty), Eugene Lipinski (J. Battle Hand)

While investigating the mysterious events surrounding the shooting of a union boss, Wade Whitehouse, a police officer in a tiny, snowbound town, finds his personal life unraveling. 1998 Academy Award-winner for Best Supporting Actor (James Coburn). This film received an additional nomination for actor (Nick Nolte).

©Lions Gate

THE HI-LO COUNTRY

Billy Crudup, Woody Harrelson

(GRAMERCY) Producers, Barbara De Fina, Martin Scorsese, Eric Fellner, Tim Bevan; Executive Producer, Rudd Simmons; Director, Stephen Frears; Screenplay, Walon Green; Based on the novel by Max Evans; Photography, Oliver Stapleton; Designer/Costumes, Patricia Norris; Editor, Masahiro Hirakubo; Music, Carter Burwell; Co-Producer, Liza Chasin; Casting, Victoria Thomas; a PolyGram Filmed Entertainment presentation in association with Martin Scorsese of a Working Title production with Cappa/De Fina productions; Dolby; Eastman color; Rated R; 114 minutes; December release

CAST

Big Boy Matson	Woody Harrelson
Pete Calder	Billy Crudup
Mona	Patricia Arquette
Little Boy "L.B." Matson	Cole Hauser
Hoover Young	James Gammon
Josepha O'Neil	Penelope Cruz
Jim Ed Love	Sam Elliott
Levi Gomez	Enrique Castillo
Les Birk	John Diehl
Billy Harte	Darren Burrows
Delfino Mondragon	Jacob Vargas
Jack Couffer	Robert Knott
Henchman	Sandy Baron
Art Logan	Craig Carter
Auctioneer	Walter C. Hall
Chickie Cobain	Will Cascio
Steve Shaw	Lane Smith
Meesa	Katy Jurado

and Richard Purdy (Bartender), Keith Walters (Man on Horse), Sarge McGraw (Nick the Bartender), Rosaleen Linehan (Mrs. Matson), Rose Maddox (Grandmother), Bob Tallman (Rodeo Announcer), Buff Douthitt, H.P. Evetts (Rodeo Wranglers), Kate Williamson (Mrs. Young), Don Pope (Sheriff Fitts), Leslie Cook (Dancer), Monica Sundown, Amanda Cordova (Singers at Sano Dance), Gaye Grant, Leon Rausch, Chris O'Connell, Marty Stuart, Donald R. Walser (Singers at Rodeo Dance)

Sam Elliott

Penelope Cruz

Following World War II, two cowboys, Pete Calder and the rambunctious Big Boy Matson, team to start a cattle business which is soon threatened by a wealthy baron who wants to gain control of smaller enterprises to expand his own.

©Gramercy Pictures

Patricia Arquette, Woody Harrelson

Billy Crudup, Woody Harrelson

Vincent Kartheiser

Melanie Griffith, James Woods

ANOTHER DAY IN PARADISE

(TRIMARK) Producers, Stephen Chin, Larry Clark, James Woods; Director, Larry Clark; Screenplay, Christopher Landon, Stephen Chin; Based on the book by Eddie Little; Photography, Eric Edwards; Designer, Aaron Osborne; Editor, Luis Colina; Co-Producer, Scott Shiffman; Costumes, Kathryn Morrison; Casting, John Papsidera; a Chinese Bookie Pictures presentation; Dolby; CFI color; Rated R; 101 minutes; December release

CAST

Mel	James Woods
Sid	Melanie Griffith
Bobbie	Vincent Kartheiser
Rosie	Natasha Gregson Wagner
Jewels	Lou Diamond Phillips
Reverend	James Otis
Danny	Branden Williams
Clem	Brent Briscoe
Ty	Peter Sarsgaard
Richard Johnson	Paul Hipp
Bonnie Johnson	Kim Flowers
Phil	John Gatins
Barry	Ryan Donahue
Conan	Christopher Doyle
Breather	Dick Hancock
Waitress	Pamela Gordon

and Jay Leggett (Security Guard), Michael Jeffrey Woods (Big Man), Karen Lee Sheperd (Big Man's Wife), Mitchell Orr, Jr. (Big Man's Boy), Leo Fitzpatrick (Guard at Reverend's Gate), Simon Williams (Maitre'd), Steven Gererd Connell (Gas Station Attendant), Clarence Carter (Himself), Roosevelt Bitten, Greg Dalton, Donald Hayes, Ishma Isreal, Maurice James, Eddie Lott, Will Miller, Darryl Richards, Isaac Smith (Band Members)

Mel and Sid, a pair of petty thieves and drug addicts, pick up a younger couple, Bobbie and Rosie, and take them on their warped and out-of-control adventures.

©Trimark Pictures

James Woods

James Woods, Melanie Griffith, Natasha Gregson Wagner, Vincent Kartheiser

PLAYING BY HEART

(MIRAMAX) formerly *Dancing About Architecture*; Producers, Willard Carroll, Meg Liberman, Tom Wilhite; Executive Producers, Paul Feldsher, Bob Weinstein, Harvey Weinstein, Guy East, Nigel Sinclair; Director/Screenplay, Willard Carroll; Co-Producer, Kurt Albrecht; Co-Executive Producer, David Witz; Photography, Vilmos Zsigmond; Designer, Missy Stewart; Music, John Barry; Costumes, April Ferry; an Intermedia Films presentation in association with Morpheus of a Hyperion Production; Dolby; Panavision; Color; Rated R; 120 minutes; December release

Ryan Phillippe, Angelina Jolie

CAST

Meredith	Gillian Anderson
Mildred	Ellen Burstyn
Paul	Sean Connery
Roger	Anthony Edwards
Joan	Angelina Jolie
Mark	Jay Mohr
Keenan	Ryan Phillippe
Hugh	Dennis Quaid
Hannah	Gena Rowlands
Trent	Jon Stewart
Gracie	Madeleine Stowe
Allison	Patricia Clarkson
Melanie	Nastassja Kinski
Martin	David Clennon
Lana	Alec Mapa
Malcolm	Jeremy Sisto

and Matt Malloy (Desk Clerk), Christian Mills (Philip), Kellie Waymire (Jane), April Grace (Valery), Tim Halligan (Director—Cook Show), Michael Emerson (Bosco), John Patrick White (Pete), Amanda Peet (Amber), David Ferguson (Drag Queen), Joel McCrary (Bartender—Drag Queen), Worthie Meacham (2nd Drag Queen Performer), Michael Buchman Silver (Max), Hal Landon, Jr. (Actor "Commissioner"), Marc Allen Lewis (Actor "Harpagon"), Ron Boussom (Actor "Jacques"), Daniel Chodos (Actor "Anselme"), Mark Lewis (Waiter), Jim Abele (Doctor), Chris Conner (Harry), Marcus Printop (Trumpet Player), Larry Antonio (Bass Player), Tom Chuchvara (Drummer), Robert English (Saxophonist), Ryo Okumuto (Pianist)

A look at the romantic ups and downs of various diverse couples and pairings in the Los Angeles area.

©Miramax Films

Sean Connery, Gena Rowlands

Madeleine Stowe, Anthony Edwards

Jon Stewart, Gillian Anderson

Irving Kristol (r) in *Arguing the World*
©First Run Features

Michael Rapaport, Lili Taylor, Kevin Corrigan in *Illtown*
©The Shooting Gallery

ARGUING THE WORLD (First Run Features) Producer/Director/Screenplay, Joseph Dorman; Executive Producer, Arnold Labaton; Photography, Peter Brownscombe, Barrin Bonet, Wayne DeLaRoche, Boyd Estus; Editor, Jonathan Oppenheim; Music, Adam Guettel; Narrator, Alan Rosenberg; a Riverside Film Prod. and Thirteen/WNET production; funded by the National Endowment for the Humanities, 1997; Color; Not rated; 109 minutes; January release. Documentary in which four leading intellectuals, Irving Howe, Daniel Bell, Nathan Glazer and Irving Kristol, discuss how ideas can change the world.

FIRESTORM (20th Century Fox) Producers, Joseph Loeb III, Matthew Weisman, Thomas M. Hammel; Executive Producer, Louise Rosner; Director, Dean Semler; Screenplay, Chris Soth; Photography, Stephen F. Windon; Designers, Richard Paris, Linda Del Rosario; Music, J. Peter Robinson; Editor, Jack Hofstra; Co-Producer, Douglas C. Metzger; Casting, Allison Gordon Kohler; Stunts, Glenn Wilder; a Loeb/Weisman production; Dolby; Deluxe color; Rated R; 89 minutes; January release. **CAST:** Howie Long (Jesse Graves), Scott Glenn (Wynt Perkins), William Forsythe (Shaye), Suzy Amis (Jennifer), Christianne Hirt (Monica), Garwin Sanford (Pete), Sebastian Spence (Cowboy), Michael Greyeyes (Andy), Barry Pepper (Packer), Vladimir Kulich (Karge), Tom McBeath (Loomis), Benjamin Ratner (Wilkins), Jonathon Young (Sherman), Chilton Crane (Tina's Mom), Robyn Driscoll (Tina's Dad), Alexandria Mitchell (Tina), Terry Kelly (Lawyer), David Fredericks (Guard), Gavin Buhr (Childs), Danny Wattley (Moody), Derek Hamilton (Dwyer), Adrian Dorval (Belcher), Jon Cuthbert (Davis), Sean Campbell (Deputy), Deryl Hayes (Sheriff Garrett)

ILLTOWN (The Shooting Gallery) Producer, David L. Bushell; Executive Producers, Larry Meistrich, Donald C. Carter; Director/Screenplay, Nick Gomez; Based on the book *The Cocaine Kids* by Terry Williams; Photography, Jim Denault; Editor, Tracy Granger; Designer, Susan Bolles; Music, Brian Keane; Associate Producer, Peter T. Dapuzzo; Casting, Sheila Jaffe, Georgianne Walken; a Donald C. Carter presentation; Dolby; Color; Rated R; 97 minutes; January release. **CAST:** Michael Rapaport (Dante), Lili Taylor (Micky), Adam Trese (Gabriel), Kevin Corrigan (Francis "Cisco"), Angela Featherstone (Lilly), Tony Danza (D'Avalon), Isaac Hayes (George), Paul Schulze (Lucas), Saul Stein (Gunther), Vernon Campbell (Sarge), Adam Cartwright, Eddie Kaye Thomas, Ian Marioles

STAR KID (Trimark) Producer, Jennie Lew Tugend; Executive Producer, Mark Amin; Director/Screenplay, Manny Coto; Co-Executive Producer, Andrew Hersh; Photography, Ronn Schmidt; Designer, C.J. Strawn; Editor, Bob Ducsay; Co-Producers, Jonathon Komack, Cami Winikoff; Costumes, Ileane Meltzer; Music, Nicholas Pike; Special Make-up Effects, Thomas R. Burman, Bari Dreiband-Burman; Visual Effects Supervisor, Thomas C. Rainone; a Jennie Lew Tugend/Trimark Pictures production; Dolby; FotoKem color; Rated PG; 101 minutes; January release. **CAST:** Joseph Mazzello (Spencer Griffith), Joey Simmrin (Turbo Bruntley), Alex Daniels (Cyborsuit), Arthur Burghardt (Cyborsuuit Voice), Brian Simpson (Broodwarrior), Richard Gilliland (Roland Griffith), Corinne Bohrer (Janet Holloway), Ashlee Levitch (Stacey Griffith), Danny Masterson (Kevin), Lauren Eckstrom (Michelle), Christine Weatherup (Nadia), Yumi Adachi (Mika), Jack McGee (Hank Bruntley), Alissa Ann Smego (Burgerworld Girl), Fred Kronenberg (Officer #1), Joshua Fardon (Rookie Cop), Bobby Porter (Trelkin/"Nath"), Larry Nicholas (Trelkin/"Tenris"), Rusty Hanson, Terry Castillo-Faass (Trelkins)

Howie Long, Suzy Amis in *Firestorm*
©Twentieth Century Fox

Joey Simmrin, Joseph Mazzello in *Star Kid*
©Trimark Pictures, Inc.

Renée Zellweger, Tim Roth in *Deceiver*
©Metro-Goldwyn-Mayer Inc.

Peter O'Toole in *Phantoms*
©Dimension Films

DECEIVER (MGM) formerly *Liar;* Producer, Peter Glatzer; Executive Producer, Mark Damon; Director/Screenplay, Jonas and Joshua Pate; Photography, Bill Butler; Designer, John Kretschmer; Co-Producer, Don Winston; Music, Harry Gregson-Williams; Costumes, Dana Allyson Greenberg; Line Producer, John Saviano; Casting, Laurel Smith; an MDP Worldwide presentation of a Peter Glatzer production; Dolby; J-D-C Scope; Color; Rated R; 102 minutes; January release. **CAST:** Tim Roth (Wayland), Chris Penn (Braxton), Michael Rooker (Kennesaw), Renée Zellweger (Elizabeth), Ellen Burstyn (Mook), Rosanna Arquette (Mrs. Kennesaw), Michael Parks (Dr. Banyard), Mark Damon (Wayland's Father), J.C. Quinn (Priest), Jody Wilhelm (Mrs. Wayland), Don Winston (Warren), Ocie Pouncie (Boogie), Bob Hungerford (Jebby), Genevieve Butler (Mary Kennesaw), Chelsea Butler (Chelsea Kennesaw), David Alan Pickelsimer II (Billy Kennesaw), Paul Smith (Wayland's Girlfriend's Father), George Nannerello (Laughing Officer), Mike Flippo, James Middleton (Police Officers), Karina Logue (Sorority Girl), Ashley Rogers (Woman in Park)

SLAPPY AND THE STINKERS (TriStar) Producers, Sid, Bill and Jon Sheinberg; Executive Producer, Martha Chang; Director, Barnet Kellman; Screenplay, Bob Wolterstorff, Mike Scott; Photography, Paul Maibaum; Designer, Ivo Cristante; Editor, Jeff Wishengrad; Costumes, Jami Burrows; Music, Craig Safan; Casting, Shari Rhodes, Joseph Middleton, Ronnie Yeskel, Mary Vernieu; a presentation of The Bubble Factory of a Sheinberg production; Dolby; Technicolor; Rated PG; 78 minutes; January release. **CAST:** B.D. Wong (Morgan Brinway), Bronson Pinchot (Roy), Jennifer Coolidge (Harriet), Joseph Ashton (Sonny), Gary LeRoi Gray (Domino), Carl Michael Lindner (Witz), Scarlett Pomers (Lucy), Travis Tedford (Loaf), David Dukes (Spencer Dane, Sr.), Spencer Klein (Spencer

Dane, Jr.), Sam McMurray (Boccoli), Terry Cain (Nancy), Bodhi Pine Elfman (Tag), Terri Garber (Witz's Mom), Rick Lawless (Tommy), Richard Taylor Olson (Max Straus), Fred Asparagus (Dockhand), Jamie Donnelly (Aquarium Information Woman), Arturo Gil (Goateed Man), Barbara Howard (Sonny's Mom), Tim Hutchinson (Domino's Dad), Thomas H. Middleton (Aquarium Security Guard), Jill Remez (Newsweek Reporter), Jonathan Slavin (Fish n' Chips Delivery Boy), Marina Vain (Tattooed Woman), Craig Rudnick (Special Animal Voices)

PHANTOMS (Dimension) Producers, Joel Soisson, Michael Leahy, Robert Pringle, Steve Lane; Executive Producers, Bob Weinstein, Harvey Weinstein, Dean Koontz; Director, Joe Chappelle; Screenplay, Dean Koontz, based on his book; Photography, Richard Clabaugh; Editor, Randolph K. Bricker; Music, David Williams; Designers, Deborah Raymond, Dorian Vernacchio; Costumes, Dana C. Litwack; Casting, Don Phillips; a Neo Motion Pictures production in association with Raven House, Inc.; Distributed by Miramax Films; Dolby; Color; Rated R; 93 minutes; January release. **CAST:** Peter O'Toole (Timothy Flyte), Rose McGowan (Lisa Pailey), Joanna Going (Jenny Pailey), Liev Schreiber (Deputy Stu Wargle), Ben Affleck (Sheriff Bryce Hammond), Nicky Katt (Deputy Steve Shanning), Clifton Powell (Gen. Copperfield), Rick Otto (Scientist Lockland), Rachel Shane (Scientist Yamaguci), Adam Nelson (Scientist Burke), John Hammil (Scientist Talbot), John Scott Clough (Scientist Shane), Michael DeLorenzo (Soldier Velazquez), William Hahn (Scientist Borman), Robert Himber (Scientist Walker), Bo Hopkins (Agent Hawthorne),

Travis Tedford, Carl Michael Lindner, Joseph Ashton, Scarlett Pomers, Gary LeRoi Gray, with Slappy in *Slappy and the Stinkers*
©TriStar Pictures

Gary Cooper, Ayn Rand in *Ayn Rand: A Sense of Life*
©Strand Releasing

Miguel Ferrer in *The Night Flier*
©New Line Cinema

Paul Monette in *Paul Monette: The Brink of Summer's End*
©First Run Features

Rob Knepper (Agent Wilson), Paul Schmidt (Church Soldier), Dean Hallo (Sgt. Harker), Clive Rosengren (Commanding Officer), Edmund Wilson (Guthrie), Luke Eberl (Tunnel Boy), Rich Beall (Security Guard), Judith Drake (Hilda), Yvette Nipar (Cowgirl), Ruger (Phantom Dog)

AYN RAND: A SENSE OF LIFE (Strand) Producer/Director/ Screenplay, Michael Paxton; Photography, Alik Sakharov; Editors, Lauren Schaffer, Christopher Earl; Music/Associate Producer, Jeff Britting; Line Producer, Ellen Raphael; Narrator, Sharon Gless; an AG Media Corporation Limited in association with Copasetic Inc. presentation; Dolby; Color; Not rated; 145 minutes; February release. Documentary on author-philosopher Ayn Rand; featuring Dr. Michael S. Berliner, Dr. Harry Binswanger, Sylvia Bokor, Daniel E. Greene, Cynthia Peikoff, Dr. Leonard Peikoff, Al Ramrus, Dr. John Ridpath, and Mike Wallace. (This film received an Oscar nomination as feature documentary for 1997).

KURT AND COURTNEY (Roxie) Producers, Tine Van Den Brande, Michael D'Acotsa; Executive Producer, Nick Frazer; Director, Nick Broomfield; Photography, Joan Churchill, Alex Vendor; Music, David Bergeaud; Editor, Mark Atkins; Dolby; Color; Not rated; 95 minutes; February release. Documentary on rock stars Kurt Cobain and his wife Courtney Love.

STEPHEN KING'S THE NIGHT FLIER (New Line Cinema) Producers, Richard P. Rubinstein, Mitchell Galin, Mark Pavia; Director, Mark Pavia; Screenplay, Mark Pavia, Jack O'Donnell; Based on a story by Stephen King; Executive Producer, David Kappes; Co-Producer, Alfredo Cuomo; Photography, David Connell; Designer, Burton Rencher; Costumes, Pauline White; Editor, Elizabeth Schwartz; Special Effects Make-up, KNB EFX Group Inc.; Music, Brian Keane; Casting, Leonard Finger, Lyn Richmond; a New Amsterdam Entertainment Inc. in association with Stardust International Ltd. & Medusa Film SpA presentation of a Richard P. Rubinstein production; Dolby; Color; Rated R; 99 minutes; February release. **CAST:** Miguel Ferrer (Richard Dees), Julie Entwisle (Katherine Blair), Dan Monahan (Merton Morrison), Michael H. Moss (Dwight Renfield), John Bennes (Ezra Hannon), Beverly Skinner (Selida McCamon), Rob Wilds (Buck Kendall), Richard Olsen (Claire Bowie), Elizabeth McCormick (Ellen Sarch), J.R. Rodriguez, Bob Casey (Terminal Cops), Ashton Stewart (Nate Wilson), William Neely (Ray Sarch), Windy Wenderlich (Henry Gates), General Fermon Judd, Jr. (Policeman), Deann Korbutt (Linda Ross), Rachel Lewis (Libby Grant), Kristen Leigh (Dottie Walsh), Simon Elsworth (Duffery Bartender), Jim Grimshaw (Gas Station Attendant), Matthew Johnson (Caretaker), Terry Neil Edlefsen (Drunk), Joy Knox, Randal Brown, Laurie Wolf, Keith Shepard, Ruth Reid (Dream Vampires), Matt Webb, David Zum Brunnen, April Turner, Manya K. Rubinstein (Reporters), Kelley Sims (Intern)

PAUL MONETTE: THE BRINK OF SUMMER'S END (First Run Features) Producer, Lesli Klainberg; Director/Screenplay, Monte Bramer; Music, Jon Ehrlich; Readings, Jonathan Fried; Narrator, Linda Hunt; Color; Not rated; 90 minutes; February release. Documentary on gay writer and activist Paul Monette.

LOVE WALKED IN (TriStar) formerly *The Bitter End;* Producer, Ricardo Freixa; Executive Producer, Jorge Estrada Mora; Director, Juan J. Campanella; Screenplay, Lynn Geller, Larry Golin, Juan J. Campanella; Based on a novel by Jose Pablo Feinmann; Co-Executive Producer, Jim Serpico; Photography, Daniel Shulman; Designer, Michael Shaw; Editor, Darren Kloomok; Music, Wendy Blackstone; Costumes, David Robinson; Casting, Pat McCorkle; a Jempsa Entertainment and Apostle Pictures production; U.S.-Argentinian; Dolby; Color; Rated R; 90 minutes; February release. **CAST:** Denis Leary (Jack Morrisey), Terence Stamp (Fred Moore), Aitana Sanchez-Gijon (Vicky Rivas), Danny Nucci (Cousin Matt), Moira Kelly (Vera), Michael Badalucco (Eddie Bianco), Gene Canfield (Joey), Marj Dusay (Judith Moore), Neal Huff (Howard), Rocco Sisto (Jim Zamsky), J.K. Simmons (Mr. Shulman), Justin Lazard (Lenny), Jimmy McQuaid (Young Howard), Murphy Guyer (Howard's Boss), Paul Eagle (Landlord), Fiddle Viracola (Aunt Ethel), Jeremy Webb (Hampton's Waiter), Gregory Scanlon (Valet), Gary DeWitt Marshall (Broken Ivory Bartender), D.C. Benny (Comedian), Patrick Boll (Porter)

Terence Stamp, Aitana Sanchez-Gijon in *Love Walked In*
©TriStar Pictures

Marla Schaffel, Michael Harris in *I Love You, Don't Touch Me!*
©MGM Distribution Co.

I LOVE YOU, DON'T TOUCH ME! (Goldwyn) Producers, Julie Davis, Scott Chosed; Director/Screenplay/Editor, Julie Davis; Co-Producer, Meredith Scott Lynn; Executive Producer, Jennifer Chaiken; Photography, Mark Putnam; Designer, Carol Strober; Original Songs, Jane Ford; Costumes, Wend Greiner; Casting, Karen Church; a Westie Films presentation in association with Big Hair Productions; Distributed by MGM; Dolby; Panavision; Foto-Kem color; Rated R; 90 minutes; February release. **CAST:** Marla Schaffel (Katie), Mitchell Whitfield (Ben), Michael Harris (Richard Webber), Meredith Scott Lynn (Janet), Darryl Theirse (Jones), Nancy Sorel (Elizabeth), Wally Kurth (David Barclay), Jack McGee (Lou Candela), Julie Ariola (Mom), Victor Raider-Wexler (Dad), Sara Van Horn (Analyst), Debbie Munroe (Margo), Tim deZarn (Vagrant), Janine Venable (Deirdre), George P. Saunders (Ted), Michael Candela (Audition Man), Ramesh Pandey (Bob Yager), Jackie Debatin (Jenny), Nell Balaban (Nina), Julie Davis (Lisa), Michael Dell, Matthew R. Eyraud, Tom Hodges, Mitchell Rose (Assholes), Geoffrey Infeld, Mark St. James (Club Sin Hunks), Shannon McLeod (Ben's Dream Date), Melanie Wachsman (Naked Blonde), Julia Bruglio (Naked Woman in Shower), Andrew Camp (Clark's Lover)

NOTES FROM UNDERGROUND (Northern Arts) Producers, Frank J. Gruber, Alicia Dollard, Chris Beckman; Executive Producer/Director/Screenplay, Gary Walkow; Based on the novel by Fyodor Dostoevsky; Photography, Dan Gillham; Editor, Peter B. Ellis; Music, Mark Governor; Designer, Michael Rizzo; Costumes, Alina Panova; Casting, Bonita Pietila; Ultra-Stereo; Foto-Kem color; Not rated; 88 minutes; February release. **CAST:** Henry Czerny (The Underground Man), Sheryl Lee (Liza), Eammon Roche (Simon), Charlie Stratton (Jerry), Geoffrey Rivas (Tom), Jon Favreau (Zerkov), Vic Polizos (Howard the Contractor), James Troesh (Anthony), Kasey Fallo (Attractive Architect), Jack Heller (Maitre D'), Fredrik Nilsen (Waiter), Ivan Migel (Cabbie), Erica Fox (Mrs. Zerkov—

fantasy), Hannah Bernstein (Zerkov's Daughter—fantasy), Theodore Siegel (Zerkov's son—fantasy), Pamala Tyson (Madam), Seth Green (Nerdsy Boy), Tony Abatemarco, Gary Walkow (Lucky Architects)

LEATHER JACKET LOVE STORY (Jour de Fete) Producer, Jerry Goldberg; Executive Producer, Bruce Baker; Director, David DeCoteau; Screenplay, Rondo Mieczkowski; Photography, Howard Wexler; Editor, Jeffrey Schwarz; Designer, Jeannie Lomma; Costumes, Edward Hibbs; a Leather Jacket Prods. presentation; Black & white; Not rated; 85 minutes; February release. **CAST:** Christopher Bradley (Mike), Sean Tataryn (Kyle), Geoff Moody (Ian), Hector Mercado (Sam), Stephen J. McCarthy/Madame Dish (Madge), Erin Krystle (Charella), Craig Olsen (Amanda), Mink Stole (Martine), Nicholas Worth (Jack), William Butler (Julian), Momma (Counterperson), Daniel Escobar (Zana), Arlene Golonka (Mom), Dennis Larkin (Youth), Bob Prest (Piercer), David Wolfson (Dan), Morris Kight (Grumpy Poet), Ruby Tuesday (Applicant), Steve Mateo (Doorman), Sophie Poster (Grandma), Moist Towelette (Fashion Girl)

THE MAN IN THE IRON MASK (Fastest Cheapest Best Film Corp.) Producer/Director/Screenplay, William Richert; Based on the story and characters of Alexandre Dumas; Executive Producers, Jerry Seltzer, Mark Terry; Co-Producer, Gloria Pryor; Photography, William Barber; Designer, Jacques Hebert; Editor, Andrew Vaillancourt; Music, Jim Ervin; Costumes, Salvador Perez; an Invisible Studio presentation; Deluxe color; Not rated; 85 minutes; February release. **CAST:** Edward Albert (Athos), Dana Barron (Valliere), Timothy Bottoms (Fouquet), Brigid Brannah (Molly Pichon), Fannie Brett (Henriette), Meg Foster (Queen Anne), James Gammon (The Commandment), Dennis Hayden (D'Artagnan), William Richert (Count Aramis), Nick Richert (King Louis XIV/Phillipe), Rex Ryon (Porthos), R.G. Armstrong, Robert Littman.

CAUGHT UP (LIVE Entertainment) Producer, Peter Heller; Director/Screenplay, Darin Scott; Co-Producer, Elaine Dysinger; Photography, Tom Callaway; Designer, Terrence Foster; Editor, Charles Bornstein; Music, Marc Bonilla; Costumes, Tracey White; Casting, Tony Lee; a Heller Highwater Production in association with LIVE Film and Mediaworks; Dolby; Color; Rated R; 95 minutes; February release. **CAST:** Bokeem Woodbine (Daryl Allen), Cynda Williams (Vanessa/Trish), Joseph Lindsey (Billy Grimm), Clifton Powell (Herbert/Frank Lowden), Tony Todd (Jake), Basil Wallace (Ahmad), Jeffrey Combs (Security Guard), Snoop Doggy Dogg (Kool Kat Daddy), LL Cool J (Roger), Damon Saleem (Trip), Shedric Hunter, Jr. (Jerome), Jeris Poindexter (Larry), Doug Kruse (Freeway Cop), Darin Scott (TV Field Reporter), Marcus Johnson (Strap), Jerry Boyd (Mayor Skrote), Michael Clarke Duncan (BB), Courtney McLean (Bob), Jason Carmichael (Rob), Mather Zickel (Rocker), George Anthony Baker (Young Brotha), Tracy James (Young Sista)

THE ONLY THRILL (Moonstone Entertainment) Producers, Yael Stroh, James Holt, Gabriel Grunfeld; Executive Producers, Etchie Stroh, Peter Masterson, Carl Baum, Erin Martin Gorman; Director, Peter Masterson; Screenplay, Larry Ketron, based on his play *The Trading Post*; Photography, Don E. Fauntleroy; Designer, John Frick; Editor, Jeff Freeman; Music, Peter Rodgers Melnick; Costumes, Jean Pierre Dorléac; Casting, Ellie Kanner; a Prestige Productions and Laureate Films production; Dolby; Color; Rated R; 108 minutes; February release. **CAST:** Diane Keaton (Carol Fritzsimmons), Sam Shepard (Reece McHenry), Diane Lane (Katherine Fritzsimmons), Robert Patrick (Tom McHenry), Tate Donovan (Eddie), Stacey Travis (Lola Jennings), Brad Leland (Louis Quillet), Brandon Smith (Mike), Sharon Lawrence (Joleen Quillet), Richard Nance, Fred Ellis (Poker Players), Robert S. Lott (Charlie), B.A. Woods (Ruth), Mona Lee (Mother), Jessica Looney (Daughter)

A PARALYZING FEAR: THE STORY OF POLIO IN AMERICA (Independent-Film Forum) Producers, Paul Wagner, Nina Gilden Seavey; Director/Screenplay, Nina Gilden Seavey; Photography, Allen Moore, Reuben Aaronson; Editor, Catherine Shields; Music, Paul Christianson; Narration Written by Stephan Chodorov; Narrator, Olympia Dukakis; Color; Not rated; 90 minutes; March release. Documentary on the 1954 discovery of the vaccine for polio.

Bokeem Woodbine, Cynda Williams in *Caught Up*
©LIVE Entertainment

Diane Keaton, Sam Shepard in *The Only Thrill*
©Moonstone Entertainment

Jason Patric in *Incognito*
©Morgan Creek Productions, Inc.

INCOGNITO (Warner Bros.) Producer, James G. Robinson; Director, John Badham; Screenplay, Jordan Katz; Executive Producer, Bill Todman, Jr.; Co-Producer, William P. Cartlidge; from Morgan Creek productions; Panavision; Color; Rated R; 107 minutes; March release. **CAST:** Jason Patric (Harry Donovan), Irène Jacob (Prof. Marieke van den Broeck), Thomas Lockyer (Alastair), Ian Richardson (Turley), Simon Chandler (Iain Ill), Pip Torrens (White), Michael Cochrane (Turley, Deeks), Rod Steiger (Milton A. Donovan), Togoigawa (Agachi), Joseph Blatchley (Prof. Scheerding), Paul Brennen (Det. Sgt. Steed), Oliver Pierre (Lecuyer), Peter Gale (Westerbrook), David Marrick (Bright), Dudley Sutton (Halifax/Offul), Adam Fogerty (Ugo), Ricardo Montez (Juan Del Campo), Antonio Elliott (Grandson), Jonathan Newth (Judge), Bryan Matheson (Concierge), Lex van Delden (Dehoog), Hugo Bower (Smit), Walter Van Dyk (Thoolen), Frank Nendels (Anton), John Tordoff (Bartender), Jean-Luc Caron (Cafe Intellectual), Maja Otessen (Nude Model), Danielle Allan (Museum Attendant), Anna Korwin (Museum Official), David Sibley (Whitehurst Landlord), Michael Dimitri (Landlord), John Paul Morgan (Conductor), Stephen Webber (Barrister), Keith Anderson (Cout Translator), Heike Willman (Paris Saleswoman), Miriam Karlin (Marina), Jon Cartwright (Auctioneer Grandson), Andrew Forbes (Newsreader), Nora Connolly (Barmaid), Ian Holm.

CHAIRMAN OF THE BOARD (Trimark) Producers, Peter M. Lenkov, Rupert Harvey; Co-Executive Producers, Brad L.C. Greenberg, Edward K. Phillips; Executive Producer, Mark Amin; Director, Alex Zamm; Screenplay, Al Septien, Turi Meyer, Alex Zamm; Story, Al Septien, Turi Meyer; Co-Producer, Phillip B. Goldfine; Photography, David Lewis; Designer, Aaron Osborne; Music, Chris Hajian; Editor, Jim Hill; a 101st Street Films production; Dolby; Color; Rated PG-13; 95 minutes; March release. **CAST:** Carrot Top (Edison), Courtney Thorne-Smith (Natalie), Larry Miller (Bradford), Raquel Welch (Grace Kosik), Mystro Clark (Ty), Jack Plotnick (Zak), Jack Warden (Armand), Estelle Harris (Ms. Krubavitch), Bill Erwin (Landers), M. Emmet Walsh (Freemont), Jack McGee (Harlan), Glenn Shadix (Larry), Fred Stoller (McMillan Gate Guard), Taylor Negron (Mr. Withermeyer), Patrick Clifton (Edison's Father), Stuart Damon (Doctor), Darcie Dodds (Nurse), Jake & Tyler Bratton-Ryan (Womb Edison), Courtney Hope Lenkov (Baby Edison), Michael Stadvec (Yuppie Man), Arianna Ratner, Monika Lynn Wesley (Girls at *Annie* Audition), Cory Oliver (Condom Girl), Jack Riley (Condom Boss) Johnny Cocktails (Messenger), Rance Howard (Rev. Hatley), James Rice Delano (Funeral Employee), Charles Kahlenberg (Lawyer), Stacey Silverman (Edison's Secretary), Franca Benvenuto (Bradford's Secretary), Mark Kriski (Newscaster), Kevin Scannell (Mr. Alosi), Cindy Margolis (Tennis Instructor), Butterbean (Museum Guard), The Blue Hawaiians: Tom Charles Maxwell, Mark C. Sproull, Bron Tieman, Mark Fontana (The Luau Band)

A Paralyzing Fear

Carrot Top, Mystro Clark, Larry Miller, Jack Plotnick in
Chairman of the Board
©Trimark Pictures, Inc.

Steve Van Wormer, Paul Walker in *Meet the Deedles*
©Disney Enterprises, Inc.

Lisa Gerstein, Chris Enright in *Mary Jane's Not a Virgin Anymore*
©Station Wagon

MEET THE DEEDLES (Walt Disney Pictures) Producers, Dale Pollock, Aaron Meyerson; Executive Producers, Andy Heyward, Artie Ripp; Director, Steve Boyum; Screenplay, Jim Herzfeld; Photography, David Hennings; Designer, Stephen Storer; Editor, Alan Cody; Costumes, Alexandra Welker, Karyn Wagner; Music, Steve Bartek; a DIC Entertainment production in association with Peak Productions; Dolby; Technicolor; Rated PG; 92 minutes; March release. **CAST:** Steve Van Wormer (Stew Deedle), Paul Walker (Phil Deedle), A.J. Langer (Jesse Ryan), John Ashton (Capt. Douglas Pine), Dennis Hopper (Frank Slater), Eric Braeden (Elton Deedle), Richard Lineback (Crabbe), Robert Englund (Nemo), M.C. Gainey (Major Flower), Ana Gasteyer (Mel), Megan Cavanagh (Mo), Michael Ruud (Ludwig), Hattie Winston (Jo-Claire), Bob Eric Hart (Governor), Bart (Bear)

PUBLIC HOUSING (Zipporah Films) Producer/Director/Editor, Frederick Wiseman; Photography, John Davey; Color; Not rated; 195 minutes; March release. A look at the poor inhabitants of Chicago's Ida B. Wells public housing development.

MARY JANE'S NOT A VIRGIN ANYMORE (Station Wagon) Producer/Director/Screenplay/Editor, Sarah Jacobson; Co-Producers, Sunny Andersen, Ruth Jacobson; Photography, Adam Dodds, Sarah Jacobson; Music, Rama Kolesnikow; Color; Not rated; 96 minutes; March release. **CAST:** Lisa Gerstein (Jane), Greg Cruikshank (Dave), Beth Ramona Allen (Ericka), Andrew David DeAngelo (Matt), Chris Enright (Tom), Marny Snyder (Grace), Brandon Stepp (Ryan)

RIDE (Dimension) Producers, Reginald Hudlin, Warrington Hudlin; Executive Producers, Bob Weinstein, Harvey Weinstein, Cary Granat; Director/Screenplay, Millicent Shelton; Co-Producer, S. Bryan Hickox; Line Producer, Ernest Johnson; Photography, Frank Byers; Editor, Earl Watson;

Designer, Bryan Jones; Music, Dunn Pearson, Jr.; Costumes, Richard Owings; Casting, Eileen Mack Knight; a Hudlin Bros. production; Distributed by Miramax Films; Dolby; Deluxe color; Rated R; 95 minutes; March release. **CAST:** Malik Yoba (Poppa), Melissa De Sousa (Leta), John Witherspoon (Roscoe), Fredro Starr (Geronimo), Cedric the Entertainer (Bo), Sticky Fingaz (Brotha X), Kellie Williams (Tuesday), Idalis De Leon (Charity), Julia Garrison (Blacké), Guy Torry (Indigo), Rueben Asher (Casper), The Lady of Rage (Peaches), Dartanyan Edmonds (Byrd), Downtown Julie Brown (Bleau), Luther "Luke" Campbell (Freddy B), Doctor Dre (Eight), Ed Lover (Six), Snoop Doggy Dogg (Mente), Kirsten Camille Hill (Sexy Woman), Thalia Baudin (#65), Gary Anthony Williams (Tiny), Gene Chen (Store Owner), Glenn Morel (Groom), Fred Williamson (Casper's Dream Dad), Michael Pilver (Rest Room Attendant), Tom Chapman (Farmer), Jonathan Bergholz (Sheriff), George Collier (Mechanic) Michael Balin (James), Amber Pyfrom (Little Girl), Dave Hollister, Redman, Keith Murray, Erik Sermon (Themselves), Terri Lester (Yes Girl #40), Tonya Oliver (Montage Girl)

BARNEY'S GREAT ADVENTURE (PolyGram) Producers, Sheryl Leach, Dennis DeShazer; Director, Steve Gomer; Screenplay, Stephen White; Story, Stephen White, Sheryl Leach, Dennis DeShazer; Executive Producer, Ben Myron; Co-Producer, Jim Rowley; Photography, Sandi Sissel; Editor, Richard Halsey; Designer, Vincent Jefferds; Casting, Ronna Kress; Presented in association with Lyrick Studios; Dolby; Color; Rated

Public Housing
©Zipporah Films

Melissa De Sousa, Malik Yoba in *Ride*
©Dimension Films

Trevor Morgan, Kyla Pratt, Barney, Diana Rice in
Barney's Great Adventure
©PolyGram Company

Dylan Walsh, Joanna Going in *Eden*
©Legacy Releasing

G; 75 minutes; March release. **CAST:** George Hearn (Grandpa), Shirley Douglas (Grandma), Trevor Morgan (Cody), Kyla Pratt (Marcella), Diana Rice (Abby), Bob West (Barney—Voice), Julie Johnson (Baby Bop—Voice), Renee Madeline LeGuerrier (Mildred Goldfinch), Jeff Ayres (Baby Bop), Alan Fawcett (Dad), Steffen Foster (The Collector), Matt Holland (Waiter), David Joyner (Barney).

EDEN (Legacy) Producers, Harvey Kahn, Chip Duncan; Executive Producer, Robert Wm. Landaas; Director/Screenplay, Howard Goldberg; Co-Producer, Todd Hoffman; Photography, Hubert Taczanowski; Art Director, Philip J. Meyer; Costumes, Elizabeth Kaye; Editor, Steve Nevius; Music, Brad Feidel; Special Effects, Fantasy II Film Effects, Gene Warren; Casting, Ellie Kanner, Heidi L. Water; a Wall Street Pictures presentation; Color; Rated R; 106 minutes; April release. **CAST:** Joanna Going (Helen Kunen), Dylan Walsh (Bill Kunen), Sean Patrick Flanery (Dave), Sean Christensen (Rick), Edward O'Blenis Jr. (Sonny), John Aylward (Dr. Bryson), Anne Christianson (Milly), Marjorie Nelson (Ruth), R. Hamilton Wright (Mr. Bainbridge), Stephen Lennstrom (Johnny), Annie Michelle Price (Amy), John Billingsley (Lee), David Estrem (Dean Shays), J. Zachary Lenihan (Isherwood), Dennis Troutman (Parker), Bonnie Root (Lucy), Wally Dalton (Red Fleischer), Tony Doupe (Officer Stanley), Maggie Heffernan (Janet), Anna Faris (Dithy), Morty Gudelsky (Teacher), Caroline Smith (Nurse), Kevin O'Morrison (Rev. Alden).

MUSIC FROM ANOTHER ROOM (Orion) Producers, John Bertolli, Brad Krevoy, Steven Stabler, Bradley Thomas; Executive Producer, Jeffrey D. Ivers; Director/Screenplay, Charlie Peters; Photography, Richard Crudo; Music, Richard Gibbs; Editor, C. Timothy O'Meara; Designer, Charles Breen; Color; Rated PG-13; 104 minutes; April release. **CAST:** Jude Law (Danny), Jennifer Tilly (Nina Swan), Gretchen Mol (Anna Swan), Karen Swan (Martha Plimpton), Brenda Blethyn (Grace Swan), Jon Tenney (Eric), Jeremy Piven (Billy Swan), Vincent Laresca (Jesus), Jane Adams (Irene), Bruce Jarchow (Richard), Kevin Kilner (Hank), Jan Rubes (Louis Klammer), Judith Malina (Clara Klammer), Hillary Matthews (Sarah), Caitlin Sarah Needham (Lily), Jon Polito (Lorenzo Palmieri), Tony Abatemarco (Lucien), Josef Pilato (Carlo), Anna Shea (Cheryl), Kari Leigh Floyd (Emma), Rainey Taylor (Stage Manager), Martha Hackett (Paula), Margarita O'Quendo (Dancing Lady), Wanda-Lee Evans (Nurse), Frank Lugo (Justice), Gregg Almquist (Doctor), Brumby Broussard (Ed), Evie Pick (Betty), Lee Weaver (Porter), Cory Buck (Young Danny), Joe Pichler (Young Billy), Sara Paxton (Young Karen), David Carpenter (Konrad), Barbara Howard (Denise), Cynthia Mace (Roberta), Don Pugsley (Taxi Driver), Thomas Rosales (Jose), Mel Green (Abel), Richard Ruccolo (Nick), Al Berman (Norman), Fred Sanders (Driver), Daniel Passer (Dominic), Jennifer Christopher (Jennifer), Paula J. Newman (Lucy), Dana Edwards (Train Patron), Tria Katz (Girl with Luggage), Jane L. Moore (Kate).

3 NINJAS: HIGH NOON AT MEGA MOUNTAIN (TriStar) Producers, James Kang, Yoram Ben-Ami; Executive Producers, Simon Sheen, Arthur Leeds; Director, Sean McNamara; Screenplay, Sean McNamara, Jeff Phillips; Photography, Blake T. Evans; Designer, Chuck Connor; Music, John Coda; Editor, Annamaria Szanto; Costumes, Miye Matsumoto; Casting, Joey Paul; a Sheen Production in association with Leeds/Ben-Ami productions; Color; Rated PG; 93 minutes; April release. **CAST:** Hulk Hogan (Dave Dragon), Loni Anderson (Medusa), Jim Varney (Lothar Zogg), Mathew Botuchis (Rocky), Michael J. O'Laskey II (Colt), J.P. Roeske II (Tum Tum), Victor Wong (Grandpa Mori), Alan McRae (Sam), Margarita Franco (Jessica), Chelsey Earlywine (Amanda), Lindsay Felton (Jennifer), Kirk Baily (Carl), Travis McKenna (Buelow), Brendan O'Brien (Zed).

WAITING FOR THE MAN (Panorama) Producer/Director/Screenplay/Editor, John Covert; Photography, John S. Terendy, Lynda Cohen; Music, Bradley Parker Sparrow; Art Director, Robert Johnson; Associate Producers, John Harriman, Daniel Gately; an Artist View Entertainment production; Color/Black and white; Not rated; 90 minutes; April release. **CAST:** John Harriman (Lindsey McMahon), Daniel Gately (Agent William Diehl), Kendra James (Emma), Elyse Mirto (Coleen Neece), John Covert (Andrew Martel), Jock Hedblade (Tommy LaRocca), Joe LaRocca (Sean Hewlett), Michael McCullough (Marco Martel).

J.P. Roeske II, Michael J. O'Laskey II, Matthew Botuchis, Victor Wong
in *3 Ninjas: High Noon at Mega Mountain*
©Columbia TriStar

Dennis Haysbert, Takaaki Ishibashi, Scott Bakula in
Major League: Back to the Minors
©Morgan Creek Prods., Inc.

Matty Liu, Patrick Shane Dorian, Matt George in *In God's Hands*
©TriStar Pictures

MAJOR LEAGUE: BACK TO THE MINORS (Warner Bros.) Producer, James G. Robinson; Executive Producers, Michael Rachmil, Gary Barber, Bill Todman, Jr.; Director/Screenplay, John Warren; Photography, Tim Suhrstedt; Editors, O. Nicholas Brown, Bryan H. Carroll; Music, Robert Folk; Designer, David Crank; Costumes, Mary McLeod; Casting, Pam Dixon Mickelson; a James G. Robinson presentation of a Morgan Creek Production; Dolby; Technicolor; Rated PG-13; 100 minutes; April release. **CAST:** Scott Bakula (Gus Cantrell), Corbin Bernsen (Roger Dorn), Dennis Haysbert (Pedro Cerrano), Takaaki Ishibashi (Taka Tanaka), Jensen Daggett (Maggie Reynolds), Eric Bruskotter (Rube Baker), Walton Goggins (Downtown Anderson), Ted McGinley (Leonard Huff), Kenneth Johnson (Lance Pere), Judson Mills (Hog Ellis), Lobo Sebastian (Carlos Liston), Thom Barry (Pops Morgan), Peter MacKenzie (Doc Windgate), Tim DiFilippo, Tom DiFilippo (Juan #1), Ted DiFilippo (Juan #2), Bob Uecker (Harry Doyle), Steve Yeager (Coach Duke Temple), Larry Brandenburg (Chuck Swartski), Jack Baun (Chuck Ledbetter), Mike Schatz (Renegades Batter), Joe Kelly (Miracles Catcher), J. Don Ferguson (Umpire), Brian Beegle (Young Player), Ted Manson (Miracles Manager), Ronald "Buzz" Bowman (Miracles Announcer), Alex Van (Billy—Bear), Tim Ware (Hot Dog Vendor), Robert M. Egan (Rockcats Announcer), Michael A. Lynch (Chief Umpire), Richard Bruce Doughty (Boll Weevils Announcer), Al Hamacher (Diner Cook), Natalie Hendrix, Stephen Hardig, Leroy Myers, Gary P. Pozsik (Reporters), Andre Tardieu

Justin Lazard, Natasha Henstridge in *Species II*
©Metro-Goldwyn-Mayer

(Maitre D'), Brien Straw (Waiter), R.J. Kackley, Raymond Sterling (1st Base Umpires), Bradley Crable (Twins Runner), Ken Medlock (Twins Assistant Coach), Lucinda Whitaker, Kimberly Herndon (Bar Girls), Elizabeth Diane Wells (Diner Waitress), Gary Murphy (Home Umpire), Scott Foxhall (2nd Base Umpire), Warren Pepper (TV Reporter), Dee Thompson (Head Umpire), Ron Clinton Smith, Richie Dye, Dolan Wilson (Tutu Men), Laura-Shay Griffin (Stewardess), Mark Storm (Mr. Buzz)

SPECIES II (MGM) Producer, Frank Mancuso, Jr.; Executive Producer, Dennis Feldman; Director, Peter Medak; Screenplay, Chris Brancato; Based on characters created by Dennis Feldman; Photography, Matthew F. Leonetti; Designer, Miljen Kreka Kljakovic; Editor, Richard Nord; Original Spieces Design, H.R. Giger; Creatures/Special Makeup Effects Creator, Steve Johnson; Visual Effects, The Digital Magic Company, Joseph Grossberg, Ralph Maiers; Costumes, Richard Bruno; Music, Edward Shearmur; Casting, Amanda Mackey Johnson, Cathy Sandrich; an FGM Production; DTS Stereo; Panavision; Deluxe color; Rated R; 111 minutes; April release. **CAST:** Michael Madsen (Peter), Natasha Henstridge (Eve), Marg Helgenberger (Laura), Mykelti Williamson (Gamble), George Dzundza (Col. Burgess), James Cromwell (Sen. Ross), Justin Lazard (Patrick), Myriam Cyr (Anne Sampas), Sarah Wynter (Melissa), Baxter Harris (Dr. Orinsky), Scott Morgan (Harry Sampas), Nancy La Scala (Debutante), Raquel Gardner (Debutante's Sister), Henderson Forsythe, Robert Hogan, Ted Sutton (Pentagon Personnel), Gwen Briley-Strand, Valerie Karasek, Jane Beard (Biologists), Nancy Young (Tether Console Guard), Beau James (Administrator), Tracy Metro (Prostitute), Irv Ziff (Seedy Motel Clerk), Melanie Pearson (Hooker), Felicia Deel (Stripper), Norman Aronovic (Medical Examiner), Kim Adams (Darlene), Dustin Turner (Kid at Supermarket), Susan Duvall (Shopper), Andreas Kraemer, Lauren Ziemski (Teenagers), Donna Sacco (Woman in Crowd), Sondra Williamson (Woman with Gamble), Kevin Grantz (Federal Agent), Zité Bidanie (Press Asst.), Nat Benchley (Squad Leader), Mike Gartland (Cobra Pilot), John C. Pratt, John T. Scanlon, Herbert R. Schutt, Jr. (Pilots), Evelyn Ebo (Gorgeous Nurse), Bill Boggs (Himself), Richard Belzer (U.S. President), Alesia Newman-Breen (News Announcer)

BULLET ON A WIRE (Provisional) Producer/Director/Story, Jim Sikora; Screenplay, Joe Carducci, Jim Sikora; Photography, John Terendy; Color; Not rated; 84 minutes; April release. **CAST:** Jeff Strong, Lara Phillips, Paula Killen, David Yow, Rex Benson, Richard Kern, Robert Maffia.

FOLLOW THE BITCH (Gurney) Producers, Dion Luther, Julian Stone; Director/Screenplay, Julian Stone; Photography, Joe Backes; Designer, Rachel Kamerman; Music, Dane Davis; Costumes, Barbara Inglehart; a Pennant Prods. presentation; Dolby; Color; Not rated' 86 minutes; April release. **CAST:** Ray Porter (Bill), David Teitelbaum (Karl), Dion Luther (Andy), Mike Cudlitz (Ty), Thomas Napier (Gordo), Matt Foyer (Blake), Melissa Lechner (Liz), Wendell Willit (Nate), Elizabeth Rainey (Vicky)

Mischa Barton, Sam Rockwell in *Lawn Dogs*
©Strand Releasing

Catherine Kellner, Nick Veronis in *Day at the Beach*
©Arrow Releasing

IN GOD'S HANDS (TriStar) Producer, Tom Stern; Executive Producers, Zalman King, David Saunders, Aladdin Pojhan; Director, Zalman King; Screenplay, Zalman King, Matt George; Co-Executive Producer, Essy Niknejad; Photography, John Aronson; Designers, Marc Greville-Masson, Paul Holt; Editors, James Gavin Bedford, Joe Shugart; Music, Paradise; Costumes, Jolie Anna Andreatta; Casting, Cathy Henderson-Martin, Dori Zuckerman; a Tom Stern production; Dolby; Super 35 Widescreen; Technicolor; Rated PG-13; 96 minutes; April release. **CAST:** Patrick Shane Dorian (Shane), Matt George (Mickey), Matty Liu (Keoni), Shaun Tomson (Wyatt), Maylin Pultar (Serena), Bret Michaels (Phillips), Brion James (Captain), Brian L. Keaulana (Brian), Darrick Doerner (Darrick), Pete Cabrinha (Pete), Rush Randle (Rush), Mike Stewart (Stewart), Brock Little (Brock), Tom Stern (Shane's Father), Amy Hathaway (Girl on Train), Vince Klyn (Madagascar Prince), Leontina Santos Miranda (Madagascar Princess), Chad Randall (Boxer), Buffalo Keaulana (Chief of Police), Monica Kuhon (Lily), Joey Van Hekken, Jessie Ryan, Marielle Landi (Wyatt's Children), James K. Kaina (Piano Player), Titus Kinimaka, Alekai Kinimaka (Kauai Boys Band), Darren D. Foy (Hugh), Tahitia Hicks (Sunshine), Judge (The Poet), Tim Skold, Duke Decter (Rockers), The Bali Lifeguard Team (Princess Bodyguards), Camerina Arvizu (Maria), Ayesha Moreno (Lady of the Night), Jade Sun (Prostitute), Jimmy Helen (Chieftain), Maria Sviland (Soul Alley Follower), Philip Boston (Agressive Australian), Mario Heras (Fisherman), Gwyne Redner (Nurse), Henric Nieminen (Orderly), Kimo Hugho, Michael Moore (Sheriffs), Carl A. McGee (Longshoreman George)

LAWN DOGS (Strand) Producer, Duncan Kenworthy; Director, John Duigan; Screenplay, Naomi Wallace; Co-Producer, David Rubin; Line Producer, Amy Kaufman; Photography, Elliot Davis; Designer, John Myhre; Editor, Humphrey Dixon; Costumes, John Dunn; Music, Trevor Jones; Casting, Ronna Kress; a Duncan Kenworthy production; Dolby; Color; Not rated; 101 minutes; May release. **CAST:** Mischa Barton (Devon Stockard), Sam Rockwell (Trent Burns), Kathleen Quinlan (Clare Stockard), Christopher McDonald (Morton Stockard), Bruce McGill (Nash), Eric Mabius (Sean), David Barry Gray (Brett), Miles Meehan (Billy), Beth Grant (Beth), Tom Aldredge (Jake), Angie Harmon (Pam), Jose Orlando Araque (Mailman)

DAY AT THE BEACH (Arrow) Producer/Director/Screenplay, Nick Veronis; Executive Producers, Sophie Marr, Michael Feldman; Photography, Nils Kenaston; Editor, Mark Juergens; Designers, Petra Barchi, Charlotte Bourke; Music, Tony Saracene; a Bushwhacked Productions and Miravista Films presentation; Color; Not rated; 93 minutes; May release. **CAST:** Jane Adams (Marie), Patrick Fitzgerald (John), Paul Gleason (Det. Johnson), Neal Jones (Chuck), Catherine Kellner (Amy), Robert Maisonett (Herman), Marie Masters (Seductress), Alec Murphy (Crazy Car Owner), Joe Ragno (Antonio Gintolini), Ed Setrakian (Augie), Martin Shakar (Det .O'Leary), Elizabeth Stearns (Real Estate Woman), Nick Veronis (Jimmy)

BLACK DOG (Universal) Producers, Raffaella De Laurentiis, Peter Saphier, Mark W. Koch; Executive Producers, Mace Neufeld, Robert Rehme, Gary Levinsohn, Mark Gordon; Director, Kevin Hooks; Screenplay, William Mickelberry, Dan Vining; Co-Producer, Hester Hargett; Photography, Buzz Feitshans IV; Designer, Victoria Paul; Editors, Debra Neil-Fisher, Sabrina Plisco-Morris; Music, George S. Clinton; Costumes, Peggy Stamper; Co-Producer, Susan Solomon; Casting, Elisabeth Rudolph; a Mutual Film Company presentation of a Prelude Pictures production in association with Raffaella De Laurentiis; Dolby; Super 35 Widescreen; Deluxe color; Rated PG-13; 88 minutes; May release. **CAST:** Patrick Swayze (Jack Crews), Meat Loaf (Red), Randy Travis (Earl), Gabriel Casseus (Sonny), Brian Vincent (Wes), Graham Beckel (Cutler), Brenda Strong (Melanie), Rusty De Wees (Junior), Cyril O'Reilly (Vince), Erin Broderick (Tracy), Charles Dutton (Ford), Stephen Tobolowsky (McClaren), Lorraine Toussaint (Avery), Hester Hargett (FBI Tech), Stuart Greer, Whitt Brantley (Troopers), Mark Steven Robison (Chicken Truck Driver), Elizabeth Jaye Moore (Linda)

LET'S KILL ALL THE LAWYERS (Barrister Films) Producers, Shannon Hamed, Ron Senkowski; Director/Screenplay, Ron Senkowski; No further credits available; Color; Rated R; 85 minutes; May release. **CAST:** Rick Frederick (Foster Merkul), James Vezina (Junior Rawley), Michelle DeVuono (Satori Bunko), Lee Gusta (Pops), Cherl Roy (Larissa), Joanne Long (Penelope)

Randy Travis, Patrick Swayze, Meat Loaf in *Black Dog*
©Universal City Studios Prods.

Jada Pinkett Smith, Tommy Davidson in *Woo*
©New Line Cinema Inc.

WOO (New Line Cinema) Producers, Beth Hubbard, Michael Hubbard; Executive Producers, John Singleton, Howard Hobson, Bradford W. Smith; Director, Daisy V.S. Mayer; Screenplay, David C. Johnson; Co-Producers, Bill Carraro, David C. Johnson; Photography, Jean Lépine; Designer, Ina Mayhew; Editors, Nicholas Eliopoulos, Janice Hampton; Music, Michel Colombier; Costumes, Michael Clancy; Casting, Robi Reed-Humes; a New Deal/Gotham Entertainment production; Dolby; Deluxe color; Rated R; 83 minutes; May release. **CAST:** Jada Pinkett Smith (Woo/Off the Wall Babe), Tommy Davidson (Tim), Duane Martin (Frankie), Michael Ralph (Romaine), Darrel M. Heath (Hop), Dave Chappelle (Lenny), Paula Jai Parker (Claudette), LL Cool J (Darryl), Aida Turturro (Tookie), Lance Slaughter (Lamar), Dartanyan Edmonds (Shakim), Foxy Brown (Fiancee), Sam Moses (Cabbie), Tiffany Hall (Denise), Girlina (Celestrial), Denosh Bennett (Sister at Concert), Joanna Bacalso (Stunning Woman), Mia Pitts (Voluptuous Woman), Catherine Burdon (Alluring Woman), Lenny Solomon (Violin Player), Silvio Oliviero (Waiter #1), Nick Corri (Maitre'd), Victor Chan, Drake Thorens (Delivery Bikers), Lisa Scarola (Latina Woman), Philip Akin (Roger Smith), Stu "Large" Riley (Beast), David "Rumble" Morgan (Patron #2), Fawn Boardley (Shanay), Natalie Venetia Belcon (Hootchie), Buddy Lewis (Bartender), Nicci Gilbert (Crayola), Christian Maelen (Crayola), Desmond Campbell (Officers), Kelley Grando (Barry—Bouncer), Orlando Jones (Sticky Fingas), Esther Jones (Shorty), Tyree Michael Simpson, Roland Rothchild (Big Brothers), Martin Roach (West Indian Brother), Wilfredo A. Crispin, Jessica Nahar, James De Jesus, Eustace Dunbar IV (Salsa Band), Sergio Trujillo (Ricardo—Salsa Dancer), Shyla Marlin (Niece), Robinne Fanfair (Fine Sister at Restaurant), John Stoneham, Jr. (Fine Sister's Date), Rus-

sell Hornsby (Guy), Marc Desourdy (Waiter with Pasta), Billy Linders (Waiter with Flambée), Frank Ferrara (Construction Guy), Silvana Gatica (Rosa), David Roberts, Kirk Pickersgill (Disco Girls), Kevin Louis (Door Person), A.J. Johnson (Doorman), Pat Dias (Salsa Party Photographer)

LOU REED: ROCK AND ROLL HEART (Independent) Producer/Director, Timothy Greenfield-Sanders; Executive Producer, Susan Lacy; Co-Producer, Karen Bernstein; Photography, John Chimpeles, Frank DeMarco, Timothy Greenfield-Sanders, Cees Samson; Music, Lou Reed; Editors, Jed Parker, Kate Schmitz; from American Masters, Thirteen Prods. & WNET; Color; Not rated; 73 minutes; May release. Documentary on musician Lou Reed, featuring John Cale, Václav Havel, Thurston Moore, Sterling Morrison, Patti Smith, Maureen Tucker. (This film originally aired on PBS in April 1998.)

PLUMP FICTION (Legacy) Producer, Gary Binkow; Executive Producer, Stephen Nemeth; Director/Screenplay, Bob Koherr; Co-Producers, Lorena David, Mark Roberts; Photography, Rex Nicholson; Designer, Jacques Herbert; Editor, Neil Kirk; from Rhino Films; Foto-Kem color; Rated R; 85 minutes; May release. **CAST:** Tommy Davidson (Julius), Julie Brown (Mimi), Paul Dinello (Jimmy), Sandra Bernhard (Bunny Roberts), Dan Castellaneta (Bumpkin), Colleen Camp (Viv), Kevin Meaney (Les), Pamela Segall (Vallory), Mathew Glave (Nicky), Phillipe Bergerone (Jean-Claude), Jennifer Rubin (Kandi Kane), Robert Costanzo (Montello), Jennifer Coolidge (Sister Sister), Nada Despotovich (Sister Batril), Karla Tamburrelli (Sister Ruth), Simbi Khali (Sister Sledge), Lezlie Deane (Jodi), Paul Provenza (Crispin Marashino), Lea Delaria (Mr. Purple), Tim Kazurinsky (Priscilla), Shawn Michael Howard (Lee), Molly O'Leary (Waitress), Kane Picoy (Christopher Walken Character), Scott LaRose (Karioke Customer), Riki Rachtman (Clerk #2), Al Septien (Cop #1), Judy Tenuta (Rhonda), Jimmie Walker (Stingy Customer)

HOMEGROWN (TriStar) Producer, Jason Clark; Executive Producers, Tom Rosenberg, Sigurjon Sighvatsson, Ted Tannenbaum, Naomi Foner; Director, Stephen Gyllenhaal; Screenplay, Nicholas Kazan, Stephen Gyllenhaal; Story, Jonah Raskin, Stephen Gyllenhaal; Photography, Greg Gardiner; Designer, Richard Sherman; Editor, Michael Jablow; Costumes, Joseph Porro; Music, Trevor Rabin; Casting, Linda Lowry, John Brace; a Rollercoaster Films production, presented in association with Lakeshore Entertainment; Dolby; Technicolor; Rated R; 95 minutes; May release. **CAST:** John Lithgow (Malcolm/Robert), Jon Tenney (Pilot), Ryan Phillippe (Harlan), Hank Azaria (Carter), Billy Bob Thornton (Jack), Kelly Lynch (Lucy), Jon Bon Jovi (Danny), Kleoka Renee Sands (Girl—age 4), Matt Ross (Ben Hickson), Judge Reinhold (Policeman), Leigh French (Waitress), Christopher Dalton (Old Farmer), Jamie Lee Curtis (Sierra Kahan), Tiffany Paulsen (Heather), Jeanette H. Wilson (White Haired Woman), Matthew Winter (Shine Kahan), Jake Gyllenhaal (Jake/Blue Kahan), Michelle Bonilla (Nurse), Matt Clark (Sheriff), Maggie Gyllenhaal (Christina), Ramsay Midwood (Bill), Milo Plasil (Mafia Enforcer), Ted Danson (Gianni), Daniel Alonso (Thug Holding Dog), Tom Burke (Straight Man), Seamus McNally, Jr. (Hippie), Joe McCrackin (Cowboy), Paul Prendergast (Man—age 25)

I GOT THE HOOK-UP (Dimension) Producer, Jonathan Heuer; Director, Michael Martin; Screenplay, Master P, Leroy Douglas, Carrie Mungo; Executive Producer, Master P; Co-Executive Producer, Bryan Turner; Photography, Antonio Calvache; Designer, Michael Pearce; Editor, T. David Binns; Music, Tommy Coster, Brad Fairman, Beats By Da Pound; Presented in association with No Limit Films and Priority Films; a Shooting Star Pictures Production; Distributed by Miramax Films; Dolby; CFI color; Rated R; 93 minutes; May release. **CAST:** Master P (Black), A.J. Johnson (Blue), Gretchen Palmer (Lorraine), Frantz Turner (Dalton), Richard Keats (Jim Brady), Joe Estevez (Lamar Hunt), William Knight (Agent in Charge), Anthony Boswell (Little Brother), Mack Morris (Andrew), Mia X (Lola Mae), Tommy "Tiny" Lister, Jr. (T-Lay), Corey Miller, Edward Smith, Michael L. Taylor (T-Lay Boys), Pablo Marz (Hispanic Man), Tangie Ambrose (Nasty Mouth Carla), Harrison White (Tootsie Pop), Howard Mungo (Mr. Tucker), Laura Hayes (Mrs. Tucker), Richard Balin (Communications Trucker), Ella Mae Evans, Judy Jean Berns (Customers), Kourtney Locke (Little Girl), John Witherspoon (Mr. Mims),

Kelly Lynch, Hank Azaria, Billy Bob Thornton, Ryan Phillippe in
Homegrown
©TriStar Pictures

Sheryl Underwood, Master P, Tangie Ambrose in *I Got the Hook-Up*
© Dimension Films

Joanna Going, Brendan Fraser in *Still Breathing*
© October Films

John Wesley (Minister), Lawrence Williams, Vercy Carter (Family Members), Izetta Karp (Ms. Rose), Paula Bellamy Franklin, Dollie Butler (Old Ladies), Helen Martin (Grandmother), Tommy Chunn (Dooley), Leland Ellis (Man), Sacha Kemp (Woman), Duffy Rich, Andrew Shack (Policemen), Cindy L. Sorensen (Martha), Dana Woods (Big Daddy), Will Gill, Jr. (Black Lamar), Jerry Dixon (Black Jim), Ice Cube (Gun Runner), Fiend (Roscoe), Daniel Garcia, David Garcia (Lorraine's Lover), Eric Vidal (D.J.), Michael D. Harris (Homeless Man), Sheryl Underwood (Bad Mouth Bessie), Phil Tinley (FBI Agent), V. Lisa Brunson (Waitress), Maryam Beigi, Shantele Blackmon, Stacia Gardner, Ursula Houstin, Lori Morrissen, Dora Riestra, Shayna Ryan, Tina White (Topless Performers)

FRENCH EXIT (Cineville) Producer, Ruta K. Aras; Director, Daphna Kastner; Screenplay, Daphna Kastner, Michael A. Lerner; Music, Alex Wurman; Dolby; Color; Not rated; 92 minutes; May release. **CAST:** Mädchen Amick (Zina), Jonathan Silverman (Davis), Molly Hagan (Alice), Vince Grant (Charles), Kurt Fuller (Stubin), Rebecca Broussard (Green Sweater Bimbette), Julia Ariola (Zina's Mother), Victoria Duffy (Herbal Ecstasy Girl), Andrea Fair (Megan), Charles Finch (TV Host), Martin Donovan, Brian Gibson (Partygoers), Drew Hammond (Anthony Price), Ayiva Kastner (Davis' Mother), Gil Kastner (Cell Phone Exec), Sidney Kastner (Zina's Father), Timothy Leary (Herbal Ecstasy Guy), Michael A. Lerner (Alice's Stud), Nicole Nagel (Klexxie), Megan Odebash (Seller's Girlfriend), Cecilia Peck (Airline Ticket Agent), Richard Perry (Mr. Boxer), June Pointer (Marsha), Gil Segal (Superagent's Friend), Lawrence Siegel (Davis' Father), Alexandra Styron (Receptionist), Charles Wessler (Price Party Producer), Kevin Williamson (Studio Guard), Pao Pei Andreoli (Italian Tourist), Beth Broderick, Bruce Nozick, Craig Vincent, Steven Brill

STILL BREATHING (October) Producers, James F. Robinson, Marshall Persinger; Director/Screenplay, James F. Robinson; Executive Producer, Joyce Schweickert; Co-Executive Producer, Janet Graham; Photography, John Thomas; Designer, Denise Pizzini; Editor, Sean Albertson; Costumes, Susanna Puisto; Music, Paul Mills; Casting, Amy Lippens; a Zap Pictures production in association with Seattle Pacific Investments; Dolby; Color; Rated PG-13; 108 minutes; May release. **CAST:** Brendan Fraser (Fletcher McBracken), Joanna Going (Roz Willoughby), Celeste Holm (Ida McBracken), Ann Magnuson (Elaine), Lou Rawls (Tree Man), Angus MacFadyen (Philip), Toby Huss (Cameron), Paolo Seganti (Tomas De Leon), Michael McKean (Roz's New Mark), Chao-Li Chi (Formosa Bartender), Wendy Benson (Brigitte), Junior Brown (Wrong Texan), Jeff Schweickert (Slamm'n Sammy), Bill Gundry (Man with Painting), Joyce Schweickert (Mary), Kathleen Couser

(Frances), Melinda Martinez (Birthday Girl), Jennifer Lauray (Birthday Girl's Mother), Tom Balmos (Beer Delivery Man), Margaret Bush (Dress Shop Sales Woman), Liz Mamana (Coffee House Girl), Katie Hagan (Little Girl in Dream), A.J. Mallett (Little Boy in Dream), Steve Lambert Man n Alley), Mara (Barking Dog), Jim Cullum (Jazz Bander Leader), Evan Christopher, Howard Elkins, Don Mopsick, Mike Pittsley, John Sheridan, Ed Torres (Jazz Band)

YELLOW (Phaedra) Producers, Chris Chan Lee, David Yang, Rita Yoon; Executive Producers, Taka Arai, Theodore Kim; Director/Screenplay, Chris Chan Lee; Photography, Theodore Cohen; Editor, Kenn Kashima; Designer, Jeanne Yang; Music, Jon Oh; a Legend Filmworks presentation of a Public Works Films production; Color; Not rated; 101 minutes; May release. **CAST:** Michael Daeho Chung (Sin Lee), Burt Bulos (Alex), Angie Suh (Grace), Mia Suh (Teri), John Cho (Joey), Jason J. Tobin (Yo Yo), Mary Chen (Mina), Lela Lee (Janet), Soon-Tek Oh (Woon Lee), Emily Kuroda (Mrs. Lee), Amy Hill (Snake Ajima), June K. Lu (Aunt Omi), Susan Fukuda (Grace's Mom), Charles S. Chun (Aaron), Steven Anthony Jones (Uncle Dave), Sharon Omi (Mrs. Park)

John Cho, Burt Bulos, Jason J. Tobin in *Yellow*
©Phaedra Cinema

Aaron Williams, Michael Shawn Lucas in *Broadway Damage*
©Jour de Fête

BROADWAY DAMAGE (Jour de Fête) Producer, David Topel; Director/Screenplay/Editor, Victor Mignatti; Photography, Michael Mayers; Music, Elliot Sokolov; Designer, Dina Goldman; Costumes, Jill Kilber; Casting, Alan Filderman; Dolby; Color; Not rated; 110 minutes; May release. **CAST:** Mara Hobel (Cynthia), Michael Shawn Lucas (Marc), Hugh Panaro (David), Aaron Williams (Robert), Gary Janetti (Zola), Gerry McIntyre (Jerry), Tyagi Schwartz (Carl), Alan Filderman (Casting Director), James Lecesne (Cruise Ship Actor), Barbara Winters Pinto (Temp Agent), Benim Foster (The Super), Jean Loup (Punk), Jonathan Walker (Chuck), Richard Davidson (The John), Michael Jefferson (Drag Queen), Steven Hasley (Waiter Guy), Lucille Patton, Shirl Bernheim (Tourists), Kit Rachlin, Lovette George, Kimberly Jajuan (Back-up Singers), Jose Rodriguez (Security Guard), Rober La Croix (Hair-in-Face), Tom O'Neill (FBI Agent), Jay Hostetler (Chester), Howard Kaye ("Peter Duquett"), James Brosnan ("Jeremy")

PARALLEL SONS (Greycat) Producers, James Spione, Nancy Larsen; Director/Screenplay, John G. Young; Photography, Matthew M. Howe; Designer, Cindi Sfinas; Costumes, Leonardo Iturregui; Music, E.D. Menasche; Casting, Kathleen Chopin; a Eureka Pictures/Black Book Films presentation; Color; Not rated; 93 minutes; May release. **CAST:** Gabriel Mann (Seth Carlson), Laurence Mason (Knowledge), Heather Gottlieb (Kristen), Murphy Guyer (Sheriff Mott), Graham Alex Johnson (Peter Carlson), Josh Hopkins (Marty), Maureen Shannon (Francine), Julia Weldon (Sally Carlson), Johnathan Charles (Malik), Tim Dumas (Bud), Michael J. Allard (Lars), Jack Novak (Jay), Karren Abrams (Doris Mott), Eric P. Granger (Corrections Officer), Kim Snow (Woman on Street), Alice J. Mick (Seth's Mother), Michael Barton Sweeney (Young Seth), Dimitri Kollias (Bartender), Daniel Ferguson, Douglas B. Lansing, John Osborn, Robert Sanson, Ward K. Segrist, Lauren Singer, Theron Snow

Chris Farley, Matthew Perry in *Almost Heroes*
©Turner Pictures Worldwide Inc.

Ken Garito, Tovah Feldshuh in *Charlie Hoboken*
©Northern Arts Entertainment

(State Trooper), William Sedgwick, Charles Terry (Ambulance Drivers)

ALMOST HEROES (Warner Bros.) Producer, Denise Di Novi; Director, Christopher Guest; Screenplay, Mark Nutter, Tom Wolfe, Boyd Hale; Co-Producer, Mary Kane; Photography, Adam Kimmel, Kenneth MacMillan; Designer, Joseph Garrity; Editor, Ronald Roose; Music, Jeffrey CJ Vanston; Costumes, Durinda Wood; Casting, Mary Gail Artz, Barbara Cohen; a Turner Pictures presentation of a Di Novi Pictures production; Dolby; Technicolor; Rated PG-13; 90 minutes; May release. **CAST:** Chris Farley (Bartholomew Hunt), Matthew Perry (Leslie Edwards), Bokeem Woodbine (Jonah), Barry Del Sherman (Sergeant), Robert Tittor (Priest at Fort Adams), Franklin Cover (Nicholas Burr), Patrick Cranshaw (Jackson), Eugene Levy (Guy Fontenot), Lisa Barbuscia (Shaquinna), Christian Clemenson (Father Girard), Steven M. Porter (Higgins), David Packer (Bidwell), Hamilton Camp (Pratt), Jonathan Joss (Bent Twig), George Aguilar (Chief Two Roads), Gregory Norman Cruz (Iowa Indian), Lewis Arquette (Merchant), Don Lake (Elias), Brent Hinkley (Trapper), John Farley (Bartender), Kevin Dunn (Hidalgo), Tim DeKay (New Bartender), Keith Sellon-Wright (Meriweather Lewis), Scott Williamson (William Clark), David Barrera (Ferdinand), Jay Lacopo (Hector), Frank Sotonoma Salsedo (Old Indian), Billy Daydodge (Strong Like Mountain), T. Dan Hopkins (Running Puma), Axel Lindren (Salmon Brave), Harry Shearer (Narrator)

CHARLIE HOBOKEN (Northern Arts Entertainment) Producer, Linda Crean; Director/Screenplay, Tom Mazziotti; Photography, Mike Slovis; Designer, Dina Goldman; Music, Peter C. Lopez; Editor, Thomas R. Rondinella; Casting, Lina Todd Casting; an Only Child Production from Mazziotti Pictures; Ultra-Stereo; Color; Not rated; 85 minutes; June release. **CAST:** Austin Pendleton (Harry Cedars), Ken Garito (Charlie Hoboken), Tovah Feldshuh (Angie Cedars), Anita Gillette (Step Mother), George Morfogen (Father), Jennifer Esposito, Veanne Cox, Amanda Peet (Girlfriends), Jonathan Staci Kim (Ping), Joel Friedman (Barber), David Eigenberg (Mario), Rocko Sisto (Cook), Paula Newsome (Office Manager), Kevin Bone (Funeral Attendant/Waiter), Tara Hauptman, Mark Jupiter (Opening Couple), Tom Mazziotti (Boss' Son), Ebony Jo-Ann, Nora Carreras, Alicia Jacobson, Laura Nieves (Secretaries), Ian Rose (Hit #1—Shrink), Robert Fisher (Hit #2—Businessman), Pat Carucci (Cleaning Woman), Cletus Polk Jr., Samy Sheraf Moustafa (Diner Patrons)

Norm Macdonald, Artie Lange, Don Rickles in *Dirty Work*
©Metro-Goldwyn-Mayer

Ione Skye, Mackenzie Astin in *Dream for an Insomniac*
©Avalanche

DIRTY WORK (MGM) Producer, Robert Simonds; Executive Producers, Brad Grey, Ray Reo; Director, Bob Saget; Screenplay, Frank Sebastiano, Norm Macdonald, Fred Wolf; Photography, Arthur Albert; Co-Producers, Martin Walters, Richard Stenta; Designer, Gregory Keen; Editor, George Folsey, Jr.; Costumes, Beth Pasternak; Music, Richard Gibbs; Casting, Roger Mussenden; a Robert Simonds/Brad Grey production; Dolby; Deluxe color; Rated PG-13; 82 minutes; June release. **CAST:** Norm Macdonald (Mitch Weaver), Jack Warden (Pops McKenna), Artie Lange (Sam McKenna), Traylor Howard (Kathy), Don Rickles (Hamilton), Christopher McDonald (Travis Cole), Chevy Chase (Dr. Farthing), Bradley Reid (Mitch at 8 years old), Matthew Steinberg (Mitch at 16 years old), Joseph Sicilia (Sam at 8 years old), Austin John Pool (Sam at 16 years old), Gerry Mendicino (Manetti), A. Frank Ruffo (Aldo), Hrant Alianak (Kirkpatrick), Michael Vollans (Derek at 10 years old), Grant Nickalls (Jason), Deborah Hinderstein (Charlene), Scott Gibson (Frat Guy), Laura Stone (Veronica), Polly Shannon (Toni-Ann), Rummy Bishop (Homeless Guy at Apartment), James Carroll (Middle-Aged Guy), Henry Chan (Doctor at Fat Clinic), David Koechner (Anton Phillips), Paul O'-Sullivan (A.D.), Uni Park (Saigon Whore), Boyd Banks (Creepy Harry), B.J. McQueen (Big Wet Man), Tony Meyler (Lobby Henchman), Shane Daly (Door Henchman), James Binkley (Unaffected Henchman), Jim Downey (Martin/Homeless Guy), Fred Wolf, Wilfrid Bray (Homeless Guys), Jessica Booker (Mrs. Murphy), Johnie Chase, Conrad Bergschneider (Policemen), Kay Hawtrey (Gladys), Lloyd White (Ron), Dini Petty, Mike Anscombe, Gord Martineau, Ken Norton, Gary Coleman (Themselves), Howard Jerome (Foreman), Arturo Gil (Midget Paul), Rebecca Romijn (Bearded Lady), Joslyn Wenn (Jenkin's Fantasy Girl), Robbie Rox (Huge Prisoner), Chris Gillett (Suit Guy), Kevin Farley, Sanjay Talwar (Theater Workers), Trevor Bain (Henchman Jenkins), George Sperdakos (Opera Critic), Eleanor Davies (Opera Critic's Date), Laura Pudwell (Opera Lady), Emilio Roman (Baratone Errante), George Chuvalo (Ring Announcer), Christine Oddy (Aunt Jenny), Robert Shipman (Crossing Guard), Richard Sali (Ed), Silvio Olivero, MIF (Low Lifes), Cliff Saunders (Thief), Bess Motta, Arlaine Wright (Aerobics Instructors), Chris Farley (Jimmy "No Nose")

DREAM FOR AN INSOMNIAC (Avalanche) Executive Producers, Christopher Lloyd, Rita J. Rokisky, John Hackett; Director/Screenplay, Tiffanie Debartolo; Photography, Guillermo Navarro; Designer, Gary New; Costumes, Charles E. Winston; Editor, Tom Fries; Music, John Laraio; Casting, Melissa Skoff; a Tritone Productions presentation; Ultra-Stereo; Color; Rated R; 88 minutes; June release. **CAST:** Ione Skye (Frankie), Jennifer Aniston (Allison), Mackenzie Astin (David Shrader), Michael Landes (Rob), Robert Kelker-Kelly (Trent), Seymour Cassel (Uncle Leo), Sean San Jose Blackman (Juice), Michael Sterk (B.J.), Leslie Stevens (Molly), David "Puck" Rainey (Delivery Man). (This film premiere on cable television in early 1998)

DEAR JESSE (Cowboy Booking Intl.) Producer, Mary Beth Mann; Executive Producer, Gill Holland; Director/Screenplay, Tim Kirkman; Editor, Joe Klotz; Photography, Norwood Cheek, Ashley McKinney; Music, John Crooke; a Bang! Inc. in association with the N.C. Film Foundation presentation; Color; Not rated; 82 minutes; June release. Documentary in which gay filmmaker Tim Kirkman returns to his native North Carolina to examine his life in comparison to that of anti-gay North Carolina senator Jesse Helms, featuring Dr. Jerry McGee, Tim Kirkman, Myron Williams, Shane Webster, Porch Party, Mike Nelson, Mandy Carter, Karen Brown, Angela Brady, Andrew George, Gene Price, Jaki Shelton Greene, James McAfee, Lee Smith, Hal Crowther, Allan Gurganus, Patsy Clarke, Eloise Vaughn, Rose Vaughn Williams, Dr. H. Mitch Simpson, Jerry Kirkman.

OUT OF THE PAST (Zeitgeist/Unapix) Producer/Director, Jeff Dupre; Screenplay, Michelle Ferrari; Co-Producers, Eliza Starr Byard, Michelle Ferrari; Executive Producer, Andrew Tobias; Photography, Buddy Squires; Editors, George O'Donnell, Toby Shimin; Music, Matthias Gohl; Narrator, Linda Hunt; an Inverted Pictures presentation; Color; Not rated; 65 minutes; July release. Documentary on Kelli Peterson's efforts to form a Gay-Straight Alliance at her Salt Lake City, Utah high school and the influence of little-known gay and lesbian historical figures as voiced by Stephen Spinella (Michael Wigglesworth), Gwyneth Paltrow (Sarah Orne Jewett), Cherry Jones (Annie Adams Fields), Edward Norton (Henry Gerber), and Leland Gantt (Bayard Rustin)

Tim Kirkman, Allan Gurganus in *Dear Jesse*
©Cowboy Booking

203

Nick Stahl, Katie Holmes, James Marsden in *Disturbing Behavior*
©Metro-Goldwyn-Mayer Pictures

Mums da Schemer, Saul Williams, Jessica Care Moore,
Beau Sia in *Slamnation*

DISTURBING BEHAVIOR (MGM) Producers, Armyan Bernstein, Jon Shestack; Executive Producers, C.O. Erickson, Phillip B. Goldfine; Director, David Nutter; Screenplay, Scott Rosenberg; Photography, John S. Bartley; Designer, Nelson Coates; Editor, Randy Jon Morgan; Costumes, Trish Keating; Music, Mark Snow; Casting, Lisa Beach; a Beacon Communications production, presented in association with Village Roadshow—Hoyts Film Partnership; Dolby; Panavision; Deluxe color; Rated R; 83 minutes; July release. **CAST:** James Marsden (Steve Clark), Katie Holmes (Rachel Wagner), Nick Stahl (Gavin Strick), Bruce Greenwood (Dr. Caldicott), William Sadler (Dorian Newberry), Steve Railsback (Officer Cox), Chad E. Donella (U.V.), Ethan Embry (Allen Clark), Katharine Isabelle (Lindsay Clark), A.J. Buckley (Chug Roman), Crystal Cass (Lorna Longley), Tygh Runyan (Dickie Atkinson), Tobias Mehler (Andy Effkin), Derek Hamilton (Trent Whalen), P.J. Prinsloo (Robby Stewart), Terry David Mulligan (Nathan Clark), Susan Hogan (Cynthia Clark), Sarah-Jane Redmond (Miss Perkins), Natassia Malthe (Mary Jo Copeland), Chris Owens (Officer Kramer), Robert Moloney (Ferry Guy), Dan Zukovic (Mr. Rooney), Michelle Skalnik (Randi Sklar), Lalainia Lindbjerg (Kathy), Brendan Fehr (Brendan—Blue Ribbon), Garry Chalk (Coach), Fiona Scott (Fiona—Blue Ribbon), David Paetkau (Tom Cox), Erin Tougas (Shannon), Ryan Taylor (Ryan—Blue Ribbon), Jay Brazeau (Principal Weathers), Carly Pope (Abbey), John Destry (Middle-Aged Man), Glynis Davies (Coupon Lady), Cynde Harmon (Mrs. Atkinson), Larry Musser (Coroner), Andre Danyliu (Roscoe), Gillian Barber (Judy Effkin), Stephen James Lang (John), Peter LaCroix (Mr. Strick), Lynda Boyd (Mrs. Lucille Strick), Daniella Evangelista (Daniella—Blue Rib-

bon), Sean Smith (School Bus Boy), Zuzana Marlow (Shannon's Mom), Tamsin Kelsey (Detrice Wagner), Suzy Joachim (Doctor), Fulvio Cecere (Anesthesiologist), Bob Wilde (Shadow Man), Judith Maxie (Shadow Woman), Doug Abrahams (Security Guard), Christopher R. Sumpton (Screaming Man), Jarred Blancard (Flossing Man), Kate Braidwood (Make-Up Girl), Stephen Holmes (Toothbrush Boy), Mark Aviss (Bald Man), Julie Patzwald (Betty Caldicott), Stephen E. Miller (Frankie), MarciaRose Shestack (Reporter), Robert Lewis (Moderator), Dee Jay Jackson (Asst. Principal), Kendall Saunders (Disrespectful Student), Sean Amsing (Damon).

THE SILVER SCREEN: COLOR ME LAVENDER (Planet Pictures) Director/Screenplay/Editor, Mark Rappaport; Photography, Nancy Schreiber; Produced by Coach Potato Productions, Inc.; Color; Not rated; 100 minutes; July release. Documentary on how Hollywood dealt with the issue of homosexuality from the 1930s to the 1960s; hosted by Dan Butler.

SLAMNATION (Independent-Film Forum) Producer/Director/Editor, Paul Devlin; Photography, John Anderson; Music, Chris Parker; Color; Not rated; 91 minutes; July release. Documentary on a four-day national poetry competition held in Portland, Oregon; featuring Saul Williams, Jessica Care Moore, Beau Sia, Mums da Schemer, Taylor Mali, Daniel Ferri, Marc Smith.

POLISH WEDDING (Fox Searchlight) Producers, Tom Rosenberg, Julia Chasman, Geoff Stier; Executive Producers, Nick Wechsler, Sigurjon Sighvatsson, Ted Tannenbaum; Director/Screenplay, Theresa Connelly; Photography, Guy Dufaux; Designer, Kara Lindstrom; Editors, Curtiss Clayton, Suzanne Fenn; Costumes, Donna Zakowska; Co-Producers, Gregory Goodman, Richard S. Wright; Music, Luis Bacalov; an Addis/Wechsler production, presented in association with Lakeshore Entertainment; Dolby; Color; Rated PG-13; 101 minutes; July release. **CAST:** Lena Olin (Jadzia Pzoniak), Gabriel Byrne (Bolek Pzoniak), Claire Danes (Hala Pzoniak), Adam Trese (Russell Schuster), Mili Avital (Sofie Pzoniak), Daniel LaPaine (Ziggy Pzoniak), Rade Serbedzija (Roman Kroll), Jon Bradford (Sailor), Ramsey Krull (Kris), Rebecca Morrin, Rachel Morrin (Ziggy and Sofie's Baby), Steven Petrarca (Witek), Brian Hoyt (Kaz), Christina Romana Lypeckyj (Kaszia), Peter Carey (Piotrusz), Robert Daniels (Roman's Business Partner), Ryan Spahn (Kid), Randy Godwin (Nosey Neighbor), Jeffrey Nordling (Father Don), Mitchell Mandeberg (Stanley Mislinski), Sheldon Alkon (Man in Church), Laurie V. Logan (Helga), Joanna Woodcock (Woman in Bakery), Joseph Haynes (Mr. Schuster), Judy Dery (Mrs. Schuster), Spark of Fire (Band at Festival), Rick Thompson, Seamus McNally (Hecklers), Cassidy Cirka (Hala's Baby)

Dan Butler in *The Silver Screen: Color Me Lavender*
©Planet Pictures

Gabriel Byrne, Lena Olin in *Polish Wedding*
©Fox Searchlight Pictures

Trey Parker, Matt Stone in *BASEketball*
©Universal City Studios Prods.

HOME BEFORE DARK (Curb Entertainment) Producers, Michael Williams, David Collins, Dorothy Aufiero, Maureen Foley; Executive Producer, Robert Laubacher; Director/Screenplay, Maureen Foley; Photography, Brian Heller, Mark Petersson; Designer, Kathleen Rosen; Editor, James Rutenbeck; Costumes, Susan Anderson; Music, Jeanine Cowen; Casting, Susan Willett; a Scout Productions and Hazelwood Films presentation; Technicolor; Not rated; 110 minutes; July release. **CAST:** Katharine Ross (Rose), Stephanie Castellarin (Nora), Patricia Kalember (Dolores), Brian Delate (Martin), Helen Lloyd Breed (Sister Concilia), Peter Bubriski (Walter), Andrew Hyman (Matt), Jamie Dunphy (Marilyn), Kathleen Fasolino (Cheryl), Terrence Classen (Liam), Brooke Sheehan (May), Mara Clark (Mrs. Flynn), Diana Sheehan (Hairdresser), Grace Costa (Maddie), Timothy Sawyer (George), Ann Foskett (Dress Saleslady), Eric John Cassie (Mailman), Andrew Mittman (Mr. Reynolds), Anne Brady (Aunt Cissie), Robert Laubacher (Uncle Hall), Charles Laubacher (Brian), Grace Laubacher (Nell), Ellen Stone (School Nun), Kevin Foley, Kevin Massey, Eric Chandonnet, Greg Chandonnet, Douglas Pollander (Schoolboys)

BASEKETBALL (Universal) Producers, David Zucker, Robert LoCash, Gil Netter; Executive Producer, Cleve Landsberg; Director, David Zucker; Screenplay, David Zucker, Robert LoCash, Lewis Friedman, Jeff Wright; Photography, Steve Mason; Designer, Steven Jordan; Editor, Jeffrey Reiner; Costumes, Catherine Adair; Music, James Ira Newborn; Casting, Junie Lowry-Johnson; a David Zucker game; Dolby; Deluxe color; Rated R; 100 minutes; July release. **CAST:** Trey Parker (Joe Cooper), Matt Stone (Doug Remer), Dian Bachar (Squeak Scolari), Yasmine Bleeth (Jenna Reed), Jenny McCarthy (Yvette Denslow), Ernest Borgnine (Ted Denslow), Robert Vaughn (Baxter Cain), Trevor Einhorn (Joey), Bob Costas, Al Michaels, Robert Stack, Reggie Jackson, Dan Patrick, Kenny Mayne, Tim McCarver, Jim Lampley, Dale Earnhardt, Kareem Abdul-Jabbar, Victoria Silvstedt, Reel Big Fish (Themselves), Curt Gowdy (World Series Announcer), Justin Chapman (Little Coop), Matthew Murray (Little Remer), Mark Goodson (Dirk Jansen), Matt Sloan (Darcy), Peter Navy Tuiasosopo (Tuttle), Robert E. Lee, Greg Grunberg (New Jersey Informants), Michael Garvey (San Antonio Defender), Paul Michael Robinson (Psyche-Out Victim), Kevin Michael Richardson (Peripatetic Player), Micah McCain (Heather), Cory Oliver (Brittany), Keith Gibbs (Davis), Jayme Gallante (Redmond), Francis X. McCarthy (Dr. Kaiser), Blair Besten (Stephanie), Stanley G. Sawicki (Skidmark Steve), Bret Lewis (News Anchor), Richard Johnson, Joey "Coco" Diaz, Michael Matthys (Referees), Jill Gascoine (Hospital Nurse), Charlotte Zucker (Surgery Nurse), John Fink (Surgeon), Kato Kaelin (Driveway Announcer), David Alan Osokow (Driveway Player), Iqbal Theba (Factory Manager), Susan Breslau (Denslow's Niece Susan), Danielle Zucker, Maureen Ardolino (Inheritors), Janeane Ardolino, Jeremy Breslau, Adam Lilling, Phoebe Lipkis (Fans), Andrew Herman (Cabbie), Jeff Wright (Fireman), Ray Xifo (Riverdance Referee), Titius Napoleon (Sumo Wrestler), Julie Dolan (Beer Barrel), Alma Aver, Nancy Bates, Kelli Camarena, Brooke Moore, Heidi Schweizer, Jennifer Strovas, Andrea Wenzel (Beers Cheerleaders), Michelle Boehle, Tani Kristiansen, Rebecca Lin, Jessica Page, Raydeen Revilla, Chanel Ryan, Jeanine Orci (Felons Cheerleaders)

TALK TO ME (Northern Arts) Producer/Director, George Esguerra; Screenplay, George Esguerra, Robert Foulkes; Photography, Randy Drummond; Editor, Tom McArdle; Music, David McLary; Associate Producers, Deborah Lanino, Robert Foulkes; from Pug Films, 1996; Color; Not rated; 87 minutes; July release. **CAST:** Cheryl Clifford (Betty Cole), Peter Welch (Arnold Dowling), Elizabeth Landis (Veronica), Gary Navicoff (Michael), Ralph Romeo (Frederick), Rick Poli (Jerry), Michael Roderick (Guy with Dog)

FULL-TILT BOOGIE (Miramax) Producer, Rana Joy Glickman; Director, Sarah Kelly; Photography, Christopher Gallo; Editor, Lauren Zuckerman; Music, Cary Berger, Dominic Kelly; Presented in association with L. Driver Productions, Inc.; Color; Rated R; 97 minutes; July release. Documentary on the making of the 1996 Dimension-Miramax release *From Dusk Till Dawn,* featuring Harvey Keitel, George Clooney, Quentin Tarantino, Juliette Lewis, Michael Parks, Robert Rodriguez, Tim "Stuffy" Soronen, Rick Stribling, Amy Cohen, Ken Bondy, Victoria Lucai, Cecilia Montiel, Jason "Jake."

Robert Rodriguez, Quentin Tarantino in *Full-Tilt Boogie*
©Miramax Films

Trey Parker in *Cannibal! The Musical*
©Troma

Maggie Hadleigh-West in *War Zone*
©Film Fatale

CANNIBAL! THE MUSICAL (Troma) Producers, Alexandra Kelly, Ian Hardin, Jason McHugh, Matt Stone, Trey Parker; Director/Screenplay, Trey Parker; Photography, Robert Muratore, Chris Graves; Music, Trey Parker, Rich Sanders; Editor, Ian Hardin; Produced in association with Lloyd Kaufman and Michael Herz, 1994; an Avenging Conscience production; Color; Not rated; 95 minutes; July release. **CAST:** Trey Parker (Alferd Packer), Toddy Walters (Polly Prye), Jason McHugh (Frank Miller), Matt Stone (Humphrey), Jon Hegel (Israel Swan), Dian Bachar (George Noon), Ian Hardin (Shannon Bell), Edward Henwood (O.D. Loutzenheiser/The Cyclops), Masao Maki (Indian Chief), Brandon Gordon (Mr. Mills), Marty Leeper (Sheriff of Saguache), Steve Jackson (Sheriff of Lake City), Randy Parker (Judge Jerry), Stan Brakhage (George Noon's Father), Robert Muratore (Frenchy Cabazon), Andy Kemler (Preston Nutter). (This film was originally released on home video and to cable stations prior to its theatrical debut).

HENRY: PORTRAIT OF A SERIAL KILLER 2 (Maljack Films) Producer, Thomas J. Bush; Executive Producers, Waleed B. Ali, Malik B. Ali; Director/Screenplay, Chuck Parello; Photography, Michael Kohnhurst; Editor, Tom Keefe; Designer, Rick Paul; Casting, Suzanne Gardner; Produced in association with H-2 Prods. Ultra-Stereo; Color; Not rated; 84 minutes; August release. **CAST:** Neil Giuntoli (Henry), Rich Komenich (Kai), Kate Walsh (Cricket), Carri Levinson (Louisa), Daniel Allar (Rooter), Penelope Milford (Woman in Woods)

Josh Hartnett, Jamie Lee Curtis in *Halloween H20*
©Dimension Films

HALLOWEEN H20: 20 YEARS LATER (Dimension) Producer, Paul Freeman; Director, Steve Miner; Screenplay, Robert Zappia, Matt Greenberg; Based on characters created by Debra Hill, John Carpenter; Story, Robert Zappia; Executive Producer, Moustapha Akkad; Co-Executive Producers, Bob Weinstein, Harvey Weinstein, Kevin Williamson; Photography, Daryn Okada; Designer, John Willet; Editor, Patrick Lusser; Music, John Ottman; *Halloween* Theme, John Carpenter; Costumes, Deborah Everton; Casting, Ross Brown; a Moustapha Akkad presentation of a Nightfall production; from Miramax Films; Dolby; Super 35 Widescreen; Color; Rated R; 85 minutes; August release. **CAST:** Jamie Lee Curtis (Laurie Strode/Keri Tate), Adam Arkin (Will), Josh Hartnett (John), Michelle Williams (Molly), Adam Hann-Byrd (Charlie), Jodi Lyn O'-Keefe (Sarah), Janet Leigh (Norma), LL Cool J (Ronny), Joseph Gordon-Levitt (Jimmy), Nancy Stephens (Marion), Branden Williams (Tony), Larisa Miller (Claudia), Emmalee Thompson (Casey), Matt Winston (Matt), Beau Billingslea (Fitz), David Blanchard (Waiter), John Cassini, Jody Wood (Cops), Lisa Gay Hamilton (Shirl), Chris Durand (Michael)

WAR ZONE (Film Fatale/Hank Levine Film, GmbH) Producer, Hank Levine; Executive Producers, Maggie Hadleigh-West, Missouri Davenport Lobrano, Hank Levine; Director, Maggie Hadleigh-West; Photography, Todd Liebler, Eileen Schreiber; Editors, Kelly Korzan, Fernando Villena, Tula Goenka, Emily Gumpel, Sara Thorson; Music, Cindy Wall, Jack Wall, David Plakke, Paul Steinman; Presented by Susan Sarandon; Color; Not rated; 76 minutes; August release. Documentary in which filmmaker Maggie Hadleigh-West interviews men about their behavior on the street towards women.

AIR BUD: GOLDEN RECEIVER (Dimension) Producer, Robert Vince; Executive Producers, Michael Strange, Anne Vince, William Vince; Director, Richard Martin; Screenplay, Paul Tamasy, Aaron Mendelsohn; Based on the character "Air Bud" created by Kevin DiCicco; Photography, Mike Southon; Music, Brahm Wenger; Editors, Bruce Lange, Melinda Seabrook; Designer, Rex Reglan; Casting, Abra Edelman, Elisa Goodman; a Keystone Pictures in association with Dimension Films presentation of a Robert Vince production; Distributed by Miramax Films; Dolby; Color; Rated G; 90 minutes; August release. **CAST:** Kevin Zegers (Josh Framm), Cynthia Stevenson (Jackie Framm), Gregory Harrison (Patrick Sullivan), Nora Dunn (Natalya), Perry Anzilotti (Popov), Robert Costanzo (Coach Fanelli), Shayn Solberg (Tom), Suzanne Ristic (Principal Salter), Alyson MacLaren (Andrea Framm), Tyler Thompson (Oliver), Rhys Williams (Goose), Shahri Khaderni (Juan), Jason Anderson (Weeble), Myles Ferguson (J.D.), Cory Fry (Cole Powers), Jeff Gulka (Pudge), Marcus Turner (Giants Quarterback), Tim Conway (Fred Davis), Dick Martin (Phil Phil), Jay Brazeau, Frank C. Turner (Officials), Mark Brandon (Richard), Jaida Hay (Tammy), Richard Martin (Guy in Stands), Doreen Esary (Receptionist), Juilo Caravetta (Giants Coach), David Lewis (Herb), Monica

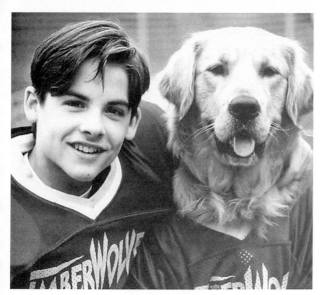

Kevin Zegers, Buddy in *Air Bud: Golden Receiver*
©Dimension Films

Richard Meier, Albert Maysles, Susan Froemke in *Concert of Wills*
©Maysles Films

Marko (Lady with Broom), Scott Ateah (Official), Ritch Renaud (Photographer), Barry MacDonald (Sportscaster), Simon Isherwood (Rams Coach), John Keelan (Ice Cream Boy), Warren Moon, Joey Galloway, Blue Edwards, Pete Chilcutt, George Lynch, Sam Mack, Lee Mayberry, Ivano Newbill (Pro Basketball Players), Rush, Zak, Chase, Chance (Buddy dogs)

STRIKE! (Miramax) formerly *The Hairy Bird*; Producers, Ira Deutchman, Peter Newman; Executive Producers, Nora Ephron, Robert Lantos, Andras Hamori; Co-Producer, Clara George; Director/Screenplay, Sarah Kernochan; Photography, Anthny Janelli; Editor, Peter C. Frank; Music, Graeme Revell; Designer, John Kasarda; Casting, Laura Rosenthal; a Redeemable Features production, in association with Alliance Communications; U.S.-Canadian; Color; Rated PG-13; 110 minutes; August release. **CAST:** Kirsten Dunst (Verena Von Stefan), Gaby Hoffmann (Odette Sinclair), Lynn Redgrave (Miss McVane), Rachael Leigh Cook (Abby), Tom Guiry (Frosty Frost), Merritt Weaver (Momo Haines), Vincent Kartheiser (Snake), Heather Matarazzo (Tweety Goldberg), Monica Keena (Tinka Parker), Matthew Lawrence (Dennis), Robert Bockstael (Mr. Dewey), Brenda Devine (Miss Phipps), Rosemary Dunsmore (Page Sawyer), Nigel Bennett (Harvey Sawyer), Jenny Parsons (Mrs. Dewey), Danny Smith (Groundhog), Dorothy Gordon (Mrs. O'Boyle), Michael Reynolds (Mr. Armstrong), Caterina Scorsone (Susie), Zachary Bennett (Skunk), Aaron Poole (Beagle), Noah Shebib (Conrad Bateman), Paul L. Nolan (Schumacher), Christopher Redmond (Danforth), Shawn Ashmore (Photographer), Jack Duffy (School Guard), Richard McMillan (Bert Chubb), Les Porter (Choirmaster), Nicu Branzea (Tomas), Barbara Radecki (Tinka's Mother), Paula Barrett (Odie's Mother), Robert Bidaman (Verena's Father), Phoebe Lapine (Tinka's Sister), Simone Rosenberg (Herald Tribune Girl), Ray Doucette (Trustee), Tino Monte (TV Reporter), Roger Dunn (Police Captain), Trevor Bain, Michael Kramer (Fathers)

CONCERT OF WILLS: MAKING THE GETTY CENTER (Maysles Films) Producer, Susan Froemke; Executive Producer, Gloria Gerace; Directors, Susan Froemke, Bob Eisenhardt, Albert Maysles; Photography, Albert Maysles, Christophe Lanzenberg, Christian Blackwood, Robert Richman, Giorgio Urbinelli; Music, Joel Goodman; Editor, Bob Eisenhardt; Co-Producer, Douglas Graves; Associate Producer, Susan Brignoli; Color; Not rated; 100 minutes; August release. Documentary on the building of the Getty Center in Los Angeles, with Richard Meier, Michael Palladino, John Walsh, Harold M. Williams, Stephen Rountree, Robert Irwin, Ada Louise Huxtable, Kurt Forster, Thierry Despont. (This film premiered on KCET-TV in Los Angeles in December, 1997)

DEAD MAN ON CAMPUS (Paramount) Producer, Gale Anne Hurd; Executive Producers, David Gale, Van Toffler; Director, Alan Cohn; Screenplay, Michael Traeger, Mike White; Story, Anthony Abrams, Adam Larson Broder; Photography, John A. Thomas; Designer, Carol Winstead Wood; Editor, Debra Chiate; Costumes, Kathleen Detoro; Co-Producer, Maggie Malina; Music, Mark Mothersbaugh; Casting, Deborah Aquila, Jane Shannon-Smith; a Pacific Western production, in association with MTV Films; Dolby; Deluxe color; Rated R; 90 minutes; August release. **CAST:** Tom Everett Scott (Josh), Mark-Paul Gosselaar (Cooper), Poppy Montgomery (Rachel), Lochlyn Munro (Cliff), Randy Pearlstein (Buckley), Corey Page (Matt), Alyson Hannigan (Lucy), Mari Morrow (Kristin), Dave Ruby (Zeke), Mark Carapezza (Hank), Jeff T (Jerry), Jason Segel (Kyle), Linda Cardellini (Kelly), Aeryk Egan (Pickle), Judyann Elder (Guidance Counselor), John Aprea (Mr. Frederickson), Michael O'Hagan (Chemistry Prof), Nancy Linehan Charles (Anatomy Prof), Shelley Malil (Biology Prof), Ann Fairlie (Mrs. Boison), Paul Collins (Prof. Durkheim), Wynn Irwin (Sonny), Johnny Dark (Henry the Drunk), Joe Barnaba (Drunk), Daniel Villarreal (Roberto), Annie O'Donnell (Merrilee), P.J. Ochlan, Bren McElroy (Bookworms), Michael Rivkin (Shhhing Student), Shawn Russell (Sky), Kenny Blank (Luke), Zoaunne LeRoy (Cafeteria Worker), Peter James Smith (Calculus Seatmate), Christy L. Medrano, Robert Michael Reilly, Jeffrey Fierson, Hope Tuck (Students), Kurt Loder (Himself), Kathleen Luong (Girl in Bed), Cory Oliver (Pam), Mary Stein (Irritated Woman), Brian Howe (Frank), Patrick T. O'Brien (Preist), Tracey Stone (Girl Groupie), Rueben Grundy, Cole Stratton (Guys), Steve Mackall (TV Show Host)

Tom Everett Scott, Mark-Paul Gosselaar in *Dead Man on Campus*
©Paramount Pictures

Leslie Nielsen, Melinda McGraw in *Wrongfully Accused*
©Morgan Creek Prods.

Randi Ingerman, Troy Beyer, Paget Brewster in *Let's Talk About Sex*
©Fine Line Features

WRONGFULLY ACCUSED (Warner Bros.) Producers, Pat Proft, James G. Robinson, Bernd Eichinger; Executive Producers, Robert L. Rosen, Gary Barber, Martin Moszkowicz; Director/Screenplay, Pat Proft; Photography, Glen MacPerson; Designer, Michael Bolton; Editor, James R. Symons; Music, Bill Conti; Casting, Karen Rea; a James G. Robinson presentation of a Morgan Creek production in a co-production with Constantin Film; Dolby; Color; Rated PG-13; 85 minutes; August release. **CAST:** Leslie Nielsen (Ryan Harrison), Richard Crenna (Fergus Falls), Kelly Le Brock (Lauren Goodhue), Melinda McGraw (Cass Lake), Michael York (Hibbing Goodhue), Sandra Bernhard (Dr. Fridley), Aaron Pearl (Sean Laughrea), Leslie Jones (Sgt. Tina Bagley), Ben Ratner (Sgt. Orono), Gerard Plunkett (Sir Robert McKintyre), Duncan Fraser (Sgt. Mc-MacDonald), John Walsh, Lambchop (Themselves), Maury Hannigan (Commissioner Hannigan), Chick Hearn (Basketball Announcer), Brian Arnold (Dan Clellan the News Reporter), Guy Bews, Alexander Boynton, Rob Daprocida (Security Guards), Mary Black (Woman with I.V.), Michael Bolton (TV Stage Manager), Jacques Bourassa (Teenager with Backpack), Ken Boyd (Usher), Johnathon Bruce (Hospital Janitor), Rick Burgess (Prisoner), Charn, Bill Tarling (Bus Convicts), Brian Cochrane (Cop#1), Arthur Corber (Percussionist), Rick Cross (Ben Hur Oarsman), Yoko Sakai, Cory Dagg, Michelle Hart, Ingrid Tesch (Reporters), Alex Daikun (Roman), Maura Nielsen Kaplan, Thea Nielsen Disney, Kanlaya-porn Neelaphamorn (Party Guests), Adrien Dorval (Proctor), Mark Fox (Butcher), Mark Francis (Abe Lincoln), Christopher L. Gibson, Charles Paynes, David Prestley, Marco Roy (Paramedics), Calvin Guo (Japanese

Gardener), Ellie Harvie (Ruth the News Anchor), Noah Heney (Parking Attendant), Ingrid Henningsen (Party Guest Out of Focus), Derek Hurst (Patient with Liquid Ears), Ellen Kennedy (Bow in the Eye Musician), P.J. Lespance (Yo Yo Double), Wallace Leung (Conductor), Bev Martin (Mary Lincoln), Mina E. Mina (Arab Diplomat), Barbaree Earl Nielsen (Fainting Pedestrian), Robin Nielsen (Party Waiter), Jason Payn (Wanted Poster Boy), Pat Proft (Window Technician), Patty Sachs (Waitress at Crash Site), Veena Sood (Nurse), Stephen Tibbetts (Patient), French Tickner (Doctor in ICU), Kenneth "Brother" Vils (Det. Van Atter), Henry O. Watson (Mayor Stopka), The Seaforth Highlanders of Canada (Drill Team)

I MARRIED A STRANGE PERSON! (Lions Gate) Producer/Director/Animator, Bill Plympton; Photography, John Donnelly; Co-Producer, John Holderried; Editor, Anthony Arcidi; Music, Maurren McElheron; Backgrounds, Greg Pais, Graham Blyth; a Bill Plympton production; Color; Not rated; 74 minutes; August release. VOICE **CAST:** Charis Michelsen (Kerry), Tom Larson (Grant), Richard Spore, Toni Rossi, J.B. Adams, John Russo, Max Brandt, Ruth Ray, Chris Cooke, Etta Valeska.

MODULATIONS (Strand) Producer, George Gund; Director, Iara Lee; Photography, Marcus Burnett, Paul Yates; Consultant Writer, Pete Shapiro; Editor, Paula Heredia; from Caipirinha Productions; Color; Not rated; 73 minutes; September release. Documentary look at electronic music, featuring Alec Empire, Alvin Toffler, Arthur Baker, Autechre, Bill Laswell, Calvin Bush, Carl Cox, Carl Craig, Christian Marclay, Coldcut, Danny Tenaglia, Darren Emerson, David Toop, DB, Derrick Carter, Derrick May, DJ Funk, DJ Sneak, DJ Spooky, Ed Rush, Eddie Fowlkes, Frankie Bones, Future Sound of London, Genesis P. Orridge, Giorgio Moroder, Grandmixer DXT, Hardfloor, Holger Czukay, Irmin Schmidt, Invisibl Skratch Piklz, Joey Beltram, Jonah Sharp, Juan Atkins, Karlheinz Stockhausen, Kevin Saunderson, Kid Koala, Kodwo Eshun, LTJ Bukem, Markus Popp, Marshall Jefferson, Meat Beat Manifesto, Mike Dearborn, Mixmaster Morris, Moby, O Yuki Conjugate, Orbital, Panacea, Pierre Henry, Photek, Prodigy, Prototype 909, Rob Playford, Robert Moog, Robert Pepperell, Roni Size, Scanner, Simon Reynolds, Stacey Pullen, Squarepusher, Surgeon, Talvin Singh, Teo Macero, Terre Thaemlitz, Tetsu Inoue, Westbam, X-Ecutioners.

LET'S TALK ABOUT SEX (Fine Line Features) Producer, Deborah Ridpath; Executive Producer, Susan Ainsworth; Director/Screenplay, Troy Beyer; Co-Producer, Sara King; Line Producer, Gary Sales; Photography, Kelly Evans; Editors, Bill Henry, Eric L. Beason; Music, Michael Carpenter; Costumes, Timothy Biel; Designer, Joe Warson; Casting, Mary Jo Slater, Ellen Jacoby; a Sphinx/Island Digital Media production; Dolby; Color; Rated R; 86 minutes; September release. **CAST:** Troy Beyer (Jazz), Paget Brewster (Michelle), Randi Ingerman (Lena), Michaline Babich (Morgan), Tina Nguyen (Drew), Joseph C. Phillips (Michael), Dale Paris (A.J.), James Hyde (Scott), Phyllis Bash (Jazz's Mother), Judith Lauro (Lena's Mother), Janis Rose Avillion (Michelle's Mother), William Walden (Box Interviewer), Luca Bestetti, James Walker (Club Doormen),

Autechre in *Modulations*
©Strand Releasing

Beastie Boys in *Free Tibet*
©The Shooting Gallery

Gillian Anderson, Kevin J. O'Connor, Paul Dillon in *Chicago Cab*

Ramon Villa (Club Owner Ramon), Bayla Kaye (Drew's Dancer Partner/Boy Toy), Daphne Duplaix (Chloe), Lauren Martin, Mona Frankel (Bathroom Girls), Christina Rumore, Melonie Mack, Diana Hulet (Topless Table Girls), Dede Rainbow (Condom Girl), Joanne Robertozzi (Saleslady), Nicholas A. Korniloff (Saleslady's Lover), Gillian Sacco (Cucumber Girl), Mercy Lopez (Pepper Girl), David Salih (Pepper Guy), Virginia Menendez (Belly Dancer), Tawnee Peaks, Rachel Rockets (Big Boob Girls), Rodi Alexander (Yorkie Peanut Butter Girl), Jessica Garvin (Ninja Girl) Juliette Gronkowski (Masturbator Girl), Geneva Cuda (Tattoo Girl), Carey Hart (Contortionist), Jessie Ride (Peacher), Norma Fontana (Sammy), Dianne Bucci (Control Girl), Joseph A. Salemi (Boy Toy), Trina Robertson (Foreplay Girl), Patrick Luh (Foreplay Guy), Linda Blaustein (Box Receptionist), Marissa Cohen, Allana Foster ("Jazz" Girls), Tania Landau (Orgasm Girl).

FREE TIBET (Shooting Gallery) Producers, The Milarepa Fund; Executive Producers, Jay Faires, Adam Yauch; Director, Sara Pirozek; Co-Executive Producer, John Sloss; Supervising Producer, Maria Ma; Supervising Editor, Paola Heredia; Photography, Evan Bernard, Roman Coppola, Spike Jonze; a Milarepa Fund production in association with Mammoth Pictures; Color; Not rated; 90 minutes; September release. Documentary focusing on the Tibetan Freedom Concert held in San Francisco's Golden Gate Park in June of 1996, featuring A Tribe Called Quest, Beastie Boys, Beck, Björk, Foo Fighters, Fugees, John Lee Hooker, Pavement, Rage Against the Machine, Red Hot Chili Peppers, Sonic Youth

CHICAGO CAB (Castle Hill) a.k.a *Hellcab;* Producers, Paul Dillon, Suzanne De Walt; Executive Producers, John Cusack, D.V. DiVincentis, Steve Pink, Gary Howsam, Kathy Morgan, Charles Weber; Directors, Mary Cybulski, John Tintori; Screenplay, Will Kern, based on his play *Hellcab*; Co-Producer, Jamie Gordon; Photography, Hubert Taczanowski; Line Producer, Paul Marcus; Costumes, Carolyn Greco; Designer, Maria Nay; Music, Page Hamilton; Casting, John Papsidera; a GFT Entertainment presentation of a Child's Will Production in association with New Crime Production; Color; Not rated; 96 minutes; September release. **CAST:** Paul Dillon (Cab Driver), Tim Gamble (Religious Father), Olivia Trevino (4-Year-Old Girl), Moira Harris (Religious Mother), Rana Khan (Pakistani), Darryl Theirse (X-Hat), Michael Ironside (Al), Shanesia Davis-Williams (Lawyer), Laura Kellogg Sandberg (Bug-Eyed Woman), Phillip Van Lear (Father-to-Be), Ora Jones (Pregnant Woman), Michael Shannon (Crack Head), Shulie Cowen (Stoner Girl), Andrew Rothenberg (Homer), Tracy Letts (Sports Fan), Carol Hall (Mega Shopper), Tim Reinhard (Geek), Hubert Taczanowski (Immigrant), Vince Green (Young Urban Man), Laura Whyte (Mom), Matt Roth, Laurie Metcalf (Ad Execs), John C. Reilly (Steve), Tara Chocol (Receptionist), Ron Dean (Old Snack Trucker), Don Julien (Nail Biter), Marc Nelson (Fat Guy), Holly Wantuch (Dog Lady), Sunni Ali Powell (Ganja Man), Troy West (Story Man), John

Morhlrein (One-Handed Man), April Grace (Shalita), Harry J. Lennix (Pissed-Off Boyfriend), Gillian Anderson (Southside Girl), Kevin J. O'Connor (Southside Guy), John Cusack (Scary Man), Mary Ann Thebus (Old Drunk Woman), Lauren Lazerine, Jeff Still (Obnoxious Guys), Julianne Moore (Distraught Woman), Reggie Hayes (Architect).

THE JEW IN THE LOTUS (Blind Dog Films) Producer/Director, Laurel Chiten; Co-Producer, Lucia Small; Based on the book by Rodger Kamenetz; Photography, Peter Wiehl; Produced in association with the Independent Television Service (ITVS) with funds provided by the Corporation for Public Broadcasting; Color; Not rated; 60 minutes; September release. Documentary in which writer Rodger Kamenetz covers the visit of eight Jewish delegates meeting with the XIV Dalai Lama of Tibet.

The Dalai Lama, Rodger Kamenetz in *The Jew in the Lotus*
©Blind Dog Films

Anthony Rapp in *David Searching*
©L4Ltd.

Robert John Burke, Sandra Bernhard in *Somewhere in the City*
©Artistic License

DAVID SEARCHING (L4Ltd. Productions/Jour de Fete) Producers, Leslie L. Smith, John P. Scholz; Director/Screenplay, Leslie L. Smith; Photography, John P. Scholz; Editor, Toni Blye; Art Director, Tina Parise; Casting, Jan Sassano; a Backpain Productions presentation; Color; Not rated; 103 minutes; September release. **CAST:** Anthony Rapp (David), Camryn Manheim (Gwen), Joseph Fuqua (Walter), David Courier (Michael), Julie Halston (Herself), Michael Rupert (Beau), Craig Chester (Mercedes Guy), Leslie L. Smith (Hotel Key Guy), Christopher Cook (Stoner Share), Chris Duva (Bungee Share), Susan Bruce (Cat Lady), Jennie Moreau (Librarian), Stephen Spinella (Humus Guy), Julio Monge (Homeboy), John Cameron Mitchell (Man with Fruit), David Pevsner (Scott), David Drake (Mark), Alicia Hurst (Usher), Kathleen Chalfant (Grandmother), Melinda Wade (Pamphlet Girl), Shane Bruce (Rambles Trick), Richard Munroe (Club 82 Doorman), Fabio Sottili, Brad Romaker (Club 82 Tricks), Brenda Cummings (Nurse Brenda), Lee Alexander (Danny), Anthony Meindl (Diner Waiter), Joe Santarelli (Gwen's Customer), Jaime D. Martinez (Taxes Truth), LaChanze (God Truth)

PHOENIX (Trimark) Producers, Victoria Nevinny, Tracie Graham Rice; Executive Producers, Tom Rosenberg, Sigurjon Sighvatsson, Ted Tannenbaum, Michael Mendelsohn; Director, Danny Cannon; Screenplay, Eddie Richey; Photography, James L. Carter; Designer, Charles Breen; Editor, Zach Staenberg; Costumes, Alexandra Welker; Music, Graeme Revell; Co-Producers, Ray Liotta, Andrew Lamal, Candace Veach; a Lakeshore

Entertainment production in association with Graham/Nevinny Productions; Dolby; Panavision; Deluxe color; Rated R; 113 minutes; September release. **CAST:** Ray Liotta (Harry Collins), Anthony LaPaglia (Mike Henshaw), Daniel Baldwin (James Nutter), Jeremy Piven (Fred Shuster), Royce D. Applegate (Dickerman), Xander Berkeley (Lt. Clyde Webber), Tamara Clatterbuck (Waitress), Vanessa Munday (Betsy), Al Sapienza (Cop), Yvette Cruise (Maria), John Henry Whitaker (Husband), Glenn Morshower (Anti-Abortionist), Brittany Murphy (Veronica), George Murdock (Sid), Kathryn Joosten (Esther), Giancarlo Esposito (Louie), Ernest M. Garcia (Chubby), David Dunard (Murray), Earl Carroll (Seymour), Anjelica Huston (Leila), Sandra Taylor (Video Game Stripper), George Aguilar (Mr. Fat), Frank Clem (Mr. Skinny), Tom Noonan (Chicago), Kari Wuhrer (Katie Shuster), Maria Stanton (Photographer), Murphy Dunn (Carl), Sibel Ergener (Carl's Wife), Giovanni Ribisi (Joey Schneider), Dig Wayne (Norm), Simi Mehta (New Girl), Annie Fitzgerald (Heist Stripper), Peter Spellos (Burt), Gordon Jennison (Manny), Carmen Filpi (Locksmith), Margaret Chavez (Dolores) (This film premiered on cable television in 1997)

SOMEWHERE IN THE CITY (Artistic License) Producers, Ramin Niami, Karen Robson; Director, Ramin Niami; Screenplay, Ramin Niami, Patrick Dillon; Photography, Igor Sunara; Music, John Cale; Designer, Lisa Albin; Costumes, Betim Balaman; Casting, Caroline Sinclair; from Sideshow; Color; Not rated; 90 minutes; September release. **CAST:** Sandra Bernhard (Betty), Robert John Burke (Frankie), Bai Ling (Lu Lu), Ornella Muti (Marta), Paul Anthony Stewart (Che), Peter Stormare (Graham), Bulle Ogier (Brigitte), Linda Dano (Casting Agent), Bill Sage (Justin), Edward I. Koch (Himself), Kim Walker (Molly), John Fugelsang (Henry), M.B. Ghaffari (Teddy), Robert Shapiro (Larry), Tom Riis Farrell (Edward), Paolina Weber (Nina), DuprE Kelly (2-Kool), David Pittu (Agent), Steven Schub (Jerry), Victoria Bastel (Johnna), Jimmy Noonan (Brain), Mike Danner (Super)

DIRTY LAUNDRY (Artistic License) Producers, Robert E. DiMilia, Robert Sherwin; Directors, Robert Sherwin, Michael Normand; Screenplay, Michael Normand; Photography, John Newby; Designer, John Paino; Editor, Andrew Morreale; Music, James Legg; from Hollywood Productions Inc.; Color; Not rated; 97 minutes; September release. **CAST:** Jay Thomas (Joey Greene), Tess Harper (Beth Greene), Tresa Hughes (Betty Greene), Michael Marcus (Max Greene), Stanley Earl Harrison (Lowel Bower), Erin Underwood (Chloe Greene), John Driver (Dr. Stoller), Michael Mulheren (Nick), Antoinette La Vecchia (Cathy), Stuart Burney (Dale Gordon), Dana Chaifetz (Amy), Ray Xifo (Jerry), Luba Mason (Ingrid)

Ray Liotta, Anthony LaPaglia in
Phoenix © Trimark Pictures

Dan Zukovic in *The Last Big Thing*
©Stratosphere

Alan Boyce, b. Wyatt in *Skin & Bone*
©Alliance

THE LAST BIG THING (Stratosphere) Producers, Vladimir Perlovich, Anthony Rubenstein; Executive Producers, David Barnett, Philip Starr; Director/Screenplay, Dan Zukovic; Photography, M. David Mullen; Designer, Martina Buckley; Editor, Markus Lofstrom; Music, Cole Coonce, Farhad Behroozi; Casting, Ann Maney; a David Barnett/Mitch Mayer/Byronic Pose production; Color; Rated R; 98 minutes; September release. **CAST:** Dan Zukovic (Simon Geist), Susan Heimbinder (Darla), Mark Ruffalo (Brent), Pamela Dickerson (Tedra), Andrew Falk (Chris), Sibel Ergener (Magda), James Lorinz (Comic), Yul Vazquez, Thomas Prisco (Interviewers), Louis Mustillo (Video Producer), Steve Kay (Video D.P.), Blaine Capatch (Band Leader), Mitch Mayer, Will Huston, Yevo (Band Members), Carl Lamb (Bennett Hames), Maria Von Hartz (Woman in Video Store), Ron Zwang (Man in Video Store), Mitch Seyfer (Neighbor Watering Lawn), Rick Askew (Man in Parking Lot).

SKIN & BONE (Jour de Fete) Producers, Claudia Lewis, Gardner Monks; Director/Editor/Screenplay, Everett Lewis; Photography, Fernando Arguelles; Music, Geoff Haba, Mark Jan Wlodarkiewicz; FotoKem color; Not rated; 114 minutes; September release. **CAST:** b. Wyatt (Harry), Alan Boyce (Dean), Susannah Melvoin (Lovely Girl), Garret Scullin (Billy), Clark Brolly (Frankie), Chad Kula (Bruno), Nicole Dillenberg (Ghislaine), Gregory Sporleder (Hadadasher), Richard Mitrani (Herb), Chris Wetzel (Asst.), Michael Nehring (Harry's Manager, Michael), Michael Haynes (Billy's Killer), Greg Jackson (Mr. Donut Audition Producer), Chris Reahm (Satanic Youth Star), Andrea Beane (Junkie with Pierced Nipples), Mark Sawicki (Powerful Casting Agent), Joseph Dalough (TV Cop), Fernando Arguelles (TV Psycho), Rebecca Little (Producer), James Michael White (Zack at the Morgue), David Arquette (Buzzhead), Wynston A. Jones (Gen. Wayne), Kimberly Cardinali (Executrix), Alexx Carroll (Insecure Female John), John Cork (Angry John), Mollena Williams (Scientist #1, Masters), Damien Kaner (Scientist #2, Johnson), Jon Leichter (George); Voices: Andrew McGarrigan (The Veteran), Mickey Cotrell (Self Esteem), Everett Lewis (Voyeur), Matt McChristy (Man in the Street).

JUST WRITE (Curb Entertainment/Heartland) Producer, Heath McLaughlin; Executive Producer, Jim Kreutzler; Co-Executive Producers, Dennis Fahey, Randy Moles; Co-Producer, Harry Knapp; Director, Andrew Gallerani; Screenplay, Stan Williamson; Photography, Michael Brown; Designer, Roger Collins; Costumes, Arlene Toback; Casting, Bruce H. Newberg; a Wind Chill Prod. of a Heath McLaughlin production; Color; Not rated; 104 minutes; September release. **CAST:** Sherilyn Fenn (Amanda Clark), Jeremy Piven (Harold McMurphy), JoBeth Williams (Sydney Stone), Jeffrey Sams (Danny), Alex Rocco (Harold's Father), Wallace Shawn (Arthur Blake), Costas Mandylor (Rich Adams), Yeardley Smith (Lulu), Holland Taylor (Emma Jeffreys), Anita Barone (Carrie), Belina Logan (Tory), Stephanie Miller (Mr. Blake's Assistant), Nancy McKeon (Bride), Ed McMahon (Luncheon Chairman), Joseph Arsenault (Joey Ace), Lara Beiner (Whisperer at Party), Lindsey Brooke, Kristin Dattilo-Hayward (Tourists), Anthony Carregal (Pizza Hut Delivery Boy), Mimi Craven (Sandy), Lou Cutell (Guest at Luncheon), John Fleck (Ex-CCI Agent/Bum), Anthony Galea (Young Harold), Callista Gallerani (Girl with Hula-Hoop), Gian-Mical Gallerani (Boy with Yo-Yo), Mary Goldman

(Psychologist at Luncheon), Mary Kathleen Gordon (Bus Tourist), Mary-Pat Green (Teenager's Mother), Dorian Gregory (Valet at Mansion Party), John Haxby (CCI Mail Clerk), Joycee Katz (Bride's Mother), Joshua Keaton (Teenager on Trolley), Jim Kreutzer (Johnny Rockets Delivery Boy), Jack Manning (George), Heath McLaughlin (Beverly Hills Cop), Robert Nelson (Fire-Eater at Carnival), Barbara Perry (Mildred), Michael Pointer (CCI Security Guard), Bill Pugin (Atilla the Hairdresser), Fred Olen Ray, Cay Mohr (Couple at Mandalay), Doug Segal, Susan Segal (Writers at Bar), Rose Shomow (Jewish Woman at Luncheon), Todd Susman (Priest), Brian To (CCI Agent Underling).

BIKER DREAMS (Castle Hill) Producer, Neil Evans; Director/Editor, Adam Berman; Photography, Andrea Ossotto; an Epicenter Films production; Dolby; Color; Not rated; 73 minutes; October release. Documentary on motorcyclists featuring Martin Tobias, Alex Landes, "Liddo" Jim Cornett, "Scorpio" Cornett, Ilene Murphy, Andy Grow.

Jeremy Piven, Sherilyn Fenn in *Just Write*
©Curb Entertainment

Elias Koteas in *Hit Me*
© Castle Hill Prods.

Kate Amend, Julie Stra, Odette Springer, Johanna Demetrakas in
Some Nudity Required
©Seventh Art Releasing

HIT ME (Castle Hill) Producers/Executive Producers, Steven Shainberg, Gregory Goodman; Director, Steven Shainberg; Screenplay, Denis Johnson; Based on the novel *A Swell-Looking Babe* by Jim Thompson; Photography, Mark J. Gordon; Designer, Amy Danger; Costumes, Karyn Wagner; Editor, Donn Aron; Music, Peter Manning Robinson; presented by the Slough Pond Company; Color; Rated R; 125 minutes; October release. **CAST:** Elias Koteas (Sonny), Laure Marsac (Monique), Jay Leggett (Leroy), Bruce Ramsay (Del), Kevin J. O'Connor (Cougar), Philip Baker Hall (Lenny Ish), J.C. Quinn (Bascomb), Haing S. Ngor (Billy), William H. Macy (The Cop)

DEE SNIDER'S STRANGELAND (Raucous Releasing) Producers, David L. Bushell, Dee Snider; Executive Producers, Larry Meistrich, Joseph DiMartino; Director, John Pieplow; Screenplay, Dee Snider; Photography, Goran Pavícevic; Designer, Debbie DeVilla; Editor, Jeff Kushner; Music, Anton Sanko; Special Effects Make-Up Designer, Michael Burnett; Costumes, Jillian Ann Kreiner; Casting, Lee Ann Groff; Dolby; Color; Rated R; 90 minutes; October release. **CAST:** Dee Snider (Captain Howdy/Carleton Hendricks), Kevin Gage (Det. Mike Gage), Brett Harrelson (Det. Steve Christian), Elizabet Peña (Toni Gage), Robert Englund (Jackson Roth), Linda Cardellini (Genevieve Gage), Amy Smart (Angela), Amal Rhoe (Tiana Moore), Brett Pirozzi, Krsztoff, R.H. Bear, Jaymz Alexander, Fort LaCourt, Bob Abuse (BiLE)

Chris Penn, Stephen Baldwin in *One Tough Cop*
©Stratosphere Entertainment

NAKED ACTS (Kindred Spirits) Producer/Director/Screenplay, Bridgett M. Davis; Executive Producer, Henry E. Norris; Photography, Herman Lew; Editor, Brunilda Torres; Music, Cecilia Smith; Designer, Donn Thompson; a Kindred Spirits, Sirron Communicatios production; Color; Not rated; 107 minutes; October release. **CAST:** Rene Cox (Diana), Patricia DeArcy (Lyida Love), Jake-ann Jones (Cicely), Sandye Wilson (Winsome), Ron Cephas Jones (Joel), John McKie (Marcel Brown), Natalie Robinson (Randi), Marantha Quick (Grandmama), Ajene Washington (Ronnie), Annette Myrie (Little Cece), Rodney Charles (Leading Man), Simone Hunt (Baby Cece), Jarius Hunt (Daddy), Sabrina Lamb (Comic), Laura Washington (Comedy Club Waitress), Jerome Bailey (Homeboy), Beatrice Brazoban (Street Artist), Peekoo A. Lewis (Bathhouse Attendant), Bridgett M. Davis (Rae)

ONE TOUGH COP (Stratosphere) Producers, Michael Bregman, Martin Bregman; Executive Producers, Michael Mendelsohn, Bo Deitl; Director, Bruno Barreto; Screenplay, Jeremy Iacone; Inspired by the book by Bo Dietl and Ken Gross; Photography, Ron Fortunato; Designer, Perri Gorrara; Co-Producers, Judith Stevens, Kathleen McGill; Costumes, Martha Mann; Music, Bruce Broughton; Casting, Mary Colquhoun; a Patriot Pictures presentation of a Bregman production; Dolby; Color; Rated R; 94 minutes; October release. **CAST:** Stephen Baldwin (Bo Dietl), Chris Penn (Duke Finnerty), Mike McGlone (Rickie La Cassa), Gina Gershon (Joey O'Hara), Christopher Bregman, Mike Santana (Gang Bangers), Vita Rezza, Marium Carvell (Cops), Luis Guzman (Gunman Popi), Dana Dietl (Little Girl), Deirdre Coleman (EMS Worker), Harvey Atkin (Andy), Paul Guilfoyle (Frankie "Hot" Salvano), Lori Alter (Wife Terry), Victor Slezak (FBI Agent Bruce Payne), Amy Irving (FBI Agent Jean Devlin), Jason Blicker (Philly Nase), Frank Gio (Sally Resio), Edmonte Salvato, Jr. (Big Jolly), Bo Dietl (Det. Benny Levine), Frank Pellegrino (Lt. Raggio), David Filippi (Uniform Cop Scarfacci), Michael Rispoli (Det. Lt. Denny Regan), Paul Calderon (Sgt. Diaz), Saundra McClain (Rowdy Woman), Ezra Knight (Toulouse), Ingrid Rogers (Toulouse's Bride), Karen Robinson (Sherese), Larry Gilliard, Jr. (Curtis Wilkins), Barbara Barnes-Hopkins (Ka'reem's Mother), Lloyd Adams (Ka'reem), David Sparrow (Uniform Cop), Mary Hammett (Frankie Hot's Girlfriend), Monica Talma (Girlfriend #2), Marlow Vella (Taxi Driver), Philip Akin (Inspector Cheney)

SOME NUDITY REQUIRED (Seventh Art) Producer/Director/Music, Odette Springer; Executive Producer, Lionel Bissoon; Screenplay, Odette Springer, Johanna Demetrakas; Photography, Alain Bertrancourt, Sandra Chandler; Editor, Kate Amend; Color; Not rated; 82 minutes; October release. Documentary on the world of straight-to-video exploitation filmmaking.

RUDOLPH THE RED-NOSED REINDEER: THE MOVIE (Legacy) Producer/Director, Bill Kowalchuk; Executive Producers, Eric Ellenbogen, Andrew Greenberg, Seth Willenson; Screenplay, Michael Aschner; Story, Robert L. May; Title song by Johnny Marks; Editor, Tom Hok; Music/Lyrics/Score, Michael Lloyd, Al Kasha; Character Design, Phil Mendez; Background Stylist, George Juhasz; Casting, Mary Jo Slater; a Goodtimes Entertainment presentation of a Cayre Borthers/Tundra pro-

Santa Claus, Rudolph in *Rudolph the Red-Nosed Reindeer*
©Legacy

David Vincent, John-Michael Lander in *All the Rage*
©Pinkplot Prods.

duction; CFI color; Rated G; 83 minutes; October release. **VOICE CAST:** John Goodman (Santa Claus), Eric Idle (Slyly the Fox), Bob Newhart (Leonard the Polar Bear), Debbie Reynolds (Mrs. Santa Claus), Richard Simmons (Boone), Whoopi Goldberg (Stormella), Eric Pospisil (Young Rudolph), Kathleen Barr (Grown-Up Rudolph)

ALL THE RAGE (Jour de Fête) Producer/Director/Screenplay/Music, Roland Tec; Co-Producer, Catherine Burns; Photography, Gretchen Widmer; Editor, John Altschuler; Designer, Louis Ashman; Costumes, Sarah Pfeiffer; a Pink Plot Prods.; Color; Not rated; 105 minutes; October release. **CAST:** John-Michael Lander (Christopher Bedford), David Vincent (Stewart), Jay Corcoran (Larry), Peter Bubriski (Tom), Paul Outlaw (Dave), Merle Perkins (Susan), Jeff Miller (John), Will Cook, Ben Robbins, Daniel Olsen, Josh Hutnak, Timothy Steiner (Shower Guys), Kate Kelly (Lori), Molly Purves (Francine), Monica Tosches, Diane W. Saunders (Realtors), John Kuntz, Rick Park, Rhys (Waiters), Bruce Ward (Bearded Cowboy), Alan Natale (Kenny), Thatcher Stevens (Timothy), Michael Pollock (Thong Boy), Mitchell Mullen (Don), Doug Brandt (Jay), Willis Emmons, Jake Sullivan (Dinner Party Guests), Ken Mason (Rick), Ellen Colton (Dr. Diva), Joe Ceriello, Jr. (Donny), Keith Brava, Jerry Kaplan, Adam Dyer (Susan's Dates), Ricardo Rodriguez (Horticultural Boy), Adam Sutton (Cruisy Guy on Dancefloor), Christopher Cause (Sam, Cruisy Guy in Men's Room), Guy Silvestro (Guy Not Cruising Larry), Jim Beller (Norbert Pennyfruger), Sylvie Stewart (Torch Singer), Ed Meradith (Pianist), Christian Matyi (Muscular Attitude Guy)

ORGAZMO (Rogue Pictures) Producers, Fran Rubel Kuzui, Jason McHugh, Matt Stone; Executive Producers, Mark Damon, Kaz Kuzui, Noriaki Nakagawa; Director/Screenplay, Trey Parker; Photography, Kenny Gioseffi; Designer, Tristan Paris Bourne; Costumes, Kristen Anacker; Associate Producers, Farrell Timlake, Anthony Mindel; Music, Paul Robb; Editors, Trey Parker, Michael R. Miller; Casting, Katy Wallin, T. Edwin Klohn; Presented in association with Kuzui Enterprises and MOP Worldwide and Avenging Conscience productions; Dolby; Color; Rated NC-17; 95 minutes; October release. **CAST:** Trey Parker (Joe Young), Dian Bachar (Ben Chapleski), Roby Lynne Raab (Lisa), Michael Dean Jacobs (Maxxx Orbison), Ron Jeremy (Clark), Andrew W. Kemler (Rodgers), David Dunn (A-Cup), Matt Stone (Dave "The Lighting Guy"), Toddy Walters (Georgi), Chasey Lain (Candi), Juli Ashton (Saffi), Masao "Maki" San (G-Flesh), Joseph Arsenault (Jimmy "The Fish"), Jeff Schubert (Tommy "The Shark"), Desi Singh (Randy "The Guppy"), Stan Sawicki (Robert White), Ken Merckx (Original Orgazmo), Buff Grey (Security Guard), Cathy Fitzpatrick (Older Porn Actress), Marcus Vaughn (White Stunt Cock), Anna Kazuki (Nasuko), Eve (Haruko), Jeffrey Bowman (Porn Actor), The Fat Lady Stripper (T-Rex), Shalya Laveaux (Greek Porno Actress), John Marlo (Sancho), Stanley L. Kaufman (Doctor), Jill Kelly (Nurse), Miyu Natsuki, Mao Yamada (G-Fresh's Daughters)

THE LAST BROADCAST (Wavelength Releasing) Producers /Directors/Screenplay, Stefan Avalos, Lance Weiler; from FFM Prods.; Color; Not rated; 86 minutes; October release. **CAST:** David Beard (David Leigh), Jim Seward (Jim Suerd), Stefan Avalos (Steven Avkast), Lance Weiler (Locus Wheeler), Rein Clabbers (Reni Clackin), Michele Pulaski

(Michelle Monarch), Tom Brunt (Video Engineer), Mark Rublee (Video Editor), A.D. Roso (Lead Investigator), Dale Worstall (Psychologist), Sam Wells (TV Director)

THE SOULER OPPOSITE (Curb Entertainment) Producer, Tani Cohen; Director/Screenplay, Bill Kalmenson; Photography, Amit Bhattacharya; Designer, Jane Anne Stewart; Music, Peter Himmelman; Editor, Timothy Snell; Costumes, Lynn Bernay; Casting, Laura Adler, Shana Landsburg; a Buffalo Jump Productions presentation; Color; Rated R; 104 minutes; October release. **CAST:** Christopher Meloni (Barry Singer), Timothy Busfield (Robert Levin), Janel Moloney (Thea Douglas), Joshua Keaton (Young Barry), Jed Rhein (Young Robert), Bruce Nozick (Barry's Dad), J.J. Rodgers (Charisse), Catrin Zack (Call Girl), Rachel Winfree (Biker Chick), Joe Rose (Biker Boyfriend), Tom McTigue (Joey Kagan), Robert Fields (Jay Smiley), Devon Meade (Sandra), Mariangela Pino (Rita), Cynthia Lynch (Yoga Instructor), Michael Kagan (Max Luckstein), Steven Kravitz (Arnold), Steve Landesberg (Himself), Buddy Winston ("A" Table Comic), Mark Clifton (Man in Clinic), Lenora May (Doctor in Clinic), Jeffrey Anderson-Gunter (Evan), Allison Mackie (Diane), Rutanya Alda (Thea's Mom), Richard Rifkin (Argus), John Putch (Lester), Jon Stafford (Bar Patron), Sarah Scott Davis, Sheila Creal (Campaign Workers), Roger Nolan (Political Analyst), Cindy Kalmenson (Folk Singer), Danny Hartigan (Van Driver), Julian Neil (Reporter), Kathleen Garret (Julianne), Suzanne Krull (Vanessa), Daran Norris (Young Man "Actor"), Gene Borkan (Father "Actor"), Casey Kalmenson (Young Girl in Hearse), Bill Kalmenson (Dad in Hearse)

David Dunn, Trey Parker in *Orgazmo*
©October Films

Christopher Meloni, Janel Moloney in *The Souler Opposite*
©Curb Entertainment

Adrien Brody, Sybil Temchen in *Ten Benny*
©Artistic License

TOUCH ME (Devin Entertainment) Producers, Greg H. Sims, David Scott Rubin; Executive Producer, Greg H. Sims; Director/Screenplay, H. Gordon Boos; Story, Greg H. Sims, H. Gordon Boos; Photography, Giles Dunning; Editor, Steve Nevius; Music, Claude Foisy; Designer, Abigail Mannox; Costumes, Denise Wingate; Casting, Dan Shaner, Michael Testa; Dolby; CFI color; Not rated; 104 minutes; October release. **CAST:** Amanda Peet (Bridgette), Michael Vartan (Adam), Peter Facinelli (Bail), Kari Wuhrer (Margot), Erica Gimpel (Kareen), Jamie Harris (Link), Greg Louganis (David), Stephen Macht (Robert)

SIX-STRING SAMURAI (Palm Pictures) Producers, Michael Burns, Leanna Creel; Director, Lance Mungia; Screenplay, Lance Mungia, Jeffrey Falcon; Photography, Kristian Bernier; Designer/Costumes, Jeffrey Falcon; Editor, James Frisa; Music, Brian Tyler; Casting, Ross Lacy; an HSX Films production; Dolby; Color; Rated PG-13; 91 minutes; October release. **CAST:** Jeffrey Falcon (Buddy), Justin McGuire (The Kid), Stephane Gauger (Death), John Sakisian (Russian General), Gabrille Pimenter (Little Man), Zuma Jay (Clint), Monti Ellison (Head Pin Pal), Kim de Angelo (Mother), Clifford Hugo (Psycho), Oleg Bernov, Igor Yuzov, Zhenya Kolykhanov, Avi Sills (Red Elvises), Richard McGuire (Cantina Owner), Alexis Lang (Voice of Death), Dan Barton (Ward Cleaver), Lora Witty (Harriet Cleaver)

Jeffrey Falcon in *Six-String Samurai*
©Palm Pictures

TEN BENNY (Palisades/Artistic License) formerly *Nothing to Lose*; Producers, H.M. Coakley, Eric Bross; Director, Eric Bross; Screenplay, Tom Cudworth, Eric Bross; Executive Producers, Paul D. Wheaton, Lisa Roberts, Michael Brysh; Photography, Horacio Marquinez; Designer, J.C. Svec; Editor, Keith Reamer; Music, Chris Hajian; Costumes, Jana Lee Fong; Casting, Lauren Nadler; Presented in association with Cubb Films and Savan Pictures; Ultra-Stereo; Color; Rated R; 98 minutes; November release. **CAST:** Adrien Brody (Ray), Michael Gallagher (Mike), Sybil Temchen (Joanne), Tony Gillan (Butchie), James E. Moriarty (Donny), Frank Vincent (Ray, Sr.), Lisa Roberts (Linda), Gayle Scott (Donna), Jill Bross (Sue), Jay Galione (Young Ray), Jason Peterson (Young Mike), Greg Zittel (Al), David Deblinger (Cosmo), Jerry Moore (Tony)

IN OUR OWN HANDS (Olin/Palm) Producers, Chuck Olin, Chuck Cooper, Matthew Palm; Director, Chuck Olin; Screenplay, Chuck Olin, Matthew Palm; Photography, Steve Rosofsky; Editor, Robert Schneiger; Music, Steve Mullan; Narrated by Peter Thomas; Color/Black and white; Not rated; 84 minutes; September release. Documentary on World War II's only all-Jewish fighting battalion.

HOME FRIES (Warner Bros.) Producers, Mark Johnson, Barry Levinson, Lawrence Kasdan, Charles Newirth; Executive Producer, Romi Lassally; Director, Dean Parisot; Screenplay, Vince Gilligan; Photography, Jerzy Zielinski; Designer, Barry Robison; Editor, Nicholas C. Smith; Music, Rachel Portman; Costumes, Jil Ohanneson; Casting, Jill Greenberg Sands, Debra Zane; a Mark Johnson/Baltimore Pictures/Kasdan Pictures production; Dolby; Technicolor; Rated PG-13; 91 minutes; November release. **CAST:** Drew Barrymore (Sally Jackson), Catherine O'Hara (Mrs. Lever), Luke Wilson (Dorian Montier), Jake Busey (Angus Montier), Shelley Duvall (Ms. Jackson), Kim Robillard (Billy), Daryl Mitchell (Roy), Lanny Flaherty (Red), Chris Ellis (Henry Lever), Blue Deckert (Sheriff), Mark Walters (Deputy), Tommy Shane Steiner (Soldier in Jeep), Theresa Merritt (Mrs. Vaughn), Jill Parker-Jones (Lamaze Instructor), Morgana Shaw (Lucy Garland), Robert Graham (Reverend), Zeke Mills (Tobacco Warehouse Supervisor), John Hawkes (Randy), Brady Coleman (Doctor), Jean Donatto, Mona Lee Fultz (Nurses), Marco Perella (Good Ol' Boy in Pickup), Meason Wiley (Photo Lab Employee), Zachary Moore (Benny)

BELLY (Artisan Entertainment) Producers, Larry Meistrich, Robert Salerno, Ron Rotholz, Hype Williams; Executive Producer, James Bigwood; Director/Screenplay, Hype Williams; Story, Anthony Bodden, Nas, Hype Williams; Photography, Malik Sayeed; Designer, Regan Jackson; Editor, David Leonard; Costumes, June Ambrose; Music, Stephen Cullo; Casting, Winsome Sinclair; a Big Dog Films production; Dolby; Deluxe color; Rated R; 95 minutes; November release. **CAST:** DMX (Tommy Brown), Nas (Sincere), Hassan Johnson (Mark), Taral Hicks (Kisha), Tionne "T-Boz" Watkins (Tionne), Power (Knowledge), Louie Rankin (Lennox), Stanley Drayton (Wise), James Parris (Lakid), Method Man (Shameek), Kurt Loder (Himself), Minister Benjamin F. Muhammed (Rev. Saviour), Tyrin Turner (Big), Jay Black (Black), John "BJ" Bryant, Prince "Blunt" Graham, Wondosas "Kilo" Martin (Thugs), Shaun Morrison (Housekeeper), Frank Vincent (Roger), Eric Keith McNeil (Shorty), Xavier Simmons (Young Tommy), Lavita Raynor (Kionna), Monica

Drew Barrymore, Luke Wilson in *Home Fries*
©Warner Bros.

Michaels (Club Manager), Jennifer "Nen" Gatien (Girl in Office), Anthony "AZ" Cruz (Born), David Edwards, Jeffrey Kaufman, Brant Spencer, Adam C. Vignola (Federal Agents), Micaal Stevens (Killer), Michael Woodhouse (Older Barber), Tyrone Lewis (Younger Barber), Carmen Yannuzzi, Jr. (Guard), Crystal N. Johnson (Knowledge's Cop Girlfriend), James Gresham (Speaker), Michael Manning (Teacher)

THE HEADHUNTER'S SISTER (Scott Sounders Prod.) Producers, Scott Saunders, Bob McGrath, Elizabeth Chae; Director/Screenplay/Editor, Scott Saunders; Story, Scott Saunders, Bob McGrath, Raquel Gutierez; Photography, Chris Bos; Music, Michael Montes; Color; Not rated; 96 minutes; November release. **CAST:** Bob McGrath (Ray), Elizabeth Schofield (Linda), Michael Harris (Harlan), Isabel Robayo (Teresa), M.W. Reid (Wayne), Richard Sheinmel (Boyd), Roberto De La Pena (Luis), James Vincent Romano (Vinnie)

RIVER RED (Castle Hill) Producers, Eric Drilling, Steven Schlueter, Avram Ludwig, Tom Everett Scott, Tischa Gomez; Executive Producers, David Miller, Gary Kaufmann; Director/Screenplay, Eric Drilling; Photography, Steven Schlueter; Designer, Roshelle Berliner; Editor, Paul Streicher; Music, Johnny Hickman; Costumes, Cindy Evans; Casting, Gabriella Leff; a Drilling Films in association with Miller Entertainment and Frontier Films presentation; Color; Rated R; 103 minutes; November release. **CAST:** Tom Everett Scott (Dave Holden), David Moscow (Tom Holden), Cara Buono (Rachel), David Lowery (Billy), Denis O'Hare (Father), Michael Kelly (Frankie), Leo Burmester (Judge Perkins), Tibor Feldman (Dr. Fields), James Murtaugh (Chief Bascomb), Michael Angarano (Young Tom), Peter Tambakis (Young Dave), Ted Travelstead (Gas Attendant), Marcia DeBonis (Sara), Christopher Cantwell (Mr. Taylor), Andrew VanDusen (Convenience Store Clerk), Jefferson Taffett (Young Store Clerk), Mella Fazzoli (Timmy the Mechanic), Charle Landry (Mike Sanel), Christopher Petrosino (Store Clerk's Son), Jenni Gallagher (Denise), Chris McGinn (Woman in Store), Andrew Sikking (Liquor Store Clerk), Louis Ludwig (Elderly Clerk), John Lally (Mr. Orton), Trudy Lally (Mrs. Orton), Gary Kauffman (Prosecutor), Pete "Conan" Winebrake (Defense Attorney), John McLaughlin (Guy in Store), Daniel Prucell (Boy at Sara's), Ceili (Mocha)

STOREFRONT HITCHCOCK (Orion/MGM) Producer, Peter Saraf; Executive Producers, Gary Goetzman, Edward Saxon; Director, Jonathan Demme; Photography, Anthony Jannelli; Editor, Andy Keir; a Clinica Estetico production; Dolby; Deluxe color; Rated PG-13; 81 minutes; November release. British singer-songwriter Robyn Hitchcock is seen in concert in a lower Manhattan storefront.

DMX in *Belly*
©Artisan Entertainment

THE DECLINE OF WESTERN CIVILIZATION PART III (Spheeris Films Inc.) Producer, Scott Wilder; Co-Producer, Ross Albert; Director, Penelope Spheeris; Photography, Jamie Thompson; Editor, Ann Trulove; Associate Producer, Guy Louthan; Dolby; Color; Not rated; 86 minutes; November release. Documentary on punk bands including Final Conflict, Litmus Green, Naked Aggression, and the Resistance.

RINGMASTER (Artisan) Producers, Jerry Springer, Brad Jenkel, Steve Stabler, Gary W. Goldstein; Executive Producers, Brent Baum, Gina Rugolo-Judd, Don Corsini, Donald Kushner, Peter Locke; Director, Neil Abramson; Screenplay, Jon Bernstein; Photography, Russell J. Lyster; Designers, Dorian Vernacchio, Deborah Raymond; Editor, Suzanne Hines; Costumes, Gail McMullen; Music, Kennard Ramsey; Casting, Carmen Tetzlaff; a Steve Stabler/Gary Goldstein production, presented in association with Kushner-Locke Company; Dolby; Color; Rated R; 90 minutes; November release. **CAST:** Jerry Springer (Jerry Farrelly), Jaime Pressly (Angel Zorzak), William McNamara (Troy), Molly Hagan (Connie Zorzak), John Capodice (Mel Riley), Wendy Raquel Robinson (Starletta), Ashley Holbrook (Willie), Tangie Ambrose (Vonda), Nick Micheaux (Leshawnette), Krista Tesreau (Catherine), Dawn Maxey (Natalie), Maximilliana (Charlie/Claire), Michael Jai White (Demond), Michael Dudikoff (Rusty), Jerry Giles (Floyd Merkel), Jason Lewis (Tim), Reamy Hall (Stage Manager), Thea Vidale (Juanita), Korrine St. Onge (Desiree), MC Gainey (Trucker), Robert H. Harvey (Businessman), Roxanne Enright (Pregnant Fan), Conrad Goode (Sexy Male Neighbor), Rebecca Broussard (Suzanne), Kimberly Pullis (Fiona), Ron Orbach (Man in Diner), Lucia Sullivan, Nicole Richard (College Girls), Joel Farar (Boy in Booth), Frank Woods (Emcee)

Tom Everett Scott, David Moscow in *River Red*
©Castle Hill Prods., Inc.

Robyn Hitchcock in *Storefront Hitchcock*
©MGM Distribution Co.

Matthew Powers, Anna Thomson in *Sue*
©AMKO Prods.

SUE (AMKO Prods.) Producer/Director/Screenplay, Amos Kollek; Co-Producers, René Bastian, Linda Moran; Photography, Ed Talavara; Designer, Charlotte Burke; Costumes, Seth Hanson; Color; Not rated; 91 minutes; November release. **CAST:** Anna Thomson (Sue), Matthew Powers (Ben), Tahnee Welch (Lola), Tracee Ross (Linda), John Ventimiglia (Larry), Edoardo Ballerini (Eddi), Matthew Faber (Sven), Robert Kya Hill (Willie), Austin Pendleton (Bob), Alice Liu (Lisa), Dechen Thurman (Interviewer), Joshua Kaplan (Sydney), Lazaro Perez (Phil)

CROSSING FIELDS (Thalia/Independent) Producers, James Rosenow, David Hannah; Director/Screenplay, James Rosenow; Photography, Dejan Georgevich; Editor, Angelo Corrao; Music, Walter Thompson; Color; Not rated; 101 minutes; November release. **CAST:** Reedy Gibbs (Carol), Gwynyth Walsh (Jessica), William James Jones (James), J.K. Simmons (Guy), Meadow Sisto (Denise), Gary Sandy

SHATTERED IMAGE (Lions Gate) Producer, Barbet Schroeder, Susan Hoffman, Lloyd A. Silverman; Executive Producers, Jack Baran, Jay Firestone, Victor Loewy, Bastiaan Gieben, James Michael Vernon; Director, Raul Ruiz; Screenplay, Duane Poole; Photography, Robby Muller; Designer, Robert De Vico; Costumes, Francine LeCoultre; Editor, Michael Duthie; Co-Producer, Lisanne Falk; Music, Jorge Arriagada; a Seven Arts/Schroeder Hoffman production in association with Fireworks Entertainment; Dolby; Color; Not rated; 103 minutes; December release. **CAST:** Anne Parillaud (Jessie), William Baldwin (Brian), Lisanne Falk (Paula/Laura), Graham Greene (Conrad/Mike), Billy Wilmott (Lamond), O'Neill Peart (Simon), Leonie Forbes (Isabel), Bulle Ogier (Mrs. Ford)

DISH DOGS (Filmwave Pictures) Producers, Richard C. Mann, Michael A. Candela; Executive Producers, David Forrest, Beau Rogers; Co-Producer, Ellen Erwin; Director, Robert Kubilos; Screenplay, Ashley Scott

Meyers, Nathan Ives; Photography, Mark Vicente; Editor, Carol Oblath; Music, Herman Beeftink; Designer, Aaron Osbourne; Casting, Candela & Assocs.; a Flashpoint Ltd. presentation of a 7.23 production; CFI color; Not rated; 95 minutes; December release. **CAST:** Sean Astin (Morgan), Matthew Lillard (Jason), Brian Dennehy (Frost), Shannon Elizabeth (Anne), Maitland Ward (Molly)

TROUBLE ON THE CORNER (Thalia/Independent) Producers, Alan Madison, Diane Kolyer; Executive Producers, Henry Eisenberg, Glenn Krevlin, Lee Schalop, Daniel Stern; Director/Screenplay, Alan Madison; Photography, Phil Abraham; Editor, Ray Hubley; Music, Robert Een; Designer, Sherri Adler; Costumes, Todd Thomas; Casting, Julie Madison; a Trouble on the Corner, LLC presentation of a Diane Kolyer/Alan Madison production; Color; Not rated; 114 minutes; December release. **CAST:** Tony Goldwyn (Jeff Stewart), Edie Falco (Vivian Stewart), Debi Mazar (Ericca Ricce), Joe Morton (Detective Bill), Tammy Grimes (Mrs. K), Giancarlo Esposito (Daryl), Roger Rees (Mr. McMurtry), Charles Busch (Ms. Ellen), Bruce MacVittie (Sandy), Mark Margolis (Mr. Borofsky), Anna Thomson (The Butcher's Wife), Daniel Von Bargen (Cecil), Phyllis Somerville (Crazy Woman), Robert Barth Sr., Rich Chew, Andrew Graham, Jonathan Kolyer, Stephen Kolyer, Craig Zakarian (Meat Packers)

HALLELUJAH! RON ATHEY: A STORY OF DELIVERANCE (Artistic License) Producer/Director/Photography, Catherine Gund Saalfield, in collaboration with Ron Athey; Editor, Aljernon Tunsil; Associate Producers, Cat Crosby, Sarah Perry; Color; Not rated; 90 minutes; December release. Documentary on performance artist Ron Athey, featuring Vaginal Davis, Julie Tolentino Wood, Darryl Carlton, James Stone, Sweet P., Myers Rifkin, Cathy Opie, Cross, Alex Binnie, Julie Fowells, Brian Murphy, Katia Esperanza, Mario Kovac, Russell McEwan, Theresa Saso.

PSYCHO (Universal) Producers, Brian Grazer, Gus Van Sant; Executive Producer, Dany Wolf; Director, Gus Van Sant; Screenplay, Joseph Stefano; Based on the novel by Robert Bloch; Photography, Chris Doyle; Designer, Tom Foden; Editor, Amy Duddleston; Costumes, Beatrix Aruna Pasztor; Music, Bernard Herrmann; Title Design, Saul Bass; an Imagine Entertainment presentation; Dolby; Deluxe color; Rated R; 100 minutes; December release. **CAST:** Vince Vaughn (Norman Bates), Anne Heche (Marion Crane), Julianne Moore (Lila Crane), Viggo Mortensen (Sam Loomis), William H. Macy (Milton Arbogast), Robert Forster (Dr. Simon), Philip Baker Hall (Sheriff Chambers), Anne Haney (Mrs. Chambers), Chad Everett (Tom Cassidy), Rance Howard (Mr. Lowery), Rita Wilson (Caroline), James Remar (Patrolman), James LeGros (Car Dealer), Steven Clark Pachosa (Police Guard), O.B. Babbs (Mechanic), Flea (Bob Summerfield), Marjorie Lovett (Customer), Ryan Cutrona (Chief of Police), Ken Jenkins (District Attorney)

OUTSIDE OZONA (TriStar) Producers, Carol Kottenbrook, Scott Einbeinder; Executive Producers, Avi Lerner, Danny Dimbort, Trevor Short, Boaz Davidson, John Thompson; Director/Screenplay, J.S. Cardone; Photography, Irek Hartowicz; Designer, Martina Buckley; Editor, Amanda Kirpaul; Music, Taj Mahal, Johnny Lee Schell; Casting, Abra Edelman, Elisa Goodman; a Millenium Films presentation in association with Nu Image of a Sandstorm Films production; Dolby; Color; Rated R; 98 min-

Jerry Springer, Jaime Pressly in *Ringmaster*
©Artisan Entertainment Inc.

Lisanne Falk, Anne Parillaud in *Shattered Image*
©Lion's Gate Films

Ron Athey in *Hallelujah! Ron Athey*
©Artistic License Films

utes; December release. **CAST:** Robert Forster (Odell Parks), Kevin Pollak (Wit Roy), Sherilyn Fenn (Marcy Duggan), David Paymer (Alan Defaux), Penelope Ann Miller (Earlene Demers), Swoosie Kurtz (Rosalee), Taj Mahal (Dix Mayal), Meat Loaf (Floyd Bibbs), Lucy Webb (Agent Deene), Lois Red Elk (Effie Twosalt), Kateri Walker (Reba Twosalt), F.J. Flynn (Percy), Beth Ann Styne (Bonnie Mimms), Kirk Baily (Agent Cole), Jack Leal (Agent Caloca), Michael Homes (Truck Stop Owner), Bert Emmett (Agent Krich), Benjamin Lum (Convenience Store Clerk), Merideth Mills (Rhonda), Ed Anders (Strip Club Patron), Matt Prescott Morton (Patrolman), Forest Freedom Guider (Garage Attendant), Tony Bernard (Red), Kendall Leigh Wyman (Lorraine), David Carpenter (Trucker), Heidi Jo Markel (Secretary), Ben McCain (Monty Radio Caller), Dylan Tarason (Strip Club D.J.), Butch McCain, Ben McCain (Radio Furniture Salesmen), Ray Pichette (Otto), Patti Duce (Margaret Chanute), Fergie (Girl)

MY KNEES WERE JUMPING: REMEMBERING THE KINDERTRANSPORTS (Independent) Producer/Director/Editor, Melissa Hacker; Photography, John Foster, Kevin Keating, Jill Johnson, Eric Schmidt; Music, Joel Goodman; Narrator, Joanne Woodward; from the National Center for Jewish Film; Black and white/color; Not rated; 76 minutes; December release. Documentary about the Jewish children who were saved from the Holocaust by emigrating to England.

GEORGE B. (WunderHund) Producers, Wade W. Danielson, Gloria Pryor; Executive Producer, Mark Terry; Director/Screenplay, Eric Lea; Photography, Wayne Kennan; Designer, Susan Karasic; Music, David Reynolds; Editor, Pamela Raymer; Costumes, Heidi Higginbotham; a Tango West presentation; Dolby; Deluxe color; Not rated; 98 minutes; December release. **CAST:** David Morse (George), Nina Siemaszko (Angela), Brad Gregg (Jerry), John Franklin (Little Mike), Grace Zabriskie (The Mother), Henry V. Brown, Jr. (Johnny), Brad Garrett (Security Guard),

Lee Tergesen (Frank), Marcelo Tubert (Ken), Dennis Hayden (Tom), Paul Dion Monte (Eddie), Gene Borkan (Lee), Richard Gross (Loan Officer)

LENA'S DREAMS (Olympia Pictures) Producer, Chip Garner; Directors/Screenplay, Heather Johnston, Gordon Eriksen; Photography, Armando Basulto; Art Director, Robert Nassau; Editor, Steve Silkensen; Music, Don Braden; Costumes, Jennifer L. Eriksen; a Lena's Film production; Color; Not rated; 85 minutes; December release. **CAST:** Marlene Forte (Lena), Gary Perez (Mike), Susan Peirez (Suze), Jeremiah Birkett (Johnny), David Zayas (Jorge), Judy Reyes (Martisa), Kai Adwoa (Angela), Pat Lucenti (Casting Director), Christine Clementson-Smith (DeeDee), Al D. Rodriguez (Reader), Suzette G. Powell (Melissa), Don Braden (Street Musician), Ronald Guttman (Bob)

The following films were inadvertently left out of Volume 48:

THE NEON BIBLE (Strand) Producers, Elizabeth Karlsen, Olivia Stewart, Victoria Westhead; Executive Producer, Nik Powell; Director/Screenplay, Terence Davies; Based on the novel by John Kennedy Toole; Photography, Michael Coulter; Editor, Charles Rees; Designer, Christopher Hobbs; U.S.-British; Color; Not rated; 92 minutes; March, 1996 release. **CAST:** Gena Rowlands (Aunt Mae), Diana Scarwid (Sarah), Denis Leary (Frank), Jacob Tierney (David, age 15), Leo Burmester (Bobbie Lee Taylor), Frances Conroy (Miss Scover), Peter McRobbie (Rev. Watkins), Joan Glover (Flora), Bob Hannah (George), Tom Turbiville (Clyde), Drake Bell (David, age 10), Jo Lynne (Dana Dick), Virgil Graham Hopkins (Mr. Williams), Jill Jane Clements (Woman), Aaron Frisch (Bruce), Sharon Blackwood (Mrs. Watkins), Charles Franzen (Tannoy), Sherry Velvet, Stephanie Astalos-Jones (Testifiers), Ian Shearer (Billy Sunday Thompson), Duncan Stewart (Head Boy)

Charles Busch, Mark Margolis, Tammy Grimes, Debi Mazar, Anna Thomson, Roger Rees in *Trouble on the Corner*

Anne Heche in *Psycho*
©Universal City Studios Prods. Inc.

Penelope Ann Miller, Kevin Pollack in *Outside Ozona*
©TriStar

My Knees Were Shaking ©Independent

UNHOOK THE STARS (Miramax) Producer, René Cleitman; Execulentive Producer, Bernard Bouix; Director, Nick Cassavetes; Screenplay, Hetive Producer, Bernard Bouix; Director, Nick Cassavetes; Screenplay, He103 minutes; October 1996 release. **CAST:** Gena Rowlands (Mildred), Marisa Tomei (Monica), Gerard Depardieu (Big Tommy), Jake Lloyd (J.J.), David Sherrill (Ethan), David Thornton (Frankie), Bridgette Wilson (Jeannie), Bobby Cooper (Bernt), Clint Howard (Gus), Moira Kelly (Ann Mary Margaret), Dave Rowlands (George), James Bozian (Jason), Christy Lenk (Miss Mannis), Brittney Lewis (Hospital Receptionist), Vinny Curto (Danny), D. Chance Williams (Bartender), Gerard L'Heureux (Mover), Tom Proctor (Duncan), Dru Homer (Par Patron), Derrick Lik, Sang Lee (Lion Dancer)

LOVE IS ALL THERE IS (Goldwyn) Producer, Elliott Kastner; Executive Producer, George Pappas; Directors/Screenplay, Joseph Bologna, Renée Taylor; Photography, Alan Jones; Editors, Nicholas Eliopoulos, Dennis M. O'Connor; Music, Jeff Beal; Designer, Ronald L. Norsworthy; Color; Rated R; 90 minutes; October 1996 release. **CAST:** Lainie Kazan (Sadie Capomezzo), Joseph Bologna (Mike Capomezzo), Barbara Carrera (Maria Malacici), Renée Taylor (Mona), William Hickey (Monsignor), Dick Van Patten (Dr. Rodino), Abe Vigoda (Rudy), Connie Stevens (Miss Deluca), Paul Sorvino (Piero Malacici), Angelina Jolie (Gina Malacici), Nathaniel Marston (Rosario Capomezzo), Joy Behar (Mary), Sal Richards (Emcee), Annie Meisels (Dottie), Bobby Alto (Joe Fasuli), Celeste Russi (Isabel), Gabriel Bologna (Tony), Edith Fields (Mrs. Frederico)

The following film was inadvertently left out of Volume 49

THE MATCHMAKER (Gramercy) Director, Mark Joffe; Screenplay, Greg Dinner, Karen Janszen, Louis Nowra, Graham Linehan; Executive Producer, Lynn Goleby; Photography, Ellery Ryan; Designer, Mark Geraghty; Working Title Films; Color; Rated R; 100 minutes; October 1997 release. **CAST:** Janeane Garofalo (Marcy Tizard), David O'Hara (Sean Kelly), Milo O'Shea (Dermot O'Brien), Denis Leary (Nick Ward), Jay O. Sanders (Sen. John McGlory), Paul Hickey (Declan), Maria Doyle Kennedy (Sarah), Saffron Burrows (Moira), Rosaleen Linehan (Millie), Olivia Caffrey (Annie), Joan Sheehy (Bus Passenger), Anne Gildea (Airport Assistant), Claude Clancy (Michael), James Ryland (Sgt. Riley), David King, Niall McDonnell (Local Lads), Sinead Murphy (Bettina), David McDonagh (Little Joe), Peter Dix (Tony), Tommy Tiernan (Vince), David Kelly (O'Connor), Akemi O'Tani (Japanese Bride), Kieran Aherne (MC), Frankie McCafferty (Jimmy), John Joe Murray (Irish Dancer), Stuart Dunne (Head Bang Man), Gerry O'Brien (Fisherman), Ned Dennehy, Donncha O'Faolain (Aran Singers), Jimmy Keogh (O'Hara), Conor McDermottroe (Paul), Linda Lee (Campaign Assistant), Joe Dillon (Aran Local), Vincent Walsh (Philip), Ellery Ryan (Phillip's Friend), Owen O'Neill (Garda), Seamus Corcoran (Local Cynic), Siobhan Vaughan (Brigid), James Hickey (Paddy Jr.), Robert Hickey (Michael), Robert Mandan (McGlory Senior), Nancy O'Neil (Journalist), David Ian ("McGlory" MC)

PROMISING NEW ACTORS OF 1998

Cate Blanchett
(Elizabeth)

Joseph Fiennes
(Elizabeth, Shakespeare in Love)

Vincent Kartheiser
(Another Day in Paradise)

Claire Forlani
(Meet Joe Black)

Natasha Lyonne
(Slums of Beverly Hills, Krippendorf's Tribe)

Ryan Phillippe
(54, Homegrown, Little Boy Blue, Playing By Heart)

Jonathan Rhys Meyers
(Velvet Goldmine, The Governess)

Natascha McElhone
(Mrs. Dalloway, Ronin, The Truman Show)

Leelee Sobieski
(*Deep Impact, A Soldier's Daughter Never Cries*)

Giovanni Ribisi
(*Saving Private Ryan, First Love Last Rites*)

Jason Schwartzman
(*Rushmore*)

Catherine Zeta-Jones
(*The Mask of Zorro*)

TOP 100 BOX OFFICE FILMS OF 1998

1. Saving Private Ryan (DW-Par/Jul) $216,180,000
2. Armageddon (BV/Jul) $201,570,000
3. There's Something About Mary (20th/Jul) $176,410,000
4. A Bug's Life (BV/Nov) $162,100,000
5. The Waterboy (BV/Nov) $161,470,000
6. Dr. Dolittle (20th/Jun) $144,160,000
7. Rush Hour (NL/Sept) $141,110,000
8. Deep Impact (Par-DW/May) $140,670,000
9. Godzilla (TriS/May) $136,320,000
10. Patch Adams (Univ/Dec) $134,990,000
11. Lethal Weapon 4 (WB/Jul) $129,450,000

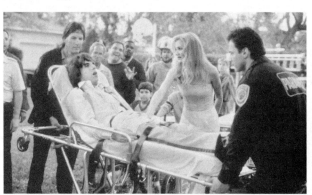

Ben Stiller, Cameron Diaz in *There's Something About Mary*
© Twentieth Century Fox

31. The Parent Trap (BV/Jul) $66,310,000
32. Ever After (20th/Jul) $65,670,000
33. Hope Floats (20th/May) $60,120,000
34. U.S. Marshals (WB/Mar) $57,840,000
35. Life is Beautiful (Mir/Oct) $57,250,000
36. The Man in the Iron Mask (MGM/Mar) $56,700,000
37. A Civil Action (BV/Dec) $56,530,000
38. Snake Eyes (Par/Aug) $55,600,000
39. What Dreams May Come (Poly/Oct) $55,390,000
40. Small Soldiers (DW/Jul) $55,150,000

Tom Hanks, Director Steven Spielberg, Edward Burns on the set of
Saving Private Ryan © Dreamworks/Paramount/Amblin

12. The Truman Show (Par/Jun) $125,620,000
13. Mulan (BV/Jun) $120,630,000
14. You've Got Mail(WB/Dec) $115,480,000
15. Enemy of the State (BV/Nov) $111,530,000
16. The Prince of Egypt (DW/Dec) $101,290,000
17. Shakespeare in Love (Mir/Dec) $100,300,000
18. The Rugrats Movie (Par/Nov) $100,190,000
19. The Mask of Zorro (TriS/Jul) $93,830,000
20. Stepmom (Col/Dec) $90,860,000
21. Antz (DW/Oct) $90,720,000
22. The X-Files (20th/Jun) $83,900,000
23. The Wedding Singer (NL/Feb) $80,250,000
24. City of Angels (WB/Apr) $78,900,000
25. The Horse Whisperer (BV/May) $75,380,000
26. Six Days, Seven Nights (BV/Jun) $73,340,000
27. Star Trek: Insurrection (Par/Dec) $70,190,000
28. Blade (NL/Aug) $70,100,000
29. Lost in Space (NL/Apr) $69,120,000
30. A Perfect Murder(WB/Jun) $67,660,000

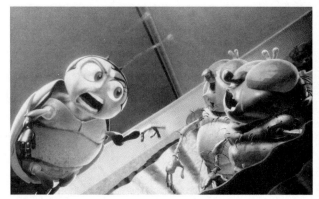

Francis in *A Bug's Life*
© Disney Enterprises/Pixar Animation Studios

41. Halloween H20 (NL/Aug) $54,100,000
42. Mighty Joe Young (BV/Dec) $50,410,000
43. Practical Magic (WB/Oct) $46,820,000
44. The Negotiator (WB/Jul) $44,750,000
45. Meet Joe Black (Univ/Nov) $44,620,000
46. Ronin (MGM/Sept) $41,560,000
47. The Siege (20th/Nov) $40,760,000
48. Pleasantville (NL/Oct) $40,530,000
49. The Faculty (Mir/Dec) $40,100,000
50. I Still Know What You Did Last Summer
    (Col/Nov) $39,590,000

51.	Primary Colors (Univ/Mar)	$39,300,000
52.	Urban Legend (TriS/Sept)	$38,100,000
53.	How Stella Got Her Groove Back (20th/Aug)	$37,670,000
54.	Out of Sight (Univ/Jun)	$37,570,000
55.	Sphere (WB/Feb)	$37,300,000
56.	The Thin Red Line (20th/Dec)	$36,300,000
57.	Jack Frost (WB/Dec)	$34,570,000
58.	Mercury Rising (Univ/Apr)	$32,990,000
59.	Bride of Chucky (Univ/Oct)	$32,410,000
60.	A Night at the Roxbury (Par/Oct)	$30,320,000
61.	Wild Things (Col/Mar)	$30,150,000
62.	Elizabeth (Gram/Nov	)$30,100,000
63.	Madeline (TriS/Jul)	$29,970,000
64.	Spice World (Col/Jan)	$29,350,000
65.	The Object of My Affection (20th/Apr)	$29,190,000

Don Knotts, Tobey Maguire in *Pleasantville*
© New Line Cinema

81.	He Got Game (BV/May)	$21,570,000
82.	Psycho (Univ/Dec)	$21,310,000
83.	John Carpenter's Vampires (Col/Oct)	$20,250,000
84.	Jane Austin's Mafia! (BV/Jul)	$19,900,000
85.	Hard Rain (Par/Jan)	$19,880,000
86.	The Replacement Killers (Col/Feb)	$19,210,000
87.	Simon Birch (BV/Sept)	$18,260,000
88.	Species II (MGM/Apr)	$18,230,000
89.	Babe: Pig in the City (Univ/Nov)	$18,130,000
90.	Disturbing Behavior (MGM/Jul)	$17,510,000
91.	The Big Lebowski (Gram/Mar)	$17,900,000
92.	Half-Baked (Univ/Jan)	$17,470,000
93.	The Odd Couple II (Par/Apr)	$17,920,000
94.	Rushmore (BV/Dec)	$16,980,000
95.	54 (Mir/Aug)	$16,760,000

Anthony Hopkins in *The Mask of Zorro* © Columbia Tristar

66.	Grease (reissue) (Par/Mar; orig: 6/78)	$28,420,000
67.	Paulie (DW/Apr)	$27,100,000
68.	The Big Hit (NL/Apr)	$27,000,000
69.	Bulworth (20th/May)	$26,530,000
70.	Great Expectations (20th/Jan)	$26,430,000
71.	Can't Hardly Wait (Col/Jun)	$25,610,000
72.	Fallen (WB/Jan)	$25,500,000
73.	Waking Ned Devine (Fox S/Nov)	$24,710,000
74.	The Avengers (WB/Aug)	$23,530,000
75.	One True Thing (Univ/Sept)	$23,340,000
76.	The Players Club (NL/Apr)	$23,100,000
77.	Quest for Camelot (WB/May)	$22,940,000
78.	Rounders (Mir/Sept)	$22,930,000
79.	Beloved (BV/Oct)	$22,750,000
80.	The Borrowers (Poly/Feb)	$22,620,000

Warren Beatty in *Bulworth*
© Twentieth Century Fox

96.	Dance With Me (Col/Aug)	$15,930,000
97.	A Simple Plan (Par/Dec)	$15,880,000
98.	Dead Man on Campus (Par/Aug)	$15,110,000
99.	Twilight (Par/Mar)	$15,000,000
100.	The Wizard of Oz (reissue) (WB/Nov; orig: MGM, 8/39)	$14,850,000

ACADEMY AWARDS FOR 1998

PRESENTED MONDAY MARCH 23, 1999

Gwyneth Paltrow, Joseph Fiennes

Judi Dench

Geoffrey Rush, Tom Wilkinson, Ben Affleck

ACADEMY AWARD WINNER FOR BEST PICTURE OF 1998

SHAKESPEARE IN LOVE

(MIRAMAX) Producers, David Parritt, Donna Gigliotti, Harvey Weinstein, Edward Zwick, Marc Norman; Executive Producers, Bob Weinstein, Julie Goldstein; Director, John Madden; Screenplay, Marc Norman, Tom Stoppard; Photography, Richard Greatrex; Designer, Martin Childs; Editor, David Gamble; Music, Stephen Warbeck; Costumes, Sandy Powell; Casting, Michelle Guish; a Universal Pictures/Bedford Falls Company presentation; Dolby; Super 35 Widescreen; Deluxe color; Rated R; 122 minutes; December release

CAST

Viola De Lesseps	Gwyneth Paltrow
Will Shakespeare	Joseph Fiennes
Earl of Wessex	Colin Firth
Philip Henslowe	Geoffrey Rush
Queen Elizabeth I	Judi Dench
Hugh Fennyman	Tom Wilkinson
Ned Alleyn	Ben Affleck
Sir Edmund Tilney, Master of the Revels	Simon Callow
Ralph Bashford	Jim Carter
Richard Burbage	Martin Clunes
The Nurse	Imelda Staunton
Christopher Marlowe	Rupert Everett
Dr. Moth	Antony Sher
Sam Gosse	Daniel Brocklebank
John Webster	Joe Roberts
William Kempe	Patrick Barlow
Wabash	Mark Williams
Lambert	Steven O'Donnell
Frees	Tim McMullen
Makepeace, the Preacher	Steven Beard
Rosaline	Sandra Reinton
Ladies in Waiting	Bridget McConnel, Georgie Glen
Henry Condell	Nicholas Boulton
Crier	Desmond McNamara
Nol	Barnaby Kay
Peter, the Stage Manager	Paul Bigley
Actor in Tavern	Jason Round
Barman	Rupert Farley
First Auditionee	Adam Barker
Second Auditionee	Harry Gostelow
Third Auditionee	Alan Cody
John Hemmings	David Curtiz
James Hemmings	Gregor Truter

and Simon Day (First Boatman), Jill Baker (Lady De Lesseps), Amber Glossop (Scullery Maid), Robin Davies (Master Plum), Hywel Simons (Servant), Nicholas Le Prevost (Sir Robert De Lesseps), Timothy Kightley (Edward Pope), Mark Saban (Augustine Philips), Bob Barrett (George Bryan), Roger Molidge (James Armitage), Roger Frost (Second Boatman), Rebecca Charles (Chambermaid), Richard Gold (Lord in Waiting), Rachel Clark, Lucy Speed, Patricia Potter (Whores), John Ramm (Makepeace's Neighbour), Martin Neeley (Paris/Lady Montague), the Choir of St. George's School, Windsor.

In 1590s London, young Will Shakespeare, experiencing writer's block, falls in love with Lady Viola, inspiring him to write one of his greatest works, Romeo and Juliet.

1998 Academy Award-winner for Best Picture, Actress (Gwyneth Paltrow), Supporting Actress (Judi Dench), Original Screenplay, Original Score—Musical or Comedy, Costume Design, and Art Direction. This film received additional nominations for supporting actor (Geoffrey Rush), director, cinematography, editing, sound, and makeup.

Gwyneth Paltrow and Joseph Fiennes

Colin Firth, Judi Dench

Ben Affleck

Colin Firth

Geoffrey Rush (center), Tom Wilkinson (r)

ROBERTO BENIGNI

in *Life is Beautiful* © Miramax Films

ACADEMY AWARD FOR BEST ACTOR OF 1998

GWYNETH PALTROW

in *Shakespeare in Love* © Miramax Films

ACADEMY AWARD FOR BEST ACTRESS OF 1998

JAMES COBURN
in *Affliction* © Lions Gate Films
ACADEMY AWARD FOR BEST SUPPORTING ACTOR OF 1998

JUDI DENCH

in *Shakespeare in Love* © Miramax Films

ACADEMY AWARD FOR BEST SUPPORTING ACTRESS OF 1998

ACADEMY AWARD NOMINEES FOR BEST ACTOR

Tom Hanks in *Saving Private Ryan*

Ian McKellen in *Gods and Monsters*

Nick Nolte in *Affliction*

Edward Norton in *American History X*

ACADEMY AWARD NOMINEES FOR BEST ACTRESS

Cate Blanchett in *Elizabeth*

Fernanda Montenegro in *Central Station*

Meryl Streep in *One True Thing*

Emily Watson in *Hilary and Jackie*

ACADEMY AWARD NOMINEES FOR BEST SUPPORTING ACTOR

Robert Duvall in *A Civil Action*

Ed Harris in *The Truman Show*

Geoffrey Rush in *Shakespeare in Love*

Billy Bob Thornton in *A Simple Plan*

ACADEMY AWARD NOMINEES FOR BEST SUPPORTING ACTRESS

Kathy Bates in *Primary Colors*

Brenda Blethyn in *Little Voice*

Rachel Griffiths in *Hilary and Jackie*

Lynn Redgrave in *Gods and Monsters*

Giorgio Cantarini, Roberto Benigni

LIFE IS BEAUTIFUL

(MIRAMAX) Producers, Elda Ferri, Gianluigi Braschi; Director, Roberto Benigni; Screenplay, Vincenzo Cerami, Roberto Benigni; Line Producer, Mario Cotone; Photography, Tonino Delli Colli; Music, Nicola Piovani; Editor, Simona Paggi; Designer/Costumes, Danilo Donati; Casting, Shaila Rubin; a Mario & Vittorio Cecchi Gori presentation of a Melampo Cinematografica production; Italian, 1997; Dolby; Color; Rated PG-13; 116 minutes; October release

CAST

Guido	Roberto Benigni
Dora	Nicoletta Braschi
Giosué	Giorgio Cantarini
Zio	Giustino Durano
Ferruccio	Sergio Bustric
Dora's Mother	Marisa Paredes
Doctor Lessing	Horst Buccholz
Guicciardini	Lydia Alfonsi
The Principal	Giuliana Lojodice
Rodolfo	Amerigo Fontani
Bartolomeo	Pietro De Silva
Vittorino	Francesco Guzzo
Elena	Raffaela Lebboroni
Rodolfo's Friend	Claudio Alfonsi
Prefect	Gil Baroni
Man with Key	Massimo Bianchi
German Orderly at Party	Jurgen Bohn
German Auxiliary	Verena Buratti, Daniela Fedtke, Inger Lise Middlethon, Laura Rudeberg
German Executioner	Robert Camero
General Graziosi	Ennio Consalvi
Waiter Ernesto	Giancarlo Cosentino
U.S. Tank Soldier	Aaron Craig
King	Alfiero Falomi
School Janitor	Antonio Fommei
Player	Stefano Frangipani
German Sergeant	Ernst Frowein Holger
Teacher	Alessandra Grassi
Vittorino	Francesco Guzzo

and Hannes Helmann (German Corporal), Wolfgang Hillinger (German Major at Party), Margareta Lucia Krauss (Soldier at Children's Diner), Patrizia Lazzarini, Maria Letizia (Women at Grand Hotel), Concetta Lomardo (Gigliola), Maria Rita Macellari (Queen), Carlotta Mangione (Eleonora), Franco Mescolini (School Inspector), Francesca Messinse (Woman at the Opera), Andrea Nardi (Upholsterer), Gunther Pfanzelter (German Soldier), Cristinia Porchiella (Old Maid Teacher), Nino Presto (Bruno), Gina Rovere (Dora's Governess), Massimo Salvianti (Book Store Policeman), Richard Sammel (German Lieutenant at Station), James Schindler (German Guard), Andrea Tidona (Grand Hotel Doorman), Dirk Karsten Van Den Berg (German Soldier), Giovanna Villa (City Hall Secretary)

Roberto Benigni, Giorgio Cantarini

In late 1930s Italy, as Mussolini forms a military alliance with Hitler, Guido woos and weds Dora, a young school teacher. Years later as antisemitism propels the Fascist government, Guido and his young son Giouse find themselves captured and taken to a concentration camp. 1998 Academy Award-winner for Best Foreign Language Film, Best Actor (Roberto Benigni), and Original Dramatic Score. This film received additional nominations for picture, director, editing, and original screenplay. Benigni became the first performer in the male acting category to win an Academy Award for a foreign language film.

©Miramax Films

Nicoletta Braschi, Roberto Benigni

ACADEMY AWARD WINNER FOR BEST FOREIGN LANGUAGE FILM

Giorgio Cantarini, Roberto Benigni, Nicoetta Braschi

Roberto Benigni, Giorgio Cantarini, Nicoletta Braschi

Annette Lantos, Tom Lantos, and their grandchildren

Alice Lok Chana

THE LAST DAYS

(OCTOBER) Prodcuers, June Beallor, Ken Lipper: Executive Producer, Steven Spielberg; Director/Editor, James Moll; Photography, Harris Done; Music, Hans Zimmer; Associate Producers, Elyse Katz, Aaron Zarrow; a Steven Spielberg and The Shoah Foundation presentation of a Ken Lipper/June Beallor production; Dolby; Color; Rated PG-13; 87 minutes; October release. Documentary focusing on five Hungarian Jews who survived the Holocaust: Tom Lantos, Alice Lok Chana, Renée Firestone, Bill Basch, Irene Zisblatt

Renée Firestone

ACADEMY AWARD WINNER FOR BEST FEATURE DOCUMENTARY

FOREIGN FILMS RELEASED IN THE U.S. IN 1998

Javier Bardem, Jose Sancho

Liberto Rabal, Angela Molina

Javier Bardem, Francesca Neri

Francesca Neri, Liberto Rabal

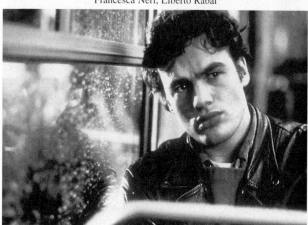

Liberto Rabal

LIVE FLESH

(GOLDWYN) Executive Producer, Agustín Almodóvar; Director/Screenplay, Pedro Almodóvar; Based on the novel by Ruth Rendell; Photography, Affonso Beato; Editor, José Salcedo; Music, Alberto Iglesias; Costumes, José M De Cossio; a El Deseo S.A. presentation of an El Deseo Ciby 2000/France 3 production; Distributed by MGM; Spanish-French, 1997; Dolby; Panavision; Eastmancolor; Rated R; 100 minutes; January release

CAST

David	Javier Bardem
Elena	Francesca Neri
Victor Plaza	Liberto Rabal
Clara	Angela Molina
Sancho	Jose Sancho

and Penelope Cruz, Pilar Bardem, Alex Angulo

A street kid, sent to prison for a crime he didn't commit, is released seven years later with the intention of seducing the industrialist's daughter he holds responsible for his condemnation.

FOUR DAYS IN SEPTEMBER

(MIRAMAX) Producer, Lucy Barreto; Director, Bruno Barreto; Screenplay, Leopoldo Serran; Based on the book *O Que é isso, Companhiero?* by Fernando Gabeira; Co-Producer, Mary Ann Braubach; Photography, Felix Monti; Art Director, Marcos Flaksman; Costumes, Emilia Duncan; Music, Stewart Copeland; Editor, Isabelle Rathery; Casting, Oliva Guimaraes (Rio de Janeiro), Sheila Jaffe, Georgianne Walken (New York); an L.C. Barreto Ltda./Filmes do Equzdor Ltda. production; Co-Produced by Sony Corporation of America/Columbia Pictures Television Trading Corporation; Presented in association with Pandora Cinema; Brazilian, 1997; Dolby; Color; Rated R; 106 minutes; January release

CAST

Charles Burke Elbrick	Alan Arkin
Fernando Gabeira/Paulo	Pedro Cardoso
Maria	Fernanda Torres
Marcão	Luiz Fernand Guimaraes
Renée	Claudia Abreu
Toledo	Nelson Dantas
Jonas	Matheus Nachtegaele
Henrique	Marco Ricca
Brandão	Mauricio Goncalves
Júlio	Caio Junqueria
César/Oswaldo	Selton Mello
Artur	Eduardo Moskovis
Elvira Elbrick	Caroline Kava
Mowinkel	Fisher Stevens

and Fernanda Montenegro, Milton Goncalves, Othon Bastos, Lulu Santos, Alessandra Negrini, Jorge Cherques, Antônio Pedro, Flávio São Thiago, Luis Armando Querioz

True story of how the U.S. Ambassador to Brazil was kidnapped in September of 1969 and held prisoner by a group of terrorists demanding justice for political prisoners. This film was nominated for an Oscar for foreign-language film (1997).

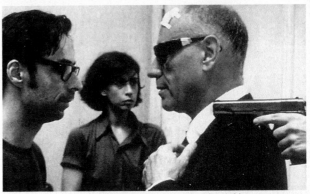

Pedro Cardosa, Fernanda Torres, Alan Arkin

Claudia Abreu

© Miramax Films

FALLEN ANGELS

(KINO) Producers, Wong Kar-Wai, Jeff Lau; Director/Screenplay, Wong Kar-Wai; Executive Producer, Chan Ye-Cheng; Photography, Christopher Doyle; Line Producer, Jacky Pang; Designer, William Chang; Editors, William Chang, Wong Ming Lam; Music, Frankie Chan, Roel A. Garcia; a Jet Tone production; Hong Kong, 1995; Color; Not rated; 96 minutes; January release

CAST

Wong Chi-Ming, the Killer	Leon Lai
He Zhiwu	Takeshi Kaneshiro
Cherry	Charlie Young
The Agent	Michelle Reis
Baby	Karen Mok
Sato, the Manager	Toru Saito
Father	Chen Wanlei
Ah-Hoi	Kong To-Hoi
Man Forced to Eat Ice Cream	Chan Fai-Hung
Woman Pressed to Buy Vegetables	Kwan Lee-Na
Man Forced to Have His Clothes Washed	Wu-Yuk Ho

The Agent becomes the linking catalyst between two diverse members of Hong Kong's underground: Wong, a hitman who wants to get out of the business, and Zhiwu, an ex-con who makes a living bullying customers into buying goods and services from him.

Michelle Reis, Leon Lai

© Kino International

SPICE WORLD

(COLUMBIA) Producers, Uri Fruchtmann, Barnaby Thompson; Executive Producer, Simon Fuller; Director, Bob Spiers; Screenplay, Kim Fuller; Based on an idea by The Spice Girls and Kim Fuller; Co-Producer, Peter McAleese; Photography, Clive Tickner; Designer, Grenville Horner; Costumes, Kate Carin; Editor, Andrea MacArthur; Music, Paul Hardcastle; Casting, Vanessa Pereira, Simone Ireland; a Spice Girls/Fragile Films production, in association with ICON Entertainment International and PolyGram Filmed Entertainment; British,1997; Dolby; Eastman Color; Rated PG; 93 minutes; January release

Victoria Adams, Melanie Chisholm, Elton John,
Melanie Brown, Emma Bunton, Geri Halliwell

CAST

Scary Spice	Melanie Brown
Baby Spice	Emma Bunton
Sporty Spice	Melanie Chisholm
Ginger Spice	Geri Halliwell
Posh Spice	Victoria Adams
Clifford	Richard E. Grant
Piers Cutherton-Smyth	Alan Cumming
Martin Barnfield, Film Producer	George Wendt
Deborah	Claire Rushbrook
Graydon	Mark McKinney
Damien	Richard O'Brien
Jess	Steven O'Donnell
Chief	Roger Moore
Jack	Devon Anderson
Mr. Step	Michael Barrymore
Bishop	Richard Briers
Enzo	David Fahm
Brad	Jason Flemyng
Judge	Stephen Fry
Kevin McMaxford	Barry Humphries
Nervous Guy	Craig Kelly
Poirot	Hugh Laurie
Dennis	Meat Loaf
Nicola	Naoko Mori
Barnaby	Neil Mullarkey
Brian	Bill Paterson
Fashionable Woman	Jennifer Saunders
Jack/Evie's Mother	Denise Stephenson
Evie	Perdita Weeks
Photographer	Dominic West

and Kevin Allen (TV Director), Simon Chandler, Marian McLoughlin (Hospital Parents), Neil Fox (Voice of Radio DJ), Llewella Gideon (Nurse), Guy Gowan (Waiter), Jools Holland (Musical Director), Kevin McNally (Policeman), Simon Shepherd (Doctor), Cathy Shipton (Midwife), Peter Sissons (Newsreader), Elvis Costello, Bob Geldof, Bob Hoskins, Elton John, Jonathan Ross, The Dream Boys (Themselves), Simon Ellis, Andy Gangadeen, Paul Gendler, Fergus Gerrand, Steve Lewison, Michael Martin (The Spice Band)

British pop singing sensations the Spice Girls make their way to their first live concert while facing their exasperated manager and a documentary filmmaker hoping to capture the group in action.

Emma Bunton, Melanie Brown, Geri Halliwell
Victoria Adams, Melanie Chisholm

The Spice Girls

The Spice Girls

NIL BY MOUTH

(SONY PICTURES CLASSICS) Producers, Luc Besson, Douglas Urbanski, Gary Oldman; Director/Screenplay, Gary Oldman; Co-Producer, Hilary Heath; Associate Producer, Marc Frydman; Photography, Ron Fortunato; Editor, Brad Fuller; Designer, Hugo Luczyc-Wyhowski; Music, Eric Clapton; Casting, Sue James; a Luc Besson presentation of an SE8 Group Production; British, 1997; Dolby; Color; Rated R; 128 minutes; February release

Ray Winstone

CAST

Raymond	Ray Winstone
Valerie	Kathy Burke
Billy	Charlie Creed-Miles
Janet	Laila Morse
Kath	Edna Dore
Paula	Chrissie Cotterill
Angus	Jon Morrison
Mark	Jamie Forman
Danny	Steve Sweeney
M.C. in Club	Terry Rowley
Club Comic	Sam Miller
Michelle	Leah Fitzgerald
Drug Dealer	Gerry Bromfield
Schmuddie	Neil Maskell
Old Guy in Window	Sid Golder

and John Blundell (Man with Knife), Kenan Hudaverdi (Laundrette Owner), Everton Nelson (Street Violinist), Ronny Fox (Peter, Pool Player), Frances Ashman (Club Singer), Dan Carey, Martin Watson, Giseppe Acunzo, Matthew Scott, Edmund Scott (Band Musicians)

A look at a dysfunctional South London family including the brutish, hard-drinking Raymond, his abused wife Valerie and her heroin-addicted younger brother Billy. This marked the debut of actor Gary Oldman as a screenwriter and director.

© Sony Pictures Entertainment

Kathy Burke, Ray Winstone

Charlie Creed-Miles

Laila Morse, Kathy Burke

Celia Imrie, Flora Newbigin, Jim Broadbent, Raymond Pickard

THE BORROWERS

(POLYGRAM) Producers, Tim Bevan, Eric Fellner, Rachel Talalay; Executive Producer, Walt DeFaria; Director, Peter Hewitt; Screenplay, Gavin Scott, John Kamps; Based on the novels by Mary Norton; Line Producer, Mary Richards; Photography, John Fenner, Trevor Brooker; Editor, David Freeman; Designer, Gemma Jackson; Visual Effects Supervisor, Peter Chiang; Costumes, Marie France; Music, Harry Gregson-Williams; Co-Producers, Debra Hayward, Liza Chasin; Casting, Nina Gold; a Working Title Films production; British, 1997; Dolby; Technicolor; Rated PG; 83 minutes; February release

Raymond Pickard, John Goodman

CAST

Ocious P. Potter	John Goodman
Exterminator Jeff	Mark Williams
Pod Clock	Jim Broadbent
Homily Clock	Celia Imrie
Arrietty Clock	Flora Newbigin
Peagreen Clock	Tom Felton
Spiller	Raymond Pickard
Pete Lender	Bradley Pierce
Joe Lender	Aden Gillett
Victoria Lender	Doon Mackichan
Officer Steady	Hugh Laurie
Town Hall Clerk	Ruby Wax
Dustbunny	Andrew Dunford
Minty	Bob Goody
Swag	Patrick Monkton
Milkman	Dick Ward
Chauffeur	George Yiassoumi
TV Gangster	Alex Winter
TV Sergeant	Michael Hewitt
TV Constables	Simon Hewitt, David Freeman

A tiny family who lives under the floor boards of the Lender's home, find their lives in danger when an evil banker evicts the Lenders and plans on demolishing the house.

© PolyGram Films

Bradley Pierce, Flora Newbigin

MRS. DALLOWAY

(FIRST LOOK PICTURES) Producers, Stephen Bayly, Lisa Katselas Paré; Co-Producers, Chris J. Ball, William Tyrer, Simon Curtis, Bill Shepherd; Director, Marleen Gorris; Screenplay, Eileen Atkins; Based on the novel by Virginia Woolf; Photography, Sue Gibson; Designer, David Richens; Costumes, Judy Pepperdine; Music, Ilona Sekacz; Editor, Michiel Reichwein; Associate Producer, Paul Frift; Casting, Celestia Fox; a Bayly/Paré production in association with Bergen Film of a Newmarket Capital Group and BBC Films presentation with the participation of the European Co-Production Fund UK, NPS Television, Dutch Co-Production Fund (Cobo) and the Dutch Film Fund; British-Dutch; Dolby; Color; Rated PG-13; 97 minutes; February release

John Standing, Vanessa Redgrave

CAST

Mrs. Clarissa Dalloway ....Vanessa Redgrave
Young Clarissa Dalloway ....Natascha McElhone
Septimus Warren Smith ....Rupert Graves
Peter Walsh ....Michael Kitchen
Young Peter ....Alan Cox
Young Sally ....Lena Headey
Rezia Warren Smith...Amelia Bullmore
Lady Rosseter (Sally Seton) ....Sarah Badel
Hugh Whitbread ....Oliver Ford Davies
Elizabeth Dalloway ....Katie Carr
Miss Kilman...Selina Cadell
Richard Dalloway...John Standing
Sir William Bradshaw ....Robert Hardy
Lady Bruton ....Margaret Tyzack
Young Richard ....Robert Portal
Young Hugh ....Hal Cruttenden
Aunt Helena..Phyllis Calvert
Lionel (Clarissa's Father) ....John Franklyn-Robbins
Herbert ....Alistair Petrie
Joseph Breitkopf ....Rupert Baker
Lucy ....Amanda Drew
and Oscar Pearce (Bookshop Assistant), Janet Henfrey (Miss Pym), Polly Pritchett (Nursemaid), Hilda Braid (Elderly Woman), Derek Smee (Man on Bench), Jane Whittenshaw, Susie Fairfax (Women by Fountain), Fanny Carby (Old Woman—Singer)

Mrs. Dalloway, whose path has crossed with a shell-shocked young man, prepares for that evening's party, while looking back on the decisions she had made as a young woman thirty years earlier.

Natascha McElhone, Lena Headey

Natascha McElhone, Lena Headey, Alan Cox

Rupert Graves, Amelia Bullmore

John Hurt, Jason Priestley

John Hurt

LOVE AND DEATH ON LONG ISLAND

(LIONS GATE) Producers, Steve Clark-Hall, Christopher Zimmer; Director/Screenplay, Richard Kwietniowski; Based on the novel by Gilbert Adair; Photography, Oliver Curtis; Designer, David McHenry; Editor, Susan Shipton; Music, The Insects, Richard Grassby-Lewis; Costumes, Andrea Galer; Casting, Kate Day, Jon Comerford; a Skyline/Imagex production; Produced with the participation of British Screen, Telefilm Canada, Arts Council of England, Nova Scottia Film Development Corporation in association with BBC Films, Mikado and the Sales Company; Canadian-British, 1997; Dolby; Color; Rated PG-13; 93 minutes; March release

CAST

Giles De'Ath	John Hurt
Ronnie Bostock	Jason Priestley
Audrey	Fiona Loewi
Mrs. Barker	Sheila Hancock
Ivring Buckmiller	Maury Chaykin
Henry	Gawn Grainger
Mrs. Reed	Elizabeth Quinn
Mrs. Abbott	Linda Busby
Eldridge	Bill Leadbitter
Maureen	Ann Reid
Video Assistant	Danny Webb
Harry	Andrew Barrow
Rob	Dean Gatiss
Video Salesman	Robert McKewley
Abigail's Mother	Tusse Silberg
Abigail	Rebecca Michael

and Jean Ainslie, Nigel Makin (Ticket Sellers), Jonathan Stratt (Taxi Driver), Magnus Magnusson (Quiz Master), Shaun Seymour (Quiz Show Consultant), Harvey Atkin (Lou), Marguerite Mc-Neil, Andrew Smith (Irv's Customers), Jocelyn Cunningham (Realtor), Jeffrey Hirschfield (Policeman), Tommy Hurst (Mailman), Lex Gigeroff, Michael Pellerin, Cecil Wright (Cab Drivers), Charlie Rhindress (Fax Assistant), Benita Ha (Weather Reporter), Vincent Corazza (Corey), Geoffrey Herod (Brad), Ryan Rogerson (Tommy), Bruce Filmore (Big Guy), Nancy Marshall (Corey's Mother), Elizabeth Murphy (The Stomper), Jenny Raymond (Molly), Charles Jannasch (Rusty), Shaun D. Richardson (Pete), Mary Allison Putnam (Girl on Bed), Gabriel Hogan (Jake), Jeremy Akerman (Father Bryson), Christine Jeffers (Sitcom Mother), Morrisssey Dunn (Sitcom Father), Swayzee (Strider), Ouzo (Mrs. Reed's Dog)

After accidentally stumbling into a cinema playing the film Hotpants College 2, erudite British writer Giles De'Ath finds himself so obsessed with young American actor Ronnie Bostock that he journeys to Long Island in order to meet him.

Jason Priestley

Fiona Loewi, Jason Priestley, John Hurt

MR. NICE GUY

(NEW LINE CINEMA) Producer, Chua Lam; Executive Producer, Leonard Ho; Director, Samo Hung; Screenplay, Edward Tang, Fibe Ma; Photography, Raymond Lam; Designer, Horace Ma; Editor, Peter Cheung; Music, J. Peter Robinson; a Raymond Chow/Golden Harvest production; Hong Kong, 1997; Dolby; Technovision; Deluxe color; Rated PG-13; 113 minutes; March release

CAST

Jackie	Jackie Chan
Giancarlo	Richard Norton
Miki	Miki Lee
Lakeisha	Karen McLymont
Diana	Gabrielle Fitzpatrick
Romeo	Vince Poletto
Baggio	Barry Otto
Cyclist	Samo Hung
Ice Cream Vendor	Emil Chau
Cook Show Audience	Mina Godenzi
Richard	Peter Houghton

and Peter Lindsay (Gronk), David No (Victor), Rachel Blakely (Sandy), Judy Green (Tina), Stephan Friedrich, Jonathan Isgar, Steve Kahlua, Matthew Meersbergen, Stuart Ritchie, Kyne Sedgman, Matt Trihey, Les Uzice (Demons), Karl Ajami, Bradley Allan, Paul Andreovski, David Baldwin, Kerry Blakeman, Mark Campbell, Terry Carter, Dennis Christensen, Tony Doherty, Cameron Douglas, Paul Douglas, Stuart Ellis, Mark Fitzpatrick, Stuart Fraser, Michael Hammad, Habby Heske, Brent Houghton, Richard Huggett, Graham Jahne, Chris Kemp, Robert Lowe, Frederick MacClure, Douglas "Rocky" MacDonald, Ian Mall, Den McCoy, Mike Menzies, Jason Murphy, Michael John Noonan, George Novak, Grant Page, Puven Pather, Harry Pavlidis, George Popovic, John Raaen, Joseph Sayah, Gary Shambrooke, Vess Svorcan, Davin Taylor, Darko Tuskan, Jade Weitering, Chris Wilson, Damon Young (Giancarlo's Men), Aaron Notarfrancesco (Sonny), Jake Notarfrancesco (Nancy), Frederick Miragliotta (NEA Head Officer), Nick Carrafa, Rod Catteral, Ben Mitchell, Mark Neal, Jerome Pride (NEA Agents), Keith Agius (Special Action Team Leader), Greg Jamieson (Priest), Matthew Dytynski (Floor Manager), Salik Silverstein (Cook Show Director), Lynn Murphy (Baby Sitter), Nicholas Bufalo (Passerby)

A cooking show host accidentally gains possession of a videotape incriminating a deadly crimelord and finds himself pursued by two rival gangs.

Jackie Chan
© *New Line Cinema*

Boris Terral, Brigitte Roüan
© *New Yorker Films*

POST COITUM

(NEW YORKER) formerly *Post Coitum, Animal Triste;* Producer, Humbert Balsan; Director, Brigitte Roüan; Screenplay, Brigitte Roüan, Santiago Amigorena, Jean-Louis Richard, Guy Zilberstein, Philippe Le Guay; Photography, Pierre Dupouey, Arnaud Leguy, Bruno Mistretta; Editor, Laurent Rouan; Costumes, Florence Emir, Marika Ingrato; Casting, Paula Chevalet, Lissa Pilu, Claire Le Saint; a co-production of Ognon Pictures Pinou-Film in association with Canal+, the Centre National de la Cinématographie, the Gan Foundation, Service Forum of the Club Méd, the region of Franche-Comté and Ad-Hoc Production; French, 1997; Dolby; Color; Not rated; 99 minutes; March release

CAST

Diane Clovier	Brigitte Roüan
Philippe Clovier	Patrick Chesnais
Emilio	Boris Terral
François Narou	Nils Tavernier
Weyoman-Lebeau	Jean-Louis Richard
Madame LePluche	Françoise Arnoul
Caroline	Emmanuelle Bach
Copine Narou	Carmen Chaplin
Isabelle	Gaëlle Le Furr
The Designer	Elodie Pong
Miguel	Roberto Plate
Victor	Oliver Lechat
Basile	Felix Dedet-Roüan
Dédé	Jean De La Valade

and Jean-Claude Chapuis (The Player on Musical Glasses), Jean-François Rouan (The Sales Manager), Bernard Budaga (Emilio's Grandfather), Nicolas Dedet (Homeless Person), Jacques Disses (Monsieur LePluche), Ali Rostand (Cafe Owner), Michel Polac, Gisele Casadesus, Lucien Pascal (Guest Stars), Nicole Garcia (Voice)

A married book editor begins an affair with a young engineer who brings a new passion and meaning to her staid existence.

FIREWORKS

(MILESTONE) a.k.a. *Hana-Bi*; Producers, Masayuki Mori, Yasushi Tsuge, Takio Yoshida, in association with Shigeru Watanabe, Kouichi Miyagawa, Hideto Osawa; Director/Screenplay, Takeshi Kitano; Co-Producers, Hiroshi Ishikawa, Kazuhiro Furukawa; Photography, Hideo Yamamoto; Art Director, Norihiro Isoda; Editors, Takeshi Kitano, Yoshinori Ota; Music, Joe Hisaishi; an Office Kitano production; Japanese; Color; Not rated; 103 minutes; March release

CAST

Yoshitaka Nishi	"Beat" Takeshi Kitano
Miyuki (Nishi's Wife)	Kayoko Kishimoto
Horibe	Ren Osugi
Nakamura	Susumu Terajima
Tezuka (Junkyard Owner)	Tetsu Watanabe
Yakuza Hitman	Hakuryu
The Criminal	Yasuei Yakushiji
Kudo	Taro Itsumi
Doctor	Kenichi Yajima
Tanaka	Makoto Ashikawa
Tanaka's Widow	Yuko Daike

After his partner is murderer detective Nishi resigns from the force and decides to take revenge on his own.

© *Milestone*

Takeshi Kitano

GENEALOGIES OF A CRIME

(STRAND) Executive Producer, Paulo Branco; Director, Raul Ruiz; Screenplay, Pascal Bonitzer, Raoul Ruiz; Photography, Stefan Ivanov; Editor, Valeria Sarmiento; Designers, Luc Chalon, Solange Zeitoun; Costumes, Elizabeth Tavernier; Music, Jorge Arriagada; from Gemini Films with the participation of Canal+ & CNC, with the support of Procirep and Madragoa Filmes; French, 1997; Dolby; Color; Not rated; 113 minutes; March release

CAST

Jeanne/Solange	Catherine Deneuve
Georges	Michel Piccoli
René	Melvil Poupaud
Christian	Andrzej Seweryn
Esther	Bernadette Lafont
Louise	Monique Melinand
Verret	Hubert Saint Macary
Mathieu	Jean-Yves Gautier
Yves	Mathieu Amalric
Soledad	Camila Mora
Bob	Patrick Modiano
L'avocat	Jean Badin

Solange, a lawyer defending young Rene, who is accused of murdering his aunt, imagines herself as the victim of his crime.

© *Strand Releasing*

Catherine Deneuve

A TASTE OF CHERRY

(ZEITGEIST), a.k.a. *The Taste Of Cherries*; Director/Producer/Screenplay/Editor, Abbas Kiarostami; Photography, Homayoun Payvar; an Abbas Kiarostami-CIBY 2000 co-production; Iranian, 1997; Color; Not rated; 95 minutes; March release

CAST

Mr. Badii	Homayoun Ershadi
The Taxidermist	Abdolhossein Bagheri
The Worker	Afshin Bakhtiari
The Soldier	Ali Moradi
The Seminarian	Hossein Noori
The Factory Guard	Ahmad Ansari
The Man in the Telephone Booth	Hamid Massomi
The Woman in Front of the Museum	Elham Imani

Mr. Badii, a middle-aged man who has decided to kill himself, meets an assortment of odd characters in his travels to the outskirts of Tehran.

© *Zeitgeist*

Homayoun Ershadi

JUNK MAIL

(LIONS GATE) Producers, Dag Nordahl, Peter Bøe; Director Pål Sletaune; Screenplay, Pål Sletaune, Jonny Halberg; Photography, Kjell Vassdal; Designer, Karl Juliusson; Music, Joachim Holbek; Editor, Pål Gengenvach; Norwegian, 1997; Color; Not rated; 79 minutes; April release

CAST

Roy	Robert Skjærstad
Line	Andrine Sæther
George	Per Egil Aske
Betsy	Eli Anne Linnestad
Sæther	Trond Høvik
Gina	Henriette Steenstrup
Per	Ådne Olav Sekkelsten

A meddlesome mailman finds himself in deep trouble when he sneaks into the home of a woman and ends up preventing her from committing suicide.

© *Lions Gate Films*

Robert Skjærstad

Bob Hoskins, Mat Hand

Danny Nussbaum

TWENTYFOURSEVEN

(OCTOBER) Producer, Imogen West; Executive Producers, Stephen Woolley, Nik Powell, George Faber, David Thompson; Director, Shane Meadows; Screenplay, Shane Meadows, Paul Fraser; Photography, Ashley Rowe; Designer, John Paul Kelley; Costumes, Phillip Crichton; Editor, Bill Diver; Music, Neil MacColl, Boo Hewerdine; Line Producer, Sally French; Casting, Abi Cohen; a BBC Films and Scalia presentation; British, 1997; Dolby; Black and white; Rated R; 96 minutes; April release

CAST

Tim	Danny Nussbaum
Alan Darcy	Bob Hoskins
Tim's Dad (Geoff)	Bruce Jones
Tim's Mum (Pat)	Annette Badland
Gadget	Justin Brady
Knighty	James Hooton
Daz	Darren Campbell
Young Darcy	Krishan Beresford
Stuart	Karl Collins
Youngy	Anthony Clarke
Benny	Johann Myers
Meggy	Jimmy Hynd
Fagash	Mat Hand
Court Security Man	Lord Dominic Dillon of Eldon
Prosecutor	Ian Smith
Sally the Judge	Tanya Myers
Ronnie	Frank Harper
Tonka	James Corden

and Tony Nyland (Gadget's Dad), Colin Higgins (Knighty's Dad), Jo Bell (Jo), Pamela Cundell (Auntie Iris), Gina Aris (Sharon), Sammy Pasha (Jimmy), Paul Fraser (Photographer), Ladene Hall (Daz's Girlfriend), Dena Smiles (Meggy's Girlfriend), John Baxter (Man Outside Shop), Maureen O'Grady (Knighty's Mum), Lord Shane Meadows of Eldon (Man with Saucepan on Head), Ben Rothwell (Man Selling Flowers), Ron Bissell, Mick Bleakley, Derek Osborne (Boxing Match Judges), Derek Groomsbridge (Staffordshire Coach), Liam Walsh, Kevin Wallace (Staffordshire Boxers), Dave Miller (Phil "The Animal" Yeats)

Hoping to restore some dignity to a small town's dissolute youths, Alan Darcy sets up a boxing club for the kids to release their anger and agression.

© *October Films*

THE BUTCHER BOY

(WARNER BROS.) Producers, Redmond Morris, Stephen Woolley; Executive Producer/Director, Neil Jordan; Screenplay, Neil Jordan, Patrick McCabe; Based upon the novel by Patrick McCabe; Photography, Adrian Biddle; Designer, Anthony Pratt; Editor, Tony Lawson; Music, Elliot Goldenthal; Costumes, Sandy Powell; Casting, Susie Figgis; a Geffen Pictures presentation; Irish-U.S.; Dolby; Technicolor; Rated R; 106 minutes; April release

Eamonn Owens, Stephen Rea

CAST

Benny Brady	Stephen Rea
Mrs. Nugent	Fiona Shaw
Francie Brady	Eamon Owens
Joe Purcell	Alan Boyle
Annie Brady	Aisling O'Sullivan
Father Bubbles	Brendan Gleeson
Father Sullivan	Milo O'Shea
Our Lady/Colleen	Sinéad O'Connor
Sergeant	Sean McGinley
Leddy	Peter Gowen
Phillip Nugent	Andrew Fullerton
Dr. Boyd	John Kavanagh
Mrs. Canning	Rosaleen Linehan
Mrs. Coyle	Anita Reeves
Mary	Gina Moxley
Father Dom	Niall Buggy
Uncle Alo	Ian Hart
Mrs. McGlone	Anne O'Neill
Charlie McGlone	Joe Pilkington
Farmer on Tractor	Pat McGrath

and Jer O'Leary (Dublin Man), Pat Leavy (Dublin Cafe Woman), Janet Moran (Dublin Shopkeeper), Paraic Breathnach (Man on Truck), John Olohan (Mr. Nugent), Ardal O'Hanlon (Mr. Purcell), Mikel Murfi (Buttsy), Brendan Conroy (Devlin), Tom Hickey (Gardener), Gregg Fitzgerald, John Finnegan, Gavin Kelty, Eoin Chaney (Bogmen), Ciaran Owens, Shane O'Connor (Boys at Fountain), Paolo Tullio (Mr. Caffolla), Siobhan McElvaney, Aine McEneaney (Girls in Shooting Gallery), Patrick McCabe (Jimmy the Skite), Sean Hughes, Gerard McSorley (Psychiatrists), Tony Rohr (Bogman in Mental Hospital), Dermot Healy (Bogman in Hospital), Birdy Sweeney (Man in Well), Marie Mullen (Mrs. Thompson), Stuart Graham (Priest at College), Macdara O'Fatharta (Alien Priest), Ronan Wilmot (Policeman), Vinnie McCabe (Detective)

Brendan Gleeson, Eamonn Owens

In a small town in 1960s Ireland, 12-year-old Francie Brady lives in a world of fantasy to escape from the hopelessness of his family life until he finally begins to lose his grip and crosses over to violence.

© Geffen Pictures

Fiona Shaw, Eamonn Owens, Andrew Fullerton

Eamonn Owens, Alan Boyle

Gong Li, Jeremy Irons

Jeremy Irons, Gong Li

Maggie Cheung, Jeremy Irons

CHINESE BOX

(**TRIMARK**) Producers, Wayne Wang, Lydia Dean Pilcher, Jean-Louis Piel; Executive Producers, Michiyo Yoshizaki, Akinori Inaba, Jean Labadie, Reinhard Brundig; Director, Wayne Wang; Screenplay, Jean-Claude Carriere, Larry Gross; Story, Jean-Claude Carriere, Paul Theroux, Wayne Wang; Photography, Vilko Filac; Music, Graeme Revell; Editor, Christopher Tellefsen; Co-Producers, Heidi Levitt, Jessinta Liu; Casting, Heidi Levitt; an NDF International Ltd. & Pony Canyon, Inc. and Le Studio Canal+ presentation; Japanese-French-U.S., 1997; Dolby; Color; Rated R; 100 minutes; April release

CAST

John	Jeremy Irons
Vivian	Gong Li
Jean	Maggie Cheung
Chang	Michael Hui
Jim	Ruben Blades
Homeless Man	Chaplin Chang
John's Friend at New Year's Party	Noel Rands
Amanda Everheart	Emma Lucia
Rick	Ken Bennett
New Year's Party MC	Russell Cawthorne
William Wong	Emotion Cheung
Weeks	Harvey Stockwin
Jonathan	Jonathan Midgley
Bruce	Bruce Walker
Baby-Lin	Angelica Lofgren
Dr. Chang	Dr. Julian Chang
Drunk Karaoke Singer	Alex Ng Hong Ling
Minibus Passenger	Chiu Wah Lee
Mamasan	Maria Cordero
Godfather	Pao Fung

and Jian Rui Chao, Wai Sing, Lo Hung (Businessmen), Shirley Hung, Michelle Yeung (Girlfriends), Hui Fan (Godfather's Wife), Lam Man Cheung (Wedding Photographer), Lee Siu Kai, Leung Chi On, Tse Yuen Fat (Gangsters), Roderick Lee (Manhattan Club Bouncer), Hui Li, Maria St. Lynne (Black Moon Hostesses), Josephine Ho (Lilly), Jared Harris (William), Gloria Wu (News Reporter)

A British journalist living in Hong Kong during its historical transferrance from British to Chinese rule, tries to sort out his frustrated love affair with Vivian after finding out he is dying from leukemia.

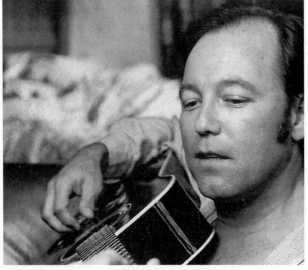

Ruben Blades

SONATINE

(ROLLING THUNDER PICTURES) Producers, Masayuki Mori, Hisao Nabeshima, Takeo Yoshida; Executive Producer, Kazuysohi Okuyama; Director/Screenplay/Editor, Takeshi Kitano; Photography, Katsumi Yanagishima; Art Director, Osamu Saseki; Music, Jo Hasaishi; a Shochiku Company production; Japanese, 1994; Color; Rated R; 94 minutes; April release

CAST

Murakama	"Beat" Takeshi (Takeshi Kitano)
Uechi	Tetsu Watanabe
Miyuki	Aya Kokumai
Ryoji	Masanobu Katsumura
Ken	Susumu Terashima
Katagiri	Ren Ohsugi
Kitajima	Tonbo Zushi
Takahashi	Kenichi Yajima
The Hit Man	Eiji Minakata

After Tokyo underboss Murakawa announces his possible retirement, he becomes suspicious of the motives behind his being assigned to a special peacekeeping mission in Okinawa.

© *Rolling Thunder*

Takeshi Kitano

Takeshi Kitano (r)

John Turturro

THE TRUCE

(MIRAMAX) Producers, Leo Pescarolo, Guido De Laurentiis; Director, Francesco Rosi; Executive Producer, Guido De Laurentiis; Screenplay, Francesco Rosi, Stefano Rulli, Sandro Petraglia; Adapted for the screen by Franesco Rosi, Tonino Guerra; Based on the book by Primo Levi; Photography, Pasqualino De Santis, Marco Pontecorvo; Designer, Andrea Crisanti; Costumes, Alberto Verso; a 3 Emme production, presented in association with Capitol Films in association with Channel Four films; Italian-Swiss-French-German-British, 1997; Dolby; Color; Rated R; 117 minutes; April release

CAST

Primo Levi	John Turturro
Cesare	Massimo Ghini
The Greek	Rade Serbedzija
Daniele	Stefano Dionisi
Col. Rovi	Teco Celio
Unverdorben	Roberto Citran
Ferrari	Claudio Bisio
D'Agata	Andy Luotto
Galina	Agnieszka Wagner
Flora	Lorenza Indovina
Maria Fiodorovna	Marina Gerasymenko
Egorov	Igor Bezgin
The Mongol	Alexandr Iljin
Lt. Sergei	Viachesslav Olhovsky
Dr. Gotlieb	Anatoliy Vassiliev

and Tatiana Meshscherkina (Irina), Franco Trevisi (Marshall), Federico Pacifici (Lieutenant), Ernesto Lama (Carmine), Gerda Maria Jurgens (Brigitte), Kasper Weiss (Kapo), Vitalij Rozstalnyj (Gen. Timoshenko), Joachim Wörmsdorf (German General)

Liberated by the Russians from Auschwitz, Primo Levi begins the long journey back to his home in Turin, Italy.

© *Miramax Films*

249

SLIDING DOORS

(MIRAMAX/PARAMOUNT) Producers, Sydney Pollack, Philippa Braithwaite, William Horberg; Executive Producers, Guy East, Nigel Sinclair; Director/Screenplay, Peter Howitt; Photography, Remi Adefarasin; Designer, Maria Djurkovic; Music, David Hirschfelder; Editor, John Smith; Costumes, Jill Taylor; Co-Producer, David Wisnievitz; Associate Producer, Sandy Poustie; Casting, Michelle Guish; Presented in association with Intermedia Films; a Mirage production; British-U.S.; Dolby; Color; Rated PG-13; 108 minutes; April release

CAST

Helen	Gwyneth Paltrow
James	John Hannah
Gerry	John Lynch
Lydia	Jeanne Tripplehorn
Anna	Zara Turner
Russel	Douglas McFerran
Clive	Paul Brightwell
Claudia	Nina Young
James' Mother	Virginia McKenna
Boss Paul	Kevin McNally
Kind Cabbie	Terry English
Man on Tube	Paul Stacey
Cheeky Bloke	Peter Howitt
Suspicious Girl	Joanna Roth
Defensive Bloke	Neil Stuke
Rachel	Theresa Kartell
James' Receptionist	Evelyn Duah
Senior Theatre Nurse	Linda Broughton
Intensive Care Doctor	Charlotte Fryer
Consultant	Pip Miller
P.R. Steve	Christopher Villiers
Mother	Merryn Jones
Child	Ella Jones
Concerned Diner	Julie McDowell

Helen, on her way home to tell her boyfriend Gerry that she has lost her job, misses the train, causing a parallel story to play out, speculating on what might have happened if Helen had made the train and come home in time to find Gerry carrying on with another woman.

© Miramax Films

John Hannah, Gwyneth Paltrow

John Lynch

Gwyneth Paltrow, John Hannah

Jeanne Tripplehorn

THE KINGDOM II

(OCTOBER) Producers, Vibeke Windeløv, Svend Abrahamsen; Directors, Lars von Trier, Morten Arnfred; Screenplay, Lars von Trier, Niels Vørsel; Photography, Eric Kress; Art Directors, Jette Lehmann, Hans Christian Lindholm; Music, Joachim Holbek; Editors, Molly Malene Stensgaard, Pernille Bech Christensen; Produced by Zentropa Entertainments ApS and DR TV, Danish Broadcasting Corporation in co-production with Liberator Productions S.a.r.l. and in association with RAI Cinema Fiction Sveriges Television, Malmö Norsk Rikskringckasting and La Sept ARTE Unite de Programmes Fictions; Danish-Swedish, 1997; Dolby; Color; Not rated; 286 minutes; May release

CAST

Stig Helmer	Ernst-Hugo Järegård
Mrs. Drusse	Kirsten Rolffes
Dr. Moesgaard	Holger Juul Hansen
Krogen	Søren Pilmark
Rigmor	Ghita Nørby
Bulder	Jens Okking
Miss Svendsen	Birthe Neumann
Hansen	Otto Brandenburg

and Erik Wedersøe (Ole), Baard Owe (Bondo), Birgitte Raaberg (Judith), Henning Jensen (Bob), John Hahn-Petersen (Nivesen), Peter Mygind (Mogge), Udo Kier (Little Brother and Aage Krüger), Vita Jensen, Morten Rotne Leffers (Dishwashers), Solbjørg Højfeldt (Camilla), Søren Elung Jensen (Man in Top Hat), Paul Hüttel (Dr. Steenbæk), Holger Perfort (Prof. Ulrich), Klaus Wegener (Doctor, Casualty), Michelle Bjørn-Andersen (Pediatrician), Timm Mehrens (Doctor, Operating Theatre), Louise Fribo (Sanne), Tine Miehe-Renard (Night Nurse), Julie Wieth (Pediatric Nurse), Annette Ketscher (Nurse, Casualty), Birthe Tove, Lise Schrøder (Nurses), Dorrit Stender-Petersen (Assisting Nurse), Ole Boisen (Christian), Thomas Stender (Student), Cecilie Brask (Young Woman in Therapy), Claus Nissen (Madsen), Thomas Bo Larsen (Falcon), Steen Svarre (Man in Overalls), Laura Christensen (Mona), Mette Munk Plum (Mona's Mother), Michael Philip Simpson (Man from Haiti), Fash Shodeinde (Philip Marco), Kim Jansson (Det. Jensen), Claus Flygare (Det. Nielsen), Nis Bank-Mikkelsen (Hospital Pastor), Britta Lillesøe (Woman in Bed), Henrik Fiig (Car Crash Victim), Birger Jensen (Janitor), Peter Hartmann (Removal Man), Lars Lunøe (Minister of Health), Jens Jørn Spottag (Attorney Bisgaard), Helle Virkner (Emma), Annevig Shelde Ebbe (Mary), Torben Zeller (Crematorium Functionary), Jannie Faurschou (Orthopedist), Stellan Skarsgård (Swedish Lawyer), Klaus Pagh (Bailiff), Vera Gebuhr (Gerda), Mette Hald (Cross Girl), Bjarne G. Nielsen (Hospital Pastor, New), Anders Hove (Celebrant), Ingolf David (Death), Philip Zandén (Jonsson from Lund), Ruth Junker, Peter Gilsfort (Voices of Dishwashers), Evald Krog (Voice of "Little Brother"), Ulrik Cold (Narrator)

A look at the various personal dramas of the staff and patients at the Kingdom Hospital in Copenhagen. Taken from four segments of the Danish television series this feature serves as a continuation of The Kingdom which was released in the U.S. in 1995 by October Films.

© October Films

Stellan Skarsgård

Ernst-Hugo Järegård

Birgitte Raaberg

INSOMNIA

(FIRST RUN FEATURES) Producer, Anne Frilseth; Executive Producers, Petter Borgli, Tomas Backström, Tom Remlov; Director, Erik Skjoldbjærg; Screenplay, Nikolaj Frobenius, Erik Skjoldbjærg; Photography, Erling Thurmann-Andersen; Set Designer, Eli Bø; Editor, Håkon Øverås; Costumes, Runa Fønne; Music, Geir Jensen; a Norsk Film/Nordic Screen production; from Castle Hill Productions; Norwegian, 1997; Dolby; Color; Not rated; 97 minutes; May release

CAST

Jonas Engström	Stellan Skarsgård
Erik Vik	Sverre Anker Ousdal
Hilde Hagen	Gisken Armand
Jon Holt	Bjørn Floberg
Ane	Maria Bonnevie
Arne Zakariassen	Kristian Figenschow
Tom Engen	Thor Michael Aamodt
Eilert	Bjørn Moan
Frøya	Marianne O. Ulrichsen
Chief of Police	Frode Rasmussen
Mia Nikolaisen	Guri Johnson
Tanja Lorentzen	Maria Mathiesen

While investigating the slaying of a young girl in a town in Northern Norway, a pair of criminal investigators are confronted with a second murder.

© First Run Features

Stephen Fry, Jude Law

Zoë Wanamaker, Vanessa Redgrave

Judy Parfitt

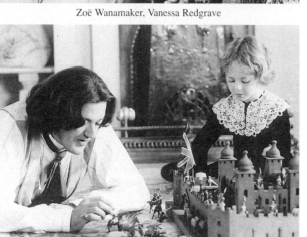

Stephen Fry, Jackson Leach

Jennifer Ehle, Laurence Owen

WILDE

(SONY PICTURES CLASSICS) Producers, Marc Samuelson, Peter Samuelson; Executive Producers, Michiyo Yoshizaki, Michael Viner, Deborah Raffin, Alex Graham, Alan Howden; Director, Brian Gilbert; Screenplay, Julian Mitchell; Based on the book *Oscar Wilde* by Richard Ellmann; Photography, Martin Fuhrer; Designer, Maria Djurkovic; Costumes, Nic Ede; Music, Debbie Wiseman; Editor, Michael Bradsell; Line Producer, Nick O'Hagan; Casting, Sarah Bird; a Dover International Inc. presentation of NDF International Ltd./Pony Canyon Inc., Pandora Film, Capitol Films, and BBC Films with the participation of the Greenlight Fund; British, 1997; Dolby; PLC Widescreen; Color; Rated R; 115 minutes; May release

CAST

Oscar Wilde ....Stephen Fry
Lord Alfred Douglas..Jude Law
Lady Speranza Wilde ....Vanessa Redgrave
Constance Wilde ....Jennifer Ehle
Lady Queensberry..Gemma Jones
Lady Mount-Temple ....Judy Parfitt
Robert Ross ....Michael Sheen
Ada Leverson ....Zoë Wanamaker
The Marquess of Queensberry ....Tom Wilkinson
John Gray ....Ioan Gruffudd
Lionel Johnson..Matthew Mills
Ernest Dowson ....Jason Morell
Charles Gill ....Peter Barkworth
C.O. Humphreys ....Robert Lang
Judge ....Philip Locke
Edward Carson..David Westhead
Cyril Wilde ....Jack Knight
Cyril Wilde (aged 4) ....Jackson Leach
Vyvyan Wilde...Laurence Owen
Alfred Wood ....Benedict Sandiford
Charles Parker ....Mark Letheren
Alfred Taylor..Michael Fitzgerald
Rentboy ....Orlando Bloom
Mine Owner ....Bob Sessions
Jones ....Adam Garcia
First Miner ....Joseph May
Friends..Jamie Leene, James D'Arcy
Undergraduate ....Orlando Wells
George Alexander ....Robin Kermode
Lady Bracknell ....Avril Elgar
Miss Prism...Jean Ainslie
Algernon ....Andrew Hav-ill
Gwendolen..Biddy Hodson
Mrs. Allonby ....Judi Maynard
Chasuble ....Hugh Munro
Lord Illingworth...Michael Simkins

The true story of how author Oscar Wilde faced disgrace and ruin once his homosexual relationship with Lord Alfred Douglas was brought to light in late 1800s Britain. Previous films on the life of Wilde include Oscar Wilde (released in the U.S. by Four City in 1960) with Robert Morley, and The Trials of Oscar Wilde (released in the U.S. by Warwick in 1960) with Peter Finch.

Jude Law, Jennifer Ehle

Stephen Fry

Tom Wilkinson

THE HANGING GARDEN

(GOLDWYN) Producers, Louise Garfield, Arnie Gelbart, Thom Fitzgerald; Director/Screenplay, Thom Fitzgerald; Photography, Daniel Jobin; Designer, Taavo Soodor; Music, John Roby; Editor, Susan Shanks; Costumes, James A. Worthen; Casting, Martha Chesley, John Dunsworth; Line Producer, Gilles Bélanger; Associate Producer, Mark Hammond; a Triptych Media/Galafilm/Emotion Pictures production; Produced with the participation of Telefilm Canada/The Harold Greenberg Fund/Channel 4/Nova Scotia Film Development Coporation; Distributed by MGM; Canadian, 1997; Dolby; Color; Rated R; 91 minutes; May release

CAST

Sweet William	Chris Leavins
Teenage Sweet William	Troy Veinotte
Rosemary	Kerry Fox
Teenage Rosemary	Sarah Polley
Iris	Seana McKenna
Whiskey Mac	Peter MacNeill
Grace	Joan Orenstein
Violet	Christine Dunsworth
Fletcher	Joel S. Keller
Laurel	Jocelyn Cunningham
Dusty Miller	Martha Irving
Basil	Ashley MacIsaac
Black Eyed Susan	Heather Rankin
Little Sweet William	Ian Parsons

and Mark Austin (Preacher), Shendi (Old Peat), Lucy (Young Peat), Jim Faraday (Mr. MacDougal), Renée Penney (Grace the Nun), Annabelle Raine Dexter (Bud), Michael Weir (Police Officer), Tom Chambers (Police Officer)

Sweet William, an attractive, openly gay man, returns to him home in Nova Scotia after a ten year absence and looks back on when he was an obese, unhappy and tormented teenager.

© MGM Distribution Co.

Chris Leavins, Peter MacNeill

Troy Veinotte, Joel S. Keller

UNDER THE SKIN

(ARROW) Producer, Kate Ogborn; Executive Producer, Ben Gibson; Director/Screenplay, Carine Adler; Photography, Barry Ackroyd; Set Designer, John-Paul Kelly; Music, Ilona Sekacz; Editor, Ewa J. Lind; Casting, Vanessa Pereira, Simone Ireland; a Strange Dog production for the British Film Institute and Channel Four Television, in association with Rouge Films and the Merseyside Film Production Fund; British, 1997; Color; Not rated; 81 minutes; May release

CAST

Iris Kelley	Samantha Morton
Rose	Claire Rushbrook
Mum	Rita Tushingham
Tom	Stuart Townsend
Vron	Christine Tremarco
Gary	Matthew Delamere
Frank	Mark Womack

and Clare Francis (Elena), Daniel O'Meara (Max), Crissy Rock (Compere), Joe Tucker (Sam), Lisa Millet (Sylvia), John Whitehall (Man at Station), Marie Jelliman (Manageress), Michelle Byatt (Mrs. Smith—Woman in Lost Property), Stella Scragg (Customer), David Brice (Man in Bed), Jack Marsden (Builder), Sean Cauldwell (Man in Club), Sandie Lavell (Woman in Phone Box), Jill Broader (Conductor), Castle Singers (Choir)

Following the unexpected death of her mother, Iris embarks on a series of self-destructive sexual experiments much to the anger and dismay of her more responsible sister Rose.

© Arrow Releasing Inc.

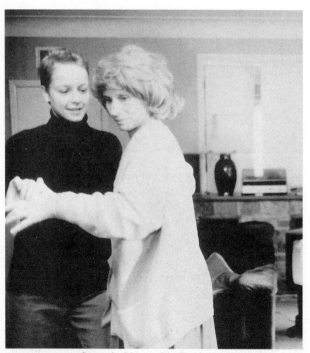

Samantha Morton, Rita Tushingham

LIFE OF JESUS (LA VIE DE JÉSUS)

(FOX LORBER) Producer, Jean Bréhat, Rachid Bouchareb; Director/Screenplay, Bruno Dumont; Photography, Philippe Van Leeuw; Set Decoration, Frédérick Suchet; Music, Richard Cuvillier; Costumes, Nathalie Raoul, Isabelle Sanchez; Editors, Guy Lecorne, Yves Dechamps; from 3B Productions/CCRAV/Norfilms/Tadrart Films; French, 1997; Color; Not rated; 95 minutes; May release

CAST

Freddy	David Douche
Marie	Marjorie Cottreel
Yvette	Geneviève Cottreel
Kader	Kader Chaatouf
Gégé	Sébastien Delbaere
Quinquin	Sébastien Bailleul
Michou	Samuel Boidin
Robert	Steve Smagghe
Rene	Rene Gilleron

and Mme. Chaatouf (Kader's Mother), M. Chaatouf (Kader's Father), Daniel Tanchon (Gégé's Father), Sophie Ruckebusch (Marjorette), Jean-Claude Lefebvre (Inspector), Gerard Wallyn (Marjorette's Father), Jean-Benoit Gros (Pierrot), Suzanne Bertelot (Nurse), Melinda Deseure (Marjorette's Leader), Jean-Paul Potteeuw (Harmonie's Leader), Bernard Fillebeen (Michou's Father), Francis Desure, Alain Lenancker (Policemen with Freddy), Helene Blaevoet (Marie's Colleague), Marie-Josee van Overbeke (Quinquin's Mother), Nadir Ghilminouni (Kader's Friend)

Freddy, a unemployed twenty-year old whose only joy in his dead-end town is his relationship with Marie, finds this threatened when Kader, an Arab teen, shows up and begins pursuing the girl.

Robert Carlyle, Oyanka Cabezas

Robert Carlyle, Scott Glenn

David Douche (foreground)

CARLA'S SONG

(SHADOW DISTRIBUTION) Producer, Sally Hibbin; Co-Producers, Ulrich Felsberg, Gerardo Herrero; Director, Ken Loach; Screenplay, Paul Laverty; Photography, Barry Ackroyd; Designer, Martin Johnson; Music, George Fenton; Editor, Jonathan Morris; Casting, Jean Bacharach, Wendy Ettinger, Florence Jaugey; a Channel Four Films presentation with the support of the Glasgow Film Fund and the Institute of Culture Nicaragua and ARD/DEGETO Film, Filmstiftung Nordrhein-Westfalen, Television Española and Alta Films of a Parallax Picture in co-production with Road Movies Dritte Produktionen and Tornasol Films S.A.; British-Scottish-Nicaraguan, 1996; Dolby; Color; Not rated; 125 minutes; June release

CAST

George	Robert Carlyle
Carla	Oyanka Cabezas
Bradley	Scott Glenn
Victor	Subash Sing Pall
McGurk	Stewart Preston
Sammy	Gary Lewis
George's Mother	Margaret McAdam
Eileen	Pamela Turner
Maureen	Louise Goodall
Keyboard Player	Greg Friel
Warden	Ann-Marie Timoney
Taxi Driver	Andy Townsley
Hospital Sister	Alicia Devine
Doctor	John Paul Leach

and Salvador Espinoza (Rafael), Richard Loza (Antonio), Norma Rivera (Norma), José Meneses (Harry), Rosa Amelia López (Carla's Mother), Keila Rodríguez (Vocals), Josefa Calderón de Calero, Azucena Figueroa, Tomasa García, Alcides Gonzales, Manuela Guevara, Karla Obando, Santos Olivas, Alison Paula Rizo, Elba Aurora Talavera, Luis Talavera (Carla's Family), Jimmy José Arguello, José Alberto Avendano, Ana Victoria Borge, Junior Escobar, Alma Blanco Medina, Tatiana Miranda, Ramón Monterrey, Santiago Neira, Belkis Ramírez, María José Silva (Brigadistas), Amy Bank, Belinda Forbes, Mark Forget, Tom Lee, Micky McKay, Ruth Pacheco, Richard Senghas, Anita Setright, Laura Tredway (Witnesses for Peace)

A Scottish bus driver finds himself attracted to Carla, a Nicaraguan refugee, and follows her back to her country at the time of the Contra rebels' assault against the Sandinista government in 1987.

THE LAND GIRLS

(GRAMERCY) Producer, Simon Relph; Executive Producer, Ruth Jackson; Co-Producer, Andrew Warren; Director, David Leland; Screenplay, Keith Dewhurst, David Leland; Based upon the novel *Land Girls* by Angela Huth; Photography, Henry Braham; Designer, Caroline Amies; Costumes, Shuna Harwood; Editor, Nick Moore; Music, Brian Lock; Casting, Jeremy Zimmerman; a PolyGram Filmed Entertainment presentation from Intermedia Films with the participation of the Greenlight Fund and Channel Four Films of a Greenpoint Film in association with West Eleven Films; British-French; Dolby; Panavision; Color; Rated R; 110 minutes; June release

CAST

Stella	Catherine McCormack
Ag	Rachel Weisz
Prue	Anna Friel
Joe Lawrence	Steven Mackintosh
Mr. Lawrence	Tom Georgeson
Mrs. Lawrence	Maureen O'Brien
Janet	Lucy Akhurst
Ratty	Gerald Down
Philip	Paul Bettany
Barry	Nick Mollo
Desmond	Michael Mantas

and Nicholas Le Prevost (Agricultural Officer), Celia Bannerman (District Commissioner), Ann Bell (Philip's Mother), Nigel Planer (Gerald), Edmund Moriarty (Harry, the Airman), Shirley Newbery (WAAF at Dance), Russell Barr (Jamie, Scottish Airman), John Gill (Doctor), Crispin Layfield (German Pilot), Grace Leland (Baby Barry), Reverend Alan Bennett (Himself), Martha Mackintosh, Felix Davis, Jacob Leland (Children at Christening), Jack O'Hampton (Jack the Dog)

During World War II, three women from different backgrounds join the Women's Land Army of England and end up working on the Lawrence farm where each of them forms a close relationship with the family's handsome son Joe.

© *Gramercy Pictures*

Anna Friel, Catherine McCormack, Rachel Weisz

Catherine McCormack, Steven Mackintosh

Vahina Giocante, Frederic Malgras

MARIE BAIE DES ANGES (MARIE FROM THE BAY OF ANGELS)

(SONY PICTURES CLASSICS) Producer, Philippe Rousselet; Executive Producer, Pascal Judelewicz; Director/Screenplay, Manuel Pradal; Photography, Christophe Pollock; Editor, Valerie Deseine; Designer, Javier Po; Music, Carlo Crivelli; Costumes, Claire Gerard-Hirne; Casting, Frank Saint Cast; French, 1997; Dolby; CinemaScope; Color; Rated R; 90 minutes; June release

CAST

Marie	Vahina Giocante
Orso	Frederic Malgras
Young Woman	Amira Casar
Larry	David Kilner
Jim	Jamie Harris
Ardito	Frederic Westerman
Goran	Nicolas Welbers
Jurec	Swan Carpio
Claude	Patrick Gomez
Hairdresser	Aladin Riebel
G.I.s	Andrew Clover, John Dowling, David Gregg

Fifteen year old Marie, determined to have a wild summer, finds herself getting involved with a volatile delinquent named Orso.

© *Sony Pictures Entertainment Inc.*

Sylvie Testud, Emmanuelle Laborit

BEYOND SILENCE

(MIRAMAX) Producers, Thomas Wöbke, Jacob Claussen, Luggi Waldleitner; Executive Producer, Uli Putz; Director, Caroline Link; Screenplay, Caroline Link, Beth Serlin; Photography, Gernot Roll; Designer, Susann Bieling; Editor, Patricia Rommel; Music, Niki Reiser; Costumes, Katharina von Martius; Casting, Risa Kes; Claussen+Wöbke Film Produktion and Roxy Film—Luggi Waldleitner production; a co-presentation of Buena Vista International; German-Swiss, 1996; Dolby; Color; Rated PG-13; 105 minutes; June release

CAST

Lara	Sylvie Testud
Lara as a Child	Tatjana Trieb
Martin	Howie Seago
Kai	Emmanuelle Laborit
Clarissa	Sibylle Canonica
Gregor	Matthias Habich
Marie	Alexandra Bolz
Tom	Hansa Czypionka
Lilli	Doris Schade
Robert	Horst Sachtleben
Mr. Gärtner	Hubert Mulzer
Ms. Mertens	Birge Schade
Bank Teller	Stephan Kampwirth
Johanna	Léa Mekhnéche
Martin as a Child	Laurel Severin
Clarissa as a Child	Selestina Stanisavijevic
Bettina	Julia Lorbeer
Uli	Alexis Segovia
Bea	Anna Bickhofer
Walter	Stefan Spreer

and Susann Bieling (Sales Clerk in Toy Store), Karin Lehmann (Secretary of Music School), Stefan von Moers (Associate of Conservatory), Marta Rodriguez (Lady at Concert), Jutta Schaad (Employee of Conservatory), Ute Cremer, Franz-Hermann Hanfstingl (Professor at Conservatory), Pfarrer Groll (Minister), Axel Hauguth (Colleague at Print Shop), Carmen Härdle, Stephan Lewetz (Pair of Lovers in Movie), Anna Müller, Caroline Otto, Benedikt Obermayer, Patrick Schleuter, Noemi Gäbelein, Christian Marschal, Ruth Obermayer (School Orchestra), Giora Feidman (Special Guest), Joe Basar (Guitarist), Tony Falanga (Bass), Annika Pages (The Voice of Lara)

When Lara is given a clarinet by her musician aunt Clarissa, her deaf parents feel as if they are further losing her to world they cannot comprehend. This film received an Oscar nomination for foreign language film (1997).

© Miramax Films

Tatjana Trieb, Emmanuelle Laborit

Tatjana Trieb, Howie Seago

Sylvie Testud, Franz-Hermann Hanfstingl

Ally Sheedy

Radha Mitchell

Patricia Clarkson, Ally Sheedy

Radha Mitchell, Ally Sheedy

Radha Mitchell

HIGH ART

(OCTOBER) Producers, Dolly Hall, Jeff Levy-Hinte, Susan A. Stover; Director/Screenplay, Lisa Cholodenko; Photography, Tami Reiker; Designer, Bernhard Blythe; Editor, Army E. Dudleston; Music Shudder to Think; Costumes, Victoria Farrell; Stills & "Lucy Berliner" Photography, Jojo Whilden; "Dieter Portfolio" Photography, Lauren Sorokin, Casting, Billy Hopkins, Suzanne Smith, Kerry Barden; a Dolly Hall production, presented in association with 391; Canadian; Color; Rated R 101 minutes; June release

Lucy Berliner	Ally Sheedy
Syd	Radha Mitchell
Greta	Patricia Clarkson
James, Syd's Boyfriend	Gabriel Mann
Arnie	Bill Sage
Dominique, Frame Editor	Anh Duong
Vera, Lucy's Mother	Tammy Grimes
Harry, Syd's Boss	David Thorton
White Hawk	Helen Mendes
Delia	Cindra Feuer
Xander	Anthony Ruivivar
Zoe	Elaine Tse
Dieter	Rudolf Martin
Waitress	Laura Ekstrand
Debby	Charis Michelson
Joan	Sarita Choudary

Syd finds her chance for advancement at Frame magazine when she discovers that her upstairs neighbor is the once-celebrated photographer Lucy Berliner who had dropped out of the scene a decade earlier.

© October Films

I WENT DOWN

(ARTISAN ENTERTAINMENT/SHOOTING GALLERY) Producer, Robert Walpole; Director, Paddy Breathnach; Screenplay, Conor McPherson; Executive Producers, Mark Shivas, David Collins, Rod Stoneman; Photography, Cian de Buitléar; Designer, Zoë MacLeod; Music, Dario Marianelli; Editor, Emer Reynolds; Costumes, Kathy Strachan; Casting, Deirdre O'Kane; a BBC Films, Bord Scannán na héireann/Irish Film Board presentation in association with Radio Telfis Éireann, Euskal Media of a Treasure Films production; British-Irish, 1997; Dolby; Color; Rated R; 107 minutes; June release

CAST

Bunny Kelly	Brendan Gleeson
Git Hynes	Peter McDonald
Frank Grogan	Peter Caffrey
Tom French	Tony Doyle
Sabrina Bradley	Antoine Byrne
Anto	David Wilmot
Johnner Doyle	Michael McElhatton
Steo Gannon	Joe Gallagher
Caroline	Carly Baker
Teresa	Carmel Callan
Caroline's Mum	Margaret Callan
Garda	Denis Conway
The Friendly Face	Donal O'Kelly

and Liam Regan (Little Boy at Teresa's), Kevin Hely (Petrol Station Attendant), Eamonn Hunt (Cork Barman), Frank O'Sullivan, Jason Byrne, Eamon A. Kelly (Cork Men), Amelia Crowley (Receptionist), Conor McPherson (Loser in Nightclub), Rachel Brady (Git's Girlfriend), Anne Kent (Bunny's Girlfriend), Johnny Murphy (Sonny Mulligan), Don Wycherley (Young Frank), John Bergin (Young Tom)

To repay a debt to crime boss Tom French, ex-con Git Hynes is reluctantly teamed up with brutish gangster Bunny Kelly to take a former associate of French's hostage.

© The Shooting Gallery

Peter McDonald, Brendan Gleeson

Agnes Jaoui

UN AIR DE FAMILLE (FAMILY RESEMBLANCES)

(LESIURE TIME FEATURES/CINEMA VILLAGE FEATURES) Executive Producer, Charles Gassot; Director, Cedric Klapisch; Screenplay, Agnes Jaoui, Jean-Pierre Bacri, Cedric Klapisch; Based on an original play by Agnes Jaoui, Jean-Pierre Bacri; Photography, Benoit Delhomme; Designer, Francois Emmanuelli; Costumes, Corinne Jorry; Editor, Francine Sandberg; Music, Philippe Eidel; a Telema, Le Studio Canal+, France 2 Cinema, Canal+ and Cofimage 7 production; French, 1996; Color; Cinemascope; Not rated; 107 minutes; June release

CAST

Henri Menard	Jean-Pierre Bacri
Betty Menard	Agnes Jaoui
Denis	Jean-Pierre Darroussin
Yolande	Catherine Frot
Mother	Claire Maurier
Philippe Menard	Wladimir Yordanoff
TV Presenter	Alain Guillo
Mother—1967	Sophie Simon
Father—1967	Cedric Klapisch

and Antoine Chappey (Neighbor), Chantal Gouard, Viviane Ordas (Mother's Friends), Aurelie Renacle (Betty—1967), Nicolas Taieb (Henri—1967), Ludovic Taieb (Philippe—1967), Romain Legrand (Kevin—Philippe's Son), Hugo Charpiot (Mikael—Philippe's Son)

A family, ruled by a domineering mother, gathers at their restaurant business for a seemingly benign get-together and begins unraveling its fragile unity, settling old scores and opening old wounds.

© Leisure Time Features

WHEN I CLOSE MY EYES

(FINE LINE) formerly *Love Letter;* Producers, Koichi Murakami, Hajime Shigemura, Juichi Horiguchi, Jiro Komaki, Tomoki Ikeda, Masahiko Nagasawa; Director/Screenplay/Editor, Shunji Iwai; Co-Producer, Takaaki Kabuto; Executive Producers, Chiaki Matsushita, Shuji Abe; Photography, Noboru Shinoda; Designer, Terumi Hosoishi; Costumes, Chikae Takahashi; Japanese, 1995; Color; Rated PG-13; 116 minutes; June release

CAST

Hiroko Watanabe/Itsuki Fujii . . . . Miho Nakayama
Shigeru Akiba. . . . . Etsushi Toyokawa
Itsuki's Mother. . . . . Bunjaku Han
Itsuki's Grandfather . . . . Katsuyuki Shinohara
Itsuki Fujii (as a Young Girl) . . . . Miki Sakai
and Takashi Kashiwabara (Male Itsuki Fujii), Ken Mitsuishi (Abekasu), Kumi Nakamura (Ms. Hamaguchi), Ranran Suzuki (Sanae Oikawa), Emiko Osada (Librarian), Kaori Oguri (Girl in Akiba's Workshop), Teppei Wataru (Yoshida), Keiichi Suzuki (Male Itsuki's Father), Sansei Shiomi (Kajioyaji), Mariko Kaga (Male Itsuki's Mother)

A woman grieving the loss of her fiancee, accidentally contacts a former classmate of his and the two begin a correspondence, remisiniscing about the man they both knew.

© Fine Line Features

Miho Nakayama

PASSION IN THE DESERT

(FINE LINE FEATURES) Producer/Director/Screenplay, Lavinia Currier: Based on the novella *A Passion in the Desert* by Honoré de Balzac: Additional Script, Martin Edmunds: Executive Producers, Joel McCleary, Stephen Dembitzer: Supervising Producer, Alton Walpole: Photography, Alexei Radionov: Editor, Nicolas Gaster; Music, José Nieto, Hamza El Din; Designer, Amanda McArthur; Leopard Trainers, Jungle Bookings, Rick Glassey, Judy Glassey; Line Producer (Jordan), Jamal Dehlavi; Casting, Daphne Becket; a Roland Films Production; British; Dolby; Color; Rated PG-13; 93 minutes; June release

CAST

Augustin . . . . Ben Daniels
Venture. . . . . Michel Piccoli
Grognard. . . . . Paul Meston
Officer. . . . . Kenneth Collard
and Nadi Odeh (Bedouin Bride), Auda Mohammed Badoul (Shepard Boy), Mohammed Ali (Medicine Man)

A French officer assigned to escort an artist on a trek through Egypt is seperated from their detachment and lost in the desert where he befriends a leopard.

© Fine Line Features

Ben Daniels

VOYAGE TO THE BEGINNING OF THE WORLD

(STRAND) a.k.a. *Journey to the Beginning of the World*; Producer, Paulo Branco; Director/Screenplay, Manoel De Oliveira; Photography, Renato Berta; Designer, Zé Branco; Editor, Valerie Loiseleux; Line Producer, António Gonçalo; a co-production of Madragoa Filmes (Lisbon), Gemini Films (Paris) with the participation of Instituto Português da Arte Cinematográfica e Audiovisual (IPACA), Radiotelevisão Portuguesa (RTP), Canal+, CNC; Portuguese-French, 1997; Color; Not rated; 95 minutes; June release

CAST

Manoel. . . . . Marcello Mastroianni
Afonso. . . . . Jean Yves Gautier
Judite. . . . . Leonor Silveira
Duarte. . . . . Diogo Dória
Maria. . . . . AfonsoIsabel de Castro
and Isabel Ruth (Olga), Cecile Sanz de Alba (Cristina), José Pinto (José Afonso)

Film director Manoel and three of his colleagues travel around Portugal with the intention of visiting an aunt Manoel has never met. This marked the last film of Marcello Mastroianni who died on Dec. 19, 1996.

© Strand Releasing

Marcello Mastroianni

THE THIEF

(STRATOSPHERE) Producer, Igor Tolstunov; Director/Screenplay, Pavel Chukhrai; Executive Producer, Sergei Kozlov; Photography, Vladimir Klimov; Designer, Victor Petrov; Music, Vladimir Dashkevich; Editors, Marina Dobryanskaya, Natalia Kucherenko; Costumes, Natalya Alexandrova, Natalya Moneva; a co-production of NTV-Profit (Russia), Productions le Pont (France), and Roissy Films (France) in association with the Russian State Committee for Cinematography, Centre National de la Cinematographie (France) and Canal+ (France); Russian-French, 1997; Color; Rated R; 94 minutes; July release

CAST

Tolyan	Vladimir Mashkov
Katya	Ekaterina Rednikova
Sanya	Misha Philipchuk
Doctor's Wife	Amalia Mordvinova
Sanya, 12 years old	Dima Shigarev
Sanya, 48 years old	Yuri Belyaev
Baby Sanya	Lidiya Savchenko
Gammy Girl	Ania Shtukaturova
Actress	Olga Peshkova
Bootmaker	Anatoliy Koscheev
Alcoholic	Lyudmila Selyanskaya
Engineer	Viktor Bunakov
Accountant's Wife	Natalia Pozdniakova
Vagrant	Yevgeni Popov
Engineer's Wife	Yulia Artamonova
Varvara	Galina Petrova
Accountant	Yervant Arzumanian

A look at the relationships between a six-year-old boy, his mother and the stranger who becomes her lover during Stalin's regime during the 1950s. This film received an Oscar nomination for foreign language film (1997).

© Stratosphere Entertainment

Vladimir Mashkov, Misha Philipchuk, Ekaterina Rednikova

WESTERN

(NEW YORKER) Producers, Maurice Bernart, Michel Saint-Jean; Director, Manuel Poirier; Screenplay, Manuel Poirier, Jean-Francois Goyet; Photography, Kara Keo Kosal; Editor, Yann Dedet; Music, Bernardo Sandoval; Designer, Roland Mabille; a Salome SA/Diaphana co-production with the participation of Canal+, CNC; French, 1997; Dolby; Widescreen; Color; Not rated; 121 minutes; July release

CAST

Paco Cazale	Sergi López
Nino	Sacha Bourdo
Marinette	Elisabeth Vitali
Nathalie (Mother with Children)	Marie Matheron
Baptiste	Basile Sieouka
Hitchhiker	Daphne Gaudefroy-Demonbyns
Policeman	Jean-Louis Dupont
Hospital Doctor	Olivier Herveet
Nurse	Alain Luc Guhur
Roland, Brother of Marinette	Bernard Mazzinghi
Voice of Mr. Letour's Secretary	Karine Lelievre
Bearded Man in Hospital Ward	Alain Denniel
Van Driver	Serge Raiboukine
Car Driver	Michel Vivier
Guenaelle	Melanie Vivier
Guenaelle's Friend	Catherine Riaux

and Carole Ledreau (Friend at Wedding), Basile Siekoua (Baptiste), Helene Foubert (Baptiste's Girlfriend), Marilyne Canto (Marilyne), Helen Berrou (Helene), Monette Cardinaux (Monette), Ghislaine Jegou (Ghislaine), Sophie Kervadel (Sophe), Angelina Pochie (Angelina), Diane Valsonne (Diane), Helene Moreau (Helene), Vanina Delannoy (Fougere—Hysterical Woman), Marie Lounici (Cafe Patron), Veronique Bellegarde (Cafe Patron), Fabien Kachev (New Salesman), Guy Abgrall (Farmer), Jean-Jacques Vanier (Dr. Yvon Le Marrec), Brigitte Legal (Pharmacist), Michel LeCossec (Bar Patron), Johan LeSaux (Johan), Tudy Bernard (Lena), Rudi Desseaux (Rudi), Maxime Guggenbuhl (Maxime), Olivier Guehenneux (Antoine), Maeva Privat (Antoine's Sister), Arthur Privat, Theo Vigouroux (Antoine's Brothers), Gerard Privat (Antoine's Father)

Paco, left stranded after Russian immigrant Nino steals his car and possessions, later encounters the thief, beats him up, then has a change of heart, becoming the man's friend.

© New Yorker Films

Sergi Lopez, Marie Matheron

Jeremy Irons, Dominique Swain

Dominique Swain

LOLITA

(SAMUEL GOLDWYN FILMS) Producers, Mario Kassar, Joel B. Michaels; Director, Adrian Lyne; Screenplay, Stephen Schiff; Based on the novel by Vladimir Nabokov; Photography, Howard Atherton: Designer, Jon Huntman; Editors, Julie Monroe, David Brenner; Costumes, Julianna Makovsky; Music, Ennio Morricone; Casting, Ellen Chenoworth; a Pathe production; British-French, 1997; Dolby; Color; Rated R; 137 minutes; July release

CAST

Humbert Humbert	Jeremy Irons
Charlotte Haze	Melanie Griffith
Clare Quilty	Frank Langella
Lolita	Dominique Swain
Miss Pratt	Suzanne Shepard
Reverand Rigger	Keith Reddin
Mona	Erin J. Dean
Miss LeBone	Joan Glover
Louise	Pat P. Perkins
Dr. Melnick	Ed Grady
Mr. Beale	Michael Goodwin
Mrs. Holmes	Angela Paton
Young Humbert	Ben Silverstone
Annabel Leigh	Emma Griffiths-Malin
Young Humbert's Father	Ronald Pickup
Mr. Leigh	Michael Culkin
Mrs. Leigh	Annabelle Apision
Don Brady	Frank McCoo
Dr. Blue	Trip Hamilton
Dick	Michael Dolan

and Hallee Hirsch (Little Girl in Bunny Suit), Scot Brian Higgs, Mert Hatfield (Policemen at Accident), Chris Jarman, Jim Grimshaw (Policeman), Hudson Lee Long (Elderly Clerk), Lenore-Banks, (Nurse at Hospital), Dorothy Deavers (Receptionist), Donnie Boswell, Sr. (Taxi Drivers), Judy Duggan (Solo Singer/Piano Player), Margaret Hammonds (Nurse), Paula Davis (Motel Clerk), Tim Gallin (Hospital Orderly)

Englishman Humbert Humbert becomes a boarder in the New England home of widow Charlotte Haze and finds himself falling hopelessly in love with her young daughter Lolita. Previous version was released by MGM in 1962 and starred James Mason (Humbert), Shelley Winters (Charlotte), Peter Sellers (Quilty), and Sue Lyon (Lolita).

© Samuel Goldwyn Films

Ben Silverstone

Jeremy Irons, Melanie Griffith

Jonathan Rhys Meyers

Florence Hoath, Minnie Driver

THE GOVERNESS

(SONY PICTURES CLASSICS) Producer, Sarah Curtis; Executive Producer, Sally Hibbin; Director/Screenplay, Sandra Goldbacher; Photography, Ashley Rowe; Designer, Sarah Greenwood; Editor, Isabel Lorente; Costumes, Caroline Harris; Music, Edward Shearmur; Casting, Michelle Guish; British; a Pandora Cinema presentation with the participation of British Screen and the Arts Council of England in association with BBC Films of a Parallax Picture; British; Dolby; Super 35 Widescreen; Color; Rated R; 112 minutes; July release

Minnie Driver

CAST

Rosina Da Silva ....Minnie Driver
Charles Cavendish ....Tom Wilkinson
Clementina Cavendish..Florence Hoath
Henry Cavendish ....Jonathan Rhys Meyers
Mrs. Cavendish...Harriet Walter
Lily Milk...Arlene Cockburn
Rebecca ....Emma Bird
Benjamin ....Adam Levy
Aunt Sofka..The Countess Koulinskyi
Rosina's Father ....Bruce Myers
Rosina's Mother ....Diana Brooks
Litnoff ....Raymond Brody
Leonora..Olga
Doctor ....Cyril Shaps
Young Rosina..Kendal Cramer
Mr. Hewlett...Ralph Riach
Prostitute ....Joe Bromley
Rabbi ....Stephen Robbins

Realizing that her Jewishness will prevent her from certain employment opportunities, Rosina Da Silva, determined to support her family, creates a new identity for herself and secures a job as a governess for the Cavendish family on a remote Scottish island.

Tom Wilkinson, Minnie Driver

Si Han, Hu Jan

BROTHER

(KINO) Producer, Sergei Selianov; Director/Screenplay, Alexei Balabanov; Photography, Sergei Astakhov; Designer, Vladimir Kartashov; Editor, Marina Lipartija; Music, Slava Butusov; from STW Film Company/GosKino of Russia; Russian, 1997; Color; Not rated; 96 minutes; July release

CAST

Danila...Sergei Bodrov, Jr.
The Brother...Victor Suhorukov
Sveta...Svetlana Pismichenko
Kat ....Maria Zhukova
Guerman ....Yury Kuznetsov
Butusov ....Slava Butusov

Danila, home after completing army service, teams up with his brother, a contract killer, to do away with a Chechen Mafia boss.

© Kino International

Koji Yakusho, Misa Shimizu

EAST PALACE, WEST PALACE

(STRAND) Producers, Zhang Yuan, Christophe Jung, Christophe Menager; Executive Producer, Willy Tsao; Director, Zhang Yuan; Screenplay, Zhang Yuan, Wang Xiabo; Photography, Zhang Jian; Music, Xiang Min; Art Director, An Bing; Editor, Vincent Levy; Produced by Amazon Entertainment Limited, Quelqu'un d'Autre Productions; Chinese-French, 1997; Dolby; Color; Not rated; 90 minutes; July release

CAST

A-Lan ....Si Han
Policeman (Shi Xiaohua)...Hu Jun
and Liu Yuxiao (Thief), Ma Wen (Yamen Runner), Wang Quan (A-Lan as a Boy), Ye Jing (A-Lan as a Youth), Zhao Wei (Streetcar), Lu Rong (A-Lan's Mother)

A-Lan, a gay writer arrested for crusing a Beijing park, is interrogated by a policeman who reacts to the young man with a combination of revulsion and fascination.

© Strand Releasing

Sergei Bodrov Jr., Victor Suhorukov

THE EEL

(NEW YORKER) Producer, Hisa Iino; Director, Shohei Imamura; Screenplay, Motofumi Tomikawa, Daisuke Tengan, Shoehi Imamura; Based on the novel *Sparkles in the Darkness* by Akira Yoshimura; Photography, Shigeru Komatsubara; Music, Shinichiro Ikebe; Editor, Hajime Okayasu; Produced by KSS, Eisei Gekijo Co. Ltd., and Groove Corp. in association with Imamura Productions; Japanese, 1997; Color; Not rated; 116 minutes; August release

CAST

Takuro Yamashita ....Koji Yakusho
Keiki Hattori ....Misa Shimizu
Jiro Nakajima ....Fujio Tsuneta
Misako Nakajima...Mitsuko Baisho
Tamotsu Takasaki ....Akira Emoto
Yuji Nozawa...Sho Aikawa
Masaki Saito ....Ken Kobayashi
Seitaro Misato ....Sabu Kawara
Fumie Hattori ....Etsuko Ichihara
Eiji Dojima...Tomoro Taguchi
The Doctor (Citizen's Hospital) ....Sansho Shinsui
The Doctor (Maternity Hospital) ....Shoichi Ozawa

Takuro, having served time in prison for stabbing his wife in a jealous rage, begins life anew as a barber in a small town and finds his emotionally cold manner being challenged by a young woman he saved from suicide.

Olivier Martinez, Aitana Sanchez-Gijon

A MERRY WAR

(FIRST LOOK PICTURES) formerly *Keep the Aspidistra Flying*; Producer, Peter Shaw; Executive Producers, Robert Bierman, John Wolstenholme; Director, Robert Bierman; Screenplay, Alan Plater; Based on the novel *Keep the Aspidistra Flying* by George Orwell; Photography, Giles Nuttgens; Associate Producer, Joyce Herlihy; Editor, Bill Wright; Designer, Sarah Greenwood; Costumes, James Keast; Music, Mike Batt; Casting, Michelle Guish; a presentation in association with the Arts Council of England and Bonaparte Films of a UBA/Sentinel Films production; British, 1997; Dolby; Rank color; Not rated; 101 minutes; August release

CAST

Gordon Comstock	Richard E. Grant
Rosemary	Helena Bonham Carter
Erskine	Jim Carter
Julia Comstock	Harriet Walter
Mrs. Trilling	Lill Roughly
Ravelston	Julian Wadham
Hermoine	Lesley Vickerage
McKechnie	John Clegg
Mrs. Wisebeach	Barbara Leigh Hunt
Beautiful Young Man	Grant Parsons
Old Woman	Dorothea Alexander
Old Man	Peter Stockbridge
Paul Doring	Malcolm Sinclair
Lecturer	Derek Smee
Ravenscroft Waiter	Ben Miles
Head Waiter	Richard Dixon
Policeman	Roger Morlidge
Magistrate Croom	Roland Oliver
Cheeseman	Bill Wallis
Mrs. Meakin	Liz Smith
Orton the Undertaker	Roger Frost
Dora	Harri Alexander
Factory Girl	Lucy Speed
Librarian	Joan Blackman
Cabby	Roy Evans
Customer	Maggie McCarthy

In 1930s London, copywriter Gordon Comstock compulsively quits his job to find his freedom and write poetry, leading his girlfriend Rosemary to worry if he will ever settle down and marry her.

© *Overseas Filmgroup*

THE CHAMBERMAID ON THE TITANIC

(SAMUEL GOLDWYN CO.) Producers, Yves Marmion, Daniel Toscan du Plantier; Director, Bigas Luna; Screenplay, Bigas Luna, Cuca Canals, Jean-Louis Benoît; Based on the novel by Didier Decoin; Photography, Patrick Blossier; Designer, Walter Caprara, Bruno Cesari; Costumes, France Squarciapino; Music, Alberto Iglesias; Editor, Kenout Peltier; a co-production of UGC YM—La Sept Cinema—France 2 Cinema—Rodeo Drive—Mate Production—Tornasol Films—Westdeutscher Rundfunk; French-Italian-Spanish, 1997; Dolby; CinecamScope: Color; Not rated; 96 minutes; August release

CAST

Zoe	Romane Bohringer
Horty	Olivier Martinez
Marie	Aitana Sánchez-Gijón
Simeon	Didier Bezace
Zeppe	Aldo Maccione
Pascal	Jean-Marie Juan
Al	Arno Chevrier
Bathilde	Marianne Groves
Simeon's Secretary	Didier Benureau
Giovanni	Alberto Cassadie
Manu	Giorgio Gobbi
Gaspard	Yves Verhoeven
Lacroix	Vincenzo De Caro
Leon	Salvador Madrid
Blanche	Barbara Lerici
Mimi	Stefania Orsola Garello
Lou	Maurizio Soldà
Chinese Photographer	Jim Adhi Limas

Horty travels to Southhampton, England where he spends an evening with Marie who is scheduled to set sail aboard the Titanic the following day.

© *Samuel Goldwyn*

Helena Bonham Carter, Richard E. Grant

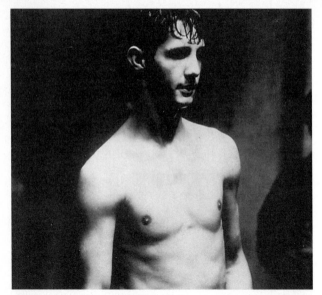

Steve Bell

Roger Daltrey, Ian Rose, Steve Bell

CUBE

(TRIMARK) Producers, Mehra Meh, Betty Orr; Executive Producer, Colin Brunton; Director, Vincenzo Natali; Screenplay, Andre Bijelic, Vincenzo Natali, Graeme Manson; Photography, Derek Rogers; Designer, Jasna Stefanovic; Editor, John Sanders; Music, Mark Korven; Special Effects and Animation, C.O.R.E. Digital Pictures; Makeup, Caligari Studio; a Cube Libre production presented by the Feature Film Project; Canadian; Ultra-Stereo; Color; Rated R; 90 minutes; September release

CAST

Leaven	Nicole de Boer
Holloway	Nicky Guadagni
Worth	David Hewlett
Kazan	Andrew Miller
Alderson	Julian Richings
Rennes	Wayne Robson
Quentin	Maurice Dean Wint

Six strangers find themselves trapped inside a surreal prison consisting of an endless maze of chambers and booby traps.

© *Trimark Pictures*

LIKE IT IS

(FIRST RUN FEATURES) Producer, Tracey Gardiner; Executive Producer, Christopher Hird; Director, Paul Oremland; Screenplay, Robert Gray; Story, Robert Gray, Paul Oremland, Kevin Sampson; Photography, Alistair Cameron; Designer, Tim Sykes; Editor, Jan Langford; Costumes, Sarah Bowern; Music, Don McGlashan; Casting, Abi Cohen; from Deep in You Ltd., Fulcrum Productions, Channel Four; British; Color; Not rated; 100 minutes; September release

CAST

Craig	Steve Bell
Matt	Ian Rose
Kelvin	Roger Daltrey
Paula	Dani Behr
Gloria	Jude Alderson
Aylon	Emile Charles
Fight Loser	Tony Van Silva
Minto	Paul Broughton
Tony, Craig's Brother	Christopher Hargreaves
Jamie	P.J. Nicholas
Jack	Sean Simpson
Amy	Suzy King
Sonya	Ursula Lea
DJ Terry	Charlie Caine
Train Girl	Suzanne Hall
Luke	Stephen Burke
Dirty Dave	Dickson Tolson
Andy	Chris Ross

Following a one-night stand with Matt, bare-knuckle fighter Craig shows up at Matt's flat in London where they begin a romance as Craig grows more comfortable with his homosexuality.

© *First Run Features*

Nicole de Boer, David Hewlett, Andrew Miller

Julian Richings

THE INHERITORS

(**STRATOSPHERE**) Producers, Danny Krausz, Kurt Stocker; Director/Screenplay, Stefan Ruzowitzky; Photography, Peter Von Haller; Art Director, Isi Wimmer; Editor, Britta Burkert-Nahler; Costumes, Nicole Fischnaller; Music, Erik Satie's Piano Compositions interpreted by Christian Heitler; a Dor Film Production with ORF and Bayerischer Rundfunk, Supported by OFI and Land Oberosterreich; Austrian; Color; Rated R; 95 minutes; October release

CAST

Lukas	Simon Schwarz
Emmy	Sophie Rois
Severin	Lars Rudolph
Old Nane	Julia Gschnitzer
Danninger	Ulrich Wildgruber
Rosalind	Elisabeth Orth
Foreman	Tilo Pruckner
Lisbeth	Susanne Silverio
Liesl	Kirstin Schwab
Sepp	Dietmar Nigsch
Policeman	Werner Prinz
Gertrud	Gertraud Maibock
Stable Boy	Christoph Gusenbauer
Florian	Eddie Fischnaller

In a small Austrian village, an unmarried farmer is found murdered, leaving behind a will which insults various locals and bequeaths his holdings to a band of peasants.

© *Stratosphere Entertainment LLC.*

Derek Jacobi

LOVE IS THE DEVIL

(STRAND) Producer, Chiara Menage; Executive Producers, Ben Gibson, Frances-Anne Solomon; Director/Screenplay, John Maybury; Line Producer, Yvonee Ibazebo; Photography, John Mathieson; Art Director, Christina Moore; Music, Ryuichi Sakamoto; Casting, Anne Laure Combris; British; Color; Not rated; 91 minutes; October release

CAST

Francis Bacon	Derek Jacobi
George Dyer	Daniel Craig
Muriel Belcher	Tilda Swinton
Isabel Rawsthorne	Anne Lambton
Daniel Farson	Adrian Scarborough
John Deakin	Karl Johnson
Henrietta Moraes	Annabel Brooks
Blonde Billy	Richard Newbold
French Official	Ariel De Ravenel
Ian Board	Tallulah
Ken Bidwell	Andy Linden

and David Kennedy (Joe Furneval), Gary Hume (Volker Dix), Damian Dibben, Antony Cotton (Brighton Rent Boys), Anthony Riding (London Rent Boy), Chrsistian Martin (Bell-Hop), Ray Olley (Boxing Referee), Wesley Morgan, Nigel Travis (Boxers), Eddie Kerr (Tailor), George Clarke, David Windle (Wrestlers), William Hoyland (Police Sergeant), Mark Umbers (PC Penham), Hamish Bowles (David Hockney)

The true story of controversial British artist Francis Bacon and his abusive, ill-fated relationship with his lover George Dwyer.

© *Strand Releasing*

Sophie Rois, Simon Schwarz

Ulrich Thomsen

THE CELEBRATION

(OCTOBER) Producer, Birgitte Hald; Director, Thomas Vinterberg; Screenplay, Thomas Vinterberg, Mogens Rukov; Based on an idea by Thomas Vinterberg; Photography, Anthony Dod Mantle; Line Producer, Moretn Kaufman; Editor, Valdis Oskarsdottir;a Nimbus Film production; Danish; Dolby; Black and white; Rated R; 101 minutes; October release

CAST

Christian	Ulrich Thomsen
Helge Klingenfeldt	Henning Moritzen
Michael	Thomas Bo Larsen
Helene	Paprika Steen
Elsa	Birthe Neumann
Pia	Trine Dyrholm
Mette	Helle Dolleris
Kim	Bjarne Henriksen
Michelle	Therese Glahn
Master of Ceremony	Klaus Bondam
Gbatokai	Gbatokai Dakinah
Grandfather	John Boas
Receptionist	Lars Brygmann
Birthe	Linda Laursen
Uncle	Lasse Lunderskov
Dead Daughter, Linda	Lene Lauboksen
Christian's Friend	Birgitte Simonsen
Guest	Poul Kajbaek

Danish patriarch Helge Klingenfeldt celebrates his sixtieth birthday with a lavish celebration at which his children gather and past family secrets begin to surface.

© *October Films*

Trine Dyrholm, Ulrich Thomsen

Hennig Moritzen, Birthe Neumann

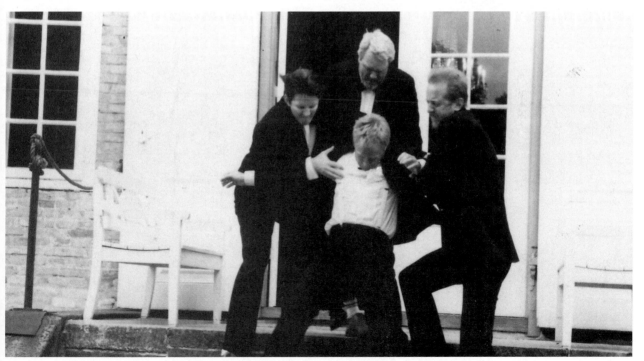

Thomas Bo Larsen, Ulrich Thomsen, Poul Kajbaek, Lasse Lunderskov

LA SÉPARATION

(PHAEDRA CINEMA) Producer, Claude Berri; Director, Christian Vincent; Screenplay, Christian Vincent, Dan Franck; Based on the novel by Dan Franck; Photography, Denis Lenoir; Editor, François Ceppi; Bach's Goldberg variations, performed by Glenn Gould; from C.M.V. Productions, Le Studio Canal+, France 2 Cinema, D.A. Films and Renn Productions; French, 1994; Color; Not rated; 88 minutes; October release

CAST

Anne	Isabelle Huppert
Pierre	Daniel Auteuil
Loulou	Louis Vincent
Victor	Jérôme Deschamps
Claire	Karin Viard
Laurence	Laurence Lerel
Marie	Nina Morato

and Jean-Jacques Vanier (Speaker at Party), Christian Benedetti (Lawyer), Frédéric Gelard (Estate Agent), Gérard Jumel (Man at Party), Estelle Larrivaz (Girl at Party), Claudine Challier (Loulou's Grandmother)

Pierre is confronted by his wife with the fact that she has grown tired of him and fallen in love with another man, a fact he at first seems to accept without opposition.

© Phaedra Cinema

Isabelle Huppert, Daniel Auteuil

Isabelle Huppert, Daniel Auteuil

Mehmet Gunsur, Alessandro Gassman

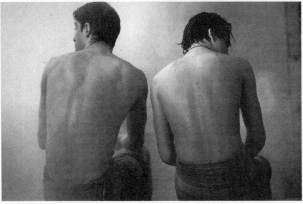

Alessandro Gassman, Mehmet Gunsur

STEAM: THE TURKISH BATH

(STRAND) a.k.a. *Hamam: The Turkish Bath*; Producers, Marco Risi, Maurizio Tedesco, Cengiz Ergun, Aldo Sanbrell; Executive Producers, Paolo Buzzi, Ozan Ergun; Director/Story, Ferzan Ozpetek; Screenplay, Stefano Tummolini, Ferzan Ozpetek; Photography, Pasquale Mari; Art Directors, Virginia Vianello, Mustafa Ziya Ulgenciler; Costumes, Metella Raboni, Selda Cicek; Editor, Mauro Bonanni; Music, Pivio & Aldo De Scalzi; a Sorpasso Film (Rome), Promete Film (Istanbul), Asbrell Productions (Madrid) production; Italian-Turkish-Spanish, 1997; Color; Not rated; 101 minutes; November release

CAST

Francesco	Alessandro Gassman
Marta	Francesca d'Aloja
Oscar	Carlo Cecchi
Osman	Halil Ergun
Perran	Serif Sezer
Mehmet	Mehmet Gunsur
Fusun	Basak Koklukaya
Paolo	Alberto Molinari
Zozo	Zozo Toledo
Voice of Aunt Anita	Ludovica Modugno

Francesco, a successful Italian designer, arrives in Turkey to oversee the disposition of an estate left him by his aunt and discovers he is the owner of a Turkish steam bath.

© Strand Releasing

DANCING AT LUGHNASA

(SONY PICTURES CLASSICS) Producer, Noel Pearson; Executive Producer, Jane Barclay; Director, Pat O'Connor; Screenplay, Frank McGuinness; Based on the play by Brian Friel; Photography, Kenneth MacMillan; Designer, Mark Geraghty; Editor, Humphrey Dixon; Music, Bill Whelan; Costumes, Joan Bergin; Choreographer, David Bolger; Line Producer, Gerrit V. Folsom; Casting, Mary Selway; a Capitol Films, Channel Four Films, Ferndale Films in association with Bord Scannan and the Irish Film Board, Radio Telefis Eireann presentation of a Noel Pearson production; British-Irish-U.S.; Dolby; Color; Rated PG; 92 minutes; November release

Meryl Streep, Brid Brennan, Sophie Thompson

CAST

Kate Mundy	Meryl Streep
Father Jack Mundy	Michael Gambon
Christina Mundy	Catherine McCormack
Maggie Mundy	Kathy Burke
Rose Mundy	Sophie Thompson
Agnes Mundy	Brid Brennan
Gerry Evans	Rhys Ifans
Michael Mundy	Darrell Johnston
Danny Bradley	Lorcan Cranitch
Austin Morgan	Peter Gowen
Sophie McLoughlin	Dawn Bradfield
Vera McLoughlin	Marie Mullen
Father Carlin	John Kavanagh
Chemist	Kate O'Toole
Narrator	Gerard McSorley

In 1936 Ireland, the five unmarried Mundy sisters prepare to meet their older brother Jack, a priest returning from Africa after twenty-five years.

Catherine McCormack, Rhys Ifans

Meryl Streep, Darrell Johnson

Kathy Burke, Meryl Streep, Michael Gambon

John Gielgud

Joseph Fiennes, Cate Blanchett

Fanny Ardant

Joseph Fiennes, Cate Blanchett

Christopher Eccleston

Kathy Burke, Valerie Gale,
Cate Blanchett

Richard Attenborough

ELIZABETH

(GRAMERCY) Producers, Alison Owen, Eric Fellner, Tim Bevan; Director, Shekhar Kapur; Screenplay, Michael Hirst; Photography, Remi Adefarasin; Designer, John Myhre; Costumes, Alexandra Byrne; Editor, Jill Bilcock; Music, David Hirschfelder; Line Producer, Mary Richards; Co-Producers, Debra Hayward, Liza Chasin; Casting, Vanessa Pereira, Simone Ireland; a PolyGram Filmed Entertainment presentation in association with Film Four of a Working Title production; British; Dolby; Technicolor; Rated R; 123 minutes; November release

Cate Blanchett

CAST

Elizabeth I	Cate Blanchett
Sir Francis Walsingham	Geoffrey Rush
Duke of Norfolk	Christopher Eccleston
Robert Dudley, Earl of Leicester	Joseph Fiennes
Sir William Cecil	Richard Attenborough
Earl of Sussex	Jamie Foreman
Alvaro de la Quadra	Joseph Fiennes
Kat Ashley	Emily Mortimer
Isabel Knollys	Kelly MacDonald
Earl of Arundel	Edward Hardwicke
Mary of Guise	Fanny Ardant
Queen Mary Tudor	Kathy Burke
Duc d'Anjou	Vincent Cassel
John Ballard	Daniel Craig
Bishop Gardiner	Terence Rigby
Lettice Howard	Amanda Ryan
Monsieur de Foix	Eric Cantona
The Pope	John Gielgud
Dance Tutor	Wayne Sleep
Waad, Chancellor of the Exchequer	Angus Deayton
Martyrs	Liz Giles, Paul Fox
Master Ridley	Rod Culbertson
Palace Chamberlain	Peter Stockbridge
King Philip II of Spain	George Yiasoumi
Mary's Dwarf	Valerie Gale
Ladies in Waiting	Sally Grey, Kate Loustau, Elika Gibbs, Sarah Owen, Lily Allen
Master of the Tower	Joe White
Norfolk's Men	Matt Andrews, Liam Foley
Young French Man	Ben Frain
Priest	Lewis Jones
Bishop Carlisle	Michael Beint
Elizabeth's Dwarf	Hayley Burroughs
Earl of Derby	Joseph O'Connor
Lord William Howard	Brendan O'Hea
Lord Harewood	Edward Highmore
Bishops	Daniel Moynihan, Jeremy Hawk, Donald Pelmear
Bishop in Cellar	James Rowe
Handsome Man	Tim Bevan
Dudley's Men	Charles Cartmell, Edward Purver
Vatican Cardinal	Vladimir Vega
Arundel's Son	Alfie Allen
Arundel's Daughter	Daisy Bevan
Arundel's Nursemaid	Jennifer Lewicki
Arundel's Wife	Viviane Horne
Walsingham's Man	Nick Smallman

Joseph Fiennes, Cate Blanchett

In 1554 Elizabeth is proclaimed queen, against the better wishes of the Duke of Norfolk, and must face the dilemmas of her country's bankruptcy, the threat of war, and the choice of marriage between two men in whom she has no interest. 1998 Academy Award-winner for Best Makeup. This film received additional nominations for picture, actress (Cate Blanchett), cinematography, original dramatic score, costume design, and art direction.

© Gramercy Pictures

Geoffrey Rush

CENTRAL STATION

(SONY PICTURES CLASSICS) Producers, Arthur Cohn, Martine De Clermont-Tonnerre; Executive Producers, Elisa Tolomelli, Lillian Birnbaum, Donald Ranvaud; Director, Walter Salles; Screenplay, João Emanuel Carneiro, Marcus Bernstein; Based on an original idea by Walter Salles; Photography, Walter Carvalho; Designer, Cassio Amarante, Carla Canteé; Editors, Isabelle Rathery, Felipe Lacerda; Music, Antonio Pinto, Jaques Morelembaum; Costumes, Cristina Camargo; Casting, Sérgio Machado; an Arthur Cohn Production in association with Martine and Antoine de Clermont-Tonnerre (MACT Prods., France), Videofilms (Brazil), Riofilme (Brazil), and Canal+ (France); Brazilian-French; Super 35 Widescreen; Dolby; Color; Rated R; 107 minutes; November release

Fernanda Montenegro, Marilia Pêra

CAST

Dora	Fernanda Montenegro
Irene	Marilia Pêra
Josué	Vinicius de Oliveira
Ana	Sôia Lira
César	Othon Bastos
Pedrão	Otávio Augusto
Yolanda	Stela Freitas
Isaias	Matheus Nachtergaele
Moisés	Caio Junqueira
Dora's Clients (Rio)	Socorro Nobre, Manoel Gomes, Roberto Andrade, Sheyla Kenia, Malcon Soares, Maria Fernandes, Maria Marlene, Chrisanto Camargo, Jorsebá-Sebastião Oliveira

A loney and cynical woman meets a boy whose mother has been killed in front of Rio de Janeiro's Central Station and makes it her duty to return him to his father in Brazil's remote Northeast. This film received Oscar nominations for actress (Fernanda Montenegro) and foreign language film.

Fernanda Montenegro, Vinicius de Oliveira

Vinicius de Oliveira, Fernanda Montenegro

BABE: PIG IN THE CITY

(**UNIVERSAL**) Producers, George Miller, Doug Mitchell, Bill Miller; Executive Producer, Barbara Gibbs; Director, George Miller; Screenplay, George Miller, Judy Morris, Mark Lamprell; Based on characters created by Dick King-Smith; Photography, Andrew Lesnie; Music, Nigel Westlake; Song: "That'll Do" by Randy Newman; Editors, Jay Friedkin, Margaret Sixel; Designer, Roger Ford; Costumes, Norma Moriceau; Visual Effects/Animation, Rhythm & Hues, The Mill, Animal Logic; Animal Action, Karl Lewis Miller; Animatronics, Neal Scanlan Studio; Associate Producers, Colin Gibson, P.J. Voeten, Catherine Barber, Guy Norris; Casting, Alison Barrett, Nicki Barrett, Barbara Harris; a Kennedy Miller Film; Australian-U.S.; Dolby; Color; Rated G; 95 minutes; November release

Babe, James Cromwell, Magda Szubanski

CAST

Mrs. Hoggett .... Magda Szubanski
Farmer Hoggett .... James Cromwell
The Landlady .... Mary Stein
Fugly Floom .... Mickey Rooney

VOICE CAST

Babe .... E.G. Daily
Ferdinand/Tug .... Danny Mann
Zootie .... Glenne Headly
Bob .... Steven Wright
Thelonius .... James Cosmo
Easy .... Nathan Kress, Myles Jeffrey
The Pitbull and the Doberman .... Stanley Ralph Ross
The Pink Poodle/Choir Cat .... Russi Taylor
Flealick .... Adam Goldberg
Nigel and Alan .... Eddie Barth
The Sniffer Dog .... Bill Capizzi
Fly .... Miriam Margolyes
Rex .... Hugo Weaving
The Narrator .... Roscoe Lee Browne
and Paul Livingston (Hot Headed Chef), Babs McMillan (Matriarch), Matthew Parkinson (Nervous Waiter), Julie Godfrey (Suspicious Neighbor), Kim Story (Judge), Richard Carter, Simon Westaway (Detectives), Margaret Christensen (Haughty Woman), Katie Leigh (Kitten), Janet Foye, Pamela Hawken (Mrs. Hoggett Friends), Basil Clarke (Doctor), Cecilia Yates (Flight Attendant), Damian Monk, Terrell Dixon (Customs Guards), Gabby Millgate (Officer), Anthony Phelan (Security Guard), Van Epperson (Night Cleaner), Mark Gerber, Ken Radley (Motorcycle Cops), John Samaha (Van Cop), Paul Moxey, Gareth Clydesdale (Tough Guys), Ken Johnson (Court Stenographer), Jennifer Kent (Lab Lady), Richard Huggett (Cop), Ric Herbert, Felix Williamson, David Allsberry, Michael Boxer, Steve Martin, Hubert Wells (Raiders), John Walton (Padded Raider), Gandhi MacIntyre, Christian Manon (Lab Technicians), Sacha Horler (Night Nurse), John Upton (Sick Boy), Peter Callan (Hospital Doctor), Dean Nottle (Doctor in Tails), Paul Maybury (Hospital Orderly), Saskia Campbell (Woman in Billowing Gown), Kristoffer Greaves (Chef), Dominic Condon (Kitchen Hand), Elizabeth Allen (Lady Zammit); Voices: Evelyn Krape (Old Ewe and Alley Cats), Charles Barlett (Cow), Michael Edward-Stevens (Horse), Al Mancini, Larry Moss (Feisty Fish), Jim Cummings (Pelican), Nathan Kress (Tough Pup)

Babe

When an injury puts Farmer Hoggett out of circulation, his prize pig Babe and Mrs. Hoggett travel to the city in hopes of cashing in on Babe's celebrity and paying the mortgage on their farm. Sequel to the 1995 Universal film Babe which also featured James Cromwell and Magda Szubanski. This film received an Oscar nomination for original song ("That'll Do").

© Universal City Studios Prods. Inc.

Babe, Easy, Zootie, Bob

David Kelly, Ian Bannen

James Nesbitt

WAKING NED DEVINE

(FOX SEARCHLIGHT) a.k.a. *Waking Ned*; Producers, Glynis Murray, Richard Holmes; Executive Producer, Alexandre Heylen; Director/Screenplay, Kirk Jones; Co-Producer, Neil Peplow; Co-Executive Producer, Stephen Margolis; Photography, Henry Braham; Designer, John Ebden; Editor, Alan Strachan; Costumes, Rosie Hackett; Associate Producer, Miara Martell; Casting, Ros and John Hubbard; a Tomboy Films presentation in association with the Gruber Brothers, Mainstream SA, Bonaparte Films Ltd., The Isle of Man Film Commission and Overseas Filmgroup with the participation of Canal+; British-Irish-French; Dolby; Panavision; Color; Rated PG; 91 minutes; November release

CAST

Jackie O'Shea	Ian Bannen
Michael O'Sullivan	David Kelly
Annie O'Shea	Fionnula Flanagan
Maggie	Susan Lynch
Pig Finn	James Nesbitt
Mrs. Kennedy	Maura O'Malley
Maurice	Robert Hickey
Brendy	Paddy Ward
Dennis Fitzgerald	James Ryland
Pat Mulligan	Fintan McKeown
Tom Tooney	Matthew Devitt
Lizzy Quinn	Eileen Dromey
Kitty	Kitty Fitzgerald
Father Patrick	Dermot Kerrigan
Ned Devine	Jimmy Keogh
Jim Kelly (Lotto Man)	Brendan F. Dempsey
Father Mulligan	Larry Randall
Dicey, the Fiddleman	Eamonn Doyle
Baudron Player	Raymond Mac Cormac
Rennie	Rennie Campbell

When Ned Devine dies hold a winning lottery ticket, life-long friends Jackie O'Shea and Michael O'Sullivan conspire to lead the authorities into believing Ned is still alive so the entire village can profit from the win.

James Ryland, Paddy Ward, David Kelly, Ian Bannen

James Nesbitt, David Kelly, Ian Bannen, Fionnula Flanagan

Ian Bannen

David Kelly

James Nesbitt, Susan Lynch

David Kelly, James Ryland, Robert Hickey, Ian Bannen, Matthew Devitt

LITTLE VOICE

(MIRAMAX) Producer, Elizabeth Karlsen; Executive Producerss, Stephen Woolley, Nik Powell; Co-Executive Producers, Bob Weinstein, Harvey Weinstein, Paul Webster; Director/Screenplay, Mark Herman; Based on the stage play *The Rise and Fall of Little Voice* by Jim Cartwright; Co-Producer, Laurie Borg; Photography, Andy Collins; Designer, Don Taylor; Editor, Michael Ellis; Music, John Altman; Costumes, Lindy Hemming; Casting, Priscilla John; a Scala presentation of a Scala Production; British; Dolby; Color; Rated R; 96 minutes; December release

Jane Horrocks, Michael Caine

CAST

Mari Hoff	Brenda Blethyn
LV	Jane Horrocks
Ray Say	Michael Caine
Mr. Boo	Jim Broadbent
Billy	Ewan McGregor
George	Philip Jackson
Sadie	Annette Badland
The Bouncers	Adam Forgerty, James Welh
Stripper	Karen Gregory
Arthur	Fred Feast
LV's Dad	Graham Turner
Pawnbroker	George Olivier
Loan Advisor	Virgil Tracy
Money Lender	Dick Van Vinkle
Talent Scout	Howard Grace
Bunnie Morris	Alex Norton
George's Girlfriend	Melodie Scales
Brenda Bailey	Kitty Roberts
Wild Trigger Smith	Fred Gaunt
Elaine	Alita Petrof
Fireman	Jonathan Clark

and George Bradley, Geoffrey Emmerson, Barry Gomersalt, Angela Harrison, Jean Hotton, David Kemp, Aiden Lawrence, Michael Lynskey, Peter Marshall, Peter Minns, Christine Quick, Len Rangley, Bob Scott, Melanie Simpson, Doug Stewart, Peter Thomson, Stan Wright (Mr. Boo's Band), Sean Hadland, Roger Neville, Michael Prior, Paul Swan, Carl Wittaker (Take Fat)

LV, a timid girl who lives with her overbearing mother Mari, has an uncanny knack for imitating famous singers, a talent which her mother's current boyfriend, sleazy talent agent Ray Say, hopes to exploit. Jane Horrocks repeats her role from the original 1992 London stage production. Hynden Welch played the part in the 1994 Broadway version. This film received an Oscar nomination for supporting actress (Brenda Blethyn).

© Miramax Films

Jane Horrocks

Ewan McGregor

Brenda Blethyn, Michael Caine

THE OGRE

(KINO) Producer, Ingrid Windisch; Executive Producers, Claude Berri, Jeremy Thomas, Lew Rywin; Director, Volker Schlondorff; Screenplay, Jean-Claude Carriere, Volker Schlondorff; Based on the novel *The Erl King (The Ogre)* by Michel Tournier; Photography, Bruno de Keyzer; Designer, Ezio Frigerio; Music, Michael Nyman; Editor, Nicolas Gaster; Associate Producers, Pierre Couveinhes, Chris Auty; a Studio Babelsberg (Germany), Renn Productions (France), Recorded Picture Company (Great Britain) coproduction; German-French-British, 1996; Super 35 Widescreen; Color/Black and white; Not rated; 117 minutes; December release

CAST

Abel	John Malkovich
Count of Kaltenborn	Armin Mueller-Stahl
Chief Forester	Gottfried John
Frau Netta	Marianne Sagebrecht
Reichsmarshall Goring	Volker Spengler
SS-Officer Raufeisen	Heino Ferch
Professor Blattchen	Dieter Laser
Rachel	Agnes Soral

During World War II, Abel, a man seemingly incapable of drawing moral distinctions, is captured by the Germans who decide to utilize his attraction to children by having him recruit youngsters for the Hitler Youth.

© Kino International

John Malkovich

Armin Mueller-Stahl, Heino Ferch

(backrow) Jimmy Nail, Helena Bergstrom, Bill Nighy, Stephen Rea
Juliet Aubrey, Timothy Spall; (front) Rachel Stirling, Hans Matheson,
Billy Connolly

STILL CRAZY

(COLUMBIA) Producer, Amanda Marmot; Director, Brian Gibson; Executive Producers/Screenplay, Dick Clement, Ian La Frenais; Photography, Ashley Rowe; Designer, Max Gottlieb; Editor, Peter Boyle; Music, Clive Langer; Song: *The Flame Still Burns* by Mick Jones, Marti Frederiksen and Chris Difford/performed by Jimmy Nail; Costumes, Caroline Harris; Line Producer, Steve Clark-Hall; Casting, Gail Stevens; a Marmont Tandy production presented with the participation of the Greenlight Fund; British- U.S.; Dolby; Deluxe color; Rated R; 91 minutes; December release

CAST

Tony Costello	Stephen Rea
Hughie	Billy Connolly
Les Wickes	Jimmy Nail
Beano Baggot	Timothy Spall
Ray Simms	Bill Nighy
Karen Knowles	Juliet Aubrey
Astrid Simms	Helena Bergström
Brian Lovell	Bruce Robinson
Luke Shand	Hans Matheson
Clare Knowles	Rachael Stirling
Neil Gaydon	Phil Daniels
Limo Driver	Phil Davis
Woman in Black	Frances Barber
Zoë	Zoë Ball

and Virginia Clay (Young Karen), Luke Garrett (Young Hughie), Sean McKenzie (Young Beano), Rupert Penry-Jones (Young Ray), Matthew Finney (Young Brian), Alex Palmer (Young Les), Gavin Kennedy (Young Tony), Lee Williams (Young Keith), Andy Nichol (Gary), Francis Magee (Hockney), Justin Grattan (Not Morrisey), Delroy Atkinson (Jason), Julian Sims (Steve Greenblatt), Peter Baynham (Kevin), Margaret Blakemore, Candida Gubbins (Waitresses), Alphonsia Emmanuel (Camille), Mikayla Jones (Natasha), Jason Green (Adam), Christopher Wild (Apprentice), Dean Lennox Kelly (Pizza Boy), Mackenzie Crook (Dutch Kid), Donna Air (Dutch Hitch-Hiker), Ralph Van Dijk (Club 4 Owner), Sabina Michael (Dutch Receptionist), Steve Ubels (Dutch Local), Danny Webb (Clive), Anita Carey (Tax Woman), David Henry (Tax Inspector), Daisy Donovan (Reporter), Bruce Byron (Snotty Reporter), Jeffrey Harmer (Dutch Policeman), Sheila Reid (Mrs. Baggot), Leelo Ross (Dutch Lady), Brian Capron (Senior Executive), Luke D'Silva (Spanish Bar Man)

Tony, the keyboard player for the long-defunct British rock band, Strange Fruit, decides to get the group members together for a reunion concert, twenty years after their bickering broke them up.

© Columbia Pictures Industries, Inc.

THE GENERAL

(SONY PICTURES CLASSICS) Producer/Director/Screenplay, John Boorman; Executive Producer, Kieran Corrigan; Photography, Seamus Deasy; Designer, Derek Wallace; Music, Richie Buckley; Editor, Ron Davis; Costumes, Maeve Paterson; Casting, Jina Jay; a Merlin Films in association with J&M Entertaiment presentation; British; Dolby; Super 35 Widescreen; Black and white; Rated R; 124 minutes; December release

CAST

Brendan Gleeson, Adrian Dunbar

Brendan Gleeson

Martin Cahill	Brendan Gleeson
Noel Curley	Adrian Dunbar
Gary	Sean McGinley
Frances	Maria Doyle Kennedy
Tina	Angeline Ball
Inspector Ned Kenny	Jon Voight
Jimmy	Eanna McLiam
Willie Byrne	Tom Murphy
Anthony	Paul Hickey
Paddy	Tommy O'Neill
Shea	John O'Toole
Tommy	Ciaran Fitzgerald
Gay	Ned Dennehy
Harry	Vinnie Murphy
Orla	Roxanna Williams
Young Martin Cahill	Eamonn Owens
Patricia	Colleen O'Neill
Sylvie	Maebh Gorby
Higgins	Pat Laffan
Lawless	Frank Melia
James Donovan	Ronan Wilmot
Arcade Woman	Lynn Cahill
Assassin	David Wilmot
Arthur Ryan	Stephen Brennan
Henry Mackie	Don Wicherley
Judge	Kevin Flood

and Pat Kinevane (Desk Guard), Barry McGovern (IRA Leader), Pat Leavy (Mrs. Duggan), Neile Conroy (Maeve), Peter Hugo Daly (Beavis), Aoife Moriarty (Young Frances), Brendan Coyle (UVF Leader), Jim Sheridan (CPAD Leader), Gavin Kelty (Young Hood #1), Owen O'Neill, David Carey (Revenue Men), Niamh Lineham, Jason Byrne (Reporters), Ann Doyle (TV Newsreader), Daragh Kelly (Young Detective), Des O'Malley (Himself)

The true story of Dublin gangster Martin Cahill who masterminded several robberies in Ireland during the 1980s.

© *Sony Pictures Entertainment Inc.*

Brendan Gleeson, Jon Voight

Maria Doyle Kennedy, Brendan Gleeson, Angeline Ball

THE THEORY OF FLIGHT

(FINE LINE FEATURES) Producers, David M. Thompson, Anant Singh, Ruth Caleb, Helena Spring; Director, Paul Greengrass; Screenplay, Richard Hawkins; Photography, Ivan Strasburg; Designer, Melanie Allen; Costumes, Dinah Collin; Editor, Mark Day; Music, Rolfe Kent; Casting, John & Ros Hubbard; a Distant Horizon and BBC Films presentation; British; Dolby; Color; Rated R;100 minutes; December release

CAST

Jane	Helena Bonham Carter
Richard	Kenneth Branagh
Anne	Gemma Jones
Julie	Holly Aird
Gigolo	Ray Stevenson
Catherine	Sue Jones Davies
Magistrate	Gwenyth Petty
Farmer	Robert Blythe
Doctor	Aneirin Hughes
Care Worker	Natasha Williams
Volunteer	Sian Naiomi
Becky	Ruth Jones

and Nia Roberts (ASDA Teller), Dilys Price (Mrs. Williams), Jill James (Mrs. Allen), Sidney Williams (Club Owner), Daryl Beeton (Disabled Man), Deborah Sheridan-Taylor (Shop Assistant)

Richard, a man who dreams of taking flight, winds up doing community services where he meets Jane, a woman with Motor Neuron Disease who hopes he can help her experience sex before it is too late.

Helena Bonham Carter, Kenneth Branagh

Isabelle Huppert, Michael Serrault

François Cluzet, Isabelle Huppert

THE SWINDLE

(NEW YORKER) Producer, Marin Karmitz; Director/Screenplay, Claude Chabrol; Photography, Eduardo Serra; Designer, Françoise Benoit-Fresco; Costumes, Corinne Jorry; Editor, Monique Fardoulis; Music, Matthieu Chabrol; Associate Producers, Jean-Louis Porchet, Gérard Ruey; a production of MK2 Productions, TF1 Films Production, CAB Productions, Television Suisse Romande, Teleclub, Rhone-Alpes Cinema, with the participation of Canal+ and the support of La Procirep and the Swiss Federal Cultural Office (DFI); French-Swiss, 1997; Dolby; Color; Not rated; 105 minutes; December release

CAST

Betty	Isabelle Huppert
Victor	Michel Serrault
Maurice	François Cluzet
Monsieur K	Jean-François Balmer
Chatillon	Jackie Berroyer
Guadeloupe Gangster	Jean Benguigui
Signora Trotti	Mony Dalmes
Swiss Desk Clerk	Thomas Chabrol
Chatty Man	Greg Germain
Blonde Woman	Nathalie Kousnetzoff

and Pierre Martot, Eric Bonicatto, Pierre-François Dumeniaud, Philippe Dana (Conventioneers), Yves Verhoeven (Pickpocket), Henri Attal (Greek Vendor), Gunther Germain (Chatty Man's Friend), Maurice Debranche (Guadeloupe Taxi Driver), Stefan Witschi (Swiss Maitre d'), Rodolphe Ittig (Belgian Dentist), Dodo Deer (Hungarian Dentist), Barbara-Magdalena Ahren (Wife of Hungarian Dentist), Alexander Seibt (Chair-Lift Worker), James Hauduroy (Barman at Hotel Waldhaus), Elie Axas (Flight Attendant), Emmanuel Guttierez (Barman at the Park Hotel), Gilbert Laumord (Tall Black Man), Yvon Crenn (Mafioso), Marie Dubois (Dédette), Brygida Ochaim (Dancer)

Betty and Victor, a pair of grifters, plot the ultimate scam when Betty seduces a young executive who is hoping to rip-off an international money launderer.

Celia Imrie, Charles Dance, Emily Watson, Rachel Griffiths, David Morrissey, Rupert Penry Jones

James Frain, Emily Watson

Emily Watson

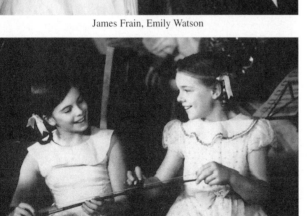

Keely Flanders, Auriol Evans

David Morrissey, Rachel Griffiths

HILARY AND JACKIE

(OCTOBER) Producers, Andy Paterson, Nicolas Kent; Executive Producers, Guy East, Nigel Sinclair, Ruth Jackson; Director, Anand Tucker; Screenplay, Frank Cottrell-Boyce; Based on the book *A Genius in the Family* by Hilary and Piers Du Pré; Photography, David Johnson; Designer, Alice Normington; Costumes, Sandy Powell; Music, Barrington Pheloung; Cellist, Caroline Dale; Casting, Simone Ireland, Vanessa Pereira; an Intermedia Films/Film Four presentation, with the participation of British Screen and the Arts Council of England of an Oxford Films production; Dolby; Super 35 Widescreen; Deluxe color; Rated R; 120 minutes; December release

Emily Watson, Rachel Griffiths

CAST

Jacqueline du Pré	Emily Watson
Hilary du Pré	Rachel Griffiths
Kiffer Finzi	David Morrissey
Daniel Barenboim	James Frain
Derek du Pré	Charles Dance
Iris du Pré	Celia Imrie
Piers du Pré	Rupert Penry Jones
Jackie's Cello Teacher	Bill Paterson
Young Hilary	Keely Flanders
Young Jackie	Auriol Evans
Teresa	Grace Chatto
Dame Margot	Nyree Dawn Porter
Margaret	Maggie McCarthy
Professor Bentley	Vernon Dobtcheff
BBC Nabob	Anthony Smee
Tweedy Woman	Delia Lindsey
Photographer	Nick Haverson
Patron	Kika Mirylees

Tamsin Pike (Harpsicord Player), David Shimwell (Man in Suit), Peter Czajkowski (German Admirer), Stella Maris (Spanish Admirer), Carla Medonca (Spanish Maid), Paul Banda (Maestro), Anna Barkan (Acolyte), Steven Atholl (Bookish Man), Heather Weeks (Guest), Ralph DeSouza (Violinist), Jon Rumney (Rabbi), Kate Hetherington (Middle Jackie), Ariana Daykin (Middle Hilary), Oliver Lee (Baby Piers), Hayley James-Gannon, Melissa James-Gannon (Hilary's Children), George Kennaway (German Concert Conductor), John Gough (Accompanist), Brian Perkins (Radio Announcer), Linda Spurrier, Robert Rietti, Andrea Chaialton

Emily Watson

The true story of world famous cellist Jacqueline Du Pré whose fame was offset by a life of unhappiness and her eventual battle with multiple sclerosis. This film received Oscar nominations for actress (Emily Watson) and supporting actress (Rachel Griffiths).

©October Films

Emily Watson, James Frain

Hayley James-Gannon, Emily Watson, Melissa James-Gannon, David Morrissey

TANGO

(SONY PICTURES CLASSICS) Producers, Luis A. Scalella, Caros A. Mentasti, Juan C. Codazzi; Co-Producers, José M. Calleja de La Fuente, Alejandro Bellaba; Director/Screenplay, Carlos Saura; Photography, Vittorio Storaro; Art Director, Emilio Basaldúa; Costumes, Beatriz Di Benedetto; Music, Lalo Schifrin; Choreographers, Juan Carlos Copes, Ana Maria Steckelman, Carlos Rivarola; Argentinian-Spanish; Dolby; Univision; Color; Rated PG-13; 114 minutes; December release

Mia Maestro, Juan Carlos Copes

CAST

Mario Suárez	Miguel Àngel Solà
Laura Fuentes	Cecilia Narova
Elena Flores	Mia Maestro
Carlos Nebbia	Juan Carlos Copes
Ernesto Landi	Carlos Rivarola
María Elman	Sandra Ballesteros
Daniel Stein	Oscar Cardozo Ocampo
Sergio Lieman	Enrique Pinti
Himself	Julio Bocca
Angelo Larroca	Juan Luis Galiardo
Andés Castro	Martín Seefeld
Waldo Norman	Ricardo Díaz Mourelle

and Antonio Soares Junior, Dante Montero (Bodyguards), Ariel Casas (Antonio), Carlos Thiel (Dr. Ramírez), Nora Zinsky, Julio Marticorena, Mabel Pessen (Investors), Johana Copes (Dance Teacher), Viviana Vigil, Héctor Pilatti (Singers), Roxana Fontan (Young Singer), Cutuli (Master of Ceremonies), Néstor Marconi, Adolfo Gómez (Bandoneón Players), Juanjo Domínguez (Guitar Player), Norberto Ramos (Pianist), Ángela Ciccone (Palmira Fuentes), Fernando Monetti (Homero Fuentes), Ángel Coria (Assistant Choreographer), Sofía Codrovich (Ana Segovia), Elvira Onetto (School Teacher)

Julio Bocca, Carlos Rivarola

A filmmaker who is having trouble making a tango movie, finds himself inspired and rejuvinated after falling in love with one of the dancers in the movie, the mistress of the gangster who is financing the project. This film received an Oscar nomination as foreign language film.

© Sony Pictures Entertainment

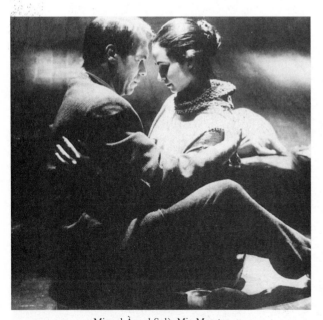

Miguel Àngel Solà, Mia Maestro

Mia Maestro, Cecilia Narova

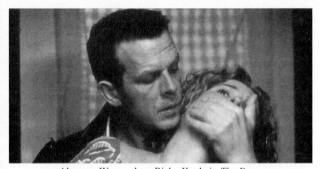

Alex van Warmerdam, Ricky Koole in *The Dress*
© Attitude Films

Fernando Torres, Leandra Leal
in *The Oyster and the Wind*

THE DRESS (Attitude Films) Producers, Marc van Warmerdam, Ton Schippers, Alex van Warmerdam; Executive Producer, Patricia McMahon; Director/Screenplay, Alex van Warmerdam; Photography, Marc Felperlaan; Editor, Rene Wiegmans; Costumes, Leonie Polak; Music, Vincent van Warmerdam; from Graniet Film; Dutch; Color; Not rated; 103 minutes; January release. **CAST:** Henri Garcin (Van Tilt), Ariane Schluter (Johanna), Alex van Warmerdam (De Smet), Ricky Koole (Chantalle), Rijk de Gooyer (Martin), Elisabeth Hoijtink (Stella), Olga Zuiderhoek (Marie), Eric van Donk (Herman), Khaldoun Elmecky (Cremer), Rudolf Lucieer (De Vet), Annet Malherbe (Woman with Gun)

GONIN (THE FIVE) (Phaedra Cinema) Producers, Kanji Miura, Taketo Niitsu, Katsuhide Motoki; Director/Screenplay, Takashi Ishii; Executive Producer, Kazuyoshi Okuyama; Photography, Yasushi Sasakibara; Music, Goro Yasukawa; from Leo Films, a Bunkasha Publishing/Image Factory Production in association with First Production Company/Kanox Company/Team Okuyama/Shochiku Company presentation; Japanese, 1995; Color; Not rated; 109 minutes; January release. **CAST:** Koichi Sato (Bandai), Masahiro Motoki (Mitsuya), Jinpachi Nezu (Hizu), Kippei Shiina (Jimmy), Naoto Takenaka (Ogiwara), Megumi Yokoyama (Nammy), Kazuya Kimura (Kazuma), Shingo Tsurumi (Hisamatsu), Toshiyuki Nagashima (Ogoshi), Takeshi "Beat" Kitano (Kyoya)

THE OYSTER AND THE WIND (Ravina/Lumiere) Producer, Flávio R. Tambellini; Director, Walter Lima Jr.; Screenplay, Walter Lima Jr., Flavio R. Tambellini; Based on the novel by Moacir C. Lopes; Photography, Pedro Farkas; Designer, Clóvis Bueno; Music, Wagner Tiso; a Ravina Files production co-produced by Rio Filmes, presented in asso-

ciation with Fabiano Canosa; Brazilian, 1997; Dolby; Color; Not rated; 112 minutes; January release. **CAST:** Lima Duarte (José), Leandra Leal (Marcela), Fernando Torres (Daniel), Floriano Peixoto (Roberto), Castrinho (Pepe), Débora Bloch (Mother), Arduíno Colasanti, Márcio Vito, Ricardo Marecos (Sailors)

VILLAGE OF DREAMS (Milestone) Producers, Tetsujiro Yamagami, Koshiro Sho; Director, Yoichi Higashi; Screenplay, Yoichi Higashi, Takehiro Nakajima; Based on the book *The Village of My Paintings* by Seizo Tashima; Photography, Yoshio Shimizu; Music, Caterina Ancient Music Ensemble; Art Director, Akira Naito; Sponsored by the Japan Arts Fund; Japan, 1996; Fujicolor; Not rated; 112 minutes; January release. **CAST:** Keigo Matsuyama (Seizo), Shogo Matsuyama (Yukihiko), Mieko Harada (Mizue Tashima), Kyozo Nagatsuka (Kenzo Tashima), Hosei Komatsu (Jimma), Kaneko Iwasaki (Toshie), Tokuko Sugiyama (Ushibamba), Koichi Ueda (The Principal), Mizuki Mamada (Ikuko), Takehiro Nakajima (The Mayor), Yukihiko Tashima, Hideko Tashima, Seizo Tashima (Themselves)

KILLING TIME (Avalanche) Producer, Richard Johns; Director, Bharat Nalluri; Screenplay, Neil Marshall, Fleur Costello, Caspar Berry; Executive Producer, Paul Brooks; Photography, Sam McCurdy; Designer, Ronald Gow; Editor, Neil Marshall; Music, Christopher Slaski; a Pilgrim Films production in association with Metrodome Films; British; Color; Not rated; 88 minutes; January release. **CAST:** Craig Fairbrass (Bryant), Kendra Torgan (Maria the Assassin), Peter Harding (Madison), Neil Armstrong (John), Ian McLaughlin (George), Stephen D. Thirkeld (Charlie), Rick Warden (Smithy), Nigel Leach (Jacob Reilly), Phil Dixon (Frank)

Masahiro Motoki, Koichi Sato in *Gonin*
© Phaedra Cinema

Keigo Matsuyama, Shogo Matsuyama
in *Village of Dreams* © Milestone Film

Romain Auger, Meziane Bardadi in *Full Speed* © Strand Releasing

Stephen Rea, Rosana Pastor in *The Break* © Castle Hill Prods, Inc.

FULL SPEED (Strand) Producer, Laurent Benegui; Director/Screenplay, Gael Morel; Adaptation and Dialogue, Gael Morel, Catherine Corsini; Photography, Jeanne Lapoirie; Editor, Catherine Schwartz; a Magouric Productions/Telema/France 2 Cinema/Rhone Alpes Cinema co-production with the participation of Cofimage 7 and Canal+; French; Dolby Stereo; Color; Not rated; 86 minutes; January release. **CAST:** Elodie Bouchez (Julie), Stephane Rideau (Jimmy), Pascal Cervo (Quentin), Meziane Bardadi (Samir), Romain Auger (Rick), Salim Kechiouche (Jamel), Mohammed Dib (Karim), Frederic Fargier, Patrice Thomas, Youcef Ninach, Missoum Laimene, Laurent Diomande, Ryad Benkouider (Jimmy's Gang), Paul Morel (Quentin's Father), Bernard Villeneuve (Journalist)

TOKYO FIST (Manga Entertainment) Executive Producer/Director/Screenplay/Photography/Editor/Art Director, Shinya Tsukamoto; Based on a story by Hisashi Saito, Shinya Tsukamoto; Costumes, Hiroko Iwasaki; Special Effects, Takashi Oda, Hiroshi Sagae; Japanese; 1997; Dolby; Color; Not rated; 90 minutes; February release. **CAST:** Shinya Tsukamoto (Tsuda Yoshiharu), Kahori Fujii (Hizuru), Koji Tsukamoto (Kojima Takuji), Naoto Takenaka (Ohizumi, trainer), Naomasa Musaka (Hase, trainer), Koichi Wajima (Shirota, gym owner), Tomoroh Taguchi (Tattoo Master), Nobu Kanaoka (Nurse)

COMRADES, ALMOST A LOVE STORY (Golden Harvest) Producer/Director, Peter Chan; Executive Producer, Raymond Chow; Co-Producer, Claudie Chung; Screenplay, Ivy Ho; Designer, Yee Chung-Man;

Koji Tsukamoto in *Tokyo Fist*
© Manga Entertainment

Photography, Jingle Ma; Costumes, Dora Ng; Music, Chiu Tsang-Hei; Editors, Chan Kei-Hop, Kwong Chi-Keung; a United Filmmakers Organization Ltd. production; Hong Kong, 1996; Color; Not rated; 116 minutes; February release. **CAST:** Maggie Cheung (Li Chiao), Leon Lai (Li Xiao-jun), Eric Tsang (Pao), Yang Kung-Yu (Xiao-ting), Irene Tsu (Aunt Rosie), Christopher Doyle (Jeremy)

THE SON OF GASCOGNE (Filmopolis) Producers, Denis Hartnagel, Daniel Vaissaire; Director, Pascal Aubier; Screenplay, Patrick Modiano, Pascal Aubier; Photography, Jean-Jacques Flori; Music, Angelo Zurzulo; Designer, Ann Chakraverty, Dominique Cluzel; editor, Dominique Roy; a Sybarite Production, in association with Cadrage Films, Fance 2; French, 1995; Color; Not rated; 106 minutes; February release. **CAST:** Gregoire Colin (Harvey), Jean-Claude Dreyfus (Marco Garciano), Dinara Droukarova (Dinara), Alexandra Stewart, Bernadette Lafont, Claude Chabrol, Otar Iosseliani, Stephane Audran, Jean-Claude Brialy, Bulle Ogier, Macha Meril, Marie-France Pisier, Marina Vlady, Anemone, Patrice Leconte, Michel Deville, Richard Leacock, Bernard Eisenschitz, Laszlo Szabo, Alain Emer, Pierre Cottrell.

GAACH (THE TREE) (Artistic License) Producer, Nayeem Hafizka; Executive Producer, Ismail Merchant; Photography, Ivan Kozelka; Editors, Catherine Poitevin, Georges-Henry Mauchant; Music, Zakir Hussain; French-British, 1997; Color; Not rated; 66 minutes; February release. Documentary on Bengali actor Soumitra Chatterjee, featuring Rabi Ghosh, Bijoya Ray, Sharmila Tagore, Madhabi Mukherjee, Aparna Sen, Mamata Shankhar, Deepa Chatterjee, Lily Chakraborty, Poulami Bose, Upma Roy.

THE BREAK (Castle Hill) formerly *A Further Gesture*; Producer, Chris Curling; Executive Producers, David Aukin, Ulrich Felsberg, Od Stoneman, Michiyo Yoshizaki; Director, Robert Dornhelm; Screenplay, Ronan Bennett; Based on an idea by Stephen Rea; Photography, Andrzej Sekula; Editor, Masahiro Hirakubo; Music, Harald Kloser, Shaun Davey; Designers, Kalina Ivanov, Tom McCullagh; Casting, Ros and John Hubbard; a Channel 4/Road Movies/Bord Scannan/NFD International production; Irish; Color; Rated R; 96 minutes; February release. **CAST:** Stephen Rea (Dowd), Alfred Molina (Tulio), Rosana Pastor (Monica), Brendan Gleeson (Richard), Jorge Sanz (Paco), Pruitt Taylor Vince (Scott), Frankie McCafferty (Danny), Sean McGinley (Tommy Breen), Paul Ronan (Liam), Richard Dormer (Joe), Roy Haybeard (Food Lorry Driver), Toby Bradford (Charlie), Maria Doyle Kennedy (Roisin), Robert Taylor (Prison Officer—Visiting Room), B.J. Hogg (Albert), Seamus Ball (First Prison Officer—Tallylodge), James Duran (Gate Prison Officer), Dierdre O'Kane (Breen's Girlfriend), Catriona Hinds (Richard's Wife), Paul Giamatti (Hotel Clerk), Brian Vincent (Lorenzo Bauch), Caroline Seymour (Junkie), Ciaran O'Reilly (Passer-by), Jerry Grayson (Restaurant Manager), Ken Solarino (Subway Man), Myra Carter (Neighbor), Shiek Mahmud-Bey (Knifeman), Esteban Fernandez (Ramon), Luis Argueta (Ramon's Bodyguard), George Bass (Ramon's Driver), Graeme Malcolm (Lattimer), Richard Council, John Rothman (FBI Agents), Ndehru Roberts (Kid Gun Dealer), Coati Mundi (Pepe), Alba Oms (Stall Owner), Barry Snider (Eamonn)

A Rat's Tale © Legacy

Arno Frisch, Susanne Lothar, Frank Giering in *Funny Games*

© Attitude Films

SHAMPOO HORNS (Elias Querejeta/Escima Prod.) Producers, Jennifer Gatien, Andrew Chiaras, Brilliant Mistake; Director/Screenplay, Manuel Toledano; Photography, Alfredo Mayo; Editor, Nacho Ruiz Capillas; Music, Angel Illarramendi; Costumes, Martha Gretsch; Spanish, 1997; Color; Not rated; 92 minutes; February release. **CAST:** Jason Reeves (Dennis), Cheyenne Besch (Cheyenne), Jonathan Lawrence (Jonathan), Jason Anthony (Mark), Andrew Gallupi (Tony), Tiffany Shepis (Amy), Brie Koyanagi (Brie)

MOTHER AND SON (International Film Circuit) Producer, Thomas Kufus; Executive Producers, Katrin Schlosser, Martin Hagemann, Aelxander Golutva; Director, Alexander Sokurov; Screenplay, Yuri Arabov; Photography, Alexei Fyodorov; Editor, Leda Semyonova; Music, Mikhail Glinka, Otmar Nussio, Giuseppe Verdi; an O Film (Berlin) Severnyj Fond (St. Petersburg) co-production; German-Russian, 1997; Dolby; Color; Not rated; 73 minutes; February release. **CAST:** Gudrun Geyer (Mother), Alexei Ananishnov (Son)

PRINCE VALIANT (20th Century Fox) Producer, Carsten H.W. Lorenz; Executive Producers, Bernd Eichinger, Tom Rosenberg; Director, Anthony Hickox; Screenplay, Anthony Hickox, Carsten H.W. Lorenz; Photography, Roger Lanser; Designer, Crispian Sallis; Music, David Bergeaud; from Constantin Film, Legacy Film Prods., Celtridge Ltd., Babelsberg Film; German-Irish-British; Color; Rated PG-13; 92 minutes; February release. **CAST:** Stephen Moyer (Prince Valiant), Katherine Heigl (Princess Ilene), Thomas Krestchmann (Thagnar), Warwick Davis (Pechet), Edward Fox (King Arthur), Zach Galligan (Sir Kay), Anthony Hickox (Prince Gawain), Jody Kidd (Lady of the Lake), Udo Kier (Sligon), Joanna Lumley (Morgana Le Fey), Ron Perlman (Boltar), Ben Pullen (Prince Arn), Marcus Schenkenberg (Tiny)

A RAT'S TALE (Legacy) Producer, Hans Peter Clahsen; Director, Michael F. Huse; Screenplay, Werner Morgenrath, Peter Scheerbaum; Based on the book by Tor Seidler; Photography, Piotr Lenar; Designer, Austen Spriggs; Music, Frederic Talgorn; Marionette Design, Hannelore Marschall-Oehmichen, Jürgen Marschall; Costumes, Eun-Young Kim; Editor, Timothy McLeish; Executive Producer, Christa-Maria Klein; a Monty Film production; German; Dolby Digital Stereo; Color; Rated G; 89 minutes; March release. **CAST:** Lauren Hutton (Evelyn Jellybean), Beverly D'Angelo (Mrs. Dollart), Jerry Stiller (Prof. Plumpingham), Josef Ostendorf (Mr. Dollart), Steffen Wink (Asst. Nick McRafferty), Andreas Herder (Assist. Tom O'Dooley), Yoshinori Yamamoto (Futon Sam), Jackie Recknitz (Mr. Adams), Natja Brunckhorst (Mrs. Lucy), Klaus Herzog (Gallery Customer), Kati Farkas (Bank Robber), Sam Morales (Taxi Driver), Michael Schreiber (Toxic Truck Driver), Stefan Frings, Erik Meyer (Toxic Sprayers), Heinz Dümbgen (Security Guard), ThermondPressley (Hot Dog Vendor); VOICES: Dee Bradley Baker (Monty Mad-Rat Jr.), Lynsey Bartilson (Isabella Noble-Rat), Ray Guth (Old Monty Senior), Scott MacDonald (Rudi Rake-Rat), Donald Arthur (Canalligator Jean-Paul/Doc Medicine-Rat/Walter Democrat), Danny Wells (Mr. Dollart), Channing Chase (Aunt Charlotte), Daamen Krall (President Noble-Rat), Chris Soldevilla (Laurat Ladida), Wally Wingert

Rat), Daran Norris (Dormouse Giuseppe/Eddi Pack-Rat), Marianne Muellerleile (Mother Noble-Rat), John Moschitta Jr. (Father Mad-Rat), Scott Weil (Asst. Nick McRafferty), Nicholas Benson (Asst. Tom O'Dooley)

FUNNY GAMES (Attitude Films) Producer, Veit Heiduschka; Director/Screenplay, Michael Haneke; Photography, Jürgen Jürges; Editor, Andreas Prochaska; Music, Georg Friedrich-Handel, Pietro Mascagni, W.A. Mozart, John Zorn; Austrian, 1997; Color; Not rated; 103 minutes; March release. **CAST:** Susanne Lothar (Anna), Ulrich Mühe (Georg), Frank Giering (Peter), Arno Frisch (Paul), Stefan Clapczynski (Georgie), Doris Kunstmann (Gerda), Christoph Bantzer (Fred), Wolfgang Glück (Robert), Susanne Meneghel (Gerda's Sister), Monika Zallinger (Eva)

THE LEADING MAN (BMG/Northern Arts) Producers, Bertil Ohlsson, Paul Raphael; Director, John Duigan; Screenplay, Virginia Duigan; Photography, Jean Francois Robin; Designer, Caroline Hanania; Costumes, Rachel Fleming; Editor Humphrey Dixon; Casting, Jina Jayawardena; from J&M Entertainment; British, 1997; Dolby; Color; Rated R; 96 minutes; March release. **CAST:** Jon Bon Jovi (Robin Grange), Lambert Wilson (Felix Webb), Anna Galiena (Elena Webb), Thandie Newton (Hilary Rule), Barry Humphries (Humphrey Beal), David Warner (Tod), Patricia Hodge (Delvene), Diana Quick (Susan), Tam Dean Burn (Henry), Harriet Walters (Liz Flett), Clare Cox (Serena), Kevin McKidd (Ant), Laura Austin Little (Miranda), Daniel Worters (Danny), Camilla Ohlsson (Jessie), Nicole Kidman (Herself)

Jon Bon Jovi, Anna Galiena in *The Leading Man*

© BMG Independents

James Elroy in *James Elroy Demon Dog...* © First Run Features

Jia Hongshen in *Frozen* © International Film Circuit

JAMES ELLROY: DEMON DOG OF AMERICAN CRIME FICTION (First Run Features) Director, Reinhard Jud; Screenplay, Reinhard Jud, Wolfgang Lehner; Photography, Wolfgang Lehner; Editor, Karina Ressler; Music, Sam Auinger, Deedee Neidhart; Narrator, Phil Tintner; Austrian, 1993; Color; Not rated; 90 minutes; March release. Documentary on author James Ellroy, featuring James Ellroy, Bill Moseley, Helen Knode, the Arroyo Varsity Cheerleaders, Barko.

MENDEL (First Run Features) Producer, Axel Helgeland; Director/Screenplay, Alexander Røsler; Co-Producers, Peter Aalbæk Jensen, Helga Bähr; Photography, Helge Semb; Designer, Jack Van Domburg; Editor, Einar Egeland; Music, Geir Bøhren, Bent Åserud; a Northern Lights presentation; Norwegian-Danish-German, 1997; Color; Not rated; 95 minutes; March release. **CAST:** Thomas Jüngling Sørensen (Mendel), Teresa Harder (Bela), Hans Kremer (Aron), Martin Meingast (David), Charlotte Trier (Mrs. Freund), Wolfgang Pintzka (Mr. Freund), John Henning Gøbring Hermstad (Markus), Bjørn Sundquist (Mitten Man), Lene Bragli (Mrs. Rosen), Geo Von Krogh (Mr. Rosen), Bjørn Jenseg (Ugland), Ketil Gudim (The Farmer)

BRIGANDS: CHAPTER VII (Piere Grise Prods.) Producer, Martine Marignac; Director/Screenplay, Otar Iosseliani; Photography, William Lubtchansky; Editors, Otar Iosseliani, Marie-Agnes Blum, Santiago Thevenet; Music, Nicolas Zourabichvili; Georgian; Color; Not rated; 129 minutes; March release. **CAST:** Amiran Amiranachvili (Vano), Dato Gogibedachvili (Sandro), Guio Tzintsadze (Spiridon), Nino Ordjonikidze (Eka), Keti Kapanadze (Lia), Alexi Djakeli (Victor), Niko Kartsivadze (Cola)

FROZEN (Intl. Film Circuit) Producers, Shu Kei, Xu Wei; Director, Wu Ming ("No Name"); Screenplay, Pang Ming, Wu Ming; Photography, Yang Shu; Editor, Qing Qing; Art Director, Li Yanxiu; Music, Roeland Dol; Produced in association with Hubert Bals Fund (Rotterdam); Chinese-Hong Kong-Netherlands, 1997; Color; Not rated; 95 minutes; March release. **CAST:** Jia Hongshen (Qi Lei), Ma Xiaoqing (Shao Yun), Bai Yu (Sister), Li Geng (Sister's Husband), Bai Yefu (Bald Guy), Wei Ye (Long Haired Guy), Zhang Yongning (Lau Ling), Qu Lixin (Doctor), Liu Jie (Dao Shi)

LITTLE DIETER NEEDS TO FLY (Werner Herzog Filmproduktion) Producer/Director/Narrator, Werner Herzog; Executive Producers, Lucki Stipetic; Photography, Peter Zeitlinger; Editors, Rainer Standke, Glen Scantlebury, Joe Bini; Presented in association with Cafe Prods. for ZDF; a ZDF Enterprises/BBC co-production; German-British; Color; Not rated; 80 minutes; April release. Documentary on German-born Dieter Dengler who moved to the U.S., learned to fly and ended up being shot down over Laos in 1966 where he was made a prisoner of war.

WHO THE HELL IS JULIETTE? (Kino) Producer/Director/Photography/Story/Editor, Carlos Marcovich; Dramatic Structure, Carlos Cuaron; English Translation, Michael Donnelly; Music, Alejandro Marcovich; Produced by December Error; Cuban-Mexican, 1997; Dolby Stereo; Color; Not rated; 91 minutes; April release. **CAST:** Yuliet Ortega (Juliette), Fabiola Quiroz (Fabiola), Oneida Ramirez, Jorge Quiroz, Obdulia Fuentes, Yolanda Barajas, Victor Ortega, Marco O Mark, Jose "Don Pepe" Breuil, Michel Ortega, Guillermo, Billy Joe Landa, Kirenia Rosa, Glenda Rayna, Salma Hayek, Benny, Francesco Clemente, Manolin.

Thomas Jüngling Sørensen in *Mendel* © First Run Features

Dieter Dengler in *Little Dieter Needs To Fly*

Yuliet Ortega in *Who the Hell is Juliette?* © Kino International Corp.

Stolen Moments © First Run Features

THE LAST OF THE HIGH KINGS (Miramax) a.k.a. *Summer Fling;* Producer, Tim Palmer; Executive Producers, John Wolstenholme, Keith Northrop; Director, David Keating; Screenplay, Gabriel Byrne, David Keating; Based on the novel by Ferdia MacAnna; Photography, Bernd Heinl; Editor, Ray Lovejoy; Music, Michael Convertino; Co-Executive Producers, Gabriel Byrne, Paul Feldsher; Co-Producers, Alan Moloney, Martha O'Neill, Lars Kolvig; Casting, Nuala Moiselle; a Parallel Film Productions/Nordisk Film/Norhtolme Entertainment production; Irish-Danish, 1996; Color; Rated R; 104 minutes; April release. **CAST:** Catherine O'Hara (Ma), Jared Leto (Frankie Griffin), Christina Ricci (Erin), Gabriel Byrne (Da), Amanda Shun (Rainbow), Stephen Rea (Taxi Driver), Colm Meaney (Jim Davern), Des Braden (Teacher), Lorraine Pilkington (Jayne Wayne), Emily Mortimer (Romy Thomas), Jason Barry (Nelson Fitzgerald), Karl Hayden (Hopper Delaney), Darren Monks (Davy Dudley), Peter Keating (Ray Griffin), Renee Weldon (Maggie Griffin), Alexandra Haughey (Dawn Griffin), Ciaran Fitzgerald (Noelie Griffin), Vincent Walsh (Bobby Gallo), Kevin & Lisa Russell (Figgis Twins), Mal Whyte (Mr. Figgis), Kay Creighton (Mrs. Figgis), Gabriel Brady (TV Reporter), Clodagh Reid (Mo), Emma Stewart (Jo), Don Wycherley (Peter Colcannon), Joe Savino (Bus Conductor), Jack Lynch (Returning Officer), Mark O'Regan (Father Michael), Oliver Maguire (Billy), Graham Wilkinson (Henchman), Luke Hayden (Fireman)

STOLEN MOMENTS (First Run Features) Director/Screenplay, Margaret Wescott; Narrator, Kate Nelligan; Canadian; Color; Not rated; 91 minutes; April release. Documentary on lesbian history featuring Joan Nestle, Leslie Feinberg, Judy Grahn, Nicole Brossard, Audre Lorde.

MIDAQ ALLEY (Northern Arts) Producer, Alfredo Ripstein, Jr.; Director, Jorge Fons; Screenplay, Vincent Lenero; Based on the novel *El Callejón de los Milagros* by Naguib Mahfouz; Photography, Carlos Marcovich; Music, Lucia Alvarez; Editor, Carlos Savage; Mexican, 1994; Color; Not rated; 140 minutes; April release. **CAST:** Ernesto Gómez Cruz (Don Ru), Salma Hayek (Alma), Bruno Bichir (Abel), Juan Manuel Bernal (Chava), Margarita Sanz (Susanita), Luis Felipe Tovar (Güicho), Delia Casanova (Eusebia), Daniel Gimenez Cacho (Jose Luis), Claudio Obregón (Don Fidel), Maria Rojo (Doña Cata), Tiare Scanda (Maru), Esteban Soberanes (Jimy), Abel Woolrich (Zacarias), Gina Morett (Doña Flor)

R.I.P.: REST IN PIECES (Prisma Film Wien) Producers, Michael Seeber, Heinz Stussak; Director/Editor, Robert-Adrian Pejo; Screenplay, Walt Michelson; Photography, Wolfgang Lehner; Music, Hasil Adkins, Charlie Feathers, Link Wray, Wanda Jackson; Austrian; Dolby; Color; Not rated; 90 minutes; April release. Documentary on artist Joe Coleman, featuring Joe Coleman, Hasil Adkins, Bill Coleman, Katharine Gates, Dian Hanson, Jim Jarmusch, Junior, Manuel De Landa, Nancy Pivar, Harold Schecter, Martin Wilner.

A NEW LIFE/UNE NOUVELLE VIE (Cowboy Intl.) Producer, Bruno Pésery; Director/Screenplay, Olivier Assayas; Photography, Denis Lenoir; Editor, Luc Barnier; French, 1993; Color; Not rated; 90 minutes; April release. **CAST:** Sophie Aubry (Tina), Judith Godreche (Lise), Bernard Giraudeau (Constantin), Christine Boisson (Laurence), Philippe Torreton (Fred), Bernard Verley (Ludovic), Nelly Borgeaud (Nadine), Antoine Basler (Kleber), Roger Dumas (Martin)

Jared Leto, Gabriel Byrne in *The Last of the High Kings*
© Miramax Films

Salma Hayek in *Midaq Alley* © Northern Arts

Rapulana Seiphemo, Jane March, Casper Van Dien in *Tarzan and the Lost City* © Edgar Rice Burroughs/Village Roadshow/Dieter Geissler

Paolo Rotondo in *The Ugly* © Trimark Pictures Inc.

FORGOTTEN LIGHT (Studio FAMA) Executive Producer, Jana Tomsová; Director, Vladimír Micháliek; Screenplay, Milena Jelínek; Story, Jakub Deml, from his book; Photography, Martin Duba; Editor, Ivana Kacírková; Music, Radim Hladík, Michael Dvorák; Czech, 1994; Color; Not rated; 101 minutes; April release. **CAST:** Boleslav Polívka (Parish Priest Holy), Veronika Zilková (Marjanka), Petr Kavan (Francek), Jiri Pecha (Klima), Simona Pekova (Klimova), Antonim Kinsky (County Kinsky), Jaromira Milova (Betina), Sona Valentova (Dr. Prokopova), Jiri Labus (Parish Priest Kubista)

TARZAN AND THE LOST CITY (Warner Bros.) Producers, Stanley Canter, Dieter Geissler, Michael Lake; Executive Producers, Greg Coote, Peter Ziegler, Kurt Silberschneider, Lawrence Mortorff; Director, Carl Schenkel; Screenplay, Bayard Johnson, J. Anderson Black; Based on the *Tarzan* stories created by Edgar Rice Burroughs; Photography, Paul Gilpin; Editor, Harry Hitner; Designer, Herbert Pinter; Music, Christopher Franke; Costumes, Jo Katsaras-Barklem; Visual Effects Supervisor, Julian Parry; Casting, Nicole Arbusto, Celestia Fox, Moonyeen Lee; a Dieter Geissler/Alta Vista production in association with Village Roadshow Pictures-Clipsal Film Partnership; Australian-German-U.S.; Dolby; Super 35 Widescreen; Technicolor; Rated PG; 105 minutes; April release. **CAST:** Casper Van Dien (Tarzan), Jane March (Jane), Steve Waddington (Ravens), Winston Ntshona (Mugambi), Rapulana Seiphemo (Kaya), Ian Roberts (Capt. Dooley), Sean Taylor (Wilkes), Gys De Villers (Schiller), Russel Savadier (Archer), Paul Buckby (Jerjynski), Zane Meas (Knowles), Barry Berk (Burke), Michael Gritten (Devlin), Dimitri Cassar (Klemmer), Tony Caprari (Ritter), Kurt Wustman (Sykes), Chris Olley (Ackerman),

Ariane Ascaride, Gerard Meylan in *Marius and Jeannette*

© New Yorker Films

Joshua Lindberg (Edwards), Henry Van Der Berg (Lucas), Pete Janschek (Laconte), Danie Van Rensburg (Devoors), Aubrey Lovett (Brooks), Paulo Tocha (Fitt), Nickie Griff (Stonehouse), Neville Strydom (Dodd), Dieter Hoffman (Lutz), Peter Spyro (Weissel), Pierre Van Rensburg (Dorr), Bismulah Mdaka (Jeremiah), Sello Sebotsane (Dube), Sello Dlamini (Chester Fukazi (Waiter), Grant Swanby (Douglas), Adam Crousdale (Douglas), Nick Rujewick (Andrew)

MARIUS AND JEANNETTE (New Yorker) Producer, Gilles Sandoz; Director, Robert Guédiguian; Screenplay, Rober Guédiguian, Jean-Louis Milesi; Photography, Bernard Cavalié; Art Director, Karim Hamzaoui; Editor, Bernard Sasia; Casting, Maya Sevleyan; a production of Agat Films & Cie in co-production with La Sept Cinema with the participation of Canal+; French; Color; Not rated; 102 minutes; April release. **CAST:** Ariane Ascaride (Jeannette), Gérard Meylan (Marius), Pascale Roberts (Caroline), Jacques Boudet (Justin), Frédérique Bonnal (Monique), Jean-Pierre Darroussin (Dédé), Laëtitia Pesenti (Magali), Miloud Nacer (Malek), Pierre Banderet (Monsieur Ebrard)

PEREIRA DECLARES (Mikado Films/Fabrica De Imagens) formerly *According to Pereira;* Producer, Elda Ferri; Director, Roberto Faenza; Screenplay, Roberto Faenza, Antonio Tabucchi; Based on the novel by Antonio Tabucchi; Photography, Blasco Giurato; Editor, Franco Casellato; Music, Ennio Morricone; a Jean Vigo International/K.G. Production; Italian-French, 1995; Color; Not rated; 104 minutes; April release. **CAST:** Marcello Mastroianni (Pereira), Daniel Auteuil (Doctor Cardoso), Stefano Dionisi (Monteiro Rossi), Nicoletta Braschi (Marta), Joaquim De Almeida (Manuel), Marthe Keller (Signora Delgado), Teresa Madruga (Portiera), Nicolau Breyner (Padre Antonio), Filipe Ferrer (Silva), Mario Viegas (Direttore del Giornale), Joâo Grosso (Capo della Polizia Politica), Teresa Gouveia (Moglie di Pereira)

HEALING BY KILLING (New Yorker) Producer/Director/Screenplay, Nitzan Aviram; Photography, Yoram Millo; Editor, Naomi Press-Aviram; Music, Oded Zehavi; Israeli, 1996; Color; Not rated; 90 minutes; April release. Documentary on the methods Nazi doctors used in their experimentation with euthanasia in an effort to realize "the final solution."

THE UGLY (Trimark) Producer, Jonathan Dowling; Director/Screenplay, Scott Reynolds; Photography, Simon Raby; Designer, Grant Major; Music, Victoria Kelly; Editor, Wayne Cook; an Essential Films in association with the New Zealand Film Commission presentation; New Zealand; Color; Not rated; 92 minutes; May release. **CAST:** Paolo Rotondo (Simon Cartwright), Rebecca Hobbs (Dr. Karen Schumaker), Jennifer Ward-Lealand (Evelyn Cartwright), Roy Ward (Dr. Marlowe), Paul Glover (Philip—Orderly #1), Chris Graham (Robert—Orderly #2), Darien Takle (Marge—Elderly Patient), Cath McWhirter (Helen Ann Miller), Carolyn Beaver (Helen's Friend), Caelem Pope (Simon—age 4), Finn Johnson, Phillip Brown, Tau Luke (Future Cops), Tim Barlow (Police

Eva Norvind in *Didn't Do It for Love* © First Run Features

Valentina Cervi, Michel Serrault in *Artemisia* © Miramax Zoë

Photographer), Sam Wallace (Simon—age 13), Aaron Buskin (Roland—Ringleader Bully), John Steemson, Oliver Hodges (Bullies), Beth Allen (Julie—age 13), Chris Bailey (Ed Daley), Gary Mackay (Man in Park), Steve Hall, Shane Bessant (Worker Thugs), Katrina Browne (Woman in the Floral Dress), Yvonne Dudman (Melinda Jackson), Frances Chan, Scott Wills, Jenny Ashton, Matt Cornelius (Simon's Victims), Hugh D'Calveley (Victim in Alleyway), Sara Pivac (Deaf Girl), Vanessa Byrnes (Julie—age 25), Jon Brazier (Vet), Micheal Dwyer (Alex), David Baxter (Clive)

DIDN'T DO IT FOR LOVE (First Run Features) Producer, Irene von Alberti; Director/Screenplay, Monika Truet; Photography, Ekkehart Pollack, Christopher Landerer; Editor, Eric Marciano; Music, Georg Kajanus; a Filmergalerie 451 production; German, 1997; Color; Not rated; 80 minutes; May release. Documentary on dominatrix-turned-sex therapist Eva Norvind, featuring Jan Baracz, Rene Cardona Jr., Jose-Luis Cuevas, Nicholas Echevarria, Juan Ferrara, Jose Flores, Juan-Jose Gurrola, Franz Harland, Georg Kajanus, Johanne Kajanus, Micheline Kinery, Nadine Markova, Ronald Moglia, Gerard O'Neal, Luz Maria Rojas, Liisa Simola, Veronica Vera, Alice Vernstad, Paul Vernstad, Esther Maria Wiig.

MARIAN (Turbulent Arts) Producers, Kristina Petrová, Petr Václav; Executive Producer, Jaroslav Stanek; Director, Petr Václav; Screenplay, Jan Sikl, Petr Václav; Photography, Stepan Kucera; Editor, Alois Fisárek; Music, Jirí Václav; Czech; Color; Not rated; minutes; May release. **CAST:** Stefan Ferko (Younger Marian), Milan Cifra (Older Marian), Radek Holub (David), Tereza Zajickova-Grygarova (eva), Jaroslava Vyslouzilova (Tosovska), Eva Hradilova (Teacher)

ARTEMISIA (Miramax Zoë) Producer, Patrice Haddad; Executive Producers, Lilian Saly, Patricia Allard, Daniel Wuhrmann; Director, Agnès Merlet; Screenplay, Agnès Merlet, Christine Miller; Adaptation and Dialogue, Agnès Merlet, Patrick Amos; Photography, Benoit Delhomme; Designer, Antonello Geleng; Music, Krishna Levy; Editor, Guy Lecorne; Costumes, Dominique Borg; Casting, Bruno Levy; a Premiere Heure Long Metràge presentation; French-Italian-German, 1997; Dolby; Color; Rated R; 96 minutes; May release. **CAST:** Valentina Cervi (Artemisia), Michel Serrault (Orazio), Miki Manojlovic (Agostino), Luca Zingaretti (Cosimo), Emmannuelle Devos (Costanza), Frederic Pierrot (Roberto), Maurice Garrel (The Judge), Brigitte Catillon (Tuzia), Yahn Tregouet (Fulvio), Jacques Nolot (The Lawyer), Silvia De Santis (Marisa), Renato Carpentieri (Nicolo), Dominique Reymond (Tassi's Sister), Liliane Rovere (The Rich Merchant's Wife), Alain Ollivier (The Duke), Patrick Lancelot (The Academy Director), Rinaldo Rocco, Enrico Salimbeni (Academy Students), Catherine Zago (The Mother Superior), Lorenzo Lavia (Orazio's Assistant), Sami Bouajila, Edoardo Ruiz, Aaron De Luca (Tassi's Assistants), Guido Roncalli (The Duke's Servant), Pierre Bechir (The Rich Merchant's Son), Massimo Pittarello (The Torturer)

A FRIEND OF THE DECEASED (Sony Pictures Classics) Producers, Mykola Machenko, Pierre Rival; Executive Producer, Jacky Ouaknine; Director, Vyacheslav Krishtofovich; Screenplay, Andreï Kourkov; Photography, Vilen Kaluta; Designer, Roman Adamovich; Editor, Eleonora Sumovska; Costumes, Lyudmila Serdinova; a Compagnie des Films/Compagnie Est-Ouest/National Dovzhenko Film Studio/Kazakhstan Aimanov Film Factory with the support of the French Ministry of Culutre (CNC) and the Ukranian MInistry of Culutre and Arts; French-Ukranian, 1997; Color; Rated R; 100 minutes; May release. **CAST:** Alexandre Lazarev (Anatoli), Tatiana Krivitska (Lena/Vika, the Prostitute), Eugen Pachin (Dima, Anatoli's Friend), Constantin Kostychin (Kostia, the Contract Killer), Elena Korikova (Marina, Kostia's Wife), Angelika Nevolina (Katia, Anatoli's Wife), Sergiy Romanyuk (Ivan, Anatoli's Contract Killer)

SHOPPING FOR FANGS (Margin Films) Producer, Quentin Lee; Directors, Quentin Lee, Justin Lin; Screenplay, Dan Alvarado, Quentin Lee, Justin Lin; Photography, Lisa Weigand; Editors, Quentin Lee, Justin Lin, Sean Yeo; Music, Steven Pranoto; Casting, Josh Diamond; A De/Center Communications production with the support of Canadian Council; Canadian-U.S., 1997; Color; Not rated; 89 minutes; May release. **CAST:** Radmar Jao (Phil), Jeanne Chin (Katherine Nguyen), Clint Jung (Jim Lee), Lela Lee (Naomi), John Cho (Clarance), Peggy Ahn (Grace), Scott Eberlein (Matt), Daniel Twyman (Dr. Suleri), Jennifer Hengstenberg (Sammi), Dana Pan (May), Roxanne Coyne (Dr. Hali)

Elena Korikova, Alexandre Lazarev in *A Friend of the Deceased*

© Sony Pictures Entertainment Inc.

Juliet Aubrey, Robert Carlyle in *Go Now* © Gramercy Pictures

Stuart Townsend, Kate Beckinsale, Dan Futterman

in *Shooting Fish* © Twentieth Century Fox

GO NOW (Gramercy) Producer, Andrew Eaton; Executive Producer, David M. Thompson; Director, Michael Winterbottom; Screenplay, Paul Henry Powell, Jimmy McGovern; Co-Producer, Roxy Spencer; Photography, Daf Hobson; Designer, Hayden Pearce; Editor, Trevor Waite; Music, Alastair Gavin; Costumes, Rachael Fleming; a PolyGram Filmed Entertainment presentation of a Revolution Films production for BBC Films; British; Dolby; Color; Not rated; 88 minutes; May release. **CAST:** Robert Carlyle (Nick Cameron), Juliet Aubrey (Karen Walker), James Nesbitt (Tony), Sophie Okonedo (Paula), Berwick Kaler (Sammy), Darren Tighe (Dell), Sean Mackenzie (George), John Brobbey (Geoff), Sara Stockbridge (Bridget), Sean Rocks (Charlie), Tom Watson (Bill Cameron), Barbara Rafferty (Madge Cameron), Tony Curran (Chris Cameron), Erin McMahon (Julie Cameron), Dave Schneider, Jenny Jules (Doctors), Anna Godsiff (Nurse), Susie Fugle (Scan Doctor), Roger McKern (Patient), James Trehearne (Male Nurse), Cal McGregor (Man in Wheelchair), Tricky (Himself)

LOUISA MAY ALCOTT'S LITTLE MEN (Legacy) Producers, Pierre David, Franco Battista; Executive Producers, Meyer Shwarzstein, Tom Berry; Director, Rodney Gibbons; Screenplay, Mark Evan Schwartz; Based on the novel by Louisa May Alcott; Co-Executive Producer, Josée Bernard; Photography, Georges Archambault; Designer, Donna Noonan; Music, Milan Kymicka; Editor, Andre Corriveau; a Brainstorm Media in association with Image Organization presentation of an Allegro Films pro

duction; Canadian; Ultra-Stereo; Color; Rated PG; 98 minutes; May release. **CAST:** Michael Caloz (Nat Blake), Mariel Hemingway (Jo Bhaer), Ben Cook (Dan), Ricky Mabe (Tommy Bangs), Chris Sarandon (Fritz Bhaer), Gabrielle Boni (Nan Harding), Michael Yarmoush (Emil), Tyler Hynes (Demi Brooke), B.J. McLellan (Jack Ford), Mathew Mackay (Franz), Daisy Brooke (Julia Garland), Serge Houde (John Brooke), Emma Campbell (Meg Brooke), Kathleen Fee (Molly/Narrator), James Bradford (Silas Blake), David Deveau (Stuffy Cole), Justin Bradley (Dolly Pettinghill), Mickey Toft (Teddy Bhaer), Frank Fontaine (Man in Market), Bill Corday (Vendor), Richard Azimov (Newspaper Boy), Mark Camacho (Police Sergeant), Michael Azeff (Boy at Xmas Party)

SHOOTING FISH (Fox Searchlight) Producers, Richard Holmes, Glynis Murray; Executive Producer, Gary Smith; Director, Stefan Schwartz; Screenplay, Stefan Schwartz, Richard Holmes; Photography, Henry Braham; Designer, Max Gottlieb; Editor, Alan Strachan; Music, Stanislas Syrewicz; a Gruber Brothers Production in association with Winchester Multimedia, the Arts Council of England and Tomboy Films; British, 1997; Dolby; Super 35 Widescreen; Color; Rated PG; 93 minutes; May release. **CAST:** Dan Futterman (Dylan), Stuart Townsend (Jez), Kate Beckinsale (Georgie), Nickolas Grace (Mr. Stratton-Luce), Claire Cox (Floss), Ralph Ineson (Mr. Ray), Dominic Mafham (Roger), Peter Capaldi (Mr. Gilzean), Annette Crosbie (Mrs. Cummins), Jane Lapotaire (Dylan's Headmistress), Phyllis Logan (Mrs. Ross)

Mariel Hemingway, Michael Caloz in *Little Men* © Legacy Releasing

Thomas Salsman, Marcel Bozonnet in *Les Desenchanteé* © First Run Features

The Saltmen of Tibet © Zeitgeist Films

Marc Richter, Udo Samel in *Killer Condom*

©Troma Entertainment, Inc.

LES DÉSENCHANTÉE (THE DISENCHANTED) (First Run Features) Producer, Philippe Carcassonne; Director/Screenplay, Benoit Jacquot; Executive Producer, Sylvie Blum; Photography, Caroline Champetier; Editor, Dominique Auvray; from Cinea/La Sept, C.N.C., Sofica Sofinergie 2; French, 1990; Color; Not rated; 78 minutes; May release. **CAST:** Judith Godreche (Beth), Marcel Bozonnet (Alphonse) ,Yvan Desny (L'Oncle), Therese Liotard (La Mere de Beth), Malcolm Conrath (L'Autre), Thomas Salsman (Remi), Hai Truhong (Chang), Francis Mage (Edouard), Marion Perry (Le Professeur de Francais), Stephane Auberghen (La Mere d'Edouard)

JUNK FOOD (Junk Food Connection for Stance Company) Producer, Toshihiro Isomi; Executive Producers, Koich Omiya, Kazunao Sakaguchi, Eisuke Ishige; Director/Screenplay, Masashi Yamamoto; Photography, Hiroshi Ito; Editor, Syuichi Kakesu; Music, DJ Krush, Ko Machida; Japanese; Color; Not rated; 84 minutes; June release. **CAST:** Miyuki Ijima (Miyuki), Akifumi Yamaguchi (Boss), Keigo Naruse (Murdered Man), Yoichi Okamura (Miyuki's Husband), Mika Kumagai (Shop Girl), Rumi Otori (Shop Manager), Arata Furuta (Yokoyama), Yoshiyuki (Hide), Onimaru (Ryo), Mia (Myan), Ali Ahmed (Cawl), Mariarna (Esther Moreno), Kanji Tuda (Sato), Choudry Ikram Ul Haq (Sarym), Tatsutoshi Kawamura (Shu), Yuta Todo (Kiku), Yoko Kobayasi (Mami), Kenta S. (Kenta), Kansai Horitatsu (Horitatsu), Nobutaka Kuwabara (Hide's Friend), Shizuko Yamamoto (Blind Woman)

AUTUMN SUN (Capitol) Producer/Director, Eduardo Mignogna; Screenplay, Eduardo Mignogna, Santiago Carlos Oves; Photography, Marcelo Camorino; Executive Producer, Lita Stantic; Art Director, Jorge Ferrari; Editors, Juan Carlos Macias, Javier Del Pino; Music, Edgardo Rudnitzky; Argentine, 1996; Color; Not rated; 90 minutes; June release. **CAST:** Noma Aleandro (Clara Goldstein), Federico Luppi (Raul Ferraro), Jorge Luz (Palomino), Cecilia Rossetto (Leticia), Roberto Carnaghi (Sr. Cohen), Gabriela Archer (Silvia), Erasmo Olivera (Nelson), Nicolas Goldschmidt (Wilson)

THE SALTMEN OF TIBET (Zeitgeist) Executive Producer, Alfi Sinniger; Director/Screenplay, Ulrike Koch; Photography, Pio Corradi; Editor, Magdolna Rokob; Music, Stefan Wulff, Frank Wulff; Co-Producers, Christophe Bicker, Knut Winkler; Produced by Catpics Coproductions (Zurich) in coproduction with Duran Film (Berlin); Swiss-German-Tibetan, 1997; Dolby; Color; Not rated; 110 minutes; July release. Documentary on a Tibetan nomadic community and their three-month pilgrimage to the holy salt lakes of the Changtang region.

KILLER CONDOM (Troma) Producers, Ralph S. Dietrich, Harald Reichebner; Executive Producer, Michael Stricker; Director, Martin Walz; Screenplay, Martin Walz, Ralf König; Based on the comic book by Ralf König; Photography, Alexander Honisch; Editor, Simone Klier; Sets, Agi Dawaach; Creative Consultant, H.R. Giger; Costumes, Anja Niehaus; Special Effects, Jorg Buttgereit; a Lloyd Kaufman and Michael Herz presentation of an Ascot-Elite Film & Ecco Film in association with the German Film Board; German; Color; Not rated; 90 minutes; July release.

CAST: Udo Samel (Luigi Mackeroni), Peter Lohmeyer (Sam O'Connery), Iris Berben (Frau Dr. Riffelson), Marc Richter (Billy), Leonard Lansink (Babette), Hennig Schlüter (Robinson), Gerd Wameling (Professor), Ralf Wolter (Boris Smirnoff), Meret Becker (Phyllis), Otto Sander (Mr. Higgins), Monika Hansen (Mrs. Higgins), Hella von Sinnen (Polizistin), Adriana Altaras (Putzfrau), Ron Williams (Boss), Evelyn Künnecke (Wilma), Inga Busch (Inga), Georg-Martin Bode (McGovern), Lillemor Malau (Edelnutte)

SEVENTH HEAVEN (Zeitgeist) Producers, Georges Benayoun, Philippe Carcassonne; Director, Benoît Jacquot; Screenplay, Benoît Jacquot, Jérôme Beaujour; Executive Producer, Françoise Guglielmi; Photography, Romain Winding; Designer, Patrice Arrat; Costumes, Caroline De Vivaise; Editor, Pascale Chavance; Casting, Frédérique Moidon; a production of Dacia Films—Cinéa in co-production with La Sept Cinema with the participation of Canal+ and the Centre National de la Cinematographie; French, 1997; Dolby; CinemaScope; Color; Not rated; 91 minutes; July release. **CAST:** Sandrine Kiberlain (Mathilde), Vincent Lindon (Nico), François Berléand (The Doctor), Francine Bergé (Mathilde's Mother), Pierre Cassignard (Etienne), Philippe Magnan (The 2nd Doctor), Florence Loiret (Chloé), Léo Le Bevillon (Arthur), Sylvie Loeillet (Nico's Assistant)

Sandrine Kiberlain, Vincent Lindon in *Seventh Heaven*

©*Zeitgeist Films*

Romain Duris, Rona Hartner in *Gadjo Dilo* © Lions Gate Films

Stephen Dillane, Sophie Marceau in *Firelight* © Hollywood Pictures

GADJO DILO (Lions Gate) Producer, Doru Mitran; Director/Screenplay/Music, Tony Gatlif; Photography, Eric Guichard; Executive Producer, Gut Marignane; Art Director, Brigitte Brassart; Editor, Monique Dartonne; Casting, Marie De Laubier; French-Romanian; Color; Not rated; 97 minutes; August release. **CAST:** Romain Duris (Stéphane), Rona Hartner (Sabina), Isidor Serban (Izidor), Ovidiu Balan (Sami), Dan Astileanu (Dimitru), Florin Moldovan (Adrjani), Mandra Ramcu (Mandra), Aurica Serban (Aurica), Radu Ramcu (Radu)

THE BEST MAN (October) Producers, Aurelio De Laurentiis, Antonio Avati; Director/Screenplay/Story, Pupi Avati; Photography, Pasquale Rachini; Designers, Alberto Cottignoli, Steno Tonelli; Costumes, Vittoria Guaita; Editor, Amadeo Salfa; Music, Riz Ortolani; a Filmauro-Duea Film production; Italian; Dolby; Color; Rated PG; 106 minutes; August release. **CAST:** Diego Abatantuono (Angelo Beliossi), Ines Sastre (Francesca Babini), Dario Cantarelli (Edgardo Osti), Cinia Mascoli (Pepina Campeggi), Valeria D'Obici (Olimpia Campeggi Babini), Toni Santagata (Manlio Lobianco), Nini Salerno (Sauro Ghinassi), Mario Erpichini (Sisto Babini), Ugo Conti (Marziano Beliossi)

REGENERATION (Alliance) Producers, Allan Scott, Peter R. Simpson; Executive Producers, Saskia Sutton, Mark Shivas; Director, Gillies

MacKinnon; Screenplay, Allan Scott; Based on the novel by Pat Barker; Photography, Glen MacPherson; Designer, Andy Harris; Editor, Pia Di Ciaula; Music, Mychael Danna; a Norstar Entertainment presentation of a Rafford Films, BBC Films, Scottish Arts Council Lottery Fund (U.K.)/Norstar Entertainment (Canada) production; British-Canadian, 1997; Dolby; Color; Not rated; 113 minutes; August release. **CAST:** Jonathan Pryce (Dr. William Rivers), James Wilby (Siegfried Sassoon), Jonny Lee Miller (Billy Prior), Stuart Bunce (Wilfred Owen), Tanya Allen (Sarah), Dougray Scott (Robert Graves), John Neville.

CHILE, OBSTINATE MEMORY (First Run/Icarus Films) Producers, Yves Jeanneau, Eric Michel; Director, Patricio Guzman; Photography, Eric Pittard; Editor, Helene Girard; Music, Robert M. Lepage; a Les Films d'Ici/National Film Board of Canada/La Sept Arte co-production; Canadian-French, 1997; Dolby; Color; Not rated; 60 minutes; September release. Documentary in which filmmaker Patricio Guzman screens his film *The Battle of Chile* and interviews participants in the 1973 coup which ended Salvador Allende's democratically elected Marxist government.

FIRELIGHT (Hollywood Pictures) Producer, Brian Eastman; Executive Producers, Susan Cartsonis, Rick Leed, Matt Williams, David McFadzean, Carmen Finestra; Director/Screenplay, William Nicholson; Photography, Nic Morris; Music, Christopher Gunning; Editor, Chris Wimble; Designer, Rob Harris; Costumes, Andrea Galer; Associate Producer, Ted Morley; Casting, John & Ros Hubbard; a Wind Dancer/Carnival Films production; British-U.S.; Dolby; Panavision: Metrocolor; Rated R; 103 minutes; September release. **CAST:** Sophie Marceau (Elisabeth), Stephen Dillane (Charles), Kevin Anderson (John Taylor), Lia Wiliams (Constance), Dominique Belcourt (Louisa), Joss Ackland (Lord Clare), Sally Dexter (Molly Holland), Emma Amos (Ellen), Maggie McCarthy (Mrs. Jago), Wolf Kahler (Sussman), Annabel Giles (Amy), John Flanagan (Robert Ames), Thomas Fischer (Davey), Valerie Minifie (Hannah), Diana Payan (Mrs. Madment), John Hodgkinson (Carlo), Anthony Dutton (Dodds), Hugh Walters (Dr. Geddes), Peter Needham (Rector), Melissa Knatchbull (Mrs. Hurst), Frank Rozelaar-Green (Dancemaster), Trevor St. John-Hacker (Fashionable Guest), Katharine Levy (French Maid), Valere Sarruf (French Patronne)

ESMERALDA COMES BY NIGHT (Fine Line) Executive Producers, Fernando do Camara, Salvador de la Fuente; Director/Screenplay, Jaime Humberto Hermosillo; Based on the short story by Elena Poniatowska; Photography, Xavier Perez Grobet; Editors, Jaime Humberto Hermosillo, Sebastian Garza; Music, Omar Guzman; Art Director, Lourdes Almeida; Costumes, Federico Castillo; Produced by Imcine, Resoncia, Monarca and Esmeralda Films; Mexican, 1997; Dolby; Color; Rated R; 106 minutes; September release. **CAST:** Maria Rojo (Esmeralda), Claudio Obregon (Victor Solorio), Martha Navarro (Lucita), Antonio Crestain (Manuel Garcia), Ignacio Retes (Don Gregorio), Humberto Pineda (Jorge Luis), Alberto Estrella (Jaime), Tito Vasconcellos (Jasefo/Josefa), Ernesto Laguardia (Pedro), Pedro Armendariz, Jr. (Antonio), Roberto Cobo (Don Virginio), Alvaro Guerrero (Carlos), Arturo Villasenor (Armando), Ana Ofelia Murguia (Dona Beatriz)

Ines Sastre, Diego Abatantuono
in *The Best Man* © October Films

Alvaro Guerrero, Maria Rojo in *Esmeralda Comes By Night*
© Fine Line Features

Franco Nero, Polly Walker, Vincent Perez in *Talk of Angels*
© Miramax Films

LILIAN'S STORY (Independent) Producer, Marian MacGowan; Executive Producers, David Court, Jeremy Bean; Director, Jerzy Domaradzki; Screenplay, Steve Wright; Based on the book by Kate Grenville; Photography, Slawomir Idziak; Editor, Lee Smith; Music, Cezary Skubiszewski; Designer, Roger Ford; Casting, Christine King; an Australian Film Finance Corp./Movieco Australia presentation of a CML production; Australian, 1996; Dolby; Atlab Color; Not rated; 94 minutes; September release. **CAST:** Ruth Cracknell (Lilian Singer), Barry Otto (John Singer/Albion Singer), Toni Collette (Young Lilian), John Flaus (Frank Stroud), Iris Shand (Aunt Kitty), Susie Lindeman (Jewel), Anne Louise Lambert (Lilian's Mother), Essie Davis (Zara), Morgan Smallbone (Young Frank), Mary Regan (Angelique), Jeff Truman (Riser), Bogdan Koca (Slav Taxi Driver), Bob Maza (Last Taxi Driver), David Argue (Spruiker)

TALK OF ANGELS (Miramax) Producer, Patrick Cassavetti; Executive Producers, Harvey Weinstein, Bob Weinstein, Donna Gigliotti; Director, Nick Hamm; Screenplay, Ann Guedes, Frank McGuinness; Based on the novel *Mary Lavelle* by Kate O'Brien; Photography, Alexei Rodionov; Designer, Michael Howells; Costumes, Liz Waller, Lala Huete; Editor, Gerry Hambling; Casting, Mary Selway, Camilla-Valentine Isola; a Polaris Films Ltd. production; British; Dolby; Color; Rated PG-13; 97 minutes; October release. **CAST:** Polly Walker (Mary Lavelle), Vincent Perez (Francisco Areavaga), Franco Nero (Dr. Vicente Areavaga), Marisa Paredes (Dona Consuelo), Leire Berrocal (Milagros), Penelope Cruz (Pilar), Frances McDormand (Conlon), Ruth McCabe (O'Toole), Francisco Rabal (Don Jorge), Ariadna Gil (Beatriz), Rossy De Palma (Elena), Britta Smith (Duggan), Anita Reeves (Harty), Veronica Duffy (Keogh), Jorge De Juan (Jaime), Ellea Ratier (Leonor)

DESTINY (Les Films du Xxeme) Producers, Humbert Balsan, Gabriel Khoury; Director, Youssef Chahine; Screenplay, Youssef Chahine, Khaled Youssef; Photography, Mohsen Nasr; Editor, Rachida Abdel Salam; Music, Kamal El Tawil, Yohia El Mougy; an Ognon Pictures (Paris)/Misr Intl. Films (Cairo) co-production in association with France 2 Cinema; French-Egyptian, 1997; Dolby; Color; Not rated; 135 minutes; October release. **CAST:** Nour El Cherif (Averroes), Laila Eloui (Gypsy), Hani Salama (Abdallah), Khaled El Nabaoui (Nasser), Mohammed Mounir (Marwan), Safia El Emary (Zeinab), MahmoudHemeida (Caliph), Magdi Idris (Sect Leader)

LA SENTINELLE (Strand) Producers, Pascal Caucheteux, Gregoire Soriat, Nicole Arbib, Veronique Marchand, Lucinda Thuillier; Director/Screenplay, Arnaud Desplechin; Adaptation, Pascale Ferran, Noemie Lvovsky, Emmanuel Salinger; Photography, Caroline Champetier; Art Director, Antoine Platteau; Music, Marc Olivier Sommer; Costumes, Valerie Pozzo Di Borgo; Editor, Francois Gedigier; Casting, Noemie Lvovsky; a Why Not production; French; Color; Not rated; 144 minutes; October release. **CAST:** Emmanuel Salinger (Mathias), Thibault De Montalembert (Jean-Jacques), Jean-Louis Richard (Bleicher), Valerie Dreville (Nathalie), Marianne Denicourt (Marie), Jean-Luc Boutte (Varins), Bruno Todeschini (William), Philippe Duclos (Macaigne), Fabrice Desplechin (Simon), Emmanuelle Devos (Claude), Philippe Laudenbach (The Priest), Laszlo Szabo (Pamiat, the Russian), Alexis Nitzer (Consul), Nadine Alari (Mme. Barillet), Jean-Pierre Ducos

(Customs Officer), Damien Eupherte (Military), Stephane Thiebot (Student), Alain Mac-Moy (Professor Waelhens), Anna Miasedova (Tamara)

CHALK (Tenderloin ActionGroup) Producers, Rand Crook, Ethan Sting; Director, Rob Nilsson; Screenplay, Don Bajema, Rob Nilsson; Photography, Mickey Freeman; Music, Tim Alexander; Editor, David Schickele; Color; Not rated; 134 minutes; October release. **CAST:** Don Bajema (Dorian James), Edwin Johnson (Earl Watson), Denise Concetta Cavaliere, Destiny Costa, Johnnie Reese, John Tidwell, Kelvin Han Yee.

A PLACE CALLED CHIAPAS (Canada Wild) Producers, Nettie Wild, Kirk Tougas, Betsy carson; Director, Nettie Wild; Screenplay, Nettie Wild, Manfred Becker; Photography, Kirk Tougas, Nettie Wild; Editor, Manfred Becker; Music, Joseph Pepe Danza, Salvador Ferreras, Celso Machado, Laurence Mallerup; Spanish; Color; Not rated; 90 minutes; November release. Documentary on Mexico's 1994 Zapatista uprising.

Emmanuel Salinger in *La Sentinelle* © Strand Releasing

Nathalie Boutefeu in *Port Djema* © Shadow Distribution

Hugh Dillon, Callum Keith Rennie in *Hard Core Logo*
© Cowboy Booking Intl.

PORT DJEMA (Shadow Distribution) Producer, Bernard Lorain; Director, Eric Heuman; Screenplay, Eric Heuman, Jacques Lebas, Lam Le; Photography, Yorgos Arvanitis; Set Designers, Danka Semenowicz, Yves Bernard; Editor, Isabelle Dedieu; Casting, Frédérique Moidon; a Paradis Films production; French, 1997; Color; Not rated; 93 minutes; November release. **CAST:** Jean-Yves Dubois (Pierre Feldman), Nathalie Boutefeu (Alice), Christophe Oden (Jérôme Delbos), Edouard Montoute (Ousman), Claire Wauthion (Soeur Marie-Françoise), Frédéric Pierrot (Antoine Barasse)

WELCOME TO WOOP WOOP (Goldwyn) Producer, Finola Dwyer; Executive Producers, Nik Powell, Stephen Woolley; Director, Stephan Elliott; Screenplay, Michael Thomas; Based on the book *The Dead Heart* by Douglas Kennedy; Co-Producer, Antonia Barnard; Photography, Mike Molloy; Designer, Owen Paterson; Costumes, Lizzy Gardiner; Editor, Martin Walsh; Music, Guy Gross; Casting, Greg Apps; a Goldwyn Entertainment Company and the Australian Film Finance Corporation in association with Scala Productions presentation of a Scala/Unthank production; Australian-British, 1997; PLC Widescreen; Dolby; Color; Rated R; 97 minutes; November release. **CAST:** Johnathon Schaech (Teddy), Rod Taylor (Daddy-O), Susie Porter (Angie), Dee Smart (Krystal), Richard Moir (Reggie), Maggie Kirkpatrick (Ginger), Barry Humphries

Johnathon Schaech, Rod Taylor, Susie Porter
in *Welcome to Woop Woop* © MGM Distribution Co.

Blind Wally), Mark Wilson (Duffy), Paul Mercurio (Midget), Stan Yarramunua (Young Lionel), Bob Oxenbould (Moose), Jan Oxenbould (Big Pat), Daniel Rigney (Small Kenny), David Hoey (Dirty Dean), Sarah Osmo (Laverne), Con Demetriou (Darren), Rachel Griffiths (Sylvia), Tina Louise (Bella), Chelsea Brown (Maud), Adryn White (Herbie), Felix Williamson (Jerome), Kevin Copeland (Plato), Shane Paxton (Sonny), Bindi Paxton (Cher), Alan Finney (Barman), Pat Gibbs (Auntie Di), Bella Cooper (Leigh Ann), Cale Morgan (Damien), Baden Jones (Leon), Breanna Sonsie (Tina), Ding (Projectionist), Kurt Murray, Patrick Gooch, Arthur Dunn, Rory Laidlaw, Rosalie Breen, Julie Dunn, Rosalie Nethercott, Cecily Palmer, Sue Hunt, Bob Oakley, Aden Oakley, Rowan Churches, Rouslan Churches, Amber Rose Poduti, Jessica Poduti, Ricki Poduti, Tara Croucher, Christopher Hunt, Bonnie Hunt, Gavin Wakefield, Chris Wakefield, Chad Wakefield, Aaron Godfrey, Lecki Taylor Smith (Woop Woopers), Chookie the Pig (Himself)

HARD CORE LOGO (Rolling Thunder Pictures) Producers, Christine Haebler, Brian Dennis; Executive Producer, James Head; Director, Bruce McDonald; Screenplay, Noel S. Baker; Based on the book by Michael Turner; Photography, Danny Nowak; Designer, David Wilson; Music, Schaun Tozer; Editor, Reginald Harkema; Associate Producer, Karen Powell; a Cowboy Booking Internatonal presentation; Produced with the participation of Telefilm Canadian association with British Columbia Film produced in association with Time Medienvertriebs GMBH and City TV; Canadian, 1996; Dolby; Color; Rated R; 92 minutes; November release. **CAST:** Hugh Dillon (Joe Dick), Callum Keith Rennie (Billy Tallent), Bernie Coulson (Pipefitter), John Pyper-Ferguson (John Oxenberger), Julian Richings (Bucky Haight)

THE MIRROR (Cowboy Booking Intl.) Producers, J. Panahi, V. Nikkhah-Azad; Director/Screenplay/Editor, Jafar Panahi; Photography, F. Jodat; Iranian; Color; Not rated; 93 minutes; November release. **CAST:** Mina Mohammad-Khani, R. Mojdehi, M. Shirzad, N. Omoumi, T. Samadpour.

Mina Mohammad-Khani in *The Mirror* © Cowboy Booking Intl,

DIVORCE IRANIAN STYLE (Women Make Movies) Directors, Kim Longinotto, Ziba Mir-Hosseini; Photography, Zahra Saiedzadeh; Editor, Barrie Vince; Iranian-British; Color; Not rated; 80 minutes; December release. Documentary about the court procedures Iranian women must go through to obtain a divorce.

THE EMPEROR'S SHADOW (Fox Lorber) Producers, Tong Gang, Hu Yuesheng, Cai Huansong; Presenters, Jimmy Tan, Chen Kunming, Zhang Pimin; Executive Producers, Ah Gui, Chen Mila; Director, Zhou Xiaowen; Screenplay, Lu Wei; Photography, Lu Gengxin; Art Directors, Cao Jiuping, Duo Guoxiang, Zhang Daqian; Music, Zhao Jiping; Editor, Zhong Furong; Costumes, Tong Huamiao; an Ocean Film Co. Ltd. & Xi'An Film Studio co-production; Chinese; Color; Not rated; 123 minutes; December release. **CAST:** Jiang Wen (Ying Zheng), Ge You (Gao Jianli), Xu Qing (Ying Yueyang), Ge Zhijun, Wang Qingxiang, Di Guogiang, Wang Ning, Shu Yaoxuan, Li Mengnan, Yuan Yuan

ZAKIR AND HIS FRIENDS (Film Forum/Independent) Producers, Lutz Leonhardt, Prof. Klaus Armbruster; Photography, Felix von Muralt; Editor, Claudia Gleisner; Music, Zakir Hussain, the Boys and Girls of Chua, others; Swiss-German, 1997; Color; Not rated; 90 minutes; December release. Documentary on percussionist Zakir Hussain.

JINNAH (Sladek) Producer, Jamil Dehlavi; Executive Producer, Akbar Ahmed; Co-Executive Producer, Nasim Ashraf; Director, Jamil Dehlavi; Screenplay, Jamil Dehlavi; Photography, Nic Knowland; Editors, Roberto Reitano, Paul Hodgson; Music, Nigle Clarke, Michael Csanyi-Wills; Deisgner, Michael Porter; Costumes, Barbara Rutter; an Akbar Ahmed production; Pakistan-British; Dolby; Technicolor; Not rated; 194 minutes; December release. **CAST:** Christopher Lee (Mohammed Ali Jinnah), James Fox (Lord Richard Mountbatten), Maria Aitken (Edwina Mountbatten), Shashi Kapoor (The Guide), Richard Lintern (Young Jinnah), Shireen Shah (Fatima Jinnah), Robert Ashby (Jawaharlal Nehru), Indira Varma (Ruttie Jinnah), Sam Dastor (Mahatma Gandhi), Shakeel (Liaquat Ali Khan)

Jiang Wen in *The Emperor's Shadow*
© Fox Lorber Associates

THE DAY OF THE BEAST (Trimark) Producer, Teresa Font; Executive Producer, Andres Vicente Gomez; Director, Alex De La Iglesia; Screenplay, Jorge Guerricaechevarria, Alex De La Iglesia, Saturnino Garcia; Photography, Flavio Mtnz. Labiano; Art Directors, Jose Luis Arrizabalaga, Biaffra; Music, B. Lena; Executive in Charge of Production, Carmen Martinez; Spanish; Color; Rated R; 104 minutes; December release. **CAST:** Álex Angulo (Priest), Armando De Razza (Professor Cavan), Santiago Segura (Jose María), Terele Pavez (Rosario), Nathalie Seseña (Mina), Maria Grazia Cucinotta (Susana), Gianni Ippoliti (TV Producer), Saturnino Garcia (Old Priest), Jaime Blanch, David Pinilla, Antonio Dechent, Ignacio Carreño (Toyotas)

Alex Angulo, Nathalie Seseña
in *The Day of the Beast* © Trimark Pictures

Ben Affleck

Suzy Amis

Armand Assante

Rowan Atkinson

Biographical Data

(Name, real name, place and date of birth, school attended)

AAMES, WILLIE (William Upton): Los Angeles, CA, July 15, 1960.
AARON, CAROLINE: Richmond, VA, Aug. 7, 1954. Catholic U.
ABBOTT, DIAHNNE: NYC, 1945.
ABBOTT, JOHN: London, June 5, 1905.
ABRAHAM, F. MURRAY: Pittsburgh, PA, Oct. 24, 1939. UTx.
ACKLAND, JOSS: London, Feb. 29, 1928.
ADAMS, BROOKE: NYC, Feb. 8, 1949. Dalton.
ADAMS, CATLIN: Los Angeles, Oct. 11, 1950.
ADAMS, DON: NYC, Apr. 13, 1926.
ADAMS, EDIE (Elizabeth Edith Enke): Kingston, PA, Apr. 16, 1927. Juilliard, Columbia.
ADAMS, JOEY LAUREN: Little Rock, AR, Jan. 6, 1971.
ADAMS, JULIE (Betty May): Waterloo, IA, Oct. 17, 1926. Little Rock, Jr. College.
ADAMS, MASON: NYC, Feb. 26, 1919. UWi.
ADAMS, MAUD (Maud Wikstrom): Lulea, Sweden, Feb. 12, 1945.
ADJANI, ISABELLE: Germany, June 27, 1955.
AFFLECK, BEN: Berkeley, CA, Aug. 15, 1972.
AGAR, JOHN: Chicago, IL, Jan. 31, 1921.
AGUTTER, JENNY: Taunton, England, Dec. 20, 1952.
AIELLO, DANNY: NYC, June 20, 1933.
AIMEE, ANOUK (Dreyfus): Paris, France, Apr. 27, 1934. Bauer-Therond.
AKERS, KAREN: NYC, Oct. 13, 1945. Hunter College.
ALBERGHETTI, ANNA MARIA: Pesaro, Italy, May 15, 1936.
ALBERT, EDDIE (Eddie Albert Heimberger): Rock Island, IL, Apr. 22, 1908. U of Minn.
ALBERT, EDWARD: Los Angeles, Feb. 20, 1951. UCLA.

ALBRIGHT, LOLA: Akron, OH, July 20, 1925.
ALDA, ALAN: NYC, Jan. 28, 1936. Fordham.
ALEANDRO, NORMA: Buenos Aires, Dec. 6, 1936.
ALEJANDRO, MIGUEL: NYC, Feb. 21, 1958.
ALEXANDER, JANE (Quigley): Boston, MA, Oct. 28, 1939. Sarah Lawrence.
ALEXANDER, JASON (Jay Greenspan): Newark, NJ, Sept. 23, 1959. Boston U.
ALICE, MARY: Indianola, MS, Dec. 3, 1941.
ALLEN, DEBBIE (Deborah): Houston, TX, Jan. 16, 1950. Howard U.
ALLEN, JOAN: Rochelle, IL, Aug. 20, 1956. EastIllU.
ALLEN, KAREN: Carrollton, IL, Oct. 5, 1951. UMd.
ALLEN, NANCY: NYC, June 24, 1950.
ALLEN, REX: Wilcox, AZ, Dec. 31, 1922.
ALLEN, STEVE: NYC, Dec. 26, 1921.
ALLEN, TIM: Denver, CO, June 13, 1953. W. MI. Univ.
ALLEN, WOODY (Allan Stewart Konigsberg): Brooklyn, Dec. 1, 1935.
ALLEY, KIRSTIE: Wichita, KS, Jan. 12, 1955.
ALLYSON, JUNE (Ella Geisman): Westchester, NY, Oct. 7, 1917.
ALONSO, MARIA CONCHITA: Cuba, June 29, 1957.
ALT, CAROL: Queens, NY, Dec. 1, 1960. HofstraU.
ALVARADO, TRINI: NYC, Jan. 10, 1967.
AMIS, SUZY: Oklahoma City, OK, Jan. 5, 1958. Actors Studio.
AMOS, JOHN: Newark, NJ, Dec. 27, 1940. Colo. U.
ANDERSON, GILLIAN: Chicago, IL, Aug. 9, 1968. DePaul U.
ANDERSON, KEVIN: Waukeegan, IL, Jan. 13, 1960.

ANDERSON, LONI: St. Paul, MN, Au[g.] 1946.
ANDERSON, MELISSA SUE: Berkeley, Sept. 26, 1962.
ANDERSON, MELODY: Edmon[ton], Canada, 1955. Carlton U.
ANDERSON, MICHAEL, JR.: Lon[don], England, Aug. 6, 1943.
ANDERSON, RICHARD DEAN: Minn[eap]olis, MN, Jan. 23, 1950.
ANDERSSON, BIBI: Stockholm, Swe[den], Nov. 11, 1935. Royal Dramatic Sch.
ANDES, KEITH: Ocean City, NJ, July 1920. Temple U., Oxford.
ANDRESS, URSULA: Bern, Switzer[land], Mar. 19, 1936.
ANDREWS, ANTHONY: London, Dec[.] 1948.
ANDREWS, JULIE (Julia Elizabeth W[ells]: Surrey, England, Oct. 1, 1935.
ANGLIM, PHILIP: San Francisco, CA, [Feb.] 11, 1953.
ANISTON, JENNIFER: Sherman Oaks, Feb. 11, 1969.
ANN-MARGRET (Olsson): Valsjobyn, [Swe]den, Apr. 28, 1941. Northwestern U.
ANSARA, MICHAEL: Lowell, MA, Ap[r.] 1922. Pasadena Playhouse.
ANSPACH, SUSAN: NYC, Nov. 23, 194[2].
ANTHONY, LYSETTE: London, 1963.
ANTHONY, TONY: Clarksburg, WV, Oc[t.] 1937. Carnegie Tech.
ANTON, SUSAN: Yucaipa, CA, Oct[.] 1950. Bernardino College.
ANTONELLI, LAURA: Pola, Italy, Nov[.] 1941.
ANWAR, GABRIELLE: Laleham[, Eng]land, Feb. 4, 1970
APPLEGATE, CHRISTINA: Holly[wood,] CA, Nov. 25, 1972.
ARCHER, ANNE: Los Angeles, Aug[.] 1947.
ARCHER, JOHN (Ralph Bowman): Osc[eola,] NB, May 8, 1915. USC.

Alec Baldwin

DANT, FANNY: Monte Carlo, Mar 22,

KIN, ADAM: Brooklyn, NY, Aug. 19,

KIN, ALAN: NYC, Mar. 26, 1934. LACC.

MSTRONG, BESS: Baltimore, MD, Dec.
953.

NAZ, DESI, JR.: Los Angeles, Jan. 19,

AZ, LUCIE: Hollywood, July 17, 1951.

NESS, JAMES (Aurness): Minneapolis,
May 26, 1923. Beloit College.

QUETTE, DAVID: Sept. 8, 1971.

QUETTE, PATRICIA: NYC, Apr. 8,

QUETTE, ROSANNA: NYC, Aug. 10,

HUR, BEATRICE (Frankel): NYC, May
924. New School.

ER, JANE: London, Apr. 5, 1946.

LEY, ELIZABETH (Elizabeth Ann
): Ocala, FL, Aug. 30, 1939.

TON, JOHN: Springfield, MA, Feb. 22,
. USC.

ER, EDWARD: Kansas City, KS, Nov.
929.

ANTE, ARMAND: NYC, Oct. 4, 1949.
A.

IN, JOHN: Baltimore, MD, Mar. 30,
. U Minn.

IN, MacKENZIE: Los Angeles, May 12,

IN, SEAN: Santa Monica, Feb. 25, 1971.

Anne Bancroft

ATHERTON, WILLIAM: Orange, CT, July 30, 1947. Carnegie Tech.

ATKINS, CHRISTOPHER: Rye, NY, Feb. 21, 1961.

ATKINS, EILEEN: London, June 16, 1934.

ATKINSON, ROWAN: England, Jan. 6, 1955. Oxford.

ATTENBOROUGH, RICHARD: Cambridge, England, Aug. 29, 1923. RADA.

AUBERJONOIS, RENE: NYC, June 1, 1940. Carnegie Tech.

AUDRAN, STEPHANE: Versailles, France, Nov. 8, 1932.

AUGER, CLAUDINE: Paris, France, Apr. 26, 1942. Dramatic Cons.

AULIN, EWA: Stockholm, Sweden, Feb. 14, 1950.

AUMONT, JEAN PIERRE: Paris, France, Jan. 5, 1909. French Nat'l School of Drama.

AVALON, FRANKIE (Francis Thomas Avallone): Philadelphia, PA, Sept. 18, 1939.

AYKROYD, DAN: Ottawa, Canada, July 1, 1952.

AZNAVOUR, CHARLES (Varenagh Aznourian): Paris, France, May 22, 1924.

AZZARA, CANDICE: Brooklyn, NY, May 18, 1947.

BACH, CATHERINE: Warren, OH, Mar. 1, 1954.

BACALL, LAUREN (Betty Perske): NYC, Sept. 16, 1924. AADA.

BACH, BARBARA: Queens, NY, Aug. 27, 1946.

BACKER, BRIAN: NYC, Dec. 5, 1956. Neighborhood Playhouse.

BACON, KEVIN: Philadelphia, PA, July 8, 1958.

BAIN, BARBARA: Chicago, IL, Sept. 13, 1934. U Ill.

BAIO, SCOTT: Brooklyn, NY, Sept. 22, 1961.

BAKER, BLANCHE: NYC, Dec. 20, 1956.

BAKER, CARROLL: Johnstown, PA, May 28, 1931. St. Petersburg, Jr. College.

BAKER, DIANE: Hollywood, CA, Feb. 25, 1938. USC.

BAKER, JOE DON: Groesbeck, TX, Feb.12, 1936.

BAKER, KATHY: Midland, TX, June 8, 1950. UC Berkley.

BAKULA, SCOTT: St. Louis, MO, Oct. 9, 1955. KansasU.

BALABAN, BOB: Chicago, IL, Aug. 16, 1945. Colgate.

BALDWIN, ADAM: Chicago, IL, Feb. 27, 1962.

BALDWIN, ALEC: Massapequa, NY, Apr. 3, 1958. NYU.

BALDWIN, STEPHEN: Long Island, NY, 1966.

BALDWIN, WILLIAM: Massapequa, NY, Feb. 21, 1963.

BALE, CHRISTIAN: Pembrokeshire, West Wales, Jan. 30, 1974.

BALLARD, KAYE: Cleveland, OH, Nov. 20, 1926.

BANCROFT, ANNE (Anna Maria Italiano): Bronx, NY, Sept. 17, 1931. AADA.

BANDERAS, ANTONIO: Malaga, Spain, Aug. 10, 1960.

BANERJEE, VICTOR: Calcutta, India, Oct. 15, 1946.

BANES, LISA: Chagrin Falls, OH, July 9, 1955. Juilliard.

BANNEN, IAN: Airdrie, Scotland, June 29, 1928.

Antonio Banderas

BARANSKI, CHRISTINE: Buffalo, NY, May 2, 1952. Juilliard.

BARBEAU, ADRIENNE: Sacramento, CA, June 11, 1945. Foothill College.

BARDOT, BRIGITTE: Paris, France, Sept. 28, 1934.

BARKIN, ELLEN: Bronx, NY, Apr. 16, 1954. Hunter College.

BARNES, CHRISTOPHER DANIEL: Portland, ME, Nov. 7, 1972.

BARR, JEAN-MARC: San Diego, CA, Sept. 1960.

BARRAULT, JEAN-LOUIS: Vesinet, France, Sept. 8, 1910.

BARRAULT, MARIE-CHRISTINE: Paris, France, Mar. 21, 1944.

BARREN, KEITH: Mexborough, England, Aug. 8, 1936. Sheffield Playhouse.

BARRETT, MAJEL (Hudec): Columbus, OH, Feb. 23. Western Reserve U.

BARRIE, BARBARA: Chicago, IL, May 23, 1931.

BARRY, GENE (Eugene Klass): NYC, June 14, 1919.

BARRY, NEILL: NYC, Nov. 29, 1965.

BARRYMORE, DREW: Los Angeles, Feb. 22, 1975.

BARRYMORE, JOHN DREW: Beverly Hills, CA, June 4, 1932. St. John's Military Academy.

BARTEL, PAUL: Brooklyn, NY, Aug. 6, 1938. UCLA.

Drew Barrymore

BARTY, BILLY: (William John Bertanzetti) Millsboro, PA, Oct. 25, 1924.

BARYSHNIKOV, MIKHAIL: Riga, Latvia, Jan. 27, 1948.

BASINGER, KIM: Athens, GA, Dec. 8, 1953. Neighborhood Playhouse.

BASSETT, ANGELA: NYC, Aug. 16, 1958.

BATEMAN, JASON: Rye, NY, Jan. 14, 1969.

BATEMAN, JUSTINE: Rye, NY, Feb. 19, 1966.

BATES, ALAN: Allestree, Derbyshire, England, Feb. 17, 1934. RADA.

BATES, JEANNE: San Francisco, CA, May 21, 1918. RADA.

BATES, KATHY: Memphis, TN, June 28, 1948. S. Methodist U.

BAUER, STEVEN (Steven Rocky Echevarria): Havana, Cuba, Dec. 2, 1956. U Miami.

BAXTER, KEITH: South Wales, England, Apr. 29, 1933. RADA.

BAXTER, MEREDITH: Los Angeles, June 21, 1947. Intelochen Acad.

BAYE, NATHALIE: Maineville, France, July 6, 1948

BEACHAM, STEPHANIE: Casablanca, Morocco, Feb. 28, 1947.

BEALS, JENNIFER: Chicago, IL, Dec. 19, 1963.

BEAN, ORSON (Dallas Burrows): Burlington, VT, July 22, 1928.

BEAN, SEAN: Sheffield, Yorkshire, England, Apr. 17, 1958.

BEART, EMMANUELLE: Gassin, France, Aug. 14, 1965.

BEATTY, NED: Louisville, KY, July 6, 1937.

BEATTY, WARREN: Richmond, VA, Mar. 30, 1937.

BECK, JOHN: Chicago, IL, Jan. 28, 1943.

BECK, MICHAEL: Memphis, TN, Feb. 4, 1949. Millsap College.

BECKINSALE, KATE: England, July 26, 1974.

BEDELIA, BONNIE: NYC, Mar. 25, 1946. Hunter College.

BEGLEY, ED, JR.: NYC, Sept. 16, 1949.

BELAFONTE, HARRY: NYC, Mar. 1, 1927.

BEL GEDDES, BARBARA: NYC, Oct. 31, 1922.

BELL, TOM: Liverpool, England, 1932.

BELLER, KATHLEEN: NYC, Feb. 10, 1957.

BELLWOOD, PAMELA (King): Scarsdale, NY, June 26, 1951.

BELMONDO, JEAN PAUL: Paris, France, Apr. 9, 1933.

BELUSHI, JAMES: Chicago, IL, June 15, 1954.

BELZER, RICHARD: Bridgeport, CT, Aug. 4, 1944.

BENEDICT, DIRK (Niewoehner): White Sulphur Springs, MT, March 1, 1945. Whitman College.

BENEDICT, PAUL: Silver City, NM, Sept. 17, 1938.

BENIGNI, ROBERTO: Tuscany, Italy, Oct. 27, 1952.

BENING, ANNETTE: Topeka, KS, May 29, 1958. SFSt. U.

BENJAMIN, RICHARD: NYC, May 22, 1938. Northwestern U.

BENNENT, DAVID: Lausanne, Sept. 9, 1966.

BENNETT, ALAN: Leeds, England, May 9, 1934. Oxford.

Alan Bates

Jennifer Beals

James Belushi

BENNETT, BRUCE (Herman Brix): Taco WA, May 19, 1909. U Wash.

BENNETT, HYWEL: Garnant, So. W. Apr. 8, 1944.

BENSON, ROBBY: Dallas, TX, Jan. 1957.

BERENGER, TOM: Chicago, IL, May 1950, U Mo.

BERENSON, MARISA: NYC, Feb. 15, 1

BERG, PETER: NYC, 1964. Malcal College.

BERGEN, CANDICE: Los Angeles, Ma 1946. U PA.

BERGEN, POLLY: Knoxville, TN, July 1930. Compton, Jr. College.

BERGER, HELMUT: Salzburg, Austria, 29, 1942.

BERGER, SENTA: Vienna, Austria, May 1941. Vienna Sch. of Acting.

BERGER, WILLIAM: Austria, Jan. 20, 1 Columbia.

BERGERAC, JACQUES: Biarritz, Fra May 26, 1927. Paris U.

BERGIN, PATRICK: Dublin, Feb. 4, 19

BERKLEY, ELIZABETH: Detroit, MI, 28, 1972.

BERKOFF, STEVEN: London, Engl Aug. 3, 1937.

BERLE, MILTON (Berlinger): NYC, July 1908.

BERLIN, JEANNIE: Los Angeles, No 1949.

BERLINGER, WARREN: Brooklyn, 31, 1937. Columbia.

BERNHARD, SANDRA: Flint, MI, Jur 1955.

BERNSEN, CORBIN: Los Angeles, Sep 1954. UCLA.

BERRI, CLAUDE (Langmann): P France, July 1, 1934.

BERRIDGE, ELIZABETH: Westche NY, May 2, 1962. Strasberg Inst.

BERRY, HALLE: Cleveland, OH, Aug 1968.

BERRY, KEN: Moline, IL, Nov. 3, 1933

BERTINELLI, VALERIE: Wilmington, Apr. 23, 1960.

BEST, JAMES: Corydon, IN, July 26, 19

BETTGER, LYLE: Philadelphia, PA, Fel 1915. AADA.

BEY, TURHAN: Vienna, Austria, Mar 1921.

BEYMER, RICHARD: Avoca, IA, Feb 1939.

BIALIK, MAYIM: San Diego, CA, Dec 1975.

BIEHN, MICHAEL: Anniston, AL, Jul 1956.

BIKEL, THEODORE: Vienna, May 2, RADA.

BILLINGSLEY, PETER: NYC, Apr 1972.

BINOCHE, JULIETTE: Paris, France, 9, 1964.

BIRCH, THORA: Los Angeles, Mar 1982.

BIRKIN, JANE: London, Dec. 14, 1947

BIRNEY, DAVID: Washington, DC, Ap 1939. Dartmouth, UCLA.

BIRNEY, REED: Alexandria, VA, Sep 1954. Boston U.

BISHOP, JOEY (Joseph Abraham Goth Bronx, NY, Feb. 3, 1918.

BISHOP, JULIE (Jacqueline Wells): De CO, Aug. 30, 1917. Westlake School.

Tom Berenger

Halle Berry

Powers Boothe

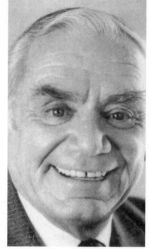
Ernest Borgnine

SET, JACQUELINE: Waybridge, Eng-, Sept. 13, 1944.

CK, KAREN (Ziegler): Park Ridge, IL, 1, 1942. Northwestern.

CKMAN, HONOR: London, Aug. 22,

DES, RUBEN: Panama City, July 16, . Harvard.

IR, BETSY (Betsy Boger): NYC, Dec. 923.

IR, JANET (Martha Jane Lafferty): Blair, Apr. 23, 1921.

IR, LINDA: Westport, CT, Jan. 22, 1959. y, NJ, Sept. 18, 1933.

KELY, SUSAN: Frankfurt, Germany, 7, 1950. U TX.

KLEY, RONEE: Stanley, ID, 1946. ord U.

NCHETT, CATE: Melbourne, Australia, 14, 1969.

THYN, BRENDA: Ramsgate, Kent, , Feb. 20, 1946.

OM, CLAIRE: London, Feb. 15, 1931. ninton School.

OM, VERNA: Lynn, MA, Aug. 7, 1939. on U.

UNT, LISA: Fayettville, AK, July 1, . UAk.

M, MARK: Newark, NJ, May 14, 1950. nn.

TH, ANN: Mt. Kisco, NY, Aug. 16, 1928. Waybum Dramatic School.

HNER, HART: Toronto, Canada, Oct. 3, , U San Diego.

HNER, LLOYD: Toronto, Canada, July 924.

ARDE, DIRK: London, Mar. 28, 1921. ow & Univ. College.

OSIAN, ERIC: Woburn, MA, Apr. 24, . Oberlin College.

RINGER, RICHARD: Paris, France, 6, 1941.

KAN, FLORINDA (Florinda Soares o): Ceara, Brazil, Feb. 15, 1941.

OGNA, JOSEPH: Brooklyn, NY, Dec. 938. Brown U.

D, DEREK: Glasgow, Scotland, Jan. 26, . Askes School.

BONET, LISA: San Francisco, CA, Nov. 16, 1967.

BONHAM-CARTER, HELENA: London, England, May 26, 1966.

BOONE, PAT: Jacksonville, FL, June 1, 1934. Columbia U.

BOOTHE, JAMES: Croydon, England, Dec.19, 1930.

BOOTHE, POWERS: Snyder, TX, June 1, 1949. So. Methodist U.

BORGNINE, ERNEST (Borgnino): Hamden, CT, Jan. 24, 1917. Randall School.

BOSCO, PHILIP: Jersey City, NJ, Sept. 26, 1930. CatholicU.

BOSLEY, TOM: Chicago, IL, Oct. 1, 1927. DePaul U.

BOSTWICK, BARRY: San Mateo, CA, Feb. 24, 1945. NYU.

BOTTOMS, JOSEPH: Santa Barbara, CA, Aug. 30, 1954.

BOTTOMS, SAM: Santa Barbara, CA, Oct. 17, 1955.

BOTTOMS, TIMOTHY: Santa Barbara, CA, Aug. 30, 1951.

BOULTING, INGRID: Transvaal, So. Africa, 1947.

BOUTSIKARIS, DENNIS: Newark, NJ, Dec. 21, 1952. CatholicU.

BOWIE, DAVID (David Robert Jones): Brixton, South London, England, Jan. 8, 1947.

BOWKER, JUDI: Shawford, England, Apr. 6, 1954.

BOXLEITNER, BRUCE: Elgin, IL, May 12, 1950.

BOYLE, LARA FLYNN: Davenport, IA, Mar. 24, 1970.

BOYLE, PETER: Philadelphia, PA, Oct. 18, 1933. LaSalle College.

BRACCO, LORRAINE: Brooklyn, NY, 1955.

BRACKEN, EDDIE: NYC, Feb. 7, 1920. Professional Children's School.

BRAEDEN, ERIC (Hans Gudegast): Kiel, Germany, Apr. 3, 1942.

BRAGA, SONIA: Maringa, Brazil, June 8, 1950.

BRANAGH, KENNETH: Belfast, No. Ireland, Dec. 10, 1960.

BRANDAUER, KLAUS MARIA: Altaussee, Austria, June 22, 1944.

BRANDIS, JONATHAN: CT, Apr. 13, 1976.

BRANDO, JOCELYN: San Francisco, Nov. 18, 1919. Lake Forest College, AADA.

BRANDO, MARLON: Omaha, NB, Apr. 3, 1924. New School.

BRANDON, CLARK: NYC, Dec. 13, 1958.

BRANDON, MICHAEL (Feldman): Brooklyn, NY.

BRANTLEY, BETSY: Rutherfordton, NC, Sept. 20, 1955. London Central Sch. of Drama.

BRENNAN, EILEEN: Los Angeles, CA, Sept. 3, 1935. AADA.

BRIALY, JEAN-CLAUDE: Aumale, Algeria, 1933. Strasbourg Cons.

BRIDGES, BEAU: Los Angeles, Dec. 9, 1941. UCLA.

BRIDGES, JEFF: Los Angeles, Dec. 4, 1949.

BRIMLEY, WILFORD: Salt Lake City, UT, Sept. 27, 1934.

BRINKLEY, CHRISTIE: Malibu, CA, Feb. 2, 1954.

BRITT, MAY (Maybritt Wilkins): Sweden, Mar. 22, 1936.

BRITTANY, MORGAN (Suzanne Cupito): Los Angeles, Dec. 5, 1950.

BRITTON, TONY: Birmingham, England, June 9, 1924.

BRODERICK, MATTHEW: NYC, Mar. 21, 1962.

BROLIN, JAMES: Los Angeles, July 18, 1940. UCLA.

BROLIN, JOSH: Los Angeles, Feb. 12, 1968.

BROMFIELD, JOHN (Farron Bromfield): South Bend, IN, June 11, 1922. St. Mary's College.

BRON, ELEANOR: Stanmore, England, 1934.

BRONSON, CHARLES (Buchinsky): Ehrenfield, PA, Nov. 3, 1920.

BROOKES, JACQUELINE: Montclair, NJ, July 24, 1930. RADA.

BROOKS, ALBERT (Einstein): Los Angeles, July 22, 1947.

BROOKS, MEL (Melvyn Kaminski): Brooklyn, NY, June 28, 1926.

BROSNAN, PIERCE: County Meath, Ireland. May 16, 1952.

Lara Flynn Boyle

Beau Bridges

Jeff Bridges

Matthew Broderick

BROWN, BLAIR: Washington, DC, Apr. 23, 1947. Pine Manor.

BROWN, BRYAN: Panania, Australia, June 23, 1947.

BROWN, GARY (Christian Brando): Hollywood, CA, 1958.

BROWN, GEORG STANFORD: Havana, Cuba, June 24, 1943. AMDA.

BROWN, JAMES: Desdemona, TX, Mar. 22, 1920. Baylor U.

BROWN, JIM: St. Simons Island, NY, Feb. 17, 1935. Syracuse U.

BROWNE, LESLIE: NYC, 1958.

BROWNE, ROSCOE LEE: Woodbury, NJ, May 2, 1925.

BUCHHOLZ, HORST: Berlin, Germany, Dec. 4, 1933. Ludwig Dramatic School.

BUCKLEY, BETTY: Big Spring, TX, July 3, 1947. TxCU.

BUJOLD, GENEVIEVE: Montreal, Canada, July 1, 1942.

BULLOCK, SANDRA: Arlington, VA, July 26, 1964.

BURGHOFF, GARY: Bristol, CT, May 24, 1943.

BURGI, RICHARD: Montclair, NJ, July 30, 1958.

BURKE, PAUL: New Orleans, July 21, 1926. Pasadena Playhouse.

BURNETT, CAROL: San Antonio, TX, Apr. 26, 1933. UCLA.

BURNS, CATHERINE: NYC, Sept. 25, 1945. AADA.

BURNS, EDWARD: Valley Stream, NY, Jan. 28, 1969.

BURROWS, DARREN E.: Winfield, KS, Sept. 12, 1966

BURSTYN, ELLEN (Edna Rae Gillhooly): Detroit, MI, Dec. 7, 1932.

BURTON, LeVAR: Los Angeles, CA, Feb. 16, 1958. UCLA.

BUSCEMI, STEVE: Brooklyn, NY, Dec. 13, 1957.

BUSEY, GARY: Goose Creek, TX, June 29, 1944.

BUSFIELD, TIMOTHY: Lansing, MI, June 12, 1957. E. Tenn. St. U.

BUTTONS, RED (Aaron Chwatt): NYC, Feb. 5, 1919.

BUZZI, RUTH: Westerly, RI, July 24, 1936. Pasadena Playhouse.

BYGRAVES, MAX: London, Oct. 16, 1922. St. Joseph's School.

BYRNE, DAVID: Dumbarton, Scotland, May 14, 1952.

BYRNE, GABRIEL: Dublin, Ireland, May 12, 1950.

BYRNES, EDD: NYC, July 30, 1933.

CAAN, JAMES: Bronx, NY, Mar. 26,1939.

CAESAR, SID: Yonkers, NY, Sept. 8, 1922.

CAGE, NICOLAS (Coppola): Long Beach, CA, Jan.7, 1964.

CAINE, MICHAEL (Maurice Micklewhite): London, Mar. 14, 1933.

CAINE, SHAKIRA (Baksh): Guyana, Feb. 23, 1947. Indian Trust College.

CALHOUN, RORY (Francis Timothy Durgin): Los Angeles, Aug. 8, 1922.

CALLAN, MICHAEL (Martin Calinieff): Philadelphia, Nov. 22, 1935.

CALLOW, SIMON: London, June 15, 1949. Queens U.

CALVERT, PHYLLIS: London, Feb. 18, 1917. Margaret Morris School.

CALVET, CORRINE (Corinne Dibos): Paris, France, Apr. 30, 1925. U Paris.

CAMERON, KIRK: Panorama City, CA, Oct. 12, 1970.

CAMP, COLLEEN: San Francisco, CA, 1953.

CAMPBELL, BILL: Chicago, IL, July 7, 1959.

CAMPBELL, GLEN: Delight, AR, Apr. 22, 1935.

CAMPBELL, NEVE: Guelph, Ontario, Canada, Oct. 3, 1973.

CAMPBELL, TISHA: Oklahoma City, OK, Oct. 13, 1968.

CANALE, GIANNA MARIA: Reggio Calabria, Italy, Sept. 12, 1927.

CANNON, DYAN (Samille Diane Friesen): Tacoma, WA, Jan. 4, 1937.

CAPERS, VIRGINIA: Sumter, SC, Sept. 25, 1925. Juilliard.

CAPSHAW, KATE: Ft. Worth, TX, Nov. 3, 1953. UMo.

CARA, IRENE: NYC, Mar. 18, 1958.

CARDINALE, CLAUDIA: Tunis, N. Af Apr. 15, 1939. College Paul Cambon.

CAREY, HARRY, JR.: Saugus, CA, May 1921. Black Fox Military Academy.

CAREY, PHILIP: Hackensack, NJ, July 1925. U Miami.

CARIOU, LEN: Winnipeg, Canada, Sept 1939.

CARLIN, GEORGE: NYC, May 12, 193

CARLYLE, ROBERT: Glasgow, Scotl Apr. 14, 1961.

CARMEN, JULIE: Mt. Vernon, NY, Ap 1954.

CARMICHAEL, IAN: Hull, England, 18, 1920. Scarborough College.

CARNE, JUDY (Joyce Botterill): Northa ton, England, 1939. Bush-Davis The School.

CARNEY, ART: Mt. Vernon, NY, No 1918.

CARON, LESLIE: Paris, France, Jul 1931. Nat'l Conservatory, Paris.

CARPENTER, CARLETON: Benning VT, July 10, 1926. Northwestern.

CARRADINE, DAVID: Hollywood, De 1936. San Francisco State.

CARRADINE, KEITH: San Mateo, Aug. 8, 1950. Colo. State U.

CARRADINE, ROBERT: San Mateo, Mar. 24, 1954.

CARREL, DANY: Tourane, Indochina, 20, 1936. Marseilles Cons.

CARRERA, BARBARA: Managua, Ni gua, Dec. 31, 1945.

CARRERE, TIA (Althea Janairo): Hono HI, Jan. 2, 1965.

CARREY, JIM: Jacksons Point, Ont Canada, Jan. 17, 1962.

CARRIERE, MATHIEU: Hannover, Germany, Aug. 2, 1950.

CARROLL, DIAHANN (Johnson): N July 17, 1935. NYU.

CARROLL, PAT: Shreveport, LA, Ma 1927. Catholic U.

CARSON, JOHN DAVID: California, M 1952. Valley College.

CARSON, JOHNNY: Corning, IA, Oct 1925. U of Neb.

Pierce Brosnan

Genevieve Bujold

Sandra Bullock

CARSTEN, PETER (Ransenthaler): Weissenberg, Bavaria, Apr. 30, 1929. Munich Akademie.

CARTER, NELL: Birmingham, AL, Sept. 13, 1948.

CARTLIDGE, KATRIN: London, 1961.

CARTWRIGHT, VERONICA: Bristol, England, Apr 20, 1949.

CARUSO, DAVID: Forest Hills, NY, Jan. 7, 1956.

CARVEY, DANA: Missoula, MT, Apr. 2, 1955. SFST.Col.

CASELLA, MAX: Washington D.C, June 6, 1967

CASEY, BERNIE: Wyco, WV, June 8, 1939.

CASS, PEGGY (Mary Margaret Cass): Boston, MA, May 21, 1924.

CASSAVETES, NICK: NYC, 1959, Syracuse U, AADA.

CASSEL, JEAN-PIERRE: Paris, France, Oct. 27, 1932.

CASSEL, SEYMOUR: Detroit, MI, Jan. 22, 1935.

CASSIDY, DAVID: NYC, Apr. 12, 1950.

CASSIDY, JOANNA: Camden, NJ, Aug. 2, 1944. Syracuse U.

CASSIDY, PATRICK: Los Angeles, CA, Jan. 4, 1961.

CATES, PHOEBE: NYC, July 16, 1962.

CATTRALL, KIM: Liverpool, England, Aug. 21, 1956. AADA.

CAULFIELD, MAXWELL: Glasgow, Scotland, Nov. 23, 1959.

CAVANI, LILIANA: Bologna, Italy, Jan. 12, 1937. U Bologna.

CAVETT, DICK: Gibbon, NE, Nov. 19, 1936.

CHAKIRIS, GEORGE: Norwood, OH, Sept. 16, 1933.

CHAMBERLAIN, RICHARD: Beverly Hills, CA, March 31, 1935. Pomona.

CHAMPION, MARGE (Marjorie Belcher): Los Angeles, Sept. 2, 1923.

CHAN, JACKIE: Hong Kong, Apr. 7, 1954

CHANNING, CAROL: Seattle, WA, Jan. 31, 1921. Bennington.

CHANNING, STOCKARD (Susan Stockard): NYC, Feb. 13, 1944. Radcliffe.

CHAPIN, MILES: NYC, Dec. 6, 1954. HB Studio.

CHAPLIN, GERALDINE: Santa Monica, CA, July 31, 1944. Royal Ballet.

CHAPLIN, SYDNEY: Los Angeles, Mar. 31, 1926. Lawrenceville.

CHARISSE, CYD (Tula Ellice Finklea): Amarillo, TX, Mar. 3, 1922. Hollywood Professional School.

CHARLES, JOSH: Baltimore, MD, Sept. 15, 1971.

CHARLES, WALTER: East Strousburg, PA, Apr. 4, 1945. Boston U.

CHASE, CHEVY (Cornelius Crane Chase): NYC, Oct. 8, 1943.

CHAVES, RICHARD: Jacksonville, FL, Oct. 9, 1951. Occidental College.

CHAYKIN, MAURY: Canada, July 27, 1954

CHEN, JOAN (Chen Chung): Shanghai, Apr. 26, 1961. CalState.

CHER (Cherilyn Sarkisian): El Centro, CA, May 20, 1946.

CHILES, LOIS: Alice, TX, Apr. 15, 1947.

CHONG, RAE DAWN: Vancouver, Canada, Feb. 28, 1962.

CHONG, THOMAS: Edmonton, Alberta, Canada, May 24, 1938.

CHRISTIAN, LINDA (Blanca Rosa Welter): Tampico, Mexico, Nov. 13, 1923.

CHRISTIE, JULIE: Chukua, Assam, India, Apr. 14, 1941.

CHRISTOPHER, DENNIS (Carrelli): Philadelphia, PA, Dec. 2, 1955. Temple U.

CHRISTOPHER, JORDAN: Youngstown, OH, Oct. 23, 1940. Kent State.

CILENTO, DIANE: Queensland, Australia, Oct. 5, 1933. AADA.

CLAPTON, ERIC: London, Mar. 30, 1945.

CLARK, CANDY: Norman, OK, June 20, 1947.

CLARK, DICK: Mt. Vernon, NY, Nov. 30, 1929. Syracuse U.

CLARK, MATT: Washington, DC, Nov. 25, 1936.

CLARK, PETULA: Epsom, England, Nov. 15, 1932.

CLARK, SUSAN: Sarnid, Ont., Canada, Mar. 8, 1943. RADA.

CLAY, ANDREW DICE (Andrew Silverstein): Brooklyn, NY, Sept. 29, 1957, Kingsborough College.

CLAYBURGH, JILL: NYC, Apr. 30, 1944. Sarah Lawrence.

CLEESE, JOHN: Weston-Super-Mare, England, Oct. 27, 1939, Cambridge.

CLOONEY, ROSEMARY: Maysville, KY, May 23, 1928.

CLOSE, GLENN: Greenwich, CT, Mar. 19, 1947. William & Mary College.

COBURN, JAMES: Laurel, NB, Aug. 31, 1928. LACC.

COCA, IMOGENE: Philadelphia, Nov. 18, 1908.

CODY, KATHLEEN: Bronx, NY, Oct. 30, 1953.

COFFEY, SCOTT: HI, May 1, 1967.

COLE, GEORGE: London, Apr. 22, 1925.

COLEMAN, GARY: Zion, IL, Feb. 8, 1968.

COLEMAN, DABNEY: Austin, TX, Jan. 3, 1932.

COLEMAN, JACK: Easton, PA, Feb. 21, 1958. Duke U.

COLIN, MARGARET: NYC, May 26, 1957.

COLLET, CHRISTOPHER: NYC, Mar. 13, 1968. Strasberg Inst.

COLLETTE, TONI: Sydney, Australia, Nov. 1, 1972.

COLLINS, JOAN: London, May 21, 1933. Francis Holland School.

COLLINS, PAULINE: Devon, England, Sept. 3, 1940.

COLLINS, STEPHEN: Des Moines, IA, Oct. 1, 1947. Amherst.

COLON, MIRIAM: Ponce, PR., 1945. UPR.

COLTRANE, ROBBIE: Ruthergien, Scotland, Mar. 30, 1950.

COMER, ANJANETTE: Dawson, TX, Aug. 7, 1942. Baylor, Tex. U.

CONANT, OLIVER: NYC, Nov. 15, 1955. Dalton.

CONAWAY, JEFF: NYC, Oct. 5, 1950. NYU.

CONNELLY, JENNIFER: NYC, Dec. 12, 1970

CONNERY, SEAN: Edinburgh, Scotland, Aug. 25, 1930.

CONNERY, JASON: London, Jan. 11, 1963.

CONNICK, HARRY, JR.: New Orleans, LA, Sept. 11, 1967.

CONNOLLY, BILLY: Glasgow, Scotland, Nov. 24, 1942.

CONNORS, MIKE (Krekor Ohanian): Fresno, CA, Aug. 15, 1925. UCLA.

Steve Buscemi

Kate Capshaw

Robert Carlyle

Katrin Cartlidge

CONRAD, ROBERT (Conrad Robert Falk): Chicago, IL, Mar. 1, 1935. Northwestern U.
CONSTANTINE, MICHAEL: Reading, PA, May 22, 1927.
CONTI, TOM: Paisley, Scotland, Nov. 22, 1941.
CONVERSE, FRANK: St. Louis, MO, May 22, 1938. Carnegie Tech.
CONWAY, GARY: Boston, Feb. 4, 1936.
CONWAY, KEVIN: NYC, May 29, 1942.
CONWAY, TIM (Thomas Daniel): Willoughby, OH, Dec. 15, 1933. Bowling Green State.
COOGAN, KEITH (Keith Mitchell Franklin): Palm Springs, CA, Jan. 13, 1970.
COOK, RACHEL LEIGH: Minneapolis, MN, Oct. 4, 1979.
COOPER, BEN: Hartford, CT, Sept. 30, 1930. Columbia U.
COOPER, CHRIS: Kansas City, MO, July 9, 1951. UMo.
COOPER, JACKIE: Los Angeles, Sept. 15, 1921.
COPELAND, JOAN: NYC, June 1, 1922. Brooklyn College, RADA.
CORBETT, GRETCHEN: Portland, OR, Aug. 13, 1947. Carnegie Tech.
CORBIN, BARRY: Dawson County, TX, Oct. 16, 1940. Texas Tech. U.
CORBY, ELLEN (Hansen): Racine, WI, June 13, 1913.
CORCORAN, DONNA: Quincy, MA, Sept. 29, 1942.
CORD, ALEX (Viespi): Floral Park, NY, Aug. 3, 1931. NYU, Actors Studio.
CORDAY, MARA (Marilyn Watts): Santa Monica, CA, Jan. 3, 1932.
COREY, JEFF: NYC, Aug. 10, 1914. Fagin School.
CORNTHWAITE, ROBERT: St. Helens, OR, Apr. 28, 1917. USC.
CORRI, ADRIENNE: Glasgow, Scot., Nov. 13, 1933. RADA.
CORT, BUD (Walter Edward Cox): New Rochelle, NY, Mar. 29, 1950. NYU.
CORTESA, VALENTINA: Milan, Italy, Jan. 1, 1924.

COSBY, BILL: Philadelphia, PA, July 12, 1937. Temple U.
COSTER, NICOLAS: London, Dec. 3, 1934. Neighborhood Playhouse.
COSTNER, KEVIN: Lynwood, CA, Jan. 18, 1955. CalStaU.
COURTENAY, TOM: Hull, England, Feb. 25, 1937. RADA.
COURTLAND, JEROME: Knoxville, TN, Dec. 27, 1926.
COX, BRIAN: Dundee, Scotland, June 1, 1946. LAMDA.
COX, COURTENEY: Birmingham, AL, June 15, 1964.
COX, RONNY: Cloudcroft, NM, Aug. 23, 1938.
COYOTE, PETER (Cohon): NYC, Oct. 10, 1941.
CRAIG, MICHAEL: Poona, India, Jan. 27, 1929.
CRAIN, JEANNE: Barstow, CA, May 25, 1925.
CRAVEN, GEMMA: Dublin, Ireland, June 1, 1950.
CRAWFORD, MICHAEL (Dumbel-Smith): Salisbury, England, Jan. 19, 1942.
CREMER, BRUNO: Paris, France, 1929.
CRENNA, RICHARD: Los Angeles, Nov. 30, 1926. USC.
CRISTAL, LINDA (Victoria Moya): Buenos Aires, Feb. 25, 1934.
CROMWELL, JAMES: Los Angeles, CA, Jan. 27, 1940.
CRONYN, HUME (Blake): Ontario, Canada, July 18, 1911.
CROSBY, DENISE: Hollywood, CA, Nov. 24, 1957.
CROSBY, HARRY: Los Angeles, CA, Aug. 8, 1958.
CROSBY, MARY FRANCES: Los Angeles, CA, Sept. 14, 1959.
CROSS, BEN: London, Dec. 16, 1947. RADA.
CROSS, MURPHY (Mary Jane): Laurelton, MD, June 22, 1950.
CROUSE, LINDSAY: NYC, May 12, 1948. Radcliffe.

CROWE, RUSSELL: New Zealand, A[p] 1964.
CROWLEY, PAT: Olyphant, PA, Sept 1932.
CRUDUP, BILLY: Manhasset, NY, Ju[ne] 1968. UNC/Chapel Hill.
CRUISE, TOM (T. C. Mapother, IV): Ju[ly] 1962, Syracuse, NY.
CRYER, JON: NYC, Apr. 16, 1965, RA[DA]
CRYSTAL, BILLY: Long Beach, NY, [Mar.] 14, 1947. Marshall U.
CULKIN, KIERAN: NYC, Sept. 30, 198[?]
CULKIN, MACAULAY: NYC, Aug [26,] 1980.
CULLUM, JOHN: Knoxville, TN, M[ar.] 1930. U Tenn.
CULLUM, JOHN DAVID: NYC, M[ar.] 1966.
CULP, ROBERT: Oakland, CA, Aug [16,] 1930. U Wash.
CUMMING, ALAN: Perthshire, Sco[t.] 1964.
CUMMINGS, CONSTANCE: Seattle, [WA,] May 15, 1910.
CUMMINGS, QUINN: Hollywood, Aug [?,] 1967.
CUMMINS, PEGGY: Prestatyn, N. W[ales,] Dec. 18, 1926. Alexandra School.
CURRY, TIM: Cheshire, England, Ap[r.] 1946. Birmingham U.
CURTIN, JANE: Cambridge, MA, Se[pt.] 1947.
CURTIS, JAMIE LEE: Los Angeles, Nov. 22, 1958.
CURTIS, KEENE: Salt Lake City, UT, [Feb.] 15, 1925. U Utah.
CURTIS, TONY (Bernard Schwartz): [NYC,] June 3, 1924.
CUSACK, JOAN: Evanston, IL, Oc[t.] 1962.
CUSACK, JOHN: Chicago, IL, June [?,] 1966.
CUSACK, SINEAD: Dalkey, Ireland, Fe[b.?,] 1948
DAFOE, WILLEM: Appleton, WI, Ju[ly] 1955.

Julie Christie   George Clooney   Glenn Close   Pauline Collins

HL, ARLENE: Minneapolis, Aug. 11, 28. U Minn.

LE, JIM: Rothwell, England, Aug. 15, 35.

LLESANDRO, JOE: Pensacola, FL, Dec. 1948.

LTON, TIMOTHY: Colwyn Bay, Wales, r. 21, 1946. RADA.

LTREY, ROGER: London, Mar. 1, 1944.

LY, TIM: NYC, Mar. 1, 1956. Bennington llege.

LY, TYNE: Madison, WI, Feb. 21, 1947. 1DA.

MON, MATT: Cambridge, MA, Oct. 8, 70.

MONE, VIC (Vito Farinola): Brooklyn, , June 12, 1928.

NCE, CHARLES: Plymouth, England, t. 10, 1946.

NES, CLAIRE: New York, NY, Apr. 12, 79.

ANGELO, BEVERLY: Columbus, OH, v. 15, 1953.

NGERFIELD, RODNEY (Jacob Cohen): bylon, NY, Nov. 22, 1921.

NIELS, JEFF: Athens, GA, Feb. 19, 1955. lichSt.

NIELS, WILLIAM: Brooklyn, NY, Mar. 1927. Northwestern.

NNER, BLYTHE: Philadelphia, PA, Feb. 1944. Bard College.

NNING, SYBIL (Sybille Johanna nninger): Vienna, Austria, May 4, 1949.

NSON, TED: San Diego, CA, Dec. 29, 47. Stanford, Carnegie Tech.

NTE, MICHAEL (Ralph Vitti): Stamford, , 1935. U Miami.

NZA, TONY: Brooklyn, NY, Apr. 21, 51. UDubuque.

ARBANVILLE-QUINN, PATTI: NYC, 51.

ARBY, KIM (Deborah Zerby): North llywood, CA, July 8, 1948.

RCEL, DENISE (Denise Billecard): Paris, nce, Sept. 8, 1925. U Dijon.

RREN, JAMES: Philadelphia, PA, June 8, 36. Stella Adler School.

RRIEUX, DANIELLE: Bordeaux, nce, May 1, 1917. Lycee LaTour.

DAVENPORT, NIGEL: Cambridge, England, May 23, 1928. Trinity College.

DAVID, KEITH: NYC, June 4, 1954. Juilliard.

DAVIDOVICH, LOLITA: Toronto, Ontario, Canada, July 15, 1961.

DAVIDSON, JAYE: Riverside, CA, 1968.

DAVIDSON, JOHN: Pittsburgh, Dec. 13, 1941. Denison U.

DAVIES, JEREMY (Boring): Rockford, IA, Oct. 28, 1969.

DAVIS, CLIFTON: Chicago, IL, Oct. 4, 1945. Oakwood College.

DAVIS, GEENA: Wareham, MA, Jan. 21, 1957.

DAVIS, HOPE: Tenafly, NJ, 1967.

DAVIS, JUDY: Perth, Australia, Apr. 23, 1955.

DAVIS, MAC: Lubbock, TX, Jan. 21,1942.

DAVIS, NANCY (Anne Frances Robbins): NYC, July 6, 1921. Smith College.

DAVIS, OSSIE: Cogdell, GA, Dec. 18, 1917. Howard U.

DAVIS, SAMMI: Kidderminster, Worcestershire, England, June 21, 1964.

DAVISON, BRUCE: Philadelphia, PA, June 28, 1946.

DAWBER, PAM: Detroit, MI, Oct. 18, 1954.

DAY, DORIS (Doris Kappelhoff): Cincinnati, Apr. 3, 1924.

DAY, LARAINE (Johnson): Roosevelt, UT, Oct. 13, 1917.

DAY LEWIS, DANIEL: London, Apr. 29, 1957. Bristol Old Vic.

DAYAN, ASSI: Israel, Nov. 23, 1945. U Jerusalem.

DEAKINS, LUCY: NYC, 1971.

DEAN, JIMMY: Plainview, TX, Aug. 10, 1928.

DEAN, LOREN: Las Vegas, NV, July 31, 1969.

DeCAMP, ROSEMARY: Prescott, AZ, Nov. 14, 1913.

DeCARLO, YVONNE (Peggy Yvonne Middleton): Vancouver, B.C., Canada, Sept. 1, 1922. Vancouver School of Drama.

DEE, FRANCES: Los Angeles, Nov. 26, 1907. Chicago U.

DEE, JOEY (Joseph Di Nicola): Passaic, NJ, June 11, 1940. Patterson State College.

DEE, RUBY: Cleveland, OH, Oct. 27, 1924. Hunter College.

DEE, SANDRA (Alexandra Zuck): Bayonne, NJ, Apr. 23, 1942.

DeGENERES, ELLEN: New Orleans, LA, Jan. 26, 1958.

DeHAVEN, GLORIA: Los Angeles, July 23, 1923.

DeHAVILLAND, OLIVIA: Tokyo, Japan, July 1, 1916. Notre Dame Convent School.

DELAIR, SUZY (Suzanne Delaire): Paris, France, Dec. 31, 1916.

DELANY, DANA: NYC, March 13, 1956. Wesleyan U.

DELPY, JULIE: Paris. Dec, 21, 1969.

DELON, ALAIN: Sceaux, France, Nov. 8, 1935.

DELORME, DANIELE: Paris, France, Oct. 9, 1926. Sorbonne.

DEL TORO, BENICIO: Santurce, Puerto Rico, Feb. 19, 1967.

DeLUISE, DOM: Brooklyn, NY, Aug. 1, 1933. Tufts College.

DeLUISE, PETER: NYC, Nov. 6, 1966.

DEMONGEOT, MYLENE: Nice, France, Sept. 29, 1938.

DeMORNAY, REBECCA: Los Angeles, Aug. 29, 1962. Strasberg Inst.

DEMPSEY, PATRICK: Lewiston, ME, Jan. 13, 1966.

DeMUNN, JEFFREY: Buffalo, NY, Apr. 25, 1947. Union College.

DENCH, JUDI: York, England, Dec. 9, 1934.

DENEUVE, CATHERINE: Paris, France, Oct. 22, 1943.

DeNIRO, ROBERT: NYC, Aug. 17, 1943. Stella Adler.

DENNEHY, BRIAN: Bridgeport, CT, Jul. 9, 1938. Columbia.

DENVER, BOB: New Rochelle, NY, Jan. 9, 1935.

DEPARDIEU, GERARD: Chateauroux, France, Dec. 27, 1948.

DEPP, JOHNNY: Owensboro, KY, June 9, 1963.

DEREK, BO (Mary Cathleen Collins): Long Beach, CA, Nov. 20, 1956.

DERN, BRUCE: Chicago, IL, June 4, 1936. UPA.

DERN, LAURA: Los Angeles, Feb. 10, 1967.

DeSALVO, ANNE: Philadelphia, Apr. 3.

DEVANE, WILLIAM: Albany, NY, Sept. 5, 1939.

DeVITO, DANNY: Asbury Park, NJ, Nov. 17, 1944.

DEXTER, ANTHONY (Walter Reinhold Alfred Fleischmann): Talmadge, NB, Jan. 19, 1919. U Iowa.

DEY, SUSAN: Pekin, IL, Dec. 10, 1953.

DeYOUNG, CLIFF: Los Angeles, CA, Feb. 12, 1945. Cal State.

DIAMOND, NEIL: NYC, Jan. 24, 1941. NYU.

DIAZ, CAMERON: Long Beach, CA, Aug. 30, 1972.

DiCAPRIO, LEONARDO: Hollywood, CA, Nov.11, 1974.

DICKINSON, ANGIE (Angeline Brown): Kulm, ND, Sept. 30, 1932. Glendale College.

DILLER, PHYLLIS (Driver): Lima, OH, July 17, 1917. Bluffton College.

DILLMAN, BRADFORD: San Francisco, Apr. 14, 1930. Yale.

DILLON, KEVIN: Mamaroneck, NY, Aug. 19, 1965.

DILLON, MATT: Larchmont, NY, Feb. 18, 1964. AADA.

DILLON, MELINDA: Hope, AR, Oct. 13, 1939. Goodman Theatre School.

DIXON, DONNA: Alexandria, VA, July 20, 1957.

DOBSON, KEVIN: NYC, Mar. 18, 1944.

DOBSON, TAMARA: Baltimore, MD, May 14, 1947. MD Inst. of Art.

DOHERTY, SHANNEN: Memphis, TN, Apr. 12, 1971.

DOLAN, MICHAEL: Oklahoma City, OK, June 21, 1965.

DOMERGUE, FAITH: New Orleans, June 16, 1925.

DONAHUE, TROY (Merle Johnson): NYC, Jan. 27, 1937. Columbia U.

DONAT, PETER: Nova Scotia, Jan. 20, 1928. Yale.

DONNELLY, DONAL: Bradford, England, July 6, 1931.

D'ONOFRIO, VINCENT: Brooklyn, NY, June 30, 1959.

DONOHOE, AMANDA: London, June 29 1962.

DONOVAN, MARTIN: Reseda, CA, Aug. 19, 1957.

DONOVAN, TATE: NYC, Sept. 25, 1963.

DOOHAN, JAMES: Vancouver, BC, Mar. 3, 1920. Neighborhood Playhouse.

DOOLEY, PAUL: Parkersburg WV, Feb. 22, 1928. U WV.

DORFF, STEPHEN: CA, July 29, 1973.

DOUG, DOUG E. (Douglas Bourne): Brooklyn, NY, Jan. 7, 1970.

DOUGLAS, DONNA (Dorothy Bourgeois): Baywood, LA, Sept. 26, 1935.

DOUGLAS, ILLEANA: MA, July 25, 1965.

DOUGLAS, KIRK (Issur Danielovitch): Amsterdam, NY, Dec. 9, 1916. St. Lawrence U.

DOUGLAS, MICHAEL: New Brunswick, NJ, Sept. 25, 1944. U Cal.

DOUGLASS, ROBYN: Sendai, Japan, June 21, 1953. UCDavis.

DOURIF, BRAD: Huntington, WV, Mar. 18, 1950. Marshall U.

DOWN, LESLEY-ANN: London, Mar. 17, 1954.

DOWNEY, ROBERT, JR.: NYC, Apr. 4, 1965.

Jennifer Connelly

Courteney Cox

Billy Crudup

DRAKE, BETSY: Paris, France, Sept. 1923.

DRESCHER, FRAN: Queens, NY, Sept. 1957.

DREW, ELLEN (formerly Terry Ray): Kan City, MO, Nov. 23, 1915.

DREYFUSS, RICHARD: Brooklyn, NY, C 19, 1947.

DRILLINGER, BRIAN: Brooklyn, NY, Ju 27, 1960. SUNY/Purchase.

DRIVER, MINNIE (Amelia Driver): Lond Jan. 31, 1971.

DUCHOVNY, DAVID: NYC, Aug. 7, 19(Yale.

DUDIKOFF, MICHAEL: Torrance, CA, O 8, 1954.

DUGAN, DENNIS: Wheaton, IL, Sept. 1946.

DUKAKIS, OLYMPIA: Lowell, MA, Ju 20, 1931.

DUKE, BILL: Poughkeepsie, NY, Feb. 1943. NYU.

DUKE, PATTY (Anna Marie): NYC, Dec. 1946.

DUKES, DAVID: San Francisco, June 1945.

DULLEA, KEIR: Cleveland, NJ, May 1936. SF State College.

DUNAWAY, FAYE: Bascom, FL, Jan. 1941, Fla. U.

DUNCAN, SANDY: Henderson, TX, Feb. 1946. Len Morris College.

DUNNE, GRIFFIN: NYC, June 8, 19. Neighborhood Playhouse.

DUNST, KIRSTEN: Point Pleasant, NJ, A 30, 1982.

DUPEREY, ANNY: Paris, France, 1947.

DURBIN, DEANNA (Edna): Winnip Canada, Dec. 4, 1921.

DURNING, CHARLES S. : Highland Fa NY, Feb. 28, 1923. NYU.

DUSSOLLIER, ANDRE: Annecy, Fran Feb. 17, 1946.

DUTTON, CHARLES: Baltimore, MD, J 30, 1951. Yale.

DUVALL, ROBERT: San Diego, CA, Jan. 1931. Principia College.

DUVALL, SHELLEY: Houston, TX, July 1949.

DYSART, RICHARD: Brighton, ME, M 30, 1929.

DZUNDZA, GEORGE: Rosenheim, Ger July 19, 1945.

EASTON, ROBERT: Milwaukee, WI, N 23, 1930. U Texas.

EASTWOOD, CLINT: San Francisco, M 31, 1931. LACC.

EATON, SHIRLEY: London, 1937. A Foster School.

EBSEN, BUDDY (Christian, Jr.): Bellevi IL, Apr. 2, 1910. U Fla.

ECKEMYR, AGNETA: Karlsborg, Swed July 2. Actors Studio.

EDELMAN, GREGG: Chicago, IL, Sept. 1958. Northwestern U.

EDEN, BARBARA (Huffman): Tucson, A Aug. 23, 1934.

EDWARDS, ANTHONY: Santa Barbara, C July 19, 1962. RADA.

EDWARDS, LUKE: Nevada City, CA, M 24, 1980.

EGGAR, SAMANTHA: London, Mar. 1939.

EICHHORN, LISA: Reading, PA, Feb. 1952. Queens Ont. U RADA.

EIKENBERRY, JILL: New Haven, CT, J 21, 1947.

LBER, JANET: Detroit, MI, July 27, 1951. Iliard.

BERG, ANITA: Malmo, Sweden, Sept. 29, 1.

LAND, BRITT: Stockholm, Sweden, Oct. 942.

DARD, RON: Long Island, NY, Feb. 20, 5.

FMAN, JENNA (Jennifer Mary Batula): s Angeles, Sept. 30, 1971.

IZONDO, HECTOR: NYC, Dec. 22, 6.

LIOTT, ALISON: San Francisco, CA, 9.

LIOTT, CHRIS: NYC, May 31, 1960.

LIOTT, PATRICIA: Gunnison, CO, July 1942. UCol.

LIOTT, SAM: Sacramento, CA, Aug. 9, 4. U Ore.

WES, CARY: London, Oct. 26, 1962.

Y, RON (Ronald Pierce): Hereford, TX, e 21, 1938.

IBRY, ETHAN (Ethan Randall): ntington Beach, CA, June 13, 1978.

GLUND, ROBERT: Glendale, CA, June 6, 9.

BE, KATHRYN: Newton, MA, July 2, 6.

DMAN, RICHARD: Enid, OK, June 1, 5.

ICSON, JOHN: Dusseldorf, Ger., Sept. 25, 6. AADA.

MEY, R. LEE (Ronald): Emporia, KS, r. 24, 1944

MOND, CARL (Willy Eichberger): nna, June 14, 1906. U Vienna.

POSITO, GIANCARLO: Copenhagen, nmark, Apr. 26, 1958.

TEVEZ, EMILIO: NYC, May 12, 1962.

TRADA, ERIK: NYC, Mar. 16, 1949.

ANS, DALE (Francis Smith): Uvalde, TX, t. 31, 1912.

ANS, JOSH: NYC, Jan. 16, 1971.

ANS, LINDA (Evanstad): Hartford, CT, v. 18, 1942.

ERETT, CHAD (Ray Cramton): South nd, IN, June 11, 1936.

ERETT, RUPERT: Norfolk, England, 9.

EVIGAN, GREG: South Amboy, NJ, Oct. 14, 1953.

FABARES, SHELLEY: Los Angeles, Jan. 19, 1944.

FABIAN (Fabian Forte): Philadelphia, Feb. 6, 1943.

FABRAY, NANETTE (Ruby Nanette Fabares): San Diego, Oct. 27, 1920.

FAHEY, JEFF: Olean, NY, Nov. 29, 1956.

FAIRBANKS, DOUGLAS, JR.: NYC, Dec. 9, 1907. Collegiate School.

FAIRCHILD, MORGAN (Patsy McClenny): Dallas, TX, Feb. 3, 1950. UCLA.

FALK, PETER: NYC, Sept. 16, 1927. New School.

FARENTINO, JAMES: Brooklyn, NY, Feb. 24, 1938. AADA.

FARGAS, ANTONIO: Bronx, NY, Aug. 14, 1946.

FARINA, DENNIS: Chicago, IL, Feb. 29, 1944.

FARINA, SANDY (Sandra Feldman): Newark, NJ, 1955.

FARNSWORTH, RICHARD: Los Angeles, Sept. 1, 1920.

FARR, FELICIA: Westchester, NY, Oct. 4. 1932. Penn State College.

FARROW, MIA (Maria): Los Angeles, Feb. 9, 1945.

FAULKNER, GRAHAM: London, Sept. 26, 1947. Webber-Douglas.

FAWCETT, FARRAH: Corpus Christie, TX, Feb. 2, 1947. TexU.

FEINSTEIN, ALAN: NYC, Sept. 8, 1941.

FELDMAN, COREY: Encino, CA, July 16, 1971.

FELDON, BARBARA (Hall): Pittsburgh, Mar. 12, 1941. Carnegie Tech.

FELDSHUH, TOVAH: NYC, Dec. 27, 1953, Sarah Lawrence College.

FELLOWS, EDITH: Boston, May 20, 1923.

FENN, SHERILYN: Detroit, MI, Feb. 1, 1965.

FERRELL, CONCHATA: Charleston, WV, Mar. 28, 1943. Marshall U.

FERRER, MEL: Elbeton, NJ, Aug. 25, 1912. Princeton U.

FERRER, MIGUEL: Santa Monica, CA, Feb. 7, 1954.

FERRIS, BARBARA: London, 1943.

FIEDLER, JOHN: Plateville, WI, Feb. 3, 1925.

FIELD, SALLY: Pasadena, CA, Nov. 6, 1946.

FIELD, SHIRLEY-ANNE: London, June 27, 1938.

FIELD, TODD (William Todd Field): Pomona, CA, Feb. 24, 1964.

FIENNES, JOSEPH: Salisbury, Wiltshire, England, May 27, 1970.

FIENNES, RALPH: Suffolk, England, Dec. 22, 1962. RADA.

FIERSTEIN, HARVEY: Brooklyn, NY, June 6, 1954. Pratt Inst.

FINCH, JON: Caterham, England, Mar. 2, 1941.

FINLAY, FRANK: Farnworth, England, Aug. 6, 1926.

FINNEY, ALBERT: Salford, Lancashire, England, May 9, 1936. RADA.

FIORENTINO, LINDA: Philadelphia, PA, Mar. 9, 1960.

FIRTH, COLIN: Grayshott, Hampshire, England, Sept. 10, 1960.

FIRTH, PETER: Bradford, England, Oct. 27, 1953.

FISHBURNE, LAURENCE: Augusta, GA, July 30, 1961.

FISHER, CARRIE: Los Angeles, CA, Oct. 21, 1956. London Central School of Drama.

FISHER, EDDIE: Philadelphia, PA, Aug. 10, 1928.

FISHER, FRANCES: Orange, TX, 1952.

FITZGERALD, TARA: London, Sept. 17, 1968.

FITZGERALD, GERALDINE: Dublin, Ireland, Nov. 24, 1914. Dublin Art School.

FLAGG, FANNIE: Birmingham, AL, Sept. 21, 1944. UAl.

FLANAGAN, FIONNULA: Dublin, Dec. 10, 1941.

FLANNERY, SUSAN: Jersey City, NJ, July 31, 1943.

FLEMING, RHONDA (Marilyn Louis): Los Angeles, Aug. 10, 1922.

FLEMYNG, ROBERT: Liverpool, England, Jan. 3, 1912. Haileybury College.

FLETCHER, LOUISE: Birmingham, AL, July 22 1934.

Tim Curry

Willem Dafoe

Claire Danes

Rodney Dangerfield

Jeremy Davies

Judy Davis

Ossie Davis

Ellen DeGeneres

FLOCKHART, CALISTA: Stockton, IL, Nov. 11, Rutgers U.

FOCH, NINA: Leyden, Holland, Apr. 20, 1924.

FOLEY, DAVE: Toronto, Canada, Jan. 4, 1963.

FOLLOWS, MEGAN: Toronto, Canada, Mar. 14, 1968.

FONDA, BRIDGET: Los Angeles, Jan. 27, 1964.

FONDA, JANE: NYC, Dec. 21, 1937. Vassar.

FONDA, PETER: NYC, Feb. 23, 1939. U Omaha.

FONTAINE, JOAN: Tokyo, Japan, Oct. 22, 1917.

FOOTE, HALLIE: NYC, 1953. UNH.

FORD, GLENN (Gwyllyn Samuel Newton Ford): Quebec, Canada, May 1, 1916.

FORD, HARRISON: Chicago, IL, July 13, 1942. Ripon College.

FOREST, MARK (Lou Degni): Brooklyn, NY, Jan. 1933.

FORLANI, CLAIRE: London, July 1, 1972.

FORREST, FREDERIC: Waxahachie, TX, Dec. 23, 1936.

FORREST, STEVE: Huntsville, TX, Sept. 29, 1924. UCLA.

FORSLUND, CONNIE: San Diego, CA, June 19, 1950. NYU.

FORSTER, ROBERT (Foster, Jr.): Rochester, NY, July 13, 1941. Rochester U.

FORSYTHE, JOHN (Freund): Penn's Grove, NJ, Jan. 29, 1918.

FORSYTHE, WILLIAM: Brooklyn, NY, June 7, 1955

FOSSEY, BRIGITTE: Tourcoing, France, Mar. 11, 1947.

FOSTER, JODIE (Ariane Munker): Bronx, NY, Nov. 19, 1962. Yale.

FOSTER, MEG: Reading, PA, May 14, 1948.

FOX, EDWARD: London, Apr. 13, 1937. RADA.

FOX, JAMES: London, May 19, 1939.

FOX, MICHAEL J.: Vancouver, BC, June 9, 1961.

FOXWORTH, ROBERT: Houston, TX, Nov. 1, 1941. Carnegie Tech.

FRAKES, JONATHAN: Bethlehem, PA, Aug. 19, 1952. Harvard.

FRANCIOSA, ANTHONY (Papaleo): NYC, Oct. 25, 1928.

FRANCIS, ANNE: Ossining, NY, Sept. 16, 1932.

FRANCIS, ARLENE (Arlene Kazanjian): Boston, Oct. 20, 1908. Finch School.

FRANCIS, CONNIE (Constance Franconero): Newark, NJ, Dec. 12, 1938.

FRANCKS, DON: Vancouver, Canada, Feb. 28, 1932.

FRANKLIN, PAMELA: Tokyo, Feb. 4, 1950.

FRANZ, ARTHUR: Perth Amboy, NJ, Feb. 29, 1920. Blue Ridge College.

FRANZ, DENNIS: Chicago, IL, Oct. 28, 1944.

FRASER, BRENDAN: Indianapolis, IN, Dec. 3, 1968.

FRAZIER, SHEILA: NYC, Nov. 13, 1948.

FRECHETTE, PETER: Warwick, RI, Oct. 1956. URI.

FREEMAN, AL, JR.: San Antonio, TX, Mar. 21, 1934. CCLA.

FREEMAN, KATHLEEN: Chicago, IL, Feb. 17, 1919.

FREEMAN, MONA: Baltimore, MD, June 9, 1926.

FREEMAN, MORGAN: Memphis, TN, June 1, 1937. LACC.

FREWER, MATT: Washington, DC, Jan. 4, 1958, Old Vic.

FRICKER, BRENDA: Dublin, Ireland, Feb. 17, 1945.

FRIELS, COLIN: Glasgow, Sept. 25, 1952.

FRY, STEPHEN: Hampstead, London, Eng., Aug. 24, 1957.

FULLER, PENNY: Durham, NC, 1940. Northwestern U.

FUNICELLO, ANNETTE: Utica, NY, Oct. 22, 1942.

FURLONG, EDWARD: Glendale, CA, Aug. 2, 1977.

FURNEAUX, YVONNE: Lille, France, 1928. Oxford U.

GABLE, JOHN CLARK: Los Angeles, Mar. 20, 1961. Santa Monica College.

GABOR, ZSA ZSA (Sari Gabor): Budapest, Hungary, Feb. 6, 1918.

GAIL, MAX: Derfoil, MI, Apr. 5, 1943.

GAINES, BOYD: Atlanta, GA, May 11, 19 Juilliard.

GALLAGHER, PETER: NYC, Aug. 1955. Tufts U.

GALLIGAN, ZACH: NYC, Feb. 14, 19 ColumbiaU.

GALLO, VINCENT: Buffalo, NY, Apr. 1961.

GAM, RITA: Pittsburgh, PA, Apr. 2, 1928.

GAMBON, MICHAEL: Dublin, Ireland, C 19, 1940.

GANZ, BRUNO: Zurich, Switzerland, M 22, 1941.

GARBER, VICTOR: Montreal, Canada, M 16, 1949.

GARCIA, ANDY: Havana, Cuba, Apr. 1956. FlaInt.

GARFIELD, ALLEN (Allen Goorwi Newark, NJ, Nov. 22, 1939. Actors Studio.

GARFUNKEL, ART: NYC, Nov. 5, 1941

GARLAND, BEVERLY: Santa Cruz, C Oct. 17, 1926. Glendale College.

GARNER, JAMES (James Baumgarn Norman, OK, Apr. 7, 1928. Okla. U.

GAROFALO, JANEANE: Newton, NJ, S 28, 1964.

GARR, TERI: Lakewood, OH, Dec. 11, 19

GARRETT, BETTY: St. Joseph, MO, M 23, 1919. Annie Wright Seminary.

GARRISON, SEAN: NYC, Oct. 19, 1937

GARY, LORRAINE: NYC, Aug. 16, 1937

GASSMAN, VITTORIO: Genoa, Italy, S 1,1922. Rome Academy of Dramatic Art.

GAVIN, JOHN: Los Angeles, Apr. 8, 19 Stanford U.

GAYLORD, MITCH: Van Nuys, CA, M 10, 1961. UCLA.

GAYNOR, MITZI (Francesca Marlene Gerber): Chicago, IL, Sept. 4, 1930.

GAZZARA, BEN: NYC, Aug. 28, 19 Actors Studio.

GEARY, ANTHONY: Coalsville, UT, M 29, 1947. UUt.

GEDRICK, JASON: Chicago, IL, Feb. 1965. Drake U.

GEESON, JUDY: Arundel, England, Sept. 1948. Corona.

GELLAR, SARAH MICHELLE: NYC, A 14, 1977.

Benicio Del Toro

Catherine Deneuve

OFFREYS, STEPHEN: Cincinnati, OH, . 22, 1964. NYU.

ORGE, SUSAN: West London, England, 26, 1950.

RARD, GIL: Little Rock, AR, Jan. 23, 0.

RE, RICHARD: Philadelphia, PA, Aug. 1949. U Mass.

RROLL, DANIEL: London, Oct. 16, 1. Central.

RSHON, GINA: Los Angeles, June 10, 2.

RTZ, JAMI: Chicago, IL, Oct. 28, 1965.

TTY, BALTHAZAR: Los Angeles, CA, 22, 1975.

TTY, ESTELLE: NYC, July 25, 1923. School.

OLSON, JULIE: Birmingham, AL, June 958.

OSTLEY, ALICE: Eve, MO, Aug. 14, 6. Okla U.

ANNINI, GIANCARLO: Spezia, Italy, . 1, 1942. Rome Acad. of Drama.

BB, CYNTHIA: Bennington, VT, Dec. 14, 3.

SON, HENRY: Germantown, PA, Sept. 1935.

SON, MEL: Peekskill, NY, Jan. 3, 1956. A.

GIBSON, THOMAS: Charleston, SC, July 3, 1962.

GIELGUD, JOHN: London, Apr. 14, 1904. RADA.

GIFT, ROLAND: Birmingham, England, May 28 1962.

GILBERT, MELISSA: Los Angeles, CA, May 8, 1964.

GILES, NANCY: NYC, July 17, 1960, Oberlin College.

GILLETTE, ANITA: Baltimore, MD, Aug. 16, 1938.

GILLIAM, TERRY: Minneapolis, MN, Nov. 22, 1940.

GILLIS, ANN (Alma O'Connor): Little Rock, AR, Feb. 12, 1927.

GINTY, ROBERT: NYC, Nov. 14, 1948. Yale.

GIRARDOT, ANNIE: Paris, France, Oct. 25, 1931.

GISH, ANNABETH: Albuquerque, NM, Mar. 13, 1971. DukeU.

GIVENS, ROBIN: NYC, Nov. 27, 1964.

GLASER, PAUL MICHAEL: Boston, MA, Mar. 25, 1943. Boston U.

GLASS, RON: Evansville, IN, July 10, 1945.

GLEASON, JOANNA: Winnipeg, Canada, June 2, 1950. UCLA.

GLEASON, PAUL: Jersey City, NJ, May 4, 1944.

GLENN, SCOTT: Pittsburgh, PA, Jan. 26, 1942. William and Mary College.

GLOVER, CRISPIN: NYC, Sept 20, 1964.

GLOVER, DANNY: San Francisco, CA, July 22, 1947. SFStateCol.

GLOVER, JOHN: Kingston, NY, Aug. 7, 1944.

GLYNN,CARLIN: Cleveland, Oh, Feb. 19, 1940. Actors Studio.

GOLDBERG, WHOOPI (Caryn Johnson): NYC, Nov. 13, 1949.

GOLDBLUM, JEFF: Pittsburgh, PA, Oct. 22, 1952. Neighborhood Playhouse.

GOLDEN, ANNIE: Brooklyn, NY, Oct. 19, 1951.

GOLDSTEIN, JENETTE: Beverly Hills, CA, 1960.

GOLDTHWAIT, BOB: Syracuse, NY, May 1, 1962.

GOLDWYN, TONY: Los Angeles, May 20, 1960. LAMDA.

GOLINO, VALERIA: Naples, Italy, Oct. 22, 1966.

GONZALEZ, CORDELIA: Aug. 11, 1958, San Juan, PR. UPR.

GONZALES-GONZALEZ, PEDRO: Aguilares, TX, Dec. 21, 1926.

GOODALL, CAROLINE: London, Nov. 13, 1959. BristolU.

GOODING, CUBA, JR.: Bronx, N.Y., Jan. 2, 1968.

GOODMAN, DODY: Columbus, OH, Oct. 28, 1915.

GOODMAN, JOHN: St. Louis, MO, June 20, 1952.

GORDON, KEITH: NYC, Feb. 3, 1961.

GORDON-LEVITT, JOSEPH: Los Angeles, Feb. 17, 1981.

GORMAN, CLIFF: Jamaica, NY, Oct. 13, 1936. NYU.

GORSHIN, FRANK: Pittsburgh, PA, Apr. 5, 1933.

GORTNER, MARJOE: Long Beach, CA, Jan. 14, 1944.

GOSSETT, LOUIS, JR.: Brooklyn, NY, May 27, 1936. NYU.

GOULD, ELLIOTT (Goldstein): Brooklyn, NY, Aug. 29, 1938. Columbia U.

GOULD, HAROLD: Schenectady, NY, Dec. 10, 1923. Cornell.

GOULD, JASON: NYC, Dec. 29, 1966.

GOULET, ROBERT: Lawrence, MA, Nov. 26, 1933. Edmonton.

GRAF, DAVID: Lancaster, OH, Apr. 16, 1950. OhStateU.

GRAFF, TODD: NYC, Oct. 22, 1959. SUNY/ Purchase.

GRAHAM, HEATHER: Milwauke, WI, Jan. 29, 1970.

GRANGER, FARLEY: San Jose, CA, July 1, 1925.

GRANT, DAVID MARSHALL: Westport, CT, June 21, 1955. Yale.

GRANT, HUGH: London, Sept. 9, 1960. Oxford.

GRANT, KATHRYN (Olive Grandstaff): Houston, TX, Nov. 25, 1933. UCLA.

GRANT, LEE: NYC, Oct. 31, 1927. Juilliard.

GRANT, RICHARD E: Mbabane, Swaziland, May 5, 1957. Cape Town U.

GRAVES, PETER (Aurness): Minneapolis, Mar. 18, 1926. U Minn.

Dom DeLuise

Laura Dern

Cameron Diaz

GRAVES, RUPERT: Weston-Super-Mare, England, June 30, 1963.
GRAY, CHARLES: Bournemouth, England, 1928.
GRAY, COLEEN (Doris Jensen): Staplehurst, NB, Oct. 23, 1922. Hamline.
GRAY, LINDA: Santa Monica, CA, Sept. 12, 1940.
GRAY, SPALDING: Barrington, RI, June 5, 1941.
GRAYSON, KATHRYN (Zelma Hedrick): Winston-Salem, NC, Feb. 9, 1922.
GREEN, KERRI: Fort Lee, NJ, Jan. 14, 1967. Vassar.
GREEN, SETH: Philadelphia, PA, Feb. 8, 1974.
GREENE, ELLEN: NYC, Feb. 22, 1950. Ryder College.
GREENE, GRAHAM: Six Nations Reserve, Ontario, June 22, 1952
GREENWOOD, BRUCE: Quebec, Canada, Aug. 12, 1956.
GREER, JANE: Washington, DC, Sept. 9, 1924.
GREER, MICHAEL: Galesburg, IL, Apr. 20, 1943.
GREIST, KIM: Stamford, CT, May 12, 1958.
GREY, JENNIFER: NYC, Mar. 26, 1960.

GREY, JOEL (Katz): Cleveland, OH, Apr. 11, 1932.
GREY, VIRGINIA: Los Angeles, Mar. 22, 1917.
GRIECO, RICHARD: Watertown, NY, Mar. 23, 1965.
GRIEM, HELMUT: Hamburg, Germany, Apr. 6, 1932. HamburgU.
GRIER, DAVID ALAN: Detroit, MI, June 30, 1955. Yale.
GRIER, PAM: Winston-Salem, NC, May 26, 1949.
GRIFFITH, ANDY: Mt. Airy, NC, June 1, 1926. UNC.
GRIFFITH, MELANIE: NYC, Aug. 9, 1957. Pierce Col.
GRIFFITHS, RACHEL: Melbourne, Australia, 1968.
GRIMES, GARY: San Francisco, June 2, 1955.
GRIMES, SCOTT: Lowell, MA, July 9, 1971.
GRIMES, TAMMY: Lynn, MA, Jan. 30, 1934. Stephens College.
GRIZZARD, GEORGE: Roanoke Rapids, NC, Apr. 1, 1928. UNC.
GRODIN, CHARLES: Pittsburgh, PA, Apr. 21, 1935.
GROH, DAVID: NYC, May 21, 1939. Brown U, LAMDA.
GROSS, MARY: Chicago, IL, Mar. 25, 1953.
GROSS, MICHAEL: Chicago, IL, June 21, 1947.
GUEST, CHRISTOPHER: NYC, Feb. 5, 1948.
GUEST, LANCE: Saratoga, CA, July 21, 1960. UCLA.
GUILLAUME, ROBERT (Williams): St. Louis, MO, Nov. 30, 1937.
GUINNESS, ALEC: London, Apr. 2, 1914. Pembroke Lodge School.
GULAGER, CLU: Holdenville, OK, Nov. 16 1928.
GUTTENBERG, STEVE: Massapequa, NY, Aug. 24, 1958. UCLA.
GUY, JASMINE: Boston, Mar. 10, 1964.
HAAS, LUKAS: West Hollywood, CA, Apr. 16, 1976.
HACK, SHELLEY: Greenwich, CT, July 6, 1952.
HACKETT, BUDDY (Leonard Hacker): Brooklyn, NY, Aug. 31, 1924.
HACKMAN, GENE: San Bernardino, CA, Jan. 30, 1930.
HAGERTY, JULIE: Cincinnati, OH, June 15, 1955. Juilliard.
HAGMAN, LARRY (Hageman): Weatherford, TX, Sept. 21, 1931. Bard.
HAID, CHARLES: San Francisco, June 2, 1943. CarnegieTech.
HAIM, COREY: Toronto, Canada, Dec. 23, 1972.
HALE, BARBARA: DeKalb, IL, Apr. 18, 1922. Chicago Academy of Fine Arts.
HALEY, JACKIE EARLE: Northridge, CA, July 14, 1961.
HALL, ALBERT: Boothton, AL, Nov. 10, 1937. Columbia.
HALL, ANTHONY MICHAEL: Boston, MA, Apr. 14, 1968.
HALL, ARSENIO: Cleveland, OH, Feb. 12, 1959.
HALL, HUNTZ: Boston, MA, Aug. 15, 1920.
HAMEL, VERONICA: Philadelphia, PA, Nov. 20, 1943.

Fran Drescher

HAMILL, MARK: Oakland, CA, Sept. 1952. LACC.
HAMILTON, CARRIE: NYC, Dec. 5, 19
HAMILTON, GEORGE: Memphis, Aug. 12, 1939. Hackley.
HAMILTON, LINDA: Salisbury, MD, S 26, 1956.
HAMLIN, HARRY: Pasadena, CA, Oct. 1951.
HAMPSHIRE, SUSAN: London, May 1941.
HAMPTON, JAMES: Oklahoma City, (July 9, 1936. NTexasStU.
HAN, MAGGIE: Providence, RI, 1959.
HANDLER, EVAN: NYC, Jan. 10, 1 Juillard.
HANKS, TOM: Concord, CA, Jul. 9, 1 CalStateU.
HANNAH, DARYL: Chicago, IL, Dec 1960. UCLA.
HANNAH, PAGE: Chicago, IL, Apr. 1964.
HARDEN, MARCIA GAY: LaJolla, (Aug. 14, 1959.
HARDIN, TY (Orison Whipple Hungerf II): NYC, June 1, 1930.
HAREWOOD, DORIAN: Dayton, OH, A 6, 1950. U Cinn.

Illeana Douglas

David Duchovny

Martin Donovan

Faye Dunaway

Clint Eastwood

Laurence Fishburne

RMON, MARK: Los Angeles, CA, Sept. 951. UCLA.

RPER, JESSICA: Chicago, IL, Oct. 10, 9.

RPER, TESS: Mammoth Spring, AK, 2. SWMoState.

RPER, VALERIE: Suffern, NY, Aug. 22, 0.

RRELSON, WOODY: Midland, TX, July 1961. Hanover College.

RRINGTON, PAT: NYC, Aug. 13, 1929. dham U.

RRIS, BARBARA (Sandra Markowitz): nston, IL, July 25, 1935.

RRIS, ED: Tenafly, NJ, Nov. 28, 1950. umbia.

RRIS, JULIE: Grosse Point, MI, Dec. 2, 5. Yale Drama School.

RRIS, MEL (Mary Ellen): Bethlehem, PA, 7. Columbia.

RRIS, RICHARD: Limerick, Ireland, Oct. 930. London Acad.

RRIS, ROSEMARY: Ashby, England, t. 19, 1930. RADA.

RRISON, GEORGE: Liverpool, England, . 25, 1943.

RRISON, GREGORY: Catalina Island, , May 31, 1950. Actors Studio.

RRISON, NOEL: London, Jan. 29, 1936.

RROLD, KATHRYN: Tazewell, VA, Aug. 950. Mills College.

RRY, DEBORAH: Miami, IL, July 1, 5.

RT, ROXANNE: Trenton, NJ, 1952, ceton.

RTLEY, MARIETTE: NYC, June 21, 1.

RTMAN, DAVID: Pawtucket, RI, May 19, 5. Duke U.

SSETT, MARILYN: Los Angeles, CA, . 17, 1947.

TCHER, TERI: Sunnyvale, CA, Dec. 8, 4.

TOSY, SHAWN: Frederick, MD, Dec. 29, 5.

UER, RUTGER: Amsterdam, Holland, 23, 1944.

HAVER, JUNE: Rock Island, IL, June 10, 1926.

HAVOC, JUNE (Hovick): Seattle, WA, Nov. 8, 1916.

HAWKE, ETHAN: Austin, TX, Nov. 6, 1970.

HAWN, GOLDIE: Washington, DC, Nov. 21, 1945.

HAWTHORNE, NIGEL: Coventry, Eng., Apr. 5, 1929.

HAYEK, SALMA: Coatzacoalcos, Veracruz, Mexico, Sept. 2, 1968.

HAYES, ISAAC: Covington, TN, Aug. 20, 1942.

HAYS, ROBERT: Bethesda, MD, July 24, 1947, SD State College.

HEADLY, GLENNE: New London, CT, Mar. 13, 1955. AmCollege.

HEALD, ANTHONY: New Rochelle, NY, Aug. 25, 1944. MIStateU.

HEARD, JOHN: Washington, DC, Mar. 7, 1946. Clark U.

HEATHERTON, JOEY: NYC, Sept. 14, 1944.

HECHE, ANNE: Aurora, OH, May 25, 1969.

HECKART, EILEEN: Columbus, OH, Mar. 29, 1919. Ohio State U.

HEDAYA, DAN: Brooklyn, NY, July 24, 1940.

HEDISON, DAVID: Providence, RI, May 20, 1929. Brown U.

HEDREN, TIPPI (Natalie): Lafayette, MN, Jan. 19, 1931.

HEGYES, ROBERT: Metuchen, NJ, May 7, 1951.

HELMOND, KATHERINE: Galveston, TX, July 5, 1934.

HEMINGWAY, MARIEL: Ketchum, ID, Nov. 22, 1961.

HEMMINGS, DAVID: Guilford, England, Nov. 18, 1941.

HEMSLEY, SHERMAN: Philadelphia, PA, Feb. 1, 1938.

HENDERSON, FLORENCE: Dale, IN, Feb. 14, 1934.

HENDRY, GLORIA: Jacksonville, FL, 1949.

HENNER, MARILU: Chicago, IL, Apr. 6, 1952.

HENRIKSEN, LANCE: NYC, May 5, 1940.

HENRY, BUCK (Henry Zuckerman): NYC, Dec. 9, 1930. Dartmouth.

HENRY, JUSTIN: Rye, NY, May 25, 1971.

HEPBURN, KATHARINE: Hartford, CT, May 12, 1907. Bryn Mawr.

HERMAN, PEE-WEE (Paul Reubenfeld): Peekskill, NY, Aug. 27, 1952.

HERRMANN, EDWARD: Washington, DC, July 21, 1943. Bucknell, LAMDA.

HERSHEY, BARBARA (Herzstein): Hollywood, CA, Feb. 5, 1948.

HESSEMAN. HOWARD: Lebanon, OR, Feb. 27, 1940.

HESTON, CHARLTON: Evanston, IL, Oct. 4, 1922. Northwestern U.

HEWITT, JENNIFER LOVE: Waco, TX, Feb. 21, 1979.

HEWITT, MARTIN: Claremont, CA, Feb. 19, 1958. AADA.

HEYWOOD, ANNE (Violet Pretty): Birmingham, England, Dec. 11, 1932.

HICKMAN, DARRYL: Hollywood, CA, July 28, 1933. Loyola U.

HICKMAN, DWAYNE: Los Angeles, May 18, 1934. Loyola U.

HICKS, CATHERINE: NYC, Aug. 6, 1951. Notre Dame.

HIGGINS, ANTHONY (Corlan): Cork City, Ireland, May 9, 1947. Birmingham Sch. of Dramatic Arts.

HIGGINS, MICHAEL: Brooklyn, NY, Jan. 20, 1926. AmThWing.

HILL, ARTHUR: Saskatchewan, Canada, Aug. 1, 1922. U Brit. College.

HILL, BERNARD: Manchester, England, Dec. 17, 1944.

HILL, STEVEN: Seattle, WA, Feb. 24, 1922. U Wash.

HILL, TERRENCE (Mario Girotti): Venice, Italy, Mar. 29, 1941. U Rome.

HILLER, WENDY: Bramhall, Cheshire, England, Aug. 15, 1912. Winceby House School.

HILLERMAN, JOHN: Denison, TX, Dec. 20, 1932.

HINES, GREGORY: NYC, Feb.14, 1946.

HINGLE, PAT: Denver, CO, July 19, 1923. Tex. U.

HIRSCH, JUDD: NYC, Mar. 15, 1935. AADA.

HOBEL, MARA: NYC, June 18, 1971.

HODGE, PATRICIA: Lincolnshire, England, Sept. 29, 1946. LAMDA.

HOFFMAN, DUSTIN: Los Angeles, Aug. 8, 1937. Pasadena Playhouse.

HOFFMAN, PHILIP SEYMOUR: Fairport, NY, 1968.

HOGAN, JONATHAN: Chicago, IL, June 13, 1951.

HOGAN, PAUL: Lightning Ridge, Australia, Oct. 8, 1939.

HOLBROOK, HAL (Harold): Cleveland, OH, Feb. 17, 1925. Denison.

HOLLIMAN, EARL: Tennesas Swamp, Delhi, LA, Sept. 11, 1928. UCLA.

HOLM, CELESTE: NYC, Apr. 29, 1919.

HOLM, IAN: Ilford, Essex, England, Sept. 12, 1931. RADA.

HOLMES, KATIE: Toledo, OH, Dec. 18, 1978.

HOMEIER, SKIP (George Vincent Homeier): Chicago, IL, Oct. 5, 1930. UCLA.

HOOKS, ROBERT: Washington, DC, Apr. 18, 1937. Temple.

HOPE, BOB (Leslie Townes Hope): London, May 26, 1903.

HOPKINS, ANTHONY: Port Talbot, So. Wales, Dec. 31, 1937. RADA.

HOPPER, DENNIS: Dodge City, KS, May 17, 1936.

HORNE, LENA: Brooklyn, NY, June 30, 1917.

HORSLEY, LEE: Muleshoe, TX, May 15, 1955.

HORTON, ROBERT: Los Angeles, July 29, 1924. UCLA.

HOSKINS, BOB: Bury St. Edmunds, England, Oct. 26, 1942.

HOUGHTON, KATHARINE: Hartford, CT, Mar. 10, 1945. Sarah Lawrence.

HOUSER, JERRY: Los Angeles, July 14, 1952. Valley, Jr. College.

HOWARD, ARLISS: Independence, MO, 1955. Columbia College.

HOWARD, KEN: El Centro, CA, Mar. 28, 1944. Yale.

HOWARD, RON: Duncan, OK, Mar. 1, 1954. USC.

HOWARD, RONALD: Norwood, England, Apr. 7, 1918. Jesus College.

HOWELL, C. THOMAS: Los Angeles, Dec. 7, 1966.

HOWELLS, URSULA: London, Sept. 17, 1922.

HOWES, SALLY ANN: London, July 20, 1930.

HOWLAND, BETH: Boston, MA, May 28, 1941.

HUBLEY, SEASON: NYC, May 14, 1951.

HUDDLESTON, DAVID: Vinton, VA, Sept. 17, 1930.

HUDSON, ERNIE: Benton Harbor, MI, Dec. 17, 1945.

HUGHES, BARNARD: Bedford Hills, NY, July 16, 1915. Manhattan College.

HUGHES, KATHLEEN (Betty von Gerkan): Hollywood, CA, Nov. 14, 1928. UCLA.

HULCE, TOM: Plymouth, MI, Dec. 6, 1953. N.C. Sch. of Arts.

HUNNICUT, GAYLE: Ft. Worth, TX, Feb. 6, 1943. UCLA.

HUNT, HELEN: Los Angeles, June 15, 1963.

HUNT, LINDA: Morristown, NJ, Apr. 1945. Goodman Theatre.

HUNT, MARSHA: Chicago, IL, Oct. 17, 1917.

HUNTER, HOLLY: Atlanta, GA, Mar. 20, 1958. Carnegie-Mellon.

HUNTER, KIM (Janet Cole): Detroit, Nov. 12, 1922.

HUNTER, TAB (Arthur Gelien): NYC, July 11, 1931.

HUPPERT, ISABELLE: Paris, France, Mar. 16, 1955.

HURLEY, ELIZABETH: Hampshire, Eng., June 10, 1965.

HURT, JOHN: Lincolnshire, England, Jan. 22, 1940.

HURT, MARY BETH (Supinger): Marshalltown, IA, Sept. 26, 1948. NYU.

HURT, WILLIAM: Washington, DC, Mar. 20, 1950. Tufts, Juilliard.

HUSSEY, RUTH: Providence, RI, Oct. 30, 1917. U Mich.

HUSTON, ANJELICA: Santa Monica, C July 9, 1951.

HUTTON, BETTY (Betty Thornberg): Ba Creek, MI, Feb. 26, 1921.

HUTTON, LAUREN (Mary): Charleston, Nov. 17, 1943. Newcomb College.

HUTTON, TIMOTHY: Malibu, CA, Aug. 1960.

HYER, MARTHA: Fort Worth, TX, Aug. 1924. Northwestern U.

ICE CUBE (O'Shea Jackson): Los Ange June 15, 1969.

IDLE, ERIC: South Shields, Durham, E land, Mar. 29, 1943. Cambridge.

INGELS, MARTY: Brooklyn, NY, Mar. 1936.

IRELAND, KATHY: Santa Barbara, C Mar. 8, 1963.

IRONS, JEREMY: Cowes, England, Sept. 1948. Old Vic.

IRONSIDE, MICHAEL: Toronto, Cana Feb. 12, 1950.

IRVING, AMY: Palo Alto, CA, Sept. 1953. LADA.

IRWIN, BILL: Santa Monica, CA, Apr. 1950.

ISAAK, CHRIS: Stockton, CA, June 1956. UofPacific.

IVANEK, ZELJKO: Lujubljana, Yugo., A 15, 1957. Yale, LAMDA.

IVEY, JUDITH: El Paso, TX, Sept. 4, 195

JACKSON, ANNE: Alleghany, PA, Sept 1926. Neighborhood Playhouse.

JACKSON, GLENDA: Hoylake, Chesh England, May 9, 1936. RADA.

JACKSON, JANET: Gary, IN, May 16, 19

JACKSON, KATE: Birmingham, AL, C 29, 1948. AADA.

JACKSON, MICHAEL: Gary, IN, Aug. 1958.

JACKSON, SAMUELL.: Atlanta, Dec. 1948.

JACKSON, VICTORIA: Miami, FL, Aug 1958.

JACOBI, DEREK: Leytonstone, Lond Oct. 22, 1938. Cambridge.

JACOBI, LOU: Toronto, Canada, Dec. 1913.

Calista Flockhart

Bridget Fonda

Brendan Fraser

Morgan Freeman

COBS, LAWRENCE-HILTON: Virgin
|nds, Sept. 14, 1953.
COBY, SCOTT: Chicago, IL, Nov. 19,
56.
GGER, MICK: Dartford, Kent, England,
y 26, 1943.
MES, CLIFTON: NYC, May 29, 1921.
e. U.
NNEY, ALLISON: Dayton, OH, Nov. 20,
50. RADA.
RMAN, CLAUDE, JR.: Nashville, TN,
ot. 27, 1934.
SON, RICK: NYC, May 21, 1926. AADA.
AN, GLORIA (Gloria Jean Schoonover):
ffalo, NY, Apr. 14, 1927.
FFREYS, ANNE (Carmichael): Goldsboro,
', Jan. 26, 1923. Anderson College.
FFRIES, LIONEL: London, June 10,
26. RADA.
RGENS, ADELE: Brooklyn, NY, Nov. 26,
22.
TER, MICHAEL: Lawrenceburg, TN,
g. 26, 1952. Memphis St.U.
LLIAN, ANN (Nauseda): Cambridge, MA,
. 29, 1951.
HANSEN, DAVID: Staten Island, NY, Jan.
1950.
HN, ELTON (Reginald Dwight): Middle-
., England, Mar. 25, 1947. RAM.
HNS, GLYNIS: Durban, S. Africa, Oct. 5,
23.
HNSON, DON: Galena, MO, Dec. 15,
50. UKan.
HNSON, PAGE: Welch, WV, Aug. 25,
30. Ithaca.
HNSON, RAFER: Hillsboro, TX, Aug. 18,
35. UCLA.
HNSON, RICHARD: Essex, England, July
1927. RADA.
HNSON, ROBIN: Brooklyn, NY, May 29,
54.
HNSON, VAN: Newport, RI, Aug. 28,
16.
LIE, ANGELINA (Angelina Jolie Voight):
s Angeles, June 4, 1975.
NES, CHRISTOPHER: Jackson, TN,
g. 18, 1941. Actors Studio.
NES, DEAN: Decatur, AL, Jan. 25, 1931.
tors Studio.
NES, GRACE: Spanishtown, Jamaica,
y 19, 1952.
NES, JACK: Bel-Air, CA, Jan. 14, 1938.
NES, JAMES EARL: Arkabutla, MS, Jan.
1931. U Mich.
NES, JEFFREY: Buffalo, NY, Sept. 28,
47. LAMDA.
NES, JENNIFER (Phyllis Isley): Tulsa,
., Mar. 2, 1919. AADA.
NES, L.Q. (Justice Ellis McQueen): Aug
1927.
NES, SAM J.: Chicago, IL, Aug. 12, 1954.
NES, SHIRLEY: Smithton, PA, March 31,
34.
NES, TERRY: Colwyn Bay, Wales, Feb. 1,
42.
NES, TOMMY LEE: San Saba, TX, Sept.
1946. Harvard.
URDAN, LOUIS: Marseilles, France, June
1920.
VOVICH, MILLA: Kiev, Ukraine, Dec.
1975.
Y, ROBERT: Montreal, Canada, Aug. 17,
51. Oxford.
DD, ASHLEY: Los Angeles, CA, Apr. 19,

Andy Garcia

Janeane Garofalo

Ben Gazzara

JURADO, KATY (Maria Christina Jurado
Garcia): Guadalajara, Mex., Jan. 16, 1927.
KACZMAREK, JANE: Milwaukee, WI,
Dec. 21, 1955.
KAHN, MADELINE: Boston, MA, Sept. 29,
1942. Hofstra U.
KANE, CAROL: Cleveland, OH, June 18,
1952.
KAPLAN, MARVIN: Brooklyn, NY, Jan. 24,
1924.
KAPOOR, SHASHI: Calcutta, India, Mar. 18,
1938.
KAPRISKY, VALERIE (Cheres): Paris,
France, Aug. 19, 1962.
KARRAS, ALEX: Gary, IN, July 15, 1935.
KARTHEISER, VINCENT: Minneapolis,
MN, May 5, 1979.
KATT, WILLIAM: Los Angeles, CA, Feb.
16, 1955.
KAUFMANN, CHRISTINE: Lansdorf, Graz,
Austria, Jan. 11, 1945.
KAVNER, JULIE: Burbank, CA, Sept. 7,
1951. UCLA.
KAZAN, LAINIE (Levine): Brooklyn, NY,
May 15, 1942.
KAZURINSKY, TIM: Johnstown, PA, March
3, 1950.
KEACH, STACY: Savannah, GA, June 2,
1941. U Cal., Yale.
KEATON, DIANE (Hall): Los Angeles, CA,
Jan. 5, 1946. Neighborhood Playhouse.
KEATON, MICHAEL: Coraopolis, PA, Sept.
9, 1951. KentStateU.
KEDROVA, LILA: Leningrad, 1918.
KEEL, HOWARD (Harold Leek): Gillespie,
IL, Apr. 13, 1919.
KEESLAR, MATT: Grand Rapids, MI, 1972.
KEITEL, HARVEY: Brooklyn, NY, May 13,
1939.
KEITH, DAVID: Knoxville, TN, May 8,
1954. UTN.
KELLER, MARTHE: Basel, Switzerland,
1945. Munich Stanislavsky Sch.
KELLERMAN, SALLY: Long Beach, CA,
June 2, 1936. Actors Studio West.
KELLEY, DeFOREST: Atlanta, GA, Jan. 20,
1920.
KELLY, MOIRA: Queens, NY, Mar. 6, 1968.
KEMP, JEREMY (Wacker): Chesterfield,
England, Feb. 3, 1935. Central Sch.
KENNEDY, GEORGE: NYC, Feb. 18, 1925.
KENNEDY, LEON ISAAC: Cleveland, OH,
1949.
KENSIT, PATSY: London, Mar. 4, 1968.
KERR, DEBORAH: Helensburg, Scotland,
Sept. 30, 1921. Smale Ballet School.
KERR, JOHN: NYC, Nov. 15, 1931. Harvard,
Columbia.
KERWIN, BRIAN: Chicago, IL, Oct. 25,
1949.
KEYES, EVELYN: Port Arthur, TX, Nov. 20,
1919.
KIDDER, MARGOT: Yellow Knife, Canada,
Oct. 17, 1948. UBC.
KIDMAN, NICOLE: Hawaii, June 20, 1967.
KIEL, RICHARD: Detroit, MI, Sept. 13,
1939.
KIER, UDO: Koeln, Germany, Oct. 14, 1944.
KILEY, RICHARD: Chicago, IL, Mar. 31,
1922. Loyola.
KILMER, VAL: Los Angeles, Dec. 31, 1959.
Juilliard.
KINCAID, ARON (Norman Neale Williams,
III): Los Angeles, June 15, 1943. UCLA.

John Gielgud

KING, ALAN (Irwin Kniberg): Brooklyn, NY, Dec. 26, 1927.

KING, PERRY: Alliance, OH, Apr. 30, 1948. Yale.

KINGSLEY, BEN (Krishna Bhanji): Snaiton, Yorkshire, England, Dec. 31, 1943.

KINNEAR, GREG: Logansport, IN, June 17, 1963.

KINSKI, NASTASSJA: Berlin, Ger., Jan. 24, 1960.

KIRBY, BRUNO: NYC, Apr. 28, 1949.

KIRK, TOMMY: Louisville, KY, Dec.10 1941.

KIRKLAND, SALLY: NYC, Oct. 31, 1944. Actors Studio.

KITT, EARTHA: North, SC, Jan. 26, 1928.

KLEIN, ROBERT: NYC, Feb. 8, 1942. Alfred U.

KLEMPERER, WERNER: Cologne, Mar. 22, 1920.

KLINE, KEVIN: St. Louis, MO, Oct. 24, 1947. Juilliard.

KLUGMAN, JACK: Philadelphia, PA, Apr. 27, 1922. Carnegie Tech.

KNIGHT, MICHAEL E.: Princeton, NJ, May 7, 1959.

KNIGHT, SHIRLEY: Goessel, KS, July 5, 1937. Wichita U.

KNOX, ELYSE: Hartford, CT, Dec. 14, 1917. Traphagen School.

Whoopi Goldberg

KOENIG, WALTER: Chicago, IL, Sept. 14, 1936. UCLA.

KOHNER, SUSAN: Los Angeles, Nov. 11, 1936. U Calif.

KORMAN, HARVEY: Chicago, IL, Feb. 15, 1927. Goodman.

KORSMO, CHARLIE: Minneapolis, MN, July, 1978.

KOTEAS, ELIAS: Montreal, Quebec, Canada, 1961. AADA.

KOTTO, YAPHET: NYC, Nov. 15, 1937.

KOZAK, HARLEY JANE: Wilkes-Barre, PA, Jan. 28, 1957. NYU.

KRABBE, JEROEN: Amsterdam, The Netherlands, Dec. 5, 1944.

KREUGER, KURT: St. Moritz, Switzerland, July 23, 1917. U London.

KRIGE, ALICE: Upington, So. Africa, June 28, 1955.

KRISTEL, SYLVIA: Amsterdam, The Netherlands, Sept. 28, 1952.

KRISTOFFERSON, KRIS: Brownsville, TX, June 22, 1936, Pomona College.

KRUGER, HARDY: Berlin, Germany, April 12, 1928.

KRUMHOLTZ, DAVID: NYC, May 15, 1978.

KUDROW, LISA: Encino, CA, July 30, 1963.

KURTZ, SWOOSIE: Omaha, NE, Sept. 6, 1944.

KWAN, NANCY: Hong Kong, May 19, 1939. Royal Ballet.

LaBELLE, PATTI: Philadelphia, PA, May 24, 1944.

LACY, JERRY: Sioux City, IA, Mar. 27, 1936. LACC.

LADD, CHERYL (Stoppelmoor): Huron, SD. July 12, 1951.

LADD, DIANE (Ladner): Meridian, MS, Nov. 29, 1932. Tulane U.

LAHTI, CHRISTINE: Detroit, MI, Apr. 4, 1950. U Mich.

LAKE, RICKI: NYC, Sept. 21, 1968.

LAMARR, HEDY (Hedwig Kiesler): Vienna, Sept. 11, 1913.

LAMAS, LORENZO: Los Angeles, Jan. 28, 1958.

LAMBERT, CHRISTOPHER: NYC, Mar. 29, 1958.

LANDAU, MARTIN: Brooklyn, NY, June 20, 1931. Actors Studio.

LANDRUM, TERI: Enid, OK, 1960.

LANE, ABBE: Brooklyn, NY, Dec. 14, 1935.

LANE, DIANE: NYC, Jan. 22, 1963.

LANE, NATHAN: Jersey City, NJ, Feb. 3, 1956.

LANG, STEPHEN: NYC, July 11, 1952. Swarthmore College.

LANGE, HOPE: Redding Ridge, CT, Nov. 28, 1931. Reed College.

LANGE, JESSICA: Cloquet, MN, Apr. 20, 1949. U Minn.

LANGELLA, FRANK: Bayonne, NJ, Jan. 1, 1940. SyracuseU.

LANSBURY, ANGELA: London, Oct. 16, 1925. London Academy of Music.

LaPAGLIA, ANTHONY: Adelaide, Australia. Jan 31, 1959.

LARROQUETTE, JOHN: New Orleans, LA, Nov. 25, 1947.

LASSER, LOUISE: NYC, Apr. 11, 1939. Brandeis U.

LATIFAH, QUEEN (Dana Owens): East Orange, NJ, 1970.

LAUGHLIN, JOHN: Memphis, TN, Apr. 3.

Louis Gossett, Jr.

LAUGHLIN, TOM: Minneapolis, MN, 19

LAUPER, CYNDI: Astoria, Queens, NY June 20, 1953.

LAURE, CAROLE: Montreal, Canada, A 5, 1951.

LAURIE, HUGH: Oxford, Eng., June 1959.

LAURIE, PIPER (Rosetta Jacobs): Detr MI, Jan. 22, 1932.

LAUTER, ED: Long Beach, NY, Oct. 1940.

LAVIN, LINDA: Portland, ME, Oct. 15 19

LAW, JOHN PHILLIP: Hollywood, C Sept. 7, 1937. Neighborhood Playhouse, Hawaii.

LAW, JUDE: Lewisham, Eng., Dec. 29, 19

LAWRENCE, BARBARA: Carnegie, C Feb. 24, 1930. UCLA.

LAWRENCE, CAROL (Laraia): Melr Park, IL, Sept. 5, 1935.

LAWRENCE, VICKI: Inglewood, CA, M 26, 1949.

LAWRENCE, MARTIN: Frankfurt, C many, Apr. 16, 1965.

LAWSON, LEIGH: Atherston, England, J 21, 1945. RADA.

LEACHMAN, CLORIS: Des Moines, Apr. 30, 1930. Northwestern U.

LEARY, DENIS: Boston, MA, Aug. 18, 19

Hugh Grant

AUD, JEAN-PIERRE: Paris, France, May 1944.

BLANC, MATT: Newton, MA, July 25, 57.

DERER, FRANCIS: Karlin, Prague, ech., Nov. 6, 1906.

E, CHRISTOPHER: London, May 27, 22. Wellington College.

E, MARK: Australia, 1958.

E, MICHELE (Dusiak): Los Angeles, June 1942. LACC.

E, PEGGY (Norma Delores Egstrom): nestown, ND, May 26, 1920.

E, SHERYL: Augsburg, Germany, Arp. 22, 57.

E, SPIKE (Shelton Lee): Atlanta, GA, Mar. 1957.

GROS, JAMES: Minneapolis, MN, Apr. 1962.

GUIZAMO, JOHN: Columbia, July 22, 55. NYU.

IBMAN, RON: NYC, Oct. 1l, 1937. Ohio esleyan.

IGH, JANET (Jeanette Helen Morrison): rced, CA, July 6, 1926. ColofPacific.

IGH, JENNIFER JASON: Los Angeles, o. 5, 1962.

MAT, PAUL: Rahway, NJ, Sept. 22, 1945.

MMON, CHRIS: Los Angeles, Jan. 22, 54.

MMON, JACK: Boston, Feb. 8, 1925. rvard.

NO, JAY: New Rochelle, NY, Apr. 28, 50. Emerson College.

NZ, KAY: Los Angeles, Mar. 4, 1953.

NZ, RICK: Springfield, IL, Nov. 21, 1939. Mich.

ONARD, ROBERT SEAN: Westwood, Feb. 28, 1969.

RNER, MICHAEL: Brooklyn, NY, June 1941.

SLIE, BETHEL: NYC, Aug. 3, 1929. earley School.

SLIE, JOAN (Joan Brodell): Detroit, Jan. 1925. St. Benedict's.

STER, MARK: Oxford, England, July 11, 58.

TO, JARED: Bossier City, LA, Dec. 26, 71.

VELS, CALVIN: Cleveland. OH, Sept. 30, 54. CCC.

VIN, RACHEL: NYC, 1954. Goddard llege.

VINE, JERRY: New Brunswick, NJ, Mar. 1957, Boston U.

VY, EUGENE: Hamilton, Canada, Dec. 1946. McMasterU.

WIS, CHARLOTTE: London, Aug.7, 57.

WIS, GEOFFREY: San Diego, CA, Jan. 1, 35.

WIS, JERRY (Joseph Levitch): Newark, Mar. 16, 1926.

WIS, JULIETTE: Los Angeles CA, June 1973.

GON, TOM: New Orleans, LA, Sept. 10, 45.

LLARD, MATTHEW: Lansing, MI, Jan. 1970.

NCOLN, ABBEY (Anna Marie Woolge): Chicago, IL, Aug. 6, 1930.

NDEN, HAL: Bronx, NY, Mar. 20, 1931. y College of NY.

NDO, DELROY: London, Nov. 18, 1952.

LINDSAY, ROBERT: Ilketson, Derbyshire, England, Dec. 13, 1951, RADA.

LINN-BAKER, MARK: St. Louis, MO, June 17, 1954, Yale.

LINNEY, LAURA: New York, NY, Feb. 5, 1964.

LIOTTA, RAY: Newark, NJ, Dec. 18, 1955. UMiami.

LISI, VIRNA: Rome, Nov. 8, 1937.

LITHGOW, JOHN: Rochester, NY, Oct. 19, 1945. Harvard.

LL COOL J (James Todd Smith): Queens, NY, Jan. 14, 1968.

LLOYD, CHRISTOPHER: Stamford, CT, Oct. 22, 1938.

LLOYD, EMILY: London, Sept. 29, 1970.

LOCKE, SONDRA: Shelbyville, TN, May, 28, 1947.

LOCKHART, JUNE: NYC, June 25, 1925. Westlake School.

LOCKWOOD, GARY: Van Nuys, CA, Feb. 21, 1937.

LOGGIA, ROBERT: Staten Island, NY, Jan. 3, 1930. UMo.

LOLLOBRIGIDA, GINA: Subiaco, Italy, July 4, 1927. Rome Academy of Fine Arts.

LOM, HERBERT: Prague, Czechoslovakia, Jan. 9, 1917. Prague U.

LOMEZ, CELINE: Montreal, Canada, May 11, 1953.

LONDON, JULIE (Julie Peck): Santa Rosa, CA, Sept. 26, 1926.

LONE, JOHN: Hong Kong, Oct 13, 1952. AADA.

LONG, SHELLEY: Ft. Wayne, IN, Aug. 23, 1949. Northwestem U.

LOPEZ, JENNIFER: Bronx, NY, July 24, 1970.

LOPEZ, PERRY: NYC, July 22, 1931. NYU.

LORDS, TRACY (Nora Louise Kuzma): Steubenville, OH, May 7, 1968.

LOREN, SOPHIA (Sophia Scicolone): Rome, Italy, Sept. 20, 1934.

LOUIS-DREYFUS, JULIA: NYC, Jan. 13, 1961.

LOUISE, TINA (Blacker): NYC, Feb. 11, 1934, Miami U.

LOVE, COURTNEY (Love Michelle Harrison): San Francisco, July 9, 1965.

LOVETT, LYLE: Klein, TX, Nov. 1, 1957.

LOVITZ, JON: Tarzana, CA, July 21, 1957.

LOWE, CHAD: Dayton, OH, Jan. 15, 1968.

LOWE, ROB: Charlottesville, VA, Mar. 17, 1964.

LOWITSCH, KLAUS: Berlin, Apr. 8, 1936, Vienna Academy.

LUCAS, LISA: Arizona, 1961.

LUCKINBILL, LAURENCE: Fort Smith, AK, Nov. 21, 1934.

LUFT, LORNA: Los Angeles, Nov. 21, 1952.

LULU (Marie Lawrie): Glasgow, Scotland, Nov. 3, 1948.

LUNA, BARBARA: NYC, Mar. 2, 1939.

LUNDGREN, DOLPH: Stockolm, Sweden, Nov. 3, 1959. Royal Inst.

LuPONE, PATTI: Northport, NY, Apr. 21, 1949, Juilliard.

LYDON, JAMES: Harrington Park, NJ, May 30, 1923.

LYNCH, KELLY: Minneapolis, MN, Jan. 31, 1959.

LYNLEY, CAROL (Jones): NYC, Feb. 13, 1942.

LYON, SUE: Davenport, IA, July 10, 1946.

LYONNE, NATASHA: NYC, 1978.

MacARTHUR, JAMES: Los Angeles, Dec. 8, 1937. Harvard.

MACCHIO, RALPH: Huntington, NY, Nov. 4, 1961.

MacCORKINDALE, SIMON: Cambridge, England, Feb. 12, 1953.

MacDOWELL, ANDIE (Rose Anderson MacDowell): Gaffney, SC, Apr. 21, 1958.

MacGINNIS, NIALL: Dublin, Ireland, Mar. 29, 1913. Dublin U.

MacGRAW, ALI: NYC, Apr. 1, 1938. Wellesley.

MacLACHLAN, KYLE: Yakima, WA, Feb. 22, 1959. UWa.

MacLAINE, SHIRLEY (Beaty): Richmond, VA, Apr. 24, 1934.

MacLEOD, GAVIN: Mt. Kisco, NY, Feb. 28, 1931.

MacNAUGHTON, ROBERT: NYC, Dec. 19, 1966.

MACNEE, PATRICK: London, Feb. 1922.

MacNICOL, PETER: Dallas, TX, Apr. 10, 1954. UMN.

MacPHERSON, ELLE: Sydney, Australia, 1965.

MacVITTIE, BRUCE: Providence, RI, Oct. 14, 1956. BostonU.

MACY, W. H. (William): Miami, FL, Mar. 13, 1950. Goddard College.

MADIGAN, AMY: Chicago, IL, Sept. 11, 1950. Marquette U.

MADONNA (Madonna Louise Veronica Cicone): Bay City, MI, Aug. 16, 1958. UMi.

MADSEN, MICHAEL: Chicago, IL, Sept. 25, 1958.

MADSEN, VIRGINIA: Winnetka, IL, Sept. 11, 1963.

MAGNUSON, ANN: Charleston, WV, Jan. 4, 1956.

MAGUIRE, TOBEY: Santa Monica, CA, June 27, 1975.

MAHARIS, GEORGE: Astoria, NY, Sept. 1, 1928. Actors Studio.

MAHONEY, JOHN: Manchester, England, June 20, 1940, WUIll.

MAILER, STEPHEN: NYC, Mar. 10, 1966. NYU.

MAJORS, LEE: Wyandotte, MI, Apr. 23, 1940. E. Ky. State College.

MAKEPEACE, CHRIS: Toronto, Canada, Apr. 22, 1964.

MAKO (Mako Iwamatsu): Kobe, Japan, Dec. 10, 1933. Pratt.

MALDEN, KARL (Mladen Sekulovich): Gary, IN, Mar. 22, 1914.

MALKOVICH, JOHN: Christopher, IL, Dec. 9, 1953, IllStateU.

MALONE, DOROTHY: Chicago, IL, Jan. 30, 1925.

MANN, TERRENCE: KY, 1945. NCSchl Arts.

MANOFF, DINAH: NYC, Jan. 25, 1958. CalArts.

MANTEGNA, JOE: Chicago, IL, Nov. 13, 1947. Goodman Theatre.

MANZ, LINDA: NYC, 1961.

MARAIS, JEAN: Cherbourg, France, Dec. 11, 1913, St. Germain.

MARCEAU, SOPHIE (Maupu): Paris, Nov. 17, 1966.

MARCHAND, NANCY: Buffalo, NY, June 19, 1928.

MARCOVICCI, ANDREA: NYC, Nov. 18, 1948.

Rupert Graves

David Alan Grier

Pam Grier

Gene Hackman

MARGULIES, JULIANNA: Spring Valley, NY, June 8, 1966.
MARIN, CHEECH (Richard): Los Angeles, July 13, 1946.
MARIN, JACQUES: Paris, France, Sept. 9, 1919. Conservatoire National.
MARINARO, ED: NYC, Mar. 31, 1950. Cornell.
MARS, KENNETH: Chicago, IL, 1936.
MARSH, JEAN: London, England, July 1, 1934.
MARSHALL, KEN: NYC, 1953. Juilliard.
MARSHALL, PENNY: Bronx, NY, Oct. 15, 1942. UN. Mex.
MARSHALL, WILLIAM: Gary, IN, Aug. 19, 1924. NYU.
MARTIN, ANDREA: Portland, ME, Jan. 15, 1947.
MARTIN, DICK: Battle Creek, MI Jan. 30, 1923.
MARTIN, GEORGE N.: NYC, Aug. 15, 1929.
MARTIN, MILLICENT: Romford, England, June 8, 1934.
MARTIN, PAMELA SUE: Westport, CT, Jan. 15, 1953.
MARTIN, STEVE: Waco, TX, Aug. 14, 1945. UCLA.
MARTIN, TONY (Alfred Norris): Oakland, CA, Dec. 25, 1913. St. Mary's College.
MASON, MARSHA: St. Louis, MO, Apr. 3, 1942. Webster College.
MASSEN, OSA: Copenhagen, Denmark, Jan. 13, 1916.
MASTERS, BEN: Corvallis, OR, May 6, 1947. UOr.
MASTERSON, MARY STUART: Los Angeles, June 28, 1966, NYU.
MASTERSON, PETER: Angleton, TX, June 1, 1934. Rice U.
MASTRANTONIO, MARY ELIZABETH: Chicago, IL, Nov. 17, 1958. UIll.
MASUR, RICHARD: NYC, Nov. 20, 1948.
MATHESON, TIM: Glendale, CA, Dec. 31, 1947. CalState.
MATHIS, SAMANTHA: NYC, May 12, 1970.
MATLIN, MARLEE: Morton Grove, IL, Aug. 24, 1965.

MATTHAU, WALTER (Matuschanskayasky): NYC, Oct. 1, 1920.
MATTHEWS, BRIAN: Philadelphia, Jan. 24. 1953. St. Olaf.
MATURE, VICTOR: Louisville, KY, Jan. 29, 1915.
MAY, ELAINE (Berlin): Philadelphia, Apr. 21, 1932.
MAYO, VIRGINIA (Virginia Clara Jones): St. Louis, MO, Nov. 30, 1920.
MAYRON, MELANIE: Philadelphia, PA, Oct. 20, 1952. AADA.
MAZURSKY, PAUL: Brooklyn, NY, Apr. 25, 1930. Bklyn College.
MAZZELLO, JOSEPH: Rhinebeck, NY, Sept. 21, 1983.
McCALLUM, DAVID: Scotland, Sept. 19, 1933. Chapman College.
McCAMBRIDGE, MERCEDES: Jolliet, IL, Mar. 17, 1918. Mundelein College.
McCARTHY, ANDREW: NYC, Nov. 29, 1962, NYU.
McCARTHY, KEVIN: Seattle, WA, Feb. 15, 1914. Minn. U.
McCARTNEY, PAUL: Liverpool, England, June 18, 1942.
McCLANAHAN, RUE: Healdton, OK, Feb. 21, 1934.
McCLORY, SEAN: Dublin, Ireland, Mar. 8, 1924. U Galway.
McCLURE, MARC: San Mateo, CA, Mar. 31, 1957.
McCLURG, EDIE: Kansas City, MO, July 23, 1950.
McCOWEN, ALEC: Tunbridge Wells, England, May 26, 1925. RADA.
McCRANE, PAUL: Philadelphia, PA, Jan. 19. 1961.
McCRARY, DARIUS: Walnut, CA, May 1, 1976.
McDERMOTT, DYLAN: Waterbury, CT, Oct. 26, 1962. Neighborhood Playhouse.
McDONALD, CHRISTOPHER: NYC, 1955.
McDONNELL, MARY: Wilkes Barre, PA, Apr. 28, 1952.
McDORMAND, FRANCES: Illinois, June 23, 1957.

McDOWELL, MALCOLM (Taylor): Leeds, England, June 19, 1943. LAMDA.
McELHONE, NATASCHA (Natasha Taylor): London, Mar. 23, 1971.
McENERY, PETER: Walsall, England, Feb. 21, 1940.
McENTIRE, REBA: McAlester, OK, Mar. 28, 1955. SoutheasternStU.
McGAVIN, DARREN: Spokane, WA, May 7, 1922. College of Pacific.
McGILL, EVERETT: Miami Beach, FL, Oct. 21, 1945.
McGILLIS, KELLY: Newport Beach, CA, July 9, 1957. Juilliard.
McGINLEY, JOHN C.: NYC, Aug. 3, 1959. NYU.
McGOOHAN, PATRICK: NYC, Mar. 19, 1928.
McGOVERN, ELIZABETH: Evanston, IL, July 18, 1961. Juilliard.
McGOVERN, MAUREEN: Youngstown, OH, July 27, 1949.
McGREGOR, EWAN: Perth, Scotland, March 31, 1971
McGUIRE, BIFF: New Haven, CT, Oct. 25, 1926. Mass. Stale College.
McGUIRE, DOROTHY: Omaha, NE, June 14, 1918.
McHATTIE, STEPHEN: Antigonish, NS, Feb. 3. Acadia U AADA.
McKAY, GARDNER: NYC, June 10, 1932. Comell.
McKEAN, MICHAEL: NYC, Oct. 17, 1947.
McKEE, LONETTE: Detroit, MI, July 22, 1955.
McKELLEN, IAN: Burnley, England, May 25, 1939.
McKENNA, VIRGINIA: London, June 7, 1931.
McKEON, DOUG: Pompton Plains, NJ, June 10, 1966.
McKERN, LEO: Sydney, Australia, Mar. 16, 1920.
McKUEN, ROD: Oakland, CA, Apr. 29, 1933.
McLERIE, ALLYN ANN: Grand Mere, Canada, Dec. 1, 1926.
McMAHON, ED: Detroit, MI, Mar. 6, 1923.
McNAIR, BARBARA: Chicago, IL, Mar. 4, 1939. UCLA.

Linda Hamilton

Tess Harper

Deborah Harry

Teri Hatcher

cNAMARA, WILLIAM: Dallas, TX, Mar. , 1965.

cNICHOL, KRISTY: Los Angeles. CA, ot. 11, 1962.

cQUEEN, ARMELIA: North Carolina, Jan. 1952. Bklyn Consv.

cQUEEN, CHAD: Los Angeles, CA, Dec. 1960. Actors Studio.

cRANEY, GERALD: Collins, MS, Aug. 19, 48.

cSHANE, IAN: Blackburn, England, Sept. , 1942. RADA.

EADOWS, JAYNE (formerly Jayne tter): Wuchang, China, Sept. 27, 1924. St. argaret's.

EANEY, COLM: Dublin, May 30, 1953.

EARA, ANNE: Brooklyn, NY, Sept. 20, 29.

EAT LOAF (Marvin Lee Aday): Dallas, TX, ot. 27, 1947.

EDWIN, MICHAEL: London, 1925. Instut cher.

EKKA, EDDIE: Worcester, MA, June 14, 52. Boston Cons.

ELATO, MARIANGELA: Milan, Italy, 41. Milan Theatre Acad.

EREDITH, LEE (Judi Lee Sauls): Oct. 22, 47. AADA.

ERKERSON, S. EPATHA: Saganaw, MI, v. 28, 1952. Wayne St. Univ.

ERRILL, DINA (Nedinia Hutton): NYC, c. 29, 1925. AADA.

ESSING, DEBRA: Brooklyn, NY, Aug. 15, 58.

ETCALF, LAURIE: Edwardsville, IL, June 1955., IIIStU.

ETZLER, JIM: Oneonda, NY, June 23. rtmouth.

ICHELL, KEITH: Adelaide, Australia, c. 1, 1926.

IDLER, BETTE: Honolulu, HI, Dec. 1, 45.

ILANO, ALYSSA: Brooklyn, NY, Dec. 19, 72.

ILES, JOANNA: Nice, France, Mar. 6, 40.

ILES, SARAH: Ingatestone, England, Dec. 1941. RADA.

ILES, SYLVIA: NYC, Sept. 9, 1934. Actors dio.

ILES, VERA (Ralston): Boise City, OK, g. 23, 1929. UCLA.

MILLER, ANN (Lucille Ann Collier): Chireno, TX, Apr. 12, 1919. Lawler Professional School.

MILLER, BARRY: Los Angeles, CA, Feb. 6, 1958.

MILLER, DICK: NYC, Dec. 25, 1928.

MILLER, JASON: Long Island City, NY, Apr. 22, 1939. Catholic U.

MILLER, JONNY LEE: Surrey, England, Nov. 15, 1972.

MILLER, LINDA: NYC, Sept. 16, 1942. Catholic U.

MILLER, PENELOPE ANN: Santa Monica, CA, Jan. 13, 1964.

MILLER, REBECCA: Roxbury, CT, 1962. Yale.

MILLS, DONNA: Chicago, IL, Dec. 11, 1945. UII.

MILLS, HAYLEY: London, Apr. 18, 1946. Elmhurst School.

MILLS, JOHN: Suffolk, England, Feb. 22, 1908.

MILLS, JULIET: London, Nov. 21, 1941.

MILNER, MARTIN: Detroit, MI, Dec. 28, 1931.

MIMIEUX, YVETTE: Los Angeles, Jan. 8, 1941. Hollywood High.

MINNELLI, LIZA: Los Angeles, Mar. 19, 1946.

MIOU-MIOU (Sylvette Henry): Paris, France, Feb. 22, 1950.

MIRREN, HELEN (Ilynea Mironoff): London, July 26, 1946.

MITCHELL, JAMES: Sacramento, CA, Feb. 29, 1920. LACC.

MITCHELL, JOHN CAMERON: El Paso, TX, Apr. 21, 1963. NorthwesternU.

MITCHUM, JAMES: Los Angeles, CA, May 8, 1941.

MODINE, MATTHEW: Loma Linda, CA, Mar. 22, 1959.

MOFFAT, DONALD: Plymouth, England, Dec. 26, 1930. RADA.

MOFFETT, D. W.: Highland Park, IL, Oct. 26, 1954. Stanford U.

MOHR, JAY: New Jersey, Aug. 23, 1971.

MOKAE, ZAKES: Johannesburg, So. Africa, Aug. 5, 1935. RADA.

MOLINA, ALFRED: London, May 24, 1953. Guildhall.

MOLL, RICHARD: Pasadena, CA, Jan. 13, 1943.

MONK, DEBRA: Middletown, OH, Feb. 27, 1949.

MONTALBAN, RICARDO: Mexico City, Nov. 25, 1920.

MONTENEGRO, FERNADA (Arlete Pinheiro): Rio de Janiero, Brazil, 1929.

MONTGOMERY, BELINDA: Winnipeg, Canada, July 23, 1950.

MONTGOMERY, GEORGE (George Letz): Brady, MT, Aug. 29, 1916. U Mont.

MOODY, RON: London, Jan. 8, 1924. London U.

MOOR, BILL: Toledo, OH, July 13, 1931. Northwestern.

MOORE, CONSTANCE: Sioux City, IA, Jan. 18, 1919.

MOORE, DEMI (Guines): Roswell, NM, Nov. 11, 1962.

MOORE, DICK: Los Angeles, Sept. 12, 1925.

MOORE, DUDLEY: Dagenham, Essex, England, Apr. 19, 1935.

MOORE, JULIANNE (Julie Anne Smith): Fayetteville, NC, Dec. 30, 1960.

MOORE, KIERON: County Cork, Ireland, 1925. St. Mary's College.

MOORE, MARY TYLER: Brooklyn, NY, Dec. 29, 1936.

MOORE, ROGER: London, Oct. 14, 1927. RADA.

MOORE, TERRY (Helen Koford): Los Angeles, Jan. 7, 1929.

MORALES, ESAI: Brooklyn, NY, Oct. 1, 1962.

MORANIS, RICK: Toronto, Canada, Apr. 18, 1954.

MOREAU, JEANNE: Paris, France, Jan. 23, 1928.

MORENO, RITA (Rosita Alverio): Humacao, P.R., Dec. 11, 1931.

MORGAN, HARRY (HENRY) (Harry Bratsburg): Detroit, Apr. 10, 1915. U Chicago.

MORGAN, MICHELE (Simone Roussel): Paris, France, Feb. 29, 1920. Paris Dramatic School.

MORIARTY, CATHY: Bronx, NY, Nov. 29, 1960.

MORIARTY, MICHAEL: Detroit, MI, Apr. 5, 1941. Dartmouth.

MORISON, PATRICIA: NYC, Mar. 19, 1915.

MORITA, NORIYUKI "PAT": Isleton, CA, June 28, 1932.

Tobey Maguire

Bruce Norris

Trey Parker

Mimi Rogers

MORRIS, GARRETT: New Orleans, LA, Feb. 1, 1937.

MORRIS, HOWARD: NYC, Sept. 4, 1919. NYU.

MORROW, ROB: New Rochelle, NY, Sept. 21, 1962.

MORSE, DAVID: Hamilton, MA, Oct. 11, 1953.

MORSE, ROBERT: Newton, MA, May 18, 1931.

MORTENSEN, VIGGO: New York, NY, 1958.

MORTON, JOE: NYC, Oct. 18, 1947. Hofstra U.

MOSES, WILLIAM: Los Angeles, Nov. 17, 1959.

MOSTEL, JOSH: NYC, Dec. 21, 1946. Brandeis U.

MOUCHET, CATHERINE: Paris, France, 1959. Ntl. Consv.

MUELLER-STAHL, ARMIN: Tilsit, East Prussia, Dec. 17, 1930.

MULDAUR, DIANA: NYC, Aug. 19, 1938. Sweet Briar College.

MULGREW, KATE: Dubuque, IA, Apr. 29, 1955. NYU.

MULHERN, MATT: Philadelphia, PA, July 21, 1960. Rutgers Univ.

MULL, MARTIN: N. Ridgefield, OH, Aug. 18, 1941. RISch. of Design.

MULLIGAN, RICHARD: NYC, Nov. 13, 1932.

MULRONEY, DERMOT: Alexandria, VA, Oct. 31, 1963. Northwestern.

MUMY, BILL (Charles William Mumy, Jr.): San Gabriel, CA, Feb. 1, 1954.

MURPHY, EDDIE: Brooklyn, NY, Apr. 3, 1961.

MURPHY, MICHAEL: Los Angeles, CA, May 5, 1938. UAz.

MURRAY, BILL: Wilmette, IL, Sept. 21, 1950. Regis College.

MURRAY, DON: Hollywood, CA, July 31, 1929.

MUSANTE, TONY: Bridgeport, CT, June 30, 1936. Oberlin College.

MYERS, MIKE: Scarborough, Canada, May 25, 1963.

NABORS, JIM: Sylacauga, GA, June 12, 1932.

NADER, GEORGE: Pasadena, CA, Oct. 19, 1921. Occidental College.

NADER, MICHAEL: Los Angeles, CA, 1945.

NAMATH, JOE: Beaver Falls, PA, May 31, 1943. UAla.

NAUGHTON, DAVID: Hartford, CT, Feb. 13, 1951.

NAUGHTON, JAMES: Middletown, CT, Dec. 6, 1945.

NEAL, PATRICIA: Packard, KY, Jan. 20, 1926. Northwestern U.

NEESOM, LIAM: Ballymena, Northern Ireland, June 7, 1952.

NEFF, HILDEGARDE (Hildegard Knef): Ulm, Germany, Dec. 28, 1925. Berlin Art Acad.

NEILL, SAM: No. Ireland, Sept. 14, 1947. U Canterbury.

NELL, NATHALIE: Paris, France, Oct. 1950.

NELLIGAN, KATE: London, Ont., Canada, Mar. 16, 1951. U Toronto.

NELSON, BARRY (Robert Nielsen): Oakland, CA, Apr. 16, 1920.

NELSON, CRAIG T.: Spokane, WA, Apr. 4, 1946.

NELSON, DAVID: NYC, Oct. 24, 1936. USC.

NELSON, JUDD: Portland, ME, Nov. 28, 1959, Haverford College.

NELSON, LORI (Dixie Kay Nelson): Santa Fe, NM, Aug. 15, 1933.

NELSON, TRACY: Santa Monica, CA, Oct. 25, 1963.

NELSON, WILLIE: Abbott, TX, Apr. 30, 1933.

NEMEC, CORIN: Little Rock, AK, Nov. 5, 1971.

NERO, FRANCO (Francisco Spartanero): Parma, Italy, Nov. 23, 1941.

NESMITH, MICHAEL: Houston, TX, Dec. 30, 1942.

NETTLETON, LOIS: Oak Park, IL, 1931. Actors Studio.

NEWHART, BOB: Chicago, IL, Sept. 5, 1929. Loyola U.

NEWLEY, ANTHONY: Hackney, London, Sept. 24, 1931.

NEWMAN, BARRY: Boston, MA, Nov. 7, 1938. Brandeis U.

NEWMAN, LARAINE: Los Angeles, Mar. 2, 1952.

NEWMAN, NANETTE: Northampton, England, 1934.

NEWMAN, PAUL: Cleveland, OH, Jan. 26, 1925. Yale.

NEWMAR, JULIE (Newmeyer): Angeles, Aug. 16, 1933.

NEWTON, THANDIE: Zambia, 1972.

NEWTON-JOHN, OLIVIA: Cambrid England, Sept. 26, 1948.

NGUYEN, DUSTIN: Saigon, Vietnam, S 17, 1962.

NICHOLAS, DENISE: Detroit, MI, July 1945.

NICHOLAS, PAUL: London, 1945.

NICHOLS, NICHELLE: Robbins, IL, D 28, 1933.

NICHOLSON, JACK: Neptune, NJ, Apr. 1937.

NICKERSON, DENISE: NYC, 1959.

NICOL, ALEX: Ossining, NY, Jan. 20, 19 Actors Studio.

NIELSEN, BRIGITTE: Denmark, July 1963.

NIELSEN, LESLIE: Regina, Saskatchew Canada, Feb. 11, 1926. Neighborhood Pl house.

NIMOY, LEONARD: Boston, MA, Mar. 1931. Boston College, Antioch College.

NIXON, CYNTHIA: NYC, Apr. 9, 19 Columbia U.

NOBLE, JAMES: Dallas, TX, Mar. 5, 19 SMU.

NOIRET, PHILIPPE: Lille, France, Oct 1930.

NOLAN, KATHLEEN: St. Louis, MO, S 27, 1933. Neighborhood Playhouse.

NOLTE, NICK: Omaha, NE, Feb. 8, 19 Pasadena City College.

NORRIS, BRUCE: Houston, TX, May 1960. Northwestern.

NORRIS, CHRISTOPHER: NYC, Oct. 1943. Lincoln Square Acad.

NORRIS, CHUCK (Carlos Ray): Ry OK,Mar. 10, 1940.

NORTH, HEATHER: Pasadena, CA, D 13, 1950. Actors Workshop.

NORTH, SHEREE (Dawn Bethel): Los geles. Jan. 17, 1933. Hollywood High.

NORTHAM, JEREMY: Cambridge, E Dec. 1, 1961.

NORTON, EDWARD: Boston, MA, Aug. 1969.

NORTON, KEN: Jacksonville, Il, Aug. 1945.

NOURI, MICHAEL: Washington, DC, D 9, 1945.

VAK, KIM (Marilyn Novak): Chicago, IL, 13, 1933. LACC.

VELLO, DON: Ashtabula, OH, Jan. 1, 3. UDayton.

YEN, FRANCE (Vannga): Marseilles, ice, July 31, 1939. Beaux Arts School.

BRIAN, HUGH (Hugh J. Krampe): Roster, N,. Apr. 19, 1928. Cincinnati U.

BRIEN, CLAY: Ray, AZ, May 6, 1961.

BRIEN, MARGARET (Angela Maxine rien): Los Angeles, Jan. 15, 1937.

BRIEN, VIRGINIA: Los Angeles, Apr. 18, 9.

CONNELL, JERRY (Jeremiah onnell): New York, NY, Feb. 17, 1974.

CONNOR, CARROLL: Bronx, NY, Aug. 924. Dublin National Univ.

CONNOR, DONALD: Chicago, IL, Aug. 1925.

CONNOR, GLYNNIS: NYC, Nov. 19, 5. NYSU.

DONNELL, CHRIS: Winetka, IL, June 27, 0.

DONNELL, ROSIE: Commack, NY, ch 21, 1961.

MARA, CATHERINE: Toronto, Canada, . 4, 1954.

MARA, MAUREEN (Maureen Fitzons): Dublin, Ireland, Aug. 17, 1920.

ERLIHY, DAN: Wexford, Ireland, May 919. National U.

KEEFE, MICHAEL: Larchmont, NY, Apr. 1955. NYU, AADA.

OMAN, GARY: New Cross, South don, England, Mar. 21, 1958.

IN, KEN: Chicago, IL, July 30, 1954. UPa.

IN, LENA: Stockholm, Sweden, Mar. 22, 5.

MOS, EDWARD JAMES: Los Angeles, . 24, 1947. CSLA.

LOUGHLIN, GERALD S.: NYC, Dec. 23, 1. U Rochester.

SON, JAMES: Evanston, IL, Oct. 8, 1930.

SON, NANCY: Milwaukee, WI, July 14, 8. UCLA.

NEAL, GRIFFIN: Los Angeles, 1965.

NEAL, RON: Utica, NY, Sept. 1, 1937. o State.

NEAL, RYAN: Los Angeles, Apr. 20, 1941.

NEAL, TATUM: Los Angeles, Nov. 5, 3.

NEIL, TRICIA: Shreveport, LA, Mar. 11, 5. Baylor U.

NEILL, ED: Youngstown, OH, Apr. 12, 6.

NEILL, JENNIFER: Rio de Janeiro, Feb. 1949. Neighborhood Playhouse.

TKEAN, MICHAEL: Vancouver, B.C., ada, Jan. 24, 1946.

QUINN, TERRY: Newbury, MI, July 15, 2.

BACH, JERRY: Bronx, NY, Oct. 20, 5.

HEA, MILO: Dublin, Ireland, June 2, 6.

MENT, HALEY JOEL: Apr. 10, 1988.

TOOLE, ANNETTE (Toole): Houston, Apr. 1, 1953. UCLA.

TOOLE, PETER: Connemara, Ireland, , 2, 1932. RADA.

ERALL, PARK: Nashville, TN, Mar. 15, 7. Tusculum College.

, FRANK (Oznowicz): Hereford, England, 25, 1944.

Isabella Rossellini

Winona Ryder

Kyra Sedgwick

PACINO, AL: NYC, Apr. 25, 1940.

PACULA, JOANNA: Tamaszow Lubelski, Poland, Jan. 2, 1957. Polish Natl. Theatre Sch.

PAGET, DEBRA (Debralee Griffin): Denver, Aug. 19, 1933.

PAIGE, JANIS (Donna Mae Jaden): Tacoma, WA, Sept. 16, 1922.

PALANCE, JACK (Walter Palanuik): Lattimer, PA, Feb. 18, 1920. UNC.

PALIN, MICHAEL: Sheffield, Yorkshire, England, May 5, 1943, Oxford.

PALMER, BETSY: East Chicago, IN, Nov. 1, 1926. DePaul U.

PALMER, GREGG (Palmer Lee): San Francisco, Jan. 25, 1927. U Utah.

PALMINTERI, CHAZZ (Calogero Lorenzo Palminteri): New York, NY, May 15, 1952.

PAMPANINI, SILVANA: Rome, Sept. 25, 1925.

PANEBIANCO, RICHARD: NYC, 1971.

PANKIN, STUART: Philadelphia, Apr. 8, 1946.

PANTOLIANO, JOE: Jersey City, NJ, Sept. 12, 1954.

PAPAS, IRENE: Chiliomodion, Greece, Mar. 9, 1929.

PAQUIN, ANNA: Winnipeg, Manitoba, Canada, July, 24, 1982.

PARE, MICHAEL: Brooklyn, NY, Oct. 9, 1959.

PARKER, COREY: NYC, July 8, 1965. NYU.

PARKER, ELEANOR: Cedarville, OH, June 26, 1922. Pasadena Playhouse.

PARKER, FESS: Fort Worth, TX, Aug. 16, 1925. USC.

PARKER, JAMESON: Baltimore, MD, Nov. 18, 1947. Beloit College.

PARKER, JEAN (Mae Green): Deer Lodge, MT, Aug. 11, 1912.

PARKER, MARY-LOUISE: Ft. Jackson, SC, Aug. 2, 1964. Bard College.

PARKER, NATHANIEL: London, 1963.

PARKER, SARAH JESSICA: Nelsonville, OH, Mar. 25, 1965.

PARKER, SUZY (Cecelia Parker): San Antonio, TX, Oct. 28, 1933.

PARKER, TREY: Auburn, AL, May 30, 1972.

PARKINS, BARBARA: Vancouver, Canada, May 22, 1943.

PARKS, MICHAEL: Corona, CA, Apr. 4, 1938.

PARSONS, ESTELLE: Lynn, MA, Nov. 20, 1927. Boston U.

PARTON, DOLLY: Sevierville, TN, Jan. 19, 1946.

PATINKIN, MANDY: Chicago, IL, Nov. 30, 1952. Juilliard.

PATRIC, JASON: NYC, June 17, 1966.

PATRICK, DENNIS: Philadelphia, Mar. 14, 1918.

PATTERSON, LEE: Vancouver, Canada, Mar. 31, 1929. Ontario College.

PATTON, WILL: Charleston, SC, June 14, 1954.

PAULIK, JOHAN: Prague, Czech., 1975.

PAVAN, MARISA (Marisa Pierangeli): Cagliari, Sardinia, June 19, 1932. Torquado Tasso College.

PAXTON, BILL: Fort Worth, TX, May. 17, 1955.

PAYMER, DAVID: Long Island, NY, Aug. 30, 1954.

PAYS, AMANDA: Berkshire, England, June 6, 1959.

PEACH, MARY: Durban, S. Africa, 1934.

PEARCE, GUY: England, Oct. 5, 1967.

PEARSON, BEATRICE: Dennison, TX, July 27, 1920.

PECK, GREGORY: La Jolla, CA, Apr. 5, 1916. U Calif.

PEÑA, ELIZABETH: Cuba, Sept. 23, 1961.

PENDLETON, AUSTIN: Warren, OH, Mar. 27, 1940. Yale U.

PENHALL, BRUCE: Balboa, CA, Aug. 17, 1960.

PENN, SEAN: Burbank, CA, Aug. 17, 1960.

PEREZ, JOSE: NYC, 1940.

PEREZ, ROSIE: Brooklyn, NY, Sept. 6, 1964.

PERKINS, ELIZABETH: Queens, NY, Nov. 18, 1960. Goodman School.

PERKINS, MILLIE: Passaic, NJ, May 12, 1938.

PERLMAN, RHEA: Brooklyn, NY, Mar. 31, 1948.

PERLMAN, RON: NYC, Apr. 13, 1950. UMn.

PERREAU, GIGI (Ghislaine): Los Angeles, Feb. 6, 1941.

PERRINE, VALERIE: Galveston, TX, Sept. 3, 1943. U Ariz.

PERRY, LUKE (Coy Luther Perry, III): Fredricktown, OH, Oct. 11, 1966.

PESCI, JOE: Newark, NJ. Feb. 9, 1943.

PESCOW, DONNA: Brooklyn, NY, Mar. 24, 1954.

PETERS, BERNADETTE (Lazzara): Jamaica, NY, Feb. 28, 1948.

PETERS, BROCK: NYC, July 2, 1927. CCNY.

PETERS. JEAN (Elizabeth): Caton, OH, Oct. 15, 1926. Ohio State U.

PETERSEN, PAUL: Glendale, CA, Sept. 23, 1945. Valley College.

PETERSEN, WILLIAM: Chicago, IL, Feb. 21, 1953.

PETERSON, CASSANDRA: Colorado Springs, CO, Sept. 17, 1951.

PETTET, JOANNA: London, Nov. 16, 1944. Neighborhood Playhouse.

PETTY, LORI: Chattanooga, TN, 1964.

PFEIFFER, MICHELLE: Santa Ana, CA, Apr. 29, 1958.

PHILLIPPE, RYAN (Matthew Phillippe): New Castle, DE, Sept. 10, 1975.

PHILLIPS, LOU DIAMOND: Phillipines, Feb. 17, 1962, UTx.

PHILLIPS, MacKENZIE: Alexandria, VA, Nov. 10, 1959.

PHILLIPS, MICHELLE (Holly Gilliam): Long Beach, CA, June 4, 1944.

PHILLIPS, SIAN: Bettws, Wales, May 14, 1934. UWales.

PHOENIX, JOAQUIN: Puerto Rico, Oct. 28, 1974.

PICARDO, ROBERT: Philadelphia, PA, Oct. 27, 1953. Yale.

PICERNI, PAUL: NYC, Dec. 1, 1922. Loyola U.

PIDGEON, REBECCA: Cambridge, MA, 1963.

PIGOTT-SMITH, TIM: Rugby, England, May 13, 1946.

PINCHOT, BRONSON: NYC, May 20, 1959. Yale.

Wallace Shawn

Christian Slater

Mira Sorvino

PINE, PHILLIP: Hanford, CA, July 16, Actors' Lab.

PISCOPO, JOE: Passaic. NJ, June 17, 1

PISIER, MARIE-FRANCE: Vietnam, 10, 1944. U Paris.

PITILLO, MARIA: Mahwah, NJ, 1965.

PITT, BRAD (William Bradley Pitt): S nee, OK, Dec. 18, 1963.

PIVEN, JEREMY: NYC, July 26, 1965.

PLACE, MARY KAY: Tulsa OK, Sept 1947. U Tulsa.

PLATT, OLIVER: Oct. 10, 1960.

PLAYTEN, ALICE: NYC, Aug. 28, NYU.

PLESHETTE, SUZANNE: NYC, Jan. 1937. Syracuse U.

PLIMPTON, MARTHA: NYC, Nov. 1970.

PLOWRIGHT, JOAN: Scunthorpe, B Lincolnshire, England, Oct. 28, 1929. Old

PLUMB, EVE: Burbank, CA, Apr. 29, 1

PLUMMER, AMANDA: NYC, Mar. 1957. Middlebury College.

PLUMMER, CHRISTOPHER: Tor Canada, Dec. 13, 1927.

PODESTA, ROSSANA: Tripoli, June 1934.

POITIER, SIDNEY: Miami, FL, Feb. 1927.

POLANSKI, ROMAN: Paris, France, 18, 1933.

POLITO, JON: Philadelphia, PA, Dec 1950. Villanova U.

POLITO, LINA: Naples, Italy, Aug. 11,

POLLACK, SYDNEY: South Bend, IN, 1, 1934.

POLLAK, KEVIN: San Francisco, Oct 1958.

POLLAN, TRACY: NYC, June 22, 1960

POLLARD, MICHAEL J.: Passaic, NJ, 30, 1939.

POLLEY, SARAH: Jan. 8, 1979.

POSEY, PARKER: Baltimore, MD, No 1968.

POSTLETHWAITE, PETE: London, Fe 1945.

POTTS, ANNIE: Nashville, TN, Oct. 1952. Stephens College.

POWELL, JANE (Suzanne Burce): Port-OR, Apr. 1, 1928.

POWELL, ROBERT: Salford, England, 1, 1944. Manchester U.

POWER, TARYN: Los Angeles, CA, 13, 1953.

POWER, TYRONE, IV: Los Angeles, Jan. 22, 1959.

POWERS, MALA (Mary Ellen): San cisco, CA, Dec. 29, 1921. UCLA.

POWERS, STEFANIE (Federkiew Hollywood, CA, Oct. 12, 1942.

PRENTISS, PAULA (Paula Ragusa): Antonio, TX, Mar. 4, 1939. Northwestern

PRESLE, MICHELINE (Micheline C sagne): Paris, France, Aug. 22, 1922. Ro Drama School.

PRESLEY, PRISCILLA: Brooklyn, NY, 24, 1945.

PRESNELL, HARVE: Modesto, CA, 14, 1933. USC.

PRESTON, KELLY: Honolulu, HI, Oct 1962. USC.

PRESTON, WILLIAM: Columbia, PA, 26, 1921. PaStateU.

PRICE, LONNY: NYC, Mar. 9, Juilliard.

James Spader

Terence Stamp

Rod Steiger

Patrick Stewart

ESTLEY, JASON: Vancouver, Canada, , 28, 1969.

MUS, BARRY: NYC, Feb. 16, 1938. ·IY.

NCE (P. Rogers Nelson): Minneapolis, , June 7, 1958.

NCIPAL, VICTORIA: Fukuoka, Japan, 3, 1945. Dade, Jr. College.

NZE, JR., FREDDIE: Los Angeles, ch 8, 1976.

OCHNOW, JURGEN: Berlin, June 10, .

OSKY, ROBERT: Philadelphia, PA, Dec. 930.

OVAL, DAVID: Brooklyn, NY, May 20, 2.

OVINE, DOROTHY: Deadwood, SD, Jan. 937. U Wash.

YCE, JONATHAN: Wales, UK, June 1, 7, RADA.

YOR, RICHARD: Peoria, IL, Dec. 1, .

LMAN, BILL: Delphi, NY, Dec. 17, 4. SUNY/Oneonta, UMass.

RCELL, LEE: Cherry Point, NC, June 15, 7. Stephens.

RDOM, EDMUND: Welwyn Garden City, land, Dec. 19, 1924. St. Ignatius College.

AID, DENNIS: Houston, TX, Apr. 9, 1954.

AID, RANDY: Houston, TX, Oct. 1, 1950. ·uston.

NLAN, KATHLEEN: Mill Valley, CA, 19, 1954.

NN, AIDAN: Chicago, IL, Mar. 8, 1959.

NN, ANTHONY: Chihuahua, Mex., Apr. 915.

FERTY, FRANCES: Sioux City, IA, 16, 1922. UCLA.

FIN, DEBORAH: Los Angeles, Mar. 13, . Valley College.

GSDALE, WILLIAM: El Dorado, AK, 19, 1961. Hendrix College.

LSBACK, STEVE: Dallas, TX, 1948.

NER, LUISE: Vienna, Austria, Jan. 12, .

RALSTON, VERA (Vera Helena Hruba): Prague, Czech., July 12, 1919.

RAMIS, HAROLD: Chicago, IL, Nov. 21, 1944. WashingtonU.

RAMPLING, CHARLOTTE: Surmer, England, Feb. 5, 1946. U Madrid.

RAMSEY, LOGAN: Long Beach, CA, Mar. 21, 1921. St. Joseph.

RANDALL, TONY (Leonard Rosenberg): Tulsa, OK, Feb. 26, 1920. Northwestern U.

RANDELL, RON: Sydney, Australia, Oct. 8, 1920. St. Mary's College.

RAPAPORT, MICHAEL: March 20, 1970.

RAPP, ANTHONY: Chicago, Oct. 26, 1971.

RASCHE, DAVID: St. Louis, MO, Aug. 7, 1944.

REA, STEPHEN: Belfast, No. Ireland, Oct. 31, 1949.

REAGAN, RONALD: Tampico, IL, Feb. 6, 1911. Eureka College.

REASON, REX: Berlin, Ger., Nov. 30, 1928. Pasadena Playhouse.

REDDY, HELEN: Melbourne, Australia, Oct. 25, 1942.

REDFORD, ROBERT: Santa Monica, CA, Aug. 18, 1937. AADA.

REDGRAVE, CORIN: London, July 16, 1939.

REDGRAVE, LYNN: London, Mar. 8, 1943.

REDGRAVE, VANESSA: London, Jan. 30, 1937.

REDMAN, JOYCE: County Mayo, Ireland, 1919. RADA.

REED, OLIVER: Wimbledon, England, Feb. 13, 1938.

REED, PAMELA: Tacoma, WA, Apr. 2, 1949.

REEMS, HARRY (Herbert Streicher): Bronx, NY, 1947. U Pittsburgh.

REES, ROGER: Aberystwyth, Wales, May 5, 1944.

REESE, DELLA: Detroit, MI, July 6, 1932.

REEVE, CHRISTOPHER: NYC, Sept. 25, 1952. Cornell, Juilliard.

REEVES, KEANU: Beiruit, Lebanon, Sept. 2, 1964.

REEVES, STEVE: Glasgow, MT, Jan. 21, 1926.

REGEHR, DUNCAN: Lethbridge, Canada, Oct. 5, 1952.

REID, ELLIOTT: NYC, Jan. 16, 1920.

REID, TIM: Norfolk, VA, Dec. 19, 1944.

REILLY, CHARLES NELSON: NYC, Jan. 13, 1931. UCt.

REILLY, JOHN C.: Chicago, IL, May 24, 1965.

REINER, CARL: NYC, Mar. 20, 1922. Georgetown.

REINER, ROB: NYC, Mar. 6, 1947. UCLA.

REINHOLD, JUDGE (Edward Ernest, Jr.): Wilmington, DE, May 21, 1957. NCSchool of Arts.

REINKING, ANN: Seattle, WA, Nov. 10, 1949.

REISER, PAUL: NYC, Mar. 30, 1957.

REMAR, JAMES: Boston, MA, Dec. 31, 1953. Neighborhood Playhouse.

REMSEN, BERT: Glen Cove, NY, Feb. 25, 1925. Ithaca.

RENFRO, BRAD: Knoxville, TN, July 25, 1982.

RENO, JEAN (Juan Moreno): Casablanca, Morocco, July 30, 1948.

REVILL, CLIVE: Wellington, NZ, Apr. 18, 1930.

REY, ANTONIA: Havana, Cuba, Oct. 12, 1927.

REYNOLDS, BURT: Waycross, GA, Feb. 11, 1935. Fla. State U.

REYNOLDS, DEBBIE (Mary Frances Reynolds): El Paso, TX, Apr. 1, 1932.

RHOADES, BARBARA: Poughkeepsie, NY, Mar. 23, 1947.

RHODES, CYNTHIA: Nashville, TN, Nov. 21, 1956.

RHYS-DAVIES, JOHN: Salisbury, England, May 5, 1944.

RHYS-MEYERS, JONATHAN: Cork, Ireland, July 27, 1977.

RIBISI, GIOVANNI: Los Angeles, CA, Mar. 31, 1976.

RICCI, CHRISTINA: Santa Monica, CA, Feb. 12, 1980.

RICHARD, CLIFF (Harry Webb)**:** India, Oct. 14, 1940.

RICHARDS, MICHAEL: Culver City, CA, July 14, 1949.

RICHARDSON, JOELY: London, Jan. 9, 1965.

RICHARDSON, LEE: Chicago, IL, Sept. 11, 1926.

RICHARDSON, MIRANDA: Southport, England, Mar. 3, 1958.

RICHARDSON, NATASHA: London, May 11, 1963.

RICKLES, DON: NYC, May 8, 1926. AADA.

RICKMAN, ALAN: Hammersmith, England, Feb. 21, 1946.

RIEGERT, PETER: NYC, Apr. 11, 1947. U Buffalo.

RIFKIN, RON: NYC, Oct. 31, 1939.

RIGG, DIANA: Doncaster, England, July 20, 1938. RADA.

RINGWALD, MOLLY: Rosewood, CA, Feb. 16, 1968.

RITTER, JOHN: Burbank, CA, Sept. 17, 1948. US. Cal.

RIVERS, JOAN (Molinsky): Brooklyn, NY, NY, June 8, 1933.

ROACHE, LINUS: Manchester, England, 1964.

ROBARDS, JASON: Chicago, IL, July 26, 1922. AADA.

ROBARDS, SAM: NYC, Dec. 16, 1963.

ROBBINS, TIM: NYC, Oct. 16, 1958. UCLA.

ROBERTS, ERIC: Biloxi, MS, Apr. 18, 1956. RADA.

ROBERTS, JULIA: Atlanta, GA, Oct. 28, 1967.

ROBERTS, RALPH: Salisbury, NC, Aug. 17, 1922. UNC.

ROBERTS, TANYA (Leigh): Bronx, NY, Oct. 15, 1954.

ROBERTS, TONY: NYC, Oct. 22, 1939. Northwestern U.

ROBERTSON, CLIFF: La Jolla, CA, Sept. 9, 1925. Antioch College.

ROBERTSON, DALE: Oklahoma City, July 14, 1923.

ROBINSON, CHRIS: West Palm Beach, FL, Nov. 5, 1938. LACC.

ROBINSON, JAY: NYC, Apr. 14, 1930.

ROBINSON, ROGER: Seattle, WA, May 2, 1940. USC.

ROCHEFORT, JEAN: Paris, France, 1930.

ROCHON, LELA (Staples):

ROCK, CHRIS: Brooklyn, NY, Feb. 7, 1966.

ROGERS, CHARLES "BUDDY": Olathe, KS, Aug. 13, 1904. U Kan.

ROGERS, MIMI: Coral Gables, FL, Jan. 27, 1956.

ROGERS, WAYNE: Birmingham, AL, Apr. 7, 1933. Princeton.

ROMAN, RUTH: Boston, Dec. 23, 1922. Bishop Lee Dramatic School.

RONSTADT, LINDA: Tucson, AZ, July 15, 1946.

ROOKER, MICHAEL: Jasper, AL, Apr. 6, 1955.

ROONEY, MICKEY (Joe Yule, Jr.): Brooklyn, NY, Sept. 23, 1920.

ROSE, REVA: Chicago, IL, July 30, 1940. Goodman.

ROSEANNE (Barr): Salt Lake City, UT, Nov. 3, 1952.

ROSS, DIANA: Detroit, MI, Mar. 26, 1944.

ROSS, JUSTIN: Brooklyn, NY, Dec. 15, 1954.

ROSS, KATHARINE: Hollywood, Jan. 29, 1943. Santa Rosa College.

ROSSELLINI, ISABELLA: Rome, June 18, 1952.

ROSSOVICH, RICK: Palo Alto, CA, Aug. 28, 1957.

ROTH, TIM: London, May 14, 1961.

ROUNDTREE, RICHARD: New Rochelle, NY, Sept. 7, 1942. Southern Ill.

ROURKE, MICKEY (Philip Andre Rourke, Jr.)**:** Schenectady, NY, Sept. 16, 1956.

ROWE, NICHOLAS: London, Nov. 22, 1966, Eton.

ROWLANDS, GENA: Cambria, WI, June 19, 1934.

RUBIN, ANDREW: New Bedford, MA, June 22, 1946. AADA.

RUBINEK, SAUL: Fohrenwold, Germany, July 2, 1948.

RUBINSTEIN, JOHN: Los Angeles, CA, Dec. 8, 1946. UCLA.

RUCK, ALAN: Cleveland, OH, July 1, 1960.

RUCKER, BO: Tampa, FL, Aug. 17, 1948.

RUDD, PAUL: Boston, MA, May 15, 1940.

RUDD, PAUL: Passaic, NJ, Apr. 6, 1969.

RUDNER, RITA: Miami, FL, Sept. 17, 1955.

RUEHL, MERCEDES: Queens, NY, Feb. 28, 1948.

RULE, JANICE: Cincinnati, OH, Aug. 15, 1931.

RUPERT, MICHAEL: Denver, CO, Oct. 23, 1951. Pasadena Playhouse.

RUSH, BARBARA: Denver, CO, Jan. 4, 1927. U Calif.

RUSH, GEOFFREY: Toowoomba, Queensland, Australia, July 6, 1951. Univ. of Queensland.

RUSSELL, JANE: Bemidji, MI, June 21, 1921. Max Reinhardt School.

RUSSELL, KURT: Springfield, MA, Mar. 17, 1951.

RUSSELL, THERESA (Paup): San Diego, CA, Mar. 20, 1957.

RUSSO, JAMES: NYC, Apr. 23, 1953.

RUTHERFORD, ANN: Toronto, Canada, Nov. 2, 1920.

RYAN, JOHN P.: NYC, July 30, 1936. CCNY.

RYAN, MEG: Fairfield, CT, Nov. 19, 1961. NYU.

RYAN, TIM (Meineslschmidt): Staten Island, NY, 1958. Rutgers U.

RYDER, WINONA (Horowitz): Winona, MN, Oct. 29, 1971.

SACCHI, ROBERT: Bronx, NY, 1941. NYU.

SÄGEBRECHT, MARIANNE: Starnberg, Bavaria, Aug. 27, 1945.

SAINT, EVA MARIE: Newark, NJ, July 4, 1924. Bowling Green State U.

SAINT JAMES, SUSAN (Suzie Jane Miller): Los Angeles, Aug. 14, 1946. Conn. College.

ST. JOHN, BETTA: Hawthorne, CA, Nov. 26, 1929.

ST. JOHN, JILL (Jill Oppenheim): Los Angeles, Aug. 19, 1940.

SALA, JOHN: Los Angeles, CA, Oct. 5, 1962.

SALDANA, THERESA: Brooklyn, NY, Aug. 20, 1954.

SALINGER, MATT: Windsor, VT, Feb. 13, 1960. Princeton, Columbia.

SALT, JENNIFER: Los Angeles, Sept. 4, 1944. Sarah Lawrence College.

SAMMS, EMMA: London, Aug. 28, 1960.

Dean Stockwell

Kiefer Sutherland

Kevin Tighe

N GIACOMO, LAURA: Orange, NJ, Nov. 1961.

NDERS, JAY O.: Austin, TX, Apr. 16, 3.

NDLER, ADAM: Bronx, NY, Sept. 9, 6. NYU.

NDS, JULIAN: Yorkshire, England, Jan 1958.

NDS, TOMMY: Chicago, IL, Aug. 27, 7.

N JUAN, OLGA: NYC, Mar. 16, 1927.

RA, MIA (Sarapocciello): Brooklyn, NY, e 19, 1967.

RANDON, CHRIS: Beckley, WV, July 24, 2. U WVa., Catholic U.

RANDON, SUSAN (Tomalin): NYC, Oct. 946. Catholic U.

RRAZIN, MICHAEL: Quebec City, ada, May 22, 1940.

VAGE, FRED: Highland Park, IL, July 9, 5.

VAGE, JOHN (Youngs): Long Island, NY, . 25, 1949. AADA.

VIOLA, CAMILLE: Bronx, NY, July 16, 0.

VOY, TERESA ANN: London, July 18, 5.

KON, JOHN (Carmen Orrico): Brooklyn, Aug. 5, 1935.

ARGE, RAPHAEL: NYC, Feb. 12, 1964.

ACCHI, GRETA: Milan, Italy, Feb. 18, 0.

ALIA, JACK: Brooklyn, NY, Nov. 10, 1.

ARWID, DIANA: Savannah, GA, Aug. 27, 5, AADA. Pace U.

HEIDER, ROY: Orange, NJ, Nov. 10, 2. Franklin-Marshall.

HEINE, RAYNOR: Emporia, VA, Nov. 10. ommonwealthU.

HELL, MARIA: Vienna, Jan. 15, 1926.

HELL, MAXIMILIAN: Vienna, Dec. 8, 0.

HLATTER, CHARLIE: Englewood, NJ, v 1, 1966. Ithaca College.

HNEIDER, JOHN: Mt. Kisco, NY, Apr. 8, 0.

HNEIDER, MARIA: Paris, France, Mar. 1952.

HREIBER, LIEV: San Francisco, CA, Oct. 967.

SCHRODER, RICK: Staten Island, NY, Apr. 13, 1970.

SCHUCK, JOHN: Boston, MA, Feb. 4, 1940.

SCHULTZ, DWIGHT: Milwaukee, WI, Nov. 10, 1938. MarquetteU.

SCHWARZENEGGER, ARNOLD: Austria, July 30, 1947.

SCHWARTZMAN, JASON: Los Angeles, June 26, 1980.

SCHWIMMER, DAVID: Queens, NY, Nov. 12, 1966.

SCHYGULLA, HANNA: Katlowitz, Germany, Dec. 25, 1943.

SCIORRA, ANNABELLA: NYC, Mar. 24, 1964.

SCOFIELD, PAUL: Hurstpierpoint, England, Jan. 21, 1922. London Mask Theatre School.

SCOGGINS, TRACY: Galveston, TX, Nov. 13, 1959.

SCOLARI, PETER: Scarsdale, NY, Sept. 12, 1956. NYCC.

SCOTT,CAMPBELL: South Salem, NY, July 19, 1962. Lawrence.

SCOTT, DEBRALEE: Elizabeth, NJ, Apr. 2, 1953

SCOTT, GEORGE C.: Wise, VA, Oct. 18, 1927. U Mo.

SCOTT, GORDON (Gordon M. Werschkul): Portland, OR, Aug. 3, 1927. Oregon U.

SCOTT, LIZABETH (Emma Matso): Scranton, PA, Sept. 29, 1922.

SCOTT, MARTHA: Jamesport, MO, Sept. 22, 1914. U Mich.

SCOTT THOMAS, KRISTIN: Redruth, Cornwall, Eng., May 24, 1960.

SEAGAL, STEVEN: Detroit, MI, Apr. 10, 1951.

SEARS, HEATHER: London, Sept. 28, 1935.

SECOMBE, HARRY: Swansea, Wales, Sept. 8, 1921.

SEDGWICK, KYRA: NYC, Aug. 19, 1965. USC.

SEGAL, GEORGE: NYC, Feb. 13, 1934. Columbia.

SELBY, DAVID: Morganstown, WV, Feb. 5, 1941. UWV.

SELLARS, ELIZABETH: Glasgow, Scotland, May 6, 1923.

SELLECK, TOM: Detroit, MI, Jan. 29, 1945. USCal.

SERBEDZIJA, RADE: Bunic, Yugoslavia, July 27, 1946.

SERNAS, JACQUES: Lithuania, July 30, 1925.

SERRAULT, MICHEL: Brunoy, France. Jan. 24, 1928. Paris Consv.

SETH, ROSHAN: New Delhi, India. 1942.

SEWELL, RUFUS: Twickenham, Eng., Oct. 29, 1967.

SEYMOUR, JANE (Joyce Frankenberg): Hillingdon, England, Feb. 15, 1952.

SHALHOUB, TONY: Oct. 7, 1953.

SHARIF, OMAR (Michel Shalhoub): Alexandria, Egypt, Apr. 10, 1932. Victoria College.

SHANDLING, GARRY: Chicago, IL, Nov. 29, 1949.

SHATNER, WILLIAM: Montreal, Canada, Mar. 22, 1931. McGill U.

SHAVER, HELEN: St. Thomas, Ontario, Canada, Feb. 24, 1951.

SHAW, FIONA: Cork, Ireland, July 10, 1955. RADA.

SHAW, STAN: Chicago, IL, 1952.

SHAWN, WALLACE: NYC, Nov. 12, 1943. Harvard.

SHEA, JOHN: North Conway, NH, Apr. 14, 1949. Bates, Yale.

SHEARER, HARRY: Los Angeles, Dec. 23, 1943. UCLA.

SHEARER, MOIRA: Dunfermline, Scotland, Jan. 17, 1926. London Theatre School.

SHEEDY, ALLY: NYC, June 13, 1962. USC.

SHEEN, CHARLIE (Carlos Irwin Estevez): Santa Monica, CA, Sept. 3, 1965.

SHEEN, MARTIN (Ramon Estevez): Dayton, OH, Aug. 3, 1940.

SHEFFER, CRAIG: York, PA, Apr. 23, 1960. E. StroudsbergU.

SHEFFIELD, JOHN: Pasadena, CA, Apr. 11, 1931. UCLA.

SHELLEY, CAROL: London, England, Aug. 16, 1939.

SHEPARD, SAM (Rogers): Ft. Sheridan, IL, Nov. 5, 1943.

SHEPHERD, CYBILL: Memphis, TN, Feb. 18, 1950. Hunter, NYU.

SHER, ANTONY: England, June 14, 1949.

SHERIDAN, JAMEY: Pasadena, CA, July 12, 1951.

SHIELDS, BROOKE: NYC, May 31, 1965.

Marisa Tomei

Dorothy Tutin

Liv Tyler

Skeet Ulrich

Brenda Vaccaro

Jean-Claude Van Damme

Mario Van Peebles

Courtney B. Vance

SHIRE, TALIA: Lake Success, NY, Apr. 25, 1946. Yale.

SHORT, MARTIN: Toronto, Canada, Mar. 26, 1950. McMasterU.

SHOWALTER, MAX (formerly Casey Adams): Caldwell, KS, June 2, 1917. Pasadena Playhouse.

SHUE, ELISABETH: S. Orange, NJ, Oct. 6, 1963. Harvard.

SHULL, RICHARD B.: Evanston, IL, Feb. 24, 1929.

SIDNEY, SYLVIA: NYC, Aug. 8, 1910. Theatre Guild School.

SIEMASZKO, CASEY: Chicago, IL, March 17, 1961.

SIKKING, JAMES B.: Los Angeles, Mar. 5, 1934.

SILVA, HENRY: Brooklyn, NY, 1928.

SILVER, RON: NYC, July 2, 1946. SUNY.

SILVERMAN, JONATHAN: Los Angeles, CA, Aug. 5, 1966. USC.

SILVERSTONE, ALICIA: San Francisco, CA, Oct. 4, 1976.

SILVERSTONE, BEN: London, Eng, 1979.

SIMMONS, JEAN: London, Jan. 31, 1929. Aida Foster School.

SIMON, PAUL: Newark. NJ, Nov. 5, 1942.

SIMON, SIMONE: Bethune, France, Apr. 23, 1910.

SIMPSON, O. J. (Orenthal James): San Francisco, CA, July 9, 1947. UCLA.

SINBAD (David Adkins): Benton Harbor, MI, Nov. 10, 1956.

SINCLAIR, JOHN (Gianluigi Loffredo): Rome, Italy, 1946.

SINDEN, DONALD: Plymouth, England, Oct. 9, 1923. Webber-Douglas.

SINGER, LORI: Corpus Christi, TX, May 6, 1962. Juilliard.

SINISE, GARY: Chicago, Mar. 17. 1955.

SIZEMORE, TOM: Detroit, MI, Sept. 29, 1964.

SKARSGÅRD, STELLAN: Gothenburg, Vastergotland, Sweden, June 13, 1951.

SKERRITT, TOM: Detroit, MI, Aug. 25, 1933. Wayne State U.

SKYE, IONE (Leitch): London, England, Sept. 4, 1971.

SLATER, CHRISTIAN: NYC, Aug. 18, 1969.

SLATER, HELEN: NYC, Dec. 15, 1965.

SMITH, CHARLES MARTIN: Los Angeles, CA, Oct. 30, 1953. CalState U.

SMITH, JACLYN: Houston, TX, Oct. 26, 1947.

SMITH, JADA PINKETT: Baltimore, MD, Sept. 18, 1971.

SMITH, KEVIN: Red Bank, NJ, Aug. 2, 1970.

SMITH, KURTWOOD: New Lisbon, WI, Jul. 3, 1942.

SMITH, LANE: Memphis, TN, Apr. 29, 1936.

SMITH, LEWIS: Chattanooga, TN, 1958. Actors Studio.

SMITH, LOIS: Topeka, KS, Nov. 3, 1930. U Wash.

SMITH, MAGGIE: Ilford, England, Dec. 28, 1934.

SMITH, ROGER: South Gate, CA, Dec. 18, 1932. U Ariz.

SMITH, WILL: Philadelphia, PA, Sept. 25, 1968.

SMITHERS, WILLIAM: Richmond, VA, July 10, 1927. Catholic U.

SMITS, JIMMY: Brooklyn, NY, July 9, 1955. Cornell U.

SNIPES, WESLEY: NYC, July 31, 1963. SUNY/Purchase.

SNODGRESS, CARRIE: Chicago, IL, Oct. 27, 1946. UNI.

SOBIEKSI, LEELEE (Liliane Sobieski): NYC, June 10, 1982.

SOLOMON, BRUCE: NYC, 1944. U Miami, Wayne State U.

SOMERS, SUZANNE (Mahoney): San Bruno, CA, Oct. 16, 1946. Lone Mt. College.

SOMMER, ELKE (Schletz): Berlin, Germany, Nov. 5, 1940.

SOMMER, JOSEF: Greifswald, Germany, June 26, 1934.

SORDI, ALBERTO: Rome, Italy, June 15, 1920.

SORVINO, MIRA: Tenafly, NJ, Sept. 28, 1967.

SORVINO, PAUL: NYC, Apr. 13, 1939. AMDA.

SOTHERN, ANN (Harriet Lake): Valley City, ND, Jan. 22, 1909.

SOTO, TALISA (Miriam Soto): Brooklyn, NY, Mar. 27, 1967.

SOUL, DAVID: Chicago, IL, Aug. 28, 19

SPACEK, SISSY: Quitman, TX, Dec. 1949. Actors Studio.

SPACEY, KEVIN: So. Orange, NJ, July 1959. Juilliard.

SPADE, DAVID: Birmingham, MS, July 1964.

SPADER, JAMES: Buzzards Bay, MA, 7, 1960.

SPANO, VINCENT: Brooklyn, NY, Oct. 1962.

SPENSER, JEREMY: Ceylon, 1937.

SPINELLA, STEPHEN: Naples, Italy, 11, 1956. NYU.

SPRINGFIELD, RICK (Richard Sp Thorpe): Sydney, Australia, Aug. 23, 1949

STACK, ROBERT: Los Angeles, Jan. 1919. USC.

STADLEN, LEWIS J.: Brooklyn, NY, Ma 1947. Neighborhood Playhouse.

STAHL, NICK: Dallas, TX, Dec. 5, 1979

STALLONE, FRANK: NYC, July 30, 19

STALLONE, SYLVESTER: NYC, Jul 1946. U Miami.

STAMP, TERENCE: London, July 23, 1

STANG, ARNOLD: Chelsea, MA, Sept. 1925.

STANLEY, KIM (Patricia Reid): Tula NM, Feb. 11, 1925. U Tex.

STANTON, HARRY DEAN: Lexington, July 14, 1926.

STAPLETON, JEAN: NYC, Jan. 19, 192

STAPLETON, MAUREEN: Troy, NY, 21, 1925.

STARR, RINGO (Richard Starkey): L pool, England, July 7, 1940.

STEEL, ANTHONY: London, May 21, 1 Cambridge.

STEELE, BARBARA: England, Dec. 1937.

STEELE, TOMMY: London, Dec. 17, 19

STEENBURGEN, MARY: Newport, 1953. Neighborhood Playhouse.

STEIGER, ROD: Westhampton, NY, Ap 1925.

STERLING, JAN (Jane Sterling Adria NYC, Apr. 3, 1923. Fay Compton School.

STERLING, ROBERT (William Ste Hart): Newcastle, PA, Nov. 13, 1917. U burgh.

Vince Vaughn

Jon Voight

Dianne Wiest

Clarence Williams III

CRN, DANIEL: Bethesda, MD, Aug. 28, 7.

CRNHAGEN, FRANCES: Washington, Jan. 13, 1932.

CVENS, ANDREW: Memphis, TN, June 1955.

CVENS, CONNIE (Concetta Ann Ingolia): oklyn, NY, Aug. 8, 1938. Hollywood Pro- ional School.

CVENS, FISHER: Chicago, IL, Nov. 27, 3. NYU.

CVENS, STELLA (Estelle Eggleston): Hot ee, MS, Oct. 1, 1936.

CVENSON, PARKER: Philadelphia, PA, 4, 1953. Princeton.

CWART, ALEXANDRA: Montreal, Cana- une 10, 1939. Louvre.

CWART, ELAINE (Elsy Steinberg): ntclair, NJ, May 31, 1929.

CWART, FRENCH (Milton French vart): Albuquerque, NM, Feb. 20, 1964.

CWART, JON (Jonathan Stewart owitz): Trenton, NJ, Nov. 28, 1962.

CWART, MARTHA (Martha Haworth): dwell, KY, Oct. 7, 1922.

CWART, PATRICK: Mirfield, England, 13, 1940.

ERS, DAVID OGDEN: Peoria, IL, Oct. 1942.

LES, JULIA: NYC, Mar. 28, 1981.

LLER, BEN: NYC, Nov. 30, 1965.

LLER, JERRY: NYC, June 8, 1931.

NG (Gordon Matthew Sumner): Wallsend, land, Oct. 2, 1951.

OCKWELL, DEAN: Hollywood, Mar. 5, 5.

OCKWELL, JOHN (John Samuels, IV): veston, TX, Mar. 25, 1961. Harvard.

OLER, SHIRLEY: Brooklyn, NY, Mar. 30, 9.

OLTZ, ERIC: Whittier, CA, Sept. 30, 1. USC.

ONE, DEE WALLACE (Deanna Bowers): sas City, MO, Dec. 14, 1948. UKS.

ORM, GALE (Josephine Cottle): Bloom- on, TX, Apr. 5, 1922.

OWE, MADELEINE: Eagle Rock, CA, 18, 1958.

RAIGHT, BEATRICE: Old Westbury, NY, 2, 1916. Dartington Hall.

RASBERG, SUSAN: NYC, May 22, 1938.

STRASSMAN, MARCIA: New Jersey, Apr. 28, 1948.

STRATHAIRN, DAVID: San Francisco, Jan. 26, 1949.

STRAUSS, PETER: NYC, Feb. 20, 1947.

STREEP, MERYL (Mary Louise): Summit, NJ, June 22, 1949. Vassar, Yale.

STREISAND, BARBRA: Brooklyn, NY, Apr. 24, 1942.

STRITCH, ELAINE: Detroit, MI, Feb. 2, 1925. Drama Workshop.

STROUD, DON: Honolulu, HI, Sept. 1, 1937.

STRUTHERS, SALLY: Portland, OR, July 28, 1948. Pasadena Playhouse.

STUDI, WES (Wesley Studie): Nofire Hollow, OK, Dec. 17, 1947.

SUMMER, DONNA (LaDonna Gaines): Boston, MA, Dec. 31, 1948.

SUTHERLAND, DONALD: St. John, New Brunswick, Canada, July 17, 1935. U Toronto.

SUTHERLAND, KIEFER: Los Angeles, CA, Dec. 18, 1966.

SVENSON, BO: Goreborg, Sweden, Feb. 13, 1941. UCLA.

SWAYZE, PATRICK: Houston, TX, Aug. 18, 1952.

SWEENEY, D. B. (Daniel Bernard Sweeney): Shoreham, NY, Nov. 14, 1961.

SWINBURNE, NORA (Elinore Johnson): Bath, England, July 24, 1902. RADA.

SWIT, LORETTA: Passaic, NJ, Nov. 4, 1937. AADA.

SYLVESTER, WILLIAM: Oakland, CA, Jan. 31, 1922. RADA.

SYMONDS, ROBERT: Bistow, AK, Dec. 1, 1926. TexU.

SYMS, SYLVIA: London, June 1, 1934. Convent School.

SZARABAJKA, KEITH: Oak Park, IL, Dec. 2, 1952. UChicago.

T, MR. (Lawrence Tero): Chicago, IL, May 21, 1952.

TABORI, KRISTOFFER (Siegel): Los Angeles, Aug. 4, 1952.

TAKEI, GEORGE: Los Angeles, CA, Apr. 20, 1939. UCLA.

TALBOT, NITA: NYC, Aug. 8, 1930. Irvine Studio School.

TAMBLYN, RUSS: Los Angeles, Dec. 30, 1934.

TARANTINO, QUENTIN: Knoxville, TN, Mar. 27, 1963.

TATE, LARENZ: Chicago, IL, Sept. 8, 1975.

TAYLOR, ELIZABETH: London, Feb. 27, 1932. Byron House School.

TAYLOR, LILI: Glencoe, IL, Feb. 20, 1967.

TAYLOR, RENEE: NYC, Mar. 19, 1935.

TAYLOR, ROD (Robert): Sydney, Aust., Jan. 11, 1929.

TAYLOR-YOUNG, LEIGH: Washington, DC, Jan. 25, 1945. Northwestern.

TEEFY, MAUREEN: Minneapolis, MN, 1954, Juilliard.

TEMPLE, SHIRLEY: Santa Monica, CA, Apr. 23, 1927.

TENNANT, VICTORIA: London, England, Sept. 30, 1950.

TERZIEFF, LAURENT: Paris, France, June 25, 1935.

TEWES, LAUREN: Braddock, PA, Oct. 26, 1954.

THACKER, RUSS: Washington, DC, June 23, 1946. Montgomery College.

THAXTER, PHYLLIS: Portland, ME, Nov. 20, 1921. St. Genevieve.

THELEN, JODI: St. Cloud, MN, 1963.

THERON, CHARLIZE: Benoni, So. Africa, Aug. 7, 1975.

THEWLIS, DAVID: Blackpool, Eng., 1963.

THOMAS, HENRY: San Antonio, TX, Sept. 8, 1971.

THOMAS, JAY: New Orleans, July 12, 1948.

THOMAS, MARLO (Margaret): Detroit, Nov. 21, 1938. USC.

THOMAS, PHILIP MICHAEL: Columbus, OH, May 26, 1949. Oakwood College.

THOMAS, RICHARD: NYC, June 13, 1951. Columbia.

THOMPSON, EMMA: London, England, Apr.15, 1959. Cambridge.

THOMPSON, FRED DALTON: Sheffield, AL, Aug. 19, 1942

THOMPSON, JACK (John Payne): Sydney, Australia, Aug. 31, 1940.

THOMPSON, LEA: Rochester, MN, May 31, 1961.

THOMPSON, REX: NYC, Dec. 14, 1942.

THOMPSON, SADA: Des Moines, IA, Sept. 27, 1929. Carnegie Tech.

THORNTON, BILLY BOB: Hot Spring, AR, Aug. 4, 1955.

THORSON, LINDA: Toronto, Canada, June 18, 1947. RADA.

Vanessa Williams

Kate Winslet

Reese Witherspoon

Noah Wyle

THULIN, INGRID: Solleftea, Sweden, Jan. 27, 1929. Royal Drama Theatre.

THURMAN, UMA: Boston, MA, Apr. 29, 1970.

TICOTIN, RACHEL: Bronx, NY, Nov. 1, 1958.

TIERNEY, LAWRENCE: Brooklyn, NY, Mar. 15, 1919. Manhattan College.

TIFFIN, PAMELA (Wonso): Oklahoma City, OK, Oct. 13, 1942.

TIGHE, KEVIN: Los Angeles, Aug. 13, 1944.

TILLY, JENNIFER: Los Angeles, CA, Sept. 16, 1958.

TILLY, MEG: Texada, Canada, Feb. 14, 1960.

TOBOLOWSKY, STEPHEN: Dallas, Tx, May 30, 1951. So. Methodist U.

TODD, BEVERLY: Chicago, IL, July 1, 1946.

TODD, RICHARD: Dublin, Ireland, June 11, 1919. Shrewsbury School.

TOLKAN, JAMES: Calumet, MI, June 20, 1931.

TOMEI, MARISA: Brooklyn, NY, Dec. 4, 1964. NYU.

TOMLIN, LILY: Detroit, MI, Sept. 1, 1939. Wayne State U.

TOPOL (Chaim Topol): Tel-Aviv, Israel, Sept. 9, 1935.

TORN, RIP: Temple, TX, Feb. 6, 1931. UTex.

TORRES, LIZ: NYC, Sept. 27, 1947. NYU.

TOTTER, AUDREY: Joliet, IL, Dec. 20, 1918.

TOWSEND, ROBERT: Chicago, IL, Feb. 6, 1957.

TRAVANTI, DANIEL J.: Kenosha, WI, Mar. 7, 1940.

TRAVIS, NANCY: Astoria, NY, Sept. 21, 1961.

TRAVOLTA, JOEY: Englewood, NJ, 1952.

TRAVOLTA, JOHN: Englewood, NJ, Feb. 18, 1954.

TREMAYNE, LES: London, Apr. 16, 1913. Northwestern, Columbia, UCLA.

TREVOR, CLAIRE (Wemlinger): NYC, March 8, 1909.

TRINTIGNANT, JEAN-LOUIS: Pont-St. Esprit, France, Dec. 11, 1930. DullinBalachova Drama School.

TRIPPLEHORN, JEANNE: Tulsa, OK, 1963.

TSOPEI, CORINNA: Athens, Greece, June 21, 1944.

TUBB, BARRY: Snyder, TX, 1963. AmConsv Th.

TUCCI, STANLEY: Katonah, NY, Jan. 11, 1960.

TUCKER, CHRIS: Atlanta, GA, 1972.

TUCKER, MICHAEL: Baltimore, MD, Feb. 6, 1944.

TUNE, TOMMY: Wichita Falls, TX, Feb. 28, 1939.

TURNER, JANINE (Gauntt): Lincoln, NE, Dec. 6, 1963.

TURNER, KATHLEEN: Springfield, MO, June 19, 1954. UMd.

TURNER, TINA (Anna Mae Bullock): Nutbush, TN, Nov. 26, 1938.

TURTURRO, JOHN: Brooklyn, NY, Feb. 28, 1957. Yale.

TUSHINGHAM, RITA: Liverpool, England, Mar. 14, 1940.

TUTIN, DOROTHY: London, Apr. 8, 1930.

TWIGGY (Lesley Hornby): London, Sept. 19, 1949.

TWOMEY, ANNE: Boston, MA, June 7, 1951. Temple U.

TYLER, BEVERLY (Beverly Jean Saul): Scranton, PA, July 5, 1928.

TYLER, LIV: Portland, ME, July 1, 1977.

TYRRELL, SUSAN: San Francisco, 1946.

TYSON, CATHY: Liverpool, England, 12, 1965. Royal Shake. Co.

TYSON, CICELY: NYC, Dec. 19, 1, NYU.

UGGAMS, LESLIE: NYC, May 25, 1, Juilliard.

ULLMAN, TRACEY: Slough, England, 30, 1959.

ULLMANN, LIV: Tokyo, Dec. 10, 1, Webber-Douglas Acad.

ULRICH, SKEET (Bryan Ray Ulrich): N Carolina, Jan. 20, 1969.

UMEKI, MIYOSHI: Otaru, Hokaido, Ja Apr. 3, 1929.

UNDERWOOD, BLAIR: Tacoma, WA, A 25, 1964. Carnegie-Mellon U.

UNGER, DEBORAH KARA: Victo British Columbia, 1966.

URICH, ROBERT: Toronto, Canada, Dec 1946.

USTINOV, PETER: London, Apr. 16, 1 Westminster School.

Renée Zellweger

Forest Whitaker

CCARO, BRENDA: Brooklyn, NY, Nov. 1939. Neighborhood Playhouse.

LANDREY, CHARLOTTE (Anne Char- Pascal): Paris, France, 1968.

LLI, ALIDA: Pola, Italy, May 31, 1921. demy of Drama.

LLONE, RAF: Riogio, Italy, Feb. 17, 6. Turin U.

N ARK, JOAN: NYC, June 16, 1943. Yale.

N DAMME, JEAN-CLAUDE (J-C nberg): Brussels, Belgium, Apr. 1, 1960.

N DE VEN, MONIQUE: Netherlands,

N DER BEEK, JAMES: Chesire, CT, ch 8, 1977.

N DEVERE, TRISH (Patricia Dressel): lewood Cliffs, NJ, Mar. 9, 1945. Ohio leyan.

N DIEN, CASPER: Ridgefield, NJ, Dec. 1968.

N DOREN, MAMIE (Joan Lucile Olan- Rowena SD, Feb. 6, 1933.

N DYKE, DICK: West Plains, MO, Dec. 1925.

NITY (Denise Katrina Smith): Niagara, , Can, Jan. 4, 1959.

N PALLANDT, NINA: Copenhagen, mark, July 15, 1932.

N PATTEN, DICK: NYC, Dec. 9, 1928.

N PATTEN, JOYCE: NYC, Mar. 9, 1934.

N PEEBLES, MARIO: NYC, Jan. 15, . Columbia U.

N PEEBLES, MELVIN: Chicago, IL, , 21, 1932.

NCE, COURTNEY B.: Detroit, MI, Mar. 1960.

RNEY, JIM: Lexington, KY, June 15, .

JGHN, ROBERT: NYC, Nov. 22, 1932.

JGHN, VINCE: Minneapolis, MN, Mar. 970.

GA, ISELA: Mexico, 1940.

JOHNSON, REGINALD: NYC, Aug. 952.

NERA, CHICK: Herkimer, NY, Mar. 27, . Pasadena Playhouse.

NORA, DIANE: Hartford, CT, 1952. ard.

RDON, GWEN: Culver City, CA, Jan. 13,

RNON, JOHN: Montreal, Canada, Feb. 932.

REEN, BEN: Miami, FL, Oct. 10, 1946.

TOR, JAMES (Lincoln Rafael Peralta): Santiago, D.R., July 27, 1939. Haaren NYC.

CENT, JAN-MICHAEL: Denver, CO, 15, 1944. Ventura.

LET, ULTRA (Isabelle Collin-Dufresne): oble, France, 1935.

ALE, MILLY: Rome, Italy, July 16, 1928. e Chateaubriand.

NS, JOAN: St. Albans, NY, July 30, 1931.

GHT, JON: Yonkers, NY, Dec. 29, 1938. olic U.

N BARGEN, DANIEL: Cincinnati, OH, 5, 1950. Purdue.

DOHLEN, LENNY: Augusta, GA, Dec. 958. UTex.

SYDOW, MAX: Lund, Sweden, July 10, . Royal Drama Theatre.

GNER, LINDSAY: Los Angeles, June 22.

WAGNER, NATASHA GREGSON: Los Angeles, CA, Sept. 29, 1970.

WAGNER, ROBERT: Detroit, Feb. 10, 1930.

WAHL, KEN: Chicago, IL, Feb. 14, 1953.

WAITE, GENEVIEVE: South Africa, 1949.

WAITE, RALPH: White Plains, NY, June 22, 1929. Yale.

WAITS, TOM: Pomona, CA, Dec. 7, 1949.

WALKEN, CHRISTOPHER: Astoria, NY, Mar. 31, 1943. Hofstra.

WALKER, CLINT: Hartfold, IL, May 30, 1927. USC.

WALLACH, ELI: Brooklyn, NY, Dec. 7, 1915. CCNY, U Tex.

WALLACH, ROBERTA: NYC, Aug. 2, 1955.

WALLIS, SHANI: London, Apr. 5, 1941.

WALSH, M. EMMET: Ogdensburg, NY, Mar. 22, 1935. Clarkson College, AADA.

WALSTON, RAY: New Orleans, Nov. 22, 1917. Cleveland Playhouse.

WALTER, JESSICA: Brooklyn, NY, Jan. 31, 1944 Neighborhood Playhouse.

WALTER, TRACEY: Jersey City, NJ, Nov. 25, 1942.

WALTERS, JULIE: London, Feb. 22, 1950.

WALTON, EMMA: London, Nov. 1962. Brown U.

WARD, BURT (Gervis): Los Angeles, July 6, 1945.

WARD, FRED: San Diego, CA, Dec. 30, 1942.

WARD, RACHEL: London, Sept. 12, 1957.

WARD, SELA: Meridian, MS, July 11, 1956.

WARD, SIMON: London, Oct. 19, 1941.

WARDEN, JACK (Lebzelter): Newark, NJ, Sept. 18, 1920.

WARNER, DAVID: Manchester, England, July 29, 1941. RADA.

WARNER, MALCOLM-JAMAL: Jersey City, NJ, Aug. 18, 1970.

WARREN, JENNIFER: NYC, Aug. 12, 1941. U Wisc.

WARREN, LESLEY ANN: NYC, Aug. 16, 1946.

WARREN, MICHAEL: South Bend, IN, Mar. 5, 1946. UCLA.

WARRICK, RUTH: St. Joseph, MO, June 29, 1915. U Mo.

WASHINGTON, DENZEL: Mt. Vernon, NY, Dec. 28, 1954. Fordham.

WASSON, CRAIG: Ontario, OR, Mar. 15, 1954. UOre.

WATERSTON, SAM: Cambridge, MA, Nov. 15, 1940. Yale.

WATLING, JACK: London, Jan. 13, 1923. Italia Conti School.

WATSON, EMILY: London, Jan. 14, 1967.

WAYANS, DAMON: NYC, Sept. 4, 1960.

WAYANS, KEENEN, IVORY: NYC, June 8, 1958. Tuskegee Inst.

WAYNE, PATRICK: Los Angeles, July 15, 1939. Loyola.

WEATHERS, CARL: New Orleans, LA, Jan. 14, 1948. Long Beach CC.

WEAVER, DENNIS: Joplin, MO, June 4, 1924. U Okla.

WEAVER, FRITZ: Pittsburgh, PA, Jan. 19, 1926.

WEAVER, SIGOURNEY (Susan): NYC, Oct. 8, 1949. Stanford, Yale.

WEBER, STEVEN: March 4, 1961.

WEDGEWORTH, ANN: Abilene, TX, Jan. 21, 1935. U Tex.

WELCH, RAQUEL (Tejada): Chicago, IL, Sept. 5, 1940.

WELD, TUESDAY (Susan): NYC, Aug. 27, 1943. Hollywood Professional School.

WELDON, JOAN: San Francisco, Aug. 5, 1933. San Francisco Conservatory.

WELLER, PETER: Stevens Point, WI, June 24, 1947. AmThWing.

WENDT, GEORGE: Chicago, IL, Oct. 17, 1948.

WEST, ADAM (William Anderson): Walla Walla, WA, Sept. 19, 1929.

WETTIG, PATRICIA: Cincinnatti, OH, Dec. 4, 1951. TempleU.

WHALEY, FRANK: Syracuse, NY, July 20, 1963. SUNY/Albany.

WHALLEY-KILMER, JOANNE: Manchester, England, Aug. 25, 1964.

WHEATON, WIL: Burbank, CA, July 29, 1972.

WHITAKER, FOREST: Longview, TX, July 15, 1961.

WHITAKER, JOHNNY: Van Nuys, CA, Dec. 13, 1959.

WHITE, BETTY: Oak Park, IL, Jan. 17, 1922.

WHITE, CHARLES: Perth Amboy, NJ, Aug. 29, 1920. Rutgers U.

WHITELAW, BILLIE: Coventry, England, June 6, 1932.

WHITMAN, STUART: San Francisco, Feb. 1, 1929. CCLA.

WHITMORE, JAMES: White Plains, NY, Oct. 1, 1921. Yale.

WHITNEY, GRACE LEE: Detroit, MI, Apr. 1, 1930.

WHITTON, MARGARET: Philadelphia, PA, Nov, 30, 1950.

WIDDOES, KATHLEEN: Wilmington, DE, Mar. 21, 1939.

WIDMARK, RICHARD: Sunrise, MN, Dec. 26, 1914. Lake Forest.

WIEST, DIANNE: Kansas City, MO, Mar. 28, 1948. UMd.

WILBY. JAMES: Burma, Feb. 20, 1958.

WILCOX, COLIN: Highlands, NC, Feb. 4, 1937. U Tenn.

WILDER, GENE (Jerome Silberman): Milwaukee, WI, June 11, 1935. UIowa.

WILLIAMS, BILLY DEE: NYC, Apr. 6, 1937.

WILLIAMS, CARA (Bernice Kamiat): Brooklyn, NY, June 29, 1925.

WILLIAMS, CINDY: Van Nuys, CA, Aug. 22, 1947. KACC.

WILLIAMS, CLARENCE, III: NYC, Aug. 21, 1939.

WILLIAMS, ESTHER: Los Angeles, Aug. 8, 1921.

WILLIAMS, JOBETH: Houston, TX, Dec 6, 1948. Brown U.

WILLIAMS, MICHELLE: Kalispell, MT, Sept. 9, 1980.

WILLIAMS, PAUL: Omaha, NE, Sept. 19, 1940.

WILLIAMS, ROBIN: Chicago, IL, July 21, 1951. Juilliard.

WILLIAMS, TREAT (Richard): Rowayton, CT, Dec. 1, 1951.

WILLIAMS, VANESSA L.: Tarrytown, NY, Mar. 18, 1963.

WILLIAMSON, FRED: Gary, IN, Mar. 5, 1938. Northwestern.

WILLIAMSON, NICOL: Hamilton, Scotland, Sept. 14, 1938.

WILLIS, BRUCE: Penns Grove, NJ, Mar. 19, 1955.

WILLISON, WALTER: Monterey Park, CA, June 24, 1947.

WILSON, DEMOND: NYC, Oct. 13, 1946. Hunter College.

WILSON, ELIZABETH: Grand Rapids, MI, Apr. 4, 1925.

WILSON, LAMBERT: Paris, France, 1959.

WILSON, SCOTT: Atlanta, GA, 1942.

WINCOTT, JEFF: Toronto, Canada, May 8, 1957.

WINCOTT, MICHAEL: Toronto, Canada, Jan. 6, 1959. Juilliard.

WINDE, BEATRICE: Chicago, IL, Jan. 6.

WINDOM, WILLIAM: NYC, Sept. 28, 1923. Williams College.

WINDSOR, MARIE (Emily Marie Bertelson): Marysvale, UT, Dec. 11, 1924. Brigham Young U.

WINFIELD, PAUL: Los Angeles, May 22, 1940. UCLA.

WINFREY, OPRAH: Kosciusko, MS, Jan. 29, 1954. TnStateU.

WINGER, DEBRA: Cleveland, OH, May 17, 1955. Cal State.

WINKLER, HENRY: NYC, Oct. 30, 1945. Yale.

WINN, KITTY: Washington, D.C., Feb, 21, 1944. Boston U.

WINNINGHAM, MARE: Phoenix, AZ, May 6, 1959.

WINSLET, KATE: Reading, Eng., Oct. 5, 1975.

WINSLOW, MICHAEL: Spokane, WA, Sept. 6, 1960.

WINTER, ALEX: London, July 17, 1965. NYU.

WINTERS, JONATHAN: Dayton, OH, Nov. 11, 1925. Kenyon College.

WINTERS, SHELLEY (Shirley Schrift): St. Louis, Aug. 18, 1922. Wayne U.

WITHERS, GOOGIE: Karachi, India, Mar. 12, 1917. Italia Conti.

WITHERS, JANE: Atlanta, GA, Apr. 12, 1926.

WITHERSPOON, REESE (Laura Jean Reese Witherspoon): Nashville, TN, Mar. 22, 1976.

WOLF, SCOTT: Newton, MA, June 4, 1968.

WONG, B.D.: San Francisco, Oct. 24,1962.

WONG, RUSSELL: Troy, NY, 1963. SantaMonica College.

WOOD, ELIJAH: Cedar Rapids, IA, Jan 28, 1981.

WOODARD, ALFRE: Tulsa, OK, Nov. 2, 1953. Boston U.

WOODLAWN, HOLLY (Harold Ajzen-berg): Juana Diaz, PR, 1947.

WOODS, JAMES: Vernal, UT, Apr. 18, 1947. MIT.

WOODWARD, EDWARD: Croyden, Surrey, England, June 1, 1930.

WOODWARD, JOANNE: Thomasville, GA, Feb. 27, 1930. Neighborhood Playhouse.

WORONOV, MARY: Brooklyn, NY, Dec. 8, 1946. Cornell.

WORTH, IRENE (Hattie Abrams): Nebraska, June 23, 1916. UCLA.

WRAY, FAY: Alberta, Canada, Sept. 15, 1907.

WRIGHT, AMY: Chicago, IL, Apr. 15, 1950.

WRIGHT, MAX: Detroit, MI, Aug. 2, 1943. WayneStateU.

WRIGHT, ROBIN: Dallas, TX, Apr. 8, 1966.

WRIGHT, TERESA: NYC, Oct. 27, 1918.

WUHL, ROBERT: Union City, NJ, Oct 1951. UHouston.

WYATT, JANE: NYC, Aug. 10, 1█ Barnard College.

WYLE, NOAH: Los Angeles, June 2, 197█

WYMAN, JANE (Sarah Jane Fulks): █ Joseph, MO, Jan. 4, 1914.

WYMORE, PATRICE: Miltonvale, KS, █ 17, 1926.

WYNN, MAY (Donna Lee Hickey): N█ Jan. 8, 1930.

WYNTER, DANA (Dagmar): London, Ju█ 1927. Rhodes U.

YORK, MICHAEL: Fulmer, England, █ 27, 1942. Oxford.

YORK, SUSANNAH: London, Jan. 9, 1█ RADA.

YOUNG, ALAN (Angus): North Sh█ England, Nov. 19, 1919.

YOUNG, BURT: Queens, NY, Apr. 30, 1█

YOUNG, CHRIS: Chambersburg, PA, █ 28, 1971.

YOUNG, LORETTA (Gretchen): Salt █ City, UT, Jan. 6, 1912. Immaculate H█ College.

YOUNG, SEAN: Louisville, KY, Nov. █ 1959. Interlochen.

YULIN, HARRIS: Los Angeles, Nov. 5, 1█

ZACHARIAS, ANN: Stockholm, Swe█ Sweden, 1956.

ZADORA, PIA: Hoboken, NJ, 1954.

ZELLWEGER, RENEE: Katy, TX, Apr█ 1969.

ZERBE, ANTHONY: Long Beach, CA, █ 20, 1939.

ZETA-JONES, CATHERINE: Swar█ Wales, Sept. 25, 1969.

ZIMBALIST, EFREM, JR.: NYC, No█ 1918. Yale.

ZUNIGA, DAPHNE: Berkeley, CA, Oct█ 1963. UCLA.

OBITUARIES 1998

PHILIP ABBOTT, 73, Nebraska-born film, stage and television character actor died of cancer in Tarzana, CA on Feb. 23, 1998. Best known for his role as "Arthur Ward" on the long-running television series "The F.B.I." he was also seen in such motion pictures as *The Invisible Boy, The Bachelor Party, Sweet Bird of Youth, The Spiral Road, The Miracle of the White Stallions,* and *Those Calloways.* Survived by his wife, two sons, and two grandchildren.

JOHN ADDISON, 78, British composer who won an Academy Award for his score for *Tom Jones,* died of a stroke in Bennington, VT, on Dec. 7, 1998. His other film credits include *Seven Days to Noon, Look Back in Anger, The Entertainer, A Taste of Honey, The Loneliness of the Long Distance Runner, The Loved One, Torn Curtain, A Fine Madness, Smashing Time, The Honey Pot, The Charge of the Light Brigade* (1968), *Sleuth* (Oscar nomination), *The Seven Percent Solution, A Bridge Too Far,* and *Grace Quigley.* He is survived by his wife, five children, six grandchildren, and a sister.

Philip Abbott   Robert Allen

ROBERT ALLEN (Irvine E. Theodore Baehr), 92, New York-born Western star died on Oct. 14, 1998 in Oyster Bay, NY after a brief battle with cancer. For Columbia he starred in a seres of Texas Ranger adventures including *Rio Grande Ranger, Unknown Ranger,* and *The Ranger Steps In.* He is survived by his son, daughter, seven grandchildren, and six great-grandchildren.

ERIC AMBLER, 89, noted best-selling author and screenwriter, died of unreported causes on Oct. 22, 1998 at his London home. In addition to *The Cruel Sea,* for which he earned an Oscar nomination, his script credits include *The October Man, The Magic Box, The Card/The Promoter, The Purple Plain, A Night to Remember,* and *The Wreck of the Mary Deare.* No reported survivors.

GENE AUTRY (Orvon Gene Autry), 91, Texas-born motion picture actor, one of the most famous of all Western movie stars, died on Oct. 2, 1998 at his home in Studio City, CA. He received his first starring role in 1935 in *Tumbling*

Gene Autry

Tumbleweeds, and this was followed by such other titles as *The Singing Cowboy, Guns and Guitars, Boots and Saddles, Prairie Moon, Western Jamboree, Home on the Prairie, Mexicali Rose, In Old Monterey, South of the Border, Melody Ranch, Back in the Saddle, The Singing Hills, Heart of the Rio Grande, Twilight on the Rio Grande,* and *Robin Hood of Texas.* As owner of various hotels, broadcasting stations and the California Angels baseball team, he became one of the wealthest men in show business. In addition to his theme song, "Back in the Saddle," he also introduced one of the best-loved Christmas songs of all time, "Rudolph the Red-Nosed Reindeer." Survived by his second wife, a sister, and several nieces and nephews.

Binnie Barnes   Sonny Bono

BINNIE BARNES (Gitelle Barnes), 95, British actress who came to Hollywood after her success playing Catherine Howard in *The Private Life of Henry VIII,* died at her Beverly Hills, CA home on July 27, 1998. Her other movie credits include *The Private Life of Don Juan, Gift of Gab, Diamond Jim, Sutter's Gold, The Last of the Mohicans* (1936), *The Magnificent Brute, Three Smart Girls, Broadway Melody of 1938, The Adventures of Marco Polo, Holiday* (1938), *Tropic Holiday, The Divorce of Lady X, Thanks for Everything, The Three Musketeers* (1939), *Froniter Marshal, This Thing Called Love, Skylark, Three Girls About Town, I Married an Angel, Up in Mabel's Room, The Hour Before the Dawn, It's in the Bag, The Spanish Main, Getting Gertie's Garter, The Time of Their Lives, The Trouble With Angels,* and *Forty Carats.* She had been married to Columbia executive-producer Mike Frankovich until his death in 1992. She is survived by two sons, a daughter, and seven grandchildren.

EVA BARTOK (Eva Ivanova Szoeke), 72, Hungarian actress died of unspecified causes on Aug. 1, 1998 in London. Her film credits include *The Venetian Bird, The Crimson Pirate, Front Page Story, Carnival Story, The Gamma People, Ten Thousand Bedrooms,* and *Operation Amsterdam.* Survived by her daughter and two grandchildren.

Lloyd Bridges

SONNY BONO (Salvatore Bono), 62, Detroit-born singer-songwriter-actor, best known for such hit records as "The Beat Goes On" and "I've Got You Babe" which he recorded in the sixties as part of the duo Sonny and Cher, was killed when he hit a tree while skiing in South Lake Tahoe, CA, on Jan. 5, 1998. He was seen in the films *Wild on the Beach, Good Times* (both with Cher); *Escape to Athena, Airplane II: The Sequel, Troll, Hairspray,* and *Under the Boardwalk;* and wrote and produced *Chastity.* He had served as mayor of Palm Springs and was a Congressional Representative for California's 44th district at the time of his death. He is survived by his fourth wife, their two children, and his daughter Chastity from his marriage to Cher.

LLOYD BRIDGES (Lloyd Vernet Bridges, Jr.), 85, California-born screen, stage and television actor who racked up a lengthy list of credits over a fifty-seven year period, died of natural causes at his home in Los Angeles on March 10, 1998.

Dane Clark   Jerome Dempsey

Following his 1941 film debut in *The Lone Wolf Takes a Chance,* he was seen in such movies as *Here Comes Mr. Jordan, Three Girls About Town, The Wife Takes a Flyer, Blondie Goes to College, Alias Boston Blackie, Sweethearts of the Fleet, The Talk of the Town, The Commandos Strike at Dawn, Sahara, The Heat's On, Once Upon a Time, A Walk in the Sun, Miss Susie Slagle's, Canyon Passage, Unconquered, Red Canyon, Home of the Brave, Colt .45, Rocketship XM, Little Big Horn, The Whistle at Eaton Falls, High Noon, Plymouth Adventure, Last of the Comanches, The Tall Texan, The Kid from Left Field, Wichita, The Rainmaker, Ride Out for Revenge, The Goddess, Around the World Under the Sea, The Happy Ending, The Daring Game, To Find a Man, Airplane!, Tucker: The Man and His Dream, Cousins, Joe vs. the Volcano, Hot Shots!, Blown Away,* and *Jane Austen's Mafia!* On television he was best remembered for playing underwater adventurer Mike Nelson on the series "Sea Hunt." He is survived by his wife of fifty-nine years, his two sons, actors Jeff and Beau Bridges, a daughter, and eleven grandchildren.

GREGG BURGE, 40, New York-born actor-dancer-choreographer, died of complications from a brain tumor, on July 4, 1998 in Atlanta. In addition to Broadway appearances in such shows as *The Wiz* and *Sophisticated Ladies,* he was seen in such movies as *A Chorus Line* and *School Daze.* Survived by his parents, two brothers, and his grandmother.

Richard Denning   John Derek

DANE CLARK (Bernard Zanville), 85, Brooklyn-born screen, stage and television actor died on Sept. 11, 1998 in Santa Monica, CA following a long illness. Making his film debut in 1942 under his real name he was first billed as "Dane Clark" in Warners' *Destination Tokyo*. This was followed by such movies as *The Very Thought of You, Hollywood Canteen, Pride of the Marines, God is My Co-Pilot, A Stolen Life, Deep Valley, Moonrise, Whiplash, Backfire* (1950), *Barricade, Highly Dangerous, Fort Defiance, The Gambler and the Lady, Go Man Go, Thunder Pass, Port of Hell, Massacre,* and *Last Rites* (1988). Survived by his wife.

BEVERLY CROSS, 69, British writer died in London on March 20, 1998 from a series of aneurysms. His credits included *Jason and the Argonauts, The Long Ships, Genghis Khan, Half a Sixpence,* and *Clash of the Titans.*

Alice Faye

DUILIO DEL PRETE, 59, Italian actor best known for appearing in the Peter Bogdanovich films *Daisy Miller* and *At Long Last Love,* died of undisclosed causes on Feb. 2, 1998 in Rome. His other movies included *Alfredo Alfredo, The Assassination of Trotsky, Massacre in Rome,* and *The Sensuous Nurse.*

JEROME DEMPSEY, 69, screen, stage and television character actor died at his New York home on Aug. 26, 1998 of heart failure. His motion picture credits include *Network, Brewster's Millions* (1985), *The Wizard of Loneliness,* and *Tune in Tomorrow.* Survived by his sister.

MICHAEL DENISON, 82, British screen and stage actor, best known for playing Algernon in the 1952 film version of *The Importance of Being Earnest,* died of cancer at his home in Amersham, England, on July 22, 1998. He was seen in such other films as *My Brother Jonathan, The Glass Mountain, The Magic Box, There Was a Young Lady, The Truth About Women,* and *Shadowlands.* He is survived by his wife of fifty-nine years, actress Dulcie Gray.

RICHARD DENNING (Louis Albert Heindrich Denninger), 84, Poughkeepsie NY-born screen and television actor, died of cardiac arrest on Oct. 11, 1998 in Escondido, CA. His movie credits include *Daughter of Shanghai, King of Alcatraz, The Arkansas Traveler, King of Chinatown, Zaza, Hotel Imperial, Union Pacific, Parole Fixer, Love Thy Neighbor, Adam Had Four Sons, Ice Capades, Beyond the Blue Horizon,* *The Glass Key* (1942), *Black Beauty* (1946), *Caged Fury, When My Baby Smiles at Me, Harbor of Missing Men, Hangman's Knot, Jivaro, The Creature from the Black Lagoon, Battle of Rogue River, The Magnificent Matador, The Creature with the Atom Brain, Day the World Ended, Girls in Prison, An Affair to Remember, The Lady Takes a Flyer, Twice Told Tales,* and *I Sailed to Tahiti with an All-Girl Crew.* On television he was known for the series "Mr. and Mrs. North" and "Hawaii Five-O" where he played the governor. Survived by a daughter from his marriage to actress Evelyn Ankers; his second wife, four stepchildren, and two granddaughters.

JOHN DEREK (Derek Harris), 71, Hollywood-born actor-director who first gained attention with his performances in the 1949 films *All the King's Men* and *Knock on Any Door,* died of heart failure on May 22, 1998 in Santa Maria, CA. As an actor he was also seen in such movies as *Rogues of Sherwood Forest, Saturday's Hero, Scandal Sheet, Mission Over Korea, Prince of Pirates, The Adventures of Hajji Baba, Prince of Players, Annapolis Story, The Leather Saint, The Ten Commandments, Omar Khayyam, Exodus, Nightmare in the Sun, Once Before I Die* (and director), and *Childish Things* (and director). He also served as director-cinematographer on three films starring his fourth wife and widow, Bo Derek, *Tarzan the Ape Man* (1981), *Bolero* (which he also wrote), and *Ghosts Can't Do It.* He is survived by a son and daughter from his first marriage to French actress Pati Behrs.

PENNY EDWARDS (Millicent Maxine Edwards), 70, New York-born actress died of lung cancer in Friendswood, Texas, on Aug. 26, 1998. Among her film credits are *My Wild Irish Rose, Adventures of Don Juan, That Hagen Girl, Trail of Robin Hood, Spoilers of the Plains, Heart of the Rockies, Woman in the Dark, Pony Soldier,* and *Powder River.* Survived by two daughters, a son, four grandchildren, two brothers, and a sister.

GENE EVANS, 75, character actor died on April 1, 1998 in Jackson, TN. His movies include *Under Colorado Skies, Crisscross* (1948), *Mother is a Freshman, It Happens Every Spring, Dallas, The Asphalt Jungle, Storm Warning, Sugarfoot, Ace in the Hole, Fixed Bayonets, Force of Arms, Donovan's Brain, Cattle Queen of Montana, The Long Wait, The Helen Morgan Story, The Sad Sack, The Bravados, Shock Corridor, The War Wagon, Support Your Local Sheriff, The Ballad of Cable Hogue,* and *Pat Garrett and Billy the Kid.* Survived by a daughter, two sons, a brother, and two grandsons.

Norman Fell   Phil Hartman

Peter Lind Hayes   Hurd Hatfield

ALICE FAYE (Alice Leppert), 86, New York City-born singer-actress who became one of the leading stars of the late thirties-early forties with her roles in such popular 20th Century Fox musicals as *In Old Chicago, Alexander's Ragtime Band,* and *The Gang's All Here,* died of cancer on May 9, 1998 in Rancho Mirage, CA. Originally a chorus girl she made her film debut in 1934 in *George White's Scandals of 1934* and soon rose to stardom under contract to Fox with such movies as *Poor Little Rich Girl, Sing Baby Sing, Stowaway, On the Avenue, Wake Up and Live, You Can't Have Everything, Sally Irene and Mary* (1938), *Hollywood Cavalcade, Rose of Washington Square, Lillian Russell, Little Old New York, Tin Pan Alley, The Great American Broadcast, Weekend in Havana, Hello Frisco Hello* (where she introduced the Oscar-winning hit "You'll Never Know"), and *Fallen Angel.* Later she was seen in *State Fair* (1962), *Won Ton Ton the Dog Who Saved Hollywood,* and *The Magic of Lassie.* Survived by her two daughters from her fifty-four year marriage to bandleader-actor Phil Harris (who died in 1995); four grandchildren; and four great-grandchildren.

NORMAN FELL, 74, Philadelphia-born character actor, perhaps best known for his role as landlord "Stanley Roper" on the series "Three's Company" and its spinoff "The Ropers," died of cancer on Dec. 14, 1998 in Woodland Hills, CA. He was seen in such films as *Pork Chop Hill, The Rat Race, Inherit the Wind, Ocean's Eleven, PT-109, It's a Mad Mad Mad Mad World, Quick Before It Melts, The Secret War of Harry Frigg, Fitzwilly, The Graduate* (as Dustin Hoffman's landlord), *Bullitt, If It's Tuesday This Must Be Belgium, The Boatniks, Catch-22, Charley Varrick, The End, Paternity,* and *For the Boys.* Survived by two daughters.

EDWIGE FEUILLÈRE (Edwige Caroline Cunati), 91, French film and stage actress, died on Nov. 13, 1998 in Paris. Her films include *Topaze, Lucrece Borgia, Duchesse de Langeais, L'Aigle a Deux Tetes,* and *La Chair de l'Orchide.* No immediate survivors.

SYLVIA FIELD, 97, Boston-born actress best remembered for playing Mrs. Wilson on the television series "Dennis the Menace," died on July 31, 1998 in Fallbrook, CA. She was seen in such films as *Her Primitive Man, Junior Miss,* and *All Mine to Give.* No reported survivors.

DOUGLAS V. FOWLEY (Daniel Vincent Fowley), 86, Bronx-born screen and television character actor, perhaps best known for playing the movie director "Roscoe Dexter" in *Singin' in the Rain,* died on May 21, 1998 in Woodland Hills, CA of natural causes. His many films include *The Mad Game,*

Operator 13, The Thin Man, Two for Tonight, On the Avenue, Wake Up and Live, Alexander's Ragtime Band, Twenty-Mule Team, Somewhere I'll Find You, The Gay Sisters, The Story of Dr. Wassell, See Here Private Hargrove, Sea of Grass, The Hucksters, Battleground, Take Me Out to the Ballgame, Mighty Joe Young (1949), *Any Number Can Play, He's a Cockeyed Wonder, Across the Wide Missouri, The Band Wagon, Barabbas, 7 Faces of Dr. Lao, The White Buffalo,* and *The North Avenue Irregulars.* He is survived by his wife, five children, three grandchildren, and a great-grandchild.

CHRISTOPHER GABLE, 58, British ballet dancer-actor best known for starring opposite Twiggy in director Ken Russell's 1971 musical *The Boy Friend,* died on Oct. 23, 1998 of cancer at his home near Halifax in Yorkshire, England. He was also seen in the films *Women in Love, The Music Lovers,* and *The Rainbow,* all directed by Russell. He is survived by his wife, a son, a daughter, and a brother.

JAMES GOLDMAN, 71, Chicago-born writer who won an Academy Award for adapting his play *The Lion in Winter* to the screen, died of a heart attack on Oct. 28, 1998 after collapsing in the lobby of his Manhattan apartment building. His other screenplays included *They Might Be Giants, Nicholas and Alexandra, Robin and Marian,* and *White Nights.* He is survived by his brother, writer William Goldman, his wife, and two children from a previous marriage.

MARIUS GORING, 86, British actor who played the composer Julian Craster in the 1948 film *The Red Shoes,* died of cancer at his home in the West Sussex county of England on Sept. 30, 1998. Following his 1935 debut in *The Amateur Gentleman* he was seen in such features as *Rembrandt, A Matter of Life and Death (Stairway to Heaven), Mr. Perin and Mr. Traill, Odette, Highly Dangerous, Pandora and the Flying Dutchman, The Magic Box, The Man Who Watched the Trains Go By, Quentin Durward, The Barefoot Contessa, Son of Robin Hood, I Was Monty's Double, Exodus, Lisa (The Inspector), The 25th Hour, Zeppelin,* and *Strike It Rich.* His is survived by his third wife.

Irene Hervey   Valerie Hobson

LEW GRADE (Lewis Winogradsky), 91, Ukraine-born British producer, impressario and founder of England's first commercially financed television company, died in London on Dec. 13, 1998. His companies ITC and Associate Film Distribution were resonsible for such movies as *The Muppet Movie, Raise the Titanic, Inside Moves, The Jazz Singer* (1980), *Legend of the Lone Ranger, The Great Muppet Caper, On Golden Pond, Barbarosa,* and *The Dark Crystal.* He is survived by his wife, a son and two grandchildren.

PHIL HARTMAN, 49, Ontario-born comedian-actor was shot to death by his wife who then committed suicide, on May 28, 1998 at his home in Encino, CA. Best known for his work on the series "Saturday Night Live" and "NewsRadio" he was also seen in such films as *Pee-wee's Big Adventure* (which he also co-wrote), *Blind Date, Coneheads, So I Married an Axe Murderer, House Guest, Sgt. Bilko, Jingle All the Way,* and his last, *Small Soldiers,* released posthumously. Survivors include his two children, two brothers and five sisters.

HURD HATFIELD (William Rukard Hurd Hatfield), 80, New York City-born screen, stage and television actor, best known for his starring role in the 1945 version of *The Picture of Dorian Gray,* died at a friend's home in Monktown, Ireland on Dec. 25, 1998 of undisclosed causes. Following his 1944 film debut in *Dragon Seed* he was seen in such films as *Diary of a Chambermaid* (1946), *The Beginning or the End?, Chinatown at Midnight, Joan of Arc, Tarzan and the Slave Girl, The Left Handed Gun, King of Kings, El Cid, Mickey One, The Boston Strangler, King David, Crimes of the Heart,* and *Her Alibi.* There were no immediate survivors.

PETER LIND HAYES (Joseph Conrad Lind), 82, San Francisco-born singer-actor died in Las Vegas on Apr. 21, 1998 from vascular problems. His movie credits include *Million Dollar Legs* (1939), *These Glamour Girls, Seventeen, Playmates, Seven Days Leave, The 5000 Fingers of Dr. T* (co-starring his wife and frequent performing partner Mary Healy-Hayes), and *Once You Kiss a Stranger.* In addition to his wife he is survived by a son, a daughter, and a grandchild.

Persis Khambatta   Jack Lord

IRENE HERVEY, 89, California-born screen and television actress died of heart failure on Dec. 20, 1998 in Woodland Hills, CA. Among her films are *Three on a Honeymoon, East Side of Heaven, Destry Rides Again* (1939), *Unseen Enemy, The Boys From Syracuse* (opposite her then-husband Allan Jones), *The Stranger's Return, Bombay Clipper, Night Monster, Chicago Deadline, Mr. Peabody and the Mermaid, A Cry in the Night, San Francisco Docks, Cactus Flower,* and *Play Misty for Me.* She is survived by her son, singer Jack Jones, and a daughter.

JOAN HICKSON, 92, British actress best known for playing Agatha Christie's amateur sleuth Jane Marple on television, died of natural causes on Oct. 17, 1998 in Colchester, Essex, England. Among her film credits are *The Man Who Could Work Miracles, The Notorious Gentleman (The Rake's Progress), The Adventuress, Seven Days to Noon, The Promoter (The Card), All at Sea (Barnacle Bill), The 39 Steps* (1959), *Murder She Said, Heavens Above!, A Day in the Death of Joe Egg,* and *Yanks.*

VALERIE HOBSON, 81, British actress, born in Northern Ireland, whose notable films include *Bride of Frankenstein, Great Expectations* (as Estella) and *Kind Hearts and Coronets,* died of a heart attack on Nov. 13, 1998 in London. She made her motion picture debut in 1933 in *Eyes of Fate* and was thereafter seen in such films as *Strange Wives, Rendezvous at Midnight, The Mystery of Edwin Drood, Werewolf of London, Chinatown Squad, Secret of Stamboul, Drums, Q Planes (Clouds Over Europe), Blackout (Contraband), Tartu, Blanche Fury, The Card (The Promoter), The Rocking Horse Winner,* and *Knave of Hearts (Lovers Happy Lovers).* She is survived by her husband, former Parliament member John Profumo, and two sons.

Akira Kurosawa

JOSEPHINE HUTCHINSON, 94, Seattle-born screen, stage and television actress died in New York on June 4, 1998, having been in failing health for some time. Her screen credits include *Happiness Ahead, Oil for the Lamps of China, The Story of Louis Pasteur, I Married a Doctor, Son of Frankenstein, Tom Brown's School Days, My Son My Son, Somewhere in the Night, Ruby Gentry, Miracle in the Rain, North by Northwest, The Adventures of Huckleberry Finn* (1960), *Baby the Rain Must Fall, Nevada Smith,* and *Rabbit Run.* No immediate survivors.

PERSIS KHAMBATTA, 49, India-born actress best known for playing the alien Lieutenant Ilia in *Star Trek: The Motion Picture,* died of a heart attack in Bombay on Aug. 18, 1998. Her other films include *The Wilby Conspiracy, Conduct Unbecoming, Nighthawks,* and *Megaforce.* She is survived by her mother and a brother.

LEONID KINSKEY, 95, Russian-born character actor died of complications from a stroke on Sept. 9, 1998 in Fountain Hills, AZ. His movies included *The Big Broadcast, Trouble in Paradise, Three-Cornered Moon, Duck Soup, Manhattan Melodrama, Goin' to Town, Hollywood Party, The Cat and the Fiddle, The Gilded Lily, Lives of a Bengal Lancer, Les Miserables* (1935), *The Garden of Allah, Rhythm on the Range, The General Died at Dawn, Nothing Sacred, Maytime, The Great Waltz* (1938), *Algiers, The Story of Vernon and Irene Castle, On Your Toes, Down Argentine Way, Ball of Fire, So Ends Our Night, I Married an Angel, Casablanca* (as Sascha the Bartender), *Presenting Lily Mars, Monsieur Beaucaire,* and *The Man with the Golden Arm.* No reported survivors.

FELIX KNIGHT, 89, Georgia-born actor-singer best known for playing Tom-Tom in the 1934 version of *Babes in Toyland (March of the Wooden Soldiers)* died on June 18, 1998 in New York. His other films include *Down to Their Last Yacht, Caravan, Springtime in Holland,* and *The Bohemian Girl.* No reported survivors.

CHARLES KORVIN (Geza Karpathi), 90, Hungarian-born American film actor died on June 18, 1998 in Manhattan. Following his 1945 film debut in *Enter Arsene Lupin* he was seen in such films as *This Love of Ours, Temptation, Berlin Express, The Killer That Stalked New York, Lydia Bailey, Sangaree, Ship of Fools,* and *Inside Out.* Survived by his wife, a daughter, a son and three grandchildren.

Joseph Maher   David Manners

AKIRA KUROSAWA, 88, Japan's greatest filmmaker, who directed such classics as *The Seven Samurai* and *Rashomon,* died of a stroke on Sept. 6, 1998 at his home in Tokyo. Among his other works were *Sanshiro Sugata, Drunken Angel, Stray Dog, The Idiot, Ikiru, Throne of Blood, The Lower Depths, The Hidden Fortress, Yojimbo, Sanjuro, Red Beard, Dodeskaden, Dersu Uzala, Kagemusha, Ran, Dreams,* and *Rhapsody in August.* He was the recipient of an honorary Academy Award in 1990, while two of his films, *Rashomon* and *Dersu Uzala* were Oscar winners for Best Foreign Language Film. Survived by his wife and son.

PHIL LEEDS, 82, stand-up comic and actor died of pneumonia on Aug. 16, 1998 in Los Angeles. He was seen in such motion pictures as *Rosemary's Baby, Beaches, Enemies a Love Story, Ghost,* and *Soapdish.* No immediate survivors.

BOBO LEWIS (Barbara Lewis), 72, screen, stage and television character actress, died of cancer on Nov. 6, 1998 in New York. Among her movie credits were *It's a Mad Mad Mad Mad World, The Wild Party, Running on Empty, The Paper,* and *One True Thing.* No reported survivors.

JACK LORD (John Joseph Patrick Ryan), 77, Brooklyn-born screen, stage and television actor, best known for his 11-year run as Detective Steve McGarrett on the series "Hawaii Five-O," died of congestive heart failure on January 21, 1998 at his home in Honolulu. His films included *Cry Murder, The Court-Martial of Billy Mitchell, The Vagabond King, Tip on a Dead Jockey, Man of the West, God's Little Acre, The Hangman, Walk Like a Dragon,* and *Dr. No.* Survived by his wife.

Jean Marais   E. G. Marshall

JOSEPH MAHER, 64, Ireland-born American character actor died of a brain tumor at his Los Angeles home on July 17, 1998. He appeared in such films as *Time After Time, Just Tell Me What You Want, Those Lips Those Eyes, Under the Rainbow, I'm Dancing as Fast as I Can, Funny Farm, My Stepmother is an Alien, The Shadow, I.Q., Surviving Picasso, Mars Attacks!,* and *In & Out.* He is survived by four sisters, and one brother.

DAVID MANNERS (Rauff de Ryther Duan Acklom), 98, Nova Scotia-born screen and stage actor, best known for portraying the hero John Harker opposite Bela Lugosi in the 1931 horror classic *Dracula,* died on Dec. 23, 1998 of natural causes in Santa Barbara, CA. His other films include *Journey's End, The Truth About Youth, The Millionaire, The Miracle Woman, The Greeks Had a Word for Them, Beauty and the Boss, Crooner, A Bill of Divorcement* (1932), *They Call It Sin, The Mummy* (1932), *From Hell to Heaven, The Warrior's Husband, The Devil's in Love, Torch Singer, Roman Scandals, The Black Cat* (1934), *The Great Flirtation, The Mystery of Edwin Drood,* and *A Woman Rebels.* Survived by a niece.

Daniel Massey   Jeanette Nolan

JEAN MARAIS, 84, French star of *Beauty and the Beast* and *Orpheus* (both directed by his off-screen companion Jean Cocteau), died of pulmonary disease on Nov. 8, 1998 in Cannes. His other credits included *Ruy Blas, Eagle With Two Heads, Les Parents Terribles (The Storm Within), Aux Yeux du Souvenir (Souvenir), The Secret of Mayerling, Royal Affair sin Versailles, The Count of Monte Cristo, Paris Does Strange Things, White Nights (Le Notti Bianche), The Testament of Orpheus, Pontius Pilate, Donkey Skin,* and *Stealing Beauty.* No reported survivors.

Roddy McDowall

E.G. MARSHALL, 84, Minnesota-born screen, stage and television character actor, died on Aug. 24, 1998 at his home in Bedford, NY following a brief illness. His films included *The House on 92nd Street* (his debut in 1945), *Call Northside 777, The Caine Mutiny, Pushover, Broken Lance, The Silver Chalice, The Left Hand of God, The Scarlet Hour, The Mountain, Twelve Angry Men, The Bachelor Party, Man on Fire, The Buccaneer* (1958), *Compulsion, Cash McCall, Town Without Pity, Is Paris Burning?, The Chase, Tora! Tora! Tora!, The Pursuit of Happiness, Interiors, Superman II, Creepshow, National Lampoon's Christmas Vacation, Two Evil Eyes, Consenting Adults, Nixon,* and *Absolute Power.* On television he won two Emmy Awards for starring in the series "The Defenders." He is survived by his wife, two daughters from his first marriage, two sons and a daughter from his second marriage; three grandchildren, and one great-grandchild.

DANIEL MASSEY, 64, London-born screen, stage and television actor, who received an Oscar nomination in 1968 for portraying Noël Coward in the film *Star!,* died of heart failure on March 25, 1998 in London. He had been suffering from Hodgkin's disease. The son of actor Raymond Massey, he had made his film debut in Coward's *In Which We Serve* in 1942 and was later seen in such movies as *The Entertainer, Go to Blazes, The Amorous Adventures of Moll Flanders, The Jokers, Mary Queen of Scots, Vault of Horror, The Incredible Sarah, Bad Timing: A Sensual Obsession, Victory* (1981), *Scandal,* and *In the Name of the Father.* He is survived by his sister, actress Anna Massey, his third wife, a son and a daughter.

LINDA McCARTNEY (Linda Louise Eastman), 56, musician-photographer who performed on many of the recordings of her husband Paul McCartney, died of breast cancer on Apr. 17, 1998 in Santa Barbara, CA. With her husband she was seen in the films *Let It Be, Rockshow, Give My Regards to Broad Street, Eat the Rich,* and *Get Back.* She is survived by her husband, a daughter from her first marriage; two daughters and a son from her marriage to McCartney, and two sisters.

RODDY McDOWALL (Andrew Roderick McDowall), 70, London-born screen, stage and television actor, who made the successful transition from child star of such classics as *How Green Was My Valley* and *Lassie Come Home,* to adult performer in *Cleopatra* (1963), *Lord Love a Duck,* and *Planet of the Apes* among others, died of cancer on Oct. 3, 1998 at his Los Angeles home. His many other motion pictures include *Murder in the Family* (his 1935 debut), *Man Hunt, The Pied Piper, Son of Fury, My Friend Flicka, The Keys of the Kingdom, The White Cliffs of Dover, Thunderhead: Son of Flicka, Molly and Me, Holiday in Mexico, Macbeth* (1948), *Kidnapped* (1948), *Killer Shark, The Subterraneans, Midnight Lace, The Longest Day, Shock Treatment, That Darn Cat!, The Greatest Story Ever Told, The Loved One, Inside Daisy Clover, The Defector, It!* (1967), *The Adventures of Bullwhip Griffin, The Cool Ones, Five Card Stud, Hello Down There, Midas Run, Escape From the Planet of the Apes, Bedknobs and Broomsticks, Pretty Maids All in a Row, The Poseidon Adventure, The Life and Times of Judge Roy Bean, Conquest of the Planet of the Apes, Battle for the Planet of the Apes, Arnold, Dirty Mary Crazy Larry, Funny Lady, Embryo, Rabbit Test, The Cat from Outer Space, Scavenger Hunt, Evil Under the Sun, Class of 1984, Fright Night, Dead of Night, Overboard, Last Summer in the Hamptons, It's My Party,* and *The Grass Harp.* He is survived by his sister.

Maureen O'Sullivan

BOB MERRILL, 74, Philadelphia-born composer-lyricist-writer, best known as the lyricist for the musical *Funny Girl* which included the hit songs "People" and "Don't Rain on My Parade," was found dead in his car at his home in Beverly Hills on Feb. 17, 1998. He had shot himself, having suffered from depression. In addition to songwriting he wrote the scripts for such movies as *Mahogany, W.C. Field and Me,* and *Chu Chu and the Philly Flash.* Survived by his second wife.

THERESA MERRITT, 75, Virginia-born screen, stage and theatre actress who starred on Broadway in *Ma Rainey's Black Bottom* and in the series "That's My Mama," died on June 12, 1998 in the Bronx after a long battle with skin cancer. Her film credits include *They Might Be Giants, The Goodbye Girl, All That Jazz, The Great Santini, The Best Little Whorehouse in Texas,* and *The Serpent and the Rainbow.* Survived by her husband and four children.

ARCHIE MOORE (Archibald Lee Wright), 84, boxer-turned-actor, best known for playing Jim in the 1960 version of *The Adventures of Huckleberry Finn,* died of heart failure on Dec. 9, 1998 in San Diego, CA. He was also seen in such other movies as *The Carpetbaggers, The Fortune Cookie,* and *Breakheart Pass.*

Alan J. Pakula   Leo Penn

JEANETTE NOLAN, 86, Los Angeles-born screen, stage and television actress died on June 5, 1998 in Los Angeles following a stroke. She was seen on screen in such movies as *Macbeth* (1948; as Lady Macbeth), *Words and Music, No Sad Songs for Me, The Secret of Convict Lake, The Happy Time, The Big Heat, Guns of Fort Petticoat, The Rabbit Trap, The Man Who Shot Liberty Valance, True Confessions, Cloak and Dagger* (1984), and *The Horse Whisperer.* She was married to actor John McIntire (who died in 1991) and was the mother of actor Tim McIntire (who died in 1986). She is survived by her daughter, her sister, and a grandson.

MAIDIE NORMAN, 85, screen and television character actress, best known for playing the maid in *What Ever Happened to Baby Jane?,* died of lung cancer on May 2, 1998 in San Jose, CA. She appeared in such other movies as *The Well, Torch Song, Bright Road, Susan Slept Here,* and *Airport '77.* Survived by a sister, a son, two stepchildren, five grandchildren, and four great-grandchildren.

MARTHA O'DRISCOLL, 76, Oklahoma-born actress died of unspecified causes on Nov. 3, 1998. Among her movie credits are *Li'l Abner* (1940, as Daisy Mae), *Forty Little Mothers, The Lady Eve, Henry Aldrich for President, Reap the Wild Wind, We've Never Been Licked, Crazy House, The Fallen Sparrow, Ghost Catchers, Under Western Skies, House of Dracula, Here Come the Co-Eds, Down Missouri Way,* and *Carnegie Hall.*

DICK O'NEILL, 70, New York-born character actor died of heart failure on Nov. 17, 1998 in Santa Monica, CA. He was seen in such films as *The Taking of Pelham One Two Three, The Jerk,* and *Prizzi's Honor.* On television he was best known for playing Charlie Cagney on the series "Cagney and Lacey." He is survived by his wife and three daughters.

MAUREEN O'SULLIVAN, 87, Ireland-born American actress best known for playing "Jane" opposite Johnny Weissmuller in the 1932 film version of *Tarzan the Ape Man* and five follow-up adventures, died of a heart attack on June 23, 1998 in Scottsdale, AZ. Following her 1930 debut in *Son o'My Heart* she was seen in such motion pictures as *Just Imagine, A Connecticut Yankee, Strange Interlude, Payment Deferred, Fast Companions, Cohens and Kellys in Trouble, Tugboat Annie, The Thin Man, The Barretts of Wimpole Street* (1934), *West Point of the Air, David Copperfield* (1935), *Cardinal Richelieu, Anna Karenina* (1935), *The Bishop Misbehaves, The Voice of Bugle Ann, The Devil Doll, A Day at the Races, The Emperor's Candlesticks, A Yank at Oxford, Hold That Kiss, Port of Seven Seas, Let Us Live, Pride and Prejudice, Maisie Was a Lady, The Big Clock, Bonzo Goes to College, Mission Over Korea, The Tall T, Never Too Late, The Phynx, Hannah and Her Sisters, Peggy Sue Got Married,* and *Stranded.* She was married to director John Farrow from 1936 to his death in 1963. She is survived by her second husband; four daughters including actress Mia Farrow; two sons; thirty-two grandchildren and thirteen great-grandchildren.

ALAN J. PAKULA, 70, Bronx-born director-writer-producer who received Oscar nominations for producing *To Kill a Mockingbird,* directing *All the President's Men* and writing *Sophie's Choice,* was killed on Nov. 19, 1998 when a metal pipe smashed through the windshield of his car, striking him in the head, while driving on the Long Island Expressway. Originally a film producer of such movies as *Love with the Proper Stranger* and *Up the Down Staircase,* he moved over to directing in 1969 with *The Sterile Cuckoo.* This was followed by such other credits as *Klute, The Parallax View, Comes a Horseman, Starting Over, Rollover, Orphans, See You in the Morning, Presumed Innocent, The Pelican Brief,* and *The Devil's Own.* He is survived by his second wife, three stepchildren, and five grandchildren.

Mae Questel   Gene Raymond

STEPHEN PEARLMAN, 63, Brooklyn-born stage and screen actor died of cancer at his Manhattan home on Sept. 30, 1998. His movies include *Quiz Show, Die Hard With a Vengeance, The First Wives Club, The Horse Whisperer,* and *Pi.* Survived by his wife, two stepdaughters, his mother and two grandchildren.

LEO PENN, 77, actor-turned-director died of lung cancer on Sept. 5, 1998 in Santa Monica, CA. As an actor he was seen in such movies as *Undercover Man* and *The Story on Page One.* Although he directed mostly for television (winning an Emmy Award in 1973 for a "Columbo" episode) he also helmed the theatrical features *A Man Called Adam, Murder in Music City,* and *Judgment in Berlin,* which featured his son, actor Sean Penn. He is survived by his wife, actress Eileen Ryan; Sean and two other sons, actor Chris and musician Michael Penn; and three grandchildren.

Jerome Robbins   Esther Rolle

NAT PERRIN, 93, screenwriter died of unspecified causes on May 9, 1998 in Los Angeles. His credits include *Roman Scandals, Duck Soup, Kid Millions, Stowaway, Pigskin Parade, The Gracie Allen Murder Case, Keep 'em Flying, Hellzapoppin', Pardon My Sarong, Miss Grant Takes Richmond, The Petty Girl,* and *I'll Take Sweden.* He also directed the film *The Great Morgan.*

MAE QUESTEL, 89, screen and stage performer whose unmistakble nasally voice was used to great effect for the animated characters "Betty Boop" and "Olive Oyl," died at her Manhattan home on Jan. 4, 1998. She was seen on screen in such movies as *A Majority of One, It's Only Money, Funny Girl, Move, New York Stories (Oedipus Wrecks),* and *National Lampoon's Christmas Vacation.* Survived by her son and three granddaughters.

Roy Rogers

GENE RAYMOND (Raymond Guion), 89, New York City-born screen, stage and television actor died of pneumonia on May 3, 1998 in Los Angeles. Following his 1931 debut in *Personal Maid* he was seen in such films as *Ladies of the Big House, The Night of June 13th, Forgotten Commandments, If I Had a Million, Red Dust, Ex-Lady, Zoo in Budapest, Flying Down to Rio, Transatlantic Merry-Go-Round, Behold My Wife, Sadie McKee, The Woman in Red, Seven Keys to Baldpate, Hooray for Love, The Smartest Girl in Town, The Bride Walks Out, Stolen Heaven, Mr. and Mrs. Smith, Smilin' Through* (opposite his wife Jeanette MacDonald to whom he was married from 1937 until her death in 1965), *Million Dollar Week-End* (which he also directed), *Hit the Deck, The Best Man,* and *I'd Rather Be Rich.* His second wife died in 1995. There were no survivors.

HUGH REILLY, 82, screen, stage and television actor best known for playing Paul Martin on the series *Lassie,* died on July 17, 1998 in Burbank, CA, of emphysema. He was seen in such movies as *Chuka, Bright Victory,* and *The Sleeping City.* Survived by his three sons.

Dorothy Stickney   Don Taylor

JEROME ROBBINS (Jerome Rabinowitz), 79, one of the theatre's greatest director-choreographers, whose Broadway works included *On the Town, Gypsy, West Side Story,* and *Fiddler on the Roof,* died at his Manhattan home on July 29, 1998 following a stroke. He received an Academy Award for co-directing (with Robert Wise) the 1961 film version of *West Side Story* and was given a special Oscar for his work as a choreographer as well. Survivors include his sister.

ROY ROGERS (Leonard Franklin Slye), 86, Ohio-born film and television actor, perhaps the most popular of the "singing cowboy" stars, who rode his trusted horse Trigger to fame, died of congestive heart failure on July 6, 1998 at his home in Apple Valley near Victorville, CA. Originally a member of the group the Sons of the Pioneers he sang on radio and in films until he starred in the 1936 feature *Under Western Skies.* This was followed by such other movies as *Billy the Kid Returns, Young Buffalo Bill, Young Bill Hickok, Jesse James at Bay, Heart of the Golden West, The Cowboy and the Senorita* (the first of many roles opposite Dale Evans who became his wife in 1947), *Hollywood Canteen* (in which he sang "Don't Fence Me In"), *Lights of Old Santa Fe, Don't Fence Me In, Along the Navajo Trail, My Pal Trigger, Roll on Prairie Moon, Pals of the Golden West, Son of Paleface,* and *Mackintosh and T.J.* He continued his success on his television series "The Roy Rogers Show" and later lent his name to a chain of fast food restaurants. In addition to Evans he is survived by two sons, four daughters, fifteen grandchildren and 33 great-grandchildren.

Frank Sinatra

ESTHER ROLLE, 78, Florida-born screen, stage and television actress, best known for her role as "Florida" on the series "Maude" and its spin-off, "Good Times," died on Nov. 17, 1998 in Los Angeles. She had been suffering from diabetes. Her film credits include *The Mighty Quinn, Driving Miss Daisy, Rosewood,* and *Down in the Delta,* released posthumously. Survived by two sisters and a brother.

HENRY G. SAPERSTEIN, 80, Chicago-born producer died of cancer in Beverly Hills, CA, on June 24, 1998. Among his fils as producer were *Gay Purr-ee, Frankenstein Conquers the World, War of the Gargantuas,*and *Hell in the Pacific.*

FRANK SINATRA, 82, Hoboken-born actor-singer whose inimitable singing style made him one of the legendary figures of the twentieth century, died of a heart attack on May 14, 1998 in Los Angeles. Starting as a singer with various bands he made his motion picture debut vocalizing with the Tommy Dorsey band in *Las Vegas Nights.* This was followed by *Ship Ahoy, Reveille with Beverly, Higher and Higher,* and *Step Lively.* By this time he had become a stage and recording sensation and thereafter was upped to starring roles starting with *Anchors Aweigh,* and continuing on through *Till the Clouds Roll By, It Happend in Brooklyn, Miracle of the Bells, The Kissing Bandit, Take Me Out to the Ball Game, On the Town, Double Dynamite,* and *Meet Danny Wilson.* In the early 1950s, after a period of decline, he made an outstanding comeback, both as a singer (with a series of hit albums, first from Capitol and then on his own label, Reprise) and film actor, in the latter department winning an Academy Award for Best Supporting Actor of 1953 for his work in *From Here to Eternity.* After this he was seen in the films *Suddenly, Young at Heart, Not as a Stranger, The Tender Trap, Guys and Dolls, The Man with the Golden Arm* (Oscar nomination), *Meet Me in Las Vegas, Johnny Concho, High Society, Around the World in 80 Days, The Pride and the Passion, The Joker is Wild, Pal Joey, Kings Go Forth, Some Came Running, A Hole in the Head, Never So Few, Can-Can, Ocean's Eleven, Pepe, The Devil at Four O'Clock, Sergeants 3, The Manchurian Candidate, The Road to Hong Kong, Come Blow Your Horn, The List of Adrian Messenger, 4 for Texas, Robin and the 7 Hoods, None But the Brave* (and director), *Von Ryan's Express, Marriage on the Rocks, The Oscar, Assault on a Queen, Cast a Giant Shadow, The Naked Runner, Tony Rome, The Detective, Lady in Cement, Dirty Dingus McGee, That's Entertainment!, The First Deadly Sin, Cannonball Run II,* and *Listen Up: The Lives of Quincy Jones.* Among the many hit songs he introduced were three Academy Award-winners, "Three Coins in the Fountain," "All the Way," and "High Hopes." He was given a special Oscar for the 1945 short film "The House I Live In" and the Jean Hersholt Humanitarian Award for his charity work. Survived by his fourth wife; his son, singer-conductor Frank Sinatra, Jr.; his two daughters, one of whom is singer-actress Nancy Sinatra; and his grandchildren.

EMIL SITKA, 83, Pennsylvania-born character actor, best known for his straight-man work in thirty-five Three Stooges shorts, died on Jan. 16, 1998 in Camarillo, CA following a stroke he'd suffered months earlier. Survived by two daughters, four sons, 13 grandchildren, and 4 great-grandchildren.

PHILIP STERLING, 76, screen, stage and television actor, died of complications from myelofibrosis, on Nov. 30, 1998 in Woodland Hills, CA. He was seen in such movies as *The Gambler, Hester Street, Audrey Rose, Meteor, The Long Walk Home,* and *My Giant.* Survived by his wife, a daughter, and a sister .

DOROTHY STICKNEY, 101, North Dakota-born stage, screen and television actress, best known for starring as "Mother" opposite her real-life husband Howard Lindsay in the original cast of the longest running straight play in Broadway history, *Life With Father,* died at her Manhattan home on June 2, 1998. In addition to her many theatrical roles she was seen in such films as *Wayward, The Little Minister, Murder at the Vanities, The Moon's Our Home, I Met My Love Again, What a Life, The Uninvited,* and *I Never Sang for My Father.* Lindsay had died in 1968. There were no immediate survivors.

DON TAYLOR, 78, Pittsburgh-born actor-turned-director, best known for playing Elizabeth Taylor's fiancee in *Father of the Bride,* died of heart failure on Dec. 29, 1998 in Los Angeles. As an actor he appeared in such movies as *The Human Comedy, Thousands Cheer, Girl Crazy, Winged Victory, Song of the Thin Man, The Naked City, Battleground, Target Unknown, Father's Little Dividend, The Blue Veil, The Girls of Pleasure Island, Stalag 17, Men of Sherwood Forest, I'll Cry Tomorrow, The Bold and the Brave,* and *The Savage Guns.* His directorial credits include *Everything's Ducky, Ride the Wild Surf, Escape from the Planet of the Apes, Tom Sawyer* (1973), *The Great Scout and Cathouse Thursday, The Island of Dr. Moreau* (1977), and *The Final Countdown.* He is survived by his wife, actress Hazel Court; two daughters, a son, a stepdaughter, a sister, and a granddaughter.

KAY THOMPSON, 95, St. Louis-born entertainer, writer and music arranger, best known as the author of the book *Eloise,* about a little girl living at the Plaza Hotel, died on July 2, 1998 in New York. She had been living with her goddaughter, performer Liza Minnelli. In addition to her other work she appeared in two movies, *Funny Face,* and *Tell Me That You Love Me Junie Moon.* Twice divorced there were no immediate survivors.

Kay Thompson

J. T. Walsh

JAMES VILLIERS, 64, British actor died of cancer on Jan. 18, 1998 in Arundel, England. His many credits include *These Are the Damned (The Damned), Murder at the Gallop, King and Country, Repulsion, The Nanny, The Wrong Box, Half a Sixpence, Otley, The Ruling Class, For Your Eyes Only, Under the Volcano, Scandal, Let Him Have It,* and *King Ralph.*

J.T. WALSH, 54, San Francisco-born screen, stage and television character actor, died of a heart attack on Feb. 27, 1998 in San Diego, CA. His motion picture credits include *Eddie Macon's Run, Hannah and Her Sisters, Tin Men, House of Games, Good Morning Vietnam, Power, Things Change, Tequila Sunrise, The Big Picture, Wired, Crazy People, The Grifters, Misery, Narrow Margin, The Russia House, Backdraft, True Identity, A Few Good Men, Hoffa, Needful Things, Blue Chips, The Client, Outbreak, Nixon, The Low Life, Executive Decision, Sling Blade, Breakdown, The Negotiator,* and his last, *Pleasantville,* released posthumously. He is survived by his son; a brother, and two sisters.

Robert Young

HELEN WESTCOTT (Myrthas Helen Hickman), 70, screen and stage actress, died of complications from cancer, on March 17, 1998 in Edmunds, WA. Her films include *A Midsummer Night's Dream* (1935), *Adventures of Don Juan, The Gunfighter, With a Song in My Heart, Abbott and Costello Meet Dr. Jekyll and Mr. Hyde, The Charge at Feather River, Hot Blood, The Last Hurrah,* and *I Love My Wife.* No reported survivors.

O.Z. WHITEHEAD, 87, New York-born character actor died of cancer on July 29, 1998 in Dublin, Ireland. His movies include *The Scoundrel, The Grapes of Wrath, My Brother Talks to Horses, A Song is Born, Family Honeymoon, Ma and Pa Kettle,* and *The Man Who Shot Liberty Valance.* No reported survivors.

FLIP WILSON (Clerow Wilson), 64, Jersey City-born comedian-actor, died of liver cancer on Nov. 25, 1998 at his home in Malibu, CA. Best known for his many television guest appearances, comedy recordings and his own hit variety series, "The Flip Wilson Show," he was also seen in such films as *Uptown Saturday Night, The Fish That Saved Pittsburgh* and *Skatetown USA.* He is survived by his two sons and three daughters.

FREDDIE YOUNG, 96, London-born cinematographer who won Academy Awards for his work on *Lawrence of Arabia, Doctor Zhivago,* and *Ryan's Daughter,* died of natural causes on Dec. 1, 1998 in London. His many other films include *Victoria the Great, Goodbye Mr. Chips* (1939), *The 49th Parallel, The Young Mr. Pitt, Caesar and Cleopatra, The Winslow Boy* (1948), *Edward My Son, Treasure Island* (1950), *Ivanhoe* (Oscar nomination), *Mogambo, Knights of the Round Table, Lust for Life, Bhowani Junction, The Inn of the Sixth Happiness, Solomon and Sheba, Lord Jim, You Only Live Twice, The Battle of Britain, Nicholas and Alexandra* (Oscar nomination), *The Tamarind Seed,* and *Bloodline.* Survived by his second wife, a son, and two children from his previous marriage.

ROBERT YOUNG, 91, Chicago-born screen and television actor whose long list of film credits, including *Tugboat Annie, Northwest Passage,* and *Crossfire,* preceeded a successful career in television, died of respiratory failure on July 21, 1998 at his home in Westlake Village, CA. Following his 1931 film debut in *The Black Camel,* he was seen in such films as *The Sin of Madelon Claudet, Hell Divers, New Morals for Old, The Wet Parade, The Kid from Spain, Strange Interlude, Today We Live, Saturday's Millions, The House of Rothschild, Spitfire, Whom the Gods Destroy, West Point of the Air, The Bride Comes Home, Remember Last Night?, Secret Agent, The Longest Night, Three Wise Guys, The Bride Walks Out, Stowaway, The Emperor's Candlesticks, The Bride Wore Red, I Met Him in Paris, Married Before Breakfast, The Toy Wife, Three Comrades, The Shining Hour, Maisie, Honolulu, The Mortal Storm, Florian, Dr. Kildare's Crisis, Lady Be Good, The Trial of Mary Dugan* (1941), *Western Union, H.M. Pulham Esq., Joe Smith—American, Cairo, Journey for Margaret, Sweet Rosie O'Grady, Claudia, The Canterville Ghost, Those Endearing Young Charms, The Enchanted Cottage, Claudia and David, The Searching Wind, They Won't Believe Me, Sitting Pretty* (1948), *Bride for Sale, Adventure in Baltimore, That Forsyte Woman, Goodbye My Fancy,* and *The Secret of the Incas.* On television he was best known for starring in two popular series, "Father Knows Best," and "Marcus Welby, M.D." His wife of more than sixty years died in 1994. He is survived by four daughters, six grandchildren, and two great-grandchildren.

Flip Wilson

Henny Youngman

HENNY YOUNGMAN (Henry Youngman), 91, London-born American nightclub and television comedian, noted for his one-liners and catchphrase "Take my wife, please," died of pneumonia on Feb. 24, 1998 in Manhattan. He was seen in such movies as *A Wave a WAC and a Marine, Silent Movie, History of the World Part 1,* and *GoodFellas.* Survived by two children and two grandchildren.

INDEX

Scanner, 208
Scantlebury, Glen, 86, 288
Scaperrotta, Jeffrey, 122, 175
Scarano, Antoni, 172
Scarborough, Adrian, 267
Scarola, Lisa, 200
Scarry, Rick, 101
Scarwid, Diana, 217, 323
Schaad, Jutta, 257
Schaaf, Normana, 122
Schaal, Wendy, 90
Schade, Birge, 257
Schade, Doris, 257
Schaech, Johnathon, 28, 296
Schaeffer, Art, 125
Schaffel, Marla, 194
Schaffer, Lauren, 193
Schalop, Lee, 216
Schanz, Heidi, 72
Scharff, William Joseph, 186
Schatz, Mike, 198
Schaub, Sally, 108
Schecter, Harold, 289
Scheer, Robert, 61, 153
Scheerbaum, Peter, 287
Scheidlinger, Rob, 75
Schell, Johnny Lee, 216
Schell, Maximilian, 58, 152, 323
Schenck, Holly, 181
Schenkel, Carl, 290
Schenkenberg, Marcus, 287
Schertler, Jean, 128-129
Schickele, David, 295
Schiff, Paul, 172
Schiff, Richard, 58, 83, 151
Schiff, Stephen, 262
Schiffer, Michael, 168
Schifrin, Lalo, 125, 284
Schifrin, William, 66
Schindler, Deborah, 107
Schindler, James, 234
Schindler, Peter, 44, 153
Schippers, Ton, 285
Schirripa, Steve, 67
Schlaikjer, Amena Lee, 116
Schleuter, Patrick, 257
Schlondorff, Volker, 18, 279
Schlosser, Katrin, 287
Schlueter, Steven, 215
Schluter, Ariane, 285
Schlüter, Hennig, 293
Schmalzbauer, Frédéric, 127
Schmidberger, Mary, 165
Schmidt, Arthur, 30
Schmidt, Dwight, 65
Schmidt, Eric, 217
Schmidt, Irmin, 208
Schmidt, Michael, 103
Schmidt, Paul, 193
Schmidt, Ronn, 191
Schmidtberger, Mary, 151
Schmidtke, Ned, 40
Schmiedt, Angel, 72, 137
Schmitt, Vincent, 127
Schmitz, Kate, 200
Schneider, Aaron E., 117
Schneider, Dave, 292
Schneider, Kelley, 92
Schneider, Marnie, 16
Schneider, Rob, 116, 158
Schneiger, Robert, 214
Schoen, Gaili, 54

Schoeny, Jeffrey, 117
Schofield, Elizabeth, 215
Scholl, Kiff, 99
Scholl, Oliver, 65
Scholz, John P., 210
Schoot, Slava, 119
Schorr, Daniel, 153
Schouweiler, John, 154
Schrader, Paul, 187
Schram, Bitty, 20
Schreiber, Eileen, 206
Schreiber, Liev, 18, 24, 192, 323
Schreiber, Michael, 287
Schreiber, Nancy, 110, 204
Schröder, Lise, 251
Schroeder, Adam, 72, 169
Schroeder, Barbet, 11, 216
Schroeder, Charlie, 91
Schroeder, Paul, 122
Schub, Steven, 11, 210
Schubert, Jeff, 213
Schull, Rebecca, 43
Schulman, Tom, 137
Schulte, Mark, 38
Schulz, Mark, 151
Schulze, Matt, 113
Schulze, Paul, 191
Schutt, Herbert R., Jr, 198
Schwab, Kirstin, 267
Schwan, J.P., 36
Schwartz, Catherine, 286
Schwartz, Elizabeth, 193
Schwartz, Kimberly, 16
Schwartz, Lloyd, 91
Schwartz, Mark Evan, 292
Schwartz, Marty Eli, 158
Schwartz, Stefan, 292
Schwartz, Stephen, 176
Schwartz, Tyagi, 202
Schwartzberg, Antoinette, 165
Schwartzman, Jason, 172-173, 221, 323
Schwartzman, John, 86
Schwartzman, Maurice, 112
Schwary, Ronald L., 159
Schwarz, Austin, 62
Schwarz, Dustin, 62
Schwarz, Jeffrey, 194
Schwarz, Simon, 267
Schweickert, Jeff, 201
Schweickert, Joyce, 201
Schweiger, Til, 14
Schweizer, Heidi, 205
Schwering, Jamie, 118
Schwimmer, David, 20, 77, 146, 323
Scialla, Fred, 151
Sciorra, Annabella, 71, 133, 323
Sclafani, James Edward, 77
Scorsese, Martin, 188
Scorsone, Caterina, 207
Scott Sounders Prod., 215
Scott, Allan, 294
Scott, Andrew, 96
Scott, Bob, 278
Scott, Byron, 9
Scott, Campbell, 41, 134-135, 170, 323
Scott, Carla, 168
Scott, Darin, 194
Scott, Donna, 162, 214
Scott, Dougray, 58, 102, 294
Scott, Edmund, 240

Scott, Eric Brice, 76
Scott, Esther, 19
Scott, Fiona, 204
Scott, Gavin, 90, 241
Scott, Gayle, 214
Scott, Helen, 54
Scott, Jason-Shane, 99
Scott, Judson, 113
Scott, Matthew, 96, 240
Scott, Mike, 192
Scott, Ridley, 130
Scott, Stuart, 55
Scott, Tom Everett, 122-123, 207, 215
Scott, Tony, 130, 134, 162
Scott Thomas, Kristin, 62-63
Scott, Willard, 137
Scotto, Rosanna, 48
Scragg, Stella, 254
Scriba, Mik, 42, 101
Scroope, Doug, 21
Scruggs, Sharon, 70
Scudder, Sam, 96
Scullin, Kevin, 106
Scullin, Garret, 211
Scurfield, Matthew, 14
Seabrook, Christine, 10
Seabrook, Melinda, 206
Seaforth Highlanders of Canada, The, 208
Seagal, Steven, 44, 323
Seago, Howie, 257
Seagraves, Douglas, 114
Seagren, Steve, 20
Seale, John, 42
Sealy-Smith, Alison, 185
Sears, Djanet, 22
Sears, Ross, 36
Seavey, Nina Gilden, 194
Sebastian, Lobo, 198
Sebastiano, Frank, 203
Sedaris, Amy, 77
Seder, Sam, 111
Sedgman, Kyne, 244
Sedgwick, William, 202
Seeber, Michael, 289
Seefeld, Martín, 284
Sefton, Gary, 96
Segal, Doug, 211
Segal, Douglas, 42
Segal, Gil, 201
Segal, Michael Ryan, 119
Segal, Susan, 211
Segall, Pamela, 200
Segalla, Kevin, 91
Segan, Allison Lyon, 8, 47, 96
Seganti, Paolo, 201
Segar, Leslie, 23
Segel, Jason, 76, 207
Segovia, Alexis, 257
Segrist, Ward K., 202
Segura, Santiago, 297
Seibt, Alexander, 281
Seiden, Ray, 91
Seidler, David, 66
Seiler, Sonny, 10
Seiphemo, Rapulana, 290
Seivwright-Adams, Troy, 185
Sekacz, Ilona, 242, 254
Sekkelsten, Ådne Olav, 246
Sekula, Andrzej, 75, 286
Seldes, Marian, 120, 165, 187
Selianov, Sergei, 264
Sellers, Stan, 83
Sellon-Wright, Keith, 202

Seltzer, David, 44
Seltzer, Jerry, 194
Selway, Mary, 20, 39, 271, 295
Selyanskaya, Lyudmila, 261
Semb, Helge, 288
Semel, Stephen, 44
Semenowicz, Danka, 296
Semler, Dean, 191
Semyonova, Leda, 287
Sen, Aparna, 286
Sender, Julie Bergman, 77
Senghas, Richard, 255
Senkowski, Ron, 199
Senseless, 19
Septien, Al, 195, 200
Serban, Aurica, 294
Serban, Isidor, 294
Serbedzija, Rade, 204, 249, 323
Serdinova, Lyudmila, 291
Seresin, Michael, 40
Sergei, Ivan, 68
Serlin, Beth, 257
Sermol, Luisa, 13
Sermon, Erik, 196
Serpico, Jim, 116, 193
Serra, Eduardo, 133, 281
Serra, Raymond, 103
Serran, Leopoldo, 238
Serrano, Nestor, 101
Serratt, Ken, Jr, 142
Serrault, Michel, 281, 291, 323
Serre, Léopoldine, 127
Servidio, Kristy Ann, 62
Servitto, Matt, 153
Seseña, Nathalie, 297
Sessions, Bob, 253
Sessions, John, 75
Setliff, Adam, 118
Setrakian, Ed, 199
Setright, Anita, 255
Settle, Matthew, 160
Seventh Art, 212
Seventh Heaven, 293
Severin, Emilie B., 57
Severin, Laurel, 257
Sevigny, Chloë, 18, 70
Sevin, Jim, 118
Sevleyan, Maya, 290
Seward, Jim, 213
Sewell, Rufus, 20-21, 323
Seweryn, Andrzej, 245
Sexton III, Brendan, 17, 128-129
Seyfer, Mitch, 211
Seymor, Brandi, 70
Seymour, Cara, 175
Seymour, Caroline, 286
Seymour, Dorin, 12
Seymour, Jane, 66, 323
Seymour, Shaun, 243
Sezer, Serif, 270
Sfinas, Cindi, 202
Shack, Andrew, 201
Shackelford, David, 92
Shadix, Glenn, 195
Shadow Distribution, 255, 296
Shadrach, 126
Shadyac, Tom, 186
Shaff, Edmund, 43
Shaffer, Dana, 57
Shaffer, Paul, 15
Shaffner, Catherine, 28

Shah, Shireen, 297
Shaifer, Andrew, 16
Shaiman, Marc, 44, 117, 186
Shainberg, Steven, 212
Shakar, Martin, 35, 199
Shakespeare In Love, 222, 224,
Shalhoub, Tony, 30, 47, 134-135, 153, 182-183, 323
Shamberg, Michael, 84, 151
Shambrooke, Gary, 244
Shamburger, Douglas, 83
Shampoo Horns, 287
Shamshak, Sam, 61
Shanahan, Mark, 103
Shand, Iris, 295
Shandling, Garry, 83, 184, 323
Shane, Rachel, 192
Shaner, Dan, 214
Shankar, Mamata, 286
Shankman, Jim, 153
Shanks, Susan, 254
Shannon, Maureen, 202
Shannon, Michael, 209
Shannon, Molly, 131, 139
Shannon, Polly, 203
Shannon, Vicellous, 19, 76
Shannon-Smith, Jane, 43, 207
Shapiro, Brent, 23
Shapiro, Grant, 23
Shapiro, Linnell, 23
Shapiro, Pete, 208
Shapiro, Robert, 23, 210
Shapiro, Theodore, 17, 103
Shaps, Cyril, 263
Shareshian, Steven, 126, 140
Sharian, John, 39, 96
Sharif, Bina, 139
Sharon Riley & Faith Corale, 15
Sharp, Colleen, 126
Sharp, Jonah, 208
Sharp, Matthew, 96
Sharpe, Trevor, 157
Shattered Image, 216-217
Shaud, Grant, 132
Shaw, Adam, 96
Shaw, Bob, 166
Shaw, Emme, 111
Shaw, Fiona, 109, 247, 323
Shaw, Michael, 193
Shaw, Morgana, 214
Shaw, Peter, 142, 265
Shaw, Stan, 104-105, 323
Shaw, Wallace, 211, 320, 323
Shawn-Williams, Nigel, 185
Shawzin, Gregg, 183
Shay, Michele, 55, 122
Shaye, Lin, 92-93, 151
Shea, Anna, 197
Shear, Claudia, 151
Shearer, Harry, 64-65, 72, 90, 202, 323
Shearer, Ian, 217
Shearer, Jack, 19, 101
Shearmur, Edward, 198, 263
Shebib, Noah, 207
Shedrick, Reamer, 136
Sheedy, Ally, 258, 323
Sheehan, Bob, 15
Sheehan, Brooke, 205
Sheehan, Diana, 205
Sheehan, Nora, 138
Sheehan, Tim, 92
Sheehy, Joan, 218